THIRD EDITION

Teaching Students with Language and Communication Disabilities

S. Jay Kuder

Rowan University

PEARSON

Boston   New York   San Francisco
Mexico City   Montreal   Toronto   London   Madrid   Munich   Paris
Hong Kong   Singapore   Tokyo   Cape Town   Sydney

Executive Editor: *Virginia Lanigan*
Series Editorial Assistant: *Matthew Buchholz*
Senior Marketing Manager: *Kris Ellis-Levy*
Production Editor: *Annette Joseph*
Editorial Production Service: *Publishers' Design and Production Services, Inc.*
Composition Buyer: *Linda Cox*
Manufacturing Buyer: *Linda Morris*
Electronic Composition: *Publishers' Design and Production Services, Inc.*
Cover Administrator: *Linda Knowles*

For related titles and support materials, visit our online catalog at www.ablongman.com.

Copyright © 2008, 2003, 1997 Pearson Education, Inc.

Between the time website information is gathered and then published, it is not unusual for some sites to have closed. Also, the transcription of URLs can result in typographical errors. The publisher would appreciate notification where these errors occur so that they may be corrected in subsequent editions.

ISBN-10: 0-205-53105-9
ISBN-13: 978-0-205-53105-9

Library of Congress Cataloging-in-Publication Data
Kuder, S. Jay.
  Teaching students with language and communication disabilities / S. Jay Kuder. —3rd ed.
      p.   cm.
  Includes bibliographical references and index.
  ISBN 0-205-53105-9 (alk. paper)
    1. Children with disabilities—Education—United States.   2. Language arts—United States.
3. Language disorders in children—United States.   4. Communicative disorders in children—
United States.   I. Title.
  LC4028.K83 2007
  371.91'4—dc22   2007013896

Printed in the United States of America

10 9 8 7 6 5 4 3 2 1 RRD-VA 11 10 09 08 07

ABOUT THE AUTHOR

Dr. S. Jay Kuder is a professor of special education and the Associate Provost for Research and Dean of the Graduate School at Rowan University in Glassboro, New Jersey. Dr. Kuder earned a doctoral degree in applied psycholinguistics from Boston University. His research interests are in the development of effective practices for enhancing the language and literacy skills of children with disabilities. He is a member of the American Speech Language Hearing Association, the Council for Exceptional Children, and a fellow of the American Association on Intellectual Disabilities.

BRIEF CONTENTS

CONTENTS

PART TWO   **Language and Communication Disorders**

P A R T   T H R E E   Language and Communication in the Classroom

13   Assessing Language and Communication   273

14   Enhancing Language and Communication   299

15   Augmentative and Alternative Communication   335

16   Language, Culture, and English Language Learners   361

PREFACE

Students with language and communication learning disorders face a number of challenges in school. In a sense, they are like visitors to a foreign country who do not speak the language. They may be reluctant to participate in class discussions because they fear being ridiculed by teachers or peers. They may misunderstand directions and fail to ask questions that would help them understand. They may shy away from interaction with other students. They have limited or nonexistent skills in reading and writing. Sometimes students with language and communication disabilities are identified as "special education students" and classified as learning disabled, speech-language disordered, or some other disability label. Many other students have language and communication disabilities but are never formally identified because other factors (such as behavior, a physical disability, or speaking a language other than English) are the focus of intervention. However, language and communication abilities often are an important part of the success (or failure) of these children.

Rising expectations for all students, including those with disabilities, means that more than ever, teachers and other education professionals must be prepared to effectively teach students with language and communication difficulties. The purpose of this book is to help teachers and other professionals who work with children identify, understand, and help children with language difficulties. To achieve these goals, it is essential that all educators, special and regular, understand language—what it is and how to help children experiencing difficulty with it. As we learn more about the role of language in learning and in learning disorders, the need for teachers and other education professionals with knowledge about language development and disorders will grow. As Moats and Lyon (1996) note, formally trained language clinicians do not have the primary instructional responsibilities for children with language disorders. It is the classroom teacher, who often has little or no knowledge of language development and disorders, who is responsible for helping the child develop language, reading, and writing skills. This book is designed to assist teachers and other education professionals in acquiring basic knowledge about language, language development, and language disorders, that will enable them to become more effective teachers and/or clinicians.

There is a growing recognition that language and literacy are closely intertwined. A recent report by the National Academy of Education's subcommittee on reading (Snow, Griffin, & Burns, 2005) states that "Reading is, at its basis, about language and thinking." This report argues that "prospective teachers of reading need to know about language structure—systems and subsystems." Unfortunately, the authors lament, most textbooks do not present information about language in a form that is usable by prospective teachers.

That is the purpose of this text: to present information about language in a form that teachers and other education professionals can use to help children with language-related learning disabilities. This book is not just for special education teachers. It is for all professionals who work with children with language difficulties, including teachers in regular education classrooms. As more and more students with special needs are included in regular education classrooms, teachers can no longer rely on "experts" to remove from their classrooms those children who are experiencing learning difficulties. Regular education teachers must develop skills in teaching all children, including those with language disorders. At the same time, it is essential that special education teachers and speech-language specialists develop skills—through collaboration and consultation with other teachers—that will enable them to support instruction in the regular education classroom.

Teaching Students with Language and Communication Disabilities is divided into three major units. Part I (Chapters 1 through 6) presents the components of speech, language, and communication and describes language development. Part II (Chapters 7 through 12) presents a description of the language abilities of students with a variety of disabilities. And Part III (Chapters 13 through 16) provides suggestions for assessment and intervention and discusses cultural factors and language.

The third edition of this book differs in significant ways from the previous editions. Greater emphasis has been placed on the language-literacy connection throughout the chapters. Coverage of both language and literacy development in early childhood as well as in school-age children has been expanded. In fact, there is a new chapter on language and literacy in the school years. In addition, there is a chapter on the language of children with neuromotor disabilities. This is an updated version of a chapter that appeared in the first edition of this book but was not included in the second edition. Reviewers' comments indicated that this was an important chapter so it was included in this edition. Research has been updated throughout the book. This research includes new ways of understanding the language disorders of students with intellectual disabilities (mental retardation), autism spectrum disorders, and students who are learning English as a second language.

In an effort to make this book useful to educators who do not have extensive backgrounds in linguistic and developmental theories, I have kept the use of technical language to a minimum, while retaining a solid base of research. My hope is that readers will feel better prepared to help their students develop those language and communication skills that are essential for success in school and in the community.

Acknowledgments

I thank my colleagues and students at Rowan University who have continued to challenge me with their questions and discussions. In addition, I thank those individuals who reviewed earlier versions of this book. Their suggestions have been very helpful in developing the third edition. I would also like to acknowledge the following individuals who reviewed this edition for Allyn & Bacon: Joe Boyle, Virginia Commonwealth University; Maryann Byrnes, University of Massachusetts, Boston; Moon K. Chang, Alabama State University; and Marie Stadler, University of Wisconsin–Stevens Point. Finally, I thank my wife, Lucy, and my children, Julia, Emily, and Suzanne, for continuing to inspire me with their love and patience.

REFERENCES

Moats, L. C., & Lyon, G. R. (1996). Wanted: Teachers with knowledge of language. *Topics in Language Disorders, 16*(2), 73–86.

Snow, C. E., Griffin, P., & Burns, M. S. (2005). *Knowledge to support the teaching of reading.* San Francisco: Jossey-Bass.

1 Language and Language Disorders

In this chapter we will explore the meaning of the terms speech, language, *and* communication. *It is important to understand the meaning of each of these terms since they will be used throughout the text. In addition, they are frequently used—and sometimes misused—to describe the difficulties experienced by some students.*

Once we are reasonably sure what we are talking about, it is possible to begin to identify children with language disorders. In this chapter we will also discuss the concept of language disorder *and consider some criteria for identifying students with language difficulties.*

After reading this chapter, you should be able to:

1. Differentiate among *speech, language,* and *communication.*
2. Explain the characteristics of a language.
3. Identify the components needed for successful communication.
4. Identify the characteristics of language disorders.

Kevin: A Case Study

Kevin is a 9-year-old student in a regular fourth-grade classroom. Kevin seems bright and usually works hard, but he is a puzzle to his teacher. Sometimes it seems as though he's just not all there. He misunderstands directions—failing to complete all of the assignment or even working on the wrong pages. He is reluctant to answer questions in class. When he does answer, he stops and starts and seems confused. Kevin is a slow, hesitant reader. His teacher, Mrs. Ross, has noticed that his comprehension of text often seems to be ahead of his ability to read the words themselves. He is a poor speller. In his writing he tends to use short, choppy sentences, and his output is often poorly organized. Although Kevin is good in math, he has difficulty with word problems. In addition to these problems with his schoolwork, Kevin often appears to be lost among his fellow students. He hangs behind the others when they go out to play and often eats by himself at lunch.

Mrs. Ross would like to help Kevin, but she is not sure what is wrong. Is he immature? Should he be referred for special education? Could there be some medical reason for Kevin's problems?

Kevin is typical of students who have problems with language and communication. He may be experiencing difficulty understanding incoming language and producing appropriate spoken responses of his own. He appears to lack some of the subtle communication skills that are critical to social acceptance by his peers. He is at risk for academic as well as social difficulties. If nothing is done, it is likely that Kevin's problems will get worse. As the pace of learning increases in middle and high school, he is likely to fall further behind. But what *should be* done? And just what is Kevin's problem?

In order to understand Kevin and children like him, it is first necessary to understand the nature of language and the related concepts of speech and communication. This may help in determining what kind of difficulty Kevin is experiencing. It may even help in the development of procedures to help Kevin and children like him to enhance their skills in language and communication.

Speech, Language, and Communication

Speech

Speech, language, and communication—all of these are words that are sometimes used in describing the language production and language difficulties of children. It may be that Kevin has a speech problem. Might he also have a language problem? Is this just another way of saying the same thing? He may well have some problems communicating with others. How can we describe the problem that Kevin, and other students like him, are having? Does it make any difference what we call his problem, or is this just a tiresome academic debate?

In order to answer these questions, it is necessary to know just what we mean by the terms *speech, language,* and *communication.* They are often used loosely, even by some professionals, in describing the difficulties many children face in learning and interacting. But each of these terms has a particular meaning that has implications for understanding and helping students. To understand what *speech, language,* and *communication* mean, we have to ask some other questions. Is it possible to have speech without language? Consider the 3-month-old baby as she begins to babble. Listen to the sounds she makes: "bah," "gah," "buh." Are these speech sounds? Linguists (people who study language) say that these *are* speech sounds because they have characteristics that are identical to the same sounds produced by adults. What about people with echolalia? This is a condition prevalent in some children with autism spectrum disorders in which they repeat what they hear. For example, I might say, "What did you have for dinner?" and a person with echolalia might respond, "What did you have for dinner?" Did this person use speech? Of course, the answer is yes.

In each of these examples it is clear that speech is being used, but most linguists would say that in neither case is true *language* being used. Although Mommy or Daddy may claim to understand what baby is saying, most outsiders would have a hard time interpreting the sounds being uttered. The baby's speech could hardly be said to be conforming to the rules of adult language. In the case of an individual with echolalia, although the speech output is certainly in the form of language, it is not being used in a meaningful way. It is not an appropriate response within the context of the conversation.

These observations can help us differentiate between speech and language. **Speech** can be defined as the neuromuscular act of producing sounds that are used in language. Not all sounds are speech sounds in a particular language. For example, I can make clicking sounds with my tongue. Although these may actually be speech sounds in some African languages, they are not speech sounds in English. Speech, then, is a physiological act in which the muscles involved in speech production are coordinated by the brain to produce the sounds of language.

Language

It has been estimated that there are nearly 7,000 languages being spoken today somewhere in the world (Gordon, 2005). So, what is language?

Before we can arrive at a definition, it is necessary to ask another question. Is it possible to have language without speech? The answer is yes. One example is American Sign Language (ASL). Most linguists agree that American Sign Language is a language. It is the primary mode of communication of many people who are deaf. It is a gestural language that has its own unique grammatical structure. But why is it considered a language? What makes it so?

One feature may be obvious: A true language *communicates.* It communicates thoughts, ideas, and meaning. Although communication is a necessary feature of language, it is not sufficient to describe language. Linguists say that in order for a system of communication to be a language, it must be shared by a group of people. They call this feature a *shared code.* That is, although not everyone may know ASL (just as not everyone knows Hungarian), those who know the language being used can communicate with each other. You might ask, How large does the group need to be? Now that is another interesting question. There have been occasional reports in the press of twins who share a "secret language." Researchers who have studied this phenomenon have concluded that, although some twins do indeed develop unique words and sentence structures, most grow out of this stage quickly (Bishop & Bishop, 1998). Even if it lasts just a short time, is this really a language? After all, it is a system of communication that is shared by more than one person. In order to answer this question, we need to know more about what makes a system of communication a language.

A third feature of language is that it consists of *arbitrary symbols.* That is, the symbols have meaning simply because we say they do. There is no reason that a tree might not be called a "smook." There is nothing green and leafy about the word *tree.* Although a few ASL signs are iconic (they look like the things they represent), most are arbitrary symbols. Therefore, ASL has this feature of language. Another feature of language is that it is *generative.* Given a finite set of words and a finite number of rules, speakers can generate an infinite number of sentences. Although you are an educated person who has read widely, there are certainly sentences in this book that you have never encountered before. This is due to the generative property of language. Finally, language is *creative*. New words are constantly entering the language while existing words drop out of usage or change their meaning. Consider some of the new words that have entered the English language—*byte, teflon, laser*. How about words that have acquired additional meanings—*gay, cool, neat?*

You can see that language is a complex phenomenon and, as such, is difficult to define. Even linguists sometimes have difficulty defining whether a communication system is a language. To take just one example, there are many regional **dialects** in Italy. Sometimes the differences between a dialect and the base language are so great that speakers from one part of the country cannot understand speakers from another region. In that case, is the dialect actually a separate language? It is hard to say. There is no definitive answer to this question, but asking questions such as this helps us better understand what defines a language.

Then there is the contentious issue of animal communication. During the past few decades, several groups of researchers have attempted to show that animals can learn language. You can read more about this research in Box 1.1, then decide for yourself whether humans are unique in their ability to understand and use language.

Because language is such a complex phenomenon and still not completely understood, there is not a single, widely accepted definition. Instead, there are many definitions of language, none of which is completely adequate. The American Speech-Language-Hearing Association (ASHA), the professional organization of speech-language specialists, has one definition (see Box 1.2). In this book we will use a definition of language that includes the features that linguists use to define a language: **Language** is a rule-governed symbol system for communicating meaning through a shared code of arbitrary symbols. Although this may not be a perfect definition, it does convey the idea that language involves communication that is shared by a community. That leads us to our final definition—the definition of communication.

Communication

Once again, a question: Is it possible to have communication without language? If you have ever been in a noisy room, the answer should be obvious. A lot of communication can go on nonlinguistically. A smile, a shift in body position, a gesture, even the raise of an eyebrow can communicate a great deal. Sometimes these communicative attempts may be misinterpreted, causing problems. But, clearly, it is possible to communicate without spoken language.

Communication is the broadest of the terms that we have attempted to define. **Communication** has been defined by one author as "the process participants use to exchange information and ideas, needs and desires" (Owens, 2005, p. 11). In order for communication to take place, there must be four elements:

1. A sender of the message
2. A receiver of the message
3. A shared intent to communicate
4. A shared means of communication

BOX **1.1**

Do Animals Have Language?

In their book titled *Apes, Language, and the Human Mind,* Savage-Rumbaugh, Shanker, and Taylor (1998) describe the remarkable language (and other accomplishments) of Kanzi, a bonobo (a species of ape from Africa). The authors recount this event:

> One day when Kanzi was visiting Austin (a chimpanzee), he wanted some cereal that had been prepared specifically for Austin. He was told, "You can have some cereal if you give Austin your monster mask to play with." Kanzi immediately found his monster mask and handed it to Austin, then pointed to Austin's cereal. When told, "Let's go to the trailer and make a water balloon," Kanzi went to the trailer, got a balloon out of the backpack, and held it under the water faucet. (p. 139)

What does an interaction such as this mean? Did Kanzi really understand what was being said to him? He certainly responded as if he did. But *what* did he understand? Did he understand the grammar of the complex sentence that he heard? Did he understand the words? Or did he just understand the situation and "figure out" what was expected of him?

These are questions that have long fascinated psychologists and linguists alike. Research has examined the so-called language abilities of many species. For example, classic studies by Karl von Frisch (1967) and Konrad Lorenz (1971) revealed that bees possess an elaborate system of communication. Through a complex dance routine, bees can tell each other about the distance and direction from the hive to a source of nectar. Although this is a remarkable achievement, the communicative abilities of bees are very limited.

There is a long history of interest in the linguistic abilities of chimpanzees. Although early attempts by Winthrop and Luella Kellogg in the 1930s and Keith and Kathy Hayes in the 1940s to induce language in chimps by raising them just as they would a human infant were largely a failure, the interest in nonhuman primate language did not disappear. Beginning in the 1960s, with research by Beatrice and Allan Gardner of the University of Nevada, interest in the potential language abilities of chimps and other nonhuman primates was revived. Using American Sign Language as the means of communication, the Gardners successfully trained a chimp named Washoe to use over 100 signs. Even more exciting, they claimed that Washoe created *new* signs by combining signs she had already learned (Gardner & Gardner, 1969).

Many of the claims put forward by the researchers on the language abilities of chimpanzees and apes have been challenged by other scientists. For example, after examining some of the Gardners' earlier research, Dr. Herbert Terrace of Columbia University (Terrace, 1980) concluded that many of the claims for evidence of chimps' language abilities were overblown and that the supposed uses of language were, in fact, merely instances of sophisticated imitation.

The debate on whether language is unique to humans will continue. It is a fascinating debate because it raises questions about what defines language as well as what it means to be human.

BOX **1.2**

ASHA Definition of Language

Language is a complex and dynamic system of conventional symbols that is used in various modes for thought and communication. Contemporary views of human language hold that:

- Language evolves within specific historical, social, and cultural contexts;
- Language, as rule-governed behavior, is described by at least five parameters—phonologic, morphologic, syntactic, semantic, and pragmatic;
- Language learning and use are determined by the interaction of biological, cognitive, psychosocial, and environmental factors;
- Effective use of language for communication requires a broad understanding of human interaction including such associated factors as nonverbal cues, motivation, and sociocultural roles.

Source: Reprinted with permission from Language. Available from www.asha.org/policy <http://www.asha.org/policy>. Copyright 1982 by American Speech-Language-Hearing Association. All rights reserved.

When all of these elements are present, communication may occur (see Figure 1.1(a)). But when one or more of these elements is missing, there may be a breakdown in communication. Figure 1.1(b) shows what may happen if you meet someone in a foreign country. You may both want to communicate, but unless you share a common language, you may be unable to do so. Although you share the intent to communicate, you lack a shared means of communication. However, if you can get your messages across with gestures and facial expressions, you may be able to communicate with each other after all. Conversely, two speakers may share the means to communicate (i.e., a common language) but not share the same communicative intent (see Figure 1.1(c)). For example, if I am teaching a class and suddenly feel hot, I may look at a student in the class who is seated near the window and say, "Gee, it's hot in here." If the student's response is to say, "Yes, it is," we have failed to communicate. My intent was for the student to open the window. The student's understanding of my message was that I was simply commenting on the room temperature. For communication to be successful, all of its elements must be in place: a speaker, a listener, a shared intent to communicate, and a shared means of communication.

We have seen that speech and language can be used for communication but are not essential for communication. Communication can take place without either speech or language being used. Similarly, language can be either spoken or nonspoken (e.g., ASL). Speech can be used to express language or for nonlanguage utterances (e.g., babble or echolalia) (see Figure 1.2).

For our purposes it is important to understand the distinctions among speech, language, and communication because these distinctions can help us be more specific about the nature of the problems of a student such as Kevin. It could be that his difficulties are primarily the result of speech problems, such as misarticulation. This could

FIGURE 1.1   Components of Communication

(a) Successful Communication

Sender   **Shared** Intent Means   Receiver

**(b) Shared Means of
    Communication Lacking**

Sender   **Shared** Intent   Receiver

(c) Shared Intent Lacking

Sender   **Shared** Means   Receiver

account for some of his reluctance to talk in class and for some of his difficulties in socializing with his peers. But a speech problem alone would not explain Kevin's difficulties in understanding language or his problems with reading and writing. Kevin clearly has some difficulty communicating with others. These could be caused by misunderstanding the communicative intentions of others or by deficiencies in the language skills that are necessary for communication. It is most likely that Kevin has a language disorder. His difficulty in using and interpreting language for learning and socialization support this conclusion.

Language Disorder

The American Speech-Language-Hearing Association has defined **language disorder** as follows:

> A language disorder is impaired comprehension and/or use of spoken, written, and/or other symbol systems. This disorder may involve (1) the form of language (phonology, morphology, syntax), (2) the content of language (semantics), and/or (3) the function of language in communication (pragmatics) in any combination. (Ad Hoc Committee on Service Delivery in the Schools, 1993, p. 40)

Let's take a look at this definition in more detail. The first major point high-lighted by the ASHA definition is that language disorder includes both *comprehension* of language and language *production.* Children who have comprehension (receptive language) difficulties may have a hard time following directions and may appear to be inattentive. Students who have problems with language production (expressive language) may be reluctant to participate in activities that require the use of language. They may use more immature language than do their peers. They might also have difficulty relating personal experiences or retelling stories. Sometimes the productive language problems are more obvious, but difficulties in comprehension can be as much as or more of a problem in the classroom.

The second major point made by the definition is that the disorder can be identified in *either spoken or written* language. Usually we think of a language disorder as referring just to *spoken* language problems. But the definition points out that language is an essential part of writing as well. Sometimes problems in writing are caused by an underlying difficulty in using language.

The third major point is that language disorders can occur in *one or more* aspects of language. We will examine these elements of language in more detail in the next chapter, but the important point is that a language disorder can be pervasive or limited in scope.

It is important to distinguish language *disorders* from language *differences.* Many students come to school speaking a language other than English as their first language or a dialect that differs from standard English. These children must not be labeled "language disordered" merely because they talk differently from their teachers or from some societal standard. However, some children may talk differently and have a language disorder. Later in this book we will see how experts have devised ways to differentiate children with language differences from those with language disorders.

FIGURE 1.2   Speech, Language, and Communication

Speech: The neuromuscular act of producing sounds that are used in language.

Language: A rule-governed symbol system for communicating meaning through a shared code of arbitrary symbols. Language:

- Communicates
- Is a shared code.
- Consists of arbitrary symbols.
- Is generative.
- Is creative.

Communication: "The process participants use to exchange information and ideas, needs and desires" (Owens, 2005). In order for communication to take place, there must be a:

- Sender of the message.
- Receiver of the message.
- Shared intent to communicate.
- Shared means of communication.

Language disorders can vary from mild (e.g., problems in using word endings but easily understood by others) to severe (e.g., extreme difficulty in understanding what others say or being understood by others). In the past, terms such as *delay* and *deviance* have also been used in relation to language disorders, in the belief that some children were simply delayed in the timing of their development while others were developing along a significantly different path. However, most researchers today (e.g., Hegde & Maul, 2006) find these terms not very useful since many children with language delays have ongoing difficulty developing some aspects of language and what might appear to be language deviance may, in fact, be a plateauing of development. In place of the terms *delay* and *deviance,* most scientists and clinicians prefer to use the generic term *language disorders.*

How prevalent are language and communication disorders? Current estimates are that about 17 percent of the total U.S. population have some type of communication disorder (Owens, Metz, & Haas, 2007). Language disorders occur in approximately 8 to 12 percent of the preschool population. This percentage decreases during the school years. On the other hand, hearing loss increases with age, probably due to exposure to noise.

Often children with language and communication disorders experience other problems as well. They may have difficulty interacting with their peers. They may be shy and reluctant to approach others. Other children may ignore them or, even worse, reject their attempts at friendship. Some children with language and communication disorders have difficulty with cognitive functioning. They may have problems organizing information for recall, may be less attentive than their peers, and may be generally slower to respond. Sometimes children with language and communication difficulties exhibit behavior problems. These problems may be the result of their own frustration with communication, or they may result from the response of others to their difficulties. Some children with language and communication disorders have physical disabilities that either cause or exacerbate their difficulty. For example, children with cleft palate often have difficulty with articulation, and children with mild, fluctuating hearing loss are at risk for a variety of language and communication disorders.

Language disorders are often associated with disabilities such as autism and intellectual disability. Children with language disorders may be called "dysphasic," "dyslexic," "dysnomic," "communication handicapped," "language learning disabled," and so on. However, language disorders are not limited to children with classifications such as mental retardation and intellectual disability. Many students with mild language difficulties are never classified or are grouped under the general term *learning disabled.* In this book, I have chosen to organize the sections on specific language disorders by category of disability. This was no easy choice, and I recognize its potential for confusion. It might seem that the book is saying that all children with a particular disability (e.g., intellectual disability) have language disorders when, in fact, this may not be the case. Alternatively, it might seem that a child has to be classified with a disability label to have a language disorder. This also is not true. However, special education tends to be organized on the basis of diagnostic categories, and much of the research on language disorders is related to diagnostic categories. So, although these categories may sometimes be misleading, they provide an organizing framework for understanding language disorders.

The key criterion in determining whether a language difficulty is serious enough to require intervention is the impact the problem has on the child and on others. Does the child appear to be concerned about the problem? Is the language difficulty interfering with the child's ability to learn and/or socialize? Do other children tease or reject the child because of difficulties the child may be experiencing with speech, language, or communication? If the answer to one or more of these questions is yes, the child may require some sort of intervention.

Because children with language and communication disorders are at risk for academic and social failure, it is important that their difficulties be identified as early as possible. In many cases it may be possible to correct or at least enhance their performance. Children with language and communication disorders may exhibit a wide variety of characteristics. Some of the more frequently occurring characteristics are listed in Figure 1.3. Students who are experiencing one or more of these characteristics for an extended period of time may have underlying difficulties with language and communication. A comprehensive evaluation should include language and communication skills to determine whether they may be contributing to the child's learning and/or behavior difficulties.

Recognizing the problem and determining the need for intervention is a necessary first step in helping children with language and communication difficulties. But it is

FIGURE 1.3   Characteristics of Children with Language and Communication Disorders

Academic Performance
Reluctance to contribute to discussions
Difficulty organizing ideas
Difficulty recognizing phonemes
Difficulty producing sounds
Failure to follow directions
Difficulty finding the right word for things

Social Interaction
Reluctance to interact with other children
Exclusion or rejection by other children
Difficulty carrying on a conversation
Problems negotiating rules for games

Cognitive Functioning
Difficulty organizing information for recall
Slow responding
Inattentiveness

Behavior
High level of frustration
Frequent arguments
Fighting with peers
Withdrawing from interaction

only a first step. Knowing *what* the child should be able to do and how to help the child get to that point is the goal of the rest of this book.

Summary

Speech, language, and communication are related to each other yet also independent. Communication is the broadest of these concepts, encompassing both verbal and non-verbal interaction. Speech refers to the neuromuscular act of sound production. Language is a complex phenomenon that involves the use of symbols that conform to rules that are used to express meaning. Language disorders are deviations from typical development and/or appropriate use of language. It is important to identify language disorders as early as possible because such disorders can cause serious problems in learning and socialization. Moreover, with early identification it may be possible to help children make significant improvement in their language skills.

REVIEW QUESTIONS

1. Is it possible to have speech without language? Why or why not? Give two examples that support your answer.

2. List and briefly explain three features that help define language.

3. When you are talking to yourself, are you communicating? Why or why not?

4. Describe the kinds of problems that a child with a language comprehension disorder might experience in a classroom situation.

5. A parent says to you, "Do you think Sharon (my 6-year-old child) should have speech therapy?" How would you respond?

6. One characteristic of human language is creativity. Give five examples of words that have entered the English language in the last 10 years.

SUGGESTED ACTIVITIES

1. In any social setting there are many opportunities to watch nonverbal communication (i.e., gestures, facial expressions, body language). Use one of these opportunities to be an observer of interaction. Look carefully. What do you see? Can you find any recurrent gestures and/or facial expressions? What do they mean? Make a list of nonverbal communication elements and what they mean. Also, watch for any misunderstandings caused by nonverbal communication.

   Does nonverbal communication constitute a language? Explain your answer with examples from your observations. What do your observations indicate about the elements that are necessary for communication to take place?

2. Ask two teachers and two adults who are not teachers to tell you what they think of when they hear the term *language disorder*. Ask them to describe the kinds of problems that children with a language disorder would face and what should be done to help such children.

   What do the responses indicate about the term *language disorder?* How closely does their understanding of this term match the definitions that were presented in the chapter?

3. Record some sounds that you make with your voice. Some of the sounds should be found in English. Others can be sounds found in other languages (e.g., a rolled *r*) or nonspeech sounds. Then ask a group of people (a) if these are speech sounds and (b) if they *could be* speech sounds.

G L O S S A R Y

communication: the process participants use to exchange information and ideas, needs and desires

dialect: a variation of a language that shares elements of structure and vocabulary with the base language but differs in significant ways

language: a rule-governed symbol system for communicating meaning through a shared code of arbitrary symbols

language disorder: impaired comprehension and/or use of spoken, written, and/or other symbol systems

speech: the neuromuscular act of producing sounds that are used in language

R E S O U R C E S O N T H E W E B

www.asha.org American Speech-Language-Hearing Association

www.aaal.org American Association for Applied Linguistics

www.lsadc.org Linguistic Society of America

www.yerkes.emory.edu Yerkes Primate Research Center

www.ethnologue.com SIL International with information on the world's languages

R E F E R E N C E S

American Speech-Language-Hearing Association. (1993). Ad Hoc Committee on Service Delivery in the Schools.

Bishop, D. V. M., & Bishop, S. J. (1998). "Twin language": A risk factor for language impairment? *Journal of Speech, Language, & Hearing Research, 41,* 150–161.

Frisch, K. von (1967). *The dance language and orientation of bees.* (L. E. Chadwick, Trans.). Cambridge, MA: Belknap.

Gardner, R., & Gardner, B. (1969). Teaching sign language to a chimpanzee. *Science, 165,* 664–672.

Gordon, R. G., Jr. (Ed.). (2005). *Ethnologue: Languages of the world* (15th ed.). Dallas, TX: SIL International. Online version: www.ethnologue.com/.

Hegde, M. N., & Maul, C. A. (2006). *Language disorders in children: An evidence-based approach to assessment and treatment.* Boston: Allyn & Bacon.

Lorenz, K. (1971). *Studies in animal behavior.* Cambridge, MA: Harvard University Press.

Owens, R. (2005). *Language development: An introduction* (6th ed.). Boston: Allyn & Bacon.

Owens, R., Metz, D. E., & Haas, A. (2007). *Introduction to communication disorders* (3rd ed.). Boston: Allyn & Bacon.

Savage-Rumbaugh, E. S., Shanker, S. G., & Taylor, T. J. (1998). *Apes, language, and the human mind.* New York: Oxford University Press.

Terrace, H. (1980). *Nim.* New York: Knopf.

2 The Elements of Language

*Language has been described as consisting of several elements. In this chapter we will look in depth at the elements of language. We will see how linguists have described each element and the rules that govern its use. Knowing these elements forms the framework for understanding language disorders and for differentiating language dis-*orders *from language* differences.

After reading this chapter, you should be able to:

1. Describe the basic elements of language.
2. Understand the terms *phoneme* and *morpheme* and know how they differ from each other.
3. Understand the rules that underlie syntax.
4. Understand some of the challenges in developing rules for semantics.
5. Understand the concept of *pragmatics* and its application in communication.

Human language is extremely complex. In order to simplify and better understand language, linguists have developed various systems for dividing language into its components (or elements). Most linguists identify five major elements: phonology, morphology, syntax, semantics, and pragmatics. Alternatively, Bloom and Lahey (1978) describe language as consisting of three components: form, content, and use. This model recognizes the interrelatedness of language elements. Within the component they call "form," Bloom and Lahey include the elements of phonology, morphology, and syntax (see Figure 2.1). It is often difficult to separate morphology from

FIGURE 2.1 Two Models of Language Elements

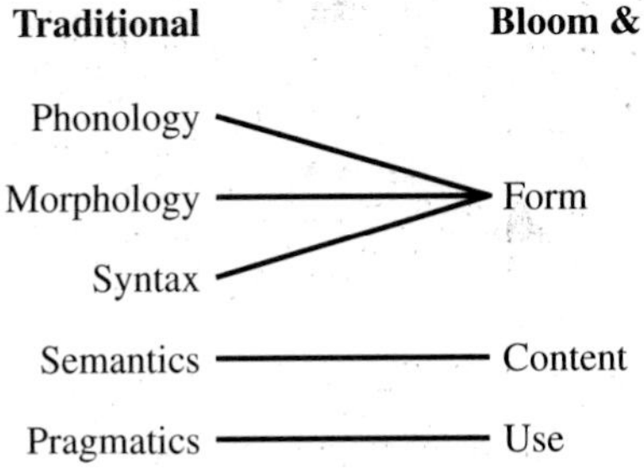

Traditional	Bloom & Lahey
Phonology	
Morphology	Form
Syntax	
Semantics	Content
Pragmatics	Use

phonology (for example, when children are learning that the plural form of *cats* makes an "s" sound but the plural of *dogs* has a "z" sound). Similarly, morphology and syntax are closely related in the emergence of language in young children. Nevertheless, in this chapter we will use the model that includes five language elements because it describes language in its most elemental form. As you read the chapter you should, however, keep in mind the interrelated nature of these elements.

Phonology

As an exercise to illustrate the interrelatedness of language elements, imagine that your task is to program a computer to understand and use spoken language—in this case, English. This is a formidable task but one that has been pursued for some time and has begun to yield very promising results. What would you include in your program? What would the computer need to know in order to process language?

Since computers work best with the most elemental sort of information, the first step might be to input the sounds of the English language. This would not be a terribly difficult task. Linguists have identified approximately 44 (some say 42, some say 45—linguistics is not always an exact science) distinctive sounds in English (see Figure 2.2) These elemental units of language are called *phonemes*. A **phoneme** is "the smallest linguistic unit of sound that can signal a difference in meaning" (Owens, 2005, p. 21).

Linguists can determine whether a sound is a phoneme in a particular language by asking native speakers of that language whether the sound, when added to a root word, makes a new word that they recognize. For example, let's say that we have already established that *bill* is a word in English. Now, if we substitute a *p* sound for the initial *b* sound, will speakers of the language recognize this as a new word? Yes, they recognize the new word as *pill*. Therefore, it appears that *p* is a phoneme in English. Now, let's say that we have determined that the word *row* is a word in English. If we substitute a rolled *r* for the flat *r* in *row,* have we made a new word that speakers of English recognize as having a different meaning? No. Although the rolled *r* is a phoneme in Spanish, it is not a phoneme in English.

Having programmed your computer with the 44 or so sounds of English, you are ready to go. The first word your computer produces is *tphj*. Oh no! Something seems to be missing. In fact, what is missing are the rules that govern phonology (there are rules that govern all of the other elements of language, as well). Remember, our definition of language said that it was a *rule-governed* system. In phonology there are rules that determine which sounds can (and cannot) occur together. There are also rules that tell when and how vowels must be used and how sound combinations are pronounced. For our computer to process language, its program must include these rules. This is not a problem, since the rules are finite and can be discovered.

Phonology, the first of the form elements of language, is the study of the sound system of language. Linguists who are interested in phonology attempt to identify the phonemes of a language and the rules that govern the combination and pronunciation of these phonemes. Knowledge of these rules enables linguists to understand how native speakers of a language know which sound combinations are possible in their language.

FIGURE 2.2 Phonemes of English

Vowels

IPA*	Example	IPA	Example
^	cup, luck	u	put, could
a:	arm, father	u:	blue, food
@	cat, black	ai	five, eye
e	met, bed	au	now, out
..	away, cinema	ou	go, home
e:(r)	turn, learn	e..(r)	where, air
i	hit, sitting	ei	say, eight
i:	see, heat	i..(r)	near, here
o	hot, rock	oi	boy, join
o:	call, four	u..(r)	pure, tourist

Consonants

IPA	Example	IPA	Example
b	bad, lab	th	think, both
d	did, lady	TH	this, mother
f	find, if	v	voice, five
g	give, flag	w	wet, window
h	how, hello	z	zoo, lazy
j	yes, yellow	Z	pleasure, vision
k	cat, back	dZ	just, large
l	leg, little		
m	man, lemon		
n	no, ten		
N	sing, finger		
p	pet, map		
r	red, try		
s	sun, miss		
S	she, crash		
t	tea, getting		

Note: IPA refers to the International Phonetic Alphabet. For more information on the IPA, go to www.arts.gla.ac.uk/IPA/ipa.html.

Morphology

So it looks as though we are ready to proceed with our task of developing a computer program to process language. With the rules governing sound, our computer is now producing combinations that look a lot more like English. Some of them may not be words that we recognize (e.g., *blif* and *ulop*), but they are at least *possible* English words. Soon we notice that we are getting some larger words, such as *unpossible* and *deerses,* and we realize that something else is missing. Although these combinations of sounds conform to the rules of phonology, speakers of the language reject these combinations.

The problem is that there must be another set of rules—a set of rules that govern how words are made. In fact there is such a group of rules. They are called *morphological rules*. **Morphology** is the study of words and how they are formed. Morphological rules determine how sounds can be put together to make words; they govern the structure of words.

Consider the word *base*. Any speaker of English would acknowledge this as a word in English. What about *baseball?* Of course this is a word, too, but it is different. It consists of two words—*base* and *ball*. Moreover, each of these words has a meaning that is related to the compound word. That is, both *bases* and *balls* are used in the game of baseball. Well, what about *basement?* Can *basement* be separated into two words? In trying to do so, we are left with *base* and *ment*. There is no problem with *base* (we have already agreed that it was a word), but just what is a *ment?* No, it appears that *basement* cannot be broken down any further. What do these examples suggest?

Based on this type of evidence, linguists have concluded that there are elemental building blocks of language called *morphemes*. A **morpheme** is the smallest unit of meaning in a language. To better understand morphemes, let's go back to the previous example. The word *base* is a morpheme. It cannot be broken into smaller pieces while retaining its original meaning. So what about *baseball?* As discussed previously, this *can* be divided into two parts that retain the meaning of the whole—*base* and *ball*. Therefore each of these words is a morpheme. Although *basement* might also be divided into two parts, doing so would leave a unit that has no meaning: *ment*. Therefore, *basement* is one morpheme.

Actually, linguists say that there are two basic kinds of morphemes. To illustrate, let's return again to the example. We have already said that *baseball* consists of two morphemes. Each of these is called a *free* morpheme. In other words, each morpheme can stand on its own as a word with meaning. Now let's add a plural *s* to create the word *baseballs*. How many morphemes do we have now? There must be three, since we have already established that *baseball* alone has two morphemes. But what is this new morpheme? What does *s* mean? In this context the *s,* since it is used as a plural, means "more than one." Therefore, there are three morphemes in the word *baseballs: base, ball,* and *s* (plural). However, the plural *s* is a special kind of morpheme. It cannot stand alone but has meaning only when it is attached to other morphemes. It is called a *bound* morpheme. Prefixes (such as *un* and *pre)* and suffixes (such as *ing* and *able)* are examples of bound morphemes.

If all of this seems a bit complicated, just consider the kind of problems that linguists have with words such as *cranberry*. For years linguists thought that this was one morpheme, since there is no such thing as a *cran*. Then along came *cranapple* juice. This demonstrated that *cran* can be separated from *berry* and still retain its meaning. Therefore, maybe *cranberry* was really two morphemes all along. This is the sort of debate that linguists love to pursue.

For our purposes, the point of this discussion is that there are rules that determine what a word is and how words can be formed. Thus, native speakers of English recognize that the word *unlikely* is fine but *inlikely* does not mean anything, and that even though *boy* is pluralized as *boys,* more than one man is not *mans* but *men*.

Morphology, then, as the study of words and how they are formed, includes the identification of morphemes (the basic *meaningful* units of language) and the rules for constructing words. With our computer programmed to identify and use morphemes, we can eliminate many of the strange letter sound combinations we were getting previously. Unfortunately, now we are getting sentences such as the following: *car the man hit the* and *the sweet is very child.* Clearly, there is still something wrong with our computer program. We need another set of rules. This additional group of rules is called *syntax.*

Syntax

Look at the following first stanza from Lewis Carroll's "Jabberwocky":

> 'Twas brillig, and _____ slithy toves
> Did _____ and gimble in the _____:
> All mimsy were the borogoves,
> And the mome raths outgrabe.

Can you guess what goes in each blank? You may not always get the exact word *(the; gyre; wabe),* but, even though this is a lot of nonsense, you probably guessed accurately about the *type* of word that must go in the blank. You undoubtedly knew that the first word was an article. You probably guessed that the second word was a verb and the third word was a noun. How did you do this? The answer is that you have rules of grammar (syntax) that help you accomplish tasks like this. You may or may not be able to formally state the rules. You may not even be aware that you possess these rules (until you are forced to use them in some ridiculous exercise), but they are there. These are *syntactic* rules. **Syntax** is the study of the rules that govern how words are put together to make phrases and sentences. What do these rules look like?

How would you describe the structure of the following sentences?

1. The dog is running.
2. The girl is reading a book.

For the first sentence, you might say that there is an article *(the)* and a noun *(dog),* an auxiliary verb *(is),* and a main verb *(running).* These are elements of the syntactic rules that linguists call **phrase structure rules.** These rules describe the structure of sentences.

Linguists have devised a shorthand code to describe these rules. For the first sentence, the code would look like the following:

S = NP + VP
NP = Art + N
VP = Aux + V

This notation says that the sentence consists of two elements—a noun phrase and a verb phrase. The noun phrase, in turn, consists of two elements—an article and a noun. The verb phrase also consists of two other elements—an auxiliary verb and a main verb.

If this were all that we knew about the English language, we could say that these were the rules of English syntax. But then we might find a sentence like the second example. Since this sentence is not completely explained by our original set of phrase structure rules, we must modify the rules somewhat. The second sentence example could be rewritten as:

$$S = NP + VP$$
$$NP = Art + N$$
$$VP = Aux + V + NP$$
$$NP = Art + N$$

This sentence introduces a new element into our phrase structure rules—a noun phrase that *follows* a verb phrase. If we were to continue examining sentences and refining our rules, we would end up with the finite (and surprisingly small) set of rules for the English language. Although small in number, these rules can be used to generate an infinite number of sentences, because of the *recursive* feature of phrase structure rules. This feature permits phrases to be joined together without limit. For example, in conjoined sentences (sentences that include a conjunction such as *and* or *but*), two or more noun phrases may be joined, as in the following example: *The boy and the girl sat outside the school.* Other nouns (e.g., *teacher, man, friend*) could be added to our sentence without limit. Similarly, more than one verb phrase may be embedded in a single sentence as in: *The girl who is here is my niece.*

For many years it was thought that phrase structure rules were all that were needed to describe a language. But there are certain kinds of sentences that are not easily explained by these rules. These include imperative sentences *(Go to bed!)* and questions *(Why are you crying?).* Such sentences bothered linguists for many years because they could not be adequately explained. Finally, Noam Chomsky (1957, 1965) developed a theory to account for these kinds of sentences. Called *transformational grammar,* his theory suggests that there are two levels in all languages—a surface structure and a deep structure. The surface structure is what we actually hear, but the deep structure is the underlying linguistic structure of the utterance. Between the deep structure and the surface structure, according to Chomsky, there is a set of rules *(transformational rules)* that can convert a deep-structure sentence to something else.

For example, take our question sentence, *Why are you crying?* The underlying (deep) structure of this sentence would be *You are crying* (deep-structure sentences are always simple, declarative sentences). In order to get the surface question, a question-transformation rule has to be applied, inverting the subject *(you)* and the auxiliary verb *(are)* and adding the appropriate *wh* word *(why).* This entire operation occurs subconsciously. In the case of the imperative, the deep-structure sentence is actually *You go to bed.* The imperative-transformation rule says that when the first noun is in the second person *(you),* it can be deleted, leaving the surface structure *(Go to bed).*

Transformational rules have served us well for many years; however, they have been found to have some limitations. Some problematic sentences can be generated by the theory and its rules. For example, the ambiguity apparent in the sentence *The duck is ready to eat* (Is it the duck that is preparing to eat or is someone about to consume the duck?) cannot be resolved by reference to phrase-structure and transformational rules. Additionally, the theory does not adequately explain the universality and learnability of languages (Leonard & Loeb, 1988). The most recent revision of transformational grammar theory, known as *government and binding theory* (Chomsky, 1981, 1982), attempts to account for the universality of language by describing the rules that relate the language we hear to the underlying mental representations we hold in our minds. In addition, Chomsky has identified additional sets of rules that provide limits to the interpretation of sentences. Although a complete discussion of this theory is beyond the scope of this book (see Shapiro, 1997, for more information), researchers in linguistics are continuing to try to describe the universal rules of grammar.

So we can now program our computer with syntactic rules, including phrase-structure and transformational rules. These will help us organize the words of English into coherent sentences that will easily be interpreted by native speakers of the language—sentences such as *Colorless green ideas sleep furiously.* Oh no! It looks like we have another problem.

The sentence *Colorless green ideas sleep furiously* was actually used by Chomsky (1957) to support his theory of the importance of structure in language. As he noted, there is nothing wrong with the syntax of this sentence. All of the words are in the right order. Still, the sentence does not mean anything (at least not in the literal sense). If we are to program our computer to understand and produce both grammatically correct and meaningful sentences, we will have to include yet another set of rules—semantic rules.

Semantics

Let's look at that sentence again—*Colorless green ideas sleep furiously*—to determine what, exactly, is wrong with this sentence. First of all, something cannot both have color *(green)* and be *colorless.* Additionally, ideas cannot have color and they cannot sleep. Even if they could sleep, it is not actually possible to sleep furiously. That this sentence makes no sense suggests that there must be rules that govern which words can meaningfully go together. These rules are called *semantic rules.* **Semantics** is the study of the meaning of words.

The search for these rules has not been easy. There are several theories of semantics, none of which seem to fully describe how words are linked to ideas. One of the most widely accepted and well-researched theories is the *semantic component theory* (Katz & Fodor, 1963). This theory claims that there are certain fundamental features of all words. For example, the word *husband* might consist of the features: + (is) male; + adult; + human; + (is not) married. There are also **selection restrictions.** These rules govern which words can appear together. For example, someone would not be described as a *married bachelor* or *my sister the bachelor* or my *2-year-old the bachelor* because of the component features of the word *bachelor.* You cannot be both married and a bachelor, nor can you be a female nor a child and also be a bachelor.

Of course, it *is* possible to talk about child bachelors and married bachelors in a nonliteral sense. Similarly, it is possible to interpret a phrase such as *colorless green ideas.* Surely many of us have had nights when we *slept furiously.* But we have to work to make sense of these expressions. They are not *literally* true; they have truth only in a metaphorical sense. It is this metaphorical feature of semantics that at times is what makes poetry interesting, and even beautiful.

Our fundamental-feature and selection-restriction rules could also be applied to the *colorless green ideas* sentence. Since one feature of green is that it is a color, it cannot be both a color and lack color. Since ideas are not animate, it is not possible for them to sleep. Fundamental-feature and selection-restriction rules help account for the contradiction that speakers find in a sentence, such as *My sister is married to a bachelor,* and for the ambiguity that we found previously in the sentence *The duck is ready to eat.* However, it is not altogether clear that children use a semantic feature approach in *learning* the meanings of words. In Chapter 4 we will examine the debate over semantic acquisition.

Now, after including some semantic rules in our computer program, we should be done. Although it may be difficult to describe all of the semantic rules, those that we have do a very good job of delivering meaningful sentences. Every once in a while, we might get a sentence that is difficult to interpret, but that happens in natural language as well.

Now, imagine trying to hold a two-way conversation with your computer. You type in statements or questions, and it types back responses. Suppose you type "Can you use a sentence with the word *dog?*" It types back "Yes." But that is not what you intended. You had wanted the computer to respond with a sentence using the word *dog.* Is there a problem? You bet there is. And you discover another problem. When you type a sentence such as "How are you today?" the computer might respond with almost anything— "The cat is on the mat," or "The car is at the shop." The response does not make any sense. What is wrong?

Pragmatics

So far, our computer programming task has been relatively simple. We tried something. When it did not work, we changed the program and added another set of rules that got us closer to our goal of simulating human language. The rules could be discovered and were relatively few. Rules for semantics turned out to be a bit more difficult, but still it was possible to include these rules. But now we are faced with a major problem. Our computer seems insensitive to some of the subtle rules that govern conversation. It is misinterpreting the intent of some sentences and not responding to the content of other sentences. In short, we are having difficulty getting our computer to *use* language in conversation, suggesting that there must be yet another element of language. In fact, there is. This element is called **pragmatics**—the use of language for communication, or, as Gleason (2005) put it, "the use of language to express one's intentions and to get things done in the world" (p. 23).

Pragmatics includes the study of the rules that govern the use of language for social interaction. There are rules that govern the reasons for communicating, as well as rules that determine the choice of codes used in communication (Bloom & Lahey, 1978). Let's look more closely at one of these rules.

I recall observing a student teacher in her placement in a classroom with 6- and 7-year-old children with language and communication disabilities. The student teacher was seated at a table at the front of the room, and the children were at their desks. Wanting the children to join her at the table, the student teacher asked, "Can you come to the table?" The children looked at the student teacher, then at each other, but they did not move. Naturally, this wanton disobedience angered the student teacher, so she raised her voice and quite sharply said, "Can you come to the table!" Once again, the only response was some puzzled looks and some foot shuffling. Finally, in exasperation the student teacher said, "Please come to the table now." The children immediately got up and went to the table. What happened in this episode? Why were these children so reluctant to come forward?

The answer is that they were probably having difficulty interpreting the communicative intent of the student teacher. Like our computer, they may have interpreted the correct answer to the question, "Can you come to the table?" as "Yes." But, in fact, this was not meant to be a question at all, even though it had the form of a question. This is an example of an *indirect speech act*—an utterance for which the syntactic form does not match the communicative intention. In the context in which this sentence was uttered, the intent was clearly that of a command. Unfortunately, the intent may not have been so clear to the children, because indirect speech acts tend to be more difficult to interpret than *direct speech acts*. Direct speech acts are those in which the communicative intention is reflected in the syntactic form, such as *Can I have some cake?* (question) and *Stop that car!* (imperative). Every utterance, however, is a speech act, and linguists such as Searle (1965) and Dore (1974) have identified speech acts and the rules that determine whether a conversation is intelligible.

Pragmatics also includes the study of the rules of conversation. You may recall what happened when we tried to engage the computer in conversation. It did not respond appropriately to what we had typed. Our computer violated one of the principles (rules) of conversation identified by Grice (1975)— specifically, the *relation principle.* This principle says that a response must be relevant to the topic. Other principles involve the *quantity* of information provided by the speaker, the *quality* (or truthfulness) of that information, and the *manner* (directness) of the information. When these principles are violated, we know that something is wrong with the conversation. Similarly, there are rules of conversation that govern how one speaks to persons of different levels of social status and rules that determine how conversations are repaired.

It would be difficult, if not impossible, to program our computer with such pragmatic rules because these require not only a solid understanding of language but also an understanding of people and their social environment. How do we tell the computer to talk one way to someone wearing a black coat and white collar and another way to someone wearing jeans and a T-shirt? The wonder is that we are able to make these subtle distinctions ourselves and that children are able to develop these skills fairly quickly.

Summary

This chapter examined the elements of language in detail—considering how form (phonology, morphology, and syntax), content (semantics), and use (pragmatics) relate to language and noting the rules characterizing each in determining the structure and use of language. The rules, considered individually, seem manageable enough, but discussion of the interrelatedness of the elements in language reveals the complexity of the language system. The next several chapters will focus on how children acquire the language system and how the system develops as children mature.

R E V I E W   Q U E S T I O N S

1. Which of the following are *possible* words in English?

   glix   nrzwt
   fmdab   flim
   smedder blumpt
   slirt   slwtr

   Make up five more possible words for English.

2. Add the appropriate ending to each of the following nonsense words

   lod (plural): _____   gack (past): _____

   lotch (plural): _____   nop (past): _____

   flim (progressive): _____   nug (plural): _____

3. Mike's teacher said to Mike, "Can you raise your hand?" Mike said "Yes," and he was given a detention. What was wrong with Mike's response?

4. List the semantic features of the following pairs of words. Compare your answers with those of a partner.

   dog/wolf   fruit/vegetable   table/desk

5. What is the message in the following statements? Is it a direct or an indirect speech act?

Statement	Message	Direct/Indirect
Can you pass the salt? (Uttered by someone seated at the dinner table)		
Can you raise your hand? (Uttered by a doctor examining a patient following an injury)		
Can you raise your hand? (Uttered by a teacher who is upset with a student who is acting out)		

SUGGESTED ACTIVITIIES

1. *Complex Sentence Activity:* Select two children between the ages of 8 and 12. One of the children should be younger than the other, or one child should have a language disorder.

    Read the following complex sentences to each child, and ask the accompanying question. Then try teaching the individual children any of the items they missed. Report on:

    a. The number of errors each child made and on which sentences they were made.

    b. What the errors indicate about the syntactic development of these children.

    c. What happened when you tried to teach the child the missed items.

    1. Before the cat was fed, the girl gave him some water.

        Q: When did the girl give some water?

        A: Before the cat was fed.

    2. The boy who kissed the girl ran down the street.

        Q: Who ran down the street?

        A: The boy.

    3. The lion that the tiger bit jumped over the giraffe.

        Q: What jumped over the giraffe?

        A: The lion.

    4. The horse jumped over the fence after the man hit him.

        Q: When did the horse jump?

        A: After the man hit him.

    5. The boy saw the man who was wearing a green hat.

        Q: Who was wearing a green hat?

        A: The man.

    6. The car that was hit by the truck was driven by the man.

        Q: What did the man drive?

        A: The car.

    7. The lady asked the man who was watching which hat to wear.

        Q: Who wore the hat?

        A: The lady.

    8. The cat that was chased by the dog was caught by the boy.

        Q: What did the boy catch?

        A: The cat.

    9. The baby crawled to the couch after her mother called her.

        Q: When did the baby crawl?

        A: After her mother called her.

    10. The girl asked the child who was sick to leave the room.

        Q: Who left the room?

        A: The child.

2. *Semantics Challenge:* In this chapter we noted some of the arguments that linguists have over the number of phonemes in words such as *cranberry.* How many morphemes are in the following words:

lamppost	television
parasailing	parachute
innocent	intake

G L O S S A R Y

morpheme: the smallest unit of meaning in a language
morphology: the study of words and how they are formed
phoneme: the smallest linguistic unit of sound that can signal a difference in meaning
phonology: the study of the sound system of language
phrase structure rules: the rules that describe the basic structure of sentences
pragmatics: the rules that govern the social use of language
selection restrictions: the rules that govern which words can appear together
semantics: the study of the rules that govern the assignment of meaning to words
syntax: the rules that govern how words are put together to make sentences

R E S O U R C E S   O N   T H E   W E B

www.linguistlist.org   General information on language theory and language research

www.pbs.org/speak/   Interesting activities related to understanding English as spoken in the United States

http://ling.bu.edu/in/the/news   News articles about language and linguistics

www.languagemuseum.org/   The national museum of language

R E F E R E N C E S

Bloom, L., & Lahey, M. (1978). *Language develop-ment and language disorders.* New York: Wiley.

Chomsky, N. (1957). *Syntactic structures.* The Hague: Mouton.

Chomsky, N. (1965). *Aspects of the theory of syntax.* Cambridge, MA: MIT Press.

Chomsky, N. (1981). *Lectures on government and binding.* Dordrecht, Netherlands: Foris.

Chomsky, N. (1982). *Some concepts and conse-quences of the theory of government and bind-ing.* Cambridge, MA: MIT Press.

Dore, J. (1974). A pragmatic description of early lan-guage development. *Journal of Psycholinguis-tic Research, 3,* 343–350.

Gleason, J. B. (2005). The development of language: An overview and a preview. In J. B. Gleason (Ed.), *The development of language* (6th ed.) (pp. 1–38). Boston: Allyn & Bacon.

Grice, H. (1975). Logic and conversation. In P. Cole & J. Morgan (Eds.), *Syntax and semantics, Vol-ume 3: Speech acts.* New York: Academic Press.

Katz, J., & Fodor, J. (1963). The structure of a se-mantic theory. *Language, 39,* 170–210.

Leonard, L., & Loeb, D. (1988). Government binding theory and some of its applications: A tutorial. *Journal of Speech and Hearing Research, 31,* 515–524.

Owens, R. E. (2005). *Language development: An in-troduction* (6th ed.). Boston: Allyn & Bacon.

Searle, J. (1965). What is a speech act? In M. Black (Ed.), *Philosophy in America.* Ithaca, NY: Cor-nell University Press.

Shapiro, L. P. (1997). Tutorial: An introduction to syn-tax. *Journal of Speech, Language, and Hearing Research, 40,* 254–273.

3 Language Acquisition

Bases

What is it about humans that enables us to learn language? What physical structures are necessary in order for language to be acquired? Are the physical structures alone sufficient for the acquisition of language? What role does cognitive development play in acquiring language? What about interaction with others? Is this a necessary part of language acquisition?

These are some of the questions that will be addressed in this chapter. The major structures of the speech and language system are described. Theories about the relationship between cognition (thought) and language are presented. Also, the role of social interaction in language acquisition is discussed.

The key question to keep in mind is: What is necessary *for language to develop and what is* sufficient *for development?*

After reading this chapter, you should be able to:

1. Understand the physical structures that produce speech.
2. Understand the role played by the central nervous system in human comprehension and production of language.
3. Explain the possible relationships between *cognition* and *language.*
4. Understand the role that social interaction plays in language acquisition.

Physiological Bases of Language Development

You might recall that despite intensive efforts to raise chimpanzees in a manner similar to that of human infants, the chimps failed to develop more than a few garbled words. Why did these experiments fail? The answer lies primarily in the physiological structures that allow humans to learn and develop language. We will look at two types of structures that contribute to language development and use: those of speech production and the regions of the brain that control language.

Speech Production Structures

The speech production system is quite complex, and a thorough discussion of the physiology of speech would go beyond the scope of this book. There are several texts, however, that give a detailed description of the physiology of the speech production system (e.g., Owens, Metz, & Haas, 2007; Anderson & Shames, 2006). Here, we will briefly look at the structures that contribute to the four processes of speech production—respiration, phonation, resonation, and articulation—and at how these processes and structures together produce speech sounds. Under the control of the brain, they function almost simultaneously in the speech production process (see Figure 3.1).

FIGURE 3.1   The Processes of Speech

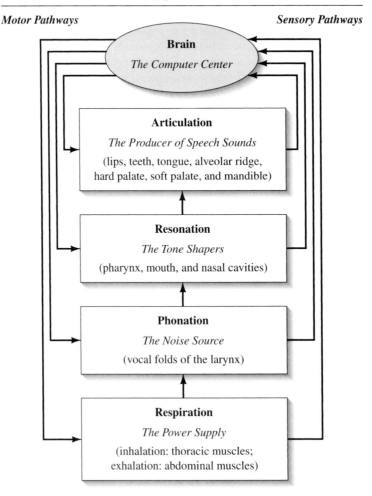

Source: From Hulit, Lloyd M. and Merle R. Howard, *Born to Talk: An Introduction to Speech and Language Development,* 4th ed. Published by Allyn and Bacon, Boston, MA. Copyright © 2006 by Pearson Education. Reprinted by permission of the publisher.

Respiration   How is sound produced? First, we need air, for it is a stream of shaped and guided air that forms sounds. When we breathe normally, about half of the breathing cycle is spent on inhaling air and about half involves exhaling (Hulit & Howard, 2006). However, during speech something very different happens. Muscles that control respiration—namely, the **diaphragm** (see Figure 3.2)—work to control the airstream so that the exhaling stage lasts close to 85 percent of the breathing cycle—15 seconds or more. Just imagine what speech would be like if we were limited to 2- or 3-second bursts.

Phonation.   In addition to maintaining a longer stream of air, the respiratory muscles allow air to be forced under pressure through structures in the **larynx.** The *vocal folds* contained in the larynx act as a valve that prevents foreign matter from entering the lungs. The vocal folds also obstruct the flow of air from the lungs, thus causing the vibrations necessary for speech. As the airstream is restricted and buffeted, it creates a buzzing sound.

FIGURE 3.2   The Human Vocal Organs

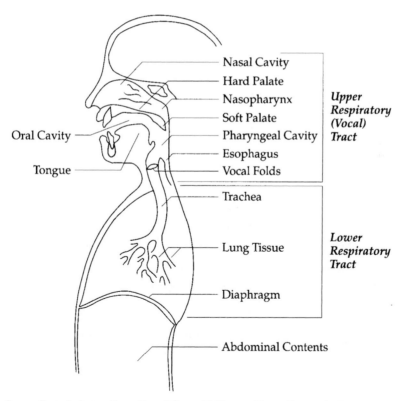

Source: From Anderson, Noma B., and George H. Shames, *Human Communication Disorders: An Introduction,* 7th ed. Published by Allyn and Bacon, Boston, MA. Copyright © 2006 by Pearson Education. Reprinted by permission of the publisher.

Resonation.   Moving upward from the larynx, the air resonates in the mouth, the nasal cavities, and/or the pharynx (see Figure 3.2). The tone of the resulting sound is affected by the size and shape of the resonating structures into which the air is expelled. In general, the larger the resonating cavity, the lower the tone. Try making a vowel sound. This is the sound created by resonated air.

Articulation.   **Articulation** of sound takes place when the airstream is further impeded by structures such as the lips, tongue, and/or teeth. The production of consonants requires the action of articulation. In fact, each phoneme has a unique combination of articulators and resonators that work together to form the sound. For example, vowel articulation can be described with respect to tongue and lip position. The tongue position varies along two dimensions: front-back and high-low (Kent & Vorperian, 2006). For example, the /ae/ sound (as in *hat*) is described as a low-front sound—that is, the tongue is the front of the mouth, in a low position when that sound is articulated. Try it. Now, say the word *heat*. What happens? You should feel your tongue move toward the roof of your mouth (the /i/ sound is high-front). Vowels are also described by lip position—rounded or unrounded.

Similarly, each consonant sound can be described by a unique combination of three sets of characteristics: **place of articulation** (where sound is formed), **manner of articulation** (how a sound is formed), and **voicing** (whether the vocal cords are vibrated). A complete discussion of consonant articulation goes beyond the scope of this book; for a more complete discussion, see Menn and Stoel-Gammon (2005). However, an example or two may help in understanding how this descriptive system works. Let's take the consonant sound /b/, as in bay. Linguists describe this sound as a bilabial, stop, voiced sound. That is, it is made with both the upper and lower lip (bilabial), there is a total obstruction of air in the vocal tract (stop), and the vocal cords are vibrated during articulation (voiced). Now try the sound /p/, as in the word, pay. Do you notice any differences between this sound and the preceding one? You should. The /p/ sound is a bilabial, stop, unvoiced sound. That is, it differs in only one feature from the /b/ sound, and that is voicing. Can you feel the difference between /b/ and /p/? With so many structures involved and such precise timing required, it is a wonder that more children do not have speech production problems.

Central Nervous System

Control of speech production is governed by the central nervous system. The human nervous system can be divided into two major divisions: the peripheral nervous system and the central nervous system.

The **peripheral nervous system** is made up of the cranial and spinal nerves that carry sensory information to the brain while relaying motor information from the brain to the muscles of the body. The 12 cranial nerves directly connect from the brain to the ears, nose, and mouth, whereas the spinal nerves are connected to the spinal cord via long pathways.

The **central nervous system** includes the brain and spinal cord. In order to better understand this complex organ, scientists often describe the brain as being comprised of three major regions: the hindbrain, the midbrain, and the forebrain (see

Figure 3.3). The **hindbrain** consists of structures of the brain stem, such as the medulla oblongata, the pons, and the cerebellum, which control functions such as respiration, digestion, and large motor movement. This part of the brain is sometimes called the most primitive, because these structures were the first to develop in animals and are the first to develop in the neonate. The **midbrain** consists of structures that assist in relaying information to and from the brain and the visual and auditory nerves.

FIGURE 3.3   View of the Brain Showing Major Regions

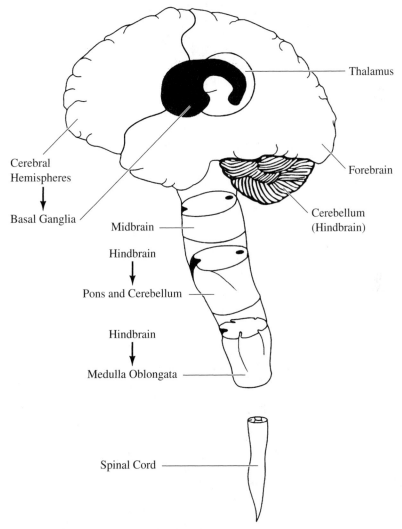

The **forebrain** (cerebrum) is the largest part of the brain. The cerebrum is divided into two nearly equal hemispheres connected by a bundle of fibers called the **corpus collosum.** For purposes of study, each hemisphere of the cerebrum is divided into four regions: frontal lobe, parietal lobe, temporal lobe, and occipital lobe (see Figure 3.4).

Each hemisphere of the cerebrum, and each region within the hemisphere, is believed to have a special function. In most people, language processing, both comprehension and production, takes place largely in the left hemisphere, although the right hemisphere *does* have a role to play in the processing of language. For example, research has shown that auditory syntactic information is processed primarily in the left temporal lobe and in part of the left frontal lobe, whereas the interpretation of paralinguistic cues such as stress and intonation takes place in the right hemisphere (Friederici, 2001). In addition, research on individuals with right hemisphere brain damage has suggested that they may have more difficulty participating in extended communicative exchanges (Obler & Gjerlow, 1999).

Two areas in the left hemisphere are thought to be especially important in language production and comprehension: Broca's area and Wernicke's area. **Broca's area** is located near the middle of the left cerebral hemisphere, where the frontal, parietal, and temporal lobes meet. This is the area where organization of the complex motor sequences necessary for speech production goes on. **Wernicke's area** lies closer to the rear of the left cerebral hemisphere in the temporal lobe and is the area involved in the

FIGURE 3.4   Left Cerebral Hemisphere

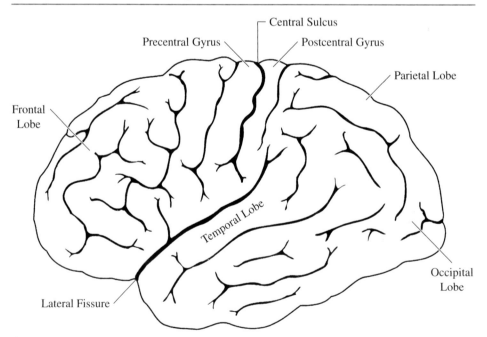

Source: From Anderson, Noma B., and George H. Shames, *Human Communication Disorders: An Introduction,* 7th ed. Published by Allyn and Bacon, Boston, MA. Copyright © 2006 by Pearson Education. Reprinted by permission of the publisher.

comprehension of language. When these regions of the brain are damaged, the effect on language use can be devastating (see Box 3.1). Recent research has suggested that similar regions located in the right hemisphere are involved in the comprehension of speech (Hickok, 2001).

Knowing what happens during a conversation helps in understanding the role of the central nervous system in language processing. Sound enters the ears and is conducted to the brain along the auditory nerve. The sound is initially processed in the midbrain and relayed to the cerebrum. Here, it is identified as speech and analyzed in Wernicke's area (and possibly in the right hemisphere). If a response is required, a message is sent to Broca's area, where the motor plan for articulation is developed. This plan is sent to the motor area of the parietal lobe, where messages are then relayed to the appropriate muscles for a response (see Figure 3.5). Of course, this is a highly simplified version of what happens in the brain during conversation.

Why is the ability to understand and use language not fully developed at birth? The most likely explanation is that the brain is not fully developed. Over time, the combination of physiological maturation and experience causes the brain to develop. However, there appears to be a time limit within which this brain development must take place. Lenneberg (1967) proposed that there is a "critical period" for brain development, as it relates to language functioning. After this period (which ends with the

---

BOX 3.1
Types of Aphasia

In his book *The Shattered Mind* (1974), Howard Gardner describes the devastating effects that brain damage can have on language. He gives some of the following examples:

David Ford (Broca's Aphasia)

Mr. Ford was a 39-year-old Coast Guardsman who had suffered a stroke. In response to a question about his work (radio operator), Mr. Ford said: "I'm a sig . . . no . . . man . . . uh, well, . . . again." When asked what had happened to his speech, Mr. Ford replied: "Head, fall, Jesus Christ, me no good, str, str . . . oh Jesus . . . stroke."

Mr. Ford's language was slow and produced with a great deal of effort. He seemed to know what he wanted to say but was not able to get it out. This is characteristic of persons with Broca's aphasia.

Philip Gorgan (Wernicke's Aphasia)

A 72-year-old retired butcher, Mr. Gorgan's language difficulties were quite different from, though no less severe than, Mr. Ford's. In response to a question about why he was in the hospital, Mr. Gorgan replied: "Boy, I'm sweating, I'm awful nervous, you know, once in a while I get caught up, I can't mention the tarripoi, a month ago, quite a while, I've done a lot well, I impose a lot, while, on the other hand, you know what I mean, I have to run around, look it over, trebbin and all that sort of stuff."

Mr. Gorgan's rambling, incoherent response is characteristic of Wernicke's aphasia, where the ability to understand and produce *meaningful* language is impaired.

FIGURE 3.5   Comprehension and Production of Speech in the Brain

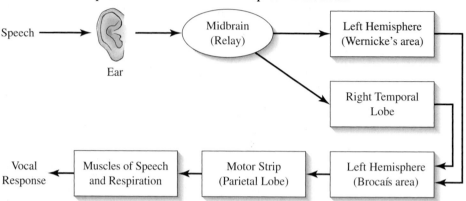

onset of puberty), acquisition of a first language is difficult, if not impossible. This theory is supported by research on individuals with brain damage that has found that adults recover language functioning much more slowly (if at all) than do children. In addition, learning a second language is much more difficult as an adult than as a child. On the other hand, recent research has discovered that some aspects of language (e.g., pragmatics and semantics) continue to develop through adolescence and beyond (Obler, 2005).

These findings about brain development and language have important implications for those interested in helping children with language learning difficulties. Since brain development continues throughout childhood, it may be possible, through appropriate experiences, to have some effect on development in those children. The critical period theory, however, suggests there is limited time to influence language acquisition, supporting the need for early intervention.

Cognitive Bases of Language Development

What do you see when you see snow? You may see a beautiful blanket of white, sparkling in the moonlight. On the other hand, you may see a gray, grungy mess that is causing monumental traffic jams. If you were an Inuit (indigenous people of Alaska), you might recognize several types of snow. In fact, the Inuit have many words to describe the different qualities of snow. Skiers make similar distinctions. They talk about *powder, granular, popcorn snow,* and the like. What determines what you see—the thing itself, or the words you have to describe it? This is one of the major problems in understanding the relationship between language and cognition.

Some researchers, such as Benjamin Whorf (1956), have argued that language affects our perception of the world. They claim that having a word to describe something makes it possible to perceive the thing itself. Consider colors, for example. When you were first learning about color, you probably learned about the primary colors—*red, blue,* and *green.* As your experience broadened, you learned to identify *purple, maroon,* and *peach.* If you have ever painted a house, you may have encountered names such as *azure, ice, melon,* and so on. Proponents of the view that *language determines thought* argue that your perception of these fine color distinctions occurred only after you had acquired a language label for these colors. According to this theory, speakers of different language actually perceive the world in different ways.

On the other hand, many theorists argue that *language is dependent on cognition,* a view whose theoretical basis was provided by the Swiss psychologist Jean Piaget and his followers (Piaget, 1954; Sinclair-DeZwart, 1973). According to this view, cognitive development precedes language development. Piaget claimed that "language is not enough to explain thought, because the structures that characterize thought have their roots in action and in sensori-motor mechanisms that are deeper than linguistics" (1954, p. 98).

Piaget believed that language was only one of several symbolic functions a child develops through growth and interaction with the environment. Language developed, Piaget claimed, only after prerequisite cognitive accomplishments had occurred. These accomplishments include development of such principles as distancing and object permanence. **Distancing** involves the gradual movement away from actual physical experiences to symbolic or representational behavior. **Object permanence** is the idea that objects exist even when they are not being touched, tasted, or seen. These and other developments of the sensorimotor period (see Table 3.1) help move the child from being dependent on the physical world to relying more on the symbolic—a necessary prerequisite to language development, according to Piaget.

The theory that language development is dependent on cognitive development has not gone unchallenged. Chomsky (1980), for example, pointed out that language comprehension begins before language production and long before the cognitive developments that Piaget claimed must precede language. Even though such criticism may be valid, Piaget's theories about cognition and language reveal the importance of cognition in the language learning process.

A third model of language and cognition claims that *language and cognition are interdependent.* The Russian psychologist Lev Vygotsky most clearly stated this view (1962). According to Vygotsky, language and cognition develop as separate and independent systems. Initially language development occurs because of interaction with others, but, eventually, language becomes internalized. It is at this point that language and thought begin to merge, allowing the child to engage in abstract thought and symbolic reasoning. Without language, according to Vygotsky, thinking could not progress beyond the earliest stages of development.

A fourth model suggests that language and cognition develop *independently,* as the result of physical maturation. The strongest statement of this position is that of the psycholinguist Steven Pinker. Pinker (1994) claims that all of the theories about cognition and language are wrong for one simple reason—language is not learned at all. He claims that language is an "instinct." By that, he means it is a skill that develops spontaneously, without conscious effort or formal instruction. Pinker further claims that what he calls the "language instinct" is a characteristic of the human species and is distinct from cognitive development. As the central nervous system matures, so too do language abilities. According to this model, disorders of language could be explained only by serious physiological disorders.

How is it that intelligent, well-educated professionals can reach such different conclusions about the relationship between thought (cognition) and language? There

TABLE 3.1 Highlights of Sensorimotor Development

Substage (and Months)	Object Permanence	Causality	Means-Ends	Imitation	Play	Communication
1 (0 to 1)	Out of sight, out of mind.	No concept of causality.	No understanding of means-ends.	None.	None.	No communicative intent.
2 (1 to 4)	Uses senses to make and maintain contact with objects.	No concept of causality.	No understanding of means-ends.	Preimitation. Repeats own behavior that has been imitated by someone else.	Produces behaviors preliminary to play including grasping and looking at objects.	Cries, coos, and laughs.
3 (4 to 8)	Watches object move and anticipates its future position. Reaches for partially hidden object.	Does not understand cause-effect. Behaves as though the cause of all actions.	Produces goal-oriented behaviors but only after activity has begun.	Imitates only behaviors has spontaneously produced at an earlier time.	Still very sensory but begins to interact with other people.	Babbles.
4 (8 to 12)	Looks for an object if sees it being hidden.	Externalizes causality. Knows other people and objects can cause activities.	Evidence of planning and the production of intentional behaviors.	Imitates behaviors has not spontaneously produced.	Uses developing concepts in his play activities.	Links gestures and vocalizations to convey fairly specific messages.
5 (12 to 18)	Follows sequential displacement to find hidden object.	Sees other people and objects as agents for causality in new situations.	Uses experimentation to solve problems.	Uninhibited imitation to facilitate own understanding.	Play reflects cognitive growth. Figures out how to make toys work.	Produces first meaningful words. Communication is intentional but still heavily nonverbal.
6 (18 to 24)	Fully developed concept of object permanence. Can now accommodate invisible displacements.	Causality enhanced by ability to represent objects and cause-effect relationships in his mind.	Can mentally represent a goal and his plan for achieving the goal.	Deferred imitation. Imitates a behavior has represented mentally and stored in his memory.	Progresses from autosymbolic to symbolic play.	Imitates and spontaneously produces multiple word utterances.

Source: From Hulit, Lloyd M., and Merle R. Howard, *Born to Talk: An Introduction to Speech and Language Development*, 4th ed. p. 434. Published by Allyn and Bacon, Boston MA. Copyright © by Pearson Education. Reprinted by permission of the publisher.

are several possible answers to this question. First, there is the complexity of both language and cognition. These are multifaceted processes that defy easy explanation. A second factor may be individual differences in development. After years of research focused on understanding how children develop over time, scientists have discovered that, although there are clearly many similarities in development, there are also differences. For example, some young children follow the usual steps in development in almost a lockstep manner, while others don't follow the usual patterns. In the end, they both reach the same goal. Therefore, trying to develop one theory that explains all human behavior may be impossible. Finally, it may be that language and cognitive development interact differently at different points in development. At six months of age, they may be developing independently, but at age 4, further language development may be dependent on cognitive development. Thus, each theory may be "right" at some stage of development. Although there is no definitive answer regarding the relationship between language and thought, all of the theoretical models have contributed to our understanding of this relationship.

So far, in examining the physiological and cognitive foundations for language acquisition, we have seen how cognitive and physical developments set the stage for language acquisition. We will now look at the role of social interaction.

Social Bases of Language Development

At the beginning of this chapter you were asked to keep in mind this question: What is *necessary* for language to develop and what is *sufficient* for development? So, what have we learned so far?

Physiological development appears to be absolutely *necessary* for the development of language. The role of cognitive development is less certain. But there is little doubt that without appropriate physical development, language is highly unlikely to develop. But is physical maturation sufficient to account for language development?

What would happen to a healthy baby who was somehow not exposed to language? Sadly, such cases have happened. Several decades ago, child welfare authorities discovered a 12-year-old girl who had been locked in a room by her parents with little or no opportunity for human interaction. When she was discovered, the girl (given the fictitious name of "Genie") seemed to be physiologically intact, but she was cognitively and socially delayed and had essentially no language development (Curtiss, 1977). After years of systematic work, speech-language specialists were able to help "Genie" develop a significant amount of language, but she never fully recovered. This, and other purported cases of children raised without human interaction (such as Victor, the "wild boy of Aveyron") suggest that human interaction is essential for language to develop.

Further evidence for the critical role of socialization comes from more systematic studies such as that by Hart and Risley (1995). These researchers studied parent–child interactions in 42 families over an extended period of time. The families were carefully chosen to provide a cross-section of socioeconomic status levels and to include both white and African American families. Observers went into the home and attempted to record every interaction that took place during the observation period. The results were stunning and disturbing. Children from the higher socioeconomic groups developed a far larger vocabulary than did children in families that received welfare. Children from middle-class families were right in the middle of vocabulary development. Similar results were found for both white and African American families. The researchers also found that parents from higher socioeconomic families engaged in more language interaction with their children than did parents of children from welfare or from middle-class families, and that the quality of their interaction differed in significant ways (see Figure 3.6). For example, parents from lower socioeconomic status families tended to

FIGURE 3.6   Child Vocabulary and Parent Utterances

a. Parent Utterances to Their Child

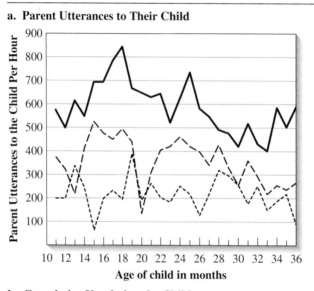

b. Cumulative Vocabulary by Children

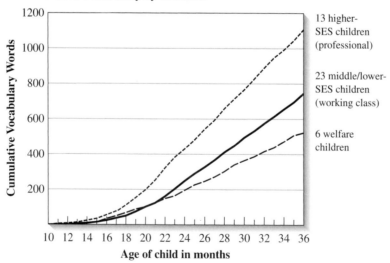

Source: B. Hart & T. Risley (1995). *Meaningful differences in the everyday experience of young American children* (pp. 234 & 235). Baltimore: Brookes.

interact with their children primarily for the purpose of behavior management. Although there are many ways to look at the results of this study, it demonstrates very clearly that early experiences are important in shaping language development. In particular, it is the amount and quality of interaction that shapes language development.

Socialization provides the third piece in the puzzle of language development. Physiological development provides the "how," cognitive development the "what," and social development the "why" of language development. All of these may be *necessary* in order for language acquisition to take place but none of them is sufficient to account for the emergence of language. In the next chapter, we will see how linguists have put this information into models that attempt to explain language development.

Summary

The physiological, cognitive, and social foundations of language acquisition were discussed in this chapter. Physiological development is a necessary prerequisite for language acquisition. However, physical development alone cannot explain the emergence of language. Children need something to talk about, and the exploration of their world that is part of cognitive development may provide that motivation. In addition, it is clear that parents and families actively provide socialization opportunities that encourage their children to interact in increasingly sophisticated ways.

REVIEW QUESTIONS

1. Describe the four major physiological processes that are required for sound production.

2. In most people, language is lateralized in the _____ hemisphere of the brain.

3. Describe the role of the right hemisphere in language processing.

4. Contrast Whorf's view of language and cognition with that of Piaget.

5. What does research indicate about the importance of social interaction for language acquisition?

SUGGESTED ACTIVITIES

1. Try making the following pairs of sounds:

    /f/   /v/
    /t/   /d/

    What is different about the sounds?

    Now try these:

    /t/   /n/
    /b/   /m/

    How do these differ?

2. Piaget described object permanence as a skill that developed over time in young children. Try this activity with children of different ages (say 2 and 4 years of age) to test object permanence:

   a. Find an object of interest to the child (e.g., a set of keys). Let the child play with the object for a few moments.

   b. Now, hide the object behind your back. What does the child do?

   c. Next, place the object in one hand and hold both hands out to the child. Ask the child to point to the hand that holds the object. Now, repeat, using the opposite hand.

   d. Continue, alternating hands. What do you observe?

3. Observe a parent and child (1 to 3 years old) in a natural setting in the home. You might ask the parent to provide some favorite toys for the child. Tape record and observe the interaction between the parent and child. As you observe, try to note what the parent and child are doing and any nonverbal interaction (gestures, facial expressions) that may be going on. Later, transcribe the tape. Try to write down *exactly* what each participant said. Analyze the tape for the following:

   a. Who takes the lead in the interaction?

   b. What does the parent do to alter spoken language to the child?

   c. What do the parent and child talk about?

GLOSSARY

articulation: shaping of the sound through impedence of airstream by the lips, tongue, and/or teeth

Broca's area: region of the cerebrum, located near the middle of the left cerebral hemisphere, where organization of the complex motor sequences necessary for speech production occur

central nervous system: major division of human nervous system that includes the brain and spinal cord

corpus callosum: bundle of fibers that connect the left and right hemispheres of the human brain

diaphragm: muscle separating the thorax and abdomen used in inhalation

distancing: in cognitive theory, the principle that involves the gradual movement away from actual physical experiences to symbolic or representational behavior

forebrain (cerebrum): region of the human brain that controls cognitive functions and language

hindbrain: region of the human brain that controls basic life functions such as respiration

larynx: structure in the neck that contains the vocal folds

manner of articulation: how a speech sound is produced

midbrain: region of the human brain that consists of structures that assist in relaying information to and from the brain and the visual and auditory nerves

object permanence: the idea that objects exist even when they are not being touched, tasted, or seen

peripheral nervous system: major division of the human nervous system that includes the nerves that carry messages to and from the extremities to the spinal cord and brain

place of articulation: where sound is formed in the mouth

voicing: presence or absence of the vocal cords' vibration during sound production

Wernicke's area: located close to the rear of the left cerebral hemisphere in the temporal lobe and is the area involved in the comprehension of language

RESOURCES ON THE WEB

www.nsf.gov/div/index.jsp?div=BCS   The National Science Foundation, Division on Social, Behavioral, and Economics research; information on current research in linguistics and neuroscience

www.neuropat.dote.hu   Provides links to information on neuroanatomy

www.aphasia.org   The National Aphasia Association; provides information on aphasia and links to other sites

www.piaget.org   The Jean Piaget Society; information about Piaget and recent research related to his theories of cognitive development

www.ohiou.edu/~scalsi   Language and social interaction division of the National Communication Association

REFERENCES

Anderson, N., & Shames, G. (2006). *Human communication disorders: An introduction* (7th ed.). Boston: Allyn & Bacon.

Chomsky, N. (1980). On cognitive structures and their development: A reply to Piaget. In M. Piattelli-Palmarini (Ed.), *Language and learning: The debate between Jean Piaget and Noam Chomsky* (pp. 35–52). Cambridge, MA: Harvard University Press.

Curtiss, S. (1977). *Genie: A psycholinguistic study of a modern-day "wild child."* New York: Academic Press.

Friederici, A. D. (2001). Syntactic, prosodic, and semantic processes in the brain: Evidence from event-related neuroimaging. *Journal of Psycholinguistic Research, 30,* 237–250.

Gardner, H. (1974). *The shattered mind.* New York: Random House.

Hart, B., & Risley, T. R. (1995). *Meaningful differences in the everyday experience of young American children.* Baltimore: Paul H. Brookes.

Hart, B., & Risley, T. R. (1999). *The social world of children learning to talk.* Baltimore: Paul H. Brookes.

Hickok, G. (2001). Functional anatomy of speech perception and speech production: Psycholinguistic implications. *Journal of Psycholinguistic Research, 30,* 225–235.

Hulit, L. M., & Howard, M. R. (2006). *Born to talk* (4th ed.). Boston: Allyn & Bacon.

Kent, R. D., & Vorperian, H. K. (2006). The biology and physics of speech. In N. B. Anderson & G.

H. Shames (Eds.), *Human communication disorders: An introduction* (7th ed.) (pp. 59–92). Boston: Allyn & Bacon.

Lenneberg, E. (1967). *Biological foundations of language.* New York: Wiley.

Menn, L., & Stoel-Gammon, C. (2005). Phonological developments learning sounds and sound patterns. In J. B. Gleason (Ed.), *The development of language* (6th ed.) (pp. 62–111). Boston: Allyn & Bacon.

Obler, L. (2005). Development in the adult years. In J. B. Gleason (Ed.), *The development of language* (6th ed.) (pp. 444–475). Boston: Allyn & Bacon.

Obler, L. K., & Gjerlow, K. (1999). *Language and the brain.* New York: Cambridge University Press.

Owens, R., Metz, D. E., & Haas, A. (2007). *Introduction to communication disorders* (3rd ed.). Boston: Allyn & Bacon.

Piaget. J. (1954). *The construction of reality in the child.* New York: Basic Books.

Pinker, S. (1994). *The language instinct: How the mind creates language.* New York: Morrow.

Sinclair-DeZwart, H. (1973). Language acquisition and cognitive development. In T. Moore (Ed.), *Cognitive development and the acquisition of language.* New York: Academic Press.

Vygotsky, L. (1962). *Thought and language.* Cambridge, MA: MIT Press.

Whorf, B. (1956). *Language, thought, and reality.* New York: Wiley.

4 Language Acquisition

Models

How do children acquire their first language? What motivates them to learn? These are questions that have challenged researchers in child language for many years.

This chapter presents theories of language acquisition, detailing how each theory explains the phenomenon of language acquisition and discussing both the contributions and limitations of each theory. Although no one model can fully explain the wonder of language acquisition, the effort to describe how children acquire language has helped us better understand the language-learning process and how we can help children with language and communication disorders.

After reading this chapter, you should be able to:

1. Understand the problems encountered in explaining language acquisition.
2. Describe five major theories of language acquisition and their limitations.
3. Explain the implications of the language-acquisition models for understanding the language acquisition of children.
4. Explain the implications of the language-acquisition models for understanding language disorders.

How do children acquire their first language? A satisfactory answer to this question has eluded linguists and psycholinguists (persons who study the relation of thought to language) for many years. The reason that this is such a difficult question lies with the phenomenon of language acquisition itself. Lindfors (1987) described the problem as follows:

> How are we to account for the fact that:
>> virtually every child
>> without special training
>> exposed to surface structures of language in many interaction contexts

builds for himself (in a short period of time and at an early stage in his cognitive development)
a deep-level, abstract, and highly complex system of linguistic structure and use.

In her statement of the problem, Lindfors challenges us to explain how it can be that *virtually every child* learns language. Not only do almost all children learn language but they also learn it at approximately the same rate. This is true, as Lindfors points out, whether children live on an isolated island or in an urban area, in primitive society or in a high-tech society. All children, no matter what their language, go through a series of very similar stages of language acquisition. As Guasti (2002) explains, regardless of their specific language, all children go through similar stages of early language development (babble; first words; multiword utterances) at about the same age.

Even more amazing is the fact that language acquisition goes on with *no direct training*. With the exception of children with significant disabilities, most children do not go to school to learn their first language. Remarkably, researchers have found that parents do not explicitly teach their children the structure of language. For example, we would hardly expect parents to begin teaching words that begin with the letter *a* and proceed through the alphabet to *z*. We would think there was something seriously wrong with parents who sat down with their 1-year-old child and said something like, "Now, the singular past tense form of the verb *be* is *was*." Rather than explicitly teaching their child, parents provide numerous opportunities for language to be used in daily interactions, responding even if their child makes a "mistake" (Hart & Risley, 1999).

What children hear from their parents is the **surface structure** of the language. They hear all the stops and starts, the ungrammatical sentences, and the colloquial and slang expressions that are a part of the language of normal conversation. Somehow, through this torrent of words, children discover the rules of language (the deep-level, abstract, and highly complex system). They do all this in a very short time (most of the important work is completed by age 5) and at a stage of cognitive development when, according to Piaget, they should not be able to form abstract rule systems at all.

This is the miracle of language acquisitions that linguists and psycholinguists have tried to explain. In developing their explanations (theories) of language acquisition, theorists have considered various factors that influence language acquisition and development:

- The linguistic environment
- Inherited abilities
- The individual's experiences
- The individual's opportunities for interaction
- The child's developing linguistic and cognitive abilities

Each of these factors has been emphasized in one of the major theories of language acquisition, and each contributes to the entire process of language acquisition. We will examine four theories or models of language acquisition. Each explains part of the phenomenon of language acquisition, but none alone gives a completely adequate explanation.

The Role of the Environment: The Behavioral Model

Most people's response to the question of how children learn language is that they learn it through imitation. When pressed to describe how this might occur, people will say that the child hears what the adult says and tries to imitate it. Cattell (2000) provides the following vignette to illustrate how this might happen:

> Mother leans over the crib and says to the baby, "Say 'Mum-Mum.'"
> After a few gurgles and splutters, the baby says something that sounds a bit like "Mum-Mum."
> Mother smiles warmly and repeats the game until the child is clearly saying "Mum-Mum."

In a very simplified form, this commonsense explanation is very similar to the actual process described in behavioral theories of language acquisition. This particular theory was set forth most completely by B. F. Skinner in his book *Verbal Behavior* (1957). As described by Skinner, the behavioral theory of language acquisition places a great deal of emphasis on the role of the environment in language acquisition. The child is seen as a relatively passive recipient of external influences—from parents, siblings, and others.

Language, according to behavioral theory, is learned like any other behavior. Children begin with no language. Gradually they begin to imitate (or model) sounds of those individuals to whom they are most frequently exposed. These individuals respond to the sound outputs (operants) by doing one of three things: reinforcing the verbal behavior *(Good!),* punishing the behavior *(Shut up!),* or ignoring the behavior. If reinforcement occurs, there is a good chance that the behavior in the child will occur again. If either of the other two responses happens, the likelihood of the verbal behavior recurring is reduced. Over time, as the child's verbal behavior is repeated, the parents (or others) become less responsive and force the child to produce a verbal output that is closer to the adult model (successive approximation). As Skinner put it, "Any response which vaguely resembles the standard behavior of the community is reinforced. When these begin to appear frequently, a closer approximation is insisted upon" (pp. 29–30). Eventually the child produces the adult word. Through the process of **chaining,** the child learns to string together several verbal behaviors to make an utterance. The actual process might go something like this:

MOTHER: See Daddy. There goes Daddy.

CHILD: *Da.*

MOTHER: Yes, there's Daddy.

　(Later)

MOTHER: Wave bye-bye to Daddy.

CHILD: Da Da.

MOTHER: Yes, that's right. There he goes.

　(Still later)

> **MOTHER:** Say good-bye to Daddy.
>
> **CHILD:** Bye-bye Da Da.
>
> **MOTHER:** Good girl.

Notice in this example how the initial simple response, "Da" becomes more fully formed ("Bye-bye Da Da") as Mother prompts a response. According to the behavioral theory, the mother is helping build a response chain in her child by reinforcing more complex language behaviors.

There is a good deal of support for the behavioral theory of language acquisition. This support comes both from structured research and from the less formal observations of parents and others. There *does* appear to be a process of imitation and reinforcement at work in the child's acquisition of language—at least for first words. Parents provide a model for these words and, when their child responds, they respond in turn with enthusiastic joy. Over time the child's verbal output does change in a way similar to that described by the theory—coming closer to the adult model. Moreover, there is a widespread belief that imitation is a critical component of language learning. Other support for the behavioral theory of language learning comes from work with people with disabilities that has claimed that children with significant language deficits can learn to acquire words through highly structured sequences based on a behavioral model (e.g., Lovaas, 1977, 1987).

There are, however, serious limitations to the behavioral explanation of language acquisition. First, the theory makes the wrong prediction about what children will learn—particularly the *order* of word acquisition. If imitation were the primary process involved in word acquisition, then one would expect that the child's first words would be those heard most frequently. In English the words *a* and *the* are the most frequently heard words. But these words are rarely, if ever, found in the language of young children. A second problem for this theory of language acquisition is its difficulty in explaining the phenomenon of *novel productions.* Young children have been found to use constructions that they have *never* heard previously. Children may say things like *I wented* when they want to use the past tense of *go* and *womans* when they want to pluralize the word *woman.* Behavioral theory alone does not account for novel productions such as these.

A third problem with the behavioral theory of language acquisition is that systematic observations of parents indicate that parents actually tend to *ignore* grammatical errors and are more concerned about the truth value of what their children say. For example, if a child says, "I eated ice cream at grandma's," the parents are more likely to respond, "No you didn't—you ate Jello," than to say, "No, we don't say *eated.* Say *ate*" (Brown & Hanlon, 1970; Hirsh-Pasek, Treiman, & Schneiderman, 1984). Behavioral theory also cannot account for the observation that comprehension usually precedes production of language in children—that is, children can understand words and sentences before they can produce them. If language learning occurs by a process of reinforcement for language production, then how can it be that children can understand language before they can produce it? What about the "evidence" derived from children with disabilities to talk using behavioral techniques? We will have more say about these studies later in the book, but at this point it is enough to say that even if children *can* be taught to imitate and acquire words through reinforcement, this does not mean that that is how they learn in natural environments.

Although behavioral theory is limited in its ability to explain all language acquisition, there is still some value to the theory. First, the theory highlights the essential role that parents and significant others play in the child's language learning. Second, the theory's description of the process of language learning, although flawed, has inspired others to develop alternative theories. Finally, the behavioral approach has been a successful tool in the development of intervention approaches to enhance the language skills of many persons with significant language disorders. For these reasons, it is important to know about the behavioral theory of language acquisition and to use the observations of behaviorists as one source of information for the language-intervention process.

The Role of Inheritance: The Linguistic (Nativist) Model

Chomsky (1968) and others developed the linguistic (or nativist) theory of language acquisition partly in response to the behavioral theory of language acquisition. In developing this theory, Chomsky noted several interesting phenomena. First, it seemed highly unlikely to him that 4-year-old children could have learned all the language they know simply by being exposed to it and remembering what they heard. The memory load required for such a feat would seem to be well beyond that available to a child. Second, Chomsky and others (e.g., Lenneberg, 1967) noted the *universality* of language. That is, they pointed out that language is learned by people of all cultures, in all environments, and in very similar stages. Moreover, language appears to be *unique* to humans—Kanzi and his cousins notwithstanding (see Box 1.1). Third, it seemed clear to Chomsky that children were doing more than memorizing chunks of language—they were also learning language *rules.* This point is evident in the cute but revealing mistakes that children make as they are learning language.

Putting these pieces of information together, Chomsky concluded that language must be innate (hence the *nativist* label). Language, according to Chomsky, is inborn in the human species—hardwired at birth. Babies are born ready to learn language. As Steven Pinker, one of Chomsky's followers, put it, "Language is not a cultural artifact that we learn the way we learn to tell time or how the federal government works. Instead, it a distinct piece of the biological makeup of our brains" (1994, p. 18).

Not only are children born ready to learn but they also possess a mechanism that Chomsky called the **language acquisition device (LAD),** which consists of basic grammatical categories and rules that are common to all languages. These basic rules might look something like the operating principles described by Slobin (1979) (see Figure 4.1). Alternatively, the LAD may consist of some inherent constraints and biases to respond to the language environment (Wexler, 1999).

In order for the LAD to operate, the child must merely be *exposed* to language. The quality of the adult language does not really matter nor do adults have to actively teach or reinforce language use. After a child's exposure to language input, according

FIGURE 4.1   Slobin's Operating Principles of Language

Principle A: Pay attention to the end of words.

Principle B: There are linguistic elements that encode relationships between words.

Principle C: Avoid exceptions.

Principle D: Underlying semantic relationships should be marked overtly and clearly.

Principle E: The use of grammatical markers should make semantic sense.

Source: Adapted from Slobin (1979).

to the theory, the child's LAD will take over to help him or her discover the underlying rules of language. Once the rules are mastered (and a certain amount of vocabulary is acquired), the child will be able to understand and produce language. The exact nature of the LAD and its physical location continues to be debated, but the idea that there is a built-in human mechanism for language acquisition continues to be a powerful theory.

The linguistic (nativist) theory addresses some of the unexplained phenomena associated with language acquisition. The nativist theory accounts for the fact that virtually all children learn language and do so without special training. The LAD model explains how children learn language rules merely by being exposed to language—that babies are programmed from birth to search out and discover the rules (generalizations) of language. The theory also accounts for the speed with which language is acquired, since it points out that children are able to process language rules right from birth.

Although the linguistic (nativist) model helps us understand many of the phenomena of language acquisition, there are some significant limitations to this theory. One of the most troublesome is the diminished role given to language input. In Wexler's (1999) view, language is not learned but develops due to the maturation of a genetic program for language learning. We will see later that recent investigations of parent–child interactions have found that parents alter their language for their children in systematic ways—simplifying and clarifying. If mere exposure to language were all that was needed for language acquisition, why would parents continue to go to the trouble of altering their language for children? In addition, there is evidence that, although parents may not be explicitly teaching language rules, they do correct their child's language "errors" by modeling the correct structure (Bohannon & Stanowicz, 1988; Bohannon, MacWhinney, & Snow, 1990; Bohannon, Padgett, Nelson, & Mark, 1996).

A second problem stems from the theoretical underpinnings of the model itself. Chomsky was interested in explaining the acquisition of *syntax* in children. He was much less interested in explaining the acquisition of the other elements of language. Although the theory adequately explains the acquisition of syntax, it does not account for the child's acquisition of semantic, morphophonological, or pragmatic rules.

Finally, the linguistic (nativist) theory poses a dilemma to those who are interested in helping children improve their language performance, as it seems to suggest that there is little hope for children experiencing significant difficulty with language.

[handwritten note in margin: "meaning of this?"]

If language is innate, perhaps these children have an innate ability to learn language. However, we know from experience supported by research that it is possible to enhance language skills. Therefore, there must be more to language learning than this biological component.

Chomsky's development of a model of language acquisition essentially marks the start of the field of *psycholinguistics*—the study of the psychology of language. His theories sparked a flood of research on language learning that continues to this day. Some of the subsequent research has supported Chomsky's claims, but some has supported competing theories of language acquisition. Although the nativist model is a no more complete explanation of language acquisition than the behavioral theory, it too has made an important contribution by addressing some of the most challenging questions about language learning and by advancing our knowledge about language and language acquisition.

The Role of the Environment: The Semantic-Cognitive Model

"Mommy, sock." These two words helped lead Lois Bloom (1970) to contribute to a new interpretation of child language acquisition. Bloom had observed a child using this expression on two occasions. One time, the child used this expression to note that the sock belonged to her mother (possessive). The second time, she appeared to be making a request (e.g., "Put my sock on, Mommy"). Although we do not know precisely what the child meant to say, it is clear from this context that the same words were being used to express two different meanings. Observations such as these led Bloom to conclude that semantics precedes syntax in child language acquisition. In other words, children develop syntax because they already have something to talk about rather than because they have the grammar to express themselves. In this case the child used one syntactic form ("Mommy, sock") to express two semantic functions (possessive and requesting).

The semantic-cognitive model of language acquisition was developed from evidence such as the above, as well as from linguistic and cognitive theory. At about the same time Bloom was conducting her observations of children, Fillmore (1968) was publishing his ideas about the role of semantics in language structure. Fillmore noted that the selection of a word to be used in a sentence is determined more by the *meaning* of the sentence than by the syntactic structure of the sentence. Thus, in a sentence such as *The _____ hit the ball,* rules of syntax tell us that the word that goes in the blank must be a noun, but semantics tells us that only certain nouns will do. The word *boy* or *girl* would be fine but *clock* or *desk* would not do. Fillmore's theory—case grammar—forced linguists to rethink their assumptions about the relationship between syntax and semantics.

While Fillmore's and Bloom's work focused on the role of semantics in language acquisition, the Swiss cognitive psychologist Jean Piaget was interested in the relationship between cognition (thought) and language. Piaget did not propose a theory of language development as such, but his work was seen as implying that language development is secondary to cognitive development. According to Piaget (1954), language is but one of many symbol systems. Also, according to Piaget and his associates (chiefly Sinclair-deZwart), cognitive developments such as object permanence must precede language development.

The combined influences of Fillmore's case grammar, Piaget's cognitive theories, and observations by researchers such as Bloom led to the development of the semantic-cognitive theory of language acquisition. This theory gives preeminence to the semantic aspect of language. The theory proposes that young children pay particular attention to the *meanings* of things. When they use language, they do so to talk *about* something they have already experienced. In other words, the experience comes first, then the language follows. According to this theory, syntax develops as the result of the need to talk about more and more things or experiences. In addition, certain cognitive accomplishments must take place before language can be acquired at all.

Like the other language-acquisition theories we have reviewed, the semantic-cognitive theory has some strong support. It seems logical that children will talk when they have something to talk *about.* As they acquire more experiences, they need more sophisticated language to express their ideas. In addition, there is evidence that certain cognitive development steps usually do precede the emergence of language. This theory helps explain why children tend to talk about the same kinds of things no matter what their socioeconomic background and environment.

The semantic-cognitive theory also has its shortcomings. Like the nativist theory, the semantic-cognitive model gives little attention to the role of input language. These theoretical models would have us believe that adult input matters little, if at all. A second problem is that the relationship between cognition and language is not as simple as Piaget claimed. Some children attain the cognitive prerequisites for language but do not develop language skills. Other children are more advanced in language than would be predicted by their cognitive skills. Therefore, it may not be essential for cognitive development to precede language.

Like the other language-acquisition models, the semantic-cognitive model has made important contributions to our understanding of language acquisition. It has forced theorists to look beyond syntax and to consider other aspects of language development. It has also had an impact on intervention practices, as we will see later. However, like the other models, although it has contributed pieces to the puzzle, it does not solve the entire enigma of language acquisition.

The Role of Communication: The Pragmatic-Interactionist Model

The pragmatic-interactionist model of language acquisition is based on a very simple observation—people talk in order to communicate. Therefore, the model places greatest emphasis on the communicative function of language. According to this theory, language development takes place as children learn to choose the linguistic form that will best express their communicative intent.

This model is grounded in two areas of research. On the one hand, linguists such as Searle (1965), and later Dore (1974) and Halliday (1975), began to identify and classify the rules of pragmatics. At the same time, psychologists and psycholinguists such as Bruner (1975) and Bates (1976) were observing and describing communication between parents and their children. These two areas of research—theoretical and applied—came together in the pragmatic-interactionist model of language acquisition.

An additional stimulus to the development of this model was the identification of a phenomenon called "motherese" or "parentese" (Newport, 1976; Newport, Gleitman, & Gleitman, 1977), or, more accurately, *child-directed speech (CDS)* (Bohannon, 2005). A number of researchers have observed that parents (and other adults) tend to alter their language in the presence of young children. These alterations include using shorter and less complex sentences, slowing the rate of their speech, using a more limited range of semantic functions, and engaging in shorter conversations (see Chapter 3). These differences have been found across languages (Fernald, 1983). Moreover, there is evidence that children who are abused and neglected and, as a consequence, receive less language interaction from their caregivers, are delayed in both receptive and expressive language (Culp, Watkins, Lawrence, Letts, Kelly, & Rice, 1991).

It is hypothesized that parents make changes in their language because they somehow intuitively know that children need this in order to learn language. In any case, children are more responsive when language is adjusted to their level. At the same time, babies have an important role in communicative interaction as well. Researchers have found that babies whose mothers followed their children's communicative lead understood more words than babies of mothers who tried to be more intrusive (Golinkoff & Hirsh-Pasek, 2000).

According to Bruner (1977), adjustments in adult language such as those described previously provide the framework, or *scaffolding,* for language development. By engaging in communication with their parents (and other significant adults), children learn that language can be used for communication and they indirectly pick up structural aspects of language. Communication—especially repetitive, routine communication—makes it possible for children to hear and model the adult language forms.

Like the behavioral model, the pragmatic-interactionist model of language acquisition puts a great deal of emphasis on events that take place in the environment around the child. Children learn language by being exposed to language. Unlike the behavioral model, however, the pragmatic-interactionist model does *not* claim that overt reinforcement is necessary in order for language to be acquired. Instead, it is similar to the nativist model in acknowledging the role of physiological maturation in determining the level of communicative interaction that can be handled by the child. The pragmatic-interactionist model can be seen as an attempt to account for both the role of the environment (nurture) and the role of biological processes (nature) in language development.

The pragmatic-interactionist model of language acquisition has much going for it. Any parent can attest to the fact that young children can communicate their needs long before they have the language to express themselves. This supports the claims of the pragmatic-interactionist model that communication precedes language. Moreover, there is evidence that children who have limited opportunities for interaction with adults have more difficulty acquiring language.

One of the limitations of the pragmatic-interactionist model, though, is in how it accounts for the acquisition of specific syntactic structures. In other words, why do almost all children follow the same sequence of language development at about the same time? If children rely primarily on the adults in their environment for language input, then it would be logical to expect that both the quality and quantity of input (and thus the child's output) would vary widely. Yet, this is not the case. Clearly there must be other factors at work. There is also limited research on just how much interaction is needed to stimulate language development. Is there a minimum amount? Is there an optimal amount? Until these questions are answered, we cannot be sure about the role of communicative interaction in early language development.

The pragmatic-interactionist model of language learning is relatively new, yet it has had a significant influence on language-intervention techniques. Today, many clinicians are emphasizing the importance of engaging children in communication—especially in repetitive, routine interactions. Rather than breaking language down into small parts and teaching each part, some clinicians are using indirect methods of language stimulation, stressing the wholeness of language and the essential role of communication in the language-learning process.

The Role of Learning: The Information-Processing Model

Information-processing models attempt to explain how learning takes place. These models originated as a way to develop machine-based learning (i.e., computers). Later, they were adapted to be applied to human learning.

Theories of **information processing** provide a more complete picture of what happens during language interaction. One of the key factors is attention. It is attention that drives the information-processing system. Imagine a lecture that contains a lot of technical terms (perhaps on the topic of neurophysiology). In this case, your attention is likely to be focused on understanding individual words, and the larger meaning may be lost. If, however, you read the text prior to the class, you might be able to focus your attention on the application of the words to understanding the topic. If you were very familiar with the content, your attention might be focused outside the classroom and you would merely monitor the classroom presentation, perhaps refocusing your attention if called on by the instructor. Attention enables you to discriminate information in short-term memory and to transfer and retrieve information from long-term memory. According to information-processing theory, metacognition guides the entire process. Metacognition is the ability to reflect on decision making and includes activities such as how much time and attention to devote to a task and how to evaluate whether a task is completed (see Figure 4.2). During language processing, the information-processing apparatus is at work, taking in new information and relating it to previously stored knowledge. Clearly, language processing is a very complex activity. Considering the speed with which all of this is happening, it is truly an amazing feat.

In an attempt to explain the phenomenal speed of information processing, researchers have developed a theory called **parallel** or **simultaneous processing.** The information-processing model of language processing previously discussed is a serial model—that is, it assumes that there is a hierarchy of steps. One step must be completed before the next takes place. But with parallel processing, several levels of analysis may take place simultaneously, thus speeding up the system. It is likely that both

FIGURE 4.2   A Schematic Model of Information Processing

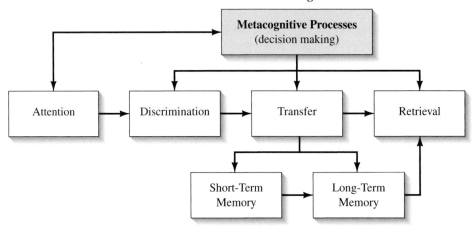

types of processing are at work in the human brain. Words that are unfamiliar may require more analysis and may be handled through serial processing, whereas more familiar words may be processed in a parallel manner.

The information-processing model of learning has been applied to language acquisition by psycholinguists such as Elizabeth Bates and Bryan MacWhinney in their competition model of language acquisition (Bates & MacWhinney, 1987). According to this model, language structures emerge from the comunicative functions that drive language acquisition. There are multilayered connections between these functions and the linguistic forms that are used to express the function. The information-processing system, operating in a parallel processing mode, makes matches between form and function. Over time, the matches that are most consistent with the language evidence the child is experiencing win out (thus, the "competition" model). These matches remain in the child's communication system.

The information-processing model has helped in understanding the complexity of the relationship between cognition and language. It recognizes that the processing of complex information is rarely done in a serial (step-by-step) manner. Instead, many levels of learning take place simultaneously. Thus, children are not only learning syntax but they are also learning meaning, and are doing so in the context of communication (pragmatics) at the same time. This model attempts to account for these many levels of learning,

Although the information-processing model has provided another view of language learning, research evidence for the operation of the model in children is limited. Most of the research thus far has been with adults or with theoretical language-processing models. In addition, the model does not appear to be able to account for the role of social interaction in language learning (Bohannon, 2005).

Conclusion

Perhaps it is not possible to completely account for the phenomena of language development described at the beginning of this chapter. Although such a conclusion may seem discouraging, it may be that what is important is the search for answers itself. As a result of this search, our ideas about language have been clarified and the debate about language learning has been sharpened. Additionally, the search for answers has led to the development of language intervention methods.

Implications for Language Intervention

Each of the language acquisition models has implications for language intervention. The *behavioral theory* of language acquisition suggests that language is learned just like any other behavior; that is, the processes of imitation, modeling, and reinforcement are critical components in the child's acquisition of language. In the behavioral model, teachers choose specific, discrete language behaviors as the focus of instruction and, through assessment, determine that the child has acquired the prerequisite skills. The child is *prompted* to make a response *(Say, "I want a cookie")* and is *reinforced* for making a correct response *(Good talking!)*. Instruction continues until mastery of the skill is achieved.

The *psycholinguistic theory* of language acquisition places most of its emphasis on biological development, on the idea that language emerges as the individual develops. Although there is little that teachers can do to directly influence biological maturation, they may still apply the psycholinguistic model to language instruction. First, this theory suggests using *developmental guidelines* for instructional goals, and second, that instruction should focus on *rule learning*. According to the psycholinguistic theory, the most important developments in early language learning involve the acquisition of the underlying rules of language. Instruction that helps children become aware of language rules, discover underlying rules, and apply these rules in new situations is most useful.

Using the *semantic-cognitive model* of language learning as a guide to teaching language involves focusing on the acquisition of cognitive prerequisites to language and on the development of semantic concepts. As discussed earlier in this chapter, some theorists (e.g., Piaget) claim that certain cognitive prerequisites (e.g., object permanence) must precede the emergence of spoken language. If children lack these prerequisites, it may be necessary to help them acquire the necessary skills. Although there has been much debate as to whether it is possible to teach cognitive skills, many researchers believe it is possible to help children who are ready to take the next step do so just a bit more quickly. The formal name for this idea is the *zone of proximal development*. As proposed by Vygotsky (1962), the notion is that when children are just at the edge of developing a new skill, experiences and instruction can help them take this step. In addition to its helping children develop cognitive prerequisites, the semantic-cognitive model suggests that language learning can be facilitated by the development of new semantic concepts. When children have something to talk about, the theory suggests, they will find a way to express their new ideas.

The *pragmatic-interactionist model* implies that the goal of language intervention should be to enhance communication. Children should be encouraged to interact with parents, peers, and teachers. Language facilitators should be responsive to the child, letting the child take the lead in language interaction by setting the conversational topic.

Finally, the *information-processing model* has been helpful in understanding the learning difficulties of children with learning disabilities. According to the model, learning difficulties can be caused by dysfunction at one or more levels of the system or in the connections between levels. In addition, the model helps us understand the important role that attention plays in learning. The implications for language learning are clear. Some children may lack specific language skills, and some may have differences or delays in cognitive processing that may interfere with their understanding and/or use of language.

Each of these models of language acquisition has contributed to the development of intervention methods. Yet none, by itself, appears to be an adequate model for intervention. In later sections of this book we will see how these models have been applied to enhance the language performance of children with disabilities and to guide classroom practice.

Summary

Language acquisition is a complex, wondrous, and still somewhat mysterious phenomenon. Five theories of language acquisition: behavioral, linguistic (nativist), semantic-cognitive, pragmatic-interactionist, and information processing were presented in this chapter (see Table 4.1). The support, both theoretical and observed, for each of

TABLE 4.1   Major Models of Language Acquisition

Model	Principles	Limitations
Behavioral	Language learned through imitation and reinforcement	Makes wrong predictions about word acquisition
	Language learned like other behaviors	Cannot explain novel utterances
	Parents reinforce meaning, not structure	
	Comprehension precedes production	
Linguistic (Nativist)	Inborn ability for language	What is role of input?
	Language acquisition device (LAD)	What about parts of language other than syntax?
Semantic-Cognitive (Filmore)	Meaning precedes structure	What is role of input?
	Same utterance can have multiple meanings (Bloom)	Relationship of cognition and language very complex
	Cognition precedes language (Piaget)	
Pragmatic-Interactionist	Need to communicate precedes language structures	How to account for specific structures
	Parents alter language for their child	What about child's role?
Information Processing	Language structures emerge from communicative functions	Limited research evidence
	Individual matches form to function	Cannot account for role of social interactor

these models was presented, as were shortcomings of the models. Each of these models has contributed something to our knowledge of language acquisition, yet none of them can completely account for the remarkable achievement that we call language.

REVIEW QUESTIONS

1. A child says, "I goded to the store." What does an utterance such as this suggest about the role of imitation in child language? What does it indicate about rule learning?

2. Chomsky proposed that children have an innate linguistic mechanism that he called a *language acquisition device.* What is the LAD? What does the LAD do?

3. What is the significance of Bloom's discovery that her child said "Mommy, sock"?

4. What are two limitations of the behavioral theory of language acquisition?

5. Match the language-acquisition model to the name of the researcher associated with that model by filling in the number of your answer next to the model:

   ___ Psycholinguistic   1. Skinner

   ___ Pragmatic-interactionist   2. Bloom

   ___ Semantic-cognitive   3. Chomsky

   ___ Behavioral   4. Bruner

SUGGESTED ACTIVITIES

1. In order to test whether receptive language does, in fact, precede expressive language, find a child (12 to 18 months old) who is just beginning to use expressive language. Ask the child's parent to choose five toys or objects that the child likes to play with or uses frequently. Place the child on the floor with the objects between yourself and the child. Say:

    (Child's Name), touch the *(Object 1)*

    (Child's Name), pick up the *(Object 2)*

    (Child's Name), get the *(Object 3)*

    Continue like this through the five objects. Now, ask the child to name each object.

    a. What happened? Did the child respond correctly when asked to touch the objects? Was the child able to say the name of each object?

    b. What do the results indicate about the child's language abilities?

    c. What do the results suggest about thought and language?

2. To determine if you can teach a new syntactic structure to a child, try this activity with a 3-year-old.

    First, teach the child to name an object that is unfamiliar to him or her (for example, a wrench). Show the object, tell the child what it is, then ask the child to repeat it.

    Now, show a picture of the object to the child. Can the child identify the picture? Next, try this with your object:

    Say: *Here is a* _____ (e.g., *wrench*). Then add a second object.

    Say: *Now I have two. I have two* _____ (use the plural).

Ask the child to repeat the phrase.

Now show the child two other objects and see if the child correctly uses the plural form. What do you think would happen if you showed two deer? What are the implications for how children acquire language?

3. Try this activity with a child about 5 years old:

Say: *I am going to read you a sentence, then I am going to ask you to tell me which of two words should go in the sentence:*

The _____ hit the ball (desk/boy).

I saw a _____ swimming in the ocean (fish/car).

The _____ looked at me (dog/train).

Ask the child to tell you why he or she chose the word. Then ask the child to help you create some more "silly sentences." What do the results indicate about the acquisition of language?

4. Tape-record someone (a parent, roommate) talking to a dog. Listen to the recording. Can you detect any elements of "parentese"? What do the results indicate?

GLOSSARY

chaining: according to behavioral theory, the process of learning to put together several verbal behaviors to create an utterance

information processing: contemporary model of human cognition that emphasizes the interconnectedness of cognitive processes

language acquisition device (LAD): consists of basic grammatical categories and rules that are common to all languages

parallel processing: a theory of information processing that suggests that multiple levels of information can be processed simultaneously

surface structure: language heard during an utterance

RESOURCES ON THE WEB

www.pbs.org/wnet/brain/episode2/babytalk/index.html Example of "parentese"

www.literacytrust.org.uk/talktoyourbaby/theories.html Information about theories of language development

REFERENCES

Bates, E. (1976). *Language and context: The acquisition of pragmatics.* New York: Academic Press.

Bates, E., & MacWhinney, B. (1987). Competition, variation, and language learning. In B. MacWhinney (Ed.), *Mechanisms of language acquisition* (pp. 157–194). Hillsdale, NJ: Erlbaum.

Bloom, L. (1970). *Language development: Form and function of emerging grammars.* Cambridge, MA: MIT Press.

Bohannon, J. (2005). Theoretical approaches to language acquisition. In J. B. Gleason (Ed.), *The development of language* (6th ed.) (pp. 230–291). Boston: Allyn & Bacon.

Bohannon, J., MacWhinney, B., & Snow, C. E. (1990). Negative evidence revisited: Beyond learnability or who has to prove what to whom? *Developmental Psychology, 26,* 221–226.

Bohannon, J., Padgett, R., Nelson, K. E., & Mark, M. (1996). Useful evidence on negative evidence. *Developmental Psychology, 32,* 551–555.

Bohannon, J., & Stanowicz, L. (1988). Adult responses to children's language errors: The issue of negative evidence. *Developmental Psychology, 24,* 684–689.

Brown, R., & Hanlon, C. (1970). Derivational complexity and order of acquisition. In J. Hayes (Ed.), *Cognition and the development of language.* New York: Wiley.

Bruner, J. (1975). The ontogenesis of speech acts. *Journal of Child Language, 2,* 1–19.

Bruner, J. (1977). Early social interaction and language acquisition. In R. Schaffer (Ed.), *Studies in mother-infant interaction.* New York: Academic Press.

Cattell, R. (2000). *Children's language: Consensus and controversy.* New York: Cassell.

Chomsky, N. (1968). *Language and mind.* New York: Harcourt, Brace, & World.

Culp, R., Watkins, R., Lawrence, H., Letts, D., Kelly, D., & Rice, M. (1991). Maltreated children's language and speech development: Abused, neglected, and abused and neglected. *First Language, 11,* 377–389.

Dore, J. (1974). A pragmatic description of early language development. *Journal of Psycholinguistic Research, 3,* 343–350.

Fernald, A. (1983). The sound of meaning in early mother-infant interaction. In L. Feagans, K. Garvey, & R. Golinkoff (Eds.), *The origins and growth of communication.* Norwood, NJ: Ablex.

Fillmore, C. (1968). The case for case. In E. Bach & R. Harmas (Eds.), *Universals in linguistic theory* (pp. 1–88). New York: Holt, Rinehart and Winston.

Golinkoff, R. M., & Hirsh-Pasek, K. (2000). *How babies talk.* New York: Plume.

Guasti, M. T. (2002). *Language acquisition: The growth of grammar.* Cambridge, MA: MIT Press.

Halliday, M. (1975). *Learning how to mean: Explorations in the development of language.* New York: Arnold.

Hart, B., & Risley, T. R. (1999). *The social world of children learning to talk.* Baltimore: Paul H. Brookes.

Hirsh-Pasek, K., Treiman, R., & Schneiderman, M. (1984). Brown and Hanlon revisited: Mother's sensitivity to ungrammatical forms. *Journal of Child Language, 11,* 81–88.

Lenneberg, E. (1967). *Biological foundations of language.* New York: Wiley.

Lindfors, J. (1987). *Children's language and learning.* Englewood Cliffs, NJ: Prentice-Hall.

Lovaas, O. I. (1977). *The autistic child: Language development through behavior modification.* New York: Irvington.

Lovaas, O. I. (1987). Behavioral treatment and normal educational and intellectual functioning in young autistic children. *Journal of Consulting and Clinical Psychology, 55,* 3–9.

Newport, E. (1976). Motherese: The speech of mothers to young children. In J. Castellan, D. Pisoni, & G. Potts (Eds.), *Cognitive theory* (Vol. 2). Hillsdale, NJ: Erlbaum.

Newport, E., Gleitman, A., & Gleitman, L. (1977). Mother I'd rather do it myself: Some effects and non-effects of maternal speech style. In C. Snow & C. Ferguson (Eds.), *Talking to children: Language input and acquisition* (pp. 109–149). New York: Cambridge University Press.

Piaget. J. (1954). *The construction of reality in the child.* New York: Basic Books.

Pinker, S. (1994). *The language instinct: How the mind creates language.* New York: Morrow.

Searle, J. (1965). What is a speech act? In M. Black (Ed.), *Philosophy in America* (pp. 221–239). New York: Allen & Unwin; Cornell University Press.

Sinclair-DeZwart, H. (1973). Language acquisition and cognitive development. In T. Moore (Ed.), *Cognitive development and the acquisition of language.* New York: Academic Press.

Skinner, B. F. (1957). *Verbal behavior.* New York: Appleton-Century-Crofts.

Slobin, D. (1979). *Psycholinguistics* (2nd ed.). Glenview, IL: Scott, Foresman.

Vygotsky, L. (1962). *Thought and language.* Cambridge, MA: MIT Press.

Wexler, K. (1999). Maturation and growth of grammar. In W. Ritchie & T. Bhatia (Eds.), *Handbook of child language acquisition* (pp. 55–110). New York: Academic Press.

5 Language Development

Birth through the Preschool Years

Language development, from birth through the preschool years, is described in this chapter. Beginning with a description of the early communicative attempts of newborns and the role of parents and other caregivers, the chapter examines the emergence of language and development in the preschool years, describing the stages of syntactic, semantic, and pragmatic development. The relationship between early language development and the emergence of literacy skills is examined and discussed.

After reading this chapter, you should be able to:

1. Describe the development of communicative skills in the newborn.
2. Understand the role of parents and other caregivers in the development of early communicative interactions.
3. Describe the stages of language development in the preschool years.
4. Understand the various perspectives on the emergence of semantic abilities.
5. Understand the relationship between language development and the emergence of literacy skills.

Having examined the physiological, cognitive, and social bases for language development, we are ready to turn our attention to describing the course of language development itself. For those interested in understanding and teaching children with language disorders, knowledge of patterns of language development is important. Imagine what it would be like if you had no idea about the progression of language development. Where would you begin teaching? What would you teach? What would you teach next? What examples would you use? How would you develop reasonable goals for instruction? Gaining knowledge of language development is the best way to answer these questions.

Before we begin to examine the course of language development in children, a note of caution is in order. There is wide variation in "typical" language development. Young children develop at different speeds and in different ways. When we refer to ages in this (and other) chapters, we really mean the *average age* at which a structure or function develops. It is important to understand that there is a range of typical development around this average and that children sometimes follow individual patterns of development. Parents and teachers are often concerned if children do not adhere closely to the "norm." They are right to be concerned, but their concern should be tempered by an understanding of the variability of child development. However, when a child deviates significantly from the typical developmental sequence, it is important to intervene as early as possible. Therefore, a knowledge of language development is essential for understanding typical development and for recognizing deviations from the norm.

Prelinguistic Development

Birth to Age 6 Months

The traditional view of infant development is that babies come into the world as a "blank slate," ready to be filled with experiences that will guide their development through childhood to become fully functioning adults. However, research conducted during the past few decades has seriously challenged this traditional view of early childhood. We now understand that infants are born ready to learn in many ways. They are not merely passive recipients of information from their environment. They are active learners who influence and even shape their environment. Even during this prelinguistic stage, when babies do not exhibit what we would call language, they are developing the necessary prerequisites to the emergence of language.

Newborns have been found to have some surprising language (comprehension) abilities. For example, they are able to distinguish their mothers' voices from those of other women (De Casper & Fifer, 1980) and can discriminate between languages. In one study, French babies who were played samples of French and Japanese speech sounds listened more attentively to the French, indicating that they recognized the language they were hearing in their environment (Nazzi, Bertoncini, & Mehler, 1998). Of course, if these babies had been exposed to Japanese, they would have showed a preference for that language. Using a technique called high-amplitude sucking, in which the frequency of sucking to stimuli is measured, researchers have found that infants as young as 1 month old can discriminate speech sound differences such as *pa* and *ba* (Eimas, Siqueland, Jusczyk, & Vigorito, 1971). Findings such as these have led some researchers to suggest that speech recognition may take place even before birth (De Casper & Spence, 1986). In this study, if the pregnant mother recited to her fetus before birth, the newborn showed a preference for these auditory patterns.

Early Communicative Interaction. From the moment of birth, and perhaps even before birth, babies communicate. Ask a pregnant woman. She is likely to tell you that her baby is telling her when he or she is awake or asleep, uncomfortable or agitated, from the movement and kicking the expectant mother experiences. This does not mean that the fetus *intends* to communicate these things, but the mere fact that mothers-to-be *interpret* the actions as communicative helps set the stage for the coming communicative interaction between mother (and father and others) and child.

How does this communicative interaction take place? Despite their limited repertoire of behavior, newborns engage their parents (and other family members) in a variety of ways. They move their head in response to the human voice. Their eyes widen and body tension increases in anticipation of attention from their caregiver. Through their wakefulness, fussiness, or other signs, infants let their parents know when they are tired or when they are ready for interaction. After a few weeks, *interactional sequences* begin to develop. The infant gazes at his or her caregiver's face and the caregiver responds with a smile and/or some comforting words (Owens, 2005). Feeding can be a wonderful interactional opportunity. The baby sucks and pauses, then gazes at her or his caregiver, who responds with a smile or a touch. The infant responds by resuming sucking. These sorts of interactions evolve into a give-and-take that begins to resemble conversational turn-taking with initiation and response (Sachs, 2005).

Vocalizations are also part of early communicative interaction. At first, most infants' sound productions are **reflexive** in nature—burps, gurgles, and other sounds that are responses to physical states. But parents respond to these vocal productions as if they were meaningful communication (Murray & Trevarthen, 1986). Look at this exchange between an English mother and her 3-month-old daughter (Ann) as described by Catherine Snow (1977):

ANN: (smiles)

MOTHER: Oh what a nice little smile.

     Yes, isn't that nice?

     There. That's a nice little smile.

ANN: (burps)

MOTHER: What a nice little wind as well!

Notice how the mother responds to her daughter's behaviors as if they were meaningful. She engages her daughter in conversational interaction (even if the conversation itself is one way). Parents typically claim that they can identify the meaning of their child's crying. They will say that their child is hungry, or wants to be changed, or is lonely. Parents may or not be accurate in identifying the meaning of their child's crying. That seems to be less important than the fact that their child's vocalizations initiate a response by the parent. In their intensive study of language development, Hart and Risley (1999) reported that long before children began saying words, they had learned essential skills of interaction such as getting and holding their parents' attention, taking turns, and maintaining interaction.

As infants move through the first six months of life, their vocal repertoire increases from reflexive sounds to cooing and babbling. At first, these are mostly vowel-like sounds. Try opening your mouth and saying, "ah." The sound produced is similar to what infants of 2 to 4 months produce. Although this may not seem like a particularly significant event, it is important because the baby is gaining control over his or her sound-production apparatus. These early sounds are the result of control of the flow of air. In addition, as the baby progresses through this stage, these sounds are increasingly produced in response to the caregiver. This is the very beginning of vocal interaction.

Somewhere between 3 and 6 months of age, babies begin to babble. Consonant sounds begin to enter the baby's vocalizations. It is as if the baby is playing with sounds. There is a common belief that babies babble all of the sounds of every language, gradually filtering out those sounds that are not actually heard in their language. However, Menn and Stoel-Gammon (2005) point out that research has found that, rather than producing every sound, babies babble a limited set of sounds—especially those that appear earlier in speech development. Children across language groups tend to produce similar sounds—some that are part of their language and some that are not. Over time, the sounds that are not part of their language are used less frequently and eventually drop out altogether (Vihman, 1992).

Parental Language Input. Our focus so far has been on the infant's role in early interaction but, of course, parents play an essential role as well. Not only do parents respond in nonverbal ways to their child (by smiling, holding, stroking) but also they talk to their baby differently from the way they talk to other people. This baby talk (sometimes called "motherese" or, more formally, "child-directed speech") is much more than "goo-goo" and "gah-gah." It is a systematic alteration in the way that parents speak to their baby. It is natural, spontaneous, and appears across a variety of cultures (Fernald, 1992; Matsaka, 1992).

Parents do not talk to their young children in the same way that they talk to older children and adults. They make a number of modifications in the way they talk, including reducing the length and complexity of their language, using a greater range of pitch in their voices, and using more limited vocabulary (Newport, Gleitman, & Gleitman, 1977, Sachs, 2005) (see Figure 5.1). These alterations have been found across a variety of languages.

In addition to making alterations to the sound of their voices, parents alter their vocal interactions to their young children in other ways. For example, they tend to pronounce labels for objects more distinctly, using exaggerated stress and higher pitch; use a high number of questions and greetings; and tend to talk about things that are present

FIGURE 5.1   Characteristics of Child-Directed Speech (Motherese)

Higher overall pitch; greater range of pitch

Exaggerated intonation and stress

Slower speech

More restricted vocabulary

More reference to here and now

Fewer broken or run-on sentences

Fewer complex sentences

More questions and imperatives

Shorter conversations

in the immediate environment. The following sample is taken from a real interaction between a mother and her 21-month-old daughter:

MOTHER: Hi baby. Want some lunch? (takes child from crib)

CHILD: Yunch! (arms outstretched to mother)

MOTHER: Would you like some turkey and cheese?

CHILD: Chee! Mmm! Cuppy? Cuppy?

MOTHER: Yes, honey, you can have your cuppy. Do you want juice or milk?

CHILD: Mook? Mook! (clapping and smiling)

MOTHER: Mommy loves you. You're such a happy baby!

CHILD: Happy. Monkey? Monkey? (looking around).

MOTHER: Where's monkey? Did you leave him upstairs?

CHILD: Up? Monkey?

What do you notice about this conversation? First, the mother is taking the lead in directing the conversation, asking questions to prompt her child to respond. But that is not always true. Note how the child requests her cup and how, toward the end of the interaction, the child changes the topic to request her monkey. Note, too, the length of the mother's utterances. They are short and simple, both in vocabulary and in sentence structure. This is clearly a rich interaction in which each partner takes an important role in the conversation.

Young children are highly responsive to talk directed to them. Studies have shown that babies prefer baby-talk patterns, even when they are only 2 days old (Cooper & Aslin, 1990). Research has also found that infants may be responding primarily to positive affect (rather than to pitch). In one study, parents spoke to their children using either baby talk or adultlike talk. In the adult-talk condition, parents used a positive affect but they did not do so in the baby-talk phase. The researchers found that babies were more responsive to positive affect (Singh, Morgan, & Best, 2002). Similar results have been found with depressed mothers. One research study revealed that depressed mothers used less exaggerated speech to their children and that babies actually responded better to unfamiliar mothers who were not depressed (Kaplan, Bachorowski, Smoski, & Hudenko, 2002).

As we noted in Chapter 4, experts in child language acquisition differ in the importance they place on parents' language input to their young child. Chomsky (1968) and his followers believe that parental input is of little importance to language learning. They point out that parents rarely correct their child's syntactic productions, instead responding to everything as if it was correct. On the other hand, the interactionist perspective is that these early language-based interactions play a critical role in later language learning. According to this perspective, parents teach their child that communication is important and meaningful. Early communicative interaction provides the basis for pragmatic and semantic development and may even provide the examples and modeling that children need to develop syntax (Bohannon & Stanowicz, 1988).

Although the debate over the significance of parent input is likely to continue, there are some conclusions that we can draw. First, so-called baby talk is not harmful. Unfortunately, there are some parents who believe that if they talk to their babies in adultlike modes right from the beginning, their child will learn language faster and be "smarter." The research evidence suggests just the opposite. Young children benefit from engaging in early interaction with parents who speak to them in the characteristic patterns of baby talk. Second, parents should be encouraged to talk to their young children as often as possible. We may not know for sure how children benefit from hearing this language input, but the evidence strongly suggests that there is a benefit.

Age 6 Months to 12 Months: The Development of Communicative Intensions

From the moment of birth (and perhaps even before birth), parents and their baby are engaging in complex behaviors that set the stage for later language development. The parent picks up the baby, makes eye contact, and smiles. The baby relaxes into the parent's arms and perhaps gurgles or burps. The parent, in turn, reacts as if this were an attempt at communication and says, "Oh, you're hungry," or, "Yes, you are sleepy. Feeding rituals and games such as "Peek-a-Boo" provide opportunities for the development of early communication skills.

During the period from 6 to 12 months there is a major change going on in the way that young children communicate. Initially, babies are dependent on their caregivers to ascribe meaning to their behavior. That is, parents act as if their child is communicating, interpreting burps and giggles as attempts to interact. This early stage of communication has been called the **perlocutionary** stage (Bates, 1979; Bates, Camaioni, & Volterra, 1975). Consider the following interaction:

> Baby cries. Mother enters the room and says, "Are you hungry? Do you want something to eat now?"
> Baby quiets and turns toward mother. Mother says, "Yes, you are hungry, aren't you?"
> Baby stretches, touching rattle lying in crib. "Do you want to play?"
> Mother picks up rattle and shakes it. Baby gurgles. "Yes, that's what you wanted, isn't it?"

Note how much the mother is reading into this conversation. She is interpreting her child's behaviors as communicative attempts. The baby is really not capable of acting intentionally at this stage, but caregivers act as if their child did intend to communicate.

By age 7 months or so, there is a significant, but subtle, change in the infant's behavior. The baby follows the parent's movements with her or his eyes and head and becomes distressed if the parent leaves the room. Children of this age have been found to show interest in toys when their caregiver is present, but stop playing when the caregiver leaves (Owens, 2005). By 8 to 10 months of age, the infant begins to respond to social gestures such as hand waving to signal "bye-bye." The young child is beginning to enter what some linguists call the **illocutionary** stage of communication. At this stage, children begin to use intentional communication.

A significant development in this period is **joint attention.** During this period, the young child shows increasing interest in objects, such as a favorite cup, a toy animal, or a set of play keys. As babies begin to reach for preferred objects and play with them, they are beginning to show some intentionality in their play. They are making more than random movements, accidentally touching an object. Rather, they are intentionally reaching for and manipulating objects. When parents respond, joint attention takes place. Parents may join in the play, shaking their child's toy monkey to get the child's attention. They may label the item, saying something like, "See the monkey? Do you want the monkey?" Researchers have found that when mothers engage in joint attention and label the objects, their babies increase their vocabulary faster (Campbell & Namy, 2003). In addition, children whose parents respond to their child's initiation of interaction have been found to have greater language development later in life (Rollins, 2003).

Throughout the illocutionary stage, young children are learning to use gestures to get what they want. Bates (1979) identified two predominant types of communicative functions expressed by early gestures: protodeclaratives and protoimperatives. When young children use gestures such as pointing at an object not to request the object but just to participate in the conversation (as if to say, "Hey, look at that!"), this is what Bates calls a **protodeclarative.** It is a precursor to the development of declarative sentences. On the other hand, when the child gestures in an attempt to control or manipulate others (such as pointing to an object and vocalizing in order to get the adult to get the object), Bates calls this a **protoimperative.**

Somewhere between 10 and 15 months (remember, there is a broad range of typical development), children begin to make the transition to the **locutionary** stage of communicative development. Now, the developing child is beginning to combine vocalizations with gesture to request, demand, and comment. At first these vocalizations may just be sounds, but gradually they begin to take on the characteristics of adult speech and language.

It seems that children and adults are engaged in communicative interaction right from the beginning. Babies are active participants in communication, performing in ways that get the adults' attention and prompt a response. Adults are engaging their children in communication by altering their own language to fit the linguistic and cognitive abilities of their child. By the time babies are 9 months old (prior to the emergence of spoken language), they can express a wide range of communicative intentions, including requests, demands, and rejection.

At the same time that the young child is developing a greater repertoire of communicative functions, their vocalizations are becoming increasingly sophisticated. Although they cannot yet produce adultlike language, their babbling gradually takes on many of the characteristics of adult language. At this stage, babbling is characterized by consonant–vowel clusters ("ba-ba") and sequences that are of a similar length as adult speech. At times, this **reduplicated babble** even sounds like adult sentences, with intonational contours that sound like questioning or demanding.

Remember, too, that babies are not just developing expressive language. At this stage, their receptive language is far ahead of their ability to express themselves. They are able to understand more and more words and respond to questions and commands. Parents often express amazement about the amount that their child can understand. Research has confirmed what parents have known to be true. In a series of studies that use a technique called a "preferential looking paradigm," Hirsh-Pasek and Golinkoff (1993, 2000) have found that children can understand a variety of language structures before they can use them.

By about 12 months of age, most children are on the verge of producing their first real words. But they have already learned a lot about language. They can understand much more than they can produce. They have learned to express a variety of intentional communicative functions and have learned how to participate in conversations. They have learned the sounds of their language and have practiced them incessantly through babbling. They are ready to take the next step in language development.

Emergence of Expressive Language

Most parents can remember the excitement of hearing their baby's first words. This remarkable achievement did not happen overnight, however. Indeed, most babies do not wake up one morning speaking in full sentences. In fact, the progression from the shrieking first heard in the hospital nursery to the controlled utterance of *da-da* or *mama* is slow, systematic, and predictable for most children.

Stark (1979) developed a framework for describing prelinguistic development consisting of five stages. We will use Stark's model to guide us through these early stages of language development. Keep in mind that, although generalizations can be made about development, these generalizations are not true of *every* child. As we noted in the beginning of this chapter, there is wide variation in language development among children.

Stage I (0–8 Weeks)

At this stage newborns are making reflexive cries and vegetative sounds. That is, they are opening their mouths and emitting whatever comes out. What comes out is generally a loud, piercing cry that does wonders for getting a parent's attention. It is difficult, even painful, to ignore this cry. The crying is typically in short, rapid bursts, although there are individual differences. Some babies are relatively quiet; others seem to cry all the time. Some have a loud, piercing cry; others whimper. In addition, babies produce sounds—such as burps, coughs, and sneezes—that parents may respond to as if they were attempts to initiate communication.

Stage II (8–20 Weeks)

This period is one in which the infant gains increasing control over her or his sound-producing apparatus. Crying becomes differentiated, and parents begin to identify different kinds of cries (hunger, discomfort, demands). The bursts of crying begin to smooth out in more sustained (but usually less frequent) occurrences. By the end of this period, most babies are making cooing sounds. These are vowel-like utterances that are often interpreted by parents as sounds of pleasure. Many babies also begin to laugh at this stage.

Stage III (16–30 Weeks)

Vocal play characterizes this stage. This is a period in which there is continued control over the vocal mechanism. Consonant sounds begin to enter the baby's vocalizations. These may be added to the cooing sounds heard previously. By the end of this stage, the baby is beginning to produce the sounds we call *babble*.

Stage IV (25–50 Weeks)

This is the true babbling stage. The baby is producing combinations of consonants and vowels such as *ba* and *na.* By the end of this period, these consonant–vowel (CV) combinations are being repeated in long strings *(ba ba ba ba),* often with changes in pitch and intonation.

Stage V (9–18 Months)

Now the child's babbling becomes increasingly complex. The range of consonant sounds increases. Jargon emerges in most children. This is a type of vocalization that produces sounds and intonation that are similar to adult language. In fact, when listening from another room, one might almost think that the baby is actually talking, since these strings of sounds take on the sound characteristics of sentences.

Stage V marks a transition to true language production. Parents detect first words being uttered, sometimes heard within the flow of jargon speech. At times the words are articulated clearly, not to be heard again for days or weeks. Some children may use *protowords,* CV combinations that are used consistently to mean something. For example, a child might use the combination "an" to indicate that she or he *wants* something. What makes this a protoword and not just babble is that the sounds are used *consistently, in appropriate contexts* to signal their meaning. Owens (2005) has suggested that the following criteria should be used in deciding whether a vocal production is actually a word:

- The utterance must have a phonetic relationship to some adult word.
- The child must use the word consistently.
- The word must occur in the presence of a referent.

Our review of early vocalizations has taken us from the reflexive crying of the newborn to the emergence of true first words. We have noted the universality of this progression, while keeping in mind the individual variations that are found in developing children. Table 5.1 summarizes the development of vocalizations (form) as well as communication (use) and content.

TABLE 5.1   Prelinguistic Development

Stage	Form	Content	Use
I (0–8 wks)	Reflexive crying Vegetative sounds Sound discrimination	Biological and physical needs	Eye contact Body movement
11 (8–20 wks)	Cooing and laughing Vowel-like sounds Cry more controlled	Differentiated crying (hunger, distress)	Games Routines

III
(16–30 wks)
	Increased control over
	    speech
	Prolonged vocalizations
	Babble
		Beginning of semantic
		    functions
			Intent to communicate

IV (25–50 wks)	Repeated syllable clusters Jargon speech Some words	Expansion of semantic functions	Illocutionary stage
V (9–18 mos)	Protowords Transition to language	Overextensions Underextensions	Locutionary stage

Source: Adapted from Stark (1979).

Language Development in the Preschool Years

In his pioneering book on language development, Harvard University psychologist Roger Brown described a longitudinal study of the language development of three children: Adam, Eve, and Sarah. Working with a group of remarkably talented assistants, Brown and his colleagues observed, recorded, and analyzed each step in the language growth of these children. Their observations were reported in the book *A First Language: The Early Stages* (Brown, 1973). This is still the most comprehensive description of language development available. One of Brown's key observations was that the *length* of a child's utterance is a better indicator of language development (especially syntactic development) than is the child's age. Brown developed a measure of syntactic development called **mean length of utterance (MLU).** MLU is relatively simple to calculate (see Box 5.1) and has become a widely used measure of language development, even though it is only a rough measure of language complexity. MLU is calculated by counting the total number of morphemes in a sample of language and dividing by the number of utterances in the sample. For example, if there were 100 morphemes used in a sample of 50 utterances, the MLU would be 2.0 (100/50). Brown and his colleagues used MLU to describe the stages of language they observed in their subjects (see Table 5.2). Brown's stages are used in the following description of language development in the preschool years.

BOX **5.1**
Measurement of Mean Length of Utterance

1. The language sample should be 50 to 100 utterances in length.
   Note: An utterance is a sentence or a shorter unit separated by a pause or signaled by a change in pitch (e.g., *Now?* with a rising pitch = an utterance).
2. Count the number of morphemes in each utterance.
   Note: Brown (1973) lists explicit rules for what to count. For example:
   a. Count as one morpheme: Compound words (e.g., *railroad*)
   Diminutives (e.g., *goggie*)
   b. Count as two morphemes: Possessive nouns (e.g., *mommy's*)
   Plural nouns (e.g., *kitties*)
   Present progressive verbs (e.g., *sleeping*)
   c. Do not count: Fillers (e.g., *um, ah*)
   Dysfluencies (e.g., *m-m-m mommy*) (only count full morpheme)
3. Divide the total number of morphemes by the total number of utterances to derive MLU:

$$MLU = \frac{\text{Total number of morphemes}}{\text{Total number of utterances}}$$

Example: 2-year-old child and grandmother

CHILD: Get donuts.
GRANDMOTHER: I know you want to get donuts. What kind of donuts do you want?
CHILD: I-I = icy.

Child's total number of morphemes = 4/2 (uttterances) = 2.0 MLU

Stage I (MLU = 1.0–2.0; Age = 12–26 Months)

Stage I marks the emergence of true words, examples of which are listed in Figure 5.2. Notice which kinds of words are (and are not) on the list. Researchers such as Nelson (1973) have found that nouns (animals, food, toys) predominate. Nelson found that approximately 65 percent of first words were nouns. These are not just any nouns, however. They fall into what we might call the "midlevel" of nouns (e.g., *dog*)—not so specific that they name just one type (e.g., *collie*) but not so general as to cover an entire category (e.g., *animal*) (Anglin, 1995). The next most frequent words are action words *(hi, bye-bye),* then modifiers *(hot, cold).*

What else do you notice about these first words? They are usually one or, at most, two syllables, and certain sounds tend to predominate *(b, p, m).* In addition, children often make systematic phonological errors at this stage. These include:

Reduction of consonant clusters *(green* becomes *geen)*
Deletion of unstressed syllables *(banana* becomes *nana)*
Devoicing of the final consonant *(bed* becomes *bet)*

TABLE 5.2   Brown's Stages of Language Development

Stage	MLU	Approximate Age (months)	Development
I	1.0–2.0	12–26	Use of semantic rules
II	2.0–2.5	27–30	Morphological development
III	2.5–3.0	31–34	Development of sentence forms
IV	3.0–3.75	35–40	Emergence of complex sentence forms
V	3.75–4.5	41–46	Elaboration and refinement of structures
VI	4.5+	47+	

FIGURE 5.2   Representative Early Words

juice (/dus/)	nose (/noɪ/)	hat
cookie (/tɪti/)	mama	all gone (/ɔdɔn/)
baby (/bibi/)	dada	more (/mɔ/)
bye-bye	doggie (/dɔdi/)	no
ball (/bɔ/)	kitty (/tldi/)	up
hi	that (/da/)	eat
car (/tɔ/)	dirty (/dɔti/)	go (/d ɔɪ/)
water (/wʌwʌ/)	hot	do
eye	shoe (/su/)	milk (/mʌk/)

Source: From Robert. E. Owens, Jr., *Language Development: An Introduction,* 6th ed., p. 231. Published by Allyn and Bacon, Boston, MA. Copyright © 2005 by Pearson Education. Reprinted by permission of the publisher.

Nelson found many similarities in the first words used by children, but she also discovered that there were clear individual differences among children. Some children tended to use language to describe and categorize, whereas others used language primarily for interpersonal interaction. These differences among children have been confirmed by other researchers (e.g., Goldfield, 1985/86).

By the end of Stage I, children are beginning to use multiword utterances. Like first words, these utterances have a typical pattern, which has often been described as *telegraphic.* That is, they are characterized by the deletion of prepositions, conjunctions, articles, and pronouns. In their early two-word utterances, children typically talk about a limited set of items-objects, agents, and actions (see Table 5.3). They point to objects (demonstrative) and they talk about where the objects are (location). They talk about who owns the object (possessive) and about the appearance of the objects (attributive). These early semantic functions are characteristic of Brown's Stage I of language development.

TABLE 5.3   **Two-Word Semantic Rules**

Semantic-Syntactic Rule	Examples
Modifier + head	
Attributive + entity	*Big doggie*
Possessor + Possession	*Daddy shoe*
Recurrent + *X*	*'Nuther cookie*
Negative + *X*	
Nonexistence or disappearance	*No juice*
Rejection (of proposal)	*No bed* (when told it is bedtime)
Denial (of statement)	*No baby* (when referred to as such)
Demonstrative (this/that) + entity	*This cup*
X + locative	*Doggie bed*
X + dative	*Give mommy*
Agent + action	*Daddy eat*
Action + object	*Throw ball*
Agent + object	*Mommy ball*

Source: From Robert. E. Owens, Jr., *Language Development: An Introduction,* 6th ed. Published by Allyn and Bacon, Boston, MA. Copyright © 2005 by Pearson Education. Reprinted by permission of the publisher. Based on Bloom (1973), Brown (1973), and Schlesinger (1971).

Stage II (MLU = 2.0–2.5; Age = 27–30 Months)

As children's utterances grow longer, they also become more complex. One of the major developments identified by Brown and his colleagues in what they called Stage II of language development is the emergence of **grammatical morphemes** (prefixes, suffixes, prepositions). As we noted in Chapter 2, morphemes are linguistic elements that carry meaning. *Grammatical* morphemes are the type that add meaning only when attached to a root word. In Stage II, young children are learning to convey more subtle meanings by adding these grammatical morphemes to words they have already acquired.

Although the use of grammatical morphemes begins in Stage II, the development of the use of grammatical morphemes continues through Stage V. Brown found that there was a highly predictable sequence of acquisition of grammatical morphemes (see Figure 5.3). Prepositions (such as *in* and *on*) and the present progressive (*-ing*) are usually acquired first. Then comes the use of the plural *s* and so on. Of course, these constructions do not emerge fully formed or in the exact order that Brown and his colleagues claimed. As children learn to use these morphemes, they make a number of errors in usage, using the endings incorrectly (e.g., *deerses*) or failing to use them at times. As children continue to develop, however, they learn to use grammatical morphemes more consistently and accurately. Pronoun use also begins to develop in Stage II. The earliest pronouns used are *I* and *my.* Later (Stage III), *he, she,* and *you* emerge in usage. By Stage V (approximately 4 years old), most children are using even the most sophisticated pronouns.

FIGURE 5.3   Average Order of Acquisition of Fourteen Grammatical Morphemes by Three Children Studied by Brown

1. Present progressive
2/3. Prepositions (in and on)
4. Plural
5. Irregular past tense
6. Possessive
7. Copula, uncontractible
8. Articles
9. Regular past tense
10. Third-person present tense, regular
11. Third-person present tense, irregular
12. Auxiliary, uncontractible
13. Copula, contractible
14. Auxiliary, contractible

Stage III (MLU = *2.5–3.0; Age = 31–34 Months*)

The major developments of Stage III are the emergence of sentence types such as negation, the imperative, and questions, and the elaboration of the basic sentence elements (noun phrase and verb phrase). Each of the sentence types has a developmental progression.

We will examine negation as an example of the steps in sentence development. Any parent can tell you that long before 31 months of age, children can express negation. They do so by pushing the bottle away, by scrunching up their faces, and by using the word *no*. However, at Stage III we begin to see the emergence of more adultlike ways of saying no. At first, the child simply adds the word *no* to the beginning of a sentence *(No the kitty eating)*. Next, the child learns to place the negative marker inside the sentence, just before the verb *(The kitty no eating)*. Still later, auxiliary verbs are used *(The kitty is not eating)*.

Development of the use of questions also follows a predictable order. Most children begin to ask questions by using a rising intonation *(Daddy?)*, where a rise in intonation at the end of the word may mean, "Is that Daddy?" As their language develops, children begin to ask more sophisticated questions. Generally, children start by asking *wh* questions—who, what, when, where, why). In order to ask such questions in English, the speaker must invert the subject and auxiliary verb and place the *wh* word at the beginning of the sentence (e.g., *Where is kitty?*). But, as they learn to use this type of construction, children typically drop the auxiliary verb, leaving something like, *Where kitty?* The next step in development is to add the auxiliary but not switch it with the subject (e.g., *Where she is going?*). Finally, children learn to use these constructions, as well as yes–no questions (e.g., *Is Daddy home?*) in the correct (adultlike) manner. The appearance of negation and questioning, like that of other sentence types, begins at Stage III and continues to develop through the preschool years (see Table 5.4).

As a variety of sentence types are beginning to emerge, the young child is adding elements to basic noun and verb phrases. Up to this point, noun phrases have generally

TABLE 5.4   Sequence of the Development of Negation and Questioning

Negation	Questioning
• No" used alone	• Yes/No questions
• "No" added to other words (placed outside sentence)	Example: *Baby drink?* (rising intonation)
Examples: *No go. No sit down. No the girl run.*	• "What" and "where" questions
• Negative moved within sentence	Example: *Where doggie?*
Example: *The girl not running.*	• "What" and "where" + NP + (going)/(doing)
• Use of auxiliary and contraction	Examples: *Where daddy going? Why you crying?*
Example: *The girl is not (isn't) running.*	• Limited inversion and use of auxiliary
• Elaboration of negative forms	Example: *What the boy is riding?*
	• Inversion of auxiliary
	Example: *What is the boy riding?*

consisted of a noun and perhaps a determiner (article). Now, the child begins to add adjectives, initiators *(all, both, only),* and postmodifiers (prepositional phrases and clauses) to the basic noun phrase. Similarly, verb use expands from simple verbs to inclusion of auxiliary verbs, the progressive *(-ing),* and modals *(can, will, may)* See Table 5.5 for details.

Stage IV *(MLU = 3.0–3.75; Age = 35–40 Months)*

Stage IV marks the emergence of complex sentence types. Complex sentences are formed when two or more *clauses* (a group of words with a subject and predicate) are joined together. The first type of complex structure to emerge is that of *coordination.* Children begin by linking ideas with the word *and (I am going to the store and my dad is going to work).* Later, the child learns to use coordination of multiple ideas as a way to *shorten* sentences *(My mom and I are going to the bank).* Still later, children begin to use other conjunctions *(but, because, since).* At Stage IV, children also typically begin to use embedded sentences. These are sentences in which a subordinate clause *(who is my friend)* is embedded in an independent clause *(The boy is here)* to form a complex sentence *(The boy who is my friend is here)* (see Table 5.6).

Stage V *(MLU = 3.75–4.5; Age = 41–46 Months)*

There are no major new structures that emerge in Stage V. Instead, this stage is marked by elaboration and refinement of structures that emerged in earlier stages. The child continues adding grammatical morphemes; more frequently uses adjectives, adverbs, and embedded sentences; and more consistently uses inversion in questions *(Are you going to the store?).* In short, the child is learning to become a more effective (and more social) communicator.

      This description of the syntactic development of children between 1 and 4 years of age is complete for the purpose intended here, although there has been no attempt to

TABLE 5.5 Expansion of Noun and Verb Phrases

Noun Phrase		Verb Phrase	
Determiners:	Articles	• Present progressive	*(is eating)*
	Possessive pronouns *(my; your)*	semi-auxiliary	*(gonna/hafta)*
	Qualifiers *(any; some)*	• True auxiliary	*(is going)*
Adjectivals:	Adjectives	overextension of	
	Ordinals *(first; last)*	regular past tense	*(he goed)*
	Quantifiers *(two; few)*	• Modals	*(may; must; can)*
Initiators:	*only; all; both*	use of "do" aux	*(I do want one)*
Postmodifiers:	*Follow* main verb	• Mastery of tense	
	prepositional phrase	(regular and irregular)	
	clause		

describe every feature that develops during this period. Instead, the goal has been to describe major accomplishments that illustrate the general course of development and provide background for an understanding of what happens when children fail to develop in the expected ways.

By the time most children enter kindergarten, they are able to understand and use quite complex and sophisticated language. They have mastered the use of pronouns and grammatical morphemes and can use all adult sentence forms, including compound and complex sentences. But they have not learned everything there is to know about language. There is still much to be learned after children enter formal schooling. Before examining syntactic development during the school years, however, we need to look at the development of two other aspects of language in the preschool years: semantics and pragmatics.

TABLE 5.6 Use of Conjunction and Embedding

Conjunction: Joining of two *main* clauses
Embedding: Joining of a *main* clause with a *subordinate* clause

Development of Conjunction	Development of Embedding
1. Single words used together	**1.** Use of prepositions
2. Use of *and* to link sentences	**2.** Use of semi-auxilliary
3. Use of *and* to link clauses (with deletion)	**3.** Object Noun Phrase complements *(I think that I will go.)*
4. Use of *but* and *if* to link clauses	**4.** Infinitive *(I gotta go home.)*
	5. Relative clause *(I am going where it is nice.)*

Learning to Mean: The Development of Semantics

By the time they are 8 years old, most children have a receptive vocabulary of about 8,000 words and can use about 5,000 in their language (Menyuk, 1999). How did they acquire so many words and how did they learn what each means?

Although no one can say exactly how children learn about word meaning, there are several prominent theories. One of these theories is the *semantic-feature* hypothesis. Eve Clark (1973) suggested that children develop meaning by adding features to their understanding of a particular concept. As they learn more, their concept becomes more like that of adults. As evidence for this theory, consider the child who calls all things with four legs either *doggy* or *kitty*. Later, the child learns that doggies not only have four legs but also bark, whereas cats meow. At first, the child will *overextend* the word to include a broad class of items. Gradually, the child refines a concept until it matches the adult meaning. Occasionally, children underextend meanings. Then they restrict a word to only one object (usually something they treasure, such as a cup or a pacifier). In this case, they will use the word only when that particular object is present.

The semantic-feature theory of the acquisition of meaning makes a lot of sense. Parents can often observe their children overextending words. However, the semantic-feature theory may not be sufficient to explain what is going on with the acquisition of meaning. In her observation of children, Katherine Nelson (1974) noted how they seemed to pay more attention to the *action* related to objects rather than to the perceptual features of the object. She pointed out that children's first words tended to be items that moved or could be manipulated by the child. Her *functional-core* hypothesis claims that children learn about meaning by interacting with things, much as Piaget claimed that cognitive growth is spurred on by experience.

Bowerman (1978) proposed still another theory of semantic development that incorporates features of both of the preceding theories. Bowerman's theory has come to be called the *prototype* hypothesis. She claimed that children learn word meanings by developing a cognitive model based on both perceptual and functional characteristics. For example, a child would learn the meaning of the word *dog* by encountering a dog and extracting features that would enable him or her to build a cognitive concept of dog. Encountering different types and sizes of dogs would then oblige the child to refine the original model through comparison of the new examples to the original model. Research by Rosch and Mervis (1975) found that adults appear to have cognitive prototypes that are quite consistent across individuals. They found, for example, that a group of adults asked to choose pictures of a "typical" dog will usually choose something that looks like a collie.

Another, more recent theory of word acquisition has found that children as young as 18 months old can acquire new words after only a few exposures to the word, often without explicit instruction from an adult (Woodward, Markman, & Fitzsimmons, 1994). This phenomenon, called **fast mapping,** indicates that children may be able to make a rough connection between a concept and a word with as little as one exposure to the word. This step may be followed by a more extended stage during which the child works out the precise meaning of the word. At first, children may learn a new word as a whole, in isolation from other words. Over time, they develop a rich inter-connected web of meanings.

Although a complete understanding of semantic development remains elusive, the four models just described give us some insights into the process children use to develop the semantic aspect of language. Each of the models views children as *active* participants in the language-learning process, constantly adding new concepts and refining old ones. As their understanding of the world changes, they develop new words or adjust the meanings of existing words to match their new knowledge. This process is gradual, at first, but builds in intensity as the child enters school.

You may wonder how researchers, observing the same phenomenon of semantic development, could have reached such different conclusions about the way children learn meaning. Several factors may explain the differing models that have been proposed. First, there are individual differences in children. Some children pay more attention to physical features of objects, whereas others are more action oriented. Second, at different stages of development, children may prefer one strategy over another. A third factor that may affect how children acquire meaning is the object itself. Some objects (e.g., pets and toys) are more likely to be discovered through action, whereas others (e.g., walls and clouds) are more likely to be viewed at some distance. So, in a sense, each of the models of semantic development may be right at a particular time, for specific children, for particular objects or items.

Learning to Converse: The Development of Pragmatics

Earlier in this chapter we discussed the development of conversational skills from infancy to the emergence of spoken language. We saw how, right from the start, infants appear to engage in exchanges that begin to take on the give-and-take characteristics of communicative interactions. Parents enhance their child's developing communication skills by responding as if they were intentionally communicating and by providing models for interaction.

With the development of spoken language comes a refinement in the use of the conversational skills, which linguists call *pragmatics.* As children develop, so too does the length of their conversational exchanges. Although the conversational interactions of 2-year-olds tend to be limited to one or two turns, 3- and 4-year-olds can maintain longer conversations and the number of utterances in each turn increases (Logan, 2003). In addition, children learn to take turns in the conversation, with fewer interruptions and overlapping language (Elias & Broerse, 1996).

Besides engaging in longer conversations, preschool children develop a number of pragmatic functions that enable them to engage in more effective conversations. For example, they develop skills in using conversational repairs, such as asking for clarification *(What?).* They become more adept at staying on topic during a conversation and at setting the topic themselves. They also begin to understand and use politeness rules (such as saying *please* and *thank you*) and begin to understand indirect requests (such as, *Why don't you play outside,* which really means, "Go play outside").

Overall, as preschool children develop more sophisticated forms of language and a wider vocabulary, they are also learning to engage in longer, more complex conversational interactions. They are beginning to learn conversational skills that will enable them to fully participate in the challenging communicative environments found in school.

Language Development and Emergent Literacy

Our focus so far has been on understanding and describing the remarkable and still somewhat mysterious phenomenon known as language development in young children. But just as remarkable (and just as mysterious) is the development of literacy skills—reading and writing—in young children.

Research over the past two decades has led to the conclusion that reading and writing skills develop long before children begin to receive formal instruction in these skills in school (see Teale & Sulzby, 1986; Dickinson & Tabors, 2001). This model of reading and writing has come to be known as **emergent literacy.** It is based on research that has found that language and literacy develop concurrently and interdependently from an early age (Whitehurst & Lonigan, 1998). In other words, language and literacy develop at the same time, and the continuing development of one skill is dependent on the other. This is very different from the "reading readiness" model that suggested that reading and writing developed only after the child had acquired sufficient language (and other) skills.

The exact relationship between language development and reading and writing is still unclear, but most researchers have concluded that early language experiences play a critical role in the development of literacy skills. In a major study using data from a national study of child development, a group of investigators from the National Institute of Child Health and Human Development Early Child Care Research Network (NICHD-ECCRN, 2005), found significant relationships between language development at age 3 and both later language development (at 54 months) and reading. Specifically, oral language skills at age 3 were directly related to both vocabulary development and the development of phonological knowledge (awareness of phonemes). The researchers did not find a direct relationship between language skills at age 3 and word recognition, but they did find such a relationship with language at 54 months. Moreover, oral language competence at 54 months of age was found to be strongly related to both first-grade word recognition and to third-grade reading comprehension. These researchers concluded that early oral language skills are critical for success in later reading.

What is the role of parents and families in the development of their child's learning of language (and literacy)? This has been a key question for researchers.

One factor that has been examined is home environment. We have already reviewed evidence (in Chapter 3) that some home environments are more conducive than others to the development of oral language skills. In the study by Hart and Risley (1995), children from lower socioeconomic families participated in fewer interactions and acquired a smaller vocabulary than children from middle or higher SES families. Interestingly, there is considerable evidence that children from lower socioeconomic families are also at risk for reading difficulties (Snow, Burns, & Griffin, 1998). A number of factors have been suggested as the cause of this phenomenon, including biological and health factors, discrimination, and home environment (Vernon-Feagans, 1996). Children from low-income families have been reported to visit libraries less often, have fewer print materials in the home, and are read to less by their parents. Although there are clearly cultural and economic forces at work here, most researchers have concluded that early literacy practices have a strong and enduring effect on children's language and literacy skills (Wasik & Hendrickson, 2004).

One of the most researched factors within the home environment is storybook reading. As Whitehurst and Lonigan (1998) pointed out, the image of a parent reading to his or her child is a cherished cultural icon. We believe it is an essential part of child rearing and have the intuitive sense that it is an important part of the child's early literacy training. In fact, a highly influential book titled *Becoming a Nation of Readers* concluded that "the single most important activity for building the knowledge required for eventual success in reading is reading aloud to children" (Anderson, Hiebert, Scott, & Wilkinson, 1985, p. 23).

Research on shared book reading has generally found that it has a positive effect on the development of early reading skills in children, although questions have been raised about the strength of the effect (Senechal, LeFevre, Thomas, & Daley, 1998). What is less in doubt is that book reading has significant effects on language development. These effects are of two types. First, shared book reading creates an opportunity for language interaction. This is a chance for parents to converse with their children and for the child to practice his or her emerging language skills. Second, children are learning new vocabulary and are being exposed to new grammatical structures as part of the book-reading experience. So, although book reading itself may not be strongly linked to later reading success, there is evidence that children who are read to more often have enhanced language skills, which, in turn, leads to more success in reading.

What can we conclude about language and the emergence of literacy? It seems clear that there is a relationship. Language skills are an important factor in the early development of literacy. At the same time, literacy experiences positively influence language development. Although there is a need for more research on the most effective ways to enhance early literacy development, there is enough evidence to suggest that parents should be encouraged to read to their children and to discuss with them what they are reading.

Summary

This chapter discussed how language development begins at birth (or even before birth) and continues through the preschool years, and reviewed evidence that babies are active participants in early communicative interaction and that parents simplify the language they use with their children. We examined the course of spoken language development, from the early vocalizations through the emergence of first words and sentences to the further refinements and elaborations that take place in early childhood. The text also considered three theories that attempt to account for semantic development. We examined the evidence that early language development both influences the emergence of literacy skills and is influenced by literacy activities (such as shared book reading).

R E V I E W   Q U E S T I O N S

1. At which stage of communicative development (perlocutionary, illocutionary, or locutionary) is each of the following children:

   a. Baby bangs on crib with rattle to get mother's attention.

   b. Baby gurgles. Mother says, "Oh, are you hungry?"

   c. Child says, "More cookie."

2. Describe what adults do to alter their language for young children.

3. What happens during the transition period as young children are beginning to use recognizable words?

4. What is MLU? How is it related to syntactic development?

5. Match the MLU stage to the appropriate syntactic development:

   a. Emergence of grammatical morphemes

   b. Emergence of negation and questions

   c. Use of telegraphic language

   d. Emergence of complex sentences

6. According to the semantic-feature theory, how does a child learn to differentiate a cow from a dog?

7. How might early language development influence the emergence of literacy skills? How do literacy activities influence language development?

S U G G E S T E D   A C T I V I T Y

1. Does receptive language really exceed expressive language in young children? Test this hypothesis by asking a young child (preferably between 12 and 18 months old) to respond to various items and utterances. Ask the parents to give you some items that are familiar to the child. Then ask the child to find a specific item from among a group.

   You say, "Show me the _____." If the child points to the correct item, say, "What is that?" How does the child respond?

   If the child can successfully perform this task, make it harder. Ask him or her to show you two objects. Say, "Show me the _____ and the _____."

   Now, try a *wh* question, such as, "Where is the _____?"

   Try this again with something (or someone) not in the room. What happens?

   What do the results indicate about the child's ability to understand and use language?

GLOSSARY

emergent literacy: a theory of reading and writing development that claims that literacy develops continuously from early childhood experiences

fast-mapping: a theory of semantics that describes the phenomenon of rapid word acquisition

grammatical morphemes: word affixes that signal a difference in grammatical usage

illocutionary stage: the stage of communication at which children begin to use intentional communication

joint attention: situation in which two individuals (e.g., parent and child) are paying attention to the same thing

locutionary stage: use of words to express communicative intentions

mean length of utterance: a measure of syntactic development that is calculated by counting the total number of morphemes in a sample of language and dividing by the number of utterances in the sample

perlocutionary stage: nonintentional communication that relies on a partner for interpretation

protodeclarative: use of objects to get the attention of adults

protoimperative: use of an adult to get a desired object

reduplicated babble: more sophisticated form of repeated babble that includes consonants

reflexive vocalizations: sounds produced by infants in response to physical needs

RESOURCES ON THE WEB

www.asha.org/public/speech/development/ Information on speech and language development, including a chart of developmental milestones

childes.psy.cmu.edu/ Information about the Child Language Data Exchange System

www.childdevelopmentinfo.com/development/language_development.shtml Information about child development, including language development, from the Child Development Institute

www.naeyc.org/ National Association for the Education of Young Children

www.srcd.org/ Society for Research in Child Development

www.famlit.org/ National Center for Family Literacy

REFERENCES

Anderson, R. C., Hiebert, E. H., Scott, J. A., & Wilkinson, I. A. G. (1985). *Becoming a nation of readers: The report of the Commission on Reading.* Washington, DC: National Academy of Education, Commission on Education and Public Policy.

Anglin, J. (1993). Vocabulary development: A morphological analysis. *Monographs of the Society for Research in Child Development,* Serial No. 238, Vol. 58, No. 10.

Anglin, J. (1995). Classifying the world through language: Functional relevance, cultural significance, and category name learning. *Inter-national Journal of Intercultural Relations, 19,* 161–181.

Bates, E. (1979). *The emergence of symbols: Cognition and communication in infancy.* New York: Academic Press.

Bates, E., Camaioni, L., & Volterra, V. (1975). The acquisition of performatives prior to speech. *Merrill-Palmer Quarterly, 21,* 205–216.

Bloom, L. (1973). *One word at a time: The use of single-word utterances before syntax.* The Hague: Mouton.

Bohannon, J., & Stanowicz, L. (1988). Adult responses to children's language errors: The issue of negative evidence. *Developmental Psychology, 24,* 684–689.

Bowerman, M. (1978). The acquisition of word meaning: An investigation in some current conflicts. In N. Waterson & C. Snow (Eds.), *The development of communication.* New York: Wiley.

Brown, R. (1973). *A first language: The early stages.* Cambridge, MA: Harvard University Press.

Campbell, A. L., & Namy, L. L. (2003). The role of social referential context and verbal and non-verbal symbol learning. *Child Development, 74,* 549–563.

Chomsky, N. (1968). *Language and mind.* New York: Harcourt, Brace, & World.

Clark, E. (1973). What's in a word: On the child's acquisition of semantics in his first language. In T. Moore (Ed.), *Cognitive development and the acquisition of language* (pp. 65–110). New York: Academic Press.

Cooper, R. P., & Aslin, R. N. (1990). Preference for infant-directed speech in the first month after birth. *Child Development, 61,* 1584–1595.

De Casper, A., & Fifer, W. (1980). Of human bonding: Newborns prefer their mothers' voices. *Science, 208,* 1174–1176.

De Casper, A., & Spence, M. (1986). Prenatal maternal speech influences newborns' perception of speech sounds. *Infant Behavior and Development, 9,* 133–150.

Dickinson, D. K., & Tabors, P. O. (2001). *Beginning literacy with language.* Baltimore: Brookes.

Eimas, P., Siqueland, E., Jusczyk, P., & Vigorito, J. (1971). Speech perception in infants. *Science, 171,* 303–306.

Elias, G., & Broerse, J. (1996). Developmental changes in the incidence and likelihood of simultaneous talk during the first two years: A question of function. *Journal of Child Language, 23,* 201–217.

Fernald, A. (1992). Human maternal vocalizations to infants as biologically relevant signals: An evolutionary perspective. In J. H. Barlow, L. Cosmides, & J. Tooby (Eds.), *The adapted mind: Evolutionary psychology and the generation of culture* (pp. 391–428). New York: Oxford University Press.

Goldfield, B. (1985/86). Referential and expressive language: A study of two mother-child dyads. *First Language, 6,* 119–131.

Golinkoff, R. M., & Hirsh-Pasek, K. (1995). Reinterpreting children's sentence comprehension: Toward a new framework. In P. Fletcher & B. MacWhinney (Eds.), *The handbook of child language* (pp. 430–461). Oxford: Blackwell.

Hart, B., & Risley, T. R. (1995). *Meaningful differences in the everyday experience of young American children.* Baltimore: Brookes.

Hart, B., & Risley, T. R. (1999). *The social world of children learning to talk.* Baltimore: Paul H. Brookes.

Hirsh-Pasek, K. (2000). Beyond Shipley, Smith, and Gleitman: Young children's comprehension of bound morphemes. In B. Landau, J. Sabini, J. Jonides, & E. Newport (Eds.), *Perception, cognition, and language: Essays in honor of Henry and Lila Gleitman* (pp. 191–208). Cambridge, MA: MIT Press.

Hirsh-Pasek, K., & Golinkoff, R. M. (1993). Skeletal supports for grammatical learning: What the infant brings to the language learning task. In C. K. Rovee-Collier (Ed.), *Advances in infancy research* (Vol. 10). Norwood, NJ: Ablex.

Kaplan, P. S., Bachorowski, J. A., Smoski, M. J., & Hudenko, W. J. (2002). Infants of depressed mothers, although competent learners, fail to learn in response to their own mothers' infant-directed speech. *Psychological Science, 13,* 268–271.

Konefal, J., & Folks, J. (1984). Linguistic analysis of children's conversational repairs. *Journal of Psycholinguistic Research, 13,* 1–11.

Logan, K. J. (2003). Language and fluency characteristics of preschoolers' multiple-utterance conversational turns. *Journal of Speech, Language, and Hearing Research, 46,* 178–188.

Matsaka, N. (1992). Pitch characteristics of Japanese maternal speech to infants. *Journal of Child Language, 19,* 213–223.

Menn, L., & Stoel-Gammon, C. (2005). Phonological development. In J. B. Gleason (Ed.), *The development of language* (6th ed.) (pp. 62–111). Boston: Allyn & Bacon.

Menyuk, P. (1999). *Reading and linguistic development.* Cambridge, MA: Brookline.

Murray, L., & Trevarthen, C. (1985). Emotional regulations of interactions between 2 month olds and their mothers. In T. Field & N. Fox (Eds.),

Social perception in infants. Norwood, NJ: Ablex.

Murray, L., & Trevarthen, C. (1986). The infant's role in mother-infant communication. *Journal of Child Language, 13,* 15–31.

National Institute of Child Health and Human Development Study of Early Child Care Research Network. (2005). Pathways to reading: The role of oral language in the transition to reading. *Developmental Psychology, 41,* 428–442.

Nazzi, T., Bertoncini, J., & Mehler, J. (1998). Language discrimination by newborns: Toward an understanding of the role of rhythm. *Journal of Experimental Psychology: Human Perception and Performance, 24,* 756–766.

Nelson, K. (1973). Some evidence for the cognitive primacy of categorization and its functional basis. *Merrill-Palmer Quarterly, 19,* 21–39.

Nelson, K. (1974). Concept, word, and sentence: Interrelations in acquisition and development. *Psychological Review, 81,* 267–285.

Newport, E., Gleitman, A., & Gleitman, L. (1977). Mother I'd rather do it myself: Some effects and non-effects of maternal speech style. In C. Snow & C. Ferguson (Eds.), *Talking to children: Language, input, and acquisition* (pp. 109–149). New York: Cambridge University Press.

Owens, R. (2005). *Language development: An introduction* (6th ed.). Boston: Allyn & Bacon.

Rollins, P. R. (2003). Caregivers' contingent comments to 9-month-old infants: Relationship with later language. *Applied Psycholinguistics, 24,* 221–234.

Rosch, E., & Mervis, C. (1975). Family resemblances: Studies in the internal structure of categories. *Cognitive Psychology, 7,* 573–605.

Sachs, J. (2005). Communication development in infancy. In J. Berko Gleason (Ed.), *The development of language* (6th ed.) (pp. 39–61). Boston: Allyn & Bacon.

Schlesinger, I. (1971). Production of utterances and language acquisition. In D. Slobin (Ed.), *The ontogenesis of grammar.* New York: Academic Press.

Senechal, M., LeFevre, J., Thomas, E. M., & Daley, K. E. (1998). Differential effects of home literacy experiences on the development of oral and written language. *Reading Research Quarterly, 33,* 96–112.

Singh, L., Morgan, J. L., & Best, C. T. (2002). Infants' listening preferences: Baby talk or happy talk? *Infancy, 3,* 365–394.

Snow, C. (1977). Mothers' speech research: From input to interaction. In C. Snow & C. Ferguson (Eds.), *Talking to children: Language input and acquisition* (pp. 31–49). Cambridge, MA: Cambridge University Press.

Snow, C., Burns, S., & Griffin, M. (1998). *Preventing reading difficulties in young children.* Washington, DC: National Academy Press.

Stark, R. (1979). Prespeech segmental feature development. In P. Fletcher & M. Garman (Eds.), *Language acquisition* (pp. 15–32). New York: Cambridge University Press.

Teale, W. H., & Sulzby, E. (Eds.). (1986). *Emergent literacy: Writing and reading.* Norwoord, NJ: Ablex.

Vernon-Feagans, L. (1996). *Children's talk in communities and classrooms.* Cambridge, MA: Blackwell.

Vihman, M. M. (1992). Early syllables and the construction of phonology. In C. A. Ferguson, L. Menn, & C. Stoel-Gammon (Eds.), *Phonological development: Models, research, implications.* Timonium, MD: York Press.

Wasik, B. H., & Hendrickson, J. S. (2004). Family literacy practices. In C. Stone, E. Silliman, B. Ehren, & K. Apel (Eds.), *Handbook of language and literacy* (pp. 154–174). New York: Guilford.

Whitehurst, G. J., & Lonigan, C. J. (1998). Child development and emergent literacy. *Child Development, 69,* 848–872.

Woodward, A., Markman, E., & Fitzsimmons, C. (1994). Rapid word learning in 13- and 18-month-olds. *Developmental Psychology, 30,* 553–566.

6 Language and Literacy in the School Years

Language development does not end when children enter school. In fact, growth in some areas of language actually accelerates during the school years. The demands of school also require that children use their knowledge of language to develop skills in reading, writing, and thinking. This chapter describes the course of language development during the school years and the important relationship between language and literacy.

After reading this chapter, you should be able to:

1. Describe the major language developments accomplished during the school years.
2. Understand the concept of metalinguistics and how it relates to school tasks.
3. Discuss the implications of ongoing language development for classroom instruction.
4. Understand the relationship between language and literacy development.
5. Discuss the implications of the language–literacy connection for identifying students at risk for literacy difficulties and for effectively teaching all students.

Language Development in the School Years

By the time most children enter school they have acquired an enormous number of language skills. They can speak in complete sentences and use many different types of sentences, including complex sentences. They can talk about past, present, and future events, and they have a large and varied vocabulary. They are competent communicators, able to take their part in a conversation. One might ask, then, whether there is anything left to learn. The answer is yes—plenty.

The beginning of formal schooling marks a period in which there are new demands on language ability. Now, the child is expected not just to talk but to *understand* language itself. In school, children are asked to study language that for several years they have used without much thought and to become aware of the sounds and structures that underlie that language. Further, they must then apply their language skills to reading and writing. Schoolchildren are presented daily with new words to learn and relate to prior knowledge. At the same time, because of the social structure of school, students face new demands on their skills as communicators. Success in classroom discussions, playground negotiations, and lunchroom conversations all require maximum skills in communication. It should come as no surprise that children with minimal language skills begin to fall behind soon after beginning school.

Morphology and Syntax

During the school years, children complete their development of many of the morphological and syntactic forms that emerged earlier. You might recall from Chapter 5 that the development of morphological endings begins around age 2 in typically developing children, but, of course, development continues for some time. In fact, during the school years, children are still adding *inflectional prefixes* (such as *un-* and *dis-*) and **derivational suffixes** (word endings that change the type of word (e.g., *-ly* added to a verb to create an adverb) (Owens, 2005). As children learn to use these sophisticated forms accurately, they increase their vocabulary significantly.

During the school year, sentence length increases as does the complexity of the sentences that are used (Nippold, 1998). Although much syntactic development during the school years can be characterized as elaboration of previous structures, Menyuk (1977) pointed out that several new language forms emerge during (and even after) the school years.

Elaboration of noun and verb phrases continues during the school years. Children learn to use noun clause structures such as **reflexives** (*myself, himself*) and to identify the subject and object pronouns in a complex sentence such as *Tom's father had two tickets for the game. He hoped that Tom wanted to go with him.* School-age children use more modifiers in their language and learn to use them in new ways (e.g., as sentence starters, *Suddenly the sun came out*). They begin to understand and use gerunds—verbs that are turned into nouns by the addition of an *-ing* ending (*Swimming is lots of fun*). During the school years, children also learn to use subtle rules such as *adjective ordering* (e.g., *The big, fat cat* not *The fat, big cat*) (Owens, 2005).

The development of verb tenses, which began in Stage III, continues into the school years as children learn to use structures such as the perfect tense (have + be + verb (e.g., *has been eaten*), modal auxiliaries (*could, should*), and enhance their use of irregular verbs (Shipley, Maddox, & Driver, 1991).

In addition to developing greater elaboration of noun and verb phrases, school-age children continue their development of the use of various sentence types and begin to use new structures. For example, it is only after age 5 that children begin to use and understand passive sentences (*The ball was hit by the girl*). Most children have begun to use compound and embedded sentences before coming to school, but during the school years they learn to use sophisticated variants of these basic sentence types, such as subordinating conjunctions (e.g., *when* and *although*) and coordinating conjunctions (*Henry likes chess and David likes checkers*) (Nippold, 1998). The use of embedded sentences (a sentence containing one independent clause and at least one dependent clause) increases during the school year and children learn to understand and use more sophisticated forms, such as center embedding ("The cat *that ate the cheese* ran away").

Although syntactic development is largely completed by the time children become adolescents, Nippold (2000) notes that syntactic development can be observed in writing—especially formal, essay writing. For example, older students tend to use longer and more complex sentences and begin to use forms such as **adverbial connectors** (words and phrases such as *although* and *finally*) to create more sophisticated writing.

Semantics

Rapid expansion of vocabulary is one of the major developments during the school years. Children are reported to have a vocabulary of about 10,000 words by the end of grade 1. increasing to about 40,000 words in grade 5 (Anglin, 1993). New vocabulary comes from exposure to a wide array of literature as well as to new concepts from the sciences and social studies. In addition to learning more words, school-age children deepen their understanding of words already in their vocabulary and are better able to define words (Litowitz, 1977). They can compare and contrast words, synthesize meanings, and begin to understand that some words have more than one meaning (e.g., *table*).

During the school years, a new development in the semantic domain is the ability to understand and use **figurative** (nonliteral) **language**. To use figurative language (metaphors, idioms, jokes, proverbs), one must have a firm grasp on the literal meanings of words, for only then can the beauty and humor of figurative language be properly used and appreciated. During the school years, children are asked to write poems and stories that go beyond the literal use of language to incorporate more and more figurative language. Social interaction also requires children to understand words used in nonliteral ways (*He is cool* does not mean that he is cold) and to understand increasingly sophisticated forms of humor.

Research has found that the ability to understand and use figurative language begins to develop around age 5 and continues through the school years (Nippold, 1998). For example, the comprehension of idioms (*He put his foot in his mouth*) has been found to develop slowly throughout childhood and even into the adult years (Nippold, 1985). Similarly, children often have a difficult time understanding proverbs (e.g., *One swallow does not a summer make*) and at first struggle to find literal explanations for them. They might say something like "It gets hot in the summer, so it is hard to swallow." Gradually, they are able to move away from the literal meaning of the words to the correct nonliteral interpretation (Billow, 1975).

The use of humor by children is a fascinating area of study (see Bernstein, 1986). If you have ever heard a 5-year-old try to tell you a joke, you know the difficulty children have learning to use humor. There is actually a developmental sequence to the understanding and use of humor. For example, Fowles and Glanz (1977) found that children begin to use riddles between ages 6 and 9 years but often do not understand what they mean. Children may say things like:

Question: Why did the chicken cross the road?
Answer: Because it was there.

This is followed by a howl of laughter from the child and a puzzled look by the adult. The child is able to understand the *form* of a riddle but does not yet understand the point of the joke. Ely and McCabe (1994) identified four levels in the development of the understanding of riddles (see Figure 6.1). They found that most 6-year-olds were at Level 1, whereas most 9-year-olds perform at Level 3.

Between 9 and 12 years of age, children begin to use and understand humor that is based on the sound and meaning of words. For example, they are able to understand the humor in the old joke:

Question: What is black and white and red (read) all over?
Answer: A newspaper.

Although the ability to tell jokes and understand humor may seem a trivial matter, in fact it is an important component of social acceptance and an essential social skill. Children who lack the language skills to appreciate humor may be at risk for social rejection.

Pragmatics

Some of the most dramatic language development in the school years is in the area of pragmatics. Although most kindergarten-age children can express their wants and needs, they are not yet truly sophisticated communicators. They do not have command of some of the subtleties of communication. For example, a preschool child may launch into a conversation about Eduardo, forgetting to tell you that Eduardo is the name of

FIGURE 6.1 Stages in Solving Riddles

Target riddle: What dog keeps the best time? Answer: A watch dog.

Level 0
Absent or minimal response: "I don't know."

Level 1
Illogical or negative attempt at explication: "Because dogs don't really have watches."

Level 2
Explanation focuses on the situation to which the language referred, not the language itself: "Because a watch dog is a kind of dog and also it keeps time."

Level 3
Incongruity is clearly attributed to the language itself: "Because, well, watch dogs are really dogs to watch and see if anybody comes in but watch dogs. . . . It's a joke 'cause it's also another word for telling time."

Source: Ely & McCabe (1994).

her teddy bear. In any case, the child's entire conversation may be irrelevant to the topic being discussed.

During the school years, children continue to develop *conversational competence* as well as increasing sophistication in the use of **narratives**—that is, a storytelling monologue. In the domain of conversational skills, school-age children improve their ability to stay on topic, to have extended dialogues, to make relevant comments, to shift between topics, and to adjust their language to the context and to the speaker (Nippold, 1998).

As you read the preceding paragraph you may have wondered who these children are who possess such good conversational skills. You may have thought about children you know who butt in to conversations, who seem insensitive to the give-and-take of conversation, or who talk to teachers just as they talk to each other. But this is the point. We *expect* school-age children to be more competent and more sensitive conversational partners. When they let us down, we are justifiably disappointed. However, keep in mind that, as with other aspects of language, *competence* may exceed *performance*. In other words, although students may possess the language *ability*, they may fail to utilize their skill—for a variety of reasons.

As children become preadolescents and adolescents, important changes in communication continue to take place. Among these changes are a greater variety of conversational partners and the addition of new topics to their conversation (Nippold, 2000). It should not be surprising that researchers have found that adolescents, especially girls, spend an increasing amount of time talking to their peers (Raffaelli & Duckett, 1989). These researchers also found that conversations with family members do not decrease, even though peer interactions take on greater importance. Adolescents tended to talk about personal issues (such as dating) and affective topics (their feelings) much more with their friends than with their families.

In addition to their developing communicative competence, school-age children are developing other pragmatic skills. For example, their ability to understand and use **indirect requests** is increasing. This is a critical skill for school success. When a teacher says, "It's getting noisy in here," she is really saying, "Be quiet." The child who is not able to *understand* indirect requests may misunderstand the message and be punished for misbehavior. Indirect requests take place when the communicative intent differs from the linguistic form. In the preceding example, the linguistic form is that of a declarative sentence *(It's getting noisy in here)*, but the communicative intent is a command *(Be quiet)*. During the school years, children become more adept at using indirect requests, recognizing that they are more likely to get what they want by saying, "Gee, I'm hungry," than by saying, "Give me another cookie."

Older children and adolescents have been found to become more effective conversational partners, especially when conversing with peers. For example, researchers have found that adolescents make fewer abrupt topic changes (Larson & McKinley, 1998). Although teens interrupt more frequently, the researchers concluded that most of these interruptions actually enhanced the conversation. When talking with peers, adolescents have been reported to ask more questions, obtain more information, and make more attempts to entertain their conversational partners. This is more evidence that the nature of communicative exchanges between adolescents and their peers is quite different from when they talk to adults.

Narrative skills are important for success in school. Children are often asked to report what they did over the weekend or on their summer vacation, or to write a story about an event that happened in the past. These activities require narrative skill. Although even young children can tell stories, as children mature, their stories take on more adult forms such as the use of beginning and end markers (e.g., *once upon a time* and *lived happily ever after*) (Owens, 2005). They also begin to use elements of story grammar—a structured form that includes setting, character, and plot.

A brief summary of the development of semantics and pragmatics in the school years appears in Table 6.1.

Metalinguistic Ability

When we ask children to sound out words, to analyze sentences into their constituent parts, to complete a map of story elements, or to identify rules of language, we are asking them to use **metalinguistic abilities**. Metalinguistic ability allows the child to go beyond language use and to *think about* language.

By the time they enter school, children have a substantial amount of language ability, but they are generally not aware of what they know. Have you ever tried asking a first-grader to differentiate grammatical from nongrammatical sentences? Many first-graders can tell you which ones are the "bad" sentences, but when asked to explain their reasoning, they encounter difficulty. They may look at you with a blank stare or say something like, "It just doesn't sound right." They *know* the rules of grammar, but they cannot *say* them. By second or third grade, however, most children can state a rule to support their answer. They can tell you that nouns must come before verbs or that word endings must agree in number. This observation has been confirmed by research such as that by Sutter and Johnson (1990).

Metalinguistic skills are important for school success. School activities such as reading, spelling, and writing often require children to use their knowledge of language in new ways. Children are asked to break words down into sounds or other units, to identify word endings, and to learn to identify the parts of speech that they have been using naturally for years.

TABLE 6.1   Development of Semantics and Pragmatics in the School Years

Semantics	Pragmatics
Rapid expansion of vocabulary	Greater variety of conversational partners
Understand multiple meaning words	More variety in conversational topics

Increase understanding of figurative language, including:
    Metaphor
    Humor
    Proverbs
	Improved understanding of indirect requests
	
	Development of narrative skills

Conclusion

Language development in the school years evolves in two ways: elaboration of existing structures and acquisition of new structures. During the school years, children build on their earlier language development—refining previous structures and broadening their use of these structures—while, at the same time, they continue to develop new structures. They can understand and use increasingly complex sentences, passive sentences, figurative language, and subtle conversational rules for a summary (see Table 6.2). School-age children also develop metalinguistic ability—the ability to think about language and apply language to other purposes (e.g., reading and writing). It would be incorrect to think of language development as ending at age 5 or 6. In fact, language continues to change and develop throughout life.

Implications for Instruction

Knowledge of language development during the school years can help teachers organize and plan for instruction. For example, the research on pragmatic language indicates that adolescents converse differently with their peers than with adults. They are more relaxed, more talkative, and more concerned that their conversation partners understand what they are saying. When older students are required to talk to adults or are asked to talk to the class, they may appear shy, be reluctant to talk, and use short responses. They probably are not interested in that type of conversational interaction. But it is important to remember that these characteristics may not represent the actual conversational competence of these students. Observing students in interaction with their peers, especially in informal settings, may give a more accurate picture of their conversational abilities. Likewise, for students with communication disorders, testing situations and structured intervention sessions with adults may be of limited value.

TABLE 6.2   Development of Language Form in the School Years

Morphology	Syntax

Increased use of inflectional prefixes	Continued expansion of Noun Phrase:
	    Reflexives
	    Modifiers
	    Gerunds
	    Adjective ordering

	Expansion of Verb Phrase:
	    Perfect tense
	    Modal auxiliary

Use of derivational suffixes	Understanding and use of passive voice Use of subordinating and coordinating conjunctions Use of center embedding

Instead, observation of informal interaction and peer interaction are more likely to expose the student's conversational skills.

Children's literature often uses many forms of figurative language, including metaphor, simile, and proverbs. These can be cognitively and linguistically difficult to understand. Nippold (1998) developed an instructional approach for enhancing proverb understanding in adolescents. Working in small groups, students learn to use contextual cues to determine the meaning of difficult words contained in the proverb (e.g., *expectation, realization*), learn to ask and answer factual and inferential questions about the proverb, and think about how the proverb could be used in their own lives.

Knowing that school-age children are still developing their understanding and use of some language structures may help teachers in their interaction with students. For example, many children in the early elementary grades would have a difficult time understanding indirect requests. Likewise, young children may have a hard time understanding humor. Older children may have difficulty understanding and using more sophisticated linguistic forms such as gerunds and the passive voice. It is not uncommon for teachers to assume that students know all they need to know to be effective readers and productive writers by third or fourth grade. But the research on language development suggests that students are continuing to develop some language skills throughout the school years

Language and Literacy

Learning to read and write is key to success in school and in life after school. Children who read well are able to acquire more knowledge, more quickly than other children. For example, researchers have reported that a middle school child who reads a lot could read as many as 10,000,000 words a year, compared to a poor reader who might read as few as 100,000 words (Nagy & Anderson, 1984). Avid readers are exposed to more new concepts and more words than unmotivated readers. As a result, the learning gap between good and poor readers widens over time.

Teachers and researchers have been searching for many years for ways to close the reading gap. The U.S. government has made the achievement of literacy skills one of the key objectives of the federal No Child Left Behind Act. The goal is for all children, including those from diverse socioeconomic groups and those with disabilities, to acquire the literacy skills that will enable them to achieve. Schools are told to adopt reading programs that have a record of success.

Despite lofty goals and the greater use of effective instructional practices, many students still struggle to acquire effective reading and writing skills. Most children with early reading problems continue to experience difficulty throughout their school careers. On the other hand, very few children who start out as good readers end up having reading difficulties later in school (Scarborough, 1998). These findings have led researchers to focus on the skills that young children bring to school. One of these skills is language. What is the relationship between language acquisition and success in reading and writing?

There can be little doubt that language ability plays an essential role in the development of reading and writing. A great deal of research has been conducted in the past 30 years that has established the language basis for literacy (e.g., NICHD-ECCRN, 2005). A number of specific language skills have been identified as critical for reading success. These include syntax, semantics, vocabulary, phonological knowledge, and linguistic awareness (Whitehurst & Lonigan, 1998). Of these specific components of language, the one that has received the most attention from researchers is **phonological awareness**. Research has established that children's sensitivity to the sounds of their language and their ability to manipulate those sounds is related to the acquisition of reading skills (Bradley & Bryant, 1985; Wagner & Torgesen, 1987).

Phonological Abilities and Reading

Phonological awareness is a term that is generally used to describe a range of skills that involve the understanding, use, and recall of sounds. **Phonemic awareness** is one kind of phonological skill that has been defined as "the ability to focus on and manipulate phonemes in spoken words" (Ehri et al., 2001, p. 253). Phonemic awareness is a key skill for learning to read and write English because a single letter may represent several different sounds. For example, the letter *c* may sound like *k* as in *cake* but sound like *s* in the word *celery*. Similarly, a single sound (such as *s*) may be represented by more than one letter. In order to figure out which sounds go with each letter, children must first learn to identify the sounds (phonemic awareness) within speech, then learn to match these sounds to letters (phonics).

Phonemic awareness involves more than recognizing the sounds within words. Children need to be able to manipulate the sounds—to move them around. Box 6.1 provides some examples of phonemic awareness tasks that help illustrate the kinds of skills involved.

By the time they enter school, most children can recognize all the phonemes of English. Once in school, they are required to become *aware* of these sounds and use them in reading. That is, they must bring to conscious awareness their underlying knowledge of the sound system of their language. This is what is meant by phonemic awareness. Children are asked to divide words into sounds, to become aware of rhyme, and to count the number of sounds in a word. In order to perform tasks such as these, children must have awareness of the phonological characteristics of their language. A great deal of research over the past 25 years has found that children who are more skilled in phonological awareness are usually better readers (Ehri et al., 2001), whereas children with reading disorders are often deficient in phonological skills (Vellutino et al., 2004).

The phonological theory of reading and reading disorders has become the dominant view among researchers interested in how children develop reading and writing skills. In fact, Stanovich (1991) went so far as to call this finding "one of the more notable scientific success stories of the last decade" (p. 78). The theory claims that children with poor phonological skills have difficulty identifying the sounds within words. As a result, these children have difficulty making the association between the sound of words and their print representations (letters). This leads to poor word recognition and, ultimately, to poor comprehension (since children cannot read the words on the page).

Phonological skills have also been found to predict reading success. For example, Storch and Whitehurst (2002) examined reading development and language skills in

BOX **6.1**

Assessing Phonological Awareness

How can phonological awareness be assessed? Kamhi and Catts (1986) used four techniques to evaluate the phonological awareness of children from 6 to 9 years of age, with and without reading and language impairments. The four methods are:

1. *Division of bisyllabic words into CVC (consonant/vowel/consonant) monosyllables.* The children were given some examples of how to divide the words into parts, using a puppet that modeled the correct response. Then the children were told to divide the following words into parts:

airplane	doctor
football	monkey
hotdog	pencil
pancake	window

2. *Division of monosyllabic words into sounds (phonemes).* The same preparation was used as that described above. Then the children were told to divide the following words into their sounds:

plane	doc
foot	key
hot	pen
cake	dow

3. *Elision task.* The children were told "I'm going to say a word to you. You say the word just like I do. Then I'm going to tell you a part to leave off, either at the beginning or the end of the word. You say the word, leaving off the part I tell you to." The children were given several examples; then were given the following words:

(t)old	sun(k)
(b)lend	bus(t)
(t)all	pin(k)
(n)ice	ten(t)
(s)top	far(m)
(n)ear	car(d)
(b)ring	for(k)
(s)pin	star(t)

4. *Segmentation (tapping) task.* The children were told "Now we're going to play a tapping game. I'm going to say something to you—some play words—and then tap them after I say them. You need to listen carefully, so you can learn how to play the game."

   Example: The tester says *oo* and taps one time. Then, the tester says *boo* and taps two times. Then *boot* and taps three times.

   The experimental items were:

ap	leb
em	kest
niz	feh
blim	sput
zan	piv
ib	kel
polt	kii
wog	mik

Source: Reprinted with permission from "Toward an Understanding of Developmental Language and Reading Disorders" by A. Kamhi & H. Catts. *Journal of Speech and Hearing Disorders,* 51(1986), pp. 346–347. Copyright 1986 by American Speech-Language-Hearing Association. All rights reserved.

626 children who attended Head Start programs. They followed the progress of these children from age 4 through fourth grade. They found that phonological skills (along with print recognition) were the most important predictors of reading in the early grades but that other language skills became more important in grades 3 and 4.

Is phonological ability the only language-based skill that is essential for reading success? It is becoming clear that, although phonological skills are critical for early reading, other language skills may also be important. In fact, other language skills may be more important than phonological skills for older readers and for more difficult reading material. What is the evidence to support this conclusion?

The language and reading development of more than 1,000 children was studied by the National Institute of Health Early Child Care Research Network (NICHD-ECCRN, 2005). These children were followed from age 36 months through grade 3. The researchers found that broad language skills, not just phonological skills, were related to first-grade word recognition and to third-grade reading comprehension. Other researchers (e.g., Tunmer, Herriman, & Nesdale, 1988; Catts et al., 1999) have also concluded that both phonological and other language abilities are important for early reading success. Scarborough (2005) has listed a number of arguments against the phonological model as the sole (or even most important) predictor of reading, including:

1. *Measures of phonological awareness are not the strongest predictors of the future reading levels of beginning students.* Phonological skills are a significant predictor, but letter-identification skills are more important and other language skills (such as expressive vocabulary and sentence recall) are also significant factors.
2. *The risk of developing a reading disability is as great for preschoolers with nonphonological language impairments as for those with impairments in phonological skills.* Children with nonphonological language disabilities have been found to be at significant risk for reading difficulties.
3. *Severe deficits in decoding and word recognition skills can emerge after third grade in children who progressed satisfactorily in reading acquisition in the primary grades.* Some children can develop phonological disabilities at later ages. These children seemed to have intact phonological skills at an early age but developed word-level processing problems in later grades.
4. *Successful reading comprehension is often accomplished by students with severe word recognition and decoding deficiencies.* Although the phonological model suggests that students with poor phonological skills will have reading comprehension difficulties, some studies have not found this to be true.

What can we conclude about phonological abilities and reading? There can be little doubt that phonological ability in particular, phonemic awareness, is strongly related to early reading success; this is especially true for word identification. Phonological ability may be an important factor in reading comprehension, but it appears that it is not the only factor. Some researchers have concluded that broad language ability, not just phonological skill, is most predictive of reading success. What are some of the specific language skills (in addition to phonological) that have been found to be related to reading?

Syntactic Skills and Reading

Earlier in this chapter, we cited research that had found that phonological knowledge, along with letter identification, was the best predictor of early reading success. However, when Scarborough (1998) reviewed a large number of research studies that examined kindergarten performance as a predictor of later reading scores, she found a number of other language measures (including general expressive and receptive language skills and sentence recall) to be as good or better predictors of reading success. Performance on these measures depends to a great degree on children's syntactic knowledge. Scarborough claims that syntactic knowledge (along with other language skills) is important for the development of reading comprehension. As children advance in reading, comprehension becomes more important, so syntactic knowledge becomes more critical. Other researchers (e.g., Tunmer et al., 1988) have found that successful reading may require both good phonological knowledge and good syntactic knowledge.

Semantic Skills and Reading

Semantic knowledge may also be a significant contributor to reading success. Research studies that have looked at factors that predict reading success have usually found that expressive and receptive vocabulary are important factors. Vocabulary knowledge becomes even more important as students begin to read in the content areas. Poor comprehenders have been found to use less effective strategies for storing semantic information (Nation & Snowling, 1999), which may affect their ability to understand what they read. The same researchers have reported that 8- and 9-year-old poor comprehenders were slower and less accurate at synonym judgments than age-matched control children (Nation & Snowling, 1998; Nation et al., 2004). These findings strongly implicate semantic knowledge as an essential factor in reading comprehension success.

Narrative Skills

In addition to being able to understand and use language structure (syntax) and meaning (semantics), there is increasing evidence that good readers and writers also have good narrative (pragmatic) skills. Students with effective narrative skills are good at understanding and composing stories. They understand that most stories have a beginning, middle, and end and that it is important to make appropriate connections so that the listener (or reader) can understand what is going on. In typically developing children, narratives become longer and more complex with age. Children who have been exposed to extended discourse have been found to be better prepared for beginning reading (Tabors, Snow, & Dickinson, 2001). On the other hand, the narrative styles of some children have been found to be related to problems in reading (Vernon-Feagans et al., 2001).

Conclusion

Today there is little question among researchers and practitioners that language skills are an essential factor in reading success. But questions remain about which language abilities are most important. It seems clear that phonological abilities are important for success in word recognition. Children with good phonological skills tend to be better (initial) readers, whereas those with poor phonological skills often struggle. But reading is more than word recognition. As children progress beyond the initial stages of reading, comprehension becomes increasingly important. We have reviewed evidence that successful reading comprehension requires that the child bring a number of language skills—syntactic, semantic, and pragmatic—to the reading task. This may explain why some studies have found that general language ability is a strong predictor of reading success.

Implications for Instruction

The research on language and literacy has important implications for educational practice. First, it is important that all teachers understand the language basis of literacy. This was one of the conclusions reached by the authors of the National Academy of Education publication, *Knowledge to Support the Teaching of Reading* (Snow, Griffin, & Burns, 2005). Unfortunately, many teachers have little or no knowledge of language development and the relationship between knowledge and literacy.

Second, knowledge about the reading–language connection can help teachers and other education professionals identify children at risk for reading and writing difficulties. Observation and assessment of language skills, especially phonological knowledge in beginning readers, can help focus instruction on children who need it the most. Similarly, knowing the language skills that are related to successful reading comprehension can help identify children with potential comprehension difficulties.

Finally, knowledge about the relationship between language and literacy can help teachers improve reading and writing success. As we noted in the beginning of this section, despite a significant focus on reading, many children continue to struggle with literacy, falling further behind their peers. We now know a great deal about how to help children learn to read. Unfortunately, this knowledge has not always made its way into the classroom. It is essential that knowledgeable teachers, working in collaboration with other professionals (such as speech-language specialists and reading specialists), apply what research has documented as effective practices to the education of all students.

Summary

Language development does not end when children enter school. Indeed, elements of language continue to develop throughout the school years. Children learn to use more complex syntactic structures and combinations of structures in novel ways. Their vocabulary expands dramatically and they become more sophisticated users of figurative language. Children become more sophisticated communicators as they expand their range of communicative partners and the topics of their interaction.

The development of reading and writing skills depends to a large extent on language. Students with better overall language skills have a greater chance for successful development of literacy skills. Phonological awareness is especially important for word recognition at the beginning stage of reading but other language skills are important as well. It is important for teachers to understand language development and how it relates to academic success in order to identify children at risk for reading and writing difficulties and to be able to help all students succeed.

REVIEW QUESTIONS

1. List three syntactic structures that are usually developed in the school years.

2. Why is the development of skill in the understanding and use of figurative language important?

3. How is metalinguistic ability related to success in school?

4. Give an example of an indirect request. Why are these structures more difficult to understand?

5. Discuss two ways that knowledge of later language development can help teachers understand and teach their students.

6. What is phonological awareness? Why is it important for beginning reading success?

7. What elements of language have been found to be important for reading comprehension?

SUGGESTED ACTIVITIES

1. Examine children's understanding of figurative (nonliteral) language. For this activity, you should use two children—one about 5 years old, the other about 8 years old. Ask each child to tell you what the following sentences mean:

   A stitch in time saves nine.

   The cat's fur was as smooth as silk.

   She put her foot in her mouth.

   People who live in glass houses shouldn't throw stones.

   What do you observe? Do the children interpret the sentences literally? Do they understand the nonliteral meaning of each statement?

2. To examine children's growth in communicative abilities, set up a *referential communication* activity. Put a barrier (a large box will do) in the middle of a table so that a person seated on one side of the table cannot see the other side. Have two piles of blocks (various sizes and shapes work best). Ask children of different ages (6 to 7 and 9 to 10) to help each other assemble the blocks into a pattern. Have the pattern set up on one side of the barrier. Ask one child to give directions to the other, using only language (no gestures or peeking allowed). After one or two attempts, switch the children so that the one giving the directions is now the listener.

   What happened?

   Was the speaker able to direct the listener to assemble the blocks accurately?

   Were directions specific?

   Did the listener ask for help?

   Did you notice any age-related differences?

3. Try the activities in Box 6.1 with two groups of students who differ in developmental level. For example, you could use students at different ages (e.g., age 6 and age 8) or students with different reading levels (e.g., grade 1 and grade 3). What do the students' responses indicate about their phonological awareness? What are the implications for teaching reading?

GLOSSARY

adverbial connectors: words and phrases that connect two phrases or sentences

derivational suffixes: word endings that change the type of word

figurative language: nonliteral use of language that uses language in more creative, imaginative ways

indirect requests: communicative form in which the syntactic form of the request (e.g., *Can you close the door?*) is different from the intent of the message (e.g., *Close the door!*)

metalinguistic ability: the ability to think about language itself

narrative: a storytelling monologue

phonemic awareness: the ability to focus on and manipulate phonemes in spoken words

phonological awareness: the ability to understand, use, and recall the phonological segment used in an alphabetic orthography

reflexives: pronouns that refer to another noun (e.g., *myself, himself*)

RESOURCES ON THE WEB

www.reading.org   International Reading Association

www.rif.org/'   "Reading Is Fundamental" literacy advocacy group

www.ed.gov/programs/readingfirst/index.html   U.S. government program to disseminate effective reading practices

REFERENCES

Anglin, J. (1993). Vocabulary development: A morphological analysis. *Monographs of the Society for Research in Child Development,* Serial No. 238, Vol. 58, No. 10.

Berko Gleason, J. (1973). Code switching in children's language. In T. Moore (Ed.), *Cognitive development and the acquisition of language* (pp. 159–167). New York: Academic Press.

Bernstein, D. (1986). The development of humor: Implications for assessment and intervention. *Folia Phoniatrica, 39,* 130–144.

Billow, R. (1975). A cognitive developmental study of metaphor comprehension. *Developmental Psychology, 11,* 415–423.

Bradley, L., & Bryant, P. (1985). *Rhyme and reason in reading and spelling.* Ann Arbor: University of Michigan Press.

Catts, H. W., Fey, M. E., Zhang, X., & Tomblin, J. B. (1999). Language basis of reading and reading disabilities. *Scientific Studies of Reading, 3,* 331–361.

Ehri, L. C., Nunes, S. R., Willows, D. M., Schuster, B. V., Yaghoub-Zadeh, Z., & Shanahan, T. (2001). Phonemic awareness instruction helps children learn to read: Evidence from the National Reading Panel's meta-analysis. *Reading Research Quarterly, 36,* 250–287.

Ely, R., & McCabe, A. (1994). The language play of kindergarten children. *First Language, 14,* 19–35.

Fowles, B., & Glanz, M. (1977). Competence and a talent in verbal riddle comprehension. *Journal of Child Language, 4,* 433–452.

Larson, V. L., & McKinley, N. L. (1998). Characteristics of adolescents' conversations: A longitudinal study. *Clinical Linguistics and Phonetics, 12,* 183–203.

Litowitz, B. (1977). Learning to make definitions. *Journal of Child Language, 4,* 289–304.

Menyuk, P. (1977). *Language and maturation.* Cambridge, MA: MIT Press.

Nagy, W. E., & Anderson, R. C. (1984). How many words are there in printed school English? *Reading Research Quarterly, 19,* 304–330.

Nation, K., Clarke, P., Marshall, C. M., & Durand, M. (2004). Hidden language impairments in children: Parallels between poor reading comprehension and specific language impairment*. Journal of Speech, Language, and Hearing Research, 47,* 199–211.

Nation, K., & Snowling, M. J. (1998). Semantic processing and the development of word recognition skills: Evidence from children with reading comprehension difficulties. *Journal of Memory and Language, 39,* 85–101.

Nation, K., & Snowling, M. J. (1999). Developmental differences in sensitivity to semantic relations among good and poor comprehenders: Evidence from semantic priming. *Cognition, 70,* B1–B13.

National Institute of Child Health and Human Development Study of Early Child Care Research Network. (2005). Pathways to reading: The role of oral language in the transition to reading. *Developmental Psychology, 41,* 428–442.

Nippold, M. (1985). Comprehension of figurative language. *Topics in Language Disorders, 3,* 1–20.

Nippold, M. (1998). *Later language development* (2nd ed.). Austin, TX: Pro-Ed.

Nippold, M. (2000). Language development during the adolescent years: Aspects of pragmatics, syntax, and semantics. *Topics in Language Disorders, 20,* 15–28.

Owens, R. (2005). *Language development: An introduction* (6th ed.). Boston: Allyn & Bacon.

Raffaelli, M., & Duckett, E. (1989). "We were just talking . . .": Conversations in early adolescence. *Journal of Youth and Adolescence, 18,* 567–582.

Scarborough, H. S. (1998). Early identification of children at risk for reading disabilities: Phonological awareness and some other promising predictors. In B. K. Shapiro, P. J. Accardo, & A. J. Capute (Eds.), *Specific reading disability: A view of the spectrum* (pp. 75–119). Timonium, MD: York Press.

Scarborough, H. S. (2005). Developmental relationships between language and reading: Reconciling a beautiful hypothesis with some ugly facts. In H. Catts & A. Kamhi (Eds.*), The connections between language and reading disabilities.* Mahwah, NJ: Lawrence Erlbaum.

Shipley, K., Maddox, M., & Driver, J. (1991). Children's development of irregular past tense forms. *Language, Speech and Hearing Services in Schools, 22,* 115–122.

Snow, C. E., Griffin, P., & Burns, M. S. (2005). *Knowledge to support the teaching of reading.* San Francisco: Jossey-Bass.

Stanovich, K. E. (1991). Cognitive science meets beginning reading. *Psychological Science, 2,* 70–81.

Storch, S. A., & Whitehurst, G. J. (2002). Oral language and code-related precursors to reading: Evidence from a longitudinal structural model. *Developmental Psychology, 38,* 934–947.

Sutter, J., & Johnson, C. (1990). School-age children's metalinguistic awareness of grammaticality in verb form. *Journal of Speech and Hearing Research, 33,* 84–95.

Tabors, P. O., Roach, K. A., & Snow, C. E. (2001). Home language and literacy environment: Final results. In D. K. Dickinson & P. O. Tabors, *Beginning literacy with language* (pp. 111–138). Baltimore: Brookes.

Tabors, P. O., Snow, C. E., & Dickinson, D. K. (2001). Home and schools together: Supporting language and literacy development. In D. K. Dickinson & P. O. Tabors (Eds.), *Beginning literacy with language* (pp. 313–334). Baltimore: Brookes.

Tunmer, W. E., Herriman, M. L., & Nesdale, A. R. (1988). Metalinguistic abilities and beginning reading. *Reading Research Quarterly, 23,* 134–158.

Vellutino, F. R., Fletcher, J. M., Snowling, M. J., & Scanlon, D. M. (2004). Specific reading disability (dyslexia): What have we learned in the past four decades*? Journal of Child Psychology and Psychiatry, 45,* 2–40.

Vernon-Feagans, L., Hammer, C. S., Miccio, A., & Manlove, E. (2001). Early language and literacy skills in low-income African-American and Hispanic Children. In S. B. Neuman & D. K. Dickinson (Eds.), *Handbook of early literacy research* (pp. 192–210). New York: Guilford.

Wagner, R. K., & Torgesen, J. K. (1987). The nature of phonological processing and its causal role in the acquisition of reading skills. *Psychological Bulletin, 101,* 192–212.

Whitehurst, G. J., & Lonigan, C. J. (1998). Child development and emergent literacy. *Child Development, 69,* 848–872.

Whitehurst, G. J., & Lonigan, C. J. (2002). Emergent literacy: Development from prereaders to readers. In S. Neuman & D. Dickinson (Eds.), *Handbook of early literacy research* (pp. 11–29). New York: Guilford.

7 Language and Students with Learning Disabilities

Students with learning disabilities comprise a large, if somewhat poorly defined, segment of the population of children with special needs. This chapter describes both the specific language characteristics of children with learning disabilities and the effects of these language difficulties on their academic and social performance. Some suggestions are provided for teaching children with language learning disabilities.

After reading this chapter you should be able to:

1. Understand the difficulties in defining *learning disabilities.*
2. Identify the major language difficulties experienced by many students with learning disabilities.
3. Discuss the effects of specific language difficulties on reading, writing, thinking, and interpersonal interaction.
4. Choose appropriate instructional approaches for students with language-learning disabilities.

Keisha W.: A Case Study

Keisha W. is an 8-year-old African American student in a regular second-grade class. Her teacher is concerned about her lack of progress in reading and her poor socialization. The teacher also reports that Keisha is pleasant and cooperative but is very shy and reluctant to participate in groups. Keisha is reading at an early first-grade level, and her reading is slow and hesitant. Her first-grade teacher noticed similar problems with reading and socialization but hoped that the child would outgrow these problems.

Mrs. W. has struggled to provide for Keisha and her two brothers since her husband left her three years ago. Mrs. W. has held a succession of low-paying jobs and has been unemployed several times. The family lives in public housing in a high-crime neighborhood. Mrs. W. has reported that Keisha's early development was normal, although she remembers that Keisha had frequent colds and earaches and was always a quiet child.

Keisha was observed in the classroom during a group reading lesson and during group work on a writing assignment that followed the reading lesson. When called on to read, she

> **Keisha W.: A Case Study Continued**
>
> read very quietly. She hesitated frequently and misread a number of words. She needed a great deal of assistance to complete a paragraph. However, when asked a question about the passage, she responded correctly. During the group activity Keisha kept to herself; she joined in only when prompted to do so by her teacher.
>
> Keisha was tested for possible classification for special educational services. Her WISC-IV scores in the major cognitive areas clustered within the average range. Within the verbal area, her results varied from the 6- to the 9-year levels. The Test of Language Development-3 (Primary) was administered and yielded a spoken language quotient (SLQ) of 84. This score placed Keisha in the below-average range. Her test profile indicated that her lowest scores were in word articulation and word discrimination—elements of phonology. Keisha scored highest in grammatic understanding and picture vocabulary.

What are we to make of a case like Keisha's? Here is a child who seems to be bright and is not a behavior problem, yet she is struggling to succeed in school. What is wrong? It is because of cases like Keisha's that the term *learning disability* was developed. Keisha must have a disability that diminishes her ability to learn, some would argue. As a result, she is not achieving to her potential. Yet, calling her "learning disabled" certainly does not solve Keisha's problems. We want to know more about her. What exactly is wrong? What can be done?

In this report there are several hints that Keisha has some sort of language-based learning disability. For example, her difficulty reading words, her reluctance to talk, and results from the language testing could indicate a language-based disability. Yet, Keisha talks normally and can communicate when she is encouraged to do so. Her language disorder, if indeed there is one, is really quite subtle. In order to better understand Keisha and other children like her, we will examine the term *learning disabilities* and the relationship between language disorders and learning disabilities.

The Dilemma of Learning Disabilities

What is a learning disability? How do we know that such a thing even exists? In 1960, there were no classes for children labeled *learning disabled.* By 2002, however, there were almost 2.9 million children classified as learning disabled in the public schools of the United States (or almost 5 percent of the entire school population). Where did all of these children with learning difficulties come from?

The answer to this question lies partly in the history of the term *learning disability* and partly in its definition. Dr. Samuel Kirk proposed the term in 1963 to describe "a group of children who have disorders in development of language, speech, reading, and associated skills needed for social interaction." (Kirk, 1963, p. 2). Kirk's proposal resonated with professionals who worked with children who had been identified by a variety of labels, including perceptually impaired, brain damaged, borderline mentally retarded, dyslexic, childhood aphasic, and so on. Now there was one label that could be used to identify children with significant learning difficulties.

Although the term *learning disabilities* helped consolidate the young field of special education and channel research funding into better understanding significant learning difficulties, it also set off a search for the "cause" of learning disabilities—a search that continues to this day.

Early theories of learning disabilities focused on perceptual deficiencies, especially auditory and visual perception, as the probable cause. It was hypothesized that students with learning disabilities had particular difficulty integrating perception with motor functions (perceptual-motor functioning).

Assessment batteries and intervention materials were developed and disseminated. Although some children may have been helped, the perceptual-motor theory of learning disabilities ultimately faltered on evidence that, in most cases, perceptual and perceptual-motor intervention simply did not work (Kavale & Mattson, 1983). Still, vestiges of the perceptual theory of learning disabilities linger to this day.

In the 1980s and 1990s, the information-processing theory of learning disabilities was predominant. This theory grew out of what was being learned about processing information in the rapidly developing computer field. Applied to humans, information-processing theory provided sophisticated models of learning that showed how information might flow and be altered during the learning process. It also helped researchers describe how learning might break down and cause the sort of learning problems seen in children identified as learning disabled. Intervention methods such as learning strategies were developed to help children overcome their information-processing deficiencies.

Although information-processing theory presented a more sophisticated explanation of what might be causing the academic and social difficulties characteristic of individuals with learning disabilities, it has proved hard to implement in practice. In addition, many children with learning disabilities exhibited no clear pattern of information-processing difficulties.

The "dilemma" of learning disabilities is that we appear to be searching for a single underlying cause for a group of disabilities that is unlikely to have a single cause. Partly as a response to this dilemma, some experts have begun to advocate for the use of **response to intervention (RTI)** as the way to identify children with probable learning disabilities. Rather than searching for internal learning difficulties, these experts advocate looking at outcomes. According to this approach, children with learning disabilities are those who fail to respond to effective instruction. Although this approach has the appeal of simplicity, there are a number of methodological and theoretical issues, including the fact that RTI requires that children fail before they can begin to be helped (Kavale, Holdnack, & Mostert, 2005).

Another approach to understanding individuals with learning disabilities is to identify subgroups within the general population. For example, children with reading disorders comprise as much as 80 percent of the learning disabled population (President's Commission on Excellence in Special Education, 2002). Although debate among researchers continues, there is a growing consensus that reading disorders are caused by difficulties with language. If true, this theory can help practitioners identify and intervene with children at risk for learning difficulties. Although there may be different causes of the learning difficulties experienced by other children labeled as learning disabled, the subgroup approach helps narrow the search for causative factors. Of course, in a sense, looking for subgroups marks a return to the days before the use of a single label, but that might be a necessary step in order to better identify and teach children with learning disabilities.

Existing definitions have done little to resolve the dilemma of learning disabilities. The definitions tend to be broad and offer little help to practitioners seeking to identify children in need of intensive remediation. For example, the federal definition of learning disabilities, incorporated in the Individuals with Disabilities Education Act (IDEA 2004), states:

> The term "specific learning disability" means a disorder in one or more of the basic psychological processes involved in understanding or in using language, spoken or written, which disorder may manifest itself in imperfect ability to listen, think, speak, read, write, spell, or to do mathematical calculations. Such disorders include such conditions as perceptual handicaps, brain injury, minimal brain dysfunction, dyslexia, and developmental aphasia. Such term does not include children who have learning problems which are primarily the result of visual, hearing, or motor handicaps, of mental retardation, of emotional disturbance, or of environmental, cultural, or economic disadvantage.

The definition was designed to be broad and inclusive, although its last section was meant to exclude other causes of learning problems from the category of learning disabilities. However, the definition has been difficult to apply in practice. Until recently, IDEA required local education agencies (school districts) to use discrepancy between achievement (usually defined as standardized test scores) and potential (IQ) to identify students with learning disabilities. The 2004 amendments to IDEA make the use of discrepancy optional and call for a process that determines if a child responds to "scientific, research based intervention" (the response to intervention (RTI) approach mentioned earlier in this chapter).

The federal definition of learning disabilities identifies disorders of language (spoken or written) as the defining feature of the disorder. The definition recognizes that most children labeled as learning disabled have difficulty understanding and using language. However, IDEA also includes the disability category of "speech or language impairment," which is defined as "a communication disorder, such as stuttering, impaired articulation, a language impairment, or a voice impairment, that adversely affects a child's educational performance." As you might imagine, there can be a lot of confusion about the terms *learning disability* and *speech or language impairment.* After all, according to the definitions, many children with "learning disabilities" have a disorder of language. But many children with "speech or language impairment" have difficulties with educational performance. To make matters worse, many speech-language specialists use an entirely different term *(specific language impairment; SLI)* to describe children who have "significant limitations in language functioning that cannot be attributed to deficits in hearing, oral structure and function, or general intelligence" (Leonard, 1987). Researchers have found that up to 50 percent of children with reading disorders (the most common type of learning disability) may also meet the criteria for specific language impairment and that a similar percentage of children with

TABLE 7.1   Definitions of Learning Disabilities and Related Disorders

Category Label	Definition	Characteristics
Learning Disabled	Disorder in one or more of the basic psychological processes involved in understanding or in using language, spoken or written.	Difficulties in thinking, listening, speaking, reading, spelling, or math.
Speech or Language Impairment	A communication disorder—such as stuttering, impaired articulation, a language impairment, or a voice impairment—that adversely affects a child's educational performance.	Speech and/or language difficulties, usually apparent early in development, that impact learning.
Specific Language Impairment	Significant limitations in language functioning that cannot be attributed to deficits in hearing, oral structure and function, or general intelligence.	Significant language difficulties, usually first identified at an early age.
Reading Disordered	Failure to learn to read despite at least average intelligence; intact perceptual abilities; no known neurological, physical, emotional, or social problems; and an adequate opportunity to learn to read.	Significant difficulty in developing reading, writing, and/or spelling skills; related language disorders.

Sources: IDEA (2004); Leonard (1987); Vellutino (1979).

SLI could be considered reading disabled (McArthur et al., 2000). See Table 7.1 for a summary of definitions of learning disabilities.

Although there is a lot of overlap between learning disabilities and specific language impairments, there may be differences as well. Children with specific speech and language impairments are typically identified prior to entering formal schooling. Their language delays and differences are so significant that they have caught the attention of their parents, preschool teachers, or family physicians. Their language disabilities are usually more significant and affect several areas of language (Bishop & Snowling, 2004). On the other hand, children with learning disabilities are not usually identified until they enter school. Their difficulties first show up in school-related tasks. Their language difficulties may be more subtle and less pervasive than those encountered by children with specific language impairments.

Most of the research on the relationship between language and learning disabilities has been conducted with students whose primary learning difficulty is in reading and writing. Children with **specific reading disability** (sometimes called **dyslexia**) have at least average intelligence, do not have general learning difficulties or sensory disabilities (hearing or vision), and are not socioeconomically disadvantaged (Vellutino, 1979). Reading disabilities have been estimated to occur in approximately 10 to 15 percent of the school-age population (Shaywitz et al., 1992). Over the years, a number of different theories about the causes of specific reading disabilities have been proposed (see Vellutino, Fletcher, Snowling, & Scanlon, 2004, for a review). But today there is a broad consensus among researchers that specific reading disabilities are caused by language difficulties (Catts, Fey, Zhang, & Tomblin, 1999; Scarborough, 2005).

Whatever we call them—learning disabled, reading disordered, dyslexic, specific language impaired—it is clear that there are a number of children who, despite normal intelligence, fail to learn adequately in typical classrooms. Although this is clearly a heterogeneous population, many, if not most, children with learning disabilities have language difficulties. That does not mean that children with learning disabilities do not have other contributing learning difficulties such as attention deficits, memory difficulties, or organizational problems. But many of these learning problems may, in fact, be mediated by underlying language difficulties.

Language and Learning Disabilities

The evidence for the relationship between learning disabilities and language comes from a variety of sources. First, children with language difficulties have been found to be at high risk for reading difficulties (Bishop & Adams, 1990; Catts, 1993; Snowling, Bishop, & Stothard, 2000). For example, in a study of approximately 200 kindergarten children with language impairments, researchers found that by fourth grade more than 50 percent of the children performed significantly below average on a test of reading comprehension—a rate more than five times greater than children with typical language development (Catts, Fey, Tomblin, & Zhang, 2002). In addition, the severity of the language impairment was found to be related to the reading deficit.

The second type of evidence for a relationship between language and learning disabilities comes from studies that have reported the existence of specific language deficiencies in children with learning disabilities. Most of these studies have been conducted with children whose primary learning difficulty was in reading. These studies have identified a variety of language-learning deficits.

Phonology. Deficits in *phonological awareness*—especially *phonemic awareness*—have been found to be highly related to reading failure. Phonological awareness is an ability that develops over time in typically developing children. By 5 years of age, most children can divide words into syllables but they are just beginning to be able to divide words into sound units (phonemes). There is a great deal of evidence that children's sensitivity to the sounds of their language and their ability to manipulate those sounds is related to the acquisition of reading skills (Bradley & Bryant, 1983; Wagner & Torgesen, 1987). Phonological skills have been identified as one of the key predictors of success in the acquisition of reading. As noted in Chapter 6, good readers tend to have good phonological skills, whereas poor readers lag behind in the development of phonological awareness.

A growing number of research studies have found that children with reading disabilities have difficulty acquiring phonological, especially phonemic, awareness. A typical study was one conducted by Fox and Routh (1980) with first-grade children who had average, mildly depressed, and severely depressed reading abilities. They asked these children to "say just a little bit" of spoken syllables. The children with severe reading problems were generally unable to divide the syllables into phonemes, whereas the other children were able to perform this task. Other studies have found that children with reading disabilities are insensitive to rhyme (Bradley & Bryant, 1978) and to the length of words (Katz, 1986). A number of other studies have found that children with reading disabilities have difficulty with phonological skills such as identification of sounds, phoneme segmentation and detecting rhyme (Blachman, 2000; Brady, Shankweiler, & Mann, 1983; Bradley & Bryant, 1983; Snowling, 2000; Torgesen, Wagner, & Rashotte, 1994; Tunmer, 1989; Vellutino, Scanlon, & Spearing, 1995).

In their review of the research, Vellutino and colleagues (2004) concluded that "there is now strong and highly convergent evidence in support of weak phonological coding as an underlying cause of the [specific reading disability] disorder" (p. 12). With so many studies reaching a similar conclusion, there can be little doubt that phonological awareness plays a very important role in reading disorders. In fact, after reviewing the research on phonological awareness and reading, the National Reading Panel (2000) concluded that "phonological awareness measured at the beginning of kindergarten is one of the two best predictors of how well children will learn to read" (p. 2–11).

Morphology.   In addition to deficits in phonological skills, there is also evidence that other language skills play a role in reading. Given the problems that many children with learning disabilities have with the sound system of the language, it should not be surprising to find that they also have difficulty with word parts. In fact, most studies of the morphological abilities of children with learning disabilities have found this is an area of difficulty (Joanisse, Manis, Keating, & Seidenberg 2000). For example, Vogel (1977) found that on two tests of morphological knowledge, 7- and 8-year-old poor readers did significantly worse than children of the same age who were good readers. The poor readers did especially poorly with the more complex rules. Casalis, Cole, and Sopo (2004) studied morphological awareness in French children with reading disorders (dyslexia). They found that morphological awareness (as well as phonological awareness) was poorer for the children with reading disorders than for their peers without reading disorders. Difficulty with morphology can affect spelling and writing. It is not uncommon to see children with learning disabilities omit word endings or use them inappropriately (e.g., writes *deerses* for *deer*).

Syntax.   Research on the syntactic skills of children with learning disabilities has been clouded by some of the issues in definition we discussed earlier in this chapter. In other words, the answer to whether children with reading and learning disabilities have deficits in syntax depends on how one identifies learning disabilities. That may explain why some researchers have reported that children with learning disabilities have deficiencies in syntactic skills, whereas others have not found such problems. For example, a number of studies that used standardized tests of language skills have found that children with learning disabilities, especially those with reading disorders, have poor syntactic skills when compared to their peers of the same age without reading disorders (e.g., Bishop & Snowling, 2004; Catts et al., 1999; Nation, Clarke, Marshall, & Durand, 2004). Students with learning disabilities have been reported to have difficulty understanding syntactic structures such as complex sentences (e.g., those that contain relative clauses and use the passive voice) (Vogel, 1974) and to use shorter and less complex sentences (Simms & Crump, 1983). Other studies have not found significant problems with syntax in children with reading and learning disabilities (Roth & Spekman, 1989; Shankweiler et al., 1995)

Why the differences in findings? Again, part of the answer lies in how one defines learning disabilities. Are we talking about students with reading disorders, language difficulties, math deficiencies, or all of the above? It would not be surprising to find different results depending on the nature of the learning problems of the children studied. In an attempt to get a more definitive picture of the syntactic skills of students with learning disabilities, Scott and Windsor (2000) carefully chose 20 children with language learning disabilities. Each student had expressive language difficulties (measured by the Test of Language Development) and a specific reading impairment. These children were matched by the researchers with children of the same chronological age and to younger, typically developing children with a similar language age as the children with language-learning disabilities. All of the children watched videotapes and then were asked either to tell or to write a story about what they had seen. The researchers evaluated the children's responses on four major criteria: productivity; lexical diversity (vocabulary); grammatical complexity; and grammatical error. The results showed that children with learning disabilities produced shorter and less complex utterances than the group of the same chronological age but were similar to the younger children matched for language age. Similar results were found for grammatical complexity and for errors, although the group with language disabilities made more errors than either of the other groups. There were no differences found on lexical diversity (vocabulary), except in writing. The students with learning disabilities used less diverse vocabulary. The researchers concluded that children with the type of syntactic difficulties found in this study would have a very difficult time functioning in a regular education classroom. Their speaking and writing would be shorter, less grammatically complex, and filled with errors.

Although there has been conflicting evidence about the syntactic functioning of students with learning disabilities, there is sufficient evidence to suggest that syntax is an area of concern. The sort of problems experienced by children with learning disabilities may not always be obvious in spoken language, but they become more identifiable in reading and in written output.

Semantics.   Since many, if not most, students with learning disabilities have difficulties with aspects of cognition such as planning, organizing, and evaluating information, it should not be surprising to find that they also have difficulty with semantic concepts. After all, semantics involves the development of relationships between ideas and language. In fact, semantics is a significant problem for many students with learning disabilities, no matter how they are defined. In particular, research has discovered two main problem areas: **word finding** and the use of figurative language. Many studies have found that the expressive vocabulary skills of children with learning disabilities lag behind those of other children (e.g., Rudel, Denckla, & Broman, 1981). Children with a variety of learning disabilities, including reading disorders, take longer to retrieve words from memory than typically developing children (Bishop & Snowling, 2004; Catts et al., 1999). Some researchers believe that this word-finding problem is characteristic of children with reading disorders (Wolf, Bowers, & Biddle, 2000). In addition to their word-finding problems, students with learning disabilities have been reported to have difficulty with word meanings. Children with reading comprehension deficits have been found to have overall deficiencies in vocabulary (Catts et al., 2006).

Studies of children with learning disabilities have also reported specific problems with **figurative** (or nonliteral) **language,** such as understanding and using metaphors (Nippold & Fey, 1983), similes (Seidenberg & Bernstein, 1986), and idioms (Qualls et al., 2004). Problems understanding and using nonliteral language may reflect the rigidity with which many students with learning disabilities seem to approach language. That is, it seems as though they become attached to the most concrete meaning of words, even when this clearly makes no sense in the context. Nonliteral language is often an important part of the curriculum; metaphors and similes are important language devices that are used in many stories. Students are asked to use such devices in their own writing (and are graded accordingly).

Pragmatics.   Although most of the research on language and learning disabilities has focused on reading disorders, there are other ways that language may affect learning. For example, many children with learning disabilities experience significant difficulty with aspects of social skill development (Bryan, Burstein, & Ergul, 2004). As a result, they often are less accepted by their peers. Since much of social interaction is language based, there is likely a relationship between social skills and the use of language for communication (pragmatics). Research has consistently found the area of pragmatics to be a major problem for children with learning disabilities (Boucher, 1986; Lapadat, 1991). Not only do these students have difficulties with language but they often lack the ability (or the knowledge) to analyze social situations, to plan their responses, and to evaluate the consequences of their actions (Bryan, 1991; Vaughn, 1991). Both language and social-cognition skills contribute to pragmatics.

Research on the pragmatic skills of children with learning disabilities has focused mostly on their conversational skills. A number of specific problems have been identified. For example, when asked to participate in a TV talk-show format, students with learning disabilities tended to be less effective interviewers than did their peers without disabilities. They asked fewer open-ended questions (i.e., questions that would give the "guest" the opportunity to discuss the topics in detail) (Bryan, Donahue, Pearl, & Sturm, 1981). Here is an example of two students who were asked to pretend to be part of such an interaction:

HOST: Welcome to the show. Today we have Doogie Howser with us.

GUEST: Hello.

H: Well, we're going to ask him a few questions. Doogie, what time did you start being a doctor?

G: When I was four.

H. What? When is the first time that you delivered a baby?

G: Twelve.

H. What time is it now?

G: 9:37.

H: Did you ever have a girlfriend?

G: Yes.

Now, contrast this example to the next one:

HOST: Good morning America! Today we have Doogie Howser on our show.

GUEST: Hello.

H: How did you do in medical school?

G: I did good. That's how I became a doctor so early. I delivered a baby when I was 12.

H. Is being a doctor scary?

G: Yeah, because you don't know what kind of patient you're going to get or if it's going to be overreactive or something like that.

These conversations were taken from two fourth-grade students. In the first sample, the host is a student who has been classified as having learning disabilities. The guest is a peer without a learning disability. In the second sample the students switched roles. You can see that the host in the second sample asked questions that elicited longer, more elaborate answers. We do not usually ask students to host talk-shows in school, but we do ask them to participate in communication with peers. These examples suggest that students with learning disabilities are less competent conversational partners.

Several studies have found students with learning disabilities to be less sensitive to the conversational needs of their partners. For example, studies of referential communication have usually found that children with learning disabilities provide incomplete and inaccurate descriptions (Spekman, 1981). In referential communication tasks, children are required to verbally guide a partner in completing a task (such as assembling blocks) when the partner is unable to see the array in front of the speaker. Although this is a somewhat artificial task, it has been found to be a good way to evaluate conversational abilities. Students with learning disabilities typically have a difficult time with this task. Other studies have found that children with learning disabilities have difficulty adjusting their language to the level of their conversational partner (Bryan & Pflaum, 1978) or to speakers of different levels of authority (Donahue, 1981). The latter difficulty can present a problem, for example, when a student needs to speak differently to the principal than to a buddy on the playground.

In addition to the research with children classified as learning disabled, a number of studies have found that children with specific language impairments are at risk for social difficulties (Brinton & Fujiki, 2004). Children with specific language impairments have been found to have difficulty with social tasks, such as cooperative learning (Brinton, Fujiki, & Higbee, 1998) and experience social rejection (Paul, Looney, & Dahm, 1991). More recently Hart, Fujiki, Brinton, and Hart (2004) found that social behavior problems were linked to the severity of language problems. Speifically, children with more severe language disorders were less prosocial (sympathetic, comforting, sharing) than their peers without language disorders. Although children with specific language impairments often have more significant language difficulties than children identified as language-learning disabled, there is considerable overlap between the two groups, adding further evidence that language difficulties may be a factor in the often reported social problems of children with learning disabilities.

In summary, it appears safe to conclude that children with learning disabilities frequently have significant difficulties with pragmatics, especially with conversational skills. They have difficulty clearly expressing themselves to others, they frequently fail to adjust their language to the needs and/or level of their listener, and they are not sure what to do when they do not understand something being said to them. These difficulties have consequences for classroom interaction, social relationships, and the ability to understand and use written language.

Metalinguistic Skills   **Metalinguistic skill** refers to "the ability to reflect consciously on the nature and properties of language" (van Kleeck, 1994, p. 53). When children play word games, use rhyme, or recognize nongrammatical sentences, they are using metalinguistic skills. As van Kleeck points out, metalinguistic skills are not essential for the development of spoken language. We don't ask young children to tell us what parts of speech they just used (at least not before they enter school). However, many researchers believe that metalinguistic skills are essential for learning how to read and write.

We have already discussed one type of metalinguistic skill—phonological awareness. As children progress from the initial stages of reading to become more proficient readers, other types of metalinguistic skills become important. For example, children develop an awareness of the grammatical rules that underlie language and the pragmatic rules that govern conversation.

Children with learning disabilities have frequently been found to have difficulty developing metalinguistic skills, especially phonological awareness. But researchers have also found that children with learning disabilities have difficulty recognizing grammatical and morphological errors and making the appropriate corrections (Kamhi & Koenig, 1985). In a study of predictors of reading difficulty, Menyuk and colleagues (1991) found that measures of metalinguistic abilities (including word retrieval, phonological, and semantic) were the best predictors of later reading problems, but that different metalinguistic skills predicted the performance of different children. Although the relationship between higher-order metalinguistic skills and reading is not entirely clear, some research (e.g., Menyuk & Flood, 1981) has suggested that these skills are an important contributor to success in reading and writing.

The research evidence suggests that children with learning disabilities, especially those with reading disorders, have a variety of language-learning deficits. Difficulty with phonological processing is the most often reported language difficulty, but a variety of other language problems are associated with reading and learning disabilities.

The strongest source of evidence for a relationship between language and learning disabilities comes from intervention studies. Although children with language disorders may be more likely to have reading difficulties, and students with reading disorders may have language difficulties, neither of these findings is conclusive evidence that language and reading are causally related. In order to show cause, we need to see evidence that enhancing language skills improves reading outcomes. Fortunately, a number of studies have found just such a result. For example, Bradley and Bryant (1983) looked at the effects of sound-categorization training on the reading development of beginning readers. Children who were poor at sound categorization were taught to recognize and group words by their sounds. Children who were taught this skill did better on reading and spelling tests than other children who were taught to group by word meaning or who received no training. Blachman (1987) taught students with learning disabilities how to enhance their phonological awareness. As a result, their reading scores increased significantly. A number of other researchers have found that training in phonological awareness skills leads to improvements in both those skills and in reading (Adams, 1990; Scanlon & Vellutino, 1996; Torgesen, Rose, Lindamood, Conway, & Garvan, 1999).

Results such as these support the conclusion that phonological awareness difficulties are a cause of reading disabilities. A comprehensive review of those studies led Ehri, Nunes, and Willows (2001) to conclude that phonological awareness instruction is more effective than other forms of instruction (or no instruction) in helping children acquire reading skills. Similarly, the National Reading Panel (2000) concluded that "phonological awareness training improves reading performance in preschoolers and elementary students, and in normally progressing students, as well as in older disabled readers and younger children at risk for reading difficulties" (p. 2–19).

Unfortunately, there is little research on the effects that training in specific language skills has on reading. As Catts and colleagues (1999) note, although there is evidence that early language intervention can enhance language performance, children with language-based reading disorders are often not identified as candidates for language intervention. Typically, their language-learning difficulties are more subtle than those of most children who are identified at an early age for speech and language intervention. Children with language-based reading disorders usually have problems with receptive language more than with expressive language. That is, they talk normally and seem to understand adequately but, in fact, their language-learning difficulties are interfering with their ability to develop adequate literacy skills.

Effects of Language Impairments

Research has found that children with language disabilities are clearly at risk for academic failure, especially in reading. In fact, the incidence of reading disabilities in children with early language difficulties has been estimated to be between 4 and 75 percent (Bashir & Scavuzzo, 1992). There is some evidence that children with language-learning disabilities are also at risk for emotional problems (Baker & Cantwell, 1982).

Therefore, it is essential that teachers and other professionals intervene as soon as possible to help these students.

For those who think that if we just wait long enough, children with language disabilities will get better, the news is not good. Although some studies have found that children with early language problems improve over time, most researchers have concluded that these children continue to be significantly impaired in their learning when compared to that of their peers (Rissman, Curtiss, & Tallal, 1990). In one study (Aram, Ekelman, & Nation, 1984), a group of children with early identified language disorders was examined 10 years later. Most adolescents (70 percent) continued to have difficulties with academic tasks and social acceptance. Although some children with early language problems do, indeed, grow out of them (30 percent of the children in the study just cited), it appears that most continue to experience significant problems. Therefore, it is important for teachers to recognize language disorders and use effective intervention approaches.

Instruction

So, just what *are* some effective instructional approaches for enhancing the language skills of students with learning disabilities? This section will focus on instruction in two specific areas known to be problematic for students with learning disabilities: phonological processing and cognitive strategies. The methods discussed in this chapter were designed primarily to address the needs of students with learning disabilities, but they can be applied to other children experiencing similar problems. An overview of instructional approaches and methods for children with language and communication disorders is presented in Chapter 14 of this text, but specific methods developed primarily for specific populations of students with disabilities are presented within the chapter that addresses that disability.

Training in Phonological Awareness

Earlier in this chapter we discussed the large research base that has implicated phonological awareness as a cause of the reading difficulties faced by most students with learning disabilities. As we noted, research studies have found that it is possible to teach phonological skills and have a positive effect on reading. Due to the strong and consistent findings linking phonological awareness to reading, a large number of phonological training programs have been developed during the past two decades (see Table 7.2 for examples). As a result, teachers and other educators are finding it increasingly difficult to decide which program to use. In their review of phonological training programs, Torgesen and Mathes (2000) suggested that any program should follow these principles:

1. *Instruction in phonological awareness should begin with easier tasks and move toward more difficult tasks.*

    Example: Instruction should begin with segmenting words, then sounds within words, then beginning and ending sounds.

TABLE 7.2 **Phonemic Awareness Instructional Programs**

Program	Developer/Date	Brief Description
Programs for Regular Classroom Instruction		
Ladders to Literacy	Notari-Syverson, O'Connor, & Vadsey (1998)	Activity books for phonological awareness and oral language skills for preschool and kindergarten ages.
Phonemic Awareness in Young Children	Adams, Foorman, Lundberg, & Beeler (1997)	Complete curriculum in phonological awareness activities for kindergarten and first grade using gamelike activities.
Programs for Small Group or Individualized Training		
Launch into Reading Success through Phonological Awareness Training	Bennett & Ottley (1996)	Small group activities for kindergarten children at risk for reading failure. Highly scripted series of 66 lessons.
Phonological Awareness Training for Reading	Torgesen & Bryant (1993)	Small group activities for children with weaknesses in phonological awareness. Highly scripted lessons and activities.
Road to the Code	Blachman, Ball, Black, & Tangel (1999)	Small group instruction for children in kindergarten and first grade having difficulty learning to read.

Source: Torgesen and Mathes (2000).

2. *Instruction in phonological awareness should be a regular part of the curriculum.*
   Example: The authors suggest that phonological awareness activities should take place for 15 to 20 minutes a day in regular kindergarten classrooms.
3. *Teachers should expect that children will respond at widely varying rates to instruction in phonological awareness.*
   Example: Instruction should begin with segmenting words, then sounds within words, then beginning and ending sounds.
4. *Instruction in phonological awareness should involve both* analytic *and* synthetic *activities.*
   Example: Analytic activities require children to identify individual sounds within whole words (e.g., "What is the first sound in the word *dog?*"). Synthetic activities involve blending together individual phonemes (e.g., "What word do these sounds make: /b/-/a/-/t/?").
5. *Because the first goal of instruction in phonological awareness is to help children notice the individual sounds in words, teachers should speak slowly and carefully, and should pronounce individual sounds correctly.*
   Example: Many teachers confuse the letter name with the sound made by the letter (e.g., the letter *p* makes the sound *puh,* not *pee*). Also, words with blends can be confusing (e.g., *church* has six letters but just three sounds (/ch/-/ur/-ch).

6. *It is not easy to pronounce individual phonemes correctly without some careful practice.*

    Example: Teachers need to be aware of issues such as regional and local accents and the distortion that takes place when sounds are used in context (e.g., /b/ sounds different in *beet* and *bought*).

7. *Methods to stimulate phonological awareness in students are limited only by the creativity of teachers.*

    Example: Good teachers embed phonological activities within many types of activities such as spelling and writing.

8. *Instruction in phonological awareness should be fun for teachers and students.*

    Example: Imagine the delight that a child in a kindergarten class for children with special needs experiences when he recognizes the letter *b* and identifies the sound it makes while participating in a story-reading activity.

Box 7.1 provides an example of a phonological training program first developed and tested by Blachman (1991) and now available for use in the classroom as "Road to the Code" (Blachman, Ball, Black, & Tangel, 1999). This program uses a variety of classroom-based instructional activities that are both fun and effective. When Blachman taught teachers to use these techniques, their kindergarten students outperformed others on several measures of phonological awareness and letter names.

Now that it is well established that phonological training can improve the phonological processing and reading of some children with disabilities, the question becomes which instructional methods are most effective. Although research has not yet found a definitive answer to this question (and may never do so, given the heterogeneous nature of learning disabilities), the results do provide research evidence that will enable teachers and other professionals to select instructional methods for students with phonological processing problems. These methods have been shown to be effective and to meet the mandate of legislation, such as the No Child Left Behind Act, that requires the use of evidence-based practices.

For example, Torgesen and colleagues (2001) assigned 60 students with reading disorders, ages 8 to 10 years old, to two groups. Each group received one-on-one instruction for two 50-minute sessions each day for eight to nine weeks for a total of 67.5 hours of instruction. This was followed by generalization training, during which the teacher supported the children in their regular classrooms. One group was taught with the Auditory Discrimination in Depth (ADD) program (now known as the Lindamood Phoneme Sequencing program; LiPS) (Lindamood & Lindamood, 1998). This program provides intensive instruction in phonological and reading skills using a multisensory approach in which students learn to use sensory information from the ear, eye, and mouth to identify, label, and classify sounds. Children are taught to identify and label the place and manner of articulation of phonemes using a special "language" (e.g., "lip popper" for the unvoiced, plosive sound /p/). The other group was taught using a program called Embedded Phonics, which was designed by Torgesen and colleagues (2001). Children in this program received intensive practice in word reading that was immediately applied to connected text. Instructional sessions included introduction of new words, spelling practice, word games, oral reading, and writing. The primary difference between the two approaches was in the amount of time spent on

BOX **7.1**

Example of a Phonological Training Program

1. *Say-It-and-Move-It Activity.* This is a phonological segmentation task in which children are taught to represent sounds by using manipulatives (such as disks, tiles, or buttons). The children are taught to represent, with a disk, each sound they hear. Each child is given a card that is divided in half. The top half is a disk storage area. On the bottom half of the card there is an arrow pointing from left to right. If the teacher says, "Show me the *a*," the children are to move a disk from the top half of the card to the left-hand end of the arrow and say the sound. After demonstrating mastery of this skill, the teacher progresses to two-phoneme words *(up, it, am)* and three-phoneme words *(sun, fat, zip).*

2. *Segmentation-Related Activity.* One of several segmentation activities is used in the second step of this lesson. For example, children might learn to group words based on rhyme, or they are taught to segment words using *Elkonin* cards. In this activity, the children are taught to identify the number of sounds in words using picture cards developed by the Russian psychologist Daniel Elkonin. The cards have a picture of a common word at the top (e.g., *sun)* and a series of boxes below the picture that represent the number of *phonemes* (not letters) in the word. Children are taught to move a disk along the boxes that correspond to each sound as they say the word.

Example of an "Elkonin" card

Sun

3. *Letter Names/Letter Sounds.* Children are taught to use keywords and phrases to help them remember the sounds made by each letter. For example, they might see a card for the letter *t* that showed two teenagers talking on a telephone. Another activity described by Blachman is a post office game in which children select a picture that illustrates a word with a target letter (e.g., *pot* for *p)* and place it in the correct letter pouch. Later, as children learn the letter-sound relationships, letters are placed on the manipulatives used in the Say-It-and Move-It activity.

Source: Adapted from Blachman (1991).

phonemic activities and on using phonemic skills in reading and writing. The ADD (LiPS) program emphasized learning phonemes out of context, whereas children in the Embedded Phonics program learned about sounds in the context of reading and writing activities.

The researchers found that children in both programs made substantial progress in both phonological processing and in reading. In fact, approximately half of the children in each group were reading at an average reading level one year after the intervention. Considering the severity of the reading deficiencies of the children in this study, this is an excellent result. Of course, that means that the other children were still behind their peers, even though their rate of reading progress did improve significantly. Surprisingly, there was no significant difference between the two approaches. The authors concluded that intensive remediation programs in phonological skills that are based on sound instructional practices, as were both of the programs in this study, can be effective for many children with significant reading difficulties.

Several phonological training programs utilize some form of technology in the delivery of instruction. Two that have received some attention by researchers are the Fast ForWord program (Scientific Learning Corporation) and Earobics (Cognitive Concepts). Fast ForWord is the general name for a series of programs that feature computer-based activities designed to build language and reading skills in individuals with language-learning difficulties, including, but not limited to, individuals with learning disabilities. The original program was designed for children between kindergarten age and 12 years old who have a wide range of language-learning difficulties. There are now six programs that cover the age range from preschool through high school. Scientific Learning Corporation (the program's distributors) claims that the program has been shown to "build a wide range of critical cognitive and foundational reading skills in just a few short weeks. Working with Fast ForWord software produces a positive and lasting effect on a student's ability to learn and read proficiently" (Scientific Learning Corporation, 2006).

Most of the research on Fast ForWord has focused on the language program, since this was the first program developed and has been in use for the longest time. Fast ForWord Language consists of seven computer games designed to teach specific language skills. Children play five computer games a day for a total of 100 minutes. The computer constantly monitors their success, adjusting the difficulty level upward or downward as necessary. Children progress through five levels on each of the seven games. One of the unique (and controversial) aspects of Fast ForWord is that at the first level of each game, acoustic input is modified. That is, the sounds that the child hears are digitally manipulated to increase the duration and the intensity of the sound. It is hypothesized that children with language-learning difficulties can not process incoming auditory input as quickly as other children. Therefore, slowing down this input should enhance their language-learning abilities. As the children progress through the levels, these sound enhancements are reduced until the child is hearing normal auditory input (see Box 7.2)

Research on Fast ForWord has generally been mixed. Initial studies by Paula Tallal (the developer of the program) and her colleagues (1996) found that children with speech and language difficulties who played computer games that utilized modified au-

---

BOX **7.2**

Fast ForWord Activities

1. *Circus Sequence:* In a circus format, the student must discriminate between sounds with higher or lower tones.
2. *Old MacDonald's Flying Farm:* Student clicks and holds the flying animal, then releases the animal when the acoustically modified speech sound changes.
3. *Phoneme Identification:* Student must discriminate between syllables in which only one phoneme differs (e.g., /dah/ and /lah/).
4. *Phonic Match:* Students play a game in which they must match sounds that they hear when they click on a block.
5. *Phonic Word:* Students click on a picture that matches a target word that they hear.
6. *Block Commander:* Student sees a board with color blocks. The student must follow increasingly complex commands (e.g., *Touch the green circle* [Easy] to *Before touching the white circle, touch the blue square* [Difficult]).
7. *Language Comprehension Builder:* Student hears a sentence and must click on the picture that shows the sentence.

Source: Adapted from www.scilearn.com

---

ditory input outperformed similar children who played games without modifications. Later studies, however, generally failed to confirm the very dramatic results reported by the early studies. For example, in an intensive study of five children with significant language-learning difficulties, Friel-Patti, DesBarres, and Thibodeau (2001) reported significant gains in phonological processing for two of the participants but little improvement for the other three. In a study with a much larger number of children with language impairments, Cohen and colleagues (2005) compared the effectiveness of intervention using (1) Fast ForWord, (2) another series of computer-based language intervention activities, and (3) traditional speech and language therapy. Although children in all three groups benefited from instruction, those who received either of the computer-based intervention activities did no better than children who received traditional therapies. Thus far, research indicates that the Fast ForWord Language program can improve the phonological processing ability of many (but not all) children with language-learning disabilities. However, it may be no more effective than other intensive language intervention programs.

In addition to improvements in language skills, the developers of the Fast ForWord programs claimed that children could improve their reading ability by participating in the program. Again, studies of these claims have yielded, at best, mixed results. For example, in a study comparing Fast ForWord with training based on the Orton-Gillingham program (a multisensory, structured language approach that emphasizes instruction in the alphabetic code), children with reading and language disorders made significant improvements in both language and reading with both approaches. Children trained using the Fast ForWord program did improve their reading skills, but not more than children using the other approach. Another study of children with learning disabilities found that Fast ForWord did not significantly improve either the language or the reading scores of most of the children. However, children with more severe learning problems did benefit from instruction using the program (Troia & Whitney, 2003). As is the case with language outcomes, it is not clear whether Fast ForWord can improve reading skills as significantly as the program developers have claimed. However, new Fast ForWord products targeting reading have recently been developed that have not yet been tested in large-scale research studies.

Another computer-based program that has been used to teach language skills to children with language-learning disabilities is the Earobics Literacy Launch program (Cognitive Concepts). Earobics uses a series of computer-based activities to teach phonological awareness, auditory processing, and phonics skills. There are three versions of the program: one for children 4 to 7 years old, one for children ages 7 to 10, and a third program for adolescents and adults. In each program the participant moves through a series of levels while playing interactive games. The computer automatically adjusts the difficulty level in response to the participant's answers. The authors claim, "Elementary school students across the country are making dramatic, statistically significant gains in essential literacy skills." The company's website (www.earobics.com/research/proven/) presents reports from several school districts that have successfully used the Earobics Literarcy Launch program.

The effectiveness of Earobics Literacy Launch, Fast ForWord, and the LiPS programs were compared in a study of 60 children with reading and language deficits (Pokorni, Worthington, & Jamison, 2004). Children received three hours of instruction in one of the programs each day in a summer program. The authors found that the LiPS program was the most effective in improving phonological skills. The Earobics program was also effective but the Fast ForWord program was not effective. None of the programs significantly improved reading skills.

All of the phonological training programs discussed so far were designed for use with individuals or small groups. But a number of programs have now been developed to use in regular education classes with the entire class (see Table 7.2 for some examples). There is now some research that shows that the use of such programs with kindergarten and first-grade classes can help children develop phonological skills (Hatcher, Hulme, & Snowling, 2004) and may be particularly beneficial for children at risk for reading disorders.

In summary, there is now overwhelming evidence that phonological training programs can improve the phonological skills and perhaps the reading skills of many children with learning disabilities. There is, as yet, no clear evidence that technology-based programs such as Fast ForWord or Earobics Literacy Launch are superior to other programs. However, the research does suggest that intensive, long-lasting intervention can work.

Learning Strategies

Phonological training has generally been used with young children who are beginning readers. What about older children with language learning problems? What can we do for them? One type of approach that has been frequently found to be useful in helping older students learn a variety of skills is **strategy training.** With this approach, students are taught *how* to learn, not just *what* to learn. In other words, the children are taught a strategy to use as they are learning.

Many students with learning disabilities have difficulty learning new vocabulary words. Mastropieri (1988) described a strategy for vocabulary learning that she and her colleagues have applied successfully in a number of academic areas (Scruggs & Mastropieri, 1992). The key word strategy includes the following steps:

1. *Recoding.* The new vocabulary word is recoded into a keyword that sounds similar to the target word, is familiar to the student, and can be easily pictured. For example, *forte* (meaning "loud") could be recoded as *fort.*
2. *Relating.* The student relates the keyword to the target word, using an illustration. A sentence that relates the word to the drawing is created. In our example, a picture of a fort during a battle might show guns firing. The sentence might read *The guns at the fort are loud.*
3. *Retrieving.* The definition of the new vocabulary is recalled by thinking of the keyword, creating the drawing (either actual or imagined), thinking of the related sentence, and stating the definition—*forte* means "loud."

Although this technique may seem slow and cumbersome, it works. It has been applied successfully in a number of studies to improve the vocabulary learning of students with learning disabilities (e.g., Mastropieri, Scruggs, Levin, Gaffney, & McLoone, 1985; Condus, Marshall, & Miller, 1986). Use of the keyword mnemonic method does not have to be limited to students with disabilities. Uberti, Scruggs, and Mastropieri (2003) reported the results of a study in which the keyword approach was compared to more traditional vocabulary instruction—providing either a picture to illustrate a word or providing a definition only—in classrooms that included both disabled and typically developing 8- to 10-year-old students. The typically developing students learned about equally in all three conditions, but the students with learning disabilities did far better with the keyword approach—actually outperforming their peers.

The keyword method is just one example of a learning strategy that may be used to help older students with language-learning difficulties. The research on this and other instructional techniques suggests that it is possible to help these students overcome at least some of their learning difficulties.

Technological Innovations

Emerging technologies show promise in helping children with learning disabilities overcome their learning difficulties. These technologies include word processing, word prompting, and speech recognition programs. These and other technologies can be combined to enhance the opportunities for students with learning disabilities to be successful in regular education classrooms.

Word Processing.　Word-processing programs have become a common feature in offices and homes throughout the world. Indeed, it is difficult to imagine what we would do without them. Yet, their use in most classrooms has been limited and the research on their effectiveness has been mixed. It would be logical to suppose that students using word-processing programs write more and better than students using handwriting, but research has not always found this to be the case for typically developing children (Masterson, Apel, & Wood, 2002). Other factors—such as the writing task, the quality of instruction, and children's writing styles and preferences—factor into the success of word-processing programs.

Although research on the use of word-processing programs with typically developing children may be unclear, the findings for students with learning disabilities more clearly support the use of word processing to enhance writing (and reading) skills. Studies have reported that students with learning disabilities can improve their writing skills (Margalit & Roth, 1989; Owston & Wideman, 1997). Word-processing programs enable students with handwriting difficulties to be more productive and, with their spell-checking and grammar-checking features, enable students with difficulties in these skill areas to produce writing that has fewer errors. In a study that intensively examined the writing performance of three junior high school-aged students with learning disabilities, the handwritten classroom output of the students was compared to that produced when students used a word-processing program (Hetzroni & Schreiber, 2004). The researchers found that when the students used a word processor in the classroom, they made fewer spelling mistakes, used more organization and structure, and made fewer reading errors when reading their own written outcomes.

Despite these potential advantages, word-processing programs are still not used as widely in the classroom as they could be. In some cases, teachers believe that word processing is a "crutch" that will prevent students from learning spelling and handwriting skills. According to research, however, students with learning disabilities can benefit from using this readily available technology and may increase their potential for successful inclusion in the regular classroom.

Word Prompting.   Word prompt programs use word prediction tools that provide a list of words after a particular letter has been entered into the computer. For example, if the student entered the letter *a,* he or she would get a list of words such as *and, at, all,* and so on, based on the frequency with which such words appear in written text. The user can choose the desired word and enter it into her or his writing. Little research has been conducted on the outcomes of the use of this technology, but one study did report that students with disabilities increased both the length and the quality (better spelling) of their writing when they used a word prompt program (Newell et al., 1992). Therefore, it may be a good idea to look for this feature in literacy programs for students with disabilities.

Speech Recognition Software.   Speech recognition is an emerging technology that holds a lot of promise for students with reading and writing difficulties. Speech recognition programs translate the spoken word into text on the computer screen. Early systems were expensive and difficult to use, but current programs, such as Dragon Naturally Speaking (Nuance Communications, www.nuance.com/naturallyspeaking/) and IBM's Via Voice (www306.ibm.com/software/voice/viavoice/) are making speech recognition more practical and accessible than ever. Speech recognition software (along with voice output programs that translate words on the computer into speech) will make computers more functional for children with a wide range of learning disorders.

Since word recognition software is relatively new, research on its use in classroom situations with children with disabilities is limited. However, the research in existence points out both the potential benefits as well as the limitations of this emerging technology. Higgins and colleagues (Higgins & Raskind, 2000, 2004; Raskind & Higgins, 1999) have conducted the most extensive research on the use of speech recognition programs with students with learning disabilties. They have found that students who use this technology can improve their word recognition, spelling, reading comprehension, and phonological processing.

Despite the positive results reported in these studies, speech recognition technology is not without difficulties Many of the students reported experiencing frustration with the time it took to "train" the program to recognize their voice and with the errors the software produced. Additionally, most speech recognition programs are not as accurate in recognizing children's voices, especially when the children have language and/or reading difficulties, as is the case with most students with learning disabilities.

Although speech recognition software is not a solution to the reading and writing difficulties of students with learning disabilities, it is a promising tool that should improve in the future.

Universal Design of Learning.　　The impetus to include students with mild to moderate learning disorders in regular education classrooms has prompted a search for more effective teaching and learning tools. Until recently, the main approach used to accommodate students with special needs has been to modify instructional materials and methods. But instructional modifications of existing classroom instruction and materials requires a great deal of work from teachers who already feel stretched to the limit. What if materials could be designed from the start so that they could be accessible to students with a variety of learning abilities and deficiencies? That is the promise of the **universal design of learning** approach.

The universal design approach is based on principles of design that led architects to develop accessible buildings for people with disabilities. When applied to learning, the idea is to incorporate subtle, unobtrusive aids into the curriculum that can be easily accessed by students who need them but that do not interfere with the learning of other students (Pisha & Coyne, 2001). The Center for Applied Special Technology (CAST) has worked with several publishers to incorporate universal design principles into curriculum materials for children. For example, the Wiggleworks reading program from Scholastic (http://teacher.scholastic.com/products/wiggleworks/index.htm) enables children to click on unknown words to hear them pronounced and/or defined and provides other technologies to support early reading and writing. AspireREADER (Aeques Technologies, www.aequstechnologies.com/) is designed to help struggling students improve reading and learning outcomes by providing access to digital talking books, webpages, and word processing through synchronized visual, auditory, and tracking feature functions.

Universal design of learning is still in its infancy. The principles of this approach are beginning to be applied to the design of instructional materials. Although there has been little systematic research on the outcomes of the use of this technique with students with disabilities, the approach has been found to be successfully applied to improving assessment outcomes (Dolan, Hall, Banerjee, Chun, & Strangman, 2005).

Summary

In this chapter we have examined the language difficulties of children with learning disabilities. Problems with defining *learning disabilities* present one of the biggest challenges to identifying students with learning needs. Despite the uncertainty created by problems with definition, overwhelming research shows that language difficulties are an important cause of learning disabilities and that they do not usually get better on their own. Instructional approaches, including phonological training methods to enhance word identification ability and the keyword strategy, were presented. Promising technology-based approaches to address the learning difficulties of students with learning disabilities were also discussed. After reading this chapter, you should be better able to identify language disorders in the classroom, understand some of the consequences of language disabilities, and be better prepared to teach children with learning disabilities.

R E V I E W   Q U E S T I O N S

1. How has the definition of *learning disabilities* changed from the time the term was first proposed to the present?

2. What are three sources of evidence that phonemic awareness is a significant cause of reading disorders?

3. Give two examples of techniques that could be used to evaluate phonological awareness in children.

4. Choose one of the specific language deficits associated with learning disabilities and explain how it could have an impact on a child's learning and/or behavior.

5. List and briefly describe three specific conversation-skill problems that have been identified in students with learning disabilities.

6. Choose one technological support approach and describe how it could help students with learning disabilities overcome their learning difficulties.

Alex S.: A Case Study

Student: Alex S. *Grade:* 3
Sex: Male C.A.: 9:1

Reason for Referral

Alex is a 9-year-old boy who presently attends a regular fourth-grade class. His parents have expressed concerns about his reading ability. Alex has had difficulty with reading since first grade. He repeated that grade to allow for "maturation."

Background Information

Alex is an only child who at age 6 months, was adopted by his present parents. Both parents teach at a local college. Little information is available on Alex's birth mother other than the fact that she was quite young when Alex was born. Alex fell from a horse at age 4 and was hospitalized for a few days, but his doctor's prognosis was for a complete recovery.

Alex's attainment of developmental milestones, as reported by his mother, was generally within the expected range. He crawled at 6 months, spoke his first word at 12 months, and put two words together at about 2 years. His parents describe their child as very active and energetic—he loves to play all types of games but is clumsy and a poor athlete. He particularly enjoys karate. Alex has had several broken bones from accidental falls.

Education Background

A review of Alex's school records and an interview with his present teacher provided the following school-related information: Alex attended a Montessori program between the ages of 2 and 3. He attended a public school kindergarten program and has continued to attend public school since that time. He had many adjustment problems when he began to attend school, refusing to sit in his chair and to follow normal classroom rules. Alex's academic skill development soon fell behind that of his classmates and he was retained in first grade. Alex's parents report that he enjoys art and other creative activities. He is currently being tutored in Chinese and in reading.

Since first grade, Alex's behavior has improved, although he continues to have behavior problems on occasion. His academic record is irregular. He is currently reading at a 2.5 grade level, according to his teacher, and is a slow reader. Although he is able to match letters to sounds in isolation, Alex has difficulty combining the sounds into words. His sight vocabulary is limited, but his comprehension is better than his word attack skills. Alex can recall most of the ideas he reads and is very good at inferring meaning from the text. He is achieving at a third-grade level in math and has had problems with place value and regrouping and has particular difficulty with word problems. Alex enjoys science and social studies and does well in these subjects, despite difficulties with reading the books.

Alex was observed while playing with his classmates at recess. He was seen attempting to join in activities but his attempts were frequently rejected. In the testing situation Alex was attentive and cooperative. He talked openly with the examiner and easily established rapport. He demonstrated a large vocabulary and an adequate grasp of spoken language, with excellent articulation. Alex's language, however, was somewhat formal and he did not seem to relax at any point. His approach to the various tasks presented was impulsive. He responded quickly with little thought given to the problem. He wrote equally well with both hands and said he had no hand preference.

(continued)

Alex S.: A Case Study Continued

Test Results

The WISC-IV (a test of intelligence) was administered to assess Alex's general level of intellectual functioning. Alex earned the following scores:

Subtests	Scaled Scores (with 10 representing average)
Verbal Comprehension Subtests	
Similarities	11
Vocabulary	7
Comprehension	12
Perceptual Reasoning Subtests	
Block Design	6
Picture Concepts	12
Matrix Reasoning	12
Working Memory Subtests	
Digit Span	9
Letter-Number Sequencing	10
Processing Speed Subtests	
Coding	8
Symbol Search	12

Verbal Comprehension index: 91–27th percentile (90% confidence interval 86–97)
Perceptual Reasoning index: 100–50th percentile (90% confidence interval 86–97)
Working Memory index: 97–42nd percentile (90% confidence interval 86–97)
Processing Speed index: 100–50th percentile (90% confidence interval 86–97)
Full Scale Score: 95–37th percentile (90% confidence interval 86–97)

Alex demonstrated relative strength in verbal reasoning. On tasks requiring him to formulate a definition for a word, Alex's results were in the low-average range.

The Woodcock Johnson III Test of Achievement was administered to obtain standardized measures of academic achievement. The subtest scores were as follows:

Subtest	Standard Score (68% Confidence Band)		Percentile Rank
Letter-Word Identification	87	(85–90)	20
Reading Fluency	93	(91–95)	33
Story Recall	100	(93–107)	49
Calculation	92	(87–97)	30
Math Fluency	86	(82–89)	17
Spelling	89	(85–93)	23
Passage Comprehension	91	(87–94)	27
Applied Problems	100	(95–106)	51
Writing Samples	108	(99–116)	70
Word Attack	81	(77–86)	11
Handwriting	85	(79–91)	16

Alex S.: A Case Study Continued

These achievement test scores indicate that Alex's strengths are in writing and in story recall. His scores were below average in letter-word identification, reading fluency, calculation, math fluency, spelling, passage comprehension, word attack, and handwriting.

The Peabody Picture Vocabulary Test III B was also administered to Alex. He scored in the high-average range, achieving a percentile rank of 84.

Case Questions

1. What are Alex's major problems? Use evidence from the case to support your answer.
2. What language difficulties is Alex experiencing? How are they affecting Alex's school performance?
3. What are Alex's strengths? How could these be utilized in the development of an instructional program for Alex?
4. If you were a member of a teacher assistance team that was asked to assist Alex's teacher in developing appropriate instruction for Alex, what suggestions would you make? Be specific and give examples.

SUGGESTED ACTIVITIES

1. Several techniques for the assessment of phonological skills were described in this chapter. Develop two additional techniques for assessing phonological skills. One of these could focus on detection of rhyme. The other might deal with discriminating auditory perception from phonological awareness. Try out these techniques with at least two children between 6 and 8 years of age.

2. Select two children between 9 and 12 years old. One of the children should be classified as having disabilities or be at risk. Have this child pretend to be a talk-show host. Be sure the child knows what a talk-show is and can give you an example. Tell the child to take five minutes to interview a guest. The other (without disabilities) child will play the guest. This child should be instructed to answer the questions as completely as possible. Tape record the interaction. Then have the children switch roles. Transcribe the interviews later, and report on the following:

   a. What problems (if any) did the children have asking or responding to questions?

   b. Compare the conversational methods used by the two students, including opening of the interview, types of questions asked, completeness of answers, topic maintenance, conversational repairs, and termination of the interview.

   c. What do the results say about the conversational skills of the students?

GLOSSARY

figurative language: nonliteral language such as metaphor and simile

metalinguistic skill: the ability to reflect consciously on the nature and properties of language

response to intervention (RTI):   A multi-level system that utilizes students' response to instruction in the general education classroom as the basis for identification and treatment

specific reading disability (dyslexia): severe reading disorder in children of at least average intelligence, and without general learning difficulties or sensory disabilities (hearing or vision), and who are not socioeconomically disadvantaged

strategy training: an approach to instruction in which students are taught *how* to learn, not just *what* to learn

universal design of learning: design principles for teaching and assessment that incorporate technological supports into materials and procedures for all students

word finding: the ability to recall a word from memory

RESOURCES ON THE WEB

scilearn.com Scientific Learning Corporation, producers of FastForWord program

earobics.com Cognitive Concepts, producers of Earobics program

ldanatl.org Learning Disabilities Association of America

ldonline.org Information and resources about learning disabilities for educators, parents, and children

nationalreadingpanel.org Contains reports of the National Reading Panel

ed.gov/policy/speced/guid/idea/idea2004.html U.S. Department of Education IDEA

interdys.org International Dyslexia Society

cast.org Center for Applied Special Technology; provides information about universal design of learning

REFERENCES

Adams, M. J. (1990). *Beginning to read: Thinking and learning about print.* Cambridge, MA: MIT Press.

Adams, M., Foorman, B., Lundberg, I., & Beeler, C. (1997). *Phonemic awareness in young children: A classroom curriculum.* Baltimore: Brookes.

Aram, D., Ekelman, B., & Nation, J. (1984). Preschoolers with language disorders: 10 years later. *Journal of Speech and Hearing Research, 27,* 232–244.

Baker, L., & Cantwell, D. (1982). Psychiatric disorder in children with different types of communication disorders. *Journal of Communication Disorders, 15,* 113–126.

Bashir, A., & Scavuzzo, A. (1992). Children with language disorders: Natural history and academic success. *Journal of Learning Disabilities, 25,* 53–65.

Bennett, L., & Ottley, P. (1996). *Launch into reading success through phonological awareness training.* Austin, TX: Pro-Ed.

Bishop, D. V. M., & Adams, C. (1990). A prospective study of the relationship between between specific language impairment, phonological disorders, and reading retardation. *Journal of Child Psychology and Psychiatry, 31,* 1027–1050.

Bishop, D. V. M., & Snowling, M. J. (2004). Developmental dyslexia and specific language impairment: Same or different? *Psychological Bulletin, 130,* 858–886.

Blachman, B. (1987). An alternative classroom reading program for learning disabled and other low-achieving children. In R. Bowler (Ed.), *Intimacy with language: A forgotten basic in teacher education* (pp. 49–55). Baltimore: The Orton Dyslexia Society.

Blachman, B. (1991). Early intervention for children's reading problems: Clinical applications of the research in phonological awareness. *Topics in Language Disorders, 12,* 51–65.

Blachman, B. A. (2000). Phonological awareness. In M. Kamil, P. Mosenthal, P. Pearson, & R. Barr (Eds.), *Handbook of reading research* (Vol. III) (pp. 483–502). Mahwah, NJ: Lawrence Erlbaum.

Blachman, B. A., Ball, E. W., Black, R. S., & Tangel,

D. M. (1999). *Road to the code: Small-group instruction for children.* Baltimore: Brookes.

Boucher, C. (1986). Pragmatics: The meaning of verbal language in learning disabled and nondisabled boys. *Learning Disability Quarterly, 9,* 285–295.

Bradley, L., & Bryant, P. (1978). Difficulties in auditory organization as possible cause of reading backwardness. *Nature, 271,* 746–747.

Bradley, L., & Bryant, P. (1983). Categorizing sounds and learning to read: A causal connection. *Nature, 301,* 419–421.

Brady, S., Shankweiler, D., & Mann, V. (1983). Speech perception and memory coding in relation to reading ability. *Journal of Experimental Psychology, 35,* 345–367.

Brinton, B., & Fujiki, M. (1982). A comparison of request-response sequences in the discourse of normal and language disordered children. *Journal of Speech and Hearing Disorders, 51,* 370–378.

Brinton, B., Fujiki, M., & Higbee, L. M. (1998). Participation in cooperative learning activities by children with specific language impairment. *Journal of Speech, Language, and Hearing Research, 41,* 1193–1206.

Bryan, T. (1991). Social problems and learning disabilities. In B. Wong (Ed.), *Learning about learning disabilities* (pp. 195–231). San Diego: Academic Press.

Bryan, T., & Pflaum, S. (1978). Linguistic, cognitive, and social analysis of learning disabled children's social interactions. *Learning Disability Quarterly, 1,* 70–79.

Bryan, T., Burstein, K., & Ergul, C. (2004). The social-emotional side of learning disabilities: A science-based presentation of the state of the art. *Learning Disability Quarterly, 27,* 45–51.

Bryan, T., Donahue, M., Pearl, R., & Sturm, C. (1981). Learning disabled children's conversational skills: The "TV Talk-Show." *Learning Disability Quarterly, 4,* 250–259.

Casalis, S., Cole, P., & Sopo, D. (2004). Morphological awareness in developmental dyslexia. *Annals of Dyslexia, 54,* 114–138.

Catts, H. W. (1993). The relationship between speech-language impairments and reading disabilities. *Journal of Speech, Language, and Hearing Research, 36,* 948–958.

Catts, H. W., Adlof, S. M., & Weismer, S. E. (2006). Language deficits in poor comprehenders: A case for the simple view of reading. *Journal of Speech, Language, and Hearing Research, 49,* 278–293.

Catts, H. W., Fey, M. E., Tomblin, J. B., & Zhang, X. (2002). A longitudinal investigation of reading outcomes in children with language impairments. *Journal of Speech, Language, and Hearing Research, 45,* 1142–1157.

Catts, H. W., Fey, M. E., Zhang, X., & Tomblin, J. B. (1999). Language basis of reading and reading disabilities: Evidence from a longitudinal investigation. *Scientific Studies of Reading, 3,* 331–361.

Cohen, W., Hodson, A., O'Hare, A., Boyle, J., Durrani, T., McCartney, E., Mattey, M., Naftalin, L., & Watson, J. (2005). Effects of computer-based intervention through acoustically modified speech (Fast ForWord) in severe mixed receptive-expressive language impairment: Outcomes from a randomized controlled trial. *Journal of Speech, Language, and Hearing Research, 48,* 715–729.

Condus, M. M., Marshall, K. J., & Miller, S. R. (1986). Effects of the keyword mnemonic strategy on vocabulary acquisition and maintenance by learning disabled children. *Journal of Learning Disabilities, 19,* 609–613.

Dolan, R. P., Hall, T. E., Banerjee, M., Chun, E., & Strangman, N. (2005). Applying principles of universal design to test delivery: The effect of computer-based read-aloud on test performance of high school students with learning disabilities. *Journal of Technology, Learning, and Assessment, 3,* 4–32.

Donahue, M. (1981). Requesting strategies of learning disabled children. *Applied Psycholinguistics, 2,* 213–234.

Ehri, L. C, Nunes, S. R., & Willows, D. M. (2001). Phonemic awareness instruction helps children learn to read: Evidence from the National Reading Panel's meta-analysis. *Reading Research Quarterly, 36,* 250–287.

Fox, B., & Routh, D. (1980). Phonemic analysis and severe reading disability. *Journal of Psycholinguistic Research, 9,* 115–119.

Friel-Patti, S., DesBarres, K., & Thibodeau, L. (2001). Case studies of children using Fast ForWord. *American Journal of Speech-Language Pathology, 10,* 203–215.

Hart, K. I., Fujiki, M., Brinton, B., & Hart, C. H. (2004). The relationship between social behavior and severity of language impairment. *Journal of*

Speech, Language, and Hearing Research, 47, 647–662.

Hatcher, P. J., Hulme, C., & Snowling, M. J. (2004). Explicit phoneme training combined with phonic reading instruction helps young children at risk of reading failure. *Journal of Child Psychology and Psychiatry, 45,* 338–358.

Hetzroni, O. E., & Schreiber, B. (2004). Word processing as an assistive technology tool for enhancing academic outcomes of students with writing disabilities in the general classroom. *Journal of Learning Disabilities, 37,* 143–154.

Higgins, E. L., & Raskind, M. H. (2000). Speaking to read: A comparison of continuous vs. discrete speech recognition in the remediation of learning disabilities. *Journal of Special Education Technology, 15,* 19–30.

Higgins, E. L., & Raskind, M. H. (2004). Speech recognition-based and automaticity programs to help students with severe reading and spelling problems. *Annals of Dyslexia, 54,* 365–392.

Hook, P. E., Macaruso, P., & Jones, S. (2001). Efficacy of Fast ForWord training on facilitating acquisition of reading skills by children with reading difficulties—A longitudinal study. *Annals of Dyslexia, 51.*

Individuals with Disabilities Education Act. (2004). Washington, DC: US Government Printing Office.

Joanisse, M. F., Manis, F. R., Keating, P., & Seidenberg, M. S. (2000). Language deficits in dyslexic children: Speech perception, phonology, and morphology. *Journal of Experimental Child Psychology, 77,* 30–60

Kamhi, A., & Koenig, L. (1985). Metalinguistic awareness in normal and language-disordered children. *Language, Speech, and Hearing Services in Schools, 16,* 199–210.

Katz, R. (1986). Phonological deficiencies in children with reading disability: Evidence from an object-naming task. *Cognition, 22,* 225–257.

Kavale, K. A., & Mattson, P. D. (1983). "One jumped off the balance beam": A meta-analysis of perceptual-motor training. *Journal of Learning Disabilities, 16,* 165–173.

Kavale, K. A., Holdnack, J. A., & Mostert, M. P. (2005). Responsiveness to intervention and the identification of specific learning disability: A critique and alternative proposal. *Learning Disability Quarterly, 28,* 2–16.

Kirk, S. (1963). Behavioral diagnosis and remediation of learning disabilities. In *Proceedings of the Conference on the Exploration into the Problems of the Perceptually Handicapped Child.* Evanston, IL: Fund for the Perceptually Handicapped Child.

Lapadat, J. (1991). Pragmatic language skills of students with language and/or learning disabilities: A quantitative synthesis. *Journal of Learning Disabilities, 24,* 147–158.

Leonard, L. B. (1987). Is specific language impairment a useful construct? In S. Rosenberg (Ed.), *Advances in Applied Psycholinguistics* (Vol. 1) (pp. 1–39). Cambridge, UK: Cambridge University Press.

Lindamood, P., & Lindamood, P. (1998). *The Lindamood Phoneme Sequencing program for reading, spelling, and speech (LIPS).* Austin, TX: Pro-Ed.

Margalit, M., & Roth, Y. B. (1989). Strategic keyboard training and spelling improvement among children with learning disabilities and mental retardation. *Educational Psychology, 9,* 321–329.

Masterson, J. J., Apel, K., & Wood, L. A. (2002). Technology and literacy: Decisions for the new millennium. In K. Butler & E. Silliman (Eds.), *Speaking, reading, and writing in children with language learning disabilities.* Mahwah, NJ: Lawrence Erlbaum.

Mastropieri, M. (1988). Using the keyword method. *Teaching Exceptional Children, 20,* 4–8.

Mastropieri, M. A., Scruggs, T. E., Levin, J. R., Gaffney, J., & McLoone, B. (1985). Mnemonic vocabulary instruction for learning disabled students. *Learning Disability Quarterly, 8,* 57–63.

McArthur, G. M., Hogben, J. H., Edwards, V. T., Heath, S. M. & Mengler, E. D. (2000). On the "specifics" of specific reading disability and specific language impairment. *Journal of Child Psychology and Psychiatry, 41,* 869–874.

Menyuk, P., & Flood, J. (1981). Linguistic competence, reading, and writing problems and remediation. *Bulletin of the Orton Society, 31,* 13–28.

Menyuk, P., Chesnick, M., Liebergott, J., Korngold, B., D'Agostino, R., & Belanger, A. (1991). Predicting reading problems in at-risk children. *Journal of Speech and Hearing Research, 34,* 893–903.

Nation, K., Clarke, P., Marshall, C. M., & Durand, M. (2004). Hidden language impairments in children: Parallels between poor reading comprehension and specific language impairment?

Journal of Speech, Language, and Hearing Research, 47, 199–211.

National Reading Panel. (2000). *Report of the National Reading Panel: Reports of the subgroups.* Washington, DC: National Institute of Child Health and Human Development Clearinghouse.

Newell, A. F., Arnott, J. L., Booth, L., Beattie, W., Brophy, B., & Ricketts, I. W. (1992). Effect of the "PAL" word prediction system on the quantity and quality of text generation. *Augmentative and Alternative Communication, 8,* 304–311.

Nippold, M., & Fey, S. (1983). Metaphor understanding in preadolescents having a history of language acquisition difficulty. *Language, Speech, and Hearing Services in Schools, 14,* 171–180.

Notari-Syverson, A., O'Connor, R. E., & Vadsey, P. F. (1998). *Ladders to literacy: A preschool activity book.* Baltimore: Brookes.

Owston, R. D., & Wideman, H. H. (1997). Word processors and children's writing in a high-computer-access setting. *Journal of Research on Computing in Education, 30,* 202–219.

Paul, R., Looney, S. S., & Dahm, P. S. (1991). Communication and socialization skills at ages 2 and 3 in "late-talking" young children. *Journal of Speech, Language, and Hearing Research, 34,* 858–865.

Pisha, B., & Coyne, P. (2001). Smart from the start: The promise of universal design for learning. *Remedial and Special Education, 22,* 197–203.

Pokorni, J. L., Worthington, C. K., & Jamison, P. J. (2004). Phonological awareness intervention comparison of Fast ForWord, Earobics, and LiPS. *Journal of Educational Research, 97,* 147–157.

President's Commission on Excellence in Special Education. (2002). *A new era: Revitalizing special education for children and their families.* Retrieved from www.ed.gov/inits/commissions boards/whspecialeducation/reports.html.

Qualls, C. D., Lantza, J. M., Pietrzykb, R. M., Blood, G. W., & Hammera, C. S. (2004). Comprehension of idioms in adolescents with language-based learning disabilities compared to their typically developing peers. *Journal of Communication Disorders, 37,* 295–311.

Raskind, M. H., & Higgins, E. L. (1999). Speaking to read: The effects of speech recognition technology on the reading and spelling performance of children with learning disabilities. *Annals of Dyslexia, 49,* 251–282.

Rissman, M., Curtiss, S., & Tallal, P. (1990). School placement outcomes of young language impaired children. *Journal of Speech Language Pathology and Audiology, 14,* 49–58.

Roth, F. P., & Spekman, N. J. (1989). The oral syntactic proficiency of learning disabled students: A spontaneous story sampling analysis. *Journal of Speech and Hearing Research, 32,* 67–77.

Rudel, R., Denckla, M., & Broman, M. (1981). The effect of varying stimulus context on word finding ability: Dyslexia further differentiated from other learning disabilities. *Brain and Language, 13,* 130–144.

Scanlon, D. M., & Vellutino, F. R. (1996). Prerequisite skills, early instruction, and success in first grade reading: Selected results from a longitudinal study. *Mental Retardation and Development Disabilities, 2,* 54–63.

Scarborough, H. S. (2005). Developmental relationships between language and reading: Reconciling a beautiful hypothesis with some ugly facts. In H. Catts & A. Kamhi (Eds.), *The connections between language and reading disabilities.* Mahwah, NJ: Lawrence Erlbaum.

Scientific Learning Corporation. (2006). Results. Retrieved from www.scilearn.com, August 27, 2006.

Scott, C. M., & Windsor, J. (2000). General language performance measures in spoken and written narrative and expository discourse of school-age children with language-learning disabilities. *Journal of Speech and Hearing Research, 43,* 324–339.

Scruggs, T., & Mastropieri, M. (1992). Effective mainstreaming for mildly handicapped students. *The Elementary School Journal, 92,* 389–409.

Seidenberg, P., & Bernstein, D. (1986). The comprehension of similes and metaphors by learning-disabled and nonlearning-disabled children. *Language, Speech, and Hearing Services in Schools, 17,* 219–229.

Shankweiler, D., Crain, S., Katz, L., Fowler, A. E., Liberman, A. M., Brady, S. A., Thornton, R., Lundquist, E., Dreyer, L., Fletcher, J. M., Stuebing, K. K., Shaywitz, S. E., & Shaywitz, B. A. (1995). Cognitive profiles of reading-disabled children: Comparison of language skills in phonology, morphology, and syntax. *Psychological Science, 6,* 149–155.

Shaywitz, S. E., Escobar, M. D., Shaywitz, B. A., Fletcher, J. M., & Makuch, R. W. (1992). Evidence that dyslexia may represent the lower tail of a normal distribution of reading ability. *New England Journal of Medicine, 326,* 145–150.

Simms, R., & Crump, W. (1983). Syntactic development in the language of learning disabled and normal students at the intermediate and secondary level. *Learning Disability Quarterly, 6,* 155–165.

Snowling, M. J. (2000). *Dyslexia.* Oxford: Blackwell.

Snowling, M. J., Bishop, D. V. M., & Stothard, S. E. (2000). Is pre-school language impairment a risk factor for dyslexia in adolescence? *Journal of Child Psychology and Psychiatry, 41,* 587–600.

Spekman, N. (1981). A study of the dyadic verbal communication abilities of learning disabled and normally achieving 4th and 5th grade boys. *Learning Disability Quarterly, 4,* 139–151.

Tallal, P., Miller, S. L., Bedi, G., Byma, G., Wang, X., Nagarajan, S., Schreiner, C., Jenkins, W. M., Merzenich, M. M. (1996). Fast-element enhanced speech improves language comprehension in language-learning impaired children. *Science, 271,* 81–84.

Torgesen, J. K., & Bryant, B. (1993). *Phonological awareness training for reading.* Austin, TX: Pro-Ed.

Torgesen, J. K., & Mathes, P. G. (2000). *A basic guide to understanding, assessing, and teaching phonological awareness.* Austin, TX: Pro-Ed.

Torgesen, J. K., Alexander, A. W., Wagner, R. K., Rashotte, C. A., Voeller, K. K. S., & Conway, T. (2001). Intensive remedial instruction for children with severe reading disabilities: Immediate and long-term outcomes from two instructional approaches. *Journal of Learning Disabilities, 34,* 33–58.

Torgesen, J. K., Rose, E., Lindamood, P., Conway, T., & Garvan, C. (1999). Preventing reading failure in young children with phonological processing disabilities: Group and individual responses to instruction. *Journal of Educational Psychology, 91,* 579–594

Torgesen, J. K., Wagner, R. K., & Rashotte, C. A. (1994). Longitudinal studies of phonological processing and reading. *Journal of Learning Disabilities, 27,* 276–286.

Troia, G. A., & Whitney, S. D. (2003). A close look at the efficacy of Fast ForWord language for children with academic weaknesses. *Contemporary Educational Psychology, 28,* 465–494 .

Tunmer, W. E. (1989). The role of language-related factors in reading disability. In O. Shankweiler & I. Y. Liberman (Eds.), *Phonology and reading disability: Solving the reading puzzle.* Ann Arbor: University of Michigan Press.

Uberti, H. Z., Scruggs, T. E., & Mastropieri, M. A. (2003). Keywords make the difference: Mnemonic instruction in inclusive classrooms. *Teaching Exceptional Children, 35,* 56–61.

Van Kleeck, A. (1994). Metalinguistic development. In G. Wallach and K. Butler (Eds.), *Language learning disabilities in school-age children and adolescents* (pp. 53–98). New York: Merrill.

Vaughn, S. (1991). Social skills enhancement in students with learning disabilities. In B. Wong (Ed.), *Learning about learning disabilities* (pp. 408–440). San Diego: Academic Press.

Vellutino, F. R., Fletcher, J. M., Snowling, M. J., & Scanlon, D. M. (2004). Specific reading disability (dyslexia): What have we learned in the past four decades. *Journal of Child Psychology and Psychiatry, 45,* 2–40.

Vellutino, F. R., Scanlon, D. M., & Spearing, D. (1995). Semantic and phonological coding in poor and normal readers. *Journal of Experimental Child Psychology, 59,* 76–123.

Vogel, S. (1974). Syntactic abilities in normal and dyslexic children. *Journal of Learning Disabilities, 7,* 35–43.

Vogel, S. (1977). Morphological ability in normal and dyslexic children. *Journal of Learning Disabilities, 10,* 35–43.

Wagner, R., & Torgesen, J. (1987). The nature of phonological processing and its causal role in the acquisition of reading skills. *Psychological Bulletin, 101,* 192–212.

Wolf, M., Bowers, P. G., & Biddle, K. (2000). Naming-speed processes, timing, and reading: A conceptual review. *Journal of Learning Disabilities, 33,* 387–407.

CHAPTER

8 Language and Students with Intellectual Disabilities

This chapter examines the language and communication problems associated with intellectual disabilities. Ideas about intellectual disabilities are changing, and teachers, as well as other education professionals, should be aware of these changes. Children with intellectual disabilities are a diverse group, ranging from those with relatively minor developmental delays to those with severe impairments. An examination of the range of language and communication problems experienced by students with intellectual disabilities and the factors that contribute to these impairments leads to some approaches to helping students improve their language and communication skills.

By the end of this chapter you should be able to:

1. Explain how *intellectual disabilities* are defined and how the definition has changed.
2. Describe the specific language and communication deficiencies of children with intellectual disabilities.
3. List factors that might account for these problems with language and communication.
4. Discuss the impact of language difficulties on literacy development of individuals with intellectual disabilities.
5. Explain what teachers (and other professionals) can do to enhance the language and communication skills of students with intellectual disabilities.

Karen: A Case Study

Karen, a 10-year-old girl with a measured IQ of 65, presently attends a regular third-grade class in a public school. An aide in the classroom assists Karen and two other children with mild disabilities. Karen has difficulty understanding directions, reading, and completing work independently. She reads at a late first-grade level, and her math achievement is at the second-grade level. Her teacher reports that Karen has made progress while in this classroom. She noted that Karen is reluctant to contribute during cooperative learning groups but will participate with prompting.

(continued)

Karen: A Case Study Continued

Karen's mother has reported that Karen had no apparent physical problems during her early development, although her development was a little slower than that of other children. Karen was late in crawling and could neither stand nor walk at 18 months. When Karen was about 2 years old, her parents became concerned about her lack of speech; however, the family physician told them not to worry—that Karen would catch up. Karen had persistent otitis media (middle-ear infections) as a young child and continues to experience occasional earaches.

Prior to this year, Karen was in a self-contained, special education classroom. She appeared to make considerable progress in that class. She began to read and opened up to other children in the class. Before being placed in the special education class, Karen had spent two years in a regular first-grade program. Her teachers there described Karen as quiet and a hard worker, but also as slow and immature. She had particular difficulty with beginning reading skills and with working independently. She appeared to have few friends.

Karen's parents asked that she be returned to the regular education classroom after her year in special education. Although the district was reluctant to return her to regular education (since she appeared to be progressing in the special education classroom), they agreed to do so. At this point, Karen appears to be making slow but steady progress. It is likely that she will remain in regular education in the future.

Danny: A Case Study

Danny is a 14-year-old boy with Down syndrome (Trisomy 21). He presently attends a special education class for children with moderate intellectual disabilities. Danny has a history of significant cognitive and language delays. He did not speak until he was approximately 3 years old. Even then, his speech was difficult to understand. Significant problems with articulation persist.

Danny has a measured IQ in the 40 to 45 range. However, his language age of 4 years (as measured by the Peabody Picture Vocabulary Test) is below his mental age of 5.6. A language sample analysis completed by the speech-language pathologist indicated that Danny had an mean length of utterance (MLU) of approximately 3.5. He used mostly simple, declarative sentences and he appeared to have a limited vocabulary, although his poor articulation made this difficult to determine.

Danny is a very talkative, outgoing young man. He loves to hug his teachers and to dance. His school program is focused on functional skills and community-based training. The class makes frequent trips to local malls and restaurants, where students get the opportunity to practice their math and travel skills. Danny's speech and language instruction is focused on improving his articulation and on helping him make appropriate requests. Danny's parents hope that he will be able to live in a group home or an apartment setting and perhaps work in a service-type job.

The stories of Karen and Danny illustrate the diversity of the population of children known to have intellectual disabilities. Despite the widespread popular belief that individuals with intellectual disabilities are more alike than different, they actually exhibit a diverse pattern of abilities and deficits. Today, most live at home, but some reside in state or private institutions. An increasing number are educated in regular education classrooms, but many more continue to receive their education in separate classrooms or in special schools. Some work in the community after school, and a small but increasing number go on to higher education. Although all children with intellectual disabilities have deficits in cognition, each child has an individual pattern of strengths and weaknesses. In addition to cognitive deficits, most children with intellectual disabilities have problems with language and communication (Long, 2005).

As we examine the research on the speech and language difficulties of children with intellectual disabilities, it is important to keep in mind the diverse nature of this population. In fact, as scientists learn more about the causes of intellectual disabilities, research has become more focused on specific disorders (such as **Fragile X syndrome** and **Williams syndrome**) rather than looking at the population of persons with intellectual disabilities as a whole. This may help in understanding some of the variability that has characterized the research on persons with intellectual disabilities. It is important also to consider against whom children with intellectual disabilities are being compared. Some studies compare children with intellectual disabilities to typically developing children of the same chronological age; other studies match children with intellectual disabilities to children having the same mental age (MA) but who are chronologically younger; and still other studies use some measure of language age as the means of comparison. Each of these methods has drawbacks and each can give quite different results.

The Changing View of Mental Retardation

In 2003, the President's Commission on Mental Retardation changed its name to the President's Commission for People with Intellectual Disabilities. What may seem like an insignificant name change for a government agency is, in fact, representative of an important change in our understanding of persons called mentally retarded. Although the term can still be found in law (IDEA) and in definitions such as that of the American Association on Mental Retardation (recently renamed the American Association on Intellectual and Developmental Disabilities), *mental retardation* has many negative connotations and is often associated with unpleasant and inaccurate stereotypes. As a result, there is a growing consensus among experts and advocates to eliminate general use of the term *mental retardation* and substitute *intellectual disabilities* in its place. It is very likely in the next few years that widely used definitions will follow this practice. Therefore, we will use the term *intellectual disabilities* to describe persons who may be labeled as *mentally retarded.*

Our understanding of intellectual disabilities and our expectations for persons with intellectual disabilities are undergoing rapid change. Examples of this change in attitudes and beliefs abound. In the last two decades, there has been a movement away from institutions as the primary sites for treatment and residence for persons with in-tellectual disabilities toward smaller, community-based, and even family-centered, res-idences. At the same time, there has been growing pressure on schools to educate children with intellectual disabilities in regular education classrooms. Recently, there has even been the development of some college-level programs for persons with intel-lectual disabilities (see www.heath.gwu.edu/Inteldisabilities.htm for more informa-tion). These trends challenge widely held beliefs about the ability of persons with intellectual disabilities to live and function in society. For those of us in education, these new insights challenge us to develop instructional techniques that will benefit stu-dents with intellectual disabilities without having a negative impact on the education of nondisabled students.

Changes in societal expectations for individuals with intellectual disabilities, es-pecially inclusion in regular education classrooms, have significant implications for language skills. Clearly, there are higher expectations for students with intellectual dis-abilities to have language skills that will enable them to fully participate in the class-room. Therefore, we will look at what is known about the language of persons with intellectual disabilities and what can be done to enhance their language skills.

Definitions and Causes of Intellectual Disabilities

In 1992, the American Association on Mental Retardation (AAMR) adopted a new de-finition of mental retardation that departed in significant ways from previous defini-tions. The association reduced the emphasis on IQ score as the primary defining characteristic of mental retardation, substituting a definition that placed greater em-phasis on the functioning of persons with mental retardation in various domains (Wehmeyer, 2003). The definition states:

> Mental retardation is a disability characterized by significant limitations both in intellectual functioning and in adaptive behavior as expressed in conceptual, social, and practical adap-tive skills.

In order to use the definition in practice, a matrix can be developed that includes the individual's strengths and weaknesses on one axis and the level of support he or she requires (intermittent, limited, extensive, pervasive) on the other axis (see Table 8.1). This matrix replaces the levels of retardation that have been used previously to classify persons with intellectual disabilities.

The 1992 AAMR definition of mental retardation is an attempt to recognize the individuality of each person with intellectual disabilities, as well as acknowledge that each individual with intellectual disabilities has a unique pattern of strengths and weak-nesses. In so doing, the 1992 definition eliminates the concept of levels of intellectual disabilities, replacing it with a more complex evaluation that recognizes that individu-als will need different levels of support across various domains of functioning. The fol-lowing IDEA (2004) definition of mental retardation still utilizes intellectual functioning (IQ) as the defining feature of the disorder but also suggests that adaptive

TABLE 8.1 Domains of Functioning and Levels of Support

	Intermittent Support	Limited Support	Extensive Support	Pervasive Support
Dimension I Intelligence & Adaptive Skills				
Dimension II Psych/Emotional				
Dimension III Physical/Health/ Etiology				
Dimension IV Environmental Considerations				

Note: Intermittent Support = support on an as-needed basis
Limited Support = consistent, time-limited support
Extensive Support = regular involvement, not time limited
Pervasive Support = constant, high-intensity support, across environments
Source: Adapted from AAMR (1992).

behavior should be considered as well as the impact of the disorder on educational functioning:

> Mental Retardation means significantly subaverage general intellectual functioning, existing concurrently [at the same time] with deficits in adaptive behavior and manifested during the developmental period, that adversely affects a child's educational performance. (IDEA, 2004)

One of the most significant developments in our understanding of intellectual disabilities has been increased research on and understanding of the various conditions that cause intellectual disabilities. There are, in fact, a number of conditions that cause intellectual disabilities, including:

1. *Genetic conditions.* Disorders such as phenylketonuria (a genetic disorder that causes a buildup of an enzyme called phenylalanine, causing mental retardation, **Down syndrome** (Trisomy 21) (a chromosomal anomaly in which there is an extra chromosome present on the twenty-first chromosome pair), and **Fragile X**

TABLE 8.2   Genetic Syndromes Related to Intellectual Disabilities

	Cause	Incidence	Major Characteristics
Down Syndrome (Trisomy 21)	Most children with Down syndrome have an extra 21 chromosome. Instead of the normal number of 46 chromosomes in each cell, the individual with Down syndrome has 47 chromosomes.	1 in 800 to 1 in 1,100 live births	Usually smaller. Slower physical and mental development.
			Physical features include flattening of back of head, slanting of eyelids, slightly smaller ears, small mouth with narrow palate.
			Majority function in mild to moderate range of mental retardation but wide variation in mental abilities.
Fragile X Syndrome	Mutation in the FMR-1 gene on the X chromosome		Males generally more affected than females. Physical features in males include large ears, loose joints and muscles, elongated face, and enlarged testicles.
			Mild to severe mental retardation. Hyperarousal. Significant problems with social skills and attention.
Williams Syndrome	Random genetic mutation (deletion of a small piece of chromosome 7) most often causes the disorder	1 in 20,000 live births	Mild to moderate mental retardation, a distinctive facial appearance, and a unique personality that combines overfriendliness and high levels of empathy with anxiety.

Sources: www.thearc.org (The ARC); www.ninds.nih.gov/disorders/williams/williams.htm (National Institute of Neurological Disorders and Stroke).

syndrome (caused by a mutation in one of the genes on the X chromosome) (see Table 8.2).

2. *Problems during pregnancy.* The use of alcohol (Fetal Alcohol Syndrome) and maternal drug use during pregnancy.
3. *Problems at birth.* Low birth weight and difficulties during labor and delivery that cut off oxygen to the brain.
4. *Problems after birth.* Caused by childhood diseases, such as measles and chicken pox, that may lead to serious complications such as meningitis and encephalitis or by injuries or lead or mercury poisoning.

5. *Poverty and malnutrition.* Higher risk for malnutrition, poor medical care, and exposure to environmental hazards that may cause intellectual disabilities.

The resulting syndrome of problems caused by one of more of these conditions can differ in many ways. We are just beginning to understand the effects of these various causes, but a growing research base indicates that terms such as *mental retardation* are really a generic name for a group of disorders that are characterized by limitations in intellectual functioning and adaptation to societal norms. As we review the research on the language and cognitive functioning of individuals with intellectual disabilities, you will note that some of the research studies identify specific subpopulations (such as Down syndrome or Fragile X), whereas others do not differentiate.

Language and Communication Characteristics

Impairments in the understanding and production of spoken language are frequently found among children with intellectual disabilities. In fact, language and speech disorders have been found to be the most frequent secondary disability among children with intellectual disabilities (Epstein, Polloway, Patton, & Foley, 1989). Although there is general agreement that language and communication disorders are an important characteristic of intellectual disabilities, there is less agreement about the causes of language deficits in this population and about the specific language difficulties that can be identified as characteristic of persons with intellectual disabilities.

One of the ongoing issues has been the question of whether the language and communication of individuals with intellectual disabilities is delayed or different. Is their language similar to that of typically developing individuals of a younger age or does it develop differently? Another issue is whether the language deficits of this population are a direct result of the cognitive delays that are characteristic of intellectual disabilities or whether they are a separate problem. The prevailing view has been that language disorders in this population were the direct result of the cognitive deficiencies characteristic of persons with intellectual disabilities. Those individuals with more significant cognitive deficits were thought to have more significant language and communication difficulties. But there have always been puzzling reports of individuals with more severe cognitive deficits performing better in some domains of language than others with less severe disabilities. An emerging point of view is that the language and communication difficulties of individuals with intellectual disabilities may be more closely related to the specific genetic (or other cause) of their disability, rather than the severity of their cognitive deficits (Abbeduto, Evans, & Dolan, 2001; Rondal, 2001). In other words, language and communication difficulties are one of several problems associated with a specific disorder. Individuals with this disorder may have cognitive deficits, socialization difficulties, and specific language differences that are caused by the disorder itself.

You may want to keep these issues in mind as we review the research on the language and communication of persons with intellectual disabilities. You will see that some studies identify the specific syndrome that causes the intellectual disabilities of their subject population, whereas other studies do not do so. This may help explain why there have been some inconsistencies in the research.

Prelinguistic Development

Most research on the prelinguistic development of children with intellectual disabilities has been conducted on children with Down syndrome. Young children with Down syndrome have been reported to use the same sort of nonverbal communication as other infants (e.g., smiling, laughing, reaching) but use vocalizations less often with these gestures (Chapman, 1997). When babbling emerges, it follows a pattern similar to that of typically developing young children, with early babbling that leads to more adultlike utterances over time (Stoel-Gammon, 1997). Some researchers have reported delays of up to two months in the onset of babble; others have reported no delays. Most children with Down syndrome continue to use babble longer than their typically developing peers, often continuing to babble into their second year of life.

Prelinguistic development in children with Down syndrome is similar to that of typically developing children, but the acquisition of first words is significantly delayed in most children with this condition. Children with Down syndrome have generally been found to start using first words at a later age and acquire words more slowly than typically developing children of the same age (Stoel-Gammon, 1997). However, there is a great deal of variability among these children. For example, in a study of 336 Swedish children with Down syndrome, the investigators found that 10 percent of the children began to use recognizable words by age 1 and 80 percent were using words by age 2. However, between 10 and 20 percent of the children had fewer than 10 words by age 3 and some children had not started to talk at all by age 5 (Berglund, Eriksson, & Johansson, 2001).

In general, it appears that the earliest language development of children with Down syndrome is similar to that of typically developing children, with some delays. However, the transition to more adultlike words is significantly delayed in some children with Down syndrome and, in a small number, never happens at all. There is little research on the prelinguistic development of other children with intellectual disabilities but it is likely that most have some delays.

Phonology and Morphology

Difficulties with speech production (articulation) are more common among children with intellectual disabilities than among children without (Long, 2005), but there is a good deal of variation among children. For example, estimates of the incidence of these speech production deficits have been reported as low as 5 percent and as high as 94 percent (Shriberg & Widder, 1990). Most studies have found that although there is an increased incidence of speech production problems among children with intellectual disabilities, these children appear to follow the same course of development as children without retardation and make similar phonological errors. The most common phonological errors are reduction of consonant clusters (saying *bake* for *break*) and final consonant deletion (saying *cah* for *cat*) (Klink, Gerstman, Raphael, Schlanger, & Newsome, 1986; Sommers, Patterson, & Wildgen, 1988).

Although children with intellectual disabilities may have a similar pattern of phonological development, their acquisition of phonology is significantly delayed. This is true both for children with Down syndrome (Stoel-Gammon, 1997) as well as those with Fragile X syndrome (Abbeduto & Hagerman, 1997). Children with Down syndrome are often difficult to understand and these speech production difficulties can persist into adulthood. Similarly, children with Fragile X can be difficult to understand. In addition, their rate of speaking can be highly variable. Sometimes they speak very quickly and at other times very slowly, causing difficulty for the listener who is trying to make sense of their speech.

Several factors might account for the phonological difficulties of children with intellectual disabilities. Although it does not appear that severity of intellectual disability by itself is highly related to phonological difficulties, it may be that physical problems often related to severe disabilities (such as cleft palate, protruding tongue, and the like) may cause phonological production problems. In addition, hearing problems are another possible cause of the articulation problems frequently found among children with intellectual disabilities.

The research on speech production in children with intellectual disabilities suggests that education professionals should be prepared to help these children enhance their speech skills. Many children with intellectual disabilities have articulation difficulties that interfere with their ability to be successful in school and in social interactions. Intervention that includes both individual therapy and classroom-based applications may be useful in helping children with intellectual disabilities become more successful learners.

Studies of the development of morphological skills in children with intellectual disabilities have generally found that these skills develop in a manner similar to that of children without retardation but at a significantly slower rate (Newfield & Schlanger, 1968). However, some forms, such as auxiliary verbs and the uncontractable auxiliary (e.g., *he is* in response to the question, "Who's coming to the party?") may be more difficult to acquire and may not be acquired at all (Laws & Bishop, 2004).

Syntax

Research on syntactic skills development in children with intellectual disabilities has generally found that although there are delays in development of these skills, the pattern of development is the same as that found in nondisabled children. As we have noted earlier, mean length of utterance (MLU) is an overall measure of grammatical development in children. Studies of children with Down syndrome have found that MLU generally increases with chronological age up to adolescence but at a much slower rate than that found in typically developing children (Rondal, 2001).

In a classic study, Lackner (1968) examined the syntax production of five children with intellectual disabilities, ages 6 to 16. He found that their sentence length increased with mental age and was similar to that of nondisabled children of similar mental age. Lackner also found that the order of development of syntactic rules was similar. One difference that Lackner discovered in his sample of individuals with intellectual disabilities was that they used the more advanced syntactic structures less frequently. Similar results were seen by Kamhi and Johnston (1982) in their study of the language development of children with mild intellectual disabilities. When compared to that of nondisabled children of similar mental age, the syntactic development of the children with intellectual disabilities appeared to be quite similar. Interestingly, the researchers also compared the children with intellectual disabilities to children with specific language impairments but who had IQ scores in the normal range. They concluded that the language produced by the children with language impairments was less complex and contained more errors than that produced by the children with intellectual disabilities.

Both the Kamhi and Johnston (1982) study and other studies (e.g., Naremore & Dever, 1975) showed that children with intellectual disabilities had greater difficulty with more advanced language constructs. For example, Kamhi and Johnston (1982) found that the nondisabled children produced more sentences with questions and with conjunctions. These findings suggest that there may be limits to the syntactic development of children with intellectual disabilities; that is, although their early development may be similar to that of nondisabled children (but with delays), there may be a plateau of development. However, this conclusion has been challenged by researchers who studied older (12- to 20-year-old) individuals with Down syndrome compared to much younger (2- to 4-year-old) typically developing children. The two groups were matched for MLU (Thordardottir, Chapman, & Wagner, 2002). This study found that the syntactic structures used by the people with Down syndrome were very similar to those used by the typically developing children. In fact, the individuals with Down syndrome actually used more complex sentences than the typically developing children of the same MLU level. The researchers concluded that there is no "plateau" of syntactic development for individuals with Down syndrome and that, in fact, syntax continues to develop into adulthood. These results, if confirmed by future research, suggest that intensive language instruction for persons with Down syndrome, and perhaps for other individuals with intellectual disabilities, should continue at least through adolescence.

Research on the syntactic development of non–Down syndrome persons with intellectual disabilities has found different patterns of deficits and strengths. For example, males with Fragile X syndrome have been reported to have receptive syntactic skills at about the level that would be expected for their mental age but also to have expressive syntax significantly below expectations (Abbeduto & Hagerman, 1997). In contrast, the syntactic skills of individuals with Williams syndrome have been reported to be at or even above what would be expected for their mental age. They can use a variety of grammatical forms, including complex constructions such as relative clauses and the passive voice (Bellugi, Lai, & Wang, 1997).

The research on syntactic skills of children with intellectual disabilities suggests that there is more variation in the population than might be expected. Although most, if not all, can be expected to develop syntactic skills much more slowly than do typically developing children of the same age, for some (such as children with Williams syndrome) syntax is a relative strength. The research also suggests that most children with intellectual disabilities could benefit from continued instruction in syntactic skills throughout their school years.

Semantics

Relatively little research has been conducted on the semantic abilities of children with intellectual disabilities. The research that does exist indicates that children with intellectual disabilities tend to be more concrete in their understanding of words. In other words, they have more difficulty, for example, interpreting idiomatic expressions (e.g., *he broke her heart*) (Ezell & Goldstein, 1991). This tendency to be more concrete may be the result of delays in development of semantic abilities (Rosenberg, 1982).

Some studies have found that an area of strength for children with intellectual disabilities is that of vocabulary skills. In a study of the comprehension of syntax and vocabulary conducted by Chapman, Schwartz, and Kay Raining-Bird (1991), the authors found that individuals with intellectual disabilities performed significantly better on the vocabulary-comprehension task than on tests of syntactic skills—in fact, they outscored a mental-age-matched control group on their vocabulary comprehension. Other studies have shown that examination of language produced in natural settings indicates children with Down syndrome have a more diverse vocabulary than do nondisabled children matched for mental age (Miller, 1988). On the other hand, individuals with Down syndrome have been found to use both fewer words and a less diverse vocabulary than mental-age-matched peers on narrative tasks (Chapman, 1997). To understand these conflicting results, one should consider two factors: the task and the age differences. First, the results of research suggest that individuals with intellectual disabilities may be able to perform better on structured tasks than when asked to produce open-ended narratives. Second, you should remember that students with intellectual disabilities matched for mental age will be older. As a result, they have had more exposure to diverse vocabulary. Despite this experience, their vocabulary skills are significantly below typically developing children of the same age.

Another aspect of semantics involves the organization of language information. If children are given groups of pictures and asked to remember them, they tend to organize the pictures in their minds and recall them in groups. These groups may be based on physical characteristics, function of the items, or the conceptual category to which the items belong (e.g., toys, animals). Children with intellectual disabilities have been found to lag behind in their development of organizing strategies (Stephens, 1972) and to use more concrete concepts (MacMillan, 1982), suggesting that children with intellectual disabilities have some difficulty developing and using semantic concepts.

The semantic abilities of children with Williams syndrome are significantly different from others with intellectual disabilities. They typically have an usually large and sophisticated vocabulary and may use words that not even typically developing children use. For example, one study reported that, when asked to name all the animals they could, adolescents with Williams syndrome gave responses including, "yak," "ibex," and "condor" while individuals with Down syndrome gave responses such as "dog" and "cat" (Bellugi et al., 1997).

Clearly, there are significant differences in semantic abilities among persons with intellectual disabilities, but the primary pattern seems to be one in which production lags behind comprehension. Teachers and others who work with these children should help them use a more diverse vocabulary in their speaking and writing by using techniques such as word banks to enhance their semantic production.

Pragmatics

Since there is a good deal of research on the pragmatic abilities of individuals with intellectual disabilities, we will examine the research in three areas: speech acts, referential communication, and conversational competence.

Speech Acts.   The concept of speech acts was described in Chapter 1. These acts occur whenever one has the intention to communicate. Requests, commands, and declarations are examples of speech acts. Children with intellectual disabilities have been described as being delayed in both their use and understanding of speech acts (Abbeduto & Hesketh, 1997). Although they have significant delays, their development of speech acts is similar to that of other children. That is, they can make requests, ask questions, and so on, like younger, typically developing children. In one study (Abbeduto, Furman, & Davies, 1988), children with and without intellectual disabilities were asked to interpret sentences requiring either a yes–no response or an action. For example, *Can you close the window?* could be either asking whether one is *able* to close the window or requesting that someone *actually close* the window. In their study, Abbeduto and colleagues found that in their ability to understand what the speaker actually wanted, adolescents with intellectual disabilities were similar to younger, nondisabled children matched for mental age. Although comprehension of speech acts is delayed, this has been found to be a relative strength, at least in children with Down syndrome. In fact, adults with Down syndrome may be quite good at understanding the messages that others are trying to convey.

One specific difference in speech-act usage by individuals with Down syndrome is the use of politeness. Children and adolescents with Down syndrome have been found to use less polite forms compared to typically developing children of the same mental age (Nuccio & Abbeduto, 1993). In other words, rather than saying, "May I please have the doll?" in requesting a toy, they were more likely to say, "You better gimme my doll." The study authors believe that this difference in the use of polite forms of request is not due to an inability to produce the polite form. In fact, the individuals with Down syndrome who were part of the study demonstrated the ability to use polite requests in certain contexts. Instead, the researchers concluded that individuals with Down syndrome fail to recognize the *need* to use a polite form. This finding suggests that teachers may need to monitor the conversation of students with Down syndrome and model a different form of requesting if this is a problem.

Referential Communication   In **referential-communication** tasks, children are evaluated on their ability to explain a task to another person. This procedure reveals their ability to take into account the information needed by someone else to complete the task. Individuals with intellectual disabilities have been reported to have problems with referential-communication tasks. They have difficulty producing messages that make the task clear to others. They tend to pay less attention to the important features of the task or object that would help their listener complete the task. Although they are generally better at the listener role than the speaker role, they are still delayed relative to typically developing children of the same mental age.

One way to test referential communication is with a *barrier task.* For this procedure, children are seated across from each other with a barrier between them that prevents them from seeing each other. One child is the speaker; the other is the listener. Each has an array of blocks or other items. The speaker's blocks—the model—are arranged in a design. The speaker's task is to tell the listener how to arrange the blocks to match the model, using only verbal directions. Using just such a procedure to study the referential-communication abilities of adolescents with intellectual disabilities, Longhurst (1974) found that when the individuals with intellectual disabilities were in the speaker's role, they were remarkably unsuccessful in directing the listeners to complete the task. However, when they were the listener, they were able to successfully perform the task when directions were given by nondisabled adults.

A second way to evaluate referential communication is by asking individuals to describe an activity (such as a game) to someone else. In one such study (Loveland, Tunali, McEvoy, & Kelly, 1989), adolescents and adults with Down syndrome were asked to explain a game to an experimenter. These individuals with intellectual disabilities performed quite well, giving the necessary information to the listener without a great deal of prompting. However, as Abbeduto (1991) points out, since we do not know how nondisabled persons would have handled this task, it is difficult to judge how good these results really are.

Most of the research on referential communication has been carried out with persons with Down syndrome. However, a recent study compared the referential communication of adolescents with intellectual disabilities caused by two different syndromes—Down syndrome and Fragile X syndrome—to typically developing 5-year-old children matched for mental age (Abbeduto et al., 2006). The participants in the study were asked to play a game in which they had to describe a novel shape to a listener so that he or she could pick out the shape from among several choices. The researchers found that both the adolescents with Down syndrome and those with Fragile X were less effective than the younger, typically developing children in helping their partner successfully complete the task. There were also some specific differences between the groups. Those with Down syndrome tended to give fewer descriptions to their partners, leaving it up to the partners to request more information. The individuals with Fragile X used less consistent referents—sometimes inventing new descriptions for the same item, leaving their partners confused. These results suggest that, although referential communication can be difficult for all individuals with intellectual disabilities, the pattern of difficulties may vary due to the specific syndrome related to the disability.

It appears from the research on referential communication that persons with intellectual disabilities have some difficulty getting their messages across to others. This can cause significant difficulties in social interaction. Listeners may become confused and be less interested in carrying on a conversation. Classroom activities that require the use of referential-communication skills can help children become better speakers and listeners. Guessing games, "20 Questions," and even "Show and Tell" provide opportunities for students to develop and use referential-communication skills.

Conversational Competence.   In order to communicate effectively, it is necessary to develop pragmatic language skills such as turn-taking, topic management, and conversational repair. The conversational competence of persons with intellectual disabilities has been studied in each of these areas.

In typical conversations, participants take turns talking, occasionally speaking at the same time. Persons with intellectual disabilities have been found to have few problems with taking turns in conversations. Studies of young children with intellectual disabilities (Tannock, 1988), as well as adults (Abbeduto & Rosenberg, 1980), show that they take turns in conversations and make few errors, much as typically developing people do.

Although people with intellectual disabilities appear capable of taking turns in a conversation, what is even more important is what they do when it is their turn. Typically, people with intellectual disabilities do not make significant contributions to maintaining the conversation (Abbeduto & Hesketh, 1997). They might make comments, such as *OK* or *um-um,* but do not *extend* the topic by adding new information.

Research on the conversational skills of people with intellectual disabilities has also found that they have difficulty *repairing* conversations that break down. If you are talking with someone else and do not understand what is being said, you will usually do something to clarify the conversation. You might say, "What?" or "Excuse me?" as a signal to the speaker that you do not understand. People with intellectual disabilities are *capable* of using such conversational repairs, but fail to use them when they are needed (Abbeduto, Davies, Solesby, & Furman, 1991; Robinson & Whittaker, 1986). Children with intellectual disabilities have also been found to be slow in responding to clarification requests made by others (Scherer & Owings, 1984). Moreover, researchers have found that the development of conversational repair skills appears to plateau during the school years and not improve with experience (Abbeduto, Short-Meyerson, Benson, & Dolish, 1997).

Although most of the research on conversational competence has been conducted with individuals with Down syndrome, there is a growing body of research on the conversational skills of individuals with Fragile X and Williams syndromes. Adolescents with Fragile X syndrome have been found to produce more repetitive speech during conversation (e.g., *I—I—I left the house*) and more "tangential" language (utterances that are off topic) than other persons with mental retardation or autism (Belser & Sudhalter, 2001; Sudhalter & Belser, 2001). In addition, they have been reported to use more perseverative language (inappropriate repetition) and more echoing (repeating what the other person says) (Sudhalter, Cohen, Silverman, & Wolf-Schein, 1990). Individuals with Williams syndrome have been reported to have significant difficulties in pragmatics. They are sometimes described as "overfriendly". They have difficulty with topic introduction, topic maintenance, turn taking, and maintaining appropriate eye contact in dyadic face-to-face interactions (Rondal, 2001).

In considering all of the research on the communicative abilities of persons with intellectual disabilities, Abbeduto (1991) concluded that "deficits in verbal communication are a defining feature of intellectual disabilities and should figure prominently in assessments of adaptive behavior" (p. 108). Although problems with verbal communication do seem to be quite common among people with intellectual disabilities, there is considerable variability within the population.

Obviously, the ability to engage in effective communication with others is a critical skill for classroom success. Teachers and other education professionals should be alert to the problems that students with intellectual disabilities may have in expressing themselves and understanding others. Placing students in heterogeneous groups can be a good way to encourage communicative interaction if the groups are well managed and the group activities carefully chosen.

Comparison of Language of Subgroups of Individuals with Intellectual Disabilities

In addition to looking at the general population of persons with intellectual disabilities, researchers have also studied subgroups, including individuals with Down syndrome, Fragile X syndrome, and Williams syndrome, as well as those with severe cognitive disabilities. As we have noted, there are both similarities and differences in the language and communication skills of individuals with these disorders.

For example, individuals with Down syndrome have generally been found to have more extensive language and communication difficulties than other persons with intellectual disabilities when matched for either chronological age or mental age (Kernan & Sasby, 1996). The differences have been found primarily in syntactic and morphological usage, but not in semantic skills (Marcell, Busby, Mansker, & Whelan, 1998). Researchers who have studied individuals with Fragile X syndrome have found significant deficits in language and communication to be one of the hallmarks of the disorder. Although their language and communication may be similar to that of individuals with autism, individuals with Fragile X have a variety of specific communicative problems that distinguish them both from children with autism as well as from individuals with mental retardation caused by other conditions. On the other hand, individuals with Fragile X have been found to have relative strengths in vocabulary and articulation (Santos, 1992). People with Williams syndrome generally have some specific deficiencies in communication skills, but they typically have relative strengths in both vocabulary and syntax. Their skills, however, are not equivalent to those of typically developing children of the same chronological age (Rondal, 2001).

Conclusion

Review of the research on the language and communication abilities of people with intellectual disabilities has revealed several things. First, in most cases, the language skills of this population can be described as delayed rather than different. That is, children with intellectual disabilities seem to develop through the same stages as nondisabled children, only much more slowly (see Table 8.3 for a summary). Second, there is a good deal of variation in the language and communication skills of persons with intellectual disabilities. These variations may be due to cognitive delays, physical characteristics, or the underlying cause of the individual's developmental disability. As research into the language and communication characteristics of specific syndromes continues, it is likely that we will better understand the variations in language performance among individuals with intellectual disabilities. In the section that follows we will examine some of the factors that may contribute to the language and communication difficulties of individuals with intellectual disabilities.

TABLE 8.3   Language and Communication of Individuals with Intellectual Disabilities

Prelinguistic Development	Phonology and Morphology	Syntax	Semantics	Pragmatics
Nonverbal communication similar to other infants but uses vocalizations less often with gestures	Difficulties with speech production Development similar to typical but delayed	Sentence-length similar to mental-age-matched controls Mean length of utterance of Down syndrome increases with chronological age, but more slowly	Problems understanding idiomatic expressions Delays in semantic development	Delays in understanding and use of speech acts Down syndrome: uses less polite forms
Babbling follows pattern similar to that of typically developing young children	Reduction of consonant clusters and final consonant deletion		Vocabulary a relative strength	Difficulty with speaker role Turn-taking intact
Children with Down syndrome start using first words at later age and acquire words more slowly	Delays in morphophonological development May be some specific deficits in morphology	Order of development of rules similar to typical Syntax of Williams syndrome at or above expected for mental age	Williams syndrome: have large vocabulary	Less significant contributions to conversation Difficulties with conversational repairs Fragile X: uses more tangential language and more repetition

Sources: Abbeduto et al. (1991); Abbeduto & Hesketh (1997); Bellugi et al. (1997); Chapman (1997); Ezell & Goldstein (1991); Klink et al. (1986); Lackner (1968); Laws & Bishop (2004); Long (2005); Longhurst (1974); Newfield & Schlanger (1968); Nuccio & Abbeduto (1993); Rondal (2001); Rosenberg (1982); Shriberg & Widder (1990); Sommers et al. (1988); Stoel-Gammon (1997); Sudhalter & Belser (2001); Tannock (1988).

Factors Related to Language and Communication Impairments

In most cases, it is not possible to say with certainty what causes the language and communication impairments of any individual (just as it is not possible to explain typical language development). It is true that in some individuals there are obvious physical characteristics (such as a cleft palate or protruding tongue) that can explain some of the communication difficulties of that person. But, in most cases, the best we can do is to talk about factors that may *contribute* to language and communication disorders. What are these contributing factors? We could have quite a long list, but we will limit our examination to three factors: cognitive functioning, specific language disorder, and input language.

Cognitive Functioning

Deficits in cognitive functioning are *the* defining feature of intellectual disabilities. Cognitive abilities—as measured by intelligence tests—are the first criteria in determining whether an individual is cognitively disabled. There may be a temptation to assume a person having low measured intelligence is functioning low across the board, but this is rarely the case. Each individual has a unique set of cognitive strengths and weaknesses. In addition, as we have seen with language and communication, there may be differences in cognitive function that can be attributed to the specific syndromes that can result in mental retardation. Let's look at three areas of cognitive functioning that have been researched extensively with regard to intellectual disabilities: attention, organization, and memory (see Table 8.4 for a summary).

TABLE 8.4   Research on the Cognitive Functioning of Persons with Intellectual Disabilities

Attention	Organization	Memory	Generalization
Difficulty discriminating (Zeaman & House, 1979)	Ineffective techniques of organizing information (Spitz, 1966)	Long-term memory relatively intact (Belmont, 1966)	Difficulties in the ability to apply knowledge to new settings (Stephens, 1972)
Relatively good sustained attention (Karrer et al., 1979)	Similar stages of development of organization (Stephens, 1972)	Verbal short-term memory difficulties (Laws & Gunn, 2004)	
Difficulty paying attention and sustaining attention in Fragile X (Cornish et al, 2004)		Inefficient rehearsal strategies (Bray, 1979)	
		Intact verbal short-term memory in Williams syndrome (Mervis & Klein-Tasman, 2000)	

Children with intellectual disabilities have been reported to have **discrimination** problems; that is, they have difficulty in determining the important features of a task and attending to more than one dimension at a time (Zeaman & House, 1979). For example, if asked to sort objects on the basis of both size and color, most children with intellectual disabilities would have difficulty. On the other hand, their ability to *sustain attention* has been found to be as good, or better than, mental-age-matched peers (Karrer, Nelson, & Galbraith, 1979). However, individuals with Fragile X syndrome generally have significant difficulties with attention. In fact, difficulty in paying attention and sustaining attention have been found to be characteristic of children with this disorder (Cornish, Sudhalter, & Turk, 2004). Children with Fragile X, especially boys, tend to be restless, impulsive, and easily distracted. These characteristics can interfere with learning in many domains, including language.

Many individuals with intellectual disabilities have difficulty with *organizing information* for recall (Spitz, 1966). This is an important skill. For example, if you were asked to remember the following list of items, you would probably use a *chunking* strategy to recall the list:

ball	apple	pear
orange	wrench	bike
hammer	doll	pliers

You would likely recognize that these items comprise three groups: toys, fruit, and tools. When asked to recall the items, you would probably report them in these three groups. Typically, children with intellectual disabilities do not spontaneously recognize or use these groups for recall (Stephens, 1972).

Memory difficulties have long been associated with intellectual disabilities. However, as we learn more about memory, we learn that people with intellectual disabilities have both strengths and weaknesses in this domain. Long-term memory, for example, has been found to be relatively intact in most persons with intellectual disabilities (Belmont, 1966). However, problems with short-term memory, especially verbal short-term memory, are frequently reported (Chapman & Hesketh, 2000; Laws & Gunn, 2004). The exception to this picture is Williams syndrome. Children with this disorder generally have relatively intact verbal short-term memory. However, they have significant difficulties with tasks that require them to match pictures or objects (visuospatial tasks) (Mervis & Klein-Tasman, 2000).

One explanation for the problems with short-term memory is that people with intellectual disabilities have *inefficient rehearsal strategies* (Bray, 1979). In order to remember information, one must store it. For example, if you want to remember a telephone number for just a few seconds, it is usually enough to repeat the number over and over. But if you want to remember the number for a few minutes or a few days or more, you need to store it in a way that is retrievable. A phone number with the last four digits *1488* might be remembered by recalling 1492 (the year Columbus landed in the Americas) minus 4 (1488). People with intellectual disabilities tend to use rehearsal strategies that do not enhance their recall. They tend to persist with inefficient strategies (such as repetition) that do not always work.

Another specific cognitive impairment associated with intellectual disabilities is **generalization** of information. Persons with intellectual disabilities have often been described as having difficulty applying what they have learned previously to use in new settings, with different people, or in new ways (Stephens, 1972). Generalization is a critical skill for learning. If students do not know when and where to apply their skills, they have really learned nothing. Therefore, it is essential that students with intellectual disabilities be taught in ways that will increase their likelihood of generalization.

How can the cognitive difficulties associated with intellectual disabilities affect the acquisition of language and communication? Clearly, if someone has difficulty attending to a certain task—especially a complex task such as social interaction—that person may have difficulty picking up pragmatic and perhaps syntactic aspects of language. Difficulties with organizing information may affect the child's ability to acquire new vocabulary, to differentiate new words from previously stored words, and to recall words when they are needed. Of course, memory impairments also have profound implications for language learning. To learn language, one must store and retrieve vast amounts of information. Syntactic rules, semantic rules, and vocabulary—all of these and more—must be stored in a way that they are easily retrieved. Moreover, this has to be done instantaneously. Children with impairments in memory are likely to have a difficult time with the understanding and use of language.

For teachers, there are several implications that can be drawn from the research discussed. First, attention of the child to the task at hand is critical. It is important to *limit the task dimensions.* In other words, whenever possible, only one aspect of a task (shape, size, color) should be varied, until the individual is ready to handle more. It is essential to *get and hold attention.* Using items that are familiar to the student, involving him or her in the lesson, and relating the lesson to his or her personal experience are ways to do this. Many children with intellectual disabilities will need to have *organization cues* given to them. They will need to be told how and when to use these cues for learning. Finally, teachers need to *teach for generalization.* This means using a variety of materials and examples. It also means teaching in the natural environment—the place where the skill will be applied—whenever possible.

Specific Language Disorders

There is no doubt that most people with mental retardation have impairments of cognitive functioning. They also have problems in several areas of language development. Might we conclude, then, that the cognitive impairments cause the language disabilities? Might it be just as true to assert that the language impairments cause delays in cognitive development?

These are not easy questions to answer because language and cognition are interrelated in very complex ways. To try to answer these questions, researchers have compared the language of children with mental retardation to that of nondisabled children who are matched for mental age. If their language performance is similar, this suggests that language development is dependent on cognitive development. If, on the other hand, the language development of the subjects with mental retardation is less advanced than that of the nondisabled subjects, one could conclude that people with mental retardation have a specific language disorder that cannot be explained by cognitive delays alone.

Research on the relationship between cognition and language in persons with mental retardation has yielded inconsistent results. Our review of the research has revealed that delays in most aspects of language development are characteristic of children with mental retardation. For the most part, their language development is like that of younger children matched for mental age. However, there are exceptions to this (e.g., in pragmatics and syntax). When Kamhi and Johnston (1982) studied the language and cognitive abilities of children with mental retardation, children with language impairments, and typically developing children, they found that, for the most part, the language of the children with mental retardation was similar to that of the younger, nondisabled children matched for mental age. When there were deviations from the typical pattern, they were attributed to deficits in motivation and adaptive behavior. Abbeduto, Furman, and Davies (1988) studied the receptive language skills of school-age children with mental retardation. They found that mental age (MA) was a good predictor of the language performance of children at lower levels of mental age (MA = 5). However, mental age was *not* a good predictor for their subjects with higher mental age (7 and 9). They suggested that at least some of the language impairments of their higher MA group were the result of specific language deficits.

So, what can be said about the relationship between cognitive abilities and language in persons with mental retardation? Is there a specific language disorder that goes beyond what would be predicted by mental age alone? Well, yes and no. It appears that in younger children (MA < 5), there is a close connection between cognitive development and language development. It still is not possible to say with certainty which is the cause and which the effect, but there is a close relationship. For older individuals (MA > 7), there appear to be specific language deficiencies that cannot be explained by mental age alone. Problems relating to motivation, adaptive behavior, or a specific language disorder may explain the language impairments of these individuals.

Input Language

Parent–Child Interaction.   In the search for causes of language and communication difficulties in children with intellectual disabilities, another aspect is input language. We know from research on typical language development that children learn language by participating in communicative interactions with parents and other caregivers. We also know that parents alter their language to make it more compatible with their child's ability to comprehend.

Some research has suggested that parents of children with intellectual disabilities do not provide an effective language-learning environment for their children. For example, mothers of children with intellectual disabilities have been found to use shorter, less complex sentences than do mothers of nondisabled children (Buium, Rynders, & Turnure, 1974). In addition, they tend to dominate interactions with their children by being more directive and by initiating more of the interactions with their children than do mothers of nondisabled children (Eheart, 1982). Mothers of children with intellectual disabilities have also been reported to be less focused on their child's activities (Mahoney, Fors, & Wood, 1990).

Other research, however, has found that parents of children with intellectual disabilities provide an adequate language environment for their child. They talk to their children as often as do parents of typically developing children and use similar speech acts. They respond to the communicative attempts of their children just like parents of typically developing children of the same language age. Mothers of children with intellectual disabilities alter their linguistic input appropriately for the language-development level of their children (Rondal, 1978). Although it is true that they use more directives in their communication with their children, they become less directive as their children become more linguistically advanced (Abbeduto & Hesketh, 1997).

When considered as a whole, it seems clear that parents of children with intellectual disabilities generally provide an appropriate language environment for their developing children. In most cases, differences in communicative interaction are an appropriate response by parents to their children's slower language development. On the other hand, these parents must be careful not to overcompensate for their children's language impairments. They must work hard at giving their daughters and sons the opportunity to initiate interaction and should be responsive to their children, even if they feel that the children may be acting inappropriately. It is often difficult to determine what children are trying to communicate until they are given a chance to do so.

Staff–Client Interaction   Individuals with intellectual disabilities who live in institutions or in group settings in the community receive much of their opportunity for communicative interaction from staff in those facilities. However, staff tend to communicate in ways that actually discourage interaction. Studies have reported that staff tend to use a lot of *directives*—commands and directions that require little if any verbal response (Prior, Minnes, Coyne, Golding, Hendy, & McGillivray, 1979). When residents try to communicate, they are often ignored.

Part of the explanation for staff members' low rates of responsiveness may be that the residents' communicative attempts are unclear. Kuder and Bryen (1991) found that when residents clearly identified their communicative partner and used a conversational opener that encouraged a response, staff were highly responsive. They also found that staff and residents communicated more frequently in a structured classroom setting than they did in a less structured, residential environment.

The results from research on both parent–child and staff–resident interactions suggest that to conclude that parents or residential staff cause the language impairments experienced by individuals with intellectual disabilities is too simple an explanation. More likely it is the language impairments themselves that alter the interactions between individuals with intellectual disabilities and others. As a result, communicative interaction may become less frequent and less effective. There is a danger that parents and staff may become so accustomed to a highly directive conversational role that they fail to give their children or residents the chance to communicate.

Conclusion

In the beginning of this section we noted the difficulty in finding a specific cause for the language impairments experienced by most persons with intellectual disabilities. Indeed, our search for a cause has yielded some clues but no firm answers. Cognitive disabilities clearly play a role, but do not account for all the language difficulties of people with intellectual disabilities. Parents and other caregivers may talk differently to children with intellectual disabilities, but it is likely that these differences are as much the *result* of language differences as the cause. Lack of motivation, adaptive behavior deficits, physical disabilities, and specific language impairments have been proposed as the cause of the language deficiencies of individuals with intellectual disabilities. Evidence increasingly supports the notion that genetic disorders such as Down syndrome, Fragile X, and Williams syndrome may include specific language deficits as a characteristic of the syndrome. As research on these syndromes continues, we may be better able to understand the specific patterns of language strengths and deficits within subgroups of individuals with intellectual disabilities.

Literacy and Students with Intellectual Disabilities

In addition to changing expectations for community living and inclusion in school, there have been changes in our understanding of and expectations for literacy skills in persons with intellectual disabilities. Historically, people felt somewhat ambivalent toward the whole notion of the development of literacy, and especially reading, among persons with intellectual disabilities. As Singh and Singh (1986) pointed out in their review of reading in persons with intellectual disabilities, until the 1950s, reading was not considered to be a necessary or even a desirable skill for individuals with intellectual disabilities. Whereas students with mild levels of intellectual disabilities might be expected to develop reading skills as high as the second- or third-grade level, individuals with lower measured intelligence were not expected to develop reading skills at all. However, there is now a good deal of evidence that, given appropriate instruction, students with intellectual disabilities can learn to read and write (Katims, 2000). The impetus to more fully include individuals with intellectual disabilities in the community, including in school, makes it even more important for educators to understand the literacy skills of individuals with intellectual disabilities and the most effective ways to enhance those skills.

Because the longstanding assumption has been that students with intellectual disabilities cannot learn to read and write, the prevailing approach to instruction has been "functional" in nature. Functional reading instruction typically involves teaching "survival" words through a sight-word approach. Students are taught to "read" specific words that are thought to be essential for survival in the world. For example, they might be taught to recognize the word *exit* on a sign or to read words on food labels. Research on the use of this approach has found that students with intellectual disabilities can learn to recognize a number of words using this method but their ability to use this skill in real situations may be limited (Browder & Xin, 1998). In addition, for many students with intellectual disabilities sight-word instruction is the only literacy training they receive in school. Some students learn (and relearn) the same words year after year, with little if any exposure to books or writing activities.

Currently, researchers are trying to discover more about the problems that underlie the reading and writing deficiencies of most students with intellectual disabilities. Undoubtedly, the language difficulties described in previous sections of this chapter are a factor. One of the specific skills that has been studied is phonological processing. Compared to students with learning disabilities, relatively little research has examined the phonological skills of individuals with intellectual disabilities. However, the limited research has confirmed that significant difficulties in phonological processing exist in this population and that reading instruction that incorporates phonological instruction can be effective (Conners, 1992; Joseph & Seery, 2004).

One example of this research comes from a study by Conners, Rosenquist, Sligh, Atwell, and Kiser (2006). They taught 20 children with mental retardation (mean IQ = 54), ages 7 to 12 years old, using a phonological training program of their own design. Students completed three units consisting of six to nine lessons per unit: oral practice in sound blending, letter-sound association, and sounding out. When compared to a matched group of students who did not receive this instruction, the phonological training group significantly outperformed their peers on measures of sounding out. However, there was significant variability in the results. About half of the children who received the instruction correctly sounded out 80 percent or more of the words on the posttest, whereas six students (30 percent) identified fewer than 20 percent of the words. The authors of the study found that previous instruction in phonological analysis and entering reading levels were important factors in success on the sounding-out task.

This, and other studies of phonological processing, suggest that instruction in phonological skills should be part of a comprehensive reading program for students with intellectual disabilities. In addition, a rich literacy environment in which children have an opportunity to listen to stories read to them, to talk about what they hear, and to write at the level of their ability should be part of a comprehensive literacy program for students with intellectual disabilities. The message from research and experience is that these children can develop literacy skills. They do so more slowly than their peers of the same age and may never reach the literacy levels of those peers, but they can do more than memorize lists of sight words.

Approaches to Instruction

As we have seen, finding the cause of the language and communication disabilities of children with intellectual disabilities is not always possible. Fortunately, it is not essential to know the cause of the problem in order to do something about it. This section presents some general principles for intervention with students with intellectual disabilities, discussing two specific intervention approaches for language and communication impairments.

Instructional Principles

Owens (2002) suggested seven principles that teachers and other education professionals can use in developing intervention programs for individuals with intellectual disabilities. These principles address some of the specific cognitive and language characteristics commonly found among students with intellectual disabilities.

We know, for example, that many individuals with intellectual disabilities have difficulty discriminating information. They have problems knowing what they are supposed to attend to. Teachers may address this problem by *highlighting new or relevant information*. New vocabulary words may be written in a different color, for example. In a conversational situation, the teacher could point out how people speak to children in different ways than they do to adults.

Another area of difficulty for many children with intellectual disabilities is in organization of information for recall. Owens suggests that it may be helpful if teachers *preorganize information*. To get students to remember words, for example, the teacher may find it useful to group the words in ways that will enhance recall (e.g., cluster the words for *toys* together). Of course, merely grouping the items together may not be enough. Students may have to be taught the category label and when to use it.

Since memory is problematic for most students with intellectual disabilities, Owens suggests that teachers can help students enhance their recall by teaching them to use *effective rehearsal strategies*. Different rehearsal strategies work for different situations. For students to remember for a long period of time, they may need to learn how to use a strategy to enhance their memory; for example, visual images or associating words that rhyme may enhance recall.

One of the most significant problems faced by teachers of students with intellectual disabilities is helping them generalize new learning. Owens offers two suggestions to help in this area: that teachers *use overlearning and repetition* and that teachers *train in the natural environment*. Not surprisingly, students who receive extra training and practice tend to retain more information. Moreover, a number of research studies have found that difficulties with generalization can be reduced if children are taught in the settings in which they will need the skill they are learning (e.g., Caro & Snell, 1989; Stowitschek, McConaughy, Peatross, Salzberg, & Lignngaris/Kraft, 1988). If, for example, children learn to approach others by practicing this skill in the cafeteria, then it should be easier for them to ask someone in the cafeteria to share a table if they need to do so.

Owens further suggests that *training should begin as early as possible* and that teachers *follow developmental guidelines*. Early training is especially critical for language, since these skills build on each other and there is a critical period for language learning. Developmental guidelines can be used to determine where to begin and how to sequence instruction. However, teachers who choose to follow developmental guidelines must be careful in making instructional decisions to also consider the demands of the child's environment.

Specific Instructional Approaches

The instructional principles suggested by Owens can help teachers begin to plan for the needs of their students with intellectual disabilities. These guidelines might be applied not just to language but to any domain of learning. A number of instructional methods have been developed to teach language and communication skills to students with intellectual disabilities, especially those with more severe retardation. In general, these approaches differ along a continuum from highly structured, didactic teaching to more naturalistic, child-oriented approaches (Yoder, Kaiser, & Alpert, 1991). Among the more highly structured procedures are behavior-based methods that use imitation, modeling, and/or reinforcement. Typically, these programs come with a standardized set of instructions and materials (such as the Language for Learning program produced by SRA/McGraw-Hill). They take the child through a highly structured sequence of steps toward a goal that is set prior to instruction. Behavioral approaches have been quite successful in enhancing the language and communication of children with significant disabilities, including intellectual disabilities and autism. Such approaches use a *stimulus* to prompt a *response,* which is then *reinforced.* **Shaping** is used to mold the verbal behavior into the adult target form that is desired (see Box 8.1).

Although behavior-intervention approaches to language instruction can work (e.g., Baer & Guess, 1973), they have limitations. The biggest concerns revolve around the generalizing of verbal behavior to natural, social situations. In other words, it is one thing to train a specific verbal behavior under a one-on-one clinical condition, but it is something else to use that newly acquired skill to order a hamburger at McDonald's.

Behavioral approaches to language instruction are most useful for training specific skill sequences (such as request routines or word endings). If using behavioral techniques, teachers should pay special attention to helping the child generalize newly acquired behavior and include practice in real social situations.

At the other end of the instructional continuum are *naturalistic* (or *milieu*) approaches. A substantial amount of research indicates that naturalistic teaching procedures can be effective for enhancing the language and communication of students with disabilities. For example, in a study with four elementary-level students with moderate

---

BOX **8.1**

Example of a Behavioral Language Lesson

TRAINER: What's that? (pointing to a cup). (prompt)
CHILD: Cuh . . .
TRAINER: Right, cup. Say cup.
CHILD: Cuh.
TRAINER: Say cup (emphasizing final *p* sound). (shaping)
CHILD: Cup.
TRAINER: Good saying cup! What's that? (pointing to cup). (reinforcement)
CHILD: Cup.
TRAINER: Good job. What do you want?
CHILD: Want?
TRAINER: Do you want the cup?
CHILD: Cup.
TRAINER: Do you want the cup?
CHILD: Want cup.
TRAINER: Good job! (hands child the cup)

intellectual disabilities, Hemmeter, Ault, Collins, and Meyer (1996) found that using **incidental teaching** (a technique that utilizes the child's natural environment as the basis for instruction) and mand-model techniques significantly increased the language interaction of the children in their study.

The **mand-model procedure** was developed to teach students to use language to obtain items or to participate in social interactions. In this approach, the adult initiates the interaction using activities and objects that the student is using at the moment; the adult prompts a response by using a "mand" (a demand or request). Similar to the interrupted-chain strategy, this technique uses natural activities in the child's environment as the basis of instruction. However, modeling, rather than operant conditioning, is used to teach the language skill. Warren (1991) gives the following example:

CONTEXT: (The child is scooping rice with a spoon and pouring it into a bowl.)

ADULT: Tell me what you are doing.

CHILD: Beans.

ADULT: Well then say, "Pour beans."

CHILD: Pour beans.

ADULT: That's right, you're pouring beans into the pot.

In this example, the adult's *Tell me what you are doing* elicited a response. If the child had not responded, the adult could have told the child to say the name of the object. Since the child did respond, the adult modeled for the child a more adult form of responding. This technique helped children with significant language impairments increase their communication (Rogers-Warren & Warren, 1980).

It is also possible to combine elements of more structured and less structured approaches. One example of a procedure that combines structured and naturalistic procedures is the **interrupted-behavior-chain strategy.** In this approach, a targeted language skill is inserted in the middle of an already established sequence of behaviors. Caro and Snell (1989) give an example of the application of this strategy in grocery shopping. Having taught an individual to read a grocery list, locate items on the shelf, and pay the cashier, the teacher could interrupt the behavior sequence to ask the student to say which items had already been placed in the grocery cart, and then praise a correct response. If the student produced an incorrect response, the instructor would model the correct response and prompt the student to produce it. This is an example of the combination of a natural environment (grocery shopping) with a structured instructional technique (prompting, modeling, reinforcement).

Hunt, Goetz, Alwell, and Sailor 1986) describe the use of the interrupted behavior chain strategy with a student named Everett, a 7-year-old boy with severe intellectual disabilities. The first step in this intervention was to identify sequences of behaviors that Everett could presently perform or was currently being taught. In Everett's case, he was able to independently get a drink from the water fountain and get food from the refrigerator. He was being taught to start and listen to a record player and to play an arcade game. Then interruptions were inserted into these behavior sequences at particular points. For example, as he leaned down to take a drink, Everett would be asked *What do you want?* and then prompted to choose by pointing to the picture of the water fountain from among a group of four pictures. Using this approach, Everett increased his ability to identify the correct picture and learned to point to a picture to request water. The researchers suggested that interrupting a previously established chain of behavior may motivate students to learn the communication skill so they can continue with the activity. A review of research on the interrupted-behavior-chain strategy found that it can be an effective way of teaching language skills to students with varying degrees of mental retardation (Carter & Grunsell, 2001).

Although the results of research studies on instructional methods for teaching language and communication to individuals with intellectual disabilities and other significant disabilities may appear to be confusing and contradictory, there may be some useful instructional guidelines that can come from these studies. Effective intervention appears to include techniques that:

- Focus on a specific skill or skills that is/are needed in the child's environment.
- Utilize appropriate and desired reinforcers.
- Take place in the most naturalistic setting possible.
- Consider the need to generalize a learned skill to new environments.

Summary

In this chapter we have seen how changes in our understanding of intellectual disabilities placed new demands on language instruction for persons with intellectual disabilities. We have reviewed recent trends in literacy and in educational services. Then, in describing the specific language and communication characteristics of persons with intellectual disabilities, we noted that although delays in language development are often found in people with intellectual disabilities, there appear to be some specific differences in their language abilities. We have examined possible causes of these language and communication impairments, including discussions of cognitive delay, specific language disorder, and deficiencies of input language. A discussion of intervention techniques included both structured and naturalistic instructional methods that have been used to help individuals with intellectual disabilities enhance their language and communication skills.

REVIEW QUESTIONS

1. How does the 1992 definition of *intellectual disabilities* differ from previous definitions?

2. How has research on specific genetic disorders such as Down syndrome, Fragile X, and Williams syndrome changed our understanding of intellectual disabilities?

3. In what ways is the early communicative development of young children with Down syndrome similar to and different from that of typically developing young children?

4. Describe the syntactic skills of persons with intellectual disabilities. Are they delayed, different, or both? Explain.

5. In what ways do the semantic skills of individuals with Williams syndrome differ from those of other individuals with intellectual disabilities?

6. What is known about the conversational skills of people with intellectual disabilities in regard to turn-taking, conversational repairs, and topic management?

7. Discuss some of the implications of research on cognition for understanding the language development of individuals with intellectual disabilities.

8. Why may sight-word approaches not be sufficient to assist students with intellectual disabilities to fully develop their literacy skills?

S U G G E S T E D   A C T I V I T I E S

1. Research on the communicative interaction between parents and their children with intellectual disabilities has sometimes led to conflicting conclusions. Some researchers have concluded that parents of children with intellectual disabilities do not provide an appropriate language environment. Others have claimed that any differences in parent–child interaction may be the result of the adjustment of parents to their child's abilities and needs. This debate suggests two essential questions that can be investigated in this activity:

   a. Does the language and other communication used by parents of children with intellectual disabilities differ from that used by parents of nondisabled children?

   b. Do parents of children with intellectual disabilities alter their language appropriately for the language level of the child?

   To investigate these questions, find two parent–child dyads. The children should be between 18 months and 3 years of age, and one of them should be intellectually disabled.

   Ask the parents to play with their children using objects that are familiar to each child. It would be best to do this in the child's home. Record your observations of each parent–child interaction (on videotape, if possible) and compare the two parents on the following:

   Length of utterance

   Use of nonverbal communication

   Number of different words used

   Complexity of language (sentence structures used)

   Initiation of communication (whether child or parent)

2. We know from research on children with intellectual disabilities that for them, comprehension of idiomatic expressions is often difficult. Try teaching such expressions to an individual with intellectual disabilities. The student should have a mental age of at least 8 years. Begin by asking the student to tell you what the following idiomatic expression mean:

   Strike a bargain.
   Hit the road.
   Break a date.
   Jump the gun.

   If the student has trouble explaining any of these expressions, explain the meaning and ask the child to try again. Once the student appears to have learned the expression, repeat the exercise a few days later to check retention.

GLOSSARY

discrimination: in cognitive psychology, the ability to identify and attend to the essential elements of a task

Down syndrome: a genetic syndrome caused by an extra chromosome at pair 21

Fragile X syndrome: a genetic disorder in which the X chromosome is deficient, causing intellectual disabilities

generalization: the ability to apply previous learning to novel situations and tasks

incidental teaching: language instructional technique in which instruction is "incidental" to the communicative interaction between student and teacher

interrupted-behavior-chain strategy: inserting a target skill in the middle of an established sequence of behaviors to teach the new skill

mand-model procedure: instructional procedure in which the trainer attempts to prompt a response from the student by using a demand or request ("mand")

referential communication: a measure of communicative ability in which individuals are evaluated on their ability to explain a task to each other

shaping: behavioral instructional technique used to mold a behavior into the adult target form that is desired

Williams syndrome: a genetic disorder caused by a random genetic mutation that causes mental retardation

RESOURCES ON THE WEB

www.aamr.org American Association on Mental Retardation

www.thearc.org The ARC-an organization of and for individuals with intellectual disabilities

www.ndscenter.org National Down Syndrome Congress

www.ndss.org National Down Syndrome Society

www.nads.org National Association for Down Syndrome

www.fragilex.org National Fragile X Foundation

www.tash.org TASH—the Association for the Severely Handicapped

REFERENCES

Abbeduto, L. (1991). Development of verbal communication in persons with moderate to mild intellectual disabilities. *International Review of Research in Mental Retardation, 17,* 91–115.

Abbeduto, L., Davies, B., Solesby, S., & Furman, L.(1991). Identifying the referents of spoken messages: Use of context and clarification requests by children with and without intellectual disabilities. *American Journal on Mental Retardation, 95,* 551–562.

Abbeduto, L., Evans, J., & Dolan, T. (2001). Theoretical perspectives on language and communication problems in mental retardation and developmental disabilities. *Mental Retardation and Developmental Disabilities Research Reviews, 7,* 45–55.

Abbeduto, L., Furman, L., & Davies, B. (1988). The development of speech act comprehension in mentally retarded individuals and nonretarded children. *Child Development, 59,* 1460–1472.

Abbeduto, L., & Hagerman, R. J. (1997). Language and communication in Fragile X syndrome. *Mental Retardation and Developmental Disabilities Research Reviews, 3,* 313–322.

Abbeduto, L. & Hesketh, L. J. (1997). Pragmatic development in individuals with mental retardation: Learning to use language in social interactions. *Mental Retardation and Developmental Disabilities Research Reviews, 3,* 323–333.

Abbeduto, L., Murphy, M. M., Richmond, E. K., Amman, A., Beth, P., Weissman, M. D., Kim, J-S., Cawthon, S. W., & Karadottir, S. (2006).

Collaboration in referential communication: Comparison of youth with Down syndrome or Fragile X syndrome. *American Journal on Mental Retardation, 111,* 170–183.

Abbeduto, L., & Rosenberg, S. (1980). The communicative competence of mildly retarded adults. *Applied Psycholinguistics, 1,* 405–426.

Abbeduto, L., Short-Meyerson, K., Benson, G., & Dolish, J. (1997). Signaling of noncomprehension by children and adolescents with mental retardation: Effects of problem type and speaker identity. *Journal of Speech, Language, and Hearing Research, 40,* 20–32.

American Association on Mental Retardation. (1992). *Intellectual disabilities: Definition, classification, and systems of support* (9th ed.). Washington, DC: Author.

Baer, D. M., & Guess, D. (1973). Teaching productive noun suffixes to severely retarded children. *American Journal of Mental Deficiency, 77,* 498–505.

Bellugi, U., Lai, Z., & Wang, P. (1997). Language, communication, and neural systems in Williams syndrome. *Mental Retardation and Developmental Disabilities Research Reviews, 3,* 334–342.

Belmont, J. (1966). Long-term memory in intellectual disabilities. *International Review of Research in Mental Retardation, 1,* 219–255.

Belser, R. C., & Sudhalter, V. (2001). Conversational characteristics of children with Fragile X syndrome: Repetitive speech. *American Journal on Mental Retardation, 106,* 28–38.

Berglund, E., Eriksson, M., & Johansson, I. (2001). Parental reports of spoken language skills in children with Down syndrome. *Journal of Speech and Hearing Research, 44,* 179–191.

Bray, N. (1979). Strategy production in the retarded. In N. Ellis (Ed.), *Handbook of mental deficiency: Psychological theory and research* (pp. 699–726). Hillsdale, NJ: Erlbaum.

Browder, D. M., & Yan Ping Xin, Y. P. (1998). A meta-analysis and review of sight word research and its implications for teaching functional reading to individuals with moderate and severe disabilities. *The Journal of Special Education, 32,* 130–153.

Buium, N., Rynders, J., & Turnure, J. (1974). Early maternal linguistic environment of normal and Down's syndrome language learning children. *American Journal of Mental Deficiency, 79,* 52–58.

Caro, P., & Snell, M. (1989). Characteristics of teaching communication to people with moderate and severe disabilities. *Education and Training in Mental Retardation, 24,* 63–77.

Carter, M., & Grunsell, J. (2001). The behavior chain interruption strategy: A review of research and discussion of future directions. *Journal of the Association for Persons with Severe Handicaps, 26,* 37–49.

Chapman, R., Schwartz, S., & Kay Raining-Bird, E. (1991). Language skills of children and adolescents with Down syndrome: 1. Comprehension. *Journal of Speech and Hearing Research, 34,* 1106–1120.

Chapman, R. S. (1997). Language development in children and adolescents with Down syndrome. *Mental Retardation and Developmental Disabilities Reviews, 3,* 307–312.

Chapman, R. S., & Hesketh, L. J. (2000). Behavioral phenotype of individuals with Down syndrome. *Mental Retardation and Developmental Disabilities Reviews, 6,* 84–95.

Conners, F. A. (1992). Reading instruction for students with moderate mental retardation. Review and analysis of research. *American Journal on Mental Retardation, 96,* 577–597.

Conners, F. A., Rosenquist, C. J., Sligh, A. C., Atwell, J. A., & Kiser, T. (2006). Phonological reading skills acquisition by children with mental retardation. *Research in Developmental Disabilities, 27,* 121–137

Cornish, K., Sudhalter, V., & Turk, J. (2004). Attention and language in Fragile X. *Mental Retardation and Developmental Disabilities Reviews, 10,* 11–16.

Eheart, B. (1982). Mother-child interactions with nonretarded and mentally retarded preschoolers. *American Journal of Mental Deficiency, 87,* 20–25.

Epstein, M., Polloway, E., Patton, J., & Foley, R. (1989). Mild retardation: Student characteristics and services. *Education and Training in Mental Retardation, 24,* 7–16.

Ezell, H., & Goldstein, H. (1991). Comparison of idiom comprehension of normal children and children with mental retardation. *Journal of Speech and Hearing Research, 34,* 812–819.

Hemmeter, M., Ault, M., Collins, B., & Meyer, S. (1996). The effects of teacher-implemented language instruction within free-time activities. *Education and Training in Mental Retardation and Developmental Disabilities, 31,* 20 3–212.

Hunt, P., Goetz, L., Alwell, M., & Sailor, W. (1986). Using an interrupted behavior chain strategy to teach generalized communication responses.

Journal of the Association for Persons with Severe Handicaps, 11, 196–204.

Individuals with Disabilities Education Act. (2004). Washington, DC: US Government Printing Office.

Joseph, L. M., & Seery, M. E. (2004). Where is the phonics?: A review of the literature on the use of phonetic analysis with students with mental retardation. *Remedial and Special Education, 25,* 88–94.

Kamhi, A., & Johnston, J. (1982). Towards an understanding of retarded children's linguistic deficiencies. *Journal of Speech and Hearing Research, 25,* 435–445.

Karrer, R., Nelson, M., & Galbraith, G. (1979). Psychophysiological research with the mentally retarded. In N. Ellis (Ed.), *International review of research in intellectual disabilities* (Vol. 7). New York: Academic Press.

Katims, D. S. (2000). Literacy instruction for people with intellectual disabilities: Historical highlights and contemporary analysis. *Education and Training in Intellectual Disabilities and Developmental Disabilities, 35,* 3–15.

Kernan, K., & Sasby, S. (1996). Linguistic and cognitive ability of adults with Down syndrome and mental retardation of unknown etiology. *Journal of Communication Disorders, 29,* 401–422.

Klink, M., Gerstman, L., Raphael, L., Schlanger, B., & Newsome, L. (1986). Phonological process usage by young EMR children and nonretarded preschool children. *American Journal of Mental Deficiency, 91,* 190–195.

Kuder, S. J., & Bryen, D. N. (1991). Communicative performance of persons with intellectual disabilities in an institutional setting. *Education and Training in Intellectual Mental Retardation, 23,* 325–332.

Lackner, J. (1968). A developmental study of language behavior in retarded children. *Neuropsychologia, 6,* 301–320.

Laws, G., & Bishop, D. V. M. (2004). Vernal deficits in Down's syndrome and specific language impairment: A comparison. *International Journal of Communication Disorders, 39,* 423–451.

Laws, G., & Gunn, D. (2004). Phonological memory as a predictor of language comprehension in Down syndrome: A five-year follow-up study. *Journal of Child Psychology and Psychiatry, 45,* 326–337

Long, S. (2005). Language and children with intellectual disabilities. In V. Reed (Ed.), *Children with language disorders* (3rd ed.) (pp. 220–252). Boston: Allyn & Bacon.

Longhurst, T. (1974). Communication in retarded adolescents: Sex and intelligence level. *American Journal of Mental Deficiency, 78,* 607–618.

Loveland, K., Tunali, B., McEvoy, R., & Kelly, M. (1989). Referential communication and response adequacy in autism and Down's syndrome. *Applied Psycholinguistics, 10,* 301–313.

MacMillan, D. (1982). *Mental retardation in school and society* (2nd ed.). Boston: Little, Brown.

Mahoney, G., Fors, S., & Wood, S. (1990). Maternal directive behavior revisited. *American Journal on Mental Retardation, 94,* 398–406.

Marcell, M., Busby, E., Mansker, J., & Whelan, M. (1998). Confrontation naming of familiar sounds by individuals with Down syndrome. *American Journal on Mental Retardation, 102,* 485–499.

Mervis, C. B., & Klein-Tasman, B. P. (2000). Williams syndrome: Cognition, personality, and adaptive behavior. *Mental Retardation and Developmental Disabilities Research Reviews, 6,* 148–158.

Miller, J. (1988). The developmental asynchrony of language development in children with Down syndrome. In L. Nadel (Ed.), *The psychobiology of Down syndrome* (pp. 168–198). Cambridge, MA: MIT Press.

Naremore, R., & Dever, R. (1975). Language performance of educable mentally retarded and normal children at five age levels. *Journal of Speech and Hearing Research, 18,* 82–95.

Newfield, M., & Schlanger, B. (1968). The acquisition of English morphology in normal and educable mentally retarded children. *Journal of Speech and Hearing Research, 11,* 693–706.

Nuccio, J., & Abbeduto, L. (1993). Dynamic contextual variables and the directives of persons with mental retardation. *American Journal of Mental Retardation, 97,* 547–558.

Owens, R. (2002). Mental retardation: Difference and delay. In D. Bernstein & E. Morris (Eds.), *Language and communication disorders in children* (5th ed.) (pp. 426–509). Boston: Allyn & Bacon.

Prior, M., Minnes, P., Coyne, T., Golding, B., Hendy, J., & McGillivray, J. (1979). Verbal interactions between staff and residents in an institution for the mentally retarded. *Mental Retardation, 17,* 65–70.

Robinson, E., & Whittaker, S. (1986). Learning about verbal referential communication in the early school years. In K. Durkin (Ed.), *Language development during the school years* (pp. 155–171). London: Croom Helm.

Rogers-Warren, A., & Warren, S. (1980). Mands for verbalization: Facilitating the display of newly-taught language. *Behavior Modification, 4,* 361–382.

Rondal, J. (1978). Maternal speech to normal and Downs syndrome children matched for mean length of utterance. In C. Meyers (Ed.), *Quality of life in severely and profoundly mentally retarded people.* Washington, DC: American Association on Mental Deficiency.

Rondal, J. (2001). Language in mental retardation: Individual and syndromic differences, and neurogenetic variation. *Swiss Journal of Psychology, 60,* 161–178.

Rosenberg, S. (1982). The language of the mentally retarded: Development, processes, and intervention. In S. Rosenberg (Ed.), *Handbook of applied psycholinguistics: Major thrusts of research and theory* (pp. 329–392). Hillsdale, NJ: Erlbaum.

Santos, K. (1992). Fragile X syndrome: An educator's role in identification, prevention, and intervention. *Remedial and Special Education, 13,* 32–39.

Scherer, N., & Owings, N. (1984). Learning to be contingent: Retarded children's responses to their mother's requests. *Language and Speech, 27,* 255–267.

Shriberg, L., & Widder, C. (1990). Speech and prosody characteristics of adults with intellectual disabilities. *Journal of Speech and Hearing Research, 33,* 637–653.

Singh, J., & Singh, N. N. (1986). Reading acquisition and remediation in the mentally retarded. In N. Ellis (Ed.), *International review of research in intellectual disabilities* (Vol. 14) (pp. 165–199). New York: Academic Press.

Smith, T., Eikeseth, S., Klevstrand, M., & Lovaas, O. (1997). Intensive behavioral treatment for preschoolers with severe intellectual disabilities and pervasive developmental disorder. *American Journal on Intellectual disabilities, 102,* 238–249.

Sommers, R., Patterson, J., & Wildgen, P. (1988). Phonology of Down syndrome speakers, ages 13–22. *Journal of Childhood Communication Disorders, 12,* 65–91.

Spitz, H. (1966). The role of input organization in the learning and memory of mental retardates. In N. Ellis (Ed.), *International review of research in intellectual disabilities* (Vol. 2). New York: Academic Press.

Stephens, W. (1972). Equivalence formation by re-

tarded and nonretarded children at different mental ages. *American Journal of Mental Deficiency, 77,* 311–313.

Stoel-Gammon, C. (1997). Phonological development in Down syndrome. *Mental Retardation and Developmental Disabilities Research Reviews, 3,* 300–306.

Stowitschek, J., McConaughy, E., Peatross, D., Salzberg, C., & Lignngaris/Kraft, B. (1988). Effects of group incidental training on the use of social amenities by adults with intellectual disabilities in work settings. *Education and Training in Intellectual Disabilities, 23,* 202–212.

Sudhalter, V., & Belser, C. (2001). Conversational characteristics of children with Fragile X syndrome: Tangential language. *American Journal on Intellectual Disabilities, 106,* 389–400.

Sudhalter, V., Cohen, I. L., Silverman, W., & Wolf-Schein, E. G. (1990). Conversational analyses of males with Fragile X, Down syndrome, and autism: A comparison of the emergence of deviant language. *American Journal on Intellectual Disabilities, 94,* 431–442.

Tannock, R. (1988). Mothers' directiveness in their interactions with their children with and without Down syndrome. *American Journal on Mental Retardation, 93,* 154–165.

Thordardottir, E. T., Chapman, R. S., & Wagner, L. (2002). Complex sentence production by adolescents with Down syndrome. *Applied Psycholinguistics, 23,* 163–183.

Warren, S. (1991). Enhancing communication and language development with milieu teaching procedures. In E. Cipani (Ed.), *A guide to developing language competence in preschool children with severe and moderate handicaps* (pp. 68–93). Springfield, IL: Charles Thomas.

Wehmeyer, M. L. (2003). Defining mental retardation and ensuring access to the general curriculum. *Education and Training in Developmental Disabilities, 38,* 271–282.

Yoder, P., Kaiser, A., & Alpert, C. (1991). An exploratory study of the interaction between language teaching methods and child characteristics. *Journal of Speech and Hearing Research, 34,* 155–167.

Zeaman, D., & House, B. (1979). A review of attention theory. In N. Ellis (Ed.), *Handbook of mental deficiency: Psychological theory and research* (2nd ed.) (pp. 63–120). Hillsdale, NJ: Erlbaum.

9 Language and Students with Autism Spectrum Disorders

Individuals with autism spectrum disorders (ASD) have significant problems in both cognitive and language development. In this chapter we will examine the characteristics, definition, and impairments of cognition and language that are usually associated with autism spectrum disorders, also reviewing explanations of the cause of the disabilities associated with ASD. We will examine some intervention approaches found effective with individuals with autism spectrum disorders, as well as look at some new, controversial techniques.

After completing this chapter you should be able to:

1. List the characteristics that are shared by individuals with autism spectrum disorders.
2. Explain how *autism* is defined.
3. Describe specific language and communication impairments that are associated with autism spectrum disorders.
4. Explain what might cause the impairments of language and cognition associated with autism spectrum disorders.
5. Describe intervention approaches that have been developed to help children with autism spectrum disorders.

José: A Case Study

José is an 11-year-old boy, who, like many children on the autism spectrum, has received multiple diagnoses. His early development showed normal acquisition of motor, speech, and language development milestones. He said his first words at 12 months of age and spoke in two- to three-word phrases at 18 months of age. Both of his parents are bilingual, and Spanish was his family's first language. At approximately 22 months of age, his parents observed that José started losing language skills. At the time of his first formal communication evaluation at age 3, he had less than a five-word vocabulary (interestingly, all in English). José's pediatrician

(continued)

José: A Case Study Continued

made a referral for a speech and language evaluation and a hearing test. An audiological evaluation at 32 months showed normal hearing. A neurologic evaluation at 4 years of age suggested pervasive developmental disorder—not otherwise specified. However, José was diagnosed with Landau-Kleffner syndrome (epilepsy with acquired aphasia) when magnetic resonance imaging revealed a small arachnoid cyst on the left temporal lobe. This diagnosis was followed up with another neurologist who specialized in Landau-Kleffner syndrome. The neurologist did not confirm the diagnosis. An electroencephalogram revealed no seizure activity.

By 4 years 6 months, José and his family were left with an uncertain diagnostic picture. By this time, José's parents were fairly certain, however, that José's diagnosis was somewhere on the autism spectrum, and they decided not to pursue any further diagnostic procedures to confirm this. This decision was predicated by fear that a diagnosis of autistic disorder would drive his educational placement into a full-time classroom for children with autism. Although this was not a lawful policy at the time, it was a common practice. Without the label of autistic disorder, José's parents hoped that he would have broader educational options. José began speech and language therapy at age 3. The frequency and length of sessions in this service have been variable over the last 8 years. For the first 6 months, sessions were conducted twice a week for 30 minutes. Initially, efforts were made by the private clinic to provide José with equitable opportunities for symbol development in both Spanish and English. Therapy was initially conducted primarily in Spanish. After parents and clinicians agreed that José was not responding to language modeling when delivered in Spanish, however, therapy continued only in English. At that point, he began attending a speech and language preschool at our university's speech and hearing clinic for two full mornings a week. At age 4, he began attending public school in a class for children with "varying exceptionalities" on mornings that he was not attending the university preschool and he began receiving pullout group speech-language therapy in the schools, which has continued since that time. When José entered kindergarten, he also began receiving individual language therapy twice a week for an hour at the university's speech and hearing clinic. In school, other than being pulled out for speech-language therapy, José has been fully included in general education classrooms with his age-peers since kindergarten. He repeated third grade, however, because of failure to pass the test to assess whether students are meeting the state's standards. He is presently in the fifth grade.

Source: Diehl, S. F., Ford, C. S., & Federico, J. "The Communication Journey of a Fully Included Child with an Autism Spectrum Disorder." *Topics in Language Disorders, 25,* 375–387. Reprinted with permission of the publisher.

Casey: A Case Study

Casey had always been described as an extremely bright young student. The majority of his developmental milestones were reported to be within normal limits. His mother reported a history of early ear infections, and a speech delay was documented at 18 months. At approximately age 3, a note in the medical record appeared [that] suggested a diagnosis of Asperger's syndrome. This label afforded Casey appropriate educational and physical intervention at a young age through area health agencies. I was able to observe Casey from his early elementary years through middle school. Casey was seen by the occupational therapist and treated by the school speech therapist for an articulation disorder. During his speech and language therapy sessions, recommendations for strategies to address the oral sensitivities and pragmatic is-

Casey: A Case Study Continued

sues were integrated into his educational program through private clinic work. Academically, Casey was always at or above age level in literacy achievement activities, but this was due to his spending many hours, sometimes 4 to 5 hours a night, on homework. This is typical of most students with Asperger syndrome because of the obsessive-compulsive nature of their disorder and, as a result, their personalities.

Many aspects of the middle school environment became a source of stress and frustration for Casey and his teachers. The two main reasons for this frustration were the demands on socialization and the lack of rule-based movement. Recess, lunch, passing in the hall, and open physical education classes were all extremely difficult for Casey because of the often random nature of the required behavior. A constant source of our conversations was the fact that he had no friends. Most of his peers teased and mocked his behavior. He had found a few friends that enjoyed the same structured activities that he did—for example, Star Wars games, Pokeman, and anything on the computer. The structure of computer games and programmed activities allowed for strictly linear thinking that is typical of students with this disorder.

Because Casey had difficulty allowing others into conversations, most junior high students were not tolerant of his differences and would ignore him. This would have an impact on his participation in literacy activities that required interpretive response. Those friends toward whom he would gravitate were also interested in these same memory-heavy, organizationally rich activities. It was safe for Casey to remain immersed in his books or computers during the school day. This further explains why Casey's need for interaction in the lunchroom and recess time outside were very sore subjects for Casey. He continually denied that junior high students were allowed out of the school during the day. He would emphatically state that there was not a recess time, although his denial was unfounded. He would do everything in his power to not go outside into those situations that were so difficult for him. At the lunch table to which he was assigned, the other students were social among themselves, but not with Casey. He usually ate quietly [and sat] apart at the table. On a few occasions, Casey was invited to participate in one of several "lunch groups" specially organized by the school's social worker, but these groups were difficult situations for him. These group activities were difficult due to [students with Asperger's syndrome experiencing] problems with transitioning and with sharing perspectives (often referred to as "theory of mind").

Much of the work we did together focused on language and literacy support, using oral motor treatment. Many times movement was added, either on a swing or a large ball. This helped to improve jaw stability and improved Casey's ability to attend and organize. Through videotape feedback activities, Casey learned to identify difficulties in his handling of social situations (i.e., what went wrong and how he could alter reactions in different situations to have a more positive outcome).

Source: "Teaching and Learning Approaches for Children with Asperger's Syndrome" by F. Falk-Ross, M. Iverson, & C. Gilbert. *Teaching Exceptional Children, 36,* 48–55. Copyright 2004 by The Council for Exceptional Children. Reprinted with permission.

Cases like those of José and Casey have fascinated both researchers and the general public. Researchers are intrigued by this mysterious disorder that defies their best efforts to find a cause and a treatment. The general public's interest in autism has been raised by depictions of those with the condition in films such as *Rain Man* and in books and appearances by authors such as Barry Kauffman (1976, 1994)—the parent of a child with autism—and Temple Grandin (1996)—a person with autism. What is it about autism and related disorders that make them so elusive and fascinating?

Characteristics of Autism Spectrum Disorders

Autism is a disorder that is present from birth or very early in development that affects social interaction, communication, and the establishment of relationships with others (National Research Council, 2001). It is one of a group of disorders sometimes called **pervasive developmental disorders (PDD)** or **autism spectrum disorders (ASD).** These terms recognize that autistic behavior lies on a continuum (or spectrum) of severity. Although the number and severity of symptoms may vary, the disorders have several characteristics in common, which we will discuss next.

Impairments in Social Interaction

Withdrawal from contact with others is probably the most salient feature of autism spectrum disorders. Young children with ASD often are not responsive to parents and other caregivers. They may remain stiff when picked up and cuddled. In addition, children with autism fail to make eye contact with others. It sometimes seems as if they are "looking through" the other person. They rarely reach out to others for comfort, seeking little or no social interaction (Rutter & Schopler, 1987).

Impairments in Language and Communication

Children with autism spectrum disorders have severe disorders in language and/or communication. A significant number of children with autism (up to half, in some estimates) never develop speech (Tager-Flusberg, Paul, & Lord, 2005). Language and communication difficulties are evident in most young children with ASD and persist through adulthood, even in adults with reasonably good language development (Howlin, 2003). There are significant delays in language development, but, even more important, there are some characteristic *differences* in language development in most individuals with autistic spectrum disorders.

Restricted Repertoire of Activities and Interests

Often, children with autism spectrum disorders are described as engaging in *ritualistic* behaviors, such as spinning objects, twirling their fingers in front of their face, slapping their heads, flapping their hands, and the like. This behavior may be self-stimulating. Children with ASD are not the only individuals with disabilities who engage in such behaviors, but the behaviors seem to be particularly characteristic of autism spectrum disorders. In addition, individuals with ASD often have a compelling desire for sameness and routine. They may become upset if something in their room is out of place or if their usual schedule is disrupted (Rutter & Schopler, 1987). If you saw *Rain Man,* you may remember the discomfort that Raymond—the individual with autism portrayed by Dustin Hoffman—experienced when he discovered that there was a book out of place in his room.

Since first being identified in the 1940s, the definition and description of autism and its related disorders has changed frequently. In the next section we will examine current definitions of autism and see how these have changed as experts have learned more about this disorder.

Definition of Autism Spectrum Disorders

At one time, autism was thought to be an early version of schizophrenia (Rutter & Schopler, 1987). In fact, the major journal in the field of autism, *The Journal of Autism and Developmental Disorders,* was at one time called *The Journal of Autism and Childhood Schizophrenia.* However, over the last 20 years, there has been a growing recognition that autism and schizophrenia are two separate disorders (Rutter & Schopler, 1987). Although there is widespread agreement that autism is a distinct disorder, there remains considerable confusion about the term and its definition. It is not unusual to find children who are called *autisticlike* or *exhibiting autistic behaviors.* These descriptions reflect the difficulty of defining autism.

During the last 20 years or so, considerable progress has been made in narrowing and sharpening the definition of autism. Even the name *(Kanner's syndrome, infantile autism, autistic disorder)* has changed. One of the most widely used definitions is that contained in the *Diagnostic and Statistical Manual of Mental Disorders, (DSM-IV-TR),* published by the American Psychiatric Association (2000). In the *DSM-IV-TR, autistic disorder* is considered one of a group of disorders called *pervasive developmental disorders.* In order to be diagnosed with autistic disorder, a child must exhibit at least six of the symptoms included in the definition. These symptoms are distributed among three general categories:

1. Qualitative impairment in social interaction
2. Qualitative impairment in communication
3. Restricted repetitive and stereotyped patterns of behavior, interests, and activities

A child must have at least two symptoms from group 1, one from group 2, and one from group 3 in order to be a candidate for the autistic disorder label. In addition, the onset of the disorder must occur during infancy or childhood (before 36 months of age).

Recently, in the Individuals with Disabilities Education Act (IDEA), the federal government recognized autism as a distinct disorder. The federal definition states:

> Autism means a developmental disability significantly affecting verbal and nonverbal communication and social interaction, generally evident before age three, that adversely affects educational performance. Characteristics of autism include irregularities and impairments in communication, engagement in repetitive activities and stereotyped movements, resistance to environmental change or change in daily routines, and unusual responses to sensory experiences. (IDEA, 2004)

The definitions contained in both the *DSM-IV* and the IDEA contain specific and easily recognizable symptoms. However, in practice, even highly skilled professionals have difficulty diagnosing autism. Frequently, children with autistic characteristics act like children with other disabilities, such as children with intellectual disabilities, pervasive language disorders, hearing impairments, or psychiatric disorders. Although children with autism share some characteristics with children with other disabilities, there are some distinct differences. For example, children with autism have more severe cognitive and behavioral impairments than those found among children with pervasive language disorders. Unlike children with other disabilities, children with autism do not respond to communicative attempts by others, and unlike children with severe hearing impairments, the sensory impairments of children with autism fluctuate from one extreme to the other.

Researchers believe that autism is one of a group of related disorders that includes Asperger's syndrome, Rett syndrome, and Pervasive Developmental Disorder–Not Otherwise Specified (PDD–NOS). These other disorders share characteristics with autism but also differ in specific ways. For example, the onset of autism is prior to age 3, but PDD-NOS may occur after age 3 (Lord & Risi, 2000). There is an ongoing debate in the scientific literature about whether **Asperger's syndrome** is part of the autism spectrum or a separate disorder. Currently, Asperger's syndrome is considered by most scientists to be a less severe form of autism. Children with Asperger's syndrome usually have deficiencies in social interaction but have much better language and cognitive skills than children with autism. For most of the remainder of this chapter our focus will be on language and communication disorders associated with autism. Until recently, most of the research has focused on this population. However, we will also examine the research on the language and communicative characteristics of individuals with Asperger's syndrome because of growing interest in and identification of this population in schools.

Causes of Autism

So much has been written about the causes of autism that it is difficult to condense the research into a few paragraphs—or even a few pages. Any discussion of the causes of this disorder must attempt to explain the myriad symptoms associated with the syndrome. This is no easy matter. Even if we cannot say for certain what causes autism, understanding what does *not* cause the disorder is important.

Early theories of autism focused on the family and family interaction as the likely cause of the syndrome. Kanner (1943), and later Bettelheim (1967), suggested that autism was caused by parents who were unusually rigid and emotionally cold. Kanner talked about the "refrigerator" parents who interacted with their children in a cold, aloof manner. This behavior by parents was thought to cause emotional deprivation in the child, which, in turn, caused the child to withdraw from human interaction. Although this psychoanalytic view of the cause of autism was widely accepted for many years, it is now rejected by most professionals. The reason is that controlled studies failed to find differences in either the personality traits of parents of children with autism or in the way they relate to their children (Prior & Werry, 1986). Although some differences have been found in interactions between parents and their autistic children, these can be attributed to the behavior of the autistic child rather than to psychopathology of the parent.

If parents do not cause autism, what does? More and more evidence points to a biological disorder underlying autism. However, the specific biological problem has been difficult to pinpoint. It has been suggested, for example, that damage to the brain stem may be the cause of the fluctuations in the processing of sensory information and the stereotypical behaviors found in autism (Tanguay & Edwards, 1982; Piven et al., 1992). However, other studies have failed to find neuroanatomical differences in this structure (Akshoomoff, 2000). Others have suggested that damage to the limbic system (Bauman & Kemper, 1994) or to a combination of cortical and subcortical regions (Fein, Pennington, Markowitz, Braverman, & Waterhouse, 1986) may cause the symptoms associated with autism. There has been a good deal of research on the role of biochemical differences in autistic individuals. This research has found a wide range of differences in the brain chemistry of autistic persons (e.g., Lama & Amanb, 2006), but no single neurochemical has been clearly identified as the cause of autistic spectrum disorders. Researchers have also suggested that genetic factors may cause autism, although the precise way in which genetic disorders cause autism has yet to be determined (Folstein & Rosen-Sheidley, 2001).

Reviewing the research on the cause of autism, Folstein and Rutter (1988) reached two conclusions. First, there are many etiologies (causes) of autism. Second, the causes of autism are organic rather than psychosocial. Perhaps this is the most we can say at this point about the causes of autism. Although many causes have been found, no *single* cause has been (or is likely to be) found. It is quite possible that there are several subtypes of autism that will be found to have different causes and unique treatments. Until research clarifies the situation, the role of educators must be to use the most effective techniques with all children with autism.

Language and Communication

Deficiencies in language and communication are an important factor in autism and autism spectrum disorders—some would say the most important factor. Language and communication skills have been found to be an excellent predictor of future development (McEachin, Smith, & Lovaas, 1993). Children with better communication skills are more likely to be successfully included in school and the community and have better overall outcomes. As noted earlier in this chapter, many children with autism do not develop spoken language at all. For those who do develop spoken language, there are significant delays in development and a pattern of relatively preserved abilities and significant deficits. One of the many questions about the language and communication of individuals with autism is whether they have truly unique language deficits—different even from those of other children with language disorders. We will examine the evidence for and against the issue of "unique" language disorders.

Specific Language Differences.

Two specific language differences have been considered by some to be characteristic of autism: echolalia and pronoun reversal. **Echolalia** is the literal repetition of speech produced by others (Prizant & Duchan, 1981). Echolalia that occurs immediately (or very shortly after) another person speaks is called **immediate echolalia. Delayed echolalia** involves the repetition of words or phrases that may have been heard days,

FIGURE 9.1   Examples of Echolalia

Immediate Echolalia	Teacher says: "Gloria, what did you do last night?" Student responds: "What did you do last night?"
Delayed Echolalia	While working quietly at a desk, the child suddenly shouts: "What's the matter with you? You can't do that."
Mitigated Echolalia	Teacher says: "So, what did you do last night?" Student responds: "Night."

weeks, or even years ago. Sometimes echolalic individuals repeat exactly what they hear, but often they change the structure of the original utterance. This is called **mitigated echolalia** (see Figure 9.1 for examples). Although echolalia is found among many individuals with disabilities (and even at certain stages of normal language development), it occurs more frequently among individuals with autism (Cantwell, Baker, & Rutter, 1978) and persists for far longer than in normally developing children (Howlin, 1982). However, as Tager-Flusberg and colleagues (2005) point out, echolalia is not unique to autism. Children with other disabilities, including children who are blind and children with intellectual disabilities, echo. Furthermore, studies have found that, although a significant number of children with autism use echoloalia, many never echo.

The traditional view of echolalia has been that it indicates a lack of comprehension ability and is noncommunicative (Schreibman & Carr, 1978). Many language training programs have actively discouraged—and even punished—the use of echolalia by children with autism. However, views about echolalia have changed. Today, many believe that echolalia actually serves an important communicative role for individuals with autism. Barry Prizant (1983), for example, holds the position that people with autism may use echolalia in an intentional way to maintain social interaction. Prizant and Duchan (1981) went so far as to delineate seven communicative functions that echolalia may serve (see Table 9.1). Their research, as well as that by others, should remind us that we must look at the total context—not just at the spoken language produced—to fully understand what may be going on in an interaction.

Another language characteristic associated with autism is **pronoun reversal.** Many children with autism say *you* when referring to themselves, or *me* when referring to another person. For example, when asking for a drink of water, they might say *You want a drink of water?* Like echolalia, pronoun reversal is not unique to children with autism. Other children with disabilities, especially children who are blind, may confuse the speaker and listener and use the wrong pronoun. Pronoun reversal does seem to be more common in autistic children, however (Lee, Hobson, & Chiat, 1994).

Several explanations for the pronoun reversals of individuals with autism have been suggested, including:

1. *Echolalia.* Difficulty with pronoun usage may be the result of echolalia (Bartak & Rutter, 1976). Referring to our earlier example, the child saying *You want a drink of water?* may have been using delayed echolalia (repeating a phrase she or

TABLE 9.1   **Seven Communicative Functions of Immediate Echolalia**

Category	Description
Interactive	
Turn-taking	Utterances used as turn fillers in an alternating verbal exchange
Declarative	Utterances labeling objects, actions, or location (accompanied by demonstrative gestures)
Yes answer	Utterances used to indicate affirmation of prior utterance
Request	Utterances used to request objects or others' actions; usually involves mitigated echolalia
Noninteractive	
Nonfocused	Utterances produced with no apparent intent and often in states of high arousal (e.g., fear, pain)
Rehearsal	Utterances used as a processing aid, followed by utterance or action indicating comprehension of echoed utterance
Self-regulatory	Utterances that serve to regulate subject's own actions; produced in synchrony with motor activity

Source: Adapted from Prizant & Duchan (1981).

he heard previously) or using immediate echolalia in response to the request, "Do you want water?"

2. *Cognitive development.* Words such as *I* and *you* are *deictic* forms—that is, words that change their referent in relation to the context. A *ball* is always a *ball,* but sometimes *I* is *I* and sometimes *I* is *you,* depending on the context. Cognitively, this is a more complex notion and one that may be more difficult for children with cognitive difficulties (Tager-Flusberg, 1981).

3. *Lack of attention.* Oshima-Takane and Benaroya (1989) have claimed that children with autism have trouble with pronouns because the children fail to attend to pronoun usage by others. They found, however, that when autistic children were guided to attend to an adult model, they *could* learn to use pronouns correctly.

It is likely that each of these factors plays a role for specific children with autism and perhaps at different stages of development. One researcher who has studied the phenomenon of pronoun reversal extensively has concluded that it is the result of a combination of difficulties that individuals with autism have with concept of "self" combined with difficulty understanding the shifting roles of speakers and listeners in conversational exchanges (Tager-Flusberg, Paul, & Lord, 2005). The implication for teachers is to *recognize* pronoun reversal when it occurs, *respond* to the child's attempt to communicate, and *model* the appropriate form. In practice, the sequence might go something like this:

STUDENT: You want water.

TEACHER: Oh. You want water. I want water, too.

What can we conclude about the language differences of children with autism? Are they truly "unique"? The answer, unfortunately, is not entirely clear. Echolalia is certainly not unique to children with autism. However, it may be more widespread among the population and persist longer than in other groups of children with disabilities. Likewise, pronoun reversal can be found in children other than those identified as autistic. But it does appear to be more persistent in this population. So, although it is hard to say that either echolalia or pronoun reversal is truly "characteristic" of autism, both are clearly significant problems in this population.

As we review the research on other specific language and communication difficulties in children on the autism spectrum, keep in mind the variability within the population. Individuals who are sometimes identified as "high-functioning" autistic (higher IQ scores) and those with Asperger's syndrome may have very different patterns of language development from children with autism. Even within that group, we are discussing only those individuals who develop spoken language. That, in itself, is a subgroup among the total population.

Early Language and Communication Development

It is not easy to examine the early language development of children with autism because these children are often not identified as autistic until age 2 or 3. However, the studies that have been done suggest that right from the start, language development is a problem for children with autism. For example, some studies have been able to analyze family videos of infants who were later diagnosed with autism. These studies have found differences in communication development by the first birthday (Osterling & Dawson, 1994). When compared to children with mental retardation, 1-year-olds with autism were less responsive to their names and did not look at others as much.

Young children with autism have been found to have difficulties with two prerequisites for communication: joint attention and symbol use. You may recall from Chapter 5 of this text that one of the earliest communicative developments takes place when infants and their parents receive attention from each other. This interaction sets the foundation for the development of communication and eventually language. But children with autism have been found to have significant deficits in joint attention (Kasari, Freeman & Paparella, 2001). That is, they are less likely than typically developing children to share their attention with a caregiver over an object or activity. In addition, young children with autism use fewer vocalizations and fewer nonverbal gestures than children with language disorders and mental retardation, or typically developing children (Wetherby, Prizant, & Schuler, 2000). Clearly, both of these deficits place children with autism at significant risk for deficits in language and communication. Even when children with autism develop spoken language, they do so at a later age and develop more slowly than other children—even those with language disorders.

Some children with autism go through a period of typical early language and communication development, then regress. They may begin to use words then fail to develop additional vocabulary. These children gradually participate less often in communicative interaction. There does not seem to be any relationship between this type of regression and later language outcomes (Tager-Flusberg, Paul, & Lord, 2005). That is, these children are not at greater risk or lesser risk for significant language and communication difficulties than other children with autism.

Children with "high-functioning" autism (usually defined as those with IQ scores higher than 80) follow a pattern of early developmental difficulties that is largely similar to that of other children with autism. However, they do start to talk, on average, at about age 3 (Howlin, 2003). By age 5 they are beginning to use multiword phrases. Although this is certainly delayed compared to typically developing children, it is much better than most children with autism, many of whom develop no spoken language by age 5. In contrast, young children with Asperger's syndrome do not have significant delays in their development of spoken language. The same study found that parents of children later identified as having Asperger's syndrome reported first words emerging in their children, on average, at 14 months and phrases at 26 months—much like typically developing children.

Development in Specific Language Domains

Children with autism spectrum disorder who develop spoken language have a pattern of language and communication that ranges from areas of relatively intact development to areas of significant deficits. Overall, individuals with autism have the most significant deficits but those identified as high-functioning autistic and those having Asperger's syndrome have specific language difficulties that affect their functioning as well.

Phonology. Studies of the speech production of children with autism have found that in those children who develop spoken language, the development of phonological rules follows the same course found in normally developing children but with delays. The speech of most verbal children with autism spectrum disorders is intelligible and may even be more advanced than typically developing peers (Kjelgaard & Tager-Flusberg, 2001). Bartolucci, Pierce, Streiner, and Eppel (1976) studied the phonological production of children with autism in comparison to children with mental retardation who were matched for mental age. They found that both groups used similar phonemes and made similar errors in the production of more advanced sounds, leading the researchers to conclude that verbal autistic children have a normal, but delayed, sequence of phonological development. However, there may be some persistence of speech production errors into adulthood. In their study of high-functioning autistic and Asperger's syndrome adolescents and adults, Shriberg and colleagues (2001) found that up to one-third of those in the study continued to have some speech errors (compared to 1 percent in the general population).

Many observers have reported that individuals with autism have considerable trouble with **suprasegmental features** of sound production (stress and intonation). Children with autism have been described as speaking in a singsong pattern, having fluctuations in vocal intensity (too loud or too soft), and using intonations that are not appropriate to the meaning of the sentence (using a rising intonation for sentences that are not questions). Individuals with autism often lack expression in their voices and may speak in a monotone. The study by Shriberg and colleagues (2001) confirmed these findings among high-functioning autistic and Asperger's syndrome groups.

These researchers found that a significant number of their study participants (30 to 40 percent) had difficulty with features such as phrasing, stress, and vocal modulation. Specifically, they often repeated sounds, syllables, and/or words, making their speech harder to follow. They placed stress at the wrong place in sentences and their voices were often too loud and too high. Although some of these differences were subtle, they are significant enough to make it more difficult for a listener to understand.

Morpholohgy and Syntax.   As with phonological development, studies of the acquisition of morphological rules by children with autism have found some similarities to normally developing children and some differences. For example, when Bartolucci, Pierce, and Streiner (1980) compared the use of morphemes by children with autism, children with mental retardation, and normally developing children, they found that the children with mental retardation and those with autism acquired morphemes in a different order than did normally developing children. In addition, there was a lag in the development of morpheme usage in both groups of children with disabilities. Bartolucci and colleagues (1980) suggested that the previously mentioned problems that children with autism have with pronouns (which change their meaning with the context) may explain some of the differences in the morphological development. Difficulty in understanding and using past tense may be a particular problem for children with autism (Tager-Flusberg, 1989; Rice et al., 1994).

Studies of the syntactic development of children with autism spectrum disorders, especially those with autism, have generally found that, although there are significant delays, development follows a normal path (Tager-Flusberg, Paul, & Lord, 2005). For example, Tager-Flusberg and colleagues (1990) compared the language development of a group of children with autism to that of children with Down syndrome. They found that for most of the children with autism, MLU increased over time and was a good indicator of level of language development. However, this was not true for one of the children. In addition, Tager-Flusberg and colleagues reported that the syntactic development of the children with autism followed a developmental course similar to that of both the normally developing children and the children with Down syndrome, although in children with autism, there appeared to be a leveling out of their development at higher stages of MLU. But, once again, there were exceptions; one child actually declined in syntactic development during the study.

Bartak, Rutter, and Cox (1975) compared the syntactic development of children with autism and *dysphasia* (a specific language disorder). They found that although the children were similar in mean length of utterance, the children with autism performed much more poorly on tests of language comprehension. They also found that the language disorder of children with autism was more extensive, involving the use and understanding of gesture and written language, as well as spoken language. In a more detailed, follow-up study, Cantwell, Baker, and Rutter (1978) analyzed the tape-recorded language samples of some of the children from the original study. They found that the two groups were quite similar, both in morphological rule usage and in development of syntactic rules. Where differences were found, they were in the *use* of language in social situations. The children with autism were described as using more "abnormal" speech and less "socialized" speech.

Landa and Goldberg (2005) compared the morphological and syntactic development of high-functioning autistic children, ages 7 to 17, with a group of typically developing children matched for age and IQ score. The language skills of the children were similar on a number of measures, but the children with autism performed more poorly on a test of expressive grammar and on understanding figures of speech. The authors suggest that even though high-functioning individuals with autism may seem to have good expressive language, a careful analysis of their skills may indicate specific difficulties with some aspects of syntax.

Most of the research on the morphological and syntactic development of children with autism concludes that these domains of development are delayed. However, there also may be limits to this development (like those reported for some individuals with mental retardation). We should keep in mind that there is a great deal of variability in this population and that some children may deviate from this pattern of delayed development. In addition, several studies have reported significant problems experienced by children with autism in *applying* linguistic rules in social situations.

Semantics. As is true with most aspects of language, individuals with autism spectrum disorders have a mixed pattern of strengths and weaknesses in semantics. Baltaxe and Simmons (1975) reported on a series of studies on the speech of higher-functioning adolescents with autism. They found that these autistic adolescents, unlike individuals with Down syndrome, had most difficulty with semantic concepts. Findings such as this have led some researchers to conclude that autism may be an example of a semantic-pragmatic language disorder (Brook & Bowler, 1992).

However, studies of the semantic skills of individuals with autism have not always found deficits. For example, when Tager-Flusberg (1985) directly examined the ability of children with autism to group information by conceptual categories, she found that the children with autism were no different from the nondisabled children in their categorization abilities. She concluded that the view of the world held by the children with autism that she tested was quite similar to that of the other children in the study. Similarly, Eskes, Bryson, and McCormick (1990) found that children with autism could comprehend both concrete and abstract words (such as *life* and *time*), much like children in a normally developing control group matched for reading ability. Research with high-functioning children with autism has shown that they score well on standardized tests of vocabulary, suggesting that this is a relative strength for many children with autism (Kjelgaard & Tager-Flusberg, 2001).

At the same time. A common finding of research studies is that children with autism use more idiosyncratic language and neologisms in their language. Volden and Lord (1991) defined **idiosyncratic language** as "the use of conventional words or phrases in unusual ways to convey specific meanings" (p. 111). For example, a child with autism in their study said, *"It makes me want to go as deep as economical with it,"* which was interpreted to mean *withdraw as much as possible.* **Neologisms** are nonstandard (or invented) words. Subjects with autism in the Volden and Lord study said *bloosers* for *bruises* and *bells* for *rings.* Volden and Lord compared the frequency of idiosyncratic language and neologisms in language samples from two groups of children with autism (IQ > 80 and IQ < 80) to the language of children with mental retardation and normally developing children matched for chronological age. They found that the children with autism made more semantic errors and produced far more neologisms than either of the comparison groups. Almost all of the children with autism produced unusual words or phrases, whereas few of the other participants did so. This study suggests that individuals with autism may have difficulty using words correctly.

Although the research on the semantic skills of individuals with autism may seem to be confusing and inconsistent, one thing stands out. Individuals with autism have difficulty using semantic concepts in natural situations. As educators, we can help children with autism by modeling correct usage, by pointing out when a word is misused or when there is an opportunity to apply a semantic concept, and by teaching students to use semantic strategies for thinking and problem solving.

Pragmatics.   One of the defining features of autism is withdrawal from social interaction. So, it should not be surprising to find that children with autism have significant impairments in the pragmatic aspects of language. A good deal of research evidence supports the claim that individuals with autism have significant problems with pragmatics. Loveland, Landry, Hughes, Hall, and McEvoy (1988), for example, found that children with autism were very unresponsive to attempts by their parents to initiate communication. In addition, the children with autism rarely initiated communication spontaneously and also produced fewer communicative acts than did mental-age-matched children with language delays or normally developing children. Loveland and colleagues concluded that the pragmatic development of the children with autism in their study was below that of even the 2-year-old nondisabled children to whom they were being compared.

Researchers have found deficiencies in pragmatic language in almost every aspect that has been investigated, including speech acts, listening, using "polite" conversation, making irrelevant statements, staying on topic, and making bizarre and inappropriate comments (Tager-Flusberg, Paul, & Lord, 2005). Several studies (e.g., Baltaxe, 1977; Eales, 1993) have shown that the pragmatic problems associated with autism persist through adolescence, even in higher-IQ individuals (see Figure 9.2 for examples).

It is possible that under certain circumstances individuals with autism can communicate more than has generally been thought. Wetherby (1986) cites several pieces of research evidence to support this conclusion. For example, she notes that some research indicates that the communicative behavior of children with autism was greater with their teacher than with their classmates. Similarly, Bernard-Opitz (1982) observed a child with autism who interacted more with his mother and a clinician than he did with an unfamiliar adult. Wetherby and Prutting (1984) found that when both nonverbal and verbal means of communication were used, individuals with autism communicated as frequently as did nondisabled children matched for language ability, although they used fewer communicative acts. These findings suggest that the communication difficulties associated with autism spectrum disorders may be more apparent in certain communicative environments, with specific communication partners. This is hopeful information for practitioners because it suggests that children with autism can be helped to communicate more effectively.

FIGURE 9.2   Examples of Pragmatic Impairments in Adults with Autism

Response Does Not Address Question

Experimenter:	Catherine is your . . .
Subject:	Sister.
E:	Sister, right. Is she younger than you or older than you?
S:	Catherine O'Brien.

Irrelevant Response

E:	Is Jane married?
S:	No.
E.	Mhmm. She's got a friend and she lives in America?
S:	Museums all shut now.

Echolalia

E:	Where do Mummy and Daddy live?
S:	Mummy and Daddy live.

Source: M. Eales. (1993). Pragmatic impairments in adults with childhood diagnoses of autism or developmental receptive language disorder. *Journal of Autism and Developmental Disorders, 23,* 593–617. With kind permission of Springer Science and Business Media.

Although most elements of language of individuals with Asperger's syndrome are at or above the levels of typically developing children, there is evidence that aspects of pragmatics may be problematic. For example, researchers have found specific difficulties in taking the lead in conversations, terminating conversations appropriately, and responding to others (Chuba, Paul, Miles, Klin, & Volkmar, 2003). In a study comparing the conversational skills of adolescents with Asperger's syndrome to individuals with conduct disorder (matched for age and IQ), Adams and colleagues (2002) discovered that the Asperger's group had many more problems successfully participating in conversations. They more frequently failed to mesh their response to their conversational partners even though they tended to talk a lot. Excessive talking by persons with Asperger's syndrome has been reported by several researchers and by practitioners. Although the Adams (2002) study did not find that most of the adolescents with Asperger's syndrome inappropriately dominated the conversation, a subgroup did fit that pattern. Landa (2000) summarized the language and communication difficulties associated with Asperger's syndrome as follows:

- Failure to adjust their language production in response to the context (e.g., using a formal greeting with someone who is already familiar)
- Tendency to initiate conversation without regard to the listener's interest in the topic
- Use of socially inappropriate topics (e.g., asking someone about his or her weight/age)
- Difficulty understanding nonliteral language
- Shifting conversational topics abruptly

These difficulties in language often have a negative impact on the ability of individuals with Asperger's syndrome to develop social relationships and to be accepted in the community.

The research on pragmatic development in children with autism suggests that teachers and other education professionals can help these children with autism enhance their communication skills by interacting with them frequently, by being responsive to both verbal and nonverbal attempts to communicate, and by communicating with the children in comfortable, familiar contexts whenever possible. Children with Asperger's syndrome are likely to have more subtle conversational difficulties but these can lead to social rejection if not addressed.

Conclusion

Language and communication deficits are an important feature of autism spectrum disorders. With the exception of individuals identified with Asperger's syndrome, most young children with autism have difficulties with language development prior to age 2. Some never develop spoken language. For those who do, some aspects of language, such as phonology and syntax, are relatively intact. There are delays, but, for the most part, development progresses through the usual stages. Deficits in semantics and pragmatics are more significant and can affect academic and social success (see Table 9.2 for a summary).

TABLE 9.2   Language Development of Individuals with Autism

Early Development	Phonology	Morphology/ Syntax	Semantics	Pragmatics
Less responsive to name	Normal but delayed development	Delays in nonverbal and written as well as spoken language	Categorization may be intact	Rigid, socially inappropriate
Does not look at others as much	Impairments in suprasegmental features (stress and intonation)	Less complex language than those with mental retardation	Higher IQ and good vocabulary	Unresponsive
Difficulty with joint attention			Difficulty with pronouns	Problems persist
				Speech-act development intact
Fewer vocalizations and nonverbal gestures	Fluctuations in vocal intensity	Difficulty with some morphological rules (e.g., past tense)	Use more idiosyncratic language	
	Inappropriate Intonation			Individuals with Asperger's syndrome have difficulty with leading and terminating conversations and responding appropriately
	Errors may persist			

Causes of Language and Communication Disorders in Autism Spectrum Disorders

What causes the language impairments associated with autism? Answering this question is about as difficult as determining the cause of autism itself. But the search for the answer may help those working with children with autism focus their efforts on effective intervention approaches. Let's briefly examine a few of the hypotheses that have been suggested to explain the cause of the language and communications disorders of children with autism.

Parent–Child Interaction

As we know, one of the earliest theories on the cause of autism identified parents as the problem. Although research evidence has not generally supported this causal hypothesis, it is possible that deficiencies in parent–child interaction might have a negative effect on language development. In fact, the most problematic language domains for children with autism—semantics and pragmatics—are those that are most affected by parent–child interaction. Early research on the interaction between parents and their children with autism claimed that deficiencies in parent–child interaction caused (or at least contributed to) the language deficiencies of children with autism (Goldfarb, Goldfarb, & Scholl, 1966). However, later research failed to support this claim. In most studies, parents of children with autism have been found to interact with their children much like parents of other children with disabilities (Cantwell et al., 1977). In fact, the only differences that Cantwell and colleagues found were that mothers of children with autism used more affectionate remarks and more elaborations than did parents of children with dysphasia. Although parent–child interaction may differ in children with autism, this difference is more likely to be due to the behavior of the child than to that of the parent(s).

On the other hand, there is some research literature that reports language problems in parents of children with autism. For example, Landa, Folstein, and Isaacs (1991) found that parents of children with autism produced story narratives that were similar in length to those produced by other adults, but that a subgroup (34 percent) produced extremely poor stories. Landa and colleagues suggested that language difficulties may run in families who have children with autism. They believe that this language disorder is due to a genetic problem, however, not to deficient language interaction.

Teachers and other education professionals may help parents of children with autism enhance the quality of interaction with their children by suggesting ways parents might engage their child's attention, comment on what their child is doing, and learn how to interpret seemingly noncommunicative verbal and nonverbal behaviors. Knowing that some, but not all, parents of children with autism may themselves have language problems may help teachers be more alert to parents' needs.

Cognitive Impairments

Because most children with autism *look* "normal" and some possess unusual talents, at one time it was thought that intelligence in autistic children was average or even above average. But today, researchers believe that most children with autism have low, measured intelligence. A majority (up to 75 percent in some estimates) have IQ scores in the range of mental retardation (< 75). Although perhaps 20 to 25 percent score within the normal range of intelligence (75 to 120), the majority fall within an IQ range of about 35 to 70 (Prior & Werry, 1986; American Psychiatric Association, 1994).

In addition to having lower IQ scores, children with autism often have significant impairments in specific cognitive abilities. Some of these problems appear to be developmental in nature. For example, the memory and discrimination problems often associated with autism are likely due to the slower cognitive development of children with autism (Prior & Werry, 1986). On the other hand, there are some cognitive impairments that seem specifically characteristic of autism. In a series of studies, Hermelin (1978) and Hermelin and O'Connor (1970) found that children with autism have special difficulty using meaning to solve problems and organizing information by rules and categories. For example, when asked to put together a jigsaw puzzle, children with autism may do as well when the pieces are face down as when the picture side is visible. They fail to use or extract meaning from this experience. Instead of using pictures or words to think, they try to retain information in a raw, unorganized state. This is not an effective way to think and remember. Ricks and Wing (1975) came to a similar conclusion in their description of the language problems of children with autism. Their research led them to conclude that children with autism have specific difficulty in forming language rules.

Several cognitive-related theories have been suggested to explain the pervasive cognitive and language impairments of autism. Prizant (1983) suggested that individuals with autism may have a **gestalt processing style.** In other words, they take in information in large chunks, failing to analyze the information. As a result, they do not acquire the rules of language. As evidence, Prizant cites echolalia as an example of the memorization and repetition of whole chunks. Wetherby and Prutting (1984) claimed that persons with autism have **asynchronous development.** In other words, the timing of their development is off. They claim that individuals with autism acquire the same skills as other children but do so out of the usual order. As a result, they are ahead on some things but behind on others. Deficiencies in "executive functions" have also been suggested as the cause for the information-processing difficulties experienced by individuals with autism. Executive functions serve to initiate behavior (while inhibiting competing responses), regulate attention, and help in the manipulation of mental representations (Mundy & Markus, 1997). Many individuals with autism have difficulty selecting the correct choice among several competing choices and focusing their attention on the task.

Still another hypothesis explaining these cognitive and language impairments claims that individuals with autism lack a **theory of mind** (Baron-Cohen, Leslie, & Frith, 1985). The theory of mind hypothesis states that normally developing children possess an understanding of mental states in others; if this ability is impaired, children have difficulty understanding the behavior (including the communicative behavior) of other people. For example, in order to communicate effectively, one must be able to understand the point of view of another person. What does that person know? What does that person need to know? For example, some individuals with autism provide their names and addresses to everyone they meet—even relatives who know all this information. Others may talk about their trip to the mall with Billy—never explaining who Billy is.

A number of research studies have found that individuals with autism have difficulty with theory of mind concepts (Baron-Cohen, 1995). Difficulty understanding another's viewpoint could certainly cause significant problems with communication. But it is not clear that, even if individuals with autism have difficulty with theory of mind concepts, this is the cause of the communication difficulties in this population.

Clearly, teachers and others need to consider the possible effects that cognitive impairments could have on the language development of children with autism. These students may benefit from participation in a variety of classroom and community experiences. But even more important is that teachers understand *how* children with autism have perceived these experiences, to know that their view may be quite different from what we *thought* they would experience. It may help for the teacher to recount what the group or individual did, to model analysis of new information, and to demonstrate how this information can be integrated with prior learning.

Neurological Causes

There is little doubt that autism spectrum disorders are neurodevelopmental disorders; that is, they are caused by some difference or dysfunction in the brain and/or central nervous system. But identifying the exact cause (or, more likely, causes) of this disorder has been extremely difficult. Numerous theories have been proposed, including biochemical agents, anatomical structures, and functional differences. But, to this point, there is no prevailing single or even group of causes.

However, advances in neuroimaging techniques have brought us closer to understanding the ways in which brain anomalies may contribute to the language difficulties experienced by individuals with autism. For example, in most typically developing, right-handed persons, the left hemisphere of the brain is slightly larger than the right—particularly in a region known as the planum temporale. It is thought that this hemispheric asymmetry is related to language functioning in the left hemisphere. But there is increasing evidence that many individuals with autism do not have the left hemisphere asymmetries found in most typically developing individuals (Muller et al., 1999). Functional magnetic resonance imaging (fMRI) can examine activity in the brain during real-time activities. Using this technique, researchers have found that individuals with high-functioning autism show lower activation in regions of the brain usually associated with the processing of grammar during a sentence-comprehension task (Just, Cherkassky, Keller, & Minshew, 2004).

Although still in their early stages, investigations of the brain structure and functioning of individuals with autism may allow us to better understand the underlying problems that contribute to the language and literacy difficulties associated with autism. Ultimately, this may help us focus intervention where it may do the most good.

Literacy and Autism Spectrum Disorders

Students with autism spectrum disorders have a range of abilities that have a significant impact on their acquisition of literacy. As we have seen, most (but not all) children with autism have significant deficits in cognitive and language development that are likely to cause significant difficulties in learning to read and write. However, higher-functioning autistic children may be able to acquire literacy skills in ways that are similar to typically developing students, and children with Asperger's syndrome may actually be more advanced than their typically developing peers in at least some aspects of reading and writing.

Students with autism who have significantly delayed language and cognitive development have faced many of the same literacy challenges as students with severe cognitive disabilities (see Chapter 8). As Mirenda (2003) points out, many students with autism were denied access to literacy because of the dominance of the reading "readiness" model. Until students achieved theoretical "prerequisite" skills (which most never did), they were not given the opportunity to participate in reading and writing activities, even if they were included in regular education classes. At best, they might be pulled aside to work on memorization of individual sight words. The problem with sight-word approaches, according to Kliewer and Biklin (2001), is that they severely limit the opportunity for further literacy development.

What is the alternative? In the past few years, approaches that combine new conceptualizations of literacy development that are based on emergent literacy (rather than "readiness" models of reading) coupled with intensive use of technology have enabled many students with autism to more fully participate in literacy activities. For example, Koppenhaver and Erickson (2003) described how they increased the literacy opportunities for three young children with autism who attended a preschool program for children with special needs. Prior to the intervention, the children had little exposure to literacy. No reading or writing materials were available to the children during free-play time. In fact, these materials were kept out of the reach of the children. Although the children occasionally listened to stories read to them, they took no active part in reading or writing activities. Interviews with the classroom teacher indicated that she felt that the children had little interest in reading and writing.

Koppenhaver and Erickson (2003) introduced a number of activities into the classroom to increase literacy opportunities. For example, they created an electronic writing center with a computer and word-processing software that was appropriate for young children. They supplemented the activities that were available during free-play with a variety of toys and activities that encouraged literacy (e.g., erasable pads, letter stamps and ink pads). They increased the variety of reading materials that were available in the classroom and helped the teacher integrate reading into regular class activities. The result of increasing literacy opportunities was that the children showed more interest in books and other literacy activities and began to show improvement in their literacy skills, such as writing.

Several research studies have focused on improving the writing skills of children with autism. Bedrosian and colleagues (2003) used augmentative communication systems, story grammar maps, and peer support to enhance the written narratives of an adolescent student with autism. Blischak and Schlosser (2003) reviewed research that has found that students with autism can make progress in spelling through the use of speech-generating devices and talking word-processing software.

Although students with autism clearly face significant challenges to the acquisition of literacy, these and other studies strongly suggest that they can develop literacy skills when given the opportunity. Kluth and Darmody-Latham (2003) suggest that teachers can increase literacy opportunities for students with autism (and other severe disabilities) by taking the following steps:

- *Recognize all literacies.* Recognize and build on the skills that students demonstrate. For example, students may not be able to write letters but they can use "pretend' (or emergent) writing to draw squiggles that represent letters for them.
- *Capitalize on students' interests.* Students with autism sometimes have interests that occupy much of their time. Use these interests as the core for literacy activities in the classroom.
- *Use a range of visual supports.* In addition to verbal input, students with autism may benefit from visual inputs such as graphic or visual organizers, flowcharts, and concept maps.
- *Read aloud.* Give students many opportunities to listen to stories. Connect the listening to follow-up activities that actively involve students in thinking about what they have heard. For example, one teacher followed a story about leaves with a walk through the woods to gather leaves and then mounted and labeled the leaves in a personal leaf books.
- *Use and encourage different types of expression.* Provide students with a range of options for participation. For example, using the story about leaves, students might draw pictures, use emergent writing, or dictate words that are used in the book.

Students with Asperger's syndrome present different types of literacy challenges. Typically they are able to read words at or above the level that would be expected for their age. However, their comprehension of text usually lags behind their word-reading ability (Loveland & Tunali-Kotoski, 1997). Some individuals with Asperger's syndrome or high-functioning autism have been called **"hyperlexic";** that is, they can read words at very high levels of proficiency. This can appear to be very impressive and lead parents and teachers to ignore the reading comprehension and other learning problems that may exist in these children. Although there is, as yet, little research on the reading comprehension difficulties of students with Asperger's syndrome or high-functioning autism, it seems clear that these students will need intensive instruction in comprehension, including technology supports.

Intervention for Language and Communication Impairments

Because the language impairments of children with autism spectrum disorders are so pervasive and have such devastating effects, many intervention approaches have been developed. Some of these have been very controversial and have failed to stand up to rigorous research and clinical practice. Today, parents, teachers, and clinicians have a bewildering number of choices of language-intervention programs that claim success with children with autism spectrum disorders. The challenge is to identify those programs that have proven to be most effective. But keep in mind that there is no one program that is effective for all children. As Goldstein (2002) put it, there is no silver bullet when it comes to programs for enhancing the language and communication of individuals with autism spectrum disorders. We will look at several approaches that have a record of success with children with autism, examining their strengths and limitations. This is mere sample of the myriad of programs that are available.

Discrete Trial Training

As noted in Chapter 8, behavioral approaches have been quite successful in enhancing the language and communication of children with significant language disabilities. One type of behaviorally based intervention program that has been used extensively with individuals with autism spectrum disorders is known as **discrete trial training** (Lovaas et al., 1980). In this approach, a "trial" is a single teaching unit that begins with a stimulus (the teacher's instruction), the child's response, the consequence, and a pause before the presentation of the next stimulus. Correct responses are reinforced, whereas incorrect responses are followed by verbal feedback (e.g., "no" or "wrong") followed by a correction. According to Lovaas (1987), to be effective, this training must go on 365 days a year for 40 or more hours a week (see Box 9.1 for an example).

In several studies, Lovaas and colleagues have documented success using this type of approach with children with autism. For example, Lovaas has reported that children with autism who received early, intensive, behavioral intervention (including lan-

---

BOX 9.1

Example of Discrete-Trial Training

Lovaas (1987, p. 53) gives the following example of a child being trained with a behavioral approach:

(E is the trainer; B is Billy, a child with autism.) (There is a breakfast tray [stimulus] between them.)

E: What do you want?
B.   Egg.
E: No, what do you want? I . . .
B: I want . . .
E: Egg (pause). O.K., what do you want?
E: No, what do you want? I . . .
B: I want egg.
E: Good boy (feeds Billy).

guage) scored higher on tests of intelligence and were more successful in school than similar children who received less intensive intervention (Lovaas, 1987). A follow-up study several years later found that these differences continued to exist (McEachlin, Smith, & Lovaas, 1993). Smith, Eikeseth, Klevstrand, and Lovaas (1997) reported that preschoolers with severe intellectual disabilities and autistic features who received intensive behavioral treatment obtained a higher IQ score and had more expressive speech than similar children who received minimal treatment.

Despite the documented success of behavioral-intervention approaches such as discrete trial, some significant questions have been raised. Heflin and Simpson (1998) note four major issues that have been raised:

1. *Outcome claims.* Lovaas has sometimes claimed that intensive use of discrete trial training actually leads to autism "recovery" in up to one-half of the individuals with whom it is used. However, researchers such as Gresham and MacMillan (1997) have expressed a number of concerns about the design of the research that has led to the claims of success for discrete trial training and concluded that the Lovaas approach is "at best experimental, is far from producing a cure for autism, and awaits replication before school districts are required to provide it on a wholesale basis" (p. 196).

2. *Exclusivity.* Advocates of the use of intensive behavioral-intervention approaches argue that their method should be the only one used in treating a child with autism. Heflin and Simpson (1998) note that this argument ignores the evidence that other intervention techniques have been found to be as effective or more effective than discrete trial in addressing social skills, pragmatic language deficiencies, and other problems typically experienced by individuals with autism spectrum disorders.

3. *Extensive use.* Advocates for discrete trial training claim that, to be effective, the program must be implemented for 40 hours a week over several years. Yet, there is no empirical evidence that this level of intervention is required for all children. In fact, this requirement ignores the strengths and weaknesses of individual children that may have an impact on the effectiveness of the intervention.

4. *Personnel.* The appropriate preparation for discrete trial trainers is in dispute. Advocates for the program argue that there is no need for trainers to be certified teachers. Others argue that uncertified trainers may lack the skills to determine the appropriate intervention program for an individual child and to recommend alternative programs for children who either do not respond well to discrete trial training or who could benefit from another approach.

In addition, significant concerns revolve around the generalization of verbal behavior to natural, social situations (Prizant & Rubin, 1999) and about intensity of instruction. It remains unclear what the optimal amount of training time should be. Many educators and clinicians have raised concerns about the practicality of instruction that has to be delivered on such an intensive schedule.

Discrete trial approaches to language instruction may be useful for training specific skill sequences (such as request routines or word endings). If using discrete trial techniques, teachers should pay special attention to helping the child generalize newly acquired behavior and include practice in real social situations.

Picture Exchange Communication System (PECS)

The Picture Exchange Communication System (PECS) (Bondy & Frost, 1994) uses pictures as the means of fostering meaningful communicative exchanges. Originally developed for individuals with autism, the program has been used successfully with students with a variety of significant disabilities. The PECS program utilizes a combination of behavioral methodology and incidental teaching techniques to enhance social communication. Students progress through six phases in which they are taught to communicate with a variety of people using increasingly complex language. A typical PECS Phase I training session might go as follows:

1. The trainer places an object in front of the child that the trainer has previously observed that the child wants.
2. When the child reaches for the item, the trainer places a picture into the child's hand.
3. The trainer then guides the child to hand the picture to the trainer.
4. When the child exchanges the picture, the trainer makes a verbal response and offers a reinforcer.

In later phases of the program, the child is helped to develop more spontaneous interactions, the ability to discriminate between pictured items, the use of sentence strings, and a broader repertoire of communicative functions and language concepts.

Bondy and Frost (1994) report that of 66 children without functional speech who were taught to use PECS, 76 percent either developed speech as their means of communication or used a combination of speech and the picture system. In addition, the same authors report significant improvements in behavior for children using the PECS program. Ganz and Simpson (2004) examined the use of the PECS program with three young children with developmental disabilities who were suspected to have autism. They found that the children progressed rapidly, acquiring new words and communication skills that generalized across environments. Yoder and Stone (2006) compared the PECS program to a naturalistic, milieu-based approach called Responsive Education and Prelinguistic Milieu Teaching (RPMT; Yoder & Warren, 2002). The RPMT system is composed of two components: one for parents (responsive education) and one for children (Prelinguistic Milieu Teaching [PMT]). The PMT component is a child-led, play-based incidental teaching method designed to teach gestures, nonword vocals, gaze use, and, later, word use as forms of clear intentional communication for turn-taking, requesting, and commenting pragmatic functions. Thirty-six young children with autism (with a mean age of 33 months) were taught with one or the other program. Although children in both programs made significant progress in the acquisition of words and the use of communication in a variety of contexts, the children who were taught with the PECS program made somewhat more progress than the other group.

Research on the PECS program is limited, but the results of those studies that have been done suggest that the Picture Exchange Communication System may be a useful program for helping children with little or no functional language begin to develop communication skills.

Pivotal-Response Model

Like the Lovaas approach, the pivotal-response intervention model is based on principles of applied behavior analysis. However, this instructional approach differs in several ways from the usual applied behavior analysis methodology, such as:

- *Intervention settings.* Intervention is provided in the most inclusive settings possible, preferably in a context that includes typically developing children.
- *Amount of intervention.* The goal is to provide the most effective intervention within a relatively small number of hours. Children are not removed from their natural environment for intervention training.
- *Intervention agents.* Intervention is provided by a number of individuals, including family members.
- *Target behaviors.* These are individualized for each child and change over time. (Koegel, Koegel, Harrower, & Carter, 1999)

One of the basic concepts of the pivotal-response intervention model is that instruction should focus on so-called pivotal areas. These include responsivity to multiple cues, motivation to initiate and respond appropriately, and self-regulation of behavior. Koegel and colleagues (1999) suggest that the following techniques can be used to enhance the language interaction of individuals with autism spectrum disorders:

- *Child choice.* Materials that the child prefers should be used during instruction.
- *Interspersing previously learned tasks with new tasks.* This leads to a higher degree of success and increases the child's motivation to respond.
- *Reinforcing the child's attempts.* A loose criterion for correct responding is preferable to a more narrowly defined goal.
- *Natural reinforcers.* A natural reinforcer is one that is directly related to the task. For example, in teaching a child to open the lid of a container, the natural reinforcer could be a sticker inside the container.

A typical teaching session using the pivotal-response model might begin with the presentation of a preferred object in an opaque bag. The trainer would attempt to prompt the child to initiate an interaction by saying to the child, "Say, 'What's that?' " If the child repeats the question, the adult responds by opening the bag and showing the child what is inside. Gradually, the prompt is faded until the child spontaneously asks the question. Later, the child is taught to ask other questions and to make other verbal initiations. In preliminary research with four children with autism, Koegel, Koegel, Shoshan, and McNerney (1999) found that pivotal-response training conducted for more than two years significantly increased the number of initiations as well as the overall pragmatic language of these children. Although still relatively untested, the pivotal-response intervention model appears to be a promising technique for enhancing the functioning of children with autism spectrum disorders.

Developmental, Individual-Difference, Relationship-Based Model (DIR)

Another relatively new intervention technique for children with autism spectrum disorders is the Developmental, Individual-Difference, Relationship-Based model (DIR) (sometimes known as Floor Time). Developed by Stanley Greenspan and Serena Wieder, this intervention model attempts to facilitate understanding of children with autism spectrum disorders and their families by focusing on three elements: the child's functional-emotional developmental level; the child's individual differences in sensory reactivity, processing, and motor planning; and the child's relationships and interactions with caregivers, family members, and others. According to Greenspan and Wieder (1999), the primary goal of the DIR approach is "to enable children to form a sense of themselves as intentional, interactive individuals, to develop cognitive, language, and social capacities from this basic sense of intentionality, and to progress through the six functional emotional developmental capacities" (p. 151).

The DIR model incorporates a number of traditional intervention techniques in a comprehensive program of instruction (see Figure 9.3). One of the key elements is the "circle of communication." Circles of communication may begin with simple reactions to a child, and then progress to symbolic communication. For example, if a child is flipping a light switch on and off, an adult can initiate a circle of communication by putting his or her hand over the switch. By initiating interaction (covering the switch), the adult has opened a circle of communication. The key is to follow the child's lead and use natural opportunities to open communication.

In reviewing the case histories of some 200 children who have been exposed to at least two years of the DIR intervention model, Greenspan and Wieder (1999) claim that over 50 percent of the children progressed to a level at which they learned to be warm, emotionally expressive, flexible children with age-appropriate academic capabilities. These children went to regular schools and had many friends. Greenspan and Wieder acknowledge that there is no way to know how many of these children might have made significant improvements without intervention. However, the model appears to hold promise for helping many children with autism spectrum disorders.

Sign-Language Training

Another effective approach to enhancing the language skills of children with autism is sign-language training. Sign language has several advantages over spoken language in training for children with autism. For one, signs can be kept in the air as long as necessary to get the child's attention, whereas words disappear quickly. A child's hands may be molded into the desired sign. It would be impossible (as well as dangerous) to try to mold a child's lips, teeth, and tongue to try to form words. Sign language also requires the use of motor skills that are usually intact (if not superior) in children with autism.

FIGURE 9.3   Developmental, Individual-Difference, Relationship-Based (DIR) Intervention Program

Home based, developmentally appropriate interactions and practices (floor time)
    Spontaneous, follow the child's lead floor time (20 to 30-minute sessions, eight to ten times a
        day)
    Semistructured problem solving (15 or more minutes, five to eight times a day)
    Spatial, motor, and sensory activities (15 minutes or more, four times a day)
        Running and changing direction, jumping, spinning, swinging, deep tactile pressure
        Perceptual motor challenges, including looking and doing games
        Visual-spatial processing and motor planning games, including treasure hunts and obstacle
          courses
        The above activities can become integrated with the pretend play

Speech therapy, typically three or more times a week

Sensory integration–based occupational therapy and/or physical therapy, typically two or more
times a week

Educational program, daily
    For children who can interact and initiate gestures and/or words and engage in preverbal
        problem solving, either an integrated program or a regular preschool program with an aide
    For children not yet able to engage in preverbal problem solving or imitation, a special
        education program where the major focus is on engagement, preverbal purposeful gestural
        interaction, preverbal problem solving (a continuous flow of back-and-forth
        communication) and learning to imitate actions, sounds, and words

Biomedical interventions, including consideration of medication, to enhance motor planning and
sequencing, self-regulation, concentration, and/or auditory processing and language

A consideration of nutrition and diet

Technologies geared to improve processing abilities, including auditory processing, visual-
spatial processing, sensory modulation, and motor planning

Source: Greenspan, S., & Wieder, S. (1999). A functional developmental approach to autism spectrum
disorders. *Journal of the Association of Persons with Severe Handicaps, 24,* 147–161.

      Studies of the use of sign-language training with children with autism have
shown that it can be a useful way to enhance language and communication skills
(Yoder & Layton, 1998; Goldstein, 2002). The use of sign or total communication generally leads to more rapid learning of vocabulary than speech therapy. Children who
are nonverbal can acquire a reasonably large repertoire of signs. Even more encouraging are reports that spoken language may increase after sign-language training (Layton
& Baker, 1981). In addition, some studies have reported that improvements in social
and self-care skills follow the introduction of sign-language training (Konstantareas,
Webster, & Oxman, 1979).

The limitations of sign-language training for children with autism should be obvious. Since there are relatively few persons who can sign, the potential number of communication partners for signers is limited. Additionally, children who use sign language as their primary means of communication will have a more difficult time being included in regular education and in community activities. However, sign-language training may be a good way to begin to build communication skills. Combining signing with spoken language may be an effective way to enhance the communication skills of children with autism.

SCERTS Program

Prizant and colleagues (2003) developed a program of language intervention for individuals with autism spectrum disorders that they call the Social Communication, Emotional Regulation, and Transactional Support (SCERTS) model. This program uses effective language-intervention procedures from both more structured approaches (such as discrete trial) and programs that teach language skills in natural settings. The result is a comprehensive model that attempts to incorporate best practices in language intervention.

The SCERTS model is designed to address three major goals: social communication, emotional regulation, and transactional support (see Figure 9.4 for details). The model provides individualized treatment based on the individual child's pattern of strengths and weaknesses. As yet, there is no research on which to evaluate the outcomes of the model, but the program appears to be well designed for success.

Auditory Training

Auditory problems are commonly found among children with autism and may, in part, account for some of the language problems associated with autism. Guy Berard, a French physician, developed a technique known as *auditory integration training (AIT),* which he claims can make a significant improvement in the language and communication of individuals with autism. The auditory training program entails 10 hours of listening to electronically modulated music over a 10-day period, using a variety of music (rock, pop, reggae), with high- and low-sound frequencies dampened on a near-random basis.

Research on auditory integration has found mixed results. Rimland and Edelson (1992) found that auditory-integration training improved the behavior and reduced auditory problems of eight children with autism in comparison to nine who did not receive the training. However, other researchers (e.g., Bettison, 1996; Mudford et al., 2000; Zollweg, Palm, & Vance, 1997) failed to find any effect for auditory-integration training in children with autism or Asperger's syndrome.

Early reports on auditory-integration training appeared to be promising, but later research has failed to substantiate the effectiveness of this technique. Although auditory-integration training may turn out to be effective for some individuals with autism spectrum disorders, the technique continues to be highly experimental and should be used with caution, if at all.

FIGURE 9.4   **Education and Treatment Goals of the SCERTS Model**

I. Social Communication
   A. Enhance capacities for joint attention
      1. Expression of communicative intent
      2. Expand range of communicative functions
      3. Enhance social reciprocity (rate of communication, repair, persistence)
      4. Enhance communicative gaze, sharing emotional states
   B. Enhance capacities for symbol use (symbolic behavior)
      1. Movement from unconventional to conventional means of communication
      2. Movement from presymbolic to symbolic behavior in communication and play
      3. Movement from echolalia to creative language
      4. Enhance comprehension of language and other symbolic systems
II. Emotional Regulation
   A. Enhance capacities for self-regulation—Ability to independently use sensory motor and/or cognitive/linguistic strategies to regulate emotional arousal, and support attention and engagement
   B. Enhance capacities for mutual regulation—Ability to seek support from others or respond to partners' efforts to regulation of emotional arousal in the context of social transaction through sensory motor and/or cognitive/linguistic strategies
   C. Enhance capacity to recover from dysregulation—Ability to recover from extreme states of dysregulation either independently or with support from partners
III. Transactional Support
   A. Educational and learning supports—Use of visuals and other organizational supports; environmental modification; curriculum modification
   B. Interpersonal supports—Calibrate partner language and interactive style, and developmental support to enable child to attend, communicate, and play at more sophisticated levels; design opportunities for learning with and developing relationships with peers
   C. Family support—Emotional and educational support provided to parents to enhance their confidence and abilities in supporting their child's development
   D. Support among professionals—Provide opportunities for enhancing educational and therapeutic skills, and for emotional support to cope with work-related challenges

Source: B. Prizant, A. Wetherby., E. Rubin, & A. Laurent (2003). The SCERTS model: A transactional, family-centered approach to enhancing communication and socioemotional abilities of children with autism spectrum disorder. *Infants and Young Children, 16,* 296–316. Reprinted by permission.

Facilitated Communication

Facilitated communication (FC) is another very controversial intervention approach for children with autism. It is a technique for enhancing communication in persons having difficulty communicating in the usual ways—those with autism, mental retardation, and physical disabilities. The method is simple. A facilitator, using a special grip, holds the hand of the individual being facilitated. The facilitator is taught to provide resistance to the movement of the individual with whom he or she is working. The facilitator may place a hand over that of the other person or simply provide a light touch at the elbow or shoulder. It is hypothesized that this touch steadies the person with autism and allows the person to better focus his or her motor movements.

From the beginning, the technique has engendered both great excitement and profound skepticism. Many spectacular and controversial early claims were made about facilitated communication. For example, in one study (Biklen & Schubert, 1991), it was reported that following the implementation of FC, 20 of 21 people were able to type words. A number of research studies published since 1992 have raised significant concerns about the effectiveness of facilitated communication. Most of the studies have found that under clinical conditions, when the facilitator was "blind" to the stimulus item, the individual was unable to produce independent communication (e.g., Wheeler, Jacobson, Paglieri, & Schwartz, 1993; Eberlin, McConnachie, Ibel, & Volpe, 1993; Regal, Rooney, & Wandas, 1994). Instead, the communication appeared to be influenced, even guided, by the facilitator. This influence, although apparently unintended, nevertheless was real and pervasive. Study after study has found that when the facilitator did not know the content of the information to which the person had been exposed, the person was unable to identify the information being facilitated.

Because of concerns about claims regarding facilitated communication, the American Speech-Language-Hearing Association (ASHA) (1994) issued a position statement on facilitated communication that cautioned against using this technique. Although facilitated communication may help some students focus their attention and reduce off-task behaviors, it should not generally be part of clinical practice.

Conclusion

With so many programs available to enhance the language and communication of children with autism spectrum disorders, it can be difficult for educators, clinicians, and parents to choose the right program. As we stated in the beginning of this section, despite some claims to the contrary, there is no single program that works for every child. Prizant and Wetherby (2005) suggest that factors related to the individual child should be used in deciding which approach to use. These factors include:

- The child's current communication ability
- Development in other areas
- History of success with previous instruction
- Parental preferences

In the end, what matters most is outcomes. Is the child developing better language and communication skills? Can the child use these skills spontaneously and in a variety of communicative contexts? Is the child more successful in school and other community settings?

Summary

In this chapter we have seen that autism and the other developmental disabilities on the autism spectrum are complex and still somewhat mysterious disorders. A variety of characteristics are associated with autism spectrum disorders, but severe impairments in socialization and in language appear to be most important. Many individuals with autism develop little or no spoken language. When language does develop, there are significant differences, especially in semantics and pragmatics. Most students with autism spectrum disorders have difficulty with the development of literacy skills, although the specific problems they encounter differ depending on their specific disability. A number of intervention programs to improve the language and literacy skills of individuals with autism spectrum disorders have been developed. Although success can be slow and frustrating, advances in research and practice are helping us to better understand and teach children with autism spectrum disorders.

REVIEW QUESTIONS

1. List and briefly describe three characteristics associated with autism.

2. How does the early development of a child with autism contribute to the child's later language difficulties?

3. How might echolalia be considered functional?

4. What does the research on pragmatic language difficulties of children with autism spectrum disorders imply for instruction in the classroom?

5. Some researchers have found children with autism to have relatively good semantic skills, whereas others have found their semantic skills deficient. How can these apparent inconsistencies be explained?

6. List two advantages and two disadvantages in using the discrete-trial approach to language intervention for children with autism.

7. What factors would you consider in deciding what kind of language-intervention program to use with a child with autism spectrum disorder?

SUGGESTED ACTIVITIES

1. Pronoun reversal, which has sometimes been considered characteristic of the language of children with autism, is controversial. Part of the controversy is whether the problem is one of language or whether difficulty using pronouns reflects the cognitive problems associated with autism. If you have access to an individual with autism, try to evaluate that person's ability to use and understand pronouns. You might try the following techniques:

   a. *Method:* Assemble a number of pictures that show individual people and animals performing actions. These pictures should include boys and girls, men and women, and cats and dogs. If possible, include among these pictures photos of the person with autism, as well as photos of yourself. Ask the individual to point to the correct picture as you say a sentence. Those sentences should describe the picture (e.g., *He is going to school; She is playing ball).* Be sure to include pronouns such as *he, she, her, his, I,* and *you.* Also, include other words, such as *the boy, the dog,* and so on.

   b. *Evaluation:* How does the person perform when pronouns are used? How about when other words *(boy, girl)* are used? Is there any difference in the response for people, as compared to animals? What do the results indicate about the ability of persons with autism to use pronouns?

      c. *Alternative:* If you do not have access to an individual with autism, try this with a younger (4- to 5-year-old) and an older (7- to 8-year-old) child.

2. A number of popular books have been written about autism, describing experiences both of parents of autistic children as well as of autistic persons themselves. Read one of these books and discuss its author's experiences.

3. Visit a school or clinical program for persons with autism. If possible, observe teachers or clinicians working with autistic individuals. What kinds of intervention procedures are being used? What kind of results are being achieved?

GLOSSARY

Asperger's syndrome: less severe form of autism, characterized by difficulties with social interaction

asynchronous development: development of the child that does not follow a typical sequence

autism spectrum disorders: a group of disorders that vary in severity but share the features of impairments in social interaction, communication, and behavior differences

delayed echolalia: the repetition of words or phrases that may have been heard days, weeks, or even years ago

discrete trial training: an instructional approach based on behavioral principles developed for persons with autism

echolalia: the literal repetition of speech produced by others

gestalt processing style: a cognitive processing style in which information is taken in in large chunks with limited analysis

hyperlexia;   a condition in which individuals can read individual words with great accuracy but lag in comprehension

idiosyncratic language: the use of conventional words or phrases in unusual ways to convey specific meanings

immediate echolalia: echolalia that occurs within a brief time period after the speaker talks

mitigated echolalia: a type of echolalia in which the structure of the original utterance is changed

neologisms: nonstandard (or invented) words

pervasive developmental disorder (PDD):   A term used by the DSM-IV to describe a group of disorders that affect a wide range of abilities

pronoun reversal: use of incorrect pronoun (e.g., saying *you* for *me*)

suprasegmental features: the use of stress and intonation in speech

theory of mind: a theory about the cognitive processing style of individuals with autism that asserts that there is a reduced ability to understand the state of mind of another

RESOURCES ON THE WEB

www.nichd.nih.gov/autism/   National Institute of Child Health and Human Development Autism projects

www.autism-society.org   Autism Society of America

www.autismwebsite.com/ari/index.htm   Autism Research Institute

www.autism-pdd.net   Autism-PDD Resources network

www.asperger.org   Asperger Coalition of the United States

www.aspergersyndrome.org   O.A.S.I.S.—Online Asperger Syndrome Information and Support

www.pecs.com   Pyramid Associates, developer of the PECS system

www.scerts.com/   SCERTS model website

REFERENCES

Adams, C., Green, J., Gilchrist, A., & Cox, A. (2002). Conversational behaviour of children with Asperger syndrome and conduct disorder. *Journal of Child Psychology and Psychiatry, 43,* 679–690.

Akshoomoff, N. (2000). Neurological underpinnings of autism. In A. M. Wetherby & B. M. Prizant (Eds.), *Autism spectrum disorders: A transactional developmental perspective* (pp. 167–192). Baltimore: Brookes.

American Psychiatric Association. (1994). *Diagnostic and statistical manual of mental disorders* (4th ed, rev.). Arlington, VA: American Psychiatric Association.

American Psychiatric Association. (2000). *Diagnostic and statistical manual of mental disorders* (DSM-IV-TR). Arlington, VA: American Psychiatric Association.

American Speech-Language-Hearing Association. (1994). Position statement on facilitated communication.

Baltaxe, C. (1977). Pragmatic deficits in the language of autistic adolescents. *Journal of Pediatric Psychology, 2,* 176–180.

Baltaxe, C., & Simmons, J. (1975). Language in childhood psychosis: A review. *Journal of Speech and Hearing Disorders, 40,* 439–458.

Baron-Cohen, S (1995). *Mindblindness: An essay on autism and theory of mind.* Cambridge, MA: MIT Press.

Baron-Cohen, S., Leslie, A., & Frith, U. (1985). Does the autistic child have a "theory of mind"? *Cognition, 21,* 37–46.

Bartak, L., & Rutter, M. (1976). Differences between mentally retarded and normally intelligent autistic children. *Journal of Autism and Childhood Schizophrenia, 6,* 109–120.

Bartak, L., Rutter, M., & Cox, A. (1975). A comparative study of infantile autism and specific developmental receptive language disorder. I. The children. *British Journal of Psychiatry, 126,* 127–145.

Bartolucci, G., Pierce, S., & Streiner, D. (1980). Cross-sectional studies of grammatical morphemes in autistic and mentally retarded children. *Journal of Autism and Developmental Disorders, 10,* 39–50.

Bartolucci, G., Pierce, S., & Streiner, D., & Eppel, P. (1976). Phonological investigation of verbal autistic and mentally retarded subjects. *Journal of Autism and Childhood Schizophrenia, 6,* 303–316.

Bauman, M. L., & Kemper, J. L. (Eds.). (1994). *The neurobiology of autism.* Baltimore, MD: Johns Hopkins University Press.

Bedrosian, J., Lasker, J., Speidel, K., & Politsch, A. (2003). Enhancing the written narrative skills of an AAC student with autism: Evidence-based research issues. *Topics in Language Disorders, 23,* 305–324.

Bernard-Opitz, V. (1982). Pragmatic analysis of the communicative behavior of an autistic *child. Journal of Speech and Hearing Disorders, 47,* 99–109.

Bettelheim, B. (1967). *The empty fortress—Infantile autism and the birth of the self.* New York: Free Press.

Bettison, S. (1996). The long-term effects of auditory training on children with autism. *Journal of Autism and Developmental Disorders, 26,* 179–197.

Biklen, D., & Schubert, A. (1991). New words: The communication of students with autism. *Remedial and Special Education, 12,* 46–57.

Blischak, D. M., & Schlosser, R. W. (2003). Use of technology to support independent spelling by students with autism. *Topics in Language Disorders, 23,* 293–304.

Bondy, A. S., & Frost, L. A. (1994). The picture exchange communication system. *Focus on Autistic Behavior, 9,* 1–19.

Brook, S., & Bowler, D. (1992). Autism by another name? Semantic and pragmatic impairments in children. *Journal of Autism and Developmental Disorders, 22,* 61–81.

Cantwell, D., Baker, L., & Rutter, M. (1977). Families of autistic and dysphasic children. II. Mothers' speech to the children. *Journal of Autism and Developmental Disorders, 7,* 313–327.

Cantwell, D., Baker, L., & Rutter, M. (1978). A comparative study of infantile autism and specific developmental receptive language disorder IV: Analysis of syntax and language function. *Journal of Child Psychology and Psychiatry, 19,* 351–362.

Chuba, H., Paul, R., Miles, S., Klin, A., & Volkmar, F. (2003, November*). Assessing pragmatic skills in individuals with autism spectrum disorders.* Presentation at the National Convention of the American Speech-Language-Hearing Association, Chicago.

Diehl, S. F., Ford, C. S., & Federico, J. (2005). The communication journey of a fully included child with an autism spectrum disorder. *Topics in Language Disorders, 25,* 375–387.

Eales, M. (1993). Pragmatic impairments in adults with childhood diagnoses of autism or developmental receptive language disorder. *Journal of Autism and Developmental Disorders, 23,* 593–617.

Eberlin, M., McConnachie, G., Ibel, S., & Volpe, L. (1993). Facilitated communication: A failure to replicate the phenomenon. *Journal of Autism and Developmental Disorders, 23,* 507–530.

Eskes, G., Bryson, S., & McCormick, T. (1990). Comprehension of concrete and abstract words in autistic children. *Journal of Autism and Developmental Disorders, 20,* 61–73.

Falk-Ross, F., Iverson, M., & Gilbert, C. (2004). Teaching and learning approaches for children with Asperger's syndrome *Teaching Exceptional Children, 36,* 48–55.

Fein, D., Pennington, B., Markowitz, P., Braverman, M., & Waterhouse, L. (1986). Toward a neuropsychological model of infantile autism: Are the social deficits primary? *Journal of the American Academy of Child Psychiatry, 25,* 198–212.

Fein, D., & Waterhouse, L. (1979, February). *Autism is not a disorder of language.* Paper presented at the New England Child Language Association, Boston.

Folstein, S., & Rosen-Sheidley, B. (2001). Genetics of autism: Complex aetiology for a heterogeneous disorder. *Nature Reviews—Genetics, 2,* 943–955.

Folstein, S., & Rutter, M. (1988). Autism: Familial aggregation and genetic implications. *Journal of Autism and Developmental Disorders, 18,* 3–30.

Ganz, J. B., & Simpson, R. L. (2004). Effects on communicative requesting and speech development of the Picture Exchange Communication System in children with characteristics of autism. *Journal of Autism and Developmental Disorders, 34,* 395–409.

Goldfarb, W., Goldfarb, N., & Scholl, M. (1966). The speech of mothers of schizophrenic children. *American Journal of Psychiatry, 122,* 1220–1227.

Goldstein, H. (2002). Communication intervention for children with autism: A review of treatment efficacy. *Journal of Autism and Developmental Disorders, 32,* 373–396.

Grandin, Temple. (1996). *Thinking in pictures: And other reports from my life with autism.* New York: Vintage Books.

Greenspan, S., & Wieder, S. (1999). A functional developmental approach to autism spectrum disorders. *Journal of the Association of Persons with Severe Handicaps, 24,* 147–161.

Gresham, F., & MacMillan, D. (1997). Autistic recovery? An analysis and critique of the empirical evidence on the Early Intervention Project. *Behavioral Disorders, 22,* 185–201.

Heflin, L., & Simpson, R. (1998). Interventions for children and youth with autism: Prudent choices in a world of exaggerated claims and empty promises. Part I: Intervention and treatment option review. *Focus on Autism and Other Developmental Disabilities, 13,* 194–211.

Hermelin, B. (1978). Images and language. In M. Rutter & E. Schopler (Eds.), *Autism: A reappraisal of concepts and treatment* (pp. 141–154). New York: Plenum Press.

Hermelin, B., & O'Connor, N. (1970). *Psychological experiments with autistic children.* London: Pergamon Press.

Howlin, P. (1982). Echolalic and spontaneous phrase speech in autistic children. *Journal of Child Psychology and Psychiatry, 23,* 281–293.

Howlin, P. (2003). Outcome in high-functioning adults with autism with and without early language delays: Implications for the differentiation between autism and Asperger syndrome. *Journal of Autism and Developmental Disorders, 33,* 3–13.

Individuals with Disabilities Education Act. (2004). Washington, DC: U.S. Government Printing Office.

Just, M. A., Cherkassky, V. L., Keller, T. A., & Minshew, N. J. (2004). Cortical activation and synchronization during sentence comprehension in high-functioning autism: Evidence of under-connectivity. *Brain, 127,* 1811–1821.

Kanner, L. (1943). Autistic disturbances of affective contact. *Nervous Child, 2,* 217–250.

Kasari, C., Freeman, S. F. N., & Paparella, T. (2001). Early intervention in autism: Joint attention and symbolic play. In L. M. Glidden (Ed.), *International review of research in mental retardation: Autism* (Vol. 23), (pp. 207–232). San Diego, CA: Academic Press.

Kaufman, B. (1976). *Son rise.* New York: Harper & Row.

Kaufman, B. (1994). *Son rise: The miracle continues.* Tiburon, CA: H. J. Kramer.

Kjelgaard, M., & Tager-Flusberg, H. (2001). An investigation of language impairment in autism: Implications for genetic subgroups. *Language and Cognitive Processes, 16,* 287–308.

Kliewer, C., & Biklin, D. (2001). School's not really a place for reading: A research synthesis of the literacy lives of students with severe disabilities. *Journal of the Association for Persons with Severe Handicaps, 26,* 1–12.

Kluth, P., & Darmody-Latham, J. (2003). Beyond sight words: Literacy opportunities for students with autism. *The Reading Teacher, 56,* 532–535.

Koegel, L., Koegel, R., Harrower, J., & Carter, C. (1999). Pivotal response intervention I: Overview of approach. *Journal of the Association of Persons with Severe Handicaps, 24,* 174–185.

Koegel, L., Koegel, R., Shoshan, Y., & McNerney, E. (1999). Pivotal response intervention II: Preliminary long-term outcome data. *Journal of the Association of Persons with Severe Handicaps, 24,* 174–185.

Konstantareas, M., Webster, C., & Oxman, J. (1979). Manual language acquisition and its influence on other areas of functioning in four autistic and autistic-like children. *Journal of Child Psychology and Psychiatry, 20,* 337–350.

Koppenhaver, D. A., & Erickson, K. A. (2003). Natural emergent literacy supports for preschoolers with autism and severe communication impairments. *Topics in Language Disorders, 23,* 283–292.

Lama, K. S. L., & Amanb, M. G. (2006). Neurochemical correlates of autistic disorder: A review of the literature. *Research in Developmental Disabilities, 27,* 254–289.

Landa, R. (2000). Social language use in Asperger syndrome and high-functioning autism. In A. Klim, F. Volkmar, & S. Sparrow (Eds.), *Asperger syndrome* (pp. 125–155). New York: Guilford Press.

Landa, R., Folstein, S., & Isaacs, C. (1991). Spontaneous narrative-discourse performance of parents of autistic individuals. *Journal of Speech and Hearing Research, 34,* 1339–1345.

Landa, R. J., & Goldberg, M. C. (2005). Language, social, and executive functions in high functioning autism: A continuum of performance. *Journal of Autism and Developmental Disorders, 35,* 557–573.

Layton, T., & Baker, P. (1981). Description of semantic-syntactic relations in an autistic child. *Journal of Autism and Developmental Disorders, 11,* 385–399.

Lee, A., Hobson, R. P., & Chiat, S. (1994). I, you, me, and autism: An experimental study. *Journal of Autism and Developmental Disorders, 24,* 155–176.

Lord, C., & Risi, S. (2000). Diagnosis of autism spectrum disorders in young children. In A. Wetherby & B. Prizant (Eds.), *Autism spectrum disorders: A transactional developmental perspective* (pp. 11–30). Baltimore: Brookes.

Lovaas, O. (1987). Behavioral treatment and normal educational and intellectual functioning in young autistic children. *Journal of Consulting and Clinical Psychology, 55,* 3–9.

Lovaas, O., Ackerman, A., Alexander, D., Firestone, P., Perkins, J., & Young, D. (1980). *Teaching developmentally disabled children: The me book.* Austin, TX: Pro-Ed.

Loveland, K., Landry, S., Hughes, S., Hall, S., & McEvoy, R. (1988). Speech acts and pragmatic deficits of autism. *Journal of Speech and Hearing Research, 31,* 593–604.

Loveland, K., & Tunali-Kotoski, B. (1997). The school-age child with autism. In D. Cohen & F. Volkmar (Eds.), *Handbook of autism and pervasive developmental disorders* (pp. 283–308). New York: Wiley.

McEachin, J., Smith, T., & Lovaas, O. (1993). Long-term outcome for children with autism who received early intensive behavioral treatment. *American Journal on Mental Retardation, 97,* 359–372.

Miranda, P. (2003). He's not really a reader: Perspectives on supporting literacy development in individuals with autism. *Topics in Language Disorders, 23,* 271–282.

Mudford, O. C., Cross, B. A., Breen, S., Cullen, C., Reeves, D., Gould, J., & Douglas, J. (2000). Auditory integration training for children with autism: No behavioral benefits detected. *American Journal on Mental Retardation, 105,* 118–129.

Muller, R. A., Behen, M. E., Rothermel, R. D., Chugani, D. C., Muzik O., Mangner, T. J., and Chugani, H. T. (1999). Brain mapping of language and auditory perception in high-functioning autistic adults: A PET study. *Journal of Autism and Developmental Disorders, 29,* 19–31.

Mundy, P., & Markus, J. (1997). On the nature of communication and language impairment in autism. *Mental Retardation and Developmental Disabilities Research Reviews, 34,* 343–349.

National Research Council. (2001). *Educating children with autism.* Washington, DC: National Academy Press.

Oshima-Takane, Y., & Benaroya, S. (1989). An alternative view of pronomial errors in autistic children. *Journal of Autism and Developmental Disorders, 19,* 73–85.

Osterling, J., & Dawson, G. (1994). Early recognition of children with autism: A study of first birthday home videotapes. *Journal of Autism and Developmental Disorders, 24,* 247–258.

Piven, J., Nehme, E., Simon, J., Barta, P., Pearlson, G., & Folstein, S. (1992). Magnetic resonance imaging in autism: Measurement of the cerebellum, pons, and fourth ventricle. *Biological Psychiatry, 31,* 491–504.

Prior, M., & Werry, J. (1986). Autism, schizophrenia, and allied disorders. In H. Quay & J. Werry (Eds.), *Psychopathological disorders of childhood* (pp. 156–210). New York: Wiley.

Prizant, B. (1983). Language acquisition and communicative behavior in autism: Toward an understanding of the "whole" of it. *Journal of Speech and Hearing Disorders, 48,* 296–307.

Prizant, B., & Duchan, J. (1981). The functions of immediate echolalia in autistic children. *Journal of Speech and Hearing Disorders, 46,* 241–249.

Prizant, B., & Rubin, E. (1999). Contemporary issues in interventions for autism spectrum disorders: A commentary. *Journal of the Association for Persons with Severe Handicaps, 24,* 199–208.

Prizant, B. M. & Wetherby, A. M. (2005). Critical issues in enhancing communication abilities for persons with autism spectrum disorders. In F. R. Volkmar, R. Paul, A. Klin, & D. Cohen (Eds.), *Handbook of autism and pervasive developmental disorders* (pp. 925–945). Hoboken, NJ: Wiley.

Prizant, B. M., Wetherby, A. M., Rubin, E., & Laurent, A. C. (2003). The SCERTS model: A transactional, family-centered approach to enhancing communication and socioemotional abilities of children with autism spectrum disorder. *Infants and Young Children, 16,* 296–316.

Regal, R., Rooney, J., & Wandas, T. (1994). Facilitated communication: An experimental evaluation. *Journal of Autism and Developmental Disorders, 24,* 345–355.

Rice, M., Oetting, J., Marquis, J., Bode, J., & Pae, S. (1994). Frequency of input effects on word comprehension of children with specific language impairment. *Journal of Speech and Hearing Research, 37,* 106–122.

Ricks, D., & Wing, L. (1975). Language, communication, and the use of symbols in normal and autistic children. *Journal of Autism and Childhood Schizophrenia, 5,* 191–221.

Rimland, B., & Edelson, S. (1992, June). *Auditory integration training in autism: A pilot study.* Autism Research Institute Publication 112.

Rutter, M. (1978). Language disorder and infantile autism. In M. Rutter & E. Schopler (Eds.), *Autism: A reappraisal of concepts and treatment* (pp. 85–104). New York: Plenum.

Rutter, M., & Schopler, E. (1987). Autism and pervasive developmental disorders: Concepts and diagnostic issues. *Journal of Autism and Developmental Disorders, 17,* 159–186.

Schreibman, L., & Carr, E. (1978). Elimination of echolalic responding to questions through training of a generalized verbal response. *Journal of Applied Behavior Analysis, 11,* 453–464.

Shriberg, L. D., Paul, R., Jane, L., McSweeny, J. L., Klin, A., Cohen, D. J., & Volkmar, F. R. (2001). Speech and prosody characteristics of adolescents and adults with high-functioning autism and Asperger syndrome. *Journal of Speech, Language, and Hearing Research, 44,* 1097–1115.

Smith, T., Eikeseth, S., Klevstrand, M., & Lovaas, O. (1997). Intensive behavioral treatment for preschoolers with severe mental retardation and pervasive developmental disorder. *American Journal on Mental Retardation, 102,* 238–249.

Tager-Flusberg, H. (1981). On the nature of linguistic functioning in early infantile autism. *Journal of Autism and Developmental Disorders, 11,* 45–56.

Tager-Flusberg, H. (1985). Basic level and superordinate level categorization by autistic, mentally retarded, and normal children. *Journal of Experimental Child Psychology, 40,* 450–469.

Tager-Flusberg, H. (1989). A psycholinguistic perspective on language development in the autistic child. In G. Dawson (Ed.), *Autism: New directions in diagnosis, nature, and treatment* (pp. 92–115). New York: Guilford Press.

Tager-Flusberg, H., Calkins, S., Nolin, T., Baumberger, T., Anderson, M., & Chadwick-Dias, A. (1990). A longitudinal study of language acquisition in autistic and Down syndrome children. *Journal of Autism and Developmental Disorders, 20,* 1–21.

Tager-Flusberg, H., Paul, R., & Lord, C. (2005). Language and communication in autism. In F. R. Volkmar, R. Paul, A. Klin, & D. Cohen (Eds.), *Handbook of autism and pervasive developmental disorders* (pp. 335–364). Hoboken, NJ: Wiley.

Tanguay, P., & Edwards, R. (1982). Electrophysiological studies of autism: The whisper of the bang. *Journal of Autism and Developmental Disorders, 12,* 177–184.

Volden, J., & Lord, C. (1991). Neologisms and idiosyncratic language in autistic speakers. *Journal of Autism and Developmental Disorders, 21,* 109–130.

Wetherby, A. (1986). Ontogeny of communicative functions in autism. *Journal of Autism and Developmental Disorders, 16,* 295–316.

Wetherby, A., & Prutting, C. (1984). Profiles of communicative and cognitive-social abilities in autistic children. *Journal of Speech and Hearing Research, 27,* 364–377.

Wetherby, A. M., Prizant, B. M., & Schuler, A. L. (2000). Understanding the nature of communication and language impairments. In A. M. Wetherby & B. M. Prizant (Eds.), *Autism spectrum disorders: A transactional developmental perspective* (pp. 10–142). Baltimore: Brookes.

Wheeler, D., Jacobson, J., Paglieri, R., & Schwartz, A. (1993). An experimental assessment of facilitated communication. *Mental Retardation, 31,* 49–60.

Yoder, P. J., & Layton, T. L. (1988). Speech following sign language training in autistic children with minimal verbal language. *Journal of Autism & Developmental Disorders, 18,* 217–230.

Yoder, P. J., & Stone, W. L. (2006). A randomized comparison of the effect of two prelinguistic communication interventions on the acquisition of spoken communication in preschoolers with ASD. *Journal of Speech, Language, and Hearing Research, 49,* 698–711.

Yoder, P. J., & Warren, S. F. (2002). Effects of prelinguistic milieu teaching and parent responsivity education on dyads involving children with intellectual disabilities. *Journal of Speech, Language, and Hearing Research, 45,* 1158–1174.

Zollweg, W., Palm, D., & Vance, V. (1997). The efficacy of auditory integration training: A double blind study. *American Journal of Audiology, 6,* 39–47.

10 Language and Students with Emotional and Behavioral Disorders

Individuals with emotional and behavioral disorders often have unexpected difficulties with language and communication. In this chapter we will examine the evidence for the existence of language and communication problems in students with emotional and behavioral disorders. We will consider the implications for assessment and intervention and discuss some specific intervention approaches that may be effective with students with emotional and behavioral difficulties.

After completing this chapter you should be able to:

1. Discuss the research evidence for the existence of language and communication problems in students with emotional and behavioral disorders.
2. Explain the relationship between emotional and behavioral disorders, language impairments, and literacy.
3. Apply the research on the language and communication of individuals with emotional and behavioral disorders to the development of effective assessment and intervention.

Luis: A Case Study

Luis, aged 7 years 10 months, was referred because he has been physically violent and verbally abusive to peers and has few friends. Luis's mother described him as a difficult baby who cried a lot and was irritable and overactive. His teacher reported that he was performing at grade level, with the exception of spelling. Luis's parents have been separated for five years. Luis rarely sees his father.

    Testing indicated average intelligence. On the language assessment, Luis scored low on tests of expressive grammar and auditory verbal memory. Problems in pragmatic skills and social discourse were evident. His narrative lacked coherence and answers were often off

(continued)

> **Luis: A Case Study** Continued
>
> topic. On academic achievement tests, Luis performed poorly on reading decoding, word at-
> tack, reading comprehension, and math computation.
>
> It was concluded that language-processing problems, both expressive and receptive, had
> been overlooked and were a source of frustration to Luis. Language impairments and associ-
> ated social-cognitive deficits interfered with both achievement and social information pro-
> cessing necessary for effective social interactions. When this feedback was given, Luis's
> teacher questioned the results and continued to attribute Luis's problems to family dysfunc-
> tion and emotional problems. However, Luis was placed in a classroom for children with spe-
> cific learning disabilities.
>
> *Source:* Adapted from Cohen (1996).

Students with emotional and behavioral disorders are a challenge to schools for several reasons. First, and most obvious, their behavior can be disruptive to the school and/or unsettling for the teacher and for their peers. Second, they can be hard to identify and classify. Should a child with attention deficits be considered emotionally or behaviorally disabled? What about a child who is anxious about school, cries from time to time, or frequently becomes involved in playground fights? Are these behaviors a normal part of growing up, or a deviation from the norm? In fact, it is not even clear how these disorders should be labeled. Are these children emotionally disturbed, behavior disordered, or socially and emotionally maladjusted? Third, schools often have a difficult time providing effective intervention in the regular education setting. Therefore, many children who are identified as emotionally or behaviorally disabled are removed from the regular education setting. Alternatively, some students who could benefit from intervention may not be helped at all.

In this chapter we will examine the evidence for language and communication impairments among students with emotional and behavioral disabilities and the impact of language and behavior disorders on social and academic performance. Although there is now a considerable amount of research that indicates that language and communication difficulties are often associated with emotional and behavioral problems, intervention rarely includes attention to language and communication. We will explore some of the reasons why this may be so. In addition, we will consider what can be done to enhance the language and communication skills of students with emotional and behavioral disorders.

Defining the Population

One of the greatest challenges for researchers and practitioners is defining, identifying, and classifying students with emotional and behavioral disorders. Identification of this population can be very challenging since behavior can vary over time and by context and many assessment techniques have technical limitations. However, definition is important in order to identify those children with difficulties that are so severe as to require specialized intervention procedures and/or special educational services.

A variety of terms have been used to describe this population of students, including *emotionally disturbed, behaviorally disordered, socially maladjusted,* and *psychiatrically disordered.* The Individuals with Disabilities Education Act (IDEA) uses the term *seriously emotionally disturbed,* defined as:

(i) The term means a condition exhibiting one or more of the following characteristics over a long period of time and to a marked extent, which adversely affects educational performance:
    (A) An inability to learn which cannot be explained by intellectual, sensory, or health factors;
    (B) An inability to build or maintain satisfactory relationships with peers and teachers:
    (C) Inappropriate types of behavior or feelings under normal circumstances;
    (D) A general pervasive mood of unhappiness or depression; or
    (E) A tendency to develop physical symptoms or fears associated with personal or school problems.

(ii) The term includes children who are schizophrenic. The term does not include children who are socially maladjusted unless it is determined that they are seriously emotionally disturbed. (IDEA, 2004)

The federal definition indicates that the problems experienced by children identified as "emotionally disturbed" must be *long-lasting* and *significant* and include both learning and social impairments. At the same time, the definition raises many questions. For example, what about students with attention deficits? Should they be included in this category? What about students with learning disabilities? If one follows the definition literally, then most students with learning disabilities could also be classified as emotionally disturbed. And what about those students who are socially maladjusted? As Gresham (2005) points out, the definition indicates that "socially maladjusted" students must not be included in this population. But most educators would say that socially maladjusted students do fit the criteria for identification as emotionally disturbed.

For the purposes of this chapter, we will use the term *emotionally and behaviorally disordered (E/BD)* because this is the term preferred by the Council for Children with Behavior Disorders of the Council for Exceptional Children (CEC). Within this category we will include students with attention deficits but not students with autism. Although students with attention deficits are not supposed to be included under the federal definition of emotional disturbance, their behavior can be very disruptive.

Many professionals believe that students with serious emotional and behavior disorders have been underidentified and underserved for many years. For example, Gresham (2005) notes that although estimates suggest that about 2 percent of the school population may have significant behavior problems, only about 1 percent are identified as E/BD. There are many reasons for this, including a reluctance to use the E/BD label, unwillingness or inability by districts to offer appropriate services for students with emotional and behavioral disorders, and difficulties with assessment (Lambros, Ward, Bocian, MacMillan, & Gresham, 1998).

Students with E/BD tend to have an impact on schools far beyond their actual numbers. They are often the most difficult to include fully in regular education classrooms. When they are included, they may disrupt or distract other students. Long-term outcomes for students with E/BD are not good. One study (Greenbaum et al., 1999) reported that approximately two-thirds of adults who had been classified as E/BD in school had at least one contact with police in which they were believed to be the perpetrators of a crime and 43 percent had been arrested. Educational outcomes are also disturbing, as more than 75 percent of the adults in this study had low reading levels and 97 percent had low math levels.

Clearly, students with emotional and behavioral disorders present a significant challenge for schools. Despite a great deal of progress in the development of intervention techniques, the problems exhibited by students with E/BD remain resistant to change. Although there are, no doubt, many reasons why this is true, including family and community factors and continuing difficulties with assessment and identification, one factor that has been largely overlooked until recently is the language and communication difficulties of this population.

Why language and communication? As we will see, there is increasing evidence that children with E/BD often have significant deficiencies in spoken language. This could affect both their academic achievement and their social interaction. Moreover, these difficulties are often ignored by education professionals who are more focused on developing intervention methods for the most troubling surface problems (e.g., aggressive behavior, disruption, social withdrawal). As a result, language and communication difficulties are often unidentified or, if identified, are not included in the intervention plan for the child. In the remainder of this chapter we will examine the evidence for language and communication deficiencies in students with E/BD and consider what can be done to address these problems.

Evidence for Language and Communication Deficiencies

Until recently, the research basis for language and communication disabilities associated with emotional and behavioral disorders was limited. Although many practitioners believed that students with emotional and behavioral problems had difficulty with aspects of language, there was limited systematic research to support their observations. However, over the past 10 years or so there has been a dramatic increase in research on the language and communication of students with emotional and behavioral disorders. Researchers have found high levels of language impairments in this population. The research evidence actually comes from two types of studies: those that have found evidence for emotional and behavioral disorders in children with speech and language problems and those that directly examined the speech and language of children with emotional and behavioral problems.

Emotional and Behavioral Problems in Children with Speech and Language Disorders

A series of studies conducted by Lorian Baker and Dennis Cantwell and their colleagues at the UCLA Neuropsychiatric Clinic has reported a high incidence of emotional and behavior problems among children with speech and language disorders (Baker & Cantwell, 1987a, 1987b, 1987c, Cantwell & Baker, 1977, 1987).

As an example of this research, we will examine one study in more detail. Cantwell and Baker (1987) examined 600 children with speech and language problems for evidence of emotional and behavioral disorders. Following an initial evaluation for speech and language problems, the children were divided into three groups: children with "pure" speech disorder; children with "speech and language disorders"; and children with "pure" language disorders. Psychiatric diagnoses were made after an interview with each child's parents and completion of four behavior-rating scales (two each by the child's parents and by a teacher). The results were that 31 percent of the children with "pure" speech disorders showed evidence of psychiatric disorder as compared to 58 percent of the children with both speech and language disorders and 73 percent of the children with "pure" language disorders. Both attention deficit disorders and **affective disorders** (e.g., separation anxiety, overanxious disorder) were commonly found, with the rates rising across the three groups of children.

A follow-up study done on the same population of children five years later (Baker & Cantwell, 1987c) showed that the prevalence of speech (but not language) disorders had decreased, but the prevalence of psychiatric problems had actually increased (from 44 percent initially to 60 percent). Attention deficit disorders were the most commonly reported problem. Other researchers have continued to find that children with early language difficulties are up to 10 times more likely to exhibit antisocial behaviors than their peers (Benner, Nelson, & Epstein, 2002; Nelson, Benner, & Cheney, 2005).

Whereas Baker and Cantwell examined children who were receiving services from a university speech and language clinic, others studied children in regular school environments. For example, Beitchman and colleagues (1986) investigated the prevalence of speech and language disorders and emotional and behavioral problems in 4,965 kindergarten children. They found that approximately 3 percent (142) of the children had significant speech and/or language disorders. These children, as well as a comparison group of children without speech and language disorders, were rated for emotional and behavior difficulties. The children with speech and language disorders were much more likely to have emotional and behavioral difficulties, especially attention deficit disorders. Beichtman and colleagues (2001) have continued to follow this sample of children into adulthood. They have found significantly higher rates of psychiatric disorders in individuals with a history of early language impairments—especially social phobias and anxiety.

This and other studies indicate that behavior disorders are related to speech and language deficiencies—especially those that involve language. This may seem to be a surprising finding at first, since there seems to be no good reason why children with speech and language difficulties should have a higher incidence of emotional and behavior disorders. However, the evidence is overwhelming that this relationship does, in fact, exist. What is not clear is which problem is the cause and which is the result. In other words, do speech and language problems cause emotional and behavior problems or are language problems the result of an emotional or behavior disorder? Before attempting to answer this question, we need to look at the evidence for the existence of speech and language deficiencies in children with emotional and behavioral disorders.

Language and Communication Problems in Children with Emotional and Behavioral Disorders

A large and growing number of studies have found that a significant number of children with emotional and behavioral disorders have speech and language problems. A comprehensive review of the research on children with emotional and behavioral disorders in a variety of placements found that three out of four children identified as E/BD had language and communication impairments (Benner, Nelson, & Epstein, 2002). Much of the early research was conducted with children with significant emotional and behavioral disorders who were receiving services in psychiatric clinics or residential settings (Cohen, Davine, & Meloche-Kelly, 1989; Gualtieri et al., 1983; Mack & Warr-Leeper, 1992). However, similar results have been found for children with less severe disabilities and those placed in regular education settings (Camarata, Hughes, & Ruhl, 1988; Nelson, Benner, & Rogers-Adkinson, 2003; Nelson, Benner, & Cheney, 2005).

Although there has been wide variation in the results for the incidence of language impairments in children with emotional and behavioral disorders, research has continued to find high rates of significant language difficulties in this population. For example, Nelson and colleagues (2005) reported that 68 percent of their sample of 166 E/BD students in public school special education placements had language deficits as determined by standardized tests. They also found that girls and boys had similar rates of language deficits and that the language impairments did not improve over time.

There is now strong and consistent research evidence that many (if not most) children with emotional and behavioral disorders also have significant language and communication impairments (see Table 10.1), but in most cases the language difficulties go unrecognized because the focus of assessment and intervention is on the children's behavior. This is true both in children served in clinical settings (Cohen et al., 1989) and in school settings (Warr-Leeper, Wright, & Mack, 1994). These findings strongly suggest that it is important to identify and treat language and communication disorders both to improve language functioning and to prevent or diminish behavior problems.

Types of Language Difficulties.   Although there is a great deal of evidence that children with emotional and behavioral disorders have language and communication difficulties at unexpectedly high rates, a number of questions remain about the nature of these problems. For example, researchers want to know whether certain kinds of language and communication problems are more prevalent than others.

Most studies have found deficits in nearly every aspect of language. For example, Ruhl, Hughes, and Camarata (1992) gave a large battery of language tests to a group of 30 children who had previously been identified as emotionally disturbed and who were attending regular education classes. The researchers found that the students had deficiencies in language functioning in all areas that were measured, with particular problems in grammatical functioning and fewer problems in semantics. Specifically, the students with E/BD tended to use simple sentences that contained only one or two main ideas. Rinaldi (2003) studied what would appear to be a similar popula-

TABLE 10.1   Research Evidence for Language Deficiencies in Students with Emotional and Behavioral Disorders

Study	Findings
Emotional/Behavior Problems in Children with Speech-Language Disorders	
Baker & Cantwell (1987a)	Evaluated psychiatric status of 600 children with suspected speech-language disorders. Children with behavior disorders had significantly more language difficulties.
Baker & Cantwell (1987b)	Study of factors that might explain high incidence of psychiatric problems in children with speech-language disorders found most significant differences in language functioning.
Baker & Cantwell (1987c)	Follow-up study of 300 children with speech-language disorders found significant increase in psychiatric illness.
Beitchman et al. (1986)	Five-year-old children with speech-language disorders were more likely than a control group to have behavior disorders.
Beitchman et al. (2001)	Adults who were identified as having speech-language disorders as children had a high rate of psychiatric disorders.
Cantwell & Baker (1977)	Review of case study reports indicated that children with speech and/or language disorders have numerous speech and/or language disorders.
Cantwell & Baker (1987)	Children with language disorders had higher rates of psychiatric problems than those with speech disorders.
Language Difficulties in Children with Emotional and Behavioral Disorders	
Camarata, Hughes, & Ruhl (1988)	Examined language skills of 38 children with mild to moderate behavior disorders in regular school; 71% fell two or more standard deviations on TOLD-I.
Cohen, Davine, & Meloche-Kelly (1989)	Of 5- to 12-year-old children referred to a psychiatric clinic, 28% had a moderate to severe language disorder.
Cohen et al. (1998)	Of 380 children, aged 7 to 14 years, referred to child psychiatric services, 40% had a language impairment that had never been suspected.
Mack and Warr-Leeper (1992)	Of 10- to 14-year-old boys from a psychiatric institute, 16 of 20 performed significantly more poorly than a control group on language measures.
Nelson et al. (2003)	Of students with an emotional disorder, 45% had a language deficit; learning difficulties were associated with language deficits.
Nelson et al. (2005)	Of 166 students with emotional and behavioral disorders in public school special education placements, 68% had language deficits; language impairments were stable over time.
Ruhl, Hughes, & Camarata (1992)	Thirty students with mild/moderate behavior disorders in public school setting scored more than one standard deviation below the mean on most language measures.
Trautman, Giddan, & Jurs (1990)	Of 6- to 13-year-old children attending a day program for severe behavioral difficulties, 54% demonstrated speech and/or language difficulties.

tion—fourth- and fifth-grade students classified as E/BD who were placed in public school settings—but found somewhat different results. Although the majority of her sample of students scored significantly below the mean in all areas of language (as measured by the Test of Language Development), semantic functioning was the biggest problem area, followed by syntax then pragmatics. It is likely that inconsistencies in the identification of the E/BD population as well as variability within the population might account for some of the differences in these studies.

Several researchers have examined whether the use of pragmatic language may be a particular problem for students with emotional and behavior problems. Since pragmatic language is closely intertwined with social interaction, and many students with E/BD have significant problems in this area, it makes sense to explore pragmatic language in this population. In fact, several studies have found that students with E/BD have significant difficulty with pragmatic language. Specific problems include poor topic maintenance and inappropriate responses (McDonough, 1989) and failure to adequately consider the needs of the listener (Rosenthal & Simeonsson, 1991).

In addition to examining specific language skills, researchers have been interested in examining the incidence of expressive and receptive language impairments among E/BD children. Several studies (e.g., Hooper et al., 2003; Nelson et al., 2003; Nelson et al., 2005) have reported a greater incidence of expressive language disorders. Other researchers have reported a higher incidence of receptive language problems (Cantwell & Baker, 1987; Cohen et al., 1989). At first, these results may seem to be very confusing, but Cohen and colleagues (1989) found that students who had been previously identified as both E/BD and language impaired had lower scores on receptive language (as well as on pragmatic language). They speculated that students who have difficulty communicating are more likely to be identified as having a disability. However, there may be other children with more difficult-to-identify receptive language problems who may be just as seriously impaired as the children with expressive language difficulties. In fact, some have claimed that receptive language impairments are a significant predictor of later conduct problems (Hooper et al., 2003). These findings suggest that educators need to go beyond expressive language abilities in identifying and teaching students with emotional and behavioral disorders.

Language and Types of E/BD.   Another question that has challenged researchers is whether differences in language and communication may be related to the type of emotional or behavioral problem of an individual. In order to explore this question, researchers have examined the language functioning of individuals with specific types of E/BD. Although there is a great deal of debate between experts as to how to classify children with emotional and behavioral disorders, two broad categories that are often used are "internalized" behavior disorders (such as withdrawal and depression) and "externalized" problems (such as aggression and hyperactivity). Are there differences in the language and communication of children with these differing types of problems and, if so, what are the implications for intervention?

Children with **internalized behavior problems** often have limited social interactions. Since social interaction is an important contributor to language development, such children may be at risk for language difficulties. Research has found that children with language impairments are often more socially withdrawn. In particular, they tend to shy away from social interaction (Fujiki, Brinton, Morgan, & Hart, 1999). Additionally, depressed children have been found to have language difficulties, especially in aspects of pragmatics (Baltaxe & Simmons, 1988). Similarly, children with internalized behavior disorders have been reported to have significant language and communication difficulties—especially in pragmatic language (Hartas, 1995).

As an example of this research, Evans (1987) examined the language and communication of what she called **reticent children**—children who spoke infrequently in the classroom. She found that, when compared their peers, these children talked about fewer topics, spoke in shorter utterances, and initiated interaction less often. All of these findings led Evans to conclude that reticent children have specific deficiencies in expressive pragmatic language (see Box 10 .1).

What about children with **externalized behavior problems?** One of the first studies on the language and communication of children with conduct disorders was conducted by Mack and Warr-Leeper (1992). They administered a broad range of language tests to 20 residents of a psychiatric institute who had been referred for chronic behavior problems. The researchers reported that 13 of the participants showed evidence of significant language impairments, 3 had both language and speech impair-

---

BOX **10.1**

Transcripts of a "Reticent" Child and a Peer during Sharing Time

Transcript of "Reticent" Girl

T: Tell us what you brought today.

C: (pulls rag doll out of bag; does up buttons on doll's dress) A doll.

T: Can you tell us about it?

C: It can stand up.

T: Can you tell us anything else?

C: (no response)

T: Does she have a name?

C: (no response)

T: Where did you get her?

C: For Christmas.

T: Did you? She's very nice.

Transcript of Peer

T: Erica (fictional name)

C: (takes out and shows doll)

T: Can you tell us who you brought today?

C: Crying Baby. You give her a bottle and pull the string out (pulls string to demonstrate). And then she cries.

T: Did you get her for Christmas?

C: (nods)

T: I see you've got some more clothes for her.

C: I got a whole bunch in my room.

T: Do you have a bed for her at your house?

C: She sleeps with me.

T: Oh does she.

Source: Evans (1987), pp. 181–182.

ments, and 1 had a specific speech impairment. Language difficulties were present in every area of language tested, so no specific area of language appeared to be more impacted than another. Increasing evidence shows that students with conduct disorders are more likely to have significant difficulty with expressive language (Nelson et al., 2005). This is not surprising, given the widespread observation by teachers that such students often seem to have difficulty expressing their feelings.

Much of the research on the language of students with externalized behavior problems has been done with children with attention deficit disorders. Although such children often exhibit behavior that is very disruptive, it is not clear whether they should be included in the E/BD population. However, we will include them here in order to look at the evidence on their language and communication functioning.

Researchers have frequently noted that children with attention deficit hyperactivity disorder (ADHD) are likely to have associated language problems (Love & Thompson, 1988). In one study, 42 percent of students with ADHD were found to have some kind of speech or language difficulty (Humphries, Koltun, Malone, & Roberts, 1994). Although the ADHD students in this study had a variety of language difficulties, this and other studies have found pragmatic language to be the most significant problem area.

Students with ADHD are often observed to have significant problems with social interaction and in developing peer relationships. A variety of factors may contribute to these difficulties, but problems with social communication (i.e., pragmatic language) have been found to be an important factor in social development deficiencies. Children with ADHD have been reported to begin conversations at awkward moments, switch topics abruptly, interject unconnected thoughts, miss conversational turns, and fail to adapt their message to the listener (Westby & Cutler, 1994). For example, in one study (Whalen et al., 1979) boys with ADHD were compared with non-ADHD children on their ability to participate in a conversational task. Both groups of children were asked to participate in a "space flight" game in which one child was assigned to act as "mission control" (giving directions) and another as the "astronaut" (receiving directions). The ADHD boys did well in the message-sender role but interrupted and disagreed more frequently when they were in the role of message receiver. The researchers concluded that the ADHD boys had difficulty adjusting to the different communicative requirements of the two roles. In other words, unlike the non-ADHD participants, the ADHD boys failed to adjust their communicative strategies to match the role they were playing in the conversation. They continued to try to direct the conversation even when they were supposed to be listening. The implications of this research are that children with ADHD are likely to be ineffective conversational partners.

Recently, researchers have investigated whether the extent to which the attention and cognition problems associated with ADHD are the cause of language difficulties in this population. For example, Cohen and colleagues (2000) compared the language skills of children with ADHD with and without language impairments to children with other behavior problems. They found no specific pattern of language impairments associated with ADHD. Rather, children with language impairments, no matter what their behavior problem, had language difficulties.

On the other hand, Redmond (2004) did discover some differences in the language functioning of children with ADHD and children with specific language impairments. Using spontaneous language samples rather than standardized testing, Redmond found that children with ADHD had specific difficulties with forming conversational utterances, whereas the spoken language of children with language impairments was characterized by lower MLU and more problems with tense usage.

Although there continues to be disagreement about the specific pattern of difficulties experienced by children with attention deficit disorders, there is evidence that many children with ADHD struggle with language. In particular, the use of language in conversational situations may be problematic.

Literacy and Students with Emotional and Behavioral Disorders

Students with emotional and behavioral disorders experience a wide range of problems in school. In addition to the behavior problems that usually attract the attention of teachers and other school personnel, students with emotional and behavioral disorders also experience difficulties with social relationships and with academic skills. Since it is well established that many children with emotional and behavioral disorders have difficulty with language, it is not surprising that reading and writing skills are often poor in this population (Benner, Nelson, & Epstein, 2002). One study of children and adolescents with E/BD found that nearly 50 percent of the children (under age 13) and 36 percent of the adolescents had reading and/or writing scores well below average (Nelson, Benner, & Rogers-Adkinson, 2003). Low reading achievement has been found to be a significant risk factor in the long-term outcomes of students with emotional and behavioral disorders (Epstein, Kinder, & Bursuck, 1989). Additionally, students with reading disorders have been found to be at higher risk for psychiatric disorders (including ADHD) than good readers (Carroll, Maughan, Goodman, & Meltzer, 2005; Willcutt & Pennington, 2000).

Clearly, there is a relationship between emotional and behavior disorders, language impairments, and reading difficulties, but it is unclear which is cause and which is effect. In other words, do children who experience significant academic problems become behavior problems or do children with behavior problems have more difficulty acquiring academic skills? And what is the role of language in both disorders? These questions were investigated in a study by Tomblin, Zhang, Buckwalter, and Catts (2000). The researchers intensively examined a population of 581 children by giving them a battery of tests that measured language, reading, and behavior. Approximately half of the participants had been identified as having language impairments in a previous study of a larger sample of children. The researchers found that the children with language impairments were about six times more likely to have reading difficulties than those without language impairments. They also discovered that children with language impairments were at significantly higher risk for behavior disorders—especially the externalizing behavior and inattention problems usually associated with ADHD. Further analysis of the data indicated that children with language impairments who also had reading disabilities were most at risk for behavior disorders. The authors concluded that it was most likely that language impairments preceded behavior disorders. Students with both language impairments and behavior disorders were most at risk for behavior problems like attention deficits.

Conclusion

Although many questions remain to be answered, there is more than enough evidence to indicate that language and communication difficulties are frequently associated with emotional and behavioral disorders. This is an important finding for three reasons. First, language and communication difficulties can have an impact on many of the areas of functioning that are problematic for children with emotional and behavioral disorders. In particular, problems with pragmatic language can contribute to difficulties in social interaction, the development of peer relationships, and interaction with teachers and others in authority. Imagine the child who does not adjust his language for different social situations. It may be acceptable for him interact with his friends on the playground by slapping hands and yelling, "Hey, what's happening?" but less so when he meets the principal in the hallway or his teacher on the first day of school. Students with language difficulties may also have problems using language to mediate their behavior—for example, thinking through the consequences of their behavior—and organizing their thoughts in writing.

Second, it is important to know that children with emotional and behavioral disorders are likely to have language and communication difficulties because these problems have often not been considered as part of the profile of E/BD students. Since their behavior is what gets the attention of teachers and parents, there is a tendency not to look past the behavior to consider what factors may contribute to their problems. The danger is that, if children have significant language and communication problems, these may go undetected and untreated, with the result that interventions for behavior problems may be less effective.

This leads directly to the third factor—intervention. Knowing that a student with emotional and behavioral difficulties may also have language and communication difficulties can lead to instruction that directly addresses the language problems while also enhancing the efficacy of behavioral interventions. For example, a child who frequently calls out in class may be on a behavioral program that rewards him or her for responding when recognized. The effectiveness of this program could be enhanced through instruction that teaches the child how to initiate interaction and how to respond when called on. Likewise, the research suggests that educators may be able to reduce the incidence of behavior (and reading) disorders through early identification and intervention for language and communication difficulties.

Implications for Assessment and Instruction

Students with emotional and behavioral disorders present some formidable challenges for education professionals. Their behavior, whether internalized or externalized, can be disturbing to both teachers and their peers. This may make it more difficult to implement effective intervention that requires the cooperation of teachers and/or peers. Moreover, the behavior of students with emotional and behavioral disorders may vary considerably from day to day or within the day. Children may come to school already angry or withdrawn. On other days, they may arrive at school in an upbeat mood but leave depressed or angry. These variations of behavior make it more difficult to assess the child and to provide consistent and appropriate instruction. In addition, many students with E/BD have "unexpected" language and communication difficulties. These problems can make assessment more difficult (since many assessment procedures are language based) and make instruction less effective. What, then, can be done to enhance the effectiveness of assessment and instruction for students with emotional and behavioral disorders?

Assessment

Assessment of speech and language skills, especially communicative abilities, should be part of the evaluation of any students suspected of having emotional and behavioral disorders. By now, the reasons for this suggestion should be obvious. In many cases, these children will have previously undetected speech and/or language problems. In a few cases, it may be that what was identified as a behavioral or emotional problem could, in fact, be primarily a language or communication difficulty. Therefore, it is essential that appropriate language and communication assessment be included as part of the assessment protocol. In many cases, however, persuading team members to include language and communication assessment in the evaluation of students with suspected emotional and behavioral difficulties may be a very difficult step. Many professionals are not aware of the impact of language and communication difficulties on behavior. As a result, they might be reluctant to include assessment of language and communication in the assessment plan of a child suspected of emotional and/or behavioral problems.

Appropriate language assessment for students with suspected emotional and behavioral disorders should include assessment of speech and language skills (e.g., phonological awareness, vocabulary, syntactic knowledge) but should also include the assessment of communicative competence. Audet and Hummel (1990) define *communicative competence* as "the child's ability to use language as a tool to effectively interact with others in social contexts" (p. 61). Many students with E/BD have difficulty applying their language skills to the task of communication. For them, testing may indicate that development of speech and language skills are at normal (or near normal) levels, but their use of these skills in conversational contexts may be lacking. Therefore, assessment procedures should include the evaluation of communicative competence.

Unfortunately, communication is not easy to assess. There are no formal, standardized tests of communicative competence (although there are tests of pragmatic language—a related skill). Instead, communication is best assessed in natural settings that are, by their very nature, difficult to control. A comprehensive assessment of communicative competence should include observation in several settings at different times during the school day. For example, observations could be done both in the classroom and in the cafeteria. Classroom observation should be done during more than one activity, since students may behave differently in response to various classroom activities. The observer must be trained in both what to observe and how to observe. Observers who get too close to students, for example, may interfere with natural interactions. In addition to observations in natural settings, it may be possible to structure situations in which children interact with a peer or in a group. Although these interactions may be less spontaneous, they have the advantage of being more easily controlled and observed. For example, teachers could assign two students to work together to write a story or could assign a group to collaborate on a science project. These activities provide opportunities for interaction that can be observed by the teacher or speech-language specialist.

Of course, the behaviors associated with children with emotional and behavioral difficulties makes the assessment task more of a challenge. Their behavior may vary widely over the course of the school day. They may respond differently to various individuals and in different settings. Children who are withdrawn or depressed might be reluctant to participate at all. Students with attention deficits or conduct disorders may have a difficult time focusing on the assessment tasks. Therefore, it is very important that the individual conducting the assessment understand the need to adapt the testing conditions for the child being evaluated. Assessment may have to be speeded up or slowed down. Children might need frequent breaks or no breaks at all. Some children may need a great deal of encouragement and reinforcement for responding; others will resent such feedback. The key is for the evaluator to be alert to each child's needs and respond appropriately. If this is done, a more complete and more accurate picture of the child may be achieved.

Instruction

As with assessment, the place to begin with intervention for students with emotional and behavioral difficulties is to be sure that language and communication are included in the instructional plan for the student. Unfortunately, this is rarely the case. Intervention plans usually focus primarily on the overt behavior exhibited by the student. For a student with a conduct disorder problem, this might be a plan to reward the student for reducing calling-out during class. For a socially withdrawn student, the plan might address increased opportunities for peer interaction.

Although it is certainly important for intervention plans to address the specific problems that students are experiencing, for students with language and communication difficulties such plans may not go far enough. In both of the cases just described, the inclusion of language and communication goals could enhance the effectiveness of the behavioral intervention. For example, rewarding a student for reducing the incidence of calling-out in class may reduce disruption in the classroom, but it does not provide the student with appropriate classroom interaction skills. For this, direct instruction in pragmatic language skills—such as how to enter an ongoing conversation, how to stay on topic, and how to keep responses brief and focused—may be necessary.

Instructional Goals.   Although specific instructional goals should always be developed for each individual child, there are some general recommendations that can apply to many students with emotional and behavioral disorders (see Table 10.2). Giddan (1991) has suggested that one important instructional goal is to *help students learn vocabulary words* that they can use to identify and describe their emotional states. She suggests that helping students understand the subtle meaning differences between words such as *scared, worried,* and *embarrassed* may help them better express their feelings to others. In order to help them learn this new vocabulary, students can keep a notebook or journal in which they write down what they are feeling. Giddan suggests that the child can take this book to class, to counseling sessions, and home, where the words and the feelings they describe can be discussed.

Another important goal is to become a *more effective classroom communicator.* Students with emotional and behavioral disorders need to learn skills such as how to get the teacher's attention (without disrupting the class) and how to appropriately ask for repetition or clarification when they do not understand. In addition, they need to develop listening skills that will enable them to attend to important information in class and store it effectively. Instruction in classroom communication can take place in many

TABLE 10.2   Intervention Suggestions for Students with Emotional and Behavioral Disorders

Problem	Intervention
Student engages in inappropriate interaction in class (e.g., calls out answers, strays off topic).	1. Teach student appropriate ways of getting attention and participating in classroom discussions. 2. Assign students to peers to ask and/or answer questions. 3. Ask students to self-monitor their interaction in the classroom.
Student interacts infrequently in class.	1. Provide opportunities to respond to a peer and/or small group. 2. Use "classwide voting" as a strategy to involve all students.
Student dominates interaction when working in groups.	1. Assign a group member to keep track of who has already talked and act as the "referee"— reminding students to wait their turn. 2. Give each group member tokens that must be "spent" in order to participate.
Student interacts infrequently in groups.	1. Establish ground rules that require all group members to participate, and ask group to self-evaluate its achievement of this goal. 2. Provide training to the student outside group time on pragmatic language skills needed to participate in groups.

ways. Teachers can use opportunities in the classroom to teach children appropriate ways of asking questions and responding. In addition to the traditional approach of asking children to raise their hands, teachers can use techniques such as picking names from a hat to ensure that all students are given an opportunity to participate, sharing an answer with a peer partner, or participating in classwide "voting" on answers. These latter suggestions can be especially useful for children who may find talking in front of the class particularly stressful.

Interaction with peers is a significant problem for many students with emotional and behavioral disorders. Therefore, a third language and communication goal for these students is *enhancing peer interaction.* Many classrooms, especially at the secondary level, provide limited opportunities for peer interaction. In fact, students are often discouraged from or punished for interacting with their peers. Of course, there is an appropriate time and place for peer interaction, but that is the point. Teachers should provide that time and place where peer interaction *can* occur. However, for many students with emotional and behavioral difficulties, simply providing opportunities for interaction with peers is not enough. They need to be helped to develop skills such as how to initiate conversation, take turns (and wait their turn), and stay on topic. Teachers can help by assigning students particular roles in a group, giving students tokens to spend in order to participate in a group, and including assessment of interaction as part of an overall assessment of the group's performance. Gallagher (1999) suggests the following activities to enhance interaction:

- Teach communicative alternatives to socially penalizing behaviors.
- Build event-based/script knowledge for socially or emotionally difficult situations.
- Manipulate antecedent events to increase opportunities to display and practice positive communicative behaviors.
- Manipulate consequent events to increase frequency and salience of outcomes of socially positive communicative behaviors.
- Develop broader and more varied emotional vocabularies.

Even when additional communicative opportunities are created, many students with emotional and behavioral disorders are unable to take advantage of those opportunities because they lack skills in pragmatic language. Hyter and colleagues (2001) reported on the results of a classroom-based program to enhance the pragmatic language skills of six students, ages 8 to 12, with emotional and behavioral disorders. The students participated in 16 lessons, each lasting 30 minutes, that focused on four skill areas:

1. Describing objects
2. Giving step-by-step directions
3. Stating personal opinions about inappropriate behavior
4. Negotiating for desired outcomes

Each lesson included role-playing of the target skill. Following the instruction, all of the students increased their scores on the Test of Pragmatic Language. They also improved their skills in describing objects and giving directions. However, the students did not show significant improvement in the other areas. These results suggest that pragmatic language skills can be taught but that students need help (such as guided practice) in order to generalize these skills to real classroom situations.

Delivery of Instruction. Service delivery issues are often a concern with students with disabilities. Questions about who should provide the service and where the service should be provided often impede the effective delivery of services. In the case of students with E/BD who may also have language and communication difficulties, the issues may be particularly complex. In addition to a regular education classroom teacher, there may be a special education teacher, a therapist, a speech-language specialist, and others involved with the child.

Although educators often recognize the importance a team approach when dealing with students with learning disabilities or mental retardation, they may not recognize the need for an interdisciplinary team when working with children with emotional and behavioral disorders. As Brinton and Fujiki (1993) point out, most speech-language specialists have had little if any training in working with such students and have not usually thought of these students as within their area of expertise. Yet, the research clearly shows that language and communication impairments are an important factor in emotional and behavioral disabilities. Similarly, classroom teachers may be so focused on behavior that they lose sight of the important contribution of language skills. This is all the more reason why an interdisciplinary team can be an essential part of the intervention program for students with emotional and behavioral disorders.

The key to effective service delivery for this (or any) group of students is collaboration. Whenever possible, professionals should share their goals and methods of intervention with each other. For example, the teacher who is trying to get a withdrawn student to participate more frequently in the classroom could be assisted by a special education teacher who could prompt the student to respond. Similarly, a speech-language specialist could help by modeling a classroom interaction scenario with the child. Unfortunately, collaboration is often an elusive goal. In practice, teachers often feel that they are too busy to share their instructional goals with others. Specialists may feel that only they understand the complexities of their area of expertise and that teachers and parents would have little to contribute. Hopefully, education professionals and parents will overcome the impediments to collaboration and work together to provide an effective intervention plan for students with emotional and behavioral difficulties.

Even when instruction for students with E/BD is carefully planned and effectively delivered, there can be challenges due to the nature of the child's difficulties. Coleman and Vaughn (2000) interviewed eight teachers who work with students with emotional and behavioral disorders regarding the challenges they faced in teaching such students. Some of the themes that emerged included the following:

- *Emotional variability of students.* Progress can occur at unexpected rates due to the emotional state of the student. Long periods without progress can be followed by a sudden leap in performance followed by regression.

- *Fear of failure and trust issues.* Students will often refuse to attempt a task because fear of failure is so deeply ingrained. Since trust is often an issue, the teachers suggested establishing consistent routines in the classroom.
- *Keeping students engaged.* Many of the teachers indicated that they used games to keep their students engaged and motivated. Noncompetitive games were preferred.

Summary

A substantial amount of research evidence indicates that children with speech and language impairments are at risk for emotional and behavioral disorders and that students with E/BD often have unsuspected language and communication problems. Language and communication difficulties can interfere with classroom participation, peer interaction, and academic performance. It is important to include assessment of speech, language, and communication in the assessment plan for students with E/BD. In addition, instruction that includes language and communication goals may enhance the effectiveness of that intervention with students with emotional and behavioral disorders.

R E V I E W   Q U E S T I O N S

1. What special challenges do students with emotional and behavioral disorders present to public schools?

2. What is the significance of the research that has reported evidence showing emotional and behavioral problems in children with speech and language disorders?

3. What is the potential impact of pragmatic language deficits on students with emotional and behavioral disorders?

4. Describe some of the conversational difficulties that have been attributed to students with ADHD.

5. Give three arguments in support of including assessment of speech and language in the assessment plan for students with emotional and behavioral difficulties.

6. Give two suggestions for enhancing the classroom interaction of withdrawn students.

7. How might classroom interaction be restructured to reduce disruption by students with emotional and behavioral disorders?

S U G G E S T E D   A C T I V I T I E S

1. Observe a child who is suspected of having an emotional and/or behavioral disorder. Try to observe interaction between this child and his or her peers in at least two different environments (e.g., the classroom and the playground). Respond to the following questions:

   a. How often does the child attempt to interact with others?

   b. How often do peers attempt to interact with the child?

    c. What happens when the child attempts to interact with peers?

    d. How does the child respond when other students approach and attempt to interact?

2. Interview three different education professionals regarding their attitudes and beliefs about students with emotional and behavioral difficulties. Include in your interview questions such as:

    a. Do students with emotional and behavioral difficulties belong in the same classroom/school with other children?

    b. What is the most effective type of intervention with students with emotional and behavioral difficulties?

    c. What role (if any) do language and communication difficulties play in contributing to the problems of students with emotional and behavioral difficulties?

GLOSSARY

affective disorders: behavioral disorders that affect mood and feelings

externalized behavior problems: behavior disorders such as aggression in which the individual acts on others

internalized behavior problems: behavior disorders such as depression in which the individual turns his or her feelings inward

reticent children: children who are reluctant to speak in class

RESOURCES ON THE WEB

www.nimh.nih.gov   National Institute of Mental Health, provides information on research on behavior disorders

www.ccbd.net   Council for Children with Behavioral Disorders

www.add.org   National Attention Deficit Disorder Association

www.chadd.org   Children and Adults with Attention Deficit Disorders

REFERENCES

Audet, L. R., & Hummel, L. J. (1990). A framework for assessment and treatment of language-learning disabled children with psychiatric disorders. *Topics in Language Disorders, 10,* 57–74.

Baker, L., & Cantwell, D. P. (1987a) Comparison of well, emotionally disturbed, and behaviorally disordered children with linguistic problems. *Journal of the American Academy of Child and Adolescent Psychiatry, 26,* 193–196.

Baker, L., & Cantwell, D. P. (1987b). Factors associated with the development of psychiatric illness in children with early speech/language problems.

Journal of Autism and Developmental Disorders, 17, 499–510.

Baker, L., & Cantwell, D. P. (1987c). A prospective psychiatric follow-up of children with speech/language disorders. *Journal of the American Academy of Child and Adolescent Psychiatry, 26,* 193–196.

Baltaxe, C., & Simmons, J. Q. (1988). Pragmatic deficits in emotionally disturbed children and adolescents. In R. Schiefelbusch & L. Lloyd (Eds.), *Language perspectives: Acquisition, retardation, intervention* (2nd ed.). Austin, TX: Pro-Ed.

Beitchman, J. H., Nair, R., Clegg, M. A., Ferguson, B., & Patel, P. G. (1986). Prevalence of psychiatric disorders in children with speech and language disorders. *Journal of the American Academy of Child Psychiatry, 25,* 528–536.

Beitchman, J. H., Wilson, B., Jophnson, C., Atkinson, L., Young, A., Adalf, E., Escobar, M., & Douglas, L. (2001). Fourteen-year follow-up of speech/language impaired and control children. *Journal of the American Academy of Child Psychiatry, 40,* 75–82.

Benner, G. J., Nelson, J. R., & Epstein, M. H. (2002). The language skills of children with emotional and behavioral disorders: A review of the literature. *Journal of Emotional and Behavioral Disorders, 10,* 43–59.

Brinton, B., & Fujiki, M. (1993). Language, social skills and socioemotional behavior. *Language, Speech and Hearing Services in Schools, 24,* 194–198.

Camarata, S., Hughes, C., & Ruhl, K. (1988). Mild/moderate behaviorally disorders students: A population at risk for language disorders. *Language, Speech and Hearing Services in Schools, 19,* 191–200.

Cantwell, D. P., & Baker, L. (1977). Psychiatric disorder in children with speech and language retardation: A critical review. *Archives of General Psychiatry, 34,* 583–591.

Cantwell, D. P., & Baker, L. (1987). Prevalence and type of psychiatric disorders in three speech and language groups. *Journal of Communication Disorders, 20,* 151–160.

Carroll, J. M., Maughan, B., Goodman, R., & Meltzer, H. (2005). Literacy difficulties and psychiatric disorders: Evidence for comorbidity. *Journal of Child Psychology and Psychiatry, 46,* 524–532.

Cohen, N. J. (1996). Unsuspected language impairments in psychiatrically disturbed children: Developmental issues and associated conditions. In J. H. Beitchman, N. J. Cohen, M. M. Konstantareas, & R. Tannock (Eds.), *Language, learning, and behavior disorders.* New York: Cambridge University Press.

Cohen, N. J., Davine, M., & Meloche-Kelly, M. (1989). Prevalence of unsuspected language disorders in a child psychiatric population. *Journal of the American Academy of Child and Adolescent Psychiatry, 28,* 107–111.

Cohen, N. J., Menna, R., Vallance, D. D., Barwick, M. A., Im, N., & Horoclezky, N. B. (1998). Language, social cognitive processing, and behavioral characteristics of psychiatrically disturbed children with previously identified and unsuspected language impairments. *Journal of Child Psychology and Psychiatry, 39,* 853–864.

Cohen, N. J., Vallance, D. D., Barwick, M., Im, N., Menna, R., Horodezky, N. B., & Isaacson, L. (2000). The interface between ADHD and language impairment: An examination of language, achievement, and cognitive processing. *Journal of Child Psychology and Psychiatry, 41,* 353–362.

Coleman, M., & Vaughn, S. (2000). Reading interventions for students with emotional/behavioral disorders. *Behavioral Disorders, 25,* 93–104.

Epstein, M. H., Kinder, D., & Bursuck, B. (1989). The academic status of adolescents with behavioral disorders. *Behavioral Disorders, 14,* 157–165.

Evans, M. A. (1987). Discourse characteristics of reticent children. *Applied Psycholinguistics, 8,* 171–184.

Fujiki, M., Brinton, B., Morgan, M., & Hart, C. H. (1999). Withdrawn and sociable behavior of children with language impairmen. *Language, Speech, and Hearing Services in Schools, 11,* 183–195.

Gallagher, T. M. (1999). Interrelationships among children's language, behavior, and emotional problems. *Topics in Language Disorders, 19,* 1–15.

Giddan, J. L. (1991). School children with emotional problems and communication deficits: Implications for speech-language pathologists. *Language, Speech, and Hearing Services in Schools, 22,* 291–295.

Greenbaum, P. E., Dedrick, R. F., Friedman, R. M., Kutash, K., Brown, E. C., Lardieri, S. P., & Pugh, A. M. (1999). National adolescent and child treatment study (NACTS): Outcomes for children with serious emotional behavioral disturbance. In M. H. Epstein, K. Kutash, & A. Duchnowski (Eds.), *Outcomes for children and youth with emotional and behavioral disorders and their families: Programs and evaluation best practices* (pp. 21–54). Austin, TX: Pro-Ed.

Gresham, F. M. (2005). Response to intervention: An alternative means of identifying students as emotionally disturbed. *Education and Treatment of Children, 28,* 328–344.

Gualtieri, C. T., Koriath, U., Bourgondien, M., & Saleeby, N. (1983). Language disorders in children referred for psychiatric services. *Journal of the*

American Academy of Child Psychiatry, 22, 165–171.

Hartas, D. (1995). Verbal interactions of children with internalizing behavior disorders. *B.C. Journal of Special Education, 19,* 11–19.

Hooper, S. R., Roberts, J. F., Zeisel, S. A., & Poe, M. (2003). Core language predictors of behavioral functioning in early elementary school children: Concurrent and longitudinal findings. *Behavioral Disorders, 29,* 10–24.

Humphries, T., Koltun, H., Malone, M., & Roberts, W. (1994). Teacher-identified oral language difficulties among boys with attention problems. *Developmental and Behavioral Pediatrics, 15,* 92–98.

Hyter, Y. D., Rogers-Adkinson, D. L., Self, T. L., Simmins, B. F., & Jantz, J. (2001). Pragmatic language intervention for children with language and emotional/behavioral disorders. *Communication Disorders Quarterly, 23,* 4–16.

Individuals with Disabilities Education Act. (2004). Washington, DC: U.S. Government Printing Office.

Lambros, K. M., Ward, S. L., Bocian, K. M., MacMillan, D. L., & Gresham, F. M. (1998). Behavioral profiles of children at-risk for emotional and behavioral disorders: Implications for assessment and classification. *Focus on Exceptional Children, 30*(5), 1–16.

Love, A. J., & Thompson, M. G. G. (1988). Language disorders and attention deficit disorders in young children referred for psychiatric services. *American Journal of Orthopsychiatry, 58,* 52–63.

Mack, A., & Warr-Leeper, G. (1992). Language abilities in boys with chronic behavior disorders. *Language, Speech, and Hearing Services in Schools, 23,* 214–223.

McDonough, J. M. (1989). Analysis of the expressive language characteristics of emotionally handicapped students in social interactions. *Behavioral Disorders, 14,* 127–149.

Nelson, J. R., Benner, J. R., & Cheney, D. (2005). An investigation of the language skills of students with emotional disturbance served in public school settings. *The Journal of Special Education, 39,* 97–105.

Nelson, J. R., Benner, J. R., & Rogers-Adkinson, D. (2003). An investigation of the characteristics of K–12 students with comorbid emotional distur-bance and significant language deficits served in public school settings. *Behavioral Disorders, 29,* 25–33.

Redmond, S. M. (2004). Conversational profiles of children with ADHD, SLI and typical development. *Clinical Linguistics & Phonetics, 18,* 107–125.

Rinaldi, C. (2003). Language competence and social behavior of students with emotional or behavioral disorders. *Behavioral Disorders, 29,* 34–42.

Rosenthal, S., & Simeonsson, R. (1991). Communication skills in emotionally disturbed and nondisturbed adolescents. *Behavioral Disorders, 16,* 192–199.

Ruhl, K. L., Hughes, C. A., & Camarata, S. T. (1992). Analysis of the expressive and receptive language characteristics of emotionally handicapped students served in public school settings. *Journal of Childhood Communication Disorders, 14,* 165–176.

Tomblin, J. B., Zhang, X., Buckwalter, P., & Catts, H. (2000). The association of reading disability, behavioral disorders, and language impairment among second-grade children. *Journal of Child Psychology and Psychiatry, 41,* 473–482.

Trautman, R., Giddan, J., & Jurs, S. (1990). Language risk factors in emotionally disturbed children within a school and day treatment program. *Journal of Childhood Communication Disorders, 13,* 123–133.

Warr-Leeper, G., Wright, N. A., & Mack, A. (1994). Language disabilities of antisocial boys in residential treatment. *Behavioral Disorders, 19,* 159–169.

Westby, C. E., & Cutler, S. K. (1994). Language and ADHD: Understanding the bases and treatment of self-regulatory deficits. *Topics in Language Disorders, 14,* 58–76.

Whalen, C. K., Henker, B., Collins, B. E., McAuliffe, S., & Vaux, A. (1979). Peer interaction in a structured communication task: Comparison of normal and hyperactive boys and of methylphenidate (Ritalin) and placebo effects. *Child Development, 50,* 388–401.

Willcutt, E. G., & Pennington, B. F. (2000). Comorbidity of reading disability and attention-deficit/hyperactivity disorder: Differences by gender and subtype. *Journal of Learning Disabilities, 33,* 179–191.

11 Language and Students with Sensory Disabilities

Children with sensory disabilities, including hearing impairments and visual impairments, present significant challenges for education professionals. Sensory disabilities can have an impact on a number of areas of functioning, including language and communication. For children with hearing impairments, the problems are apparent. However, individuals with vision disabilities frequently have difficulties with language and communication that may limit their ability to fully participate in school and society. This chapter examines the impact of sensory impairments on language and cognitive development and on academic and social performance. The chapter also includes instructional methods that have been used effectively with children with sensory and motor impairments.

After completing this chapter, you should be able to:

1. Describe how sensory impairments have been defined and classified.
2. Describe the impact of sensory impairments on:
   cognitive development
   language development
   educational performance
   social interaction
3. List the advantages and disadvantages of various intervention techniques for children with sensory impairments.

John A.: A Case Study

Student: John A. Grade: 3
Sex: Male Age: 9:5

Reason for Referral
John presently attends a special class for children with hearing impairments. Because he has made good progress in the development of communication skills, he is being considered as a candidate for inclusion in a regular education classroom.

John A.: A Case Study Continued

Background Information

John is the second child of Mr. and Mrs. A. At birth, John was small, weighing 5 pounds, 2 ounces. John spent two days in an intensive care nursery, but his parents were told that he would probably have no long-term problems. Mrs. A. reports that John was often sick, running high fevers several times. Following one of John's more severe bouts of fever and illness at age 3, Mrs. A. began to notice some changes in his behavior. It seemed as if he sometimes did not hear things. He was slow to respond or did not respond at all. His speech, which had begun to develop, became harder to understand and did not develop as quickly as that of other children.

When John was 4 years old, he was taken for a speech and hearing examination. The results indicated that John had both a moderate, high-frequency hearing loss and receptive aphasia. It was suggested that John use a hearing aid and begin speech therapy; however, he did not begin to use a hearing aid until entering school at the age of 6 because his parents were concerned about social rejection.

School Background

John's educational difficulties began in kindergarten. His teacher observed that he was often slow in following directions. When told to line up, for example, John seemed to move slowly, as if he did not know what to do. Although he excelled at physical games, he was shy and was often teased by the other children. At the end of kindergarten, John was placed in a class for children with hearing impairments because of his difficulty in communicating with others and his slow development in reading.

John has made considerable progress in this class: His speech has become more intelligible. He has adapted to his hearing aid and can generally understand the teacher. Although he excels in math, John continues to lag behind in reading and writing. He has several friends among his hearing-impaired peers but has few friends outside the classroom.

Test Results

Audiology

John was recently given an audiological exam. He had a 50-decibel (dB) hearing loss in the right ear and a 60-dB loss in the left ear. These results suggest that he has a moderate hearing disability.

Speech

John's test results from the Goldman-Fristoe Test of Articulation indicated an overall percentile rank of 20. John had difficulty producing several consonant sounds in initial and medial positions, and he also had difficulty with consonant blends.

Aptitude

John took the WISC-III (a test of intelligence), achieving a verbal-scale score of 75 and a performance score of 105. Although he did not do well on the information and vocabulary subtests, he did perform well on the block-design and object-assembly tests. These results indicate that John has measured intelligence in the average range, with performance scores significantly higher than verbal scores.

(continued)

John A.: A Case Study Continued

Achievement
The Peabody Individual Achievement Test (PIAT) was administered, and John achieved the following results:

	Standard Score	Percentile Rank
Mathematics:	112	52
Reading recognition:	83	13
Reading comprehension:	84	14
Spelling:	70	2
General information:	99	35

The results of the PIAT indicate that John has academic achievement significantly below the norm in reading and in spelling. His achievement level in mathematics indicates an area of relative strength.

Conclusion

John is a 9-year-old boy with a moderate hearing impairment. His excellent progress in a self-contained class suggests that he may be a good candidate for inclusion in a regular education classroom.

Marisol: A Case Study

Marisol is a six-year-old girl who is a student in Mrs. Wright's first-grade classroom. Marisol was born two months premature and developed retinopathy of immaturity, which left her with little residual vision. Marisol can see shadows but cannot see images.

Marisol has received intervention almost since the day she left the hospital. As a preschooler, Marisol attended a program that emphasized interaction with peers, hands-on learning, and play activities to promote language acquisition.

Marisol attended a regular kindergarten program in her community. She received support in the classroom from a full-time instructional aide. Marisol made very good progress in kindergarten both academically and socially. In addition to participating in classwide activities such as circle-time and listening to stories, Marisol began to learn to read Braille with the assistance of a part-time instructor provided by the State Commission on the Blind. Although Marisol is still reluctant to initiate interactions with her peers, she was included in social activities both within and outside the classroom.

Now that she is in first grade, Marisol continues to receive Braille instruction from a part-time teacher. Unfortunately, there have been some problems with coordinating the Braille lessons with classroom instruction provided by the regular first-grade teacher. The two teachers have found it difficult to find time to plan together so Marisol receives a consistent program. Since there are no Braille versions available for the math book used in class, Marisol's aide has been tape-recording those lessons. She is finding it difficult to keep the recordings up to date.

Marisol: A Case Study Continued

Marisol tends to be reluctant to initiate interactions with peers. She does have one friend in the classroom who she also sees out of school. However, most of the rest of the children in the classroom rarely interact with her.

Marisol's language skills seem to be close to those that would be expected for a child of her age. She is able to understand almost everything said to her. She can ask questions and initiate interactions, although she is often reluctant to do so. She has been receiving speech therapy for some lingering speech production problems but not for language skills. Marisol's teacher, Mrs. Wright, has reported that Marisol has some difficulty learning new words but can do so if given enough time.

Marisol is continuing to make good progress in the regular education classroom. Her aide assists her with mobility and with lessons that require reading. Her Braille teacher reports that Marisol is making excellent progress in acquiring Braille. Marisol's overall language skills are good. Her most significant challenge is in socialization. She is reluctant to initiate interactions and has few friends in the classroom. This will need to be a focus for intervention in the future.

Defining Hearing Impairment

Children with hearing impairments run the gamut from those with mild impairments to the profoundly deaf. They may have a disability that fluctuates, is stable, gets progressively worse, or is either hard to identify in the classroom or easily recognizable. With this much variation in the population with hearing impairments, it is essential that teachers have a clear definition of hearing impairment.

The Individuals with Disabilities Education Act (IDEA, 2004) defines two categories of students with hearing impairments as follows:

> *Deafness:* means a hearing impairment so severe that a child is impaired in processing linguistic information through hearing, with or without amplification, that adversely affects a child's educational performance.
>
> *Hearing impairment:* means an impairment in hearing, whether permanent or fluctuating, that adversely affects a child's educational performance but is not included under the definition of "deafness."

If you think these definitions are not very specific, you are correct. There is no "legal" definition of deafness (as there is for blindness). As Karchmer and Mitchell (2003) note, the definitions of *deafness* and *hearing impairment* are "amorphous and contested" (p. 22). The Conference of Executives of American Schools for the Deaf (CEAD) adopted the following definitions to classify persons with hearing impairments:

> **Hearing impairment:** This generic term indicates a hearing disability that can range from mild to profound. It includes the subsets of deaf and hard-of-hearing.
>
> **Deaf:** A person who is deaf is one whose hearing disability precludes successful processing of linguistic information through audition, with or without a hearing aid.
>
> **Hard-of-hearing:** A hard-of-hearing person has residual hearing sufficient for successful processing of linguistic information through audition, generally with the use of a hearing aid.

The most important distinction made by these definitions involves the ability to process language. Children who are deaf are *unable* to use hearing to process language. Hard-of-hearing children can process spoken language, although they may experience delays and differences in development.

Another approach to the classification and definition of hearing impairments is by the type of hearing loss. There are three major types of hearing impairments. **Conductive hearing loss** is caused by a problem with transmission of sound from the outer to the middle ear (see Figure 11.1). This hearing loss is usually mild to moderate. The most common cause of conductive hearing loss is *otitis media (middle-ear infection)*. Conductive hearing losses are usually treatable but, if left untreated, may cause significant problems. **Sensorineural hearing loss** results from damage to structures that transmit sound from the ear to the brain and often involves auditory nerve damage. This condition usually results in moderate to severe hearing losses and is usually not reversible. **Central hearing loss** is caused by damage to the brain resulting from many factors, including tumors, disease, or stroke. Central hearing losses are often difficult to identify because a child may seem to hear normally but may have problems in interpretation and integration of acoustic information.

The most commonly used approach to the classification of hearing impairments is the *degree of hearing loss.* With this approach, hearing impairments are classified according to the results of audiometric testing. The speech-language clinician evaluates the child's hearing by determining how loud a sound or word must be in order for the child to recognize it. The results are recorded on an **audiogram** (see Figure 11.2). The audiogram shows the hearing threshold (the point at which the child can identify sounds) and the pitch frequencies of those sounds.

FIGURE 11.1   The Human Ear

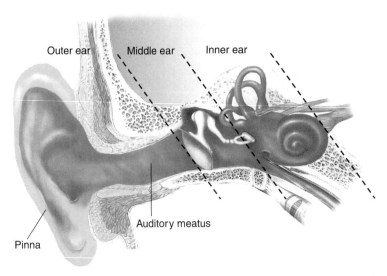

Source: From Owens, Robert E., et al. *Introduction to Communication Disorders: A Lifespan Perspective,* 3rd ed. Published by Allyn and Bacon, Boston, MA. Copyright © 2007 by Pearson Education. Reprinted by permission of the publisher.

FIGURE 11.2   Two Audiograms

A. Moderate Conductive Hearing Loss

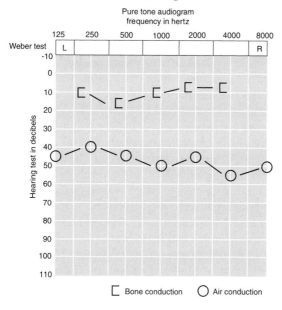

B. Severe Sensorineural Hearing Loss

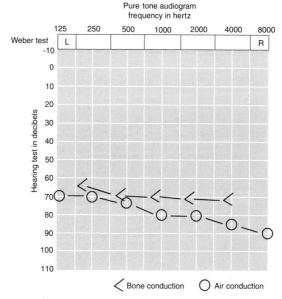

Source: From Owens, Robert E., et al. *Introduction to Communication Disorders: A Lifespan Perspective,* 3rd ed. Published by Allyn and Bacon, Boston, MA. Copyright © 2007 by Pearson Education. Reprinted by permission of the publisher.

When the results for several different types of audiometric testing are averaged, that average indicates how seriously the child's hearing is impaired. Knowing the child's level of hearing impairment allows for predictions about that child's ability to learn and interact in the classroom (see Table 11.1). For example, children with **mild hearing loss** (15–30 dB) have minimal difficulty hearing, although they may have some problems hearing faint speech. However, these children may have some articulation difficulties, language delays, and difficulty with reading and writing. It is important that teachers learn to recognize those with mild hearing disorders, since relatively simple interventions (such as preferential seating and the use of visual cues) may help these children.

Children with **moderate hearing loss** (31–60 dB) have more significant hearing and speech disorders. Many of these children experience significant delays in speech and language development, and they may have difficulty hearing in noisy environments or when speech is not directed at them. Children with moderate hearing losses may benefit from hearing aids and intensive speech and language instruction.

Children with **severe hearing loss** (61–90 dB) have considerable difficulty hearing normal speech and frequently have significant delays in speech and language development. Many have abnormal voice quality as well. Children with severe hearing losses will usually require some sort of amplification system. Therefore, early identification and intervention is important so these children can learn to utilize their residual hearing.

TABLE 11.1   Levels of Hearing Impairment

Classification	Hearing Threshold Level	Impact	Intervention
Mild	15–30 dB	Minimal difficulty hearing Some articulation problems Possible reading/writing delays	Preferential seating Visual cues
Moderate	31–60 dB	Delays in speech and language Difficulty hearing with background interference	Amplification Speech/language instruction
Severe	61–90 dB	Considerable difficulty with normal speech Significant delays in speech/language Abnormal voice quality	May benefit from amplification Speech reading or sign language
Profound	91 + dB	Little residual hearing Reliance on visual/tactile cues	Manual communication or total communication

Source: Adapted from S. Shaw. (1994). Language and hearing-impaired children. *An introduction to children with language disorders.* New York: Macmillan.

Children with **profound hearing loss** (91+ dB) can hear little if anything. They learn to rely heavily on visual and tactile cues, and amplification is usually of little help to them. These children are most likely to benefit from training in the use of a manual communication system.

In addition to the degree of hearing loss, several other factors should be considered to understand the effects of a hearing impairment on a particular child. The *age of onset* of the disability is critical. Children who acquire hearing disabilities after the initial stages of language learning usually have less impairment than children whose disability is present at birth. *Age of identification of the hearing loss* is also very important. Children who are identified early and who receive appropriate intervention services are usually able to progress more quickly than children who are not identified early. *Stability of the hearing loss* should also be considered. Children with fluctuating or progressive hearing losses may require different types of instruction than children with stable hearing losses.

Cognitive Characteristics

Moores (1996) described three stages in the development of understanding of the cognitive abilities of persons who are deaf. In the first stage, which lasted from the beginning of the twentieth century until the 1950s, the prevailing notion was that persons who were deaf had deficient intellectual abilities. The development of intelligence testing in the early part of the twentieth century confirmed the assumptions about the intellectual abilities of deaf persons. Although there were inconsistencies in the findings, most researchers concluded that persons who were deaf functioned below the norm on most tests of cognitive skills.

The second stage of research on the cognitive development of the deaf was called the "deaf as concrete" phase by Moores (1996). The theory was that deaf persons were not cognitively deficient but exhibited thinking in different ways (more "concretely" than hearing individuals). For example, Myklebust (1960) examined the research on the intellectual functioning of deaf people and concluded that they were not intellectually inferior to hearing persons but that they thought in qualitatively *different* ways. He claimed that deafness caused differences in perception, which, in turn, caused persons with hearing loss to think in a more concrete manner. Myklebust's work strongly influenced educational practices for children with deafness. There was more emphasis on using concrete materials and examples and less emphasis on having these children use abstract thinking.

Since the 1960s, the prevailing view has been that persons with hearing loss are neither intellectually inferior nor do they think in different ways. As part of this third stage of research, psychometric testing has been reevaluated and reinterpreted, with the result that most researchers believe that the intellectual abilities of persons who are deaf cover the same range as those of the hearing population. For example, when Vernon (1968) reviewed a number of studies on the intellectual functioning of persons with deafness, he found that in a majority of the studies, the deaf individuals equaled or exceeded the performance of hearing individuals. In those cases where the performance of persons who were deaf was found to be below the norm, the results may have been invalidated by the testing procedures. In such cases, even when nonverbal tests were used, directions were often given via spoken language or test items may have assumed prior experience with spoken language.

More recently, however, research on the cognitive development of deaf persons has focused on the cognitive differences between this population and hearing persons and the factors that contribute to these differences. Rather than absolute differences in ability, researchers are finding that factors such as early home experiences, exposure to language, and educational experiences can have an impact on cognitive development (Marschark, Lang, & Albertini, 2002). For example, research on the intelligence of deaf and hard-of-hearing persons has found that children with hereditary deafness tend to have higher IQ scores than those with acquired deafness (Kusche, Greenberg, & Garfield 1983). Deaf children with deaf parents have also been found to score higher on intelligence tests (Zweibel, 1987). These results suggest that early experiences and exposure to language (especially manual language) may have a strong influence on the development of intelligence in deaf persons.

Contemporary research on the cognitive abilities of deaf persons has focused on their ability to receive, store, and process information. As an example, researchers have been interested in whether visual processing abilities are superior in deaf persons. For a long time it has been assumed that deaf persons compensate for their lack of hearing through enhanced visual skills. However, research has generally not supported this assumption. In fact, there is some evidence that young deaf children have poorer visual attention (Spencer, 2000). On the other hand, some research has suggested that deaf persons who use sign language have superior visual skills to those who use spoken language (e.g., Emmorey & Kosslyn, 1996). Marschark and colleagues (2002) concluded that, depending on the nature of the visual task, deaf persons may perform better, worse, or the same as hearing individuals. Similarly, various results have been found regarding the memory abilities of deaf persons. Research has found some subtle differences in the ways in which deaf persons organize information but memory appears to be generally intact.

Another focus of research on the cognitive abilities of deaf persons has been on problem solving. Researchers such as Hans Furth and colleagues (Furth, 1973; Furth & Youniss, 1971) evaluated the ability of deaf children to perform Piagetian tasks. They found that children with hearing loss progressed through the same stages of development at about the same times as those Piaget had found in hearing children. However, they also found that development lagged at the latter stages of concrete operations and in formal operations. If true, these delays may be the result of the lack of spoken language or less opportunity to engage in abstract thinking.

So, what can we conclude about the cognitive abilities of persons who are deaf? It is likely that their intellectual abilities are similar to those found in the hearing population; that is, some persons with hearing loss have higher than average intellectual skills, most falling around the norm and a few ranging below normal (assuming no other disabilities are involved). There may be some delays in the development of higher-order thinking skills. These delays could result from a lack of spoken language or a lack of opportunity to engage in challenging problem-solving tasks.

Language Characteristics

Impairments in understanding and using spoken language are the most important consequence of deafness. But what does that mean for the development of language itself? Can deaf children develop language skills with limited or nonexistent auditory input? What is the impact of spoken language deficits on the development of academic skills such as reading and writing? In this section we will review some of the research on the language development and language characteristics of hearing-impaired persons. We will look at spoken language first, then at manual language development. Finally, we will examine several factors that may help explain the language impairments associated with significant hearing loss.

Spoken Language

The development of spoken language is usually delayed in children who are deaf. Some children fail to develop spoken language at all. Even children with relatively mild hearing impairments often experience delays in some aspects of language development.

Early Development of Language and Communication.   The early language and communication development of children with mild to moderate hearing impairments appears to follow a typical developmental sequence and pace (Yoshinaga-Itano & Seedy, 1999). Early communicative interaction with parents is intact, as is the early development of cooing and babble (Oller, Eilers, Bull, & Carney, 1985). The intelligibility of early speech is also high for children with mild to moderate hearing impairments.

But what about children with severe and profound deafness? Experts know that early parent–child interaction sets the stage for language development. What is the impact of severe deafness on this interaction? Interestingly, research studies have found that hearing mothers produce comparable amounts of speech to their deaf and hearing children and modify their language in ways that are typical of parent–infant interaction (Gallaway & Woll, 1994; Lederberg & Everhart, 1998). But deaf babies are limited in their ability to benefit from spoken language input. They may benefit from the nonverbal communicative interaction sequences and from facial expressions, but they can learn little from the spoken language itself.

The early vocalizations of deaf babies have been found to be similar to those of hearing infants, but that changes when babbling begins. Deaf babies babble less frequently and use fewer different sounds in their babble, even when they have hearing aids and when parents emphasize spoken language (Oller & Eilers, 1988). Vocalization differences increase as deaf babies approach the emergence of first words.

Phonology and Speech.   Most of the research on the phonological abilities of children who are deaf has focused on their ability to *produce* language sounds. For the most part, researchers have found that speech production is delayed in these children and follows a developmental course that is similar to that of hearing infants. However, there may be some sounds that never fully develop (Blamey, 2003).

Studies of older children have also found delays in the development of speech production. Children who are deaf or hard-of-hearing have been found to make more phonological errors and substitutions than do hearing children (Ratner, 2005). However, researchers have also discovered that children who are deaf develop the same phonological rules as do hearing children. These rules may develop more slowly, but when they do emerge they are similar to those used by hearing children (Oller, Jensen, & Lafayette, 1978).

It is important for hearing-impaired children to acquire phonological rules, but it is even more important that these children be understood. Most people find the speech of children with significant hearing impairments difficult to understand. Intelligibility seems to be related to the degree of hearing impairment; that is, children with more serious impairments generally are more difficult to understand. However, several factors may affect a child's ability to be understood, one of the most important being the experience of the listener. Several studies indicate that those listeners who are more experienced in interacting with persons who are deaf are better able to understand such speakers (McGarr, 1983; Monsen, 1983). Other factors that affect speech intelligibility are the context of the conversation and the ability of the listener to see the face of the speaker (Monsen, 1983).

Research on the speech capabilities of children who are deaf or hard of hearing suggests that these children will have significant delays in speech development. These delays often result in speech that is difficult to understand, thus creating significant problems in the classroom. But research also suggests that teachers and others who work with these children can help them be better understood by seating them so they can be seen and by having listeners use context clues as an aid to understanding.

Morphology and Syntax.   Word parts such as prefixes and suffixes are a rather subtle aspect of language and are sometimes hard to acquire, even for children without disabilities. In English, word parts are often unstressed, a situation making it all the more difficult for children with hearing disabilities to acquire these structures. Children with hearing impairments, not surprisingly, have been found to be delayed in their acquisition of morphological rules. This is true of both children with profound hearing impairments (Russell, Power, & Quigley, 1976) as well as individuals with less serious difficulties (Brown, 1984). Although researchers have generally found that children who are deaf follow the same sequence of morphological development as do hearing children, their delays in development can be up to 6 years or more.

A good deal of research has been conducted on the syntactic skills of persons who are deaf. Most of these studies have found that these children experience significant delays, relative to hearing children. For example, Schirmer (1985) examined the spontaneous spoken language of 20 children between the ages of 3 and 5 with severe to profound hearing impairments. The children were videotaped during a 1-hour play session. Analysis of their spoken-language production indicated that the children with hearing impairments were developing a syntactic-rule system similar to that of hearing children, but with significant delays.

Some researchers have concluded that these delays are so great that some syntactic structures fail to develop at all. In their summary of a series of studies of the syntactic development of persons who are deaf, Quigley, Power, and Steinkamp (1977) reported that many of the syntactic structures usually acquired by hearing children between the ages of 10 and 18 had not been acquired by most 18-year-old persons who are deaf. These include the passive and embedded clauses. Quigley and colleagues also noted that persons who are deaf produce unique syntactic structures that are rarely if ever produced by hearing persons. For example, individuals who are deaf place the negative marker (*no*) outside the sentence, as in *Beth made candy no* (for other examples, see Table 11.2). These structures appear to be rule based, since they are used consistently. Quigley and colleagues suggested adapting reading materials for those who are deaf to include these unique syntactic structures, to facilitate their reading. This would be a difficult and time-consuming task. Alternatively, teachers who are aware that hearing-impaired children may produce unusual syntactic structures can be alert for these constructions and can point out to the children how their language differs from that of standard English.

So, are children who are deaf *delayed* in their development of syntax or is their language *different* from the norm? This is not an easy question to answer. One reason is that researchers have used different methods to study the language development of persons who are deaf. Schirmer's study examined spontaneous spoken language. The studies by Quigley and colleagues gave deaf children a paper-and-pencil test of syntactic skills. Still other studies have analyzed written language samples. Despite these methodology limitations, teachers and other educators can expect that most children with serious hearing impairments will be delayed in their development of syntax. Some structures may not develop at all, whereas some structures may be unique to children with hearing impairments.

Semantic and Pragmatic Development

Research on the emergence of semantic and pragmatic functions in young children with hearing impairment has typically found that pragmatic functions are more fully developed. Skarakis and Prutting (1977), for example, studied the spoken language of four children with hearing impairments (2 to 4 years old) who were being taught to use spoken language. They found that the children used the same semantic and pragmatic

TABLE 11.2 Syntactic Structures of Deaf Students

Structural Environment	Description of Structure	Example Sentences
Conjunction	Marking only first verb	*Beth threw the ball and jean catch it.*
Complementation	Extra "for"	*For to play baseball is fun.*
	Infinitive in place of gerund	*John goes to fish.*
Question formation	Incorrect inversion	*Who TV watched?*
Relativization	Object-subject deletion	*The dog chased the girl had on a red dress.*

Source: Adapted from Quigley, Power, & Steinkamp (1977).

functions as younger, hearing children. However, some higher-order semantic functions were not used by the children with hearing impairment. Similarly, in their study of 12 children with severe and profound hearing impairments, Curtiss, Prutting, and Lowell (1979) found that pragmatic development was very similar to that of hearing children, whereas semantic development lagged far behind. Curtiss and colleagues attributed their results to the fact that the children were primarily using gestures to communicate. They noted that it is very difficult to use gestures to express semantic notions.

Studies directly examining the development of semantic skills in children with hearing impairment have also generally found significant delays and difficulties with receptive vocabulary (Davis, Elfenbein, Schum, & Bentler, 1986), with expressive vocabulary (Easterbrooks, 1987), and with the use of abstract language (Moeller, Osberger, & Morford, 1987). Blamey (2003) has estimated that deaf persons learn vocabulary at about half the rate of hearing children. What causes these difficulties is not known. They may result from the fact that many children who are deaf have not had the range of experiences available to hearing children and that their educational programs have failed to challenge them with language activities and reading materials that enhance semantic skills. Regardless, semantic development appears to be a particular problem for children with serious hearing impairments and should be a focus of instruction.

We have already seen that some studies have found that pragmatic development is relatively intact in young children who are deaf. Although the emergence of pragmatic functions may be delayed, the sequence of development is similar to that of hearing children. Nicholas, Geers, and Kozak (1994) looked at the use of communicative functions by 2-year-old children with hearing impairments compared to two control groups—one matched for chronological age, the other matched for language ability. The researchers found that the children with hearing impairments lagged well behind their same-age hearing peers but were actually ahead of the language-age-matched group. In other words, although they were delayed in the development of communicative functions, children with hearing impairments were ahead of where they should be for their level of language development. The authors suggested that these results may have been due to the fact that the children with hearing impairments participated in an educational program that emphasized communicative interaction.

What about later pragmatic development? There is really very little research in this area. One reason is that many persons who are deaf develop little if any spoken language. Therefore, they have very few opportunities to develop the elusive rules of pragmatics.

This brief review of the spoken-language development of persons who are deaf suggests that significant delays, as well as some language differences, can be expected. There may be several causes of these language impairments. Obviously, the major factor is the hearing impairment itself. With limited opportunity to participate in oral-verbal conversations, children who are deaf do not have the same chance to learn the rules of language. This just seems like common sense. However, the relation between hearing impairments and language development may not be so simple. Some studies (e.g., Davis et al., 1986) have failed to find a clear link between the degree of hearing loss and language and cognitive impairments, while others (e.g., Davis, Shepard, Stelma-chowicz, & Gorga, 1981) *have* reported such a link. In addition to degree of hearing impairment, factors such as parents' efforts, educational programming, and individual differences intrinsic to the child may have significant effects on the language and cognitive development of a child with hearing impairments.

Manual Language

So far we have focused on the development of spoken language in children who are deaf. But some would argue that this focus is entirely wrong, that manual communication (i.e., sign language), not spoken language, is the natural language of those who are deaf. To understand the language development of children who are deaf, the argument goes, look at their development of manual language.

Support for the claim that manual language is the natural language of those who are deaf comes from studies of early communication such as that of Goldin-Meadow and Feldman (1977), who videotaped interaction between hearing parents and their children with hearing impairment. The parents were selected for the study because they had decided that their children should not acquire a manual sign language; therefore, the children were attending an educational program that emphasized spoken language. Yet, when the children were observed interacting with their parents, the researchers found something quite amazing. These children had acquired a number of gestures that could be called signs. They used these gestures consistently and even combined them into "multiword" phrases. Even more surprising was the discovery that the parents themselves, who were opponents of manual language, were unknowingly communicating via sign language. Through careful analysis of their videotapes, Goldin-Meadow and Feldman concluded that the children had developed the signs on their own, while their parents had unconsciously acquired signing from their children.

Researchers who have looked at manual-language development in children who are deaf have found the development following a course similar to that found in hearing children as they acquire a spoken language (Bonvillian, Nelson, & Charrow, 1976; Klima & Bellugi, 1979). For example, deaf children developing a sign language appear to progress through similar stages of "manual babbling" as hearing children learning to speak (Petitto & Marantette, 1991). When first words (signs) develop, they have errors similar to those made by young children learning a vocal language (Schick, 2003). In fact, some researchers have claimed that deaf children learning sign begin to use "words" from three to four months earlier than hearing children developing spoken language (e.g., Anderson & Reilly, 2002). The research on the early development of deaf children learning to sign suggests that language development itself is not impaired in children who are deaf, but rather, the development of *spoken* language is delayed.

It is interesting that a number of studies have found that the later development of English language of deaf children whose parents are deaf is superior to that of deaf children of hearing parents (e.g., Bonvillian, Charrow, & Nelson, 1973; Brasel & Quigley, 1977). It may be that parents who are deaf are more accepting of their deaf child or that early exposure to a manual language sets the stage for acquiring a second (English) language. Geers and Schick (1988) suggest that the *type* of language used by parents (manual or English) is not as important as the opportunity to receive language stimulation. This is an important point for teachers who work with children who are deaf. If Geers and Schick are right, giving children who are deaf the opportunity to engage in language interaction, whether with spoken or manual language, may be most important.

Research on the language development of children who are deaf has led to several important findings. First, spoken-language delays and even some language differences are characteristic of most children who are deaf. However, these delays are *not* found when manual-language development is observed. Therefore, although hearing impairment is clearly an important contributing factor to impairments in spoken-language development, teachers must recognize that other contributing factors (such as parental input and educational programming) are important, as well. Perhaps the most significant consideration is that language needs *stimulation*. When children are exposed to a rich language environment and given the opportunity to interact, they are more likely to develop language skills.

Manual Language versus Spoken Language

There is an ongoing and highly emotional debate in the deaf community about whether children should learn a spoken language or a manual language as their first language. Part of the debate is based on issues of culture and power. The most significant issue is what is best for the ultimate language development of deaf children.

One important question is whether the acquisition of a manual language interferes with the acquisition of spoken language. Marschark and colleagues (2002) note that, although there is evidence that the unique syntactic structure of American Sign Language can affect the speech and writing of deaf children, there is no research evidence that the acquisition of manual language interferes with spoken language acquisition. On the contrary, it may enhance spoken language acquisition. The best advice for parents of deaf children is to interact frequently with their children using every modality available—spoken language, gesture, and sign. Over time, children tend to prefer one mode of communication over another but there appears to be no harm in exposing them to multiple forms of communicative interaction.

Cochlear Implants and Language Development

Cochlear implants are one of those recent innovations that hold great promise for individuals with hearing impairments. These devices work by directly stimulating the auditory nerve fibers, unlike conventional hearing aids that merely amplify sound. A microphone is contained within a wearable speech processor that filters out background noise while enhancing speech signals. These signals are transferred to a receiver implanted in the mastoid bone behind the ear and then to electrodes that have been implanted into the *cochlea,* (inner ear), which, in turn, delivers the sound to the auditory nerve.

Cochlear implants can improve auditory perception and spoken language production but there is still disagreement about the extent of improvements. For example, one study of 70 children who had received cochlear implants found minimal improvement on a test of auditory perception (Meyer et al., 1998). On the other hand, a number of studies have found significant improvements in language skills, especially in younger children who received cochlear implants (Svirsky et al., 2000; Tomblin et al., 2005). In addition to age of implantation, other factors, such as parental interaction and language instruction, can have an impact on the eventual language development of children who receive cochlear implants.

Educational Performance

Since cognitive ability and language development (with the exception of spoken language) is intact in most children with hearing impairments, there is no reason to expect that the educational performance of the children should be below normal. Yet, study after study has found that the educational performance of students with moderate to severe hearing impairments is below that of hearing students, especially in reading and language arts (e.g., Davis et al., 1981; Davis et al., 1986; Gentile, 1972; Phelps & Branyan, 1990). These results have been consistent for many years (LaSasso & Mobley, 1998).

What factors cause the educational deficiencies of deaf and hard-of-hearing students? More importantly, what can be done to improve academic achievement in this population?

Reading

The reading achievement of students who are deaf is an area of particular concern. The average deaf high school graduate reads at a level equal to the average 8- to 9-year-old hearing student, and about 30 percent leave school functionally illiterate (Paul, 1998; Traxler, 2000). Moreover, the average growth rate has been found to be about 0.3 grade level per year (Allen, 1986). That is, with each year of schooling, deaf and hard-of-hearing children appear to fall further behind their hearing peers. This does not mean that every deaf person has poor literacy skills, but a significant portion of the population has literacy deficiencies that can affect subsequent employment and quality of life.

What might account for the reading difficulties of deaf persons? From their review of the literature, Luckner and colleagues (2005/2006) identified five factors:

1. *Obstructed access to the phonological code.* Deaf persons have been found to develop phonological skills more slowly than hearing children and may be less able to use those skills in reading (Sterne & Goswami, 2000).
2. *Limited fluency at the onset of formal schooling.* Many deaf students have limited (or no) experience with the English language. Therefore, they are like second language learners who are simultaneously learning a new language while learning to read the language.
3. *Inadequate literacy experiences in early childhood.* Many deaf children come to school with inadequate experience with print and with books. Their parents read to them less often than parents of hearing children (Paul, 1998). When parents of

deaf children do read to their children, they tend to be more directive with their child, providing less opportunity for interaction with the text (Aram, Most, & Mayafit, 2006).

4. *Delayed acquisition of vocabulary.* Research has found that students who are deaf or hard-of-hearing experience delays in developing their vocabulary knowledge, have smaller lexicons, and acquire new words at slower rates (Lederberg & Spencer, 2001).

5. *Problems with lower-level skills.* Skills such as word recognition, syntax, and morphology skills are inadequate. These form building blocks for reading success.

In addition to these, two other factors may contribute to the reading difficulties of deaf and hard-of-hearing persons—prior knowledge and affect. In order to understand what one reads, it is necessary to refer to previous knowledge. Paul (2003) has suggested that difficulties with the use of prior knowledge may have an impact on reading comprehension. Although there is limited research on affective factors (such as motivation and interest) in deaf readers, it may be that problems in this domain contribute to the poor performance of deaf persons as well.

What can teachers do to help deaf and hard-of-hearing children develop their reading skills? Marschark and colleagues (2002) suggest the use of a balanced literacy approach that combines the teaching of skills emphasized in a basal reader approach with the authentic text reading associated with whole-word approaches to literacy. Unfortunately, there is little research to indicate that this and other approaches commonly used with deaf and hard-of-hearing students (e.g., the language experience approach, bilingual approaches, dialogue journals, predictable books, teaching sight words, teaching figurative language, the use of story retelling) are consistently effective (Luckner et al., 2005/2006). So, the best advice may be to simply provide as many literacy experiences as possible in the classroom, including shared book reading and writing activities while working on the improvement of English language skills.

One approach that has been documented to be effective in a few studies is the use of the Reading Recovery program. Reading Recovery is a one-to-one intervention individually designed to accelerate literacy learning of children identified as "at risk" for reading difficulties. In a study in which first-grade students with severe and profound hearing impairments were included in a Reading Recovery program, all of the students made significant improvements in reading, and nine of the children were on grade level by the end of the year (Charlesworth et al., 2005). Although it is not known if these improvements will hold up over time, the Reading Recovery program may prove useful for some children with significant hearing impairments.

Writing

Writing is another area of concern for students who are deaf. Difficulties in written language are well documented (see Moores, 1996; Yoshinaga-Itano, 1986; Quigley & Paul, 1990). Typically, the writing of students who are deaf is shorter and less complex than that of hearing students (Marschark et al., 2002). In addition, these students make more errors in their writing, including using unnecessary words, omitting essential words, substituting the wrong word, and using incorrect word order (Quigley & Paul, 1990).

When Everhart and Marschark (1988) asked deaf and hearing students, ages 8 to 15 years old, to write a story about what they would do if they were picked up by a UFO, they found that the deaf children produced stories that were shorter, used simpler sentences, and used fewer modifiers. It is especially interesting that the written output of the deaf children was more literal and less imaginative than when they were asked to tell the story through sign language. Clearly, the deaf students had thoughts that were more sophisticated than they were able to express through written language.

What accounts for the poor educational performance of deaf and hard-of-hearing students? Interestingly, one factor that has not proved to be that important is the degree of hearing loss. Instead, the critical factors appear to be language ability (Davis et al., 1986) and educational program. Moores (1992) has pointed out that children who are deaf spend less time than hearing children do on academic subject matter. He cautions that magic solutions to this problem are not likely. The answer, he says, is that "teachers and children must work harder on academic tasks" (p. 3).

Research on the academic achievement of students who are deaf can be viewed in two ways. The pessimistic view is that despite years of effort, the academic achievement of these students has not significantly improved. Children who are deaf still struggle with reading and writing, and the gap between their performance and that of hearing children generally widens with time. The optimistic view is that the factors that appear to cause these academic deficiencies also appear to be subject to remediation. Early intervention, consistent language development, and appropriate educational programs can make a difference. In the next section we will take a look at some of the educational programs that have been developed for children with hearing impairments.

Educational Programs

Although there is general agreement that appropriate educational intervention is essential for children who are deaf, there continues to be a lack of consensus as to what constitutes an appropriate education. For decades there has been a raging debate over the best way to enhance language development. Now there is a new debate about where children who are deaf should be educated. In this section we will examine three aspects of educational programming for these children: language instruction, educational placement, and technological innovations.

Language Instruction—The Great Debate

In her review of the history of U.S. educational programs for persons who are deaf, Lou (1988) divided the history into four periods. In the first period (1817–1860), **manual-language programs** were established. In 1815, Thomas Gallaudet traveled to Europe to learn about the instructional methods developed there for persons who are deaf. It was his intention to visit both types of programs: those emphasizing the development of spoken language and those employing sign language. But, denied access to oral schools, he observed only French schools that emphasized sign language. When he returned to the United States, he established the American School for the Deaf in Hartford, Connecticut. This school became the model for education for people in the United States who are deaf. Since there was no instruction in spoken language, there was complete reliance on sign language for communication. In the first half of the nineteenth century, a significant proportion of the teachers at this and other such schools were themselves deaf.

By the middle part of the century, however, there was a growing interest in the **oral approach** to language development for people with hearing impairments. According to Lou (1988), among the causes of this interest were reports by Horace Mann about the wonderful results European schools for people who are deaf were achieving with the oral approach. By 1867, the first schools emphasizing the oral approach were established in the United States. Meanwhile, even advocates of the manual approach, such as Edward M. Gallaudet (the son of Thomas Gallaudet), were suggesting that oral methods of instruction, such as lipreading and articulation instruction, should be included in the curriculums of manual-based schools. Another strong and influential supporter of the oral-instruction approach was Alexander Graham Bell. Bell opposed any use of sign language, believing that use of it interfered with the development of spoken language.

By the end of the nineteenth century, the "oralists" had won. Both in the United States and around the world, oral programs predominated. For this reason, Lou (1988) called the period from 1900 to 1960 "the period of oral domination" (p. 86). More and more schools for people who were deaf used spoken English as the basis of instruction in their programs. Most schools discouraged students from using manual language. Some even punished students who dared to communicate through sign language. Gallaudet, who had earlier sought to include oral instruction in manual training programs, now argued for the need to retain sign language. One of the unfortunate side effects of the dominance of oral programs was the parallel reduction in the number of teachers who were deaf. In fact, discrimination against these teachers grew to the point where, in the 1920s, Gallaudet College actively discouraged students who were deaf from pursuing teaching careers.

Since 1960, the tide has again turned away from oral-only programs. Now, many educators advocate programs that include both oral and manual methods for teaching persons who are deaf. This new approach, called **total communication,** is actually not that dissimilar to what E. M. Gallaudet was suggesting in the latter part of the nineteenth century. Two developments have contributed to the ascendancy of total communication as the preferred language-instruction method for persons who are deaf. First, American Sign Language (ASL) has become accepted as a language in its own right. Today, most linguists acknowledge that although ASL has a syntactic structure all its own, it is a viable language. With the acceptance of ASL has come a recognition by many that manual language is the natural language of individuals who are deaf. The second development contributing to the rising acceptance of total communication results from research in the 1960s and 1970s reporting that children who were deaf who had parents who were deaf outperformed children who were deaf with hearing parents on academic tasks (e.g., Stevenson, 1964; Brasel & Quigley, 1977). The implication is that children who acquire manual language as their first language have a better chance for academic success.

Today, all three approaches coexist in the education of children who are deaf—oral, manual, and total communication. The goal of oral approaches is to help students become integrated into hearing society through development of skills in understanding and using spoken language. Oral programs use methods such as speech reading (lipreading), auditory training, and speech and language training to reach these goals, with mixed results. Although some programs claim to have high rates of success, many graduates have a difficult time using spoken language. Methods such as speech reading take a long time to learn and are limited in their usefulness.

The goal of manual programs is to enable children who are deaf to develop a first language as quickly as possible. Manual programs use either American Sign Language or a manual language based on English syntax such as Seeing Essential English (SEE I) or Signing Exact English (SEE II) (see Table 11.3). The idea with SEE I and SEE II is that the children with hearing impairments will make more academic progress if they are exposed to a manual-language system that is based on the same syntactic structure as English. Many advocates argue, however, that ASL should be the mode of instruction, since it is the natural language of the deaf; English, if introduced at all, should be used as a second language.

Many education programs for persons who are deaf follow a total communication approach. Quigley and Paul (1990) defined *total communication* as "the philosophy or system which permits any and all methods of communication to be used with deaf children" (p. 25). In actuality, total-communication programs usually combine spoken-language instruction with manual communication. Two examples of total-communication methods are cued speech and the Rochester method. With *cued speech,* hand signals

TABLE 11.3   Types of Sign Language

Sign System	Description	Advantages/Disadvantages
Seeing Essential English (SEE)	Uses ASL signs and invented signs with English syntactic structure	Uses some ASL signs English syntax should make transition to English easier
Signing Exact English (SEE 11)	Modification of SEE I Closer to ASL Uses English syntax	Easier for ASL users
Signed English	Uses ASL signs in English word order	Even closer to ASL Still based in English syntax
American Sign Language (ASL)	Unique syntax Uses both abstract and iconic signs	"Natural" language of deaf persons Syntax differs from English

TABLE 11.4   Intervention Approaches for Persons Who Are Deaf

Program Type	Goals	Methods	Outcomes
Oral/Aural	Development of spoken language Integration into hearing society	Amplification Speech reading Instruction in English Speech therapy	Generally poor intelligibility Reading may be better
Manual communication	Development of a first language Integration into deaf culture	ASL or other sign-language system	Good manual language development Generally poor academic outcomes
Total communication	Develop social, language, and academic skills	Uses both sign- and spoken-language development	Generally fair academic outcomes Some spoken-language development
Bilingual/Bicultural	Develop English as a second language	Builds English language skills on ASL base Emphasizes deaf culture	May be improved academic performance

are used near the face to differentiate speech sounds that look alike in speech reading. The *Rochester method* combines finger spelling with speech. Total-communication approaches can use any combination of spoken and signed language to enhance students' learning. The logic behind total communication seems appealing, but some have argued that total communication approaches can slow down the natural language development of deaf children.

An emerging approach to deaf education is the *bilingual-bicultural (bi-bi)* method. Modeled after English as a Second Language (ESL) programs, bi-bi programs use American Sign Language as the basis of instruction in order to assure that the deaf child has a firm language foundation. These programs also include experiences in deaf culture that emphasize the child's place in a wider community of deaf persons. English language skills are taught after children become competent in ASL. Bilingual-bicultural programs are growing in popularity, with over 40 percent of residential and day-school programs reporting the use of such a program (LaSasso & Lollis, 2003).

The debate about the best approach to teaching children who are deaf is likely to go on for some time. At this point there is no one approach that addresses all the problems faced by persons with hearing loss (see Table 11.4). However, total-communication and bilingual-bicultural programs have emerged as the preferred approaches to instruction because they combine the development of a manual language with the instruction in spoken English that is essential for the development of reading and writing skills.

Educational Placement Issues

Where should children with hearing impairments be educated? In separate schools, as has been the case for most children with hearing impairments for most of the history of education? In separate programs within public schools? Or should children with hearing impairments be included in regular education classes? Although the intellectual debate about inclusion for all children with disabilities has become increasingly strident, the issue is of more than theoretical importance when it comes to the population with hearing impairments. Indeed, the question of inclusion goes to the heart of the debate about the culture and education of persons who are deaf—a topic that has been an underlying theme for many years in the community of persons who are deaf.

The question is at once simple and quite complex. Should the goal of education for students with hearing impairments be to integrate them into hearing society to the maximum extent possible, or should the goal be to prepare children who are deaf to be contributing members of their own culture? Advocates of such a culture argue that most persons who are deaf can never be fully integrated and successful in a hearing society. Therefore, children who are deaf will do best when taught by teachers like themselves and using sign language in programs that respect the beauty of their particular culture. At its most extreme, this culture movement rejects the whole notion of deafness as a disability. Proponents of the movement argue that deafness is a disability only for those who attempt to learn spoken language. Otherwise, deafness is simply a difference (Solomon, 1994).

On the other hand, advocates for inclusion argue that all children, including those with hearing impairments, have the right to be included in regular education programs. Improved amplification technologies, increased use of computers, and other educational innovations increase the likelihood of success for students who are deaf. By in-

---

BOX 11.1

Desiree: A Deaf Student in the Regular Education Classroom

Deseree has a 95 percent hearing loss in each ear and has been diagnosed as "profoundly deaf." Desiree has learned American Sign Language and has also had speech therapy that included lipreading.

For first and second grade, Desiree attended a special program for children with hearing impairments in her county. Students from throughout the county went to a community school where they were included in regular education classrooms most of the day but received intensive speech and language instruction from a speech-language specialist.

Now that she is in the third grade, Desiree is fully included in a regular class in her home school. She still receives daily speech and language instruction. However, her progress has been very slow. Her speech is largely unintelligible. The speech-language specialist has recommended the use of an augmentative communication system, but Desiree's parents have been reluctant to agree so far.

Desiree is supported by a full-time instructional aide who knows some American Sign Language. Mr. Morales, Desiree's third-grade teacher, makes a special effort to face Desiree when he talks to the class. He also tries to include Desiree in the classroom by using more charts and pictures than he has been accustomed to using. He has found Desiree to be eager to learn but he is frustrated by his difficulty communicating with her.

cluding these children in regular education classes, the argument goes, the stigma of disability will be reduced, educational expectations will increase, and children with hearing impairments will have increased opportunities for socialization (see Box 11.1). Citing recommendations from the Individuals with Disabilities Education Act, Fiedler (2001) suggests that the following questions be asked when considering the appropriate educational placement for students with hearing impairments:

1. Communication needs:
   - What does the student need in order to communicate?
   - Does this student use residual hearing efficiently?
   - Does this student need training in a specific communication mode?
2. Language and communication mode
   - What is the student's proficiency in spoken English? (other spoken language?)
   - What is the student's proficiency in written English? (other written language?)
   - What is the student's proficiency in manual communication?
3. Academic level
   - What academic skills does this student have?
   - Does this student have the academic skills to compete with hearing peers?
4. Full range of needs
   - What other needs does this student have that will affect academics, socialization, and emotional development?
   - What are the social and emotional implications of an educational placement for this student?
   - What are the specific needs of this student based on age?
5. Opportunities for direct instruction in the child's language and communication mode
   - Can the student communicate effectively with the teacher?
   - Can the student communicate effectively with other staff in the school?

While the political and cultural debate over where and how to educate deaf children continues, there is clearly a trend to educate these children in more inclusive settings. Data from the 2004–2005 school year show that a majority of deaf students were educated in regular education settings (see Table 11.5) and that nearly half of all deaf students spent the majority of their time in school integrated with hearing students. This is a monumental change in deaf education that has profound implications both for the deaf community and for regular and special educators. "Regular" educators can expect to encounter more children with significant hearing loss in their classrooms. Special educators are likely to be asked to support these children and their teachers in the classroom.

Because an increasing number of deaf and hard-of-hearing children are educated in regular education settings, teachers need to know the most effective ways to successfully include such students. Williams and Finnegan (2003) suggest a number of instructional modifications, including:

1. Face the class when giving instructions.
2. Use the overhead projector, since it allows the teacher to face the class.
3. Use gestures to enhance spoken language.

TABLE 11.5 2004–2005 Educational Placements of Students with Hearing Impairments

Type of Placement	Percentage of Students
Special school	28
Self-contained special education (in regular education setting)	30
Resource room	14
Regular education	47
Home	3
Other	7

Note: Totals exceed 100 percent because respondents could choose more than one placement.
Source: Gallaudet Research Institute (2004–2005). Annual Survey of Deaf and Hard of Hearing Children and Youth. Washington, DC: Gallaudet University, Gallaudet Research Institute.

4. Address the student directly. (If the student has an interpreter, don't say, "What is her favorite book?")
5. Repeat or summarize questions or statements from another student.
6. Provide an outline of the lecture and use advance organizers.

As with all students with disabilities, it is not easy to find a solution to the question of what constitutes the *best* educational placement. Part of the answer lies in what the goals are. If integration into hearing society is expected, then inclusion, with appropriate support, would seem to be the best route. Alternatively, if the goal is integration into a culture for individuals who are deaf, then special programs will be necessary. Part of the answer to the best placement choice should be based on the individual needs and abilities of the child. How does the child currently communicate? What are the child's literacy skills? What goals do the child's parents have for their child?

Technological Aids

Advances in technology hold promise for individuals with hearing impairments. In the past 20 years, there have been remarkable advances in hearing aid technology. New developments in digital technology may mean that researchers are on the threshold of even greater advances. It is important for teachers and other education professionals to understand how to make the best use of these technological advances.

Amplification Devices.   Many types of amplification devices (hearing aids) are in use today. No matter what their shape or where they are worn, all amplification devices work in essentially the same way. A microphone picks up sound and converts it to electrical energy. An amplifier boosts the electrical signal, which is transferred to a receiver that converts the electrical signal back into sound waves. A battery supplies the electrical energy needed to power the components.

Behind-the-ear hearing aids are the most common type for children. It is essential that the hearing aid, which is shaped to fit behind the ear, be fitted properly to avoid feedback of sound. Because of this, the aid must be resized as the child grows. *In-the-*

ear hearing aids are becoming increasingly popular. Although they are small and inconspicuous, they are powerful devices that can provide good sound amplification. However, they may not always be a good choice for young children because they have to be repaired and resized frequently. **FM radio hearing aids** are group amplification devices that permit a teacher's voice to be amplified for a group of students with hearing impairments. With this system, the teacher wears a microphone that transmits on an FM radio frequency being received in an earphone worn by the child. The FM system allows the teacher to move freely around the room and reduces background interference.

All hearing aids work by amplifying the sound entering the ear. Until recently, all sounds—speech and nonspeech—were amplified to the same extent. But today, some hearing aids (such as analog programmable aids and digital signal processing devices) can be matched precisely to the individual's hearing loss. However, these devices can be expensive and may not be available to all children. Although hearing aids are not a perfect solution for every child, they can be useful in helping children in social interactions as well as in the development of language (Marschark et al., 2002).

A problem specific to children is the need to refit the hearing aid as a child grows. In addition, when batteries grow weak and the devices need to be repaired, children may go for days or weeks hearing a weak or nonexistent signal. Some individuals, especially those with more serious hearing impairments, may have hearing that is little improved by amplification. Teachers who work with children who wear amplification devices should check to see that the device is being worn properly and that it is still operational.

Cochlear Implants.   Earlier in this chapter we discussed the impact of cochlear implants on language development. Cochlear implants differ from hearing aids in that they are surgically implanted in the skull to provide a direct connection between incoming sound and the nerves that carry auditory input to the brain. The use of cochlear implants has increased rapidly. By the year 2002, more than 70,000 adults and children were using cochlear implants (Marschark & Spencer, 2003). As evidence grows regarding the positive effect of these implants on language development, children as young as 10 months old are receiving the implants. However, cochlear implants are not a magic solution. In most cases, even after the implant, children need to receive extensive speech and language training. In addition, the effects of cochlear implants on academic and social development have yet to be fully determined.

Although cochlear implants hold great promise in decreasing the effects of many types of deafness, there has been significant controversy within the deaf community about their use. Some advocates claim that the use of an invasive surgical procedure sends a message that deafness is "bad" and needs to be eradicated—with the implication that deaf people are bad. Others express concern that children who receive the operation may be caught between the deaf world and the hearing world—not fully comfortable in either one. Ultimately, parents will need to decide whether cochlear implants are the right choice for their child and their family. Teachers and other education professionals can help by providing research-based information to the family as well as support for whatever decision is made.

Otitis Media

We have seen that moderate to severe hearing disabilities interfere with the ability to understand and use spoken language. But what about milder hearing impairments? Do they also interfere with language development? This is the question posed by the occurrence of **otitis media,** commonly known as middle-ear infection.

Parents of young children sometimes experience being awakened in the middle of the night by howling children who are holding their ears. These children may have otitis media, one of the most common childhood illnesses. By 3 years of age, about two-thirds of all children have experienced at least one bout of otitis media. During the worst phase of the infection, most children experience pain, fever, and fluid in their ears *(effusion)* (Teele, Klein, & Rosner, 1980). However, some children do not exhibit these outward signs of otitis media at all.

During episodes of otitis media there may be a slight loss in hearing ability. This is of no great concern except when the child experiences frequent and long-lasting bouts of otitis media or when the infection goes untreated. Then the child may be at risk for more serious impairments. Since these fluctuating hearing losses occur just at the time when children are beginning to acquire language, there is concern about the effect of chronic, persistent otitis media on language development.

Research on the short-term effects of otitis media on the developing child has been mixed. Some studies (e.g., Wallace, Gravel, McCarton, & Ruben, 1988) have reported that children with otitis media experience delays in the development of expressive language. These delays, if they exist, may be caused by the hearing impairment that results from otitis media (Friel-Patti & Finitzo, 1990). Other studies have failed to find a relationship between otitis media and the development of language in the young child (e.g., Grievink, Peters, van Bron, & Schilder, 1993; Paul, Lynn, & Lohr-Flanders, 1993; Shriberg, Friel-Patti, Flipsen, & Brown, 2000).

While the debate continues on the short-term effects of otitis media on language development, we should still be concerned about the possible long-term effects of persistent bouts of otitis media. Some studies that failed to find a relationship between otitis media and language development at an early age did find that as the children got older, their language development lagged (Roberts, Burchinal, Boch, Footo, & Henderson, 1988). Other research suggests that children with early chronic otitis media are at higher risk for learning disabilities and behavior disorders (Silva, Chalmers, & Stewart, 1986; Reichman & Healey, 1983).

The best advice for parents is to have their child examined by a physician if they suspect their child may be having ear infections. Otitis media can often be treated with drug therapies, but when this approach is not successful, surgery may be necessary. Teachers of younger children can help by looking for the symptoms of otitis media—frequent colds, fluid from the ears, unusual crankiness, and/or difficulty hearing. Teachers of older children should be aware that a history of chronic and persistent otitis media may be related to later problems with language-related activities such as reading and writing. These children may benefit from additional practice on phonological analysis.

Visual Impairment and Language

You were probably not surprised to learn that hearing impairments can have a significant impact on language learning. After all, language is usually relayed by speech and therefore relies on hearing. But what about visual impairments?

What effect, if any, do impairments of vision have on language development? Is it possible that language abilities are actually *enhanced* in those who have visual impairments? There is a widespread belief that individuals with visual impairments develop heightened sensory abilities that enable them to compensate for their vision disability (Erin, 1990). Conversely, is it possible that visual impairments *interfere* with language development—causing delays and even developmental differences?

Defining Visual Impairment

Before examining the evidence on the language abilities of individuals with visual impairments, we first need to define this population. This is not such an easy task. Dekker and Koole (1992) note that the population with visual impairments is often divided into low vision and blind, but there is a good deal of disagreement as to just how to measure vision. The researchers go on to report that there are as many as 65 definitions of **blindness** in the professional literature. Disagreement among professionals about the best way to define visual impairments is likely to continue, but the Individuals with Disabilities Education Act (IDEA) defines *visually handicapped* as "a visual impairment which, even with correction, adversely affects educational performance." For educational purposes, however, a child who learns primarily through tactile or auditory input is considered blind. For legal purposes, a person considered to be blind must have visual acuity of 20/200 or less in the better eye, after correction. A child is generally considered to be **low vision** if the child can benefit from the use of optical aids and environmental and instructional modifications (e.g., preferential seating or enlarged print) in order to learn.

Early Development

Studies of the early development of children who are blind have generally found that the timing and sequence of their language development is very much like that of sighted children, but there are some qualitative developmental differences. For example, Bigelow (1987) studied the emergence of the first 50 words in three congenitally blind children (ages 9 to 21 months). She found that the timing and growth of these first words was quite similar to that of sighted children. In addition, Bigelow found that blind children tend to talk about the same kinds of things as sighted children. They use nouns and verbs that reflect their personal experiences. However, the specific referents named by blind children often differed from those reported in studies of sighted children. Not surprisingly, blind children tended to use words that described objects that could be heard (*piano, drum, bird*) or actually experienced (*dirt, powder*).

Other studies have discovered additional differences in the early language acquisition of blind children. For example, young blind children have been found to be slightly delayed in learning sounds that are visually distinctive (e.g., sounds that can be "seen" on the lips) (Perez-Pererira & Conti-Ramsden, 1998). Andersen, Dunlea, and Kekelis (1984) found that the children with visual impairments they studied rarely used overextensions or idiosyncratic forms of language. As children learn new words, it is not uncommon for them to extend these words incorrectly to other similar items *(overextension)* or to make up words *(idiosyncratic)*. Yet, Andersen and colleagues did not find this same phenomenon in the children they observed. They suggested that blind children were learning words as a whole—via imitation—not experimenting with words, as do sighted children. The result, they claim, is that blind children "have less understanding of words as symbolic vehicles and are slower to form hypotheses about word meaning than sighted children" (p. 661).

The early experiences of blind children may influence the subtle inconsistencies in their language development. For example, although the motor development of blind children in the first few months of life is similar to that of sighted infants, later motor development of blind children tends to be delayed. Also, blind children are often slower to crawl and walk. There may be many reasons for these delays, including lack of visual stimulation and parental overprotectiveness, but whatever the reasons, less movement means less opportunity to explore and experience the world. Limited experience may, in turn, lead to delays in the development of some cognitive concepts.

Bigelow (1990) examined the development of cognition and language in three children with vision loss. Mothers kept a record of the first 50 words spoken by their children, and the children were tested on 10 tasks that measure aspects of the development of object permanence. Bigelow found that the beginning of word usage and the rate of word acquisition by the three children were quite similar to those of sighted children. However, there were some differences in the development of object permanence. One child, who was not totally blind, showed no differences from the development of sighted children, but two other children, both of whom were totally blind, were delayed in their object permanence development. Bigelow suggested that blind children may have more difficulty *decentering*—that is, taking the perspective of another person. Consequently, it takes them longer to develop *object permanence*—the understanding that things that are not present are not gone forever. Understanding delays in object-permanence development may help us understand why at least some blind children talk primarily about present objects and events rather than those in the past and future.

In addition to some motor and cognitive differences, some researchers have reported that interaction between blind children and their parents differs from that observed between parents and their sighted children (Kekelis & Andersen, 1984; Urwin, 1984). This should come as no surprise. After all, many of the early communicative exchanges between infants and their caregivers are visual—baby looks at mom, mom smiles, baby gurgles. The baby who is blind lacks an important means of initiating interaction, while the mother is deprived of the subtle cues provided by her baby's eye contact. Blind infants do attempt to communicate, but their cues are often hard to discern and parents must be on the lookout for subtle hints that the baby wants to communicate. It is interesting to note that research has found that blind children whose parents were more responsive to them had better pragmatic language skills (Dote-Kwan & Hughes, 1994).

In their study, Kekelis and Andersen (1984) reported specific differences in the way that parents talk to their young blind children. For example, they found that parents of blind children used more commands and more requests for action, whereas parents of sighted children used more requests for information. Also, parents of blind children tended to label the objects with which their children interacted *(That's your belly)* whereas parents of sighted children provided richer, more detailed information about the objects. These differences, although subtle, may help account for the differences in early language development often found in blind children.

There appear to be some subtle, but significant, differences in the early language development of blind children (see Table 11.6 for a summary of the research). Although the timing and sequence of their development is similar to that of sighted children, there are some qualitative differences. For example, children with significant visual impairments are more likely to talk about things they have *heard and touched,* they tend to learn words as a whole, and they appear to have delays in the development of object permanence—this is especially true for children with more serious visual impairments. These differences in language development may be the result of more limited opportunities to experience the world and/or to deficient parent–child interaction. The good news is that these are factors that teachers and other education professionals can address in the classroom. Later, we will discuss some ways to increase the world experiences and communicative interactions of children with visual impairments.

TABLE 11.6   Summary of Studies of the Early Language Development of Children with Visual Impairments

Study	Subjects	Results
Bigelow (1987)	3 congenitally blind children (9–21 mo.)	Timing and growth rate of first words similar to sighted
Andersen, Dunlea, & Kekelis (1984)	6 young children (9–40 mos.) with varying degrees of blindness	Types of words similar to sighted, but specific referents differed Words used for objects that can be heard and touched
Bigelow (1990)	3 young children with visual impairments (9–26 mos.)	Rarely used overextensions and idiosyncratic words Seemed to be learning words by imitation
Kekelis & Andersen (1984)	6 children (12–36 mos.) with varying degrees of blindness	Delays in object permanence for the two blind children No delays for child with visual impairment Parents of blind children were highly directive and initiated more topics

Language Characteristics

Like other children with disabilities, children with visual impairments are a heterogeneous group. Many factors other than their disability affect their learning, including the cause of their visual impairment, home environment, educational history, and opportunities for learning; however, it is possible to make some generalizations about the language development of children with visual impairments.

Phonology

Although research on the acquisition of phonology in blind children is limited, the evidence suggests that perception of sound is not significantly different from that of sighted children. Although there may be delays in the acquisition of some sounds, the ability to perceive speech may actually be more advanced. Similarly, the rate and pattern of sound production has generally been found to be similar to that of sighted children.

Syntax

Generally, researchers have found few differences between blind and sighted persons in their development of syntax. Utterance length, a measure of syntactic development, has been found to be the same (Landau & Gleitman, 1985) or slightly shorter in blind children when compared to sighted children (Erin, 1990). However, blind children use fewer different sentence types and tend to use a few types repeatedly (Erin, 1990).

Semantics

Earlier we reviewed research by Andersen and colleagues and by Bigelow that found that the early semantic development of blind children differs in subtle ways from that of sighted children. Blind children talk about different things. They talk more about items that are immediately present in their environment and less about the past and the future. Erin (1990) reported that the children with visual loss in her study used imaginative play less frequently. One specific problem that has been frequently reported is in pronoun usage (Fraiberg, 1977; Erin, 1990). Blind children often confuse *I* and *you.*

For many years it was claimed that blind children developed *verbalisms* (Cutsforth, 1951); that is, they used words without understanding the words' meanings. When blind children used a word such as *white* or *black,* it was thought that they could not possibly understand such a word, that they must just be parroting what they had previously heard. However, more recent research has found that although blind children may develop idiosyncratic meanings, their word usage is much like that of sighted children (Civelli, 1983). Although there may be some specific differences between blind and sighted children in their semantic development, these differences appear to be subtle and limited in scope.

FIGURE 11.3   Summary of Language Development of Children with Visual Impairments

Phonology	Delays in the acquisition of some sounds
	Rate and pattern of sound production similar to that of sighted children (Perez-Pererira & Conti-Ramsden, 1998)
Syntax	Utterance length same or slightly shorter (Landau & Gleitman, 1985; Erin, 1990)
	Fewer sentence types used (Erin, 1990)
Semantics	Less imaginative play used (Erin, 1990)
	Confusion of pronouns (Fraiberg, 1977; Erin, 1990)
	Idiosyncratic meanings used (Civelli, 1983)
Pragmatics	Idiosyncratic gestures (Fraiberg, 1977)
	Misleading body postures (Urwin, 1984)
	Inappropriate and less frequent nonverbal cues (Parke, Shallcross, & Anderson, 1980)
	Less awareness of need to adjust speech to needs of listener (Freeman & Blockberger, 1987; Erin, 1990)

Pragmatics

Research on the pragmatic language of blind persons is rather sparse, but what there is again suggests some subtle differences. For example, the research literature reports the use of idiosyncratic gestures (Fraiberg, 1977) and changes in body posture (Urwin, 1984) that may cause the listener to misinterpret what a person with visual impairment is trying to communicate. Parke, Shallcross, and Anderson (1980) also found some subtle differences in nonverbal communication when they compared the videotaped interactions of 30 blind children and a similar number of sighted children. Specifically, they found that many of the blind children smiled constantly (and inappropriately), nodded less frequently to signal understanding, and raised their eyebrows inappropriately. Any one of these behaviors might seem trivial in itself, but any taken together could cause some misunderstanding of communicative intent. Differences in vocal quality have been found as well. Children who are blind often speak in a loud, strident voice (perhaps because they are not sure of the distance between them and the speaker) and show less awareness of the need to adapt their speech to the needs of the listener (Freeman & Blockberger, 1987; Erin, 1990) (see Figure 11.3 for a summary of the research).

The effects of visual impairments on language, as we have seen, tend to be subtle but widespread. In particular, there are delays in the development of some semantic concepts (pronouns and words that require vision) and in several aspects of pragmatics. These language differences may have an impact on the academic and social development of children with visual impairment.

Literacy Development

There is surprisingly little research on the acquisition and development of literacy skills by blind and visually impaired children. Clearly, children with mild to moderate visual impairments face significant challenges in learning to read. If their impairments are identified early and appropriate compensatory methods are used, they should be able to acquire reading and writing skills at a similar rate as sighted children. Teachers need to be aware of resources that are available from organizations such as the American Printing House for the Blind (www.aph.org) and the National Library Service for the Blind (www.loc.gov/nls).

Children with significant visual impairments are often taught to read braille. Braille is a written language system that uses a series of raised dots to represent words (see Figure 11.4). As Dodd and Conn (2000) point out, children learning to read braille start out at a disadvantage, since they would generally not have had any experience reading braille prior to starting school. In their own studies of 7- to 12-year-old blind children learning to read braille, Dodd and Conn found an average delay of 9 months in reading compared to sighted children, However, they attributed most of this difference to the structure of braille itself rather than to the effects of blindness.

Children with significant visual impairments are at risk for difficulties with reading comprehension. As Steinman, LeJeune, and Kimbrough (2006) note, blind children typically lack the early experiences available to sighted children. So, when they read a story about an firetruck, for example, they have no direct experience with this concept. Teachers should be aware of this potential problem and take the time to explain crucial concepts in text.

The limited research on the effects of visual impairments on reading and writing skills suggests that blind children may experience some delays, especially in comprehension, but that, with appropriate instruction and accommodations, they can attain high levels of literacy.

FIGURE 11.4 Braille Alphabet

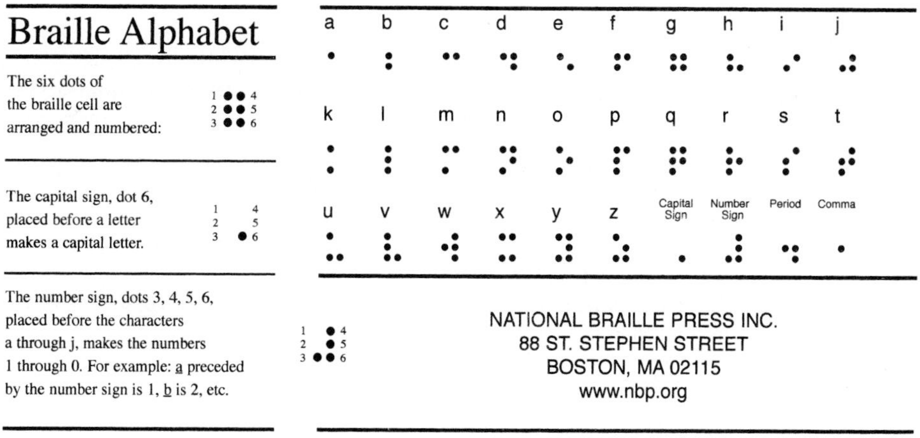

Source: Used with Permission of National Braille Press, www.braille.com <http://www.braille.com>

Implications for Teaching

Since there is a good deal of variation in the language and communication skills of children with visual impairments, teachers and other education professionals should be careful to observe and assess individual children. Do they have delays in development? Are essential vocabulary words missing? Do they have difficulty conveying their messages and understanding what others say? Freeman and Blockberger (1987) caution that some language differences may reflect an adaptation to blindness. At times language differences may be caused by other disabilities the child may have, in addition to impairment of vision. When intervention is necessary, they suggest that strategies should focus on:

- Helping the child compensate for lack of visual stimulation through use of other sources of information
- Helping parents learn how to interact with their blind child
- Altering those behaviors that interfere with successful communication

Our review of the language problems associated with visual impairments suggests that the following areas may be appropriate targets for intervention:

- Vocabulary development
- Use of nonverbal communication
- Voice modulation
- Varying language for different communication situations
- Pronoun usage

One of the best ways to enhance language skills is to engage the child in communicative exchanges. Kekelis and Andersen (1984) provide suggestions that parents can use to enhance their interaction with their blind children (see Figure 11.5). These suggestions would be useful for teachers to consider as well.

FIGURE 11.5   Suggestions for Enhancing Interaction with Blind Children

---

- Use rich detail and variation in language input.
- In speaking, be responsive to the child's own interests.
- Present communication in a natural manner.
- Expand the child's messages. (If the child says, *Blanket,* the parent may respond, *Here's your blanket. It's soft, isn't it.)*
- Create a stimulating environment with items that appeal to the child's interests.
- Include the child in everyday routines.
- Inform the child about what other people are doing.

Source: Adapted from Kekelis & Andersen (1984).

If teachers and parents create a stimulating environment where there is plenty of opportunity for learning about the world and for communicative interaction, it is likely that most children with visual impairment will develop good language skills. They may continue to have specific problems with words that rely on visual input (e.g., colors) and with nonverbal communication, but these difficulties should be minimized by effective teaching.

Summary

In this chapter we have examined the impact of sensory disabilities on language and communication development. Hearing impairments can have significant effects on spoken-language development. Even so, the ability to develop a language (including sign language) remains intact. Despite intact cognitive abilities, children with hearing impairments frequently have a difficult time acquiring written language skills. Although language impairments do not generally come to mind when we think about children with vision disabilities, difficulties with language are also frequently present.

A good deal of disagreement exists about the best way to teach children who have hearing impairments. Advocates of the oral approach stress the need for children who are deaf to become integrated into a hearing society. Proponents of the use of sign language claim that this is the "natural" language of individuals who are deaf. Current instructional practices attempt to combine elements of both approaches.

The impact of visual impairments on language acquisition and development is more subtle. There may be delays in early development, especially in the acquisition of words. But, in general, language develops at about the same rate as in sighted children.

Teachers and other education professionals need to understand the impact of sensory disabilities on language, especially since so many children with these disabilities are being integrated into regular education settings. Effective management of instruction for these children will be critical for their academic and social success.

REVIEW QUESTIONS

1. Briefly describe the difference between the terms *deaf* and *hard-of-hearing*.

2. Fill in the blank with the correct type of hearing impairment:

   _____ results from damage to structures that transmit sound from the ear to the brain.

   _____ is caused by damage to the brain.

   _____ is caused by problems with transmission of sound from the outer to the middle ear.

3. Contrast the educational adjustments and strategies that would be needed for a child with a mild versus a severe hearing impairment.

4. In addition to degree of hearing loss, what other factors should be considered in determining the impact of a hearing impairment?

5. What conclusions can be drawn about the cognitive abilities of persons who are deaf?

6. Some researchers have argued that the syntactic development of persons who are deaf is delayed; others have claimed that it is different from the norm. Briefly review the evidence in support of each of these positions.

7. What factors might explain the generally poor academic outcomes of persons with hearing impairments?

8. Compare and contrast the goals, methods, and outcomes of both the oral and the manual approaches to the education of individuals who are deaf.

9. Contrast the vision abilities and the implications for teaching blind children with those of children with low vision.

10. List three of the specific differences in language that have been found in persons with significant vision impairments.

11. Give three suggestions that teachers could use in the classroom to enhance the language of children with severe visual impairments.

S U G G E S T E D   A C T I V I T I E S

1. Arrange to attend a cultural activity sponsored by, or largely attended by, persons who are deaf. This might be a theater play, a social event, or some other activity.
   Report on your feelings about your participation in this activity. Did you understand what was going on? Did you feel left out?

2. Try to simulate the experience of deafness with one of the following activities:

   a. Turn off the sound as you watch television. How much can you understand about what is going on?

   b. How does your viewing differ from when you can hear the sound?

   c. Try lipreading. Put earplugs in your ears, and see how well you can read the lips of those around you. What problems do you encounter in doing this?

3. Reread the case study of Marisol—the child with a severe visual impairment who is included in a regular education classroom. Analyze the case carefully and respond to the following questions:

   a. What kinds of support has Marisol received to assist her in the classroom?

   b. What could be done to help Marisol increase interactions with her peers?

   c. What could Marisol's teachers do to improve their collaboration?

G L O S S A R Y

audiogram: a graph on which the results of a hearing examination are recorded

blindness: visual acuity of 20/200 or less in the better eye, after correction

central hearing loss: a hearing disability caused by damage to the brain

cochlear implants: a sensory aid that is implanted into the ear to stimulate the auditory nerve fibers

conductive hearing loss: a hearing disability caused by a problem with transmission of sound from the outer to the middle ear

deaf: a hearing disability that precludes successful processing of linguistic information through audition, with or without a hearing aid

FM radio hearing aid: a type of sensory aid in which the speaker uses a microphone and the listener wears headphones to receive the signal

hard-of-hearing: a hearing disability in which there is sufficient residual hearing for successful processing of linguistic information through audition, generally with the use of a hearing aid

hearing impairment: a hearing disability ranging from mild to profound; includes the subsets of deaf and hard-of-hearing

low vision: a vision disability in which the individual can generally benefit from the use of optical aids and environmental and instructional modifications in order to learn

manual language programs: an instructional approach for deaf persons that emphasizes the acquisition of a manual signing system

mild hearing loss: a hearing loss in the range of 15 to 30 dB that causes minimal hearing difficulties

moderate hearing loss: a hearing loss in the range of 31 to 60 dB in which there may be significant delays in speech and language development

oral approach: an instructional approach for deaf persons that emphasizes the maximization of residual hearing and acquisition of spoken language

otitis media: middle-ear infection that can cause mild to moderate fluctuating hearing loss

profound hearing loss: a hearing loss greater than 90 dB in which the individual can hear little if anything

sensorineural hearing loss: a hearing disability caused by damage to structures that transmit sound from the ear to the brain and often involves auditory nerve damage

severe hearing loss: a hearing disability in the range of 61 to 90 dB caused by damage to structures that transmit sound from the ear to the brain, causing considerable difficulty hearing normal speech and delays in speech and language development

total communication: an instructional approach for deaf persons that utilizes methods drawn from both the oral-aural and manual instructional models

RESOURCES ON THE WEB

www.agbell.org Alexander Graham Bell Association for the Deaf and Hard of Hearing

http://clerccenter.gallaudet.edu/ Laurent Clerc National Deaf Education Center

www.aslta.org American Sign Language Teachers Association

www.nad.org National Association of the Deaf

www.nidcd.nih.gov National Institute on Deafness and Other Communication Disorders

www.afb.org American Foundation for the Blind

www.lighthouse.org Lighthouse International, an advocacy organization for persons with vision impairments

www.nei.nih.gov National Eye Institute

REFERENCES

Allen, T. (1986). Patterns of academic achievement among hearing impaired students: 1974 and 1983. In A. Schildroth & M. Karchmer (Eds.), *Deaf children in America* (pp. 161–206). San Diego, CA: Little, Brown.

Anderson, D., & Reilly, J. S. (2002). The MacArthur Communicative Development Inventory: Normative data for American Sign Language. *Journal of Deaf Studies and Deaf Education, 7,* 83–106.

Andersen, E., Dunlea, A., & Kekelis, L. (1984). Blind children's language: Resolving some differences. *Journal of Child Language, 11,* 645–664.

Aram, D., Most, T., & Mayafit, H. (2006). Contributions of mother-child storybook telling and joint writing. *Language, Speech, and Hearing Services in Schools, 37,* 209–223.

Bigelow, A. (1987). Early words of blind children. *Journal of Child Language, 14,* 47–56.

Bigelow, A. (1990). Relationship between the development of language and thought in young blind children. *Journal of Visual Impairment and Blindness, 84,* 414–419.

Blamey, P. J. (2003). Development of spoken language by deaf children. In M. Marschark and P. Spencer (Eds.), *Deaf studies, language, and education* (pp. 232–246). New York: Oxford University Press.

Bonvillian, J., Charrow, V., & Nelson, K., (1973). Psycholinguistic and educational implications of deafness. *Human Development, 16,* 321–345.

Bonvillian, J., Nelson, K., & Charrow, V. (1976). Language and language-related skills in deaf and hearing children. *Sign Language Studies, 12,* 211–250.

Brasel, K., & Quigley, S. (1977). The influence of certain language and communication environments in early childhood on the development of language in deaf individuals. *Journal of Speech and Hearing Research, 20,* 95–107.

Brown, J. (1984). Examination of grammatical morphemes in the language of hard-of-hearing children. *Volta Review, 86,* 229–238.

Charlesworth, A., Charlesworth, R., Raban, B., & Rickards, F. (2005). Reading Recovery for children with hearing loss. *The Volta Review, 106,* 29–51.

Civelli, E. (1983). Verbalism in young blind children. *Journal of Visual Impairment and Blindness, 77,* 61–63.

Curtiss, S., Prutting, C., & Lowell, E. (1979). Pragmatic and semantic development in young children with impaired hearing. *Journal of Speech and Hearing Research, 22,* 534–552.

Cutsforth, T. (1951). *The blind in school and society: A psychological study.* American Foundation for the Blind.

Davis, J., Elfenbein, J., Schum, R., & Bentler, R. (1986). Effects of mild and moderate hearing impairments on language, educational, and psychosocial behavior of children. *Journal of Speech and Hearing Disorders, 51,* 53–62.

Davis, J., Shepard, N., Stelmachowicz, P., & Gorga, M. (1981). Characteristics of hearing impaired children in the public schools: Part II—Psychoeducational data. *Journal of Speech and Hearing Disorders, 46,* 130–137.

Dekker, R., & Koole, E. (1992). Visually impaired children's visual characteristics and language. *Developmental Medicine and Child Neurology, 34,* 123–133.

Dodd, B., & Conn, L. (2000). The effect of braille orthography on blind children's phonological awareness. *Journal of Research in Reading, 23,* 1–11.

Dote-Kwan, J., & Hughes, M. (1994). The home environments of young blind children. *Journal of Visual Impairment and Blindness, 88,* 31–42.

Easterbrooks, S. (1987). Speech/language assessment and intervention with school-age hearing-impaired children. In J. Alpiner & P. McCarthy (Eds.), *Rehabilitative audiology: Children and adults* (pp. 188–240). Baltimore: Williams and Wilkins.

Emmorey, K., & Kosslyn, S. (1996). Enhanced image generation abilities in deaf signers: A right hemispere effect. *Brain and Cognition, 32,* 28–44.

Erin, J. (1990). Language samples from visually impaired four- and five-year-olds. *Journal of Childhood Communication Disorders, 13,* 181–191.

Everhart, V., & Marschark, M. (1988). Linguistic flexibility in signed and written language productions of deaf children. *Journal of Experimental Child Psychology, 46,* 174–193.

Fiedler, B. (2001). Considering placement and educational approaches for students who are deaf and hard of hearing. *Teaching Exceptional Children, 34,* 54–59.

Fraiberg, S. (1977). *Insights from the blind.* London: Souvenir Press.

Freeman, R., & Blockberger, S. (1987). Language development and sensory disorder: Visual and hearing impairments. In W. Yule & M. Rutter (Eds.), *Language development and disorders* (pp. 234–247). Philadelphia: J. B. Lippincott.

Friel-Patti, S., & Finitzo, T. (1990). Language learning in a prospective study of otitis media with effusion in the first two years of life. *Journal of Speech and Hearing Research, 33,* 188–194.

Furth, H. (1973). *Deafness and learning: A psychosocial approach.* Belmont, CA: Wadsworth.

Furth, H., & Youniss, J. (1971). Formal operations and language: A comparison of deaf and hearing adolescents. *International Journal of Psychology, 6,* 49–64.

Gallaudet Research Institute. (2006). *2004–2005 annual survey of deaf and hard of hearing children and youth.* Washington, DC: Gallaudet University, Gallaudet Research Institute.

Gallaway, C., & Woll, B. (1994). Interaction and childhood deafness. In C. Gallaway & B. Richards (Eds.), *Input and interaction in language acquisition* (pp. 197–218). Cambridge: Cambridge University Press.

Geers, A., & Schick, B. (1988). Acquisition of spoken and signed English by hearing-impaired children of hearing-impaired or hearing parents. *Journal of Speech and Hearing Disorders, 53,* 136–143.

Gentile, A. (1972). *Academic achievement test results of a national testing program for hearing impaired students: 1971.* Annual Survey of Hearing-Impaired Children and Youth. Gallaudet College Office of Demographic Studies, Ser. D, No. 9.

Goldin-Meadow, S., & Feldman, H. (1977). The development of language-like communication without a language model. *Science, 197,* 401–403.

Grievink, E., Peters, S., van Bron, W., & Schilder, A. (1993). The effects of early bilateral otitis media with effusion on language ability: A prospective cohort study. *Journal of Speech and Hearing Research, 36,* 1004–1012.

Individuals with Disabilities Education Act. (2004). Washington, DC: U.S. Government Printing Office.

Karchmer, M. A., & Mitchell, R. E. (2003). Demographic and achievement characteristics of deaf and hard-of-hearing students. In M. Marschark & P. Spencer (Eds.), *Deaf studies, language, and education* (pp. 21–37). New York: Oxford University Press.

Kekelis, L., & Andersen, E. (1984). Family communication styles and language development. *Journal of Visual Impairment and Blindness, 78,* 54–65.

Klima, E., & Bellugi, U. (1979). *The signs of language.* Cambridge, MA: Harvard University Press.

Kusche, C. A., Greenberg, M. T., & Garfield, T. S. (1983). Nonverbal intelligence and verbal achievement in deaf adolescents: An examination of heredity and environment. *American Annals of the Deaf, 128,* 458–466.

Landau, B., & Gleitman, L. (1985). *Language and experience: Evidence from the blind child.* Cambridge, MA: Harvard University Press.

LaSasso, C., & Lollis, J. (2003). Survey of residential and day schools for deaf students in the United States that identify themselves as bilingual-bicultural. *Journal of Deaf Studies and Deaf Education, 8,* 79–91.

LaSasso, C., & Mobley, R. (1998). National survey of reading instruction for deaf or hard-of-hearing students in the U.S. *The Volta Review, 99,* 31–58.

Lederberg, A., & Everhart, V. (1998). Communication between deaf children and their hearing mothers: The role of language, gesture, and vocalizations. *Journal of Speech, Language, and Hearing Research, 41,* 887–899.

Lederberg, A. R., & Spencer, P. E. (2001). Vocabulary development of deaf and hard of hearing children. In M. D. Clark, M. Marschark, & M. Karchmer (Eds.), *Context, cognition, and deafness* (pp. 88–112). Washington, DC: Gallaudet University Press.

Lou, M. (1988). The history of language use in the education of the deaf in the United States. In M. Strong (Ed.), *Language learning and deafness* (pp. 79–98). New York: Cambridge University Press.

Luckner, J. L., Sebald, A. M., Cooney, J., Young III, J., & Muir, S. G. (2005/2006). An examination of the evidence-based literacy research in deaf education. *American Annals of the Deaf, 150,* 443–456.

Marschark, M., Lang, H. G., & Albertini, J. A. (2002). *Educating deaf students: From research to practice.* New York: Oxford University Press.

Marschark, M., & Spencer, P. (Eds.). (2003). *Deaf studies, language, and education.* New York: Oxford University Press.

McGarr, N. (1983). The intelligibility of deaf speech to experienced and inexperienced listeners. *Journal of Speech and Hearing Research, 26,* 451–458.

Meyer, T., Svirsky, M., Kirk, K., & Miyamoto, R. (1998). Improvements in speech perception with profound prelingual hearing loss: Effects of device, communication mode, and chronological age. *Journal of Speech and Hearing Research, 41,* 846–858.

Moeller, M., Osberger, M., & Morford, J. (1987). Speech-language assessment and intervention with preschool hearing-impaired children. In J. Alpiner & P. McCarthy (Eds.), *Rehabilitative audiology: Children and adults* (pp. 163–187). Baltimore: Williams and Wilkins.

Monsen, R. (1983). The oral speech intelligibility of hearing-impaired talkers. *Journal of Speech and Hearing Disorders, 48,* 286–296.

Moores, D. (1992). Take longer steps faster, work more hours harder. *American Annals of the Deaf, 137,* 3.

Moores, D. (1996). *Educating the deaf. Psychology, principles, and practices* (3rd ed.). Boston: Houghton-Mifflin.

Myklebust, H. (1960). *The psychology of deafness.* New York: Grune & Stratton.

Nicholas, J., Geers, A., & Kozak, V. (1994). Development of communicative function in young hearing-impaired and normally hearing children. *Volta Review, 96,* 113–135.

Oller, D. K., & Eilers, R. E. (1988). The role of audition in infant babbling. *Child Development, 59,* 441–449.

Oller, D., Eilers, R., Bull, D., & Carney, A. (1985). Prespeech vocalizations of a deaf infant: A comparison with normal meta-phonological development. *Journal of Speech and Hearing Research, 28,* 47–63.

Oller, D., Jensen, H., & LaFayette, R. (1978). The relatedness of phonological processes of a hearing-impaired child. *Journal of Communication Disorders, 11,* 97–105.

Owens, R. E., Metz, D. E., & Haas, A. (2007). *Communication disorders: A lifetime perspective* (3rd ed.). Boston: Allyn & Bacon.

Parke, K., Shallcross, R., & Anderson, R. (1980). Differences in coverbal behavior between blind and sighted persons during dyadic communication. *Visual Impairment and Blindness, 74,* 142–146.

Paul, P. V. (1998). *Literacy and deafness: The development of reading, writing, and literate thought.* Boston: Allyn & Bacon.

Paul, P. V. (2003). Processes and components of reading. In M. Marschark & P. Spencer (Eds.), *Deaf studies, language, and education* (pp. 97–109). New York: Oxford University Press.

Paul, R., Lynn, T., & Lohr-Flanders, M. (1993). History of middle ear involvement and speech/language development in late talkers. *Journal of Speech and Hearing Research, 36,* 1055–1062.

Perez-Pererira, M., & Conti-Ramsden, G. (1998). *Language development and social interaction in blind children.* Hove, UK: Psychology Press.

Petitto, L. A., & Marantette, P. F. (1991). Babbling in the manual mode: Evidence for the ontogeny of language. *Science, 251,* 1493–1496.

Phelps, L., & Branyan, B. (1990). Academic achievement and nonverbal intelligence in public school hearing-impaired children. *Psychology in the Schools, 27,* 210–217.

Quigley, S., & Paul, P. (1990). *Language and deafness.* San Diego, CA: Singular Publishing.

Quigley, S., Power, D., & Steinkamp, M. (1977). The language structure of deaf children. *Volta Review, 79,* 73–84.

Ratner, N. B. (2005). Atypical language development. In J. Gleason (Ed.), *The development of language* (3rd ed.) (pp. 324–394). Boston: Allyn & Bacon.

Reichman, J., & Healey, W. (1983). Learning disabilities and conductive hearing loss involving otitis media. *Journal of Learning Disabilities, 16,* 272–278.

Roberts, J., Burchinal, M., Koch, M., Footo, M., & Henderson, F. (1988). Otitis media in early childhood and its relationship to later phonological development. *Journal of Speech and Hearing Disorders, 53,* 416–424.

Russell, W., Power, D., & Quigley, S. (1976). *Linguistics and deaf children.* Washington, DC: Alexander Graham Bell Association for the Deaf.

Schick, B. (2003). The development of American Sign Language and manually coded English language systems. In M. Marschark & P. Spencer (Eds.), *Deaf studies, language, and education* (pp. 219–231). New York: Oxford University Press.

Schirmer, B. (1985). An analysis of the language of young hearing-impaired children in terms of syntax, semantics, and use. *American Annals of the Deaf, 130,* 15–19.

Shriberg, L. D., Friel-Patti, S., Flipsen, P., & Brown, R. C. (2000). Otitis media, fluctuant hearing loss, and speech-language outcomes; A preliminary structural equation model. *Journal of Speech, Language, and Hearing Research, 43,* 100–120.

Silva, P., Chalmers, D., & Stewart, I. (1986). Some audiological, psychological, educational and behavioral characteristics of children with bilateral otitis media with effusion: A longitudinal study. *Journal of Learning Disabilities, 19,* 165–169.

Skarakis, E., & Prutting, C. (1977). Early communication: Semantic functions and communicative intentions in the communication of the pre-school child with impaired hearing. *American Annals of the Deaf, 122,* 383–391.

Solomon, A. (1994). Defiantly deaf. *New York Times Magazine,* August 28, p. 38.

Spencer, P. E. (2000). Looking without listening: Is audition a prerequisite for normal development of visual attention during infancy? *Journal of Deaf Studies and Deaf Education, 5,* 291–302.

Steinman, B. A., LeJeune, B. J., & Kimbrough, B. T. (2006). Developmental stages of reading processes in children who are blind and sighted. *Journal of Visual Impairment & Blindness, 100,* 36–46.

Sterne, A., & Goswami, U. (2000). Phonological awareness of syllables, rhymes, and phonemes in deaf children. *Journal of Child Psychology and Psychiatry, 41,* 609–625.

Stevenson, E. (1964). A study of the educational achievement of deaf children of deaf parents. *California News.* Berkeley: California School for the Deaf.

Svirsky, M. A., Robbins, A. M., Kirk, K. I., Pisoni, D. B., & Miyamoto, R. T. (2000). Language development in profoundly deaf children with cochlear implants. *Psychological Science, 11,* 153–158.

Teele, D., Klein, J., & Rosner, B. (1980). Epidemiology of otitis media in children. *Annals of Otology, Rhinology, and Laryngology, 89,* 5–6.

Tomblin, J. B., Barker, B. A., Spencer, L. I., Zhang, X., & Gantz, B. J. (2005). The effect of age at cochlear implant: Initial stimulation on expressive language growth in infants and toddlers. *Journal of Speech, Language, and Hearing Research, 48,* 853–867.

Traxler, C. B. (2000). The Stanford Achievement Test, ninth edition: National norming and performance standards for deaf and hard-of hearing students. *Journal of Deaf Studies and Deaf Education, 5*(4), 337–348.

Urwin, C. (1984). Language for absent things: Learning from visually handicapped children. *Topics in Language Disorders, 4,* 24–37.

Vernon, M. (1968). Fifty years of research on the intelligence of deaf and hard of hearing children. *Journal of Rehabilitation of the Deaf, 1,* 1–12.

Wallace, I., Gravel, J., McCarton, C., & Ruben, R. (1988). Otitis media and language development at 1 year of age. *Journal of Speech and Hearing Disorders, 53,* 245–251.

Williams, C. B., & Finnegan, M. (2003). From myth to reality: Sound information for teachers about students who are deaf. *Teaching Exceptional Children, 35,* 40–45.

Yoshinaga-Itano, C. (1986). Beyond the sentence level: What's in a hearing-impaired child's story? *Topics in Language Disorders, 6,* 71–83.

Yoshinaga-Itano, C., & Seedy, A. (1999). Early speech development in children who are deaf or hard of hearing: Interrelationships with language and hearing. *The Volta Review, 100,* 181–211.

Zweibel, A. (1987). More on the effects of early manual communication on the cognitive development of deaf children. *American Annals of the Deaf, 132,* 16–20.

12 Language and Students with Neuromotor Disabilities and Brain Injury

Children with neuromotor disabilities and brain injury have disabilities that are the result of developmental neurological disorders or brain injury. In most cases, their physical disability is the primary difficulty they face. However, many individuals with neuromotor disorders and brain injury have speech and/or language difficulties as well. This chapter examines the impact of neuromotor impairments and brain injury on language and cognitive development and on academic and social performance. The chapter also includes instructional methods that have been used effectively with children with neuromotor impairments and brain injury.

After completing this chapter, you should be able to:

1. Describe how neuromotor disabilities and brain injury have been defined and classified.
2. Describe the impact of neuromotor impairments and brain injury on:
   cognitive development
   language development
   educational performance
   social interaction
3. List the advantages and disadvantages of various intervention techniques for children with neuromotor impairments and brain injury.

Alfonso: A Case Study

Alfonso is a 12-year-old student with cerebral palsy. When he was born, he suffered anoxia, or lack of oxygen, for several minutes in a protracted labor. Although his intellect is unimpaired, Alfonso's motor and speech abilities were affected. He cannot walk or control many fine motor activities, and he requires assistance with self-care activities such as dressing and feeding. His writing with a pencil or pen results in scribbles and much frustration for Alfonso. His speech is intelligible only to family, teachers, and others who have known him for at least several months.

Alfonso: A Case Study Continued

After being carefully assessed, Alfonso was provided with an augmentative communication device called a Light Talker. This device is programmed with words and phrases customized to Alfonso's school and home environment. There are switches attached both to the lapboard on Alfonso's wheelchair and near the side of his face. Alfonso presses the switches with his hand or head to direct the scanning mode of the Light Talker and select what he wants to say. Then he activates the "voice." One of the greatest benefits of a synthesized voice for Alfonso is his ability to talk with friends during recess.

Technology also assists Alfonso in his schoolwork. An adaptation on his computer allows Alfonso to access word-processing programs with his switch devices. Because of this technology, when other students turn in written assignments, so can Alfonso.

Alfonso attends a class where there is a reverse mainstreaming program: Students from an adjacent third-fourth–grade class join Alfonso's class each day for activities that include reading, spelling, writing, and readers' theater. Alfonso will soon leave this class and move to an integrated fifth-grade classroom. Although excited by this prospect, Alfonso is a little frightened, too.

Ethan: A Case Study

Ethan was 7 years old when he was hit by a car while riding his bicycle without a helmet. Minutes after the accident, medics arrived and found Ethan with an abnormal flexion motor response and no verbal or eye opening responses. A cranial CT scan showed a large subdural hematoma over the left frontal, temporal, and parietal lobes. Ethan was taken to the operating room for removal of the hematoma and placement of an intercranial pressure monitor.

Ethan remained in a coma for 10 weeks. He then began to respond to the command move your hand by moving his left hand. He also followed objects placed in his field of vision, but he did not speak. He was transferred to the neurorehabilitation service, where twice daily he received physical, occupational, and speech therapy. Gradually, over the next 12 weeks, his motor control improved, although he had spasticity on the right side of his body. He began to walk with a leg brace and was able to independently complete self-care activities. Communication remained a major problem, as both expressive and receptive difficulties were evident. Cognitive testing revealed persisting problems, with scores on both verbal and performance subtests falling more than two standard deviations below the norms.

Ethan was discharged and enrolled in an outpatient rehabilitation program, where he received physical and occupational therapy weekly and speech-language therapy three times weekly. Three months later, he returned to school, entering a self-contained communication-disability class with added physical and occupational therapy. At a one-year follow-up, both his expressive and receptive language skills had significantly improved. His individualized education plan (IEP) for the next school year included continued placement in his communication-disability class, with inclusion in a third-grade class for 20 percent of the day and continued physical and occupational therapies.

Children with motor impairments caused by brain dysfunction face a number of serious challenges. Their primary difficulties are in the areas of motor development and movement but they may have a number of other disabilities, including speech and/or language difficulties, social and emotional problems, and impairments in the development of literacy skills. Until recently these problems usually resulted in social isolation and significantly reduced opportunities for life experiences. However, with new technologies and new attitudes toward individuals with physical challenges, the emphasis today is on including these persons in society to the maximum extent possible. An increasing number of children with neuromotor impairments are likely to be found in both regular and special education classes. With higher expectations and greater inclusion comes the need for enhanced language and communication skills.

Cerebral Palsy

Cerebral palsy is the name given to a variety of disorders that cause brain damage early in life. These disorders cause difficulties with movement and posture, as well as a variety of other problems, including cognitive delays and speech and language disorders. This damage often takes place during the birth process, but it may also be caused by trauma during prenatal development or by brain injury during early childhood. Cerebral palsy is a nonprogressive disorder; that is, the damage to the brain does not get worse over time. However, the associated motor problems may worsen if they are left untreated.

Until recently, there has been no widely accepted medical definition of cerebral palsy. However, a multidisciplinary group has proposed the following definition:

> Cerebral palsy (CP) describes a group of disorders of the development of movement and posture, causing activity limitation, that are attributed to non-progressive disturbances that occurred in the developing fetal or infant brain. The motor disorders of cerebral palsy are often accompanied by disturbances of sensation, cognition, communication, perception, and/or behaviour, and/or by a seizure disorder. (Bax et al., 2005)

Approximately 10,000 babies are born with cerebral palsy each year. The incidence of cerebral palsy has remained stable in the United States and western Europe for the past 30 years. Today, there are approximately 800,000 persons with cerebral palsy living in the United States (National Institute of Neurological Disorders and Stroke ([NINDS], 2006).

The Individuals with Disabilities Education Act (IDEA) includes children with cerebral palsy in a larger category of disabilities called "orthopedic impairments." These disorders are defined as follows:

> Orthopedic Impairment: . . . means a severe orthopedic impairment that adversely affects a child's educational performance. The term includes impairments caused by a congenital anomaly (e.g., clubfoot, absence of some member, etc.), impairments caused by disease (e.g., poliomyelitis, bone tuberculosis, etc.), and impairments from other causes (e.g., cerebral palsy, amputations, and fractures or burns that cause contractures).

Types of Cerebral Palsy

Cerebral palsy can be divided into several subtypes according to two criteria: type of movement disorder and part of the body affected. Five types of movement disorders are commonly recognized. **Hypertonia** (*spasticity*) is characterized by significant limitations in the individual's range of motion. Muscle tone is increased and the muscles contract. Movement may be slow and jerky. Significant problems with posture can develop in this type of cerebral palsy. In **athetoid** (*extrapyramidal*) **cerebral palsy,** the limbs have involuntary movements. Individuals with athetoid cerebral palsy seem to have little control over their movements. They may lack head control, flail out their arms or legs when they try to move, or have writhing (choreoathetoid) movements. Individuals with **ataxic cerebral palsy** have difficulty balancing. When reaching for an object, they may overshoot their target. Bleck (1982) described the walk of children with ataxic cerebral palsy as like that of a "sailor on a rolling ship at sea, with feet apart, trunk weaving" (p. 65). **Rigidity** is an extreme form of spasticity in which there is a simultaneous contraction of all muscle groups. Movement is very limited. Ataxia and rigidity are relatively rare disorders. Often several types of movement disorders may be identified in a single individual. This is known as **mixed cerebral palsy** (Bigge, 1991) (see Table 12.1).

Disabilities other than serious motor impairments may also be associated with cerebral palsy. Up to two-thirds of individuals with cerebral palsy may be intellectually impaired (NINDS, 2006). However, since individuals with cerebral palsy can be very difficult to test, it is possible that intellectual disabilities are overestimated in this population. Many children with cerebral palsy have epilepsy. Other related disorders that may occur in some children with cerebral palsy include delayed growth and development, impaired vision, and hearing impairments.

TABLE 12.1   Subtypes of Cerebral Palsy

Subtype	Characteristic
Hypertonia (spasticity)	Significant limitations to range of motion Muscles contracted Movements slow and jerky
Athetoid (extrapyramidal)	Involuntary movement of limbs Lack head control Flail arms and legs Writhing (coreoathetoid) movement
Ataxic	Difficulty with balance Overshoot when reaching for object
Rigidity	Simultaneous contraction of all muscle groups—extreme form of spasticity
Mixed	Combination of two or more types

Sources: Adapted from Bigge (1991), Bleck (1982), McDonald (1987).

Speech and Language Impairments

Children with cerebral palsy are at significant risk for speech and language difficulties. Since speech production involves the precise control and coordination of a variety of muscle groups, it is not surprising that speech impairments are very common among children with cerebral palsy. A large-scale study found that 58 percent of children with cerebral palsy had communication difficulties (Bax, Tydeman, & Flodmark, 2006). Studies of school-age children with cerebral palsy have reported that approximately 40 percent have difficulty being understood (Kennes et al., 2002). The speech difficulties of children with cerebral palsy are extremely heterogeneous and depend, to a great extent, on the specific nature of the physical disability. Individuals with cerebral palsy may have speech production difficulties in one or several areas, including respiration (e.g., rapid, shallow breathing), phonation (inadequate airflow), resonation (hypernasality), and articulation (Owens, Metz, & Haas, 2007). Articulation is often affected because of difficulty controlling the tongue, lips, or mouth.

In addition to difficulties with speech production, differences in early development may have an impact on language. Hanzlik (1990) studied interaction between infants with cerebral palsy, ages 8 to 32 months, and their mothers. The children were described as more compliant and less responsive than typically developing infants. Although this may seem inconsistent, it can be explained by the lack of voluntary movement by the babies with cerebral palsy. The compliance was primarily in response to physical manipulations from their mothers. The mothers of babies with cerebral palsy were found to interact more frequently with their children than the mothers of typically developing babies. This interaction was both physical and communicative. However, the mothers of the children with cerebral palsy engaged in less face-to-face interaction with their children and initiated interaction less often. These early experiences may put the young child with cerebral palsy at risk for early language delays.

What is the impact of speech disorders and early experiences on speech comprehension and language development in persons with cerebral palsy? This question was posed by Bishop, Brown, and Robson (1990). In a series of studies, they examined the ability of 48 individuals with cerebral palsy to discriminate sounds and understand language. Half of their sample exhibited serious speech production difficulties. The other half had no serious speech problems. The researchers found that the group with speech impairments had considerable difficulty with a phoneme discrimination task that used nonwords, but did much better when real words were used. The group with speech impairments did poorly on a test of receptive vocabulary. However, there was no difference between the two groups on their syntactic development. After doing further testing, the authors concluded that individuals with cerebral palsy and speech impairments have more difficulty retaining meaningless strings of sounds in memory. The authors suggest that this problem may be the result of lack of opportunity to use spoken speech sounds. This may not seem like a significant problem, but Bishop and colleagues point out that this is the process children use when they are learning new words. At first, these strings of sounds are meaningless. Only later do they become meaningful words. Difficulty retaining sounds in memory may slow down vocabulary acquisition.

On the other hand, the results of the research reported by Bishop and colleagues (1990) also indicate that despite limited opportunities to use language, individuals with cerebral palsy who also have significant speech impairments can develop structural aspects of language (e.g., syntax) much like other persons. This suggests that language may be intact for these individuals. Yet many, if not most, children with cerebral palsy appear to lag behind their nondisabled peers in language development. There are several reasons why this may occur. Most significantly, cerebral palsy is often associated with other disabilities. It is not unusual to find children with cerebral palsy who also have hearing or vision problems or who have intellectual impairments. We know that all of these conditions can adversely affect language.

Redmond and Johnston (2001) examined the morphological skills of 11- to 15-year-old children with severe speech and physical impairments, three of whom had cerebral palsy. The participants in their study were asked to judge whether test sentences were correct. Although the children with speech impairments had some difficulty identifying past-tense errors, overall there was little difference between these children and typically developing peers. These findings support the view that receptive language is relatively intact in children with cerebral palsy.

In addition to their obvious difficulty in producing spoken language, students with cerebral palsy may sometimes appear to have more significant language difficulties because of the ways in which they are assessed. Many tests of language require children to perform a motor movement. For example, the Peabody Picture Vocabulary Test requires a pointing response to a verbal command. Other tests ask parents or caregivers to rate the observed performance of the child. Of course, these sorts of procedures may tell nothing about language comprehension. Cauley, Golinkoff, Hirsh-Pasek, and Gordon (1989) reported on a procedure they developed to more accurately assess the language skills of children with motor disorders. Children were shown two different pictures on screens simultaneously as a target word was spoken. An observer recorded which screen the child looked at in response to the word by noting the child's eye fixation. The results suggested that children with motor impairments seemed to be able to respond to this sort of testing. This kind of procedure may enable researchers to more accurately assess the language development of children with motor disorders.

Given the variability in physical and cognitive development in individuals with cerebral palsy and the difficulties in testing children with motor disorders, it is not surprising that there is disagreement about the language skills of this population. Research mentioned previously suggests that many persons with cerebral palsy experience significant delays in language, but for some, language is intact. Unless there is specific brain damage in regions of the brain that process language, there is reason to expect that most children with cerebral palsy will have the capacity to develop receptive language.

Literacy Development in Individuals with Cerebral Palsy

Students with cerebral palsy often experience significant difficulty developing literacy skills. In fact, their literacy development has been found to lag behind both their language skills and their cognitive development. It has been suggested that factors such as early home literacy experiences, school curriculums that focus more on physical development than literacy, and physical limitations associated with the child's disability may contribute to the literacy difficulties of children with cerebral palsy (Smith, 2001).

In addition to these factors, several studies have investigated the phonological processing skills of children with cerebral palsy. As we have seen, phonological abilities appear to be a very critical factor in reading success. Since children with cerebral palsy have great difficulty articulating the sounds of English, it would not be surprising to find that they have some problems with sound processing. Although most studies have not found significant deficits in phonological processing among children with cerebral palsy, they do appear to have difficulty applying their knowledge of the sound system to reading and spelling tasks (Sandberg, 2001).

Students with cerebral palsy clearly face significant challenges to their development of literacy skills. Some of these challenges may be the result of lack of opportunity, and some may be the result of differences in language processing that could affect the development of reading and writing skills. There is just not enough information to draw firm conclusions. However, teachers can help develop literacy skills in this population by ensuring they have frequent opportunities to participate in literacy activities, including listening to text.

Other Neuromotor Disorders

Other neuromotor disorders, such as spina bifida and muscular dystrophy, can also affect language acquisition and development. **Spina bifida** refers to a group of conditions in which a portion of the spinal cord is not completely enclosed by the vertebrae in the spinal column. In some cases, part of the spinal cord protrudes. In the most serious form of the disorder, **myelomeningocele,** damage to the spinal cord can cause sensory and motor losses. In addition, in about 80 percent of the cases, fluid accumulates in the brain, causing the condition known as **hydrocephalus.** If not treated quickly, hydrocephalus can cause mental retardation. Surgery can often correct the spinal cord abnormality in spina bifida, but some sensory and motor disabilities can remain (Bigge, 1991). **Muscular dystrophy** is a progressive disorder that produces weakness in muscles. Over time, the muscles waste away and children become unable to walk and talk. There are several forms of muscular dystrophy. The most common is the Duchenne type, which affects about 1 in 3,500 children, mostly males, and begins in early childhood. Children may have problems with balance and in climbing stairs and eventually lose the ability to walk and sit up as muscle weakness spreads and muscles deteriorate. Children with muscular dystrophy usually live only into adolescence or early adulthood (Bigge, 1991).

Impairments in language and communication, in addition to the very serious motor problems, are also associated with spina bifida and muscular dystrophy. For example, children with spina bifida who also have hydrocephalus are frequently reported to have problems with semantic and pragmatic usage. One example of these problems is the "cocktail chatter" phenomenon. As reported by Tew (1979), this difficulty in pragmatics is characterized by chatty conversations that remain at a superficial level. On the other hand, studies have generally found that syntactic development is relatively intact. Byrne, Abbeduto, and Brooks (1990) attacked some of the long-held beliefs about the language disabilities of children with spina bifida and hydrocephalus (SBH). They pointed out that in most of the previous studies, the children with SBH also had mental retardation. Therefore, it was impossible to determine whether the language deficits were the result of SBH or mental retardation. They examined the language of seven SBH children who had IQ scores in the normal range and compared them to nondisabled children of the same chronological age. They found very few differences between the groups of children in their use of language. The SBH sample of children responded appropriately to questions and stayed on task, and their language production was equal in sophistication to that of the nondisabled children. Byrne and colleagues concluded that the language deficiencies previously reported in the SBH population are likely the result of mental retardation, not spina bifida or hydrocephalus. Therefore, teachers and other education professionals should be careful about jumping to conclusions regarding intelligence or language abilities of children with one of these conditions (spina bifida or hydrocephalus). With newer surgical procedures and early intervention, many of these children can function quite normally.

Language and cognitive abilities can also be affected by *Duchenne muscular dystrophy.* Typically, researchers have found that measured intelligence is lower in children with muscular dystrophy, with language skills being especially low in younger children (Karagan & Zellweger, 1978). Dorman, Hurley, and D'Avignon (1988) reported mean IQ scores of about 87, with verbal scores lower than performance. In a more intensive analysis of 15 cases, Dorman and colleagues determined that children with Duchenne muscular dystrophy can exhibit a wide discrepancy in their abilities. They found that 6 of the 15 children had very low measured intelligence and significant problems in reading, writing, and spelling, functioning much like children with severe dyslexia. The other children had performance levels similar to those found in nondisabled children. The implication of this research is that Duchenne muscular dystrophy may manifest itself in different ways. In some cases, language-based abilities are significantly impacted, but in other cases, they remain intact. With time, however, most children with this disorder have increasing difficulty communicating because of the deterioration of muscles involved in speech production.

Epilepsy is another neurological disorder that affects movement. Epilepsy is a condition that produces brief disturbances, called *seizures,* in the electrical functioning of the brain. This disorder has a number of causes, including illness, brain damage, or abnormal brain development. However, in most cases, no cause can be identified (NINDS, 2006). Seizure disorders are generally divided into two types: generalized and partial. Generalized seizures affect both hemispheres of the brain, whereas partial seizures are focused on one side. In some cases, epilepsy can cause disturbances in thinking and in language. For example, Caplan and colleagues (2002) examined the social communication skills of children with complex, partial seizures (CPS) (a type of seizure in which a person may not lose consciousness but cannot interact with others), generalized epilepsy, and non-epileptic children. They found that the children with

CPS had significant deficits in social communication. Specifically, these children underutilized conjunctions to tie together thoughts and used fewer pronouns and definite articles to refer to people or objects in their conversation. Children with generalized epilepsy also had some difficulty with social communication, but it was not as serious.

Although most children with mild epilepsy may not have language difficulties, some children—especially those with complex, partial seizures—may have difficulty developing and using language for social communication. Teachers and other education professionals who work with children with epilepsy need to know about the type of epilepsy affecting these children and be aware of the possible impact on language, cognitive, and social development.

Implications for Intervention

Typically, intervention for individuals with motor disorders has focused on speech therapy. For children with cerebral palsy, speech therapy often focuses on developing the muscles used in eating and swallowing. Most children with neuromotor disorders at some point will need help with breathing, vocal production, and articulation. Although speech therapy is important and should not be ignored as part of an instructional program, it can often be very slow in producing results and frustrating for both the child and the therapist.

In addition to receiving speech therapy, children with motor impairments should be given numerous opportunities to engage in literacy-based activities and to communicate with a variety of people. Literacy-based activities may include listening to stories, watching movies or videotapes of stories, and using computer word-processing programs that permit the user to write with a minimum of motor movement. It is essential that children with neuromotor disorders be involved in as many communicative interactions as possible. Teachers can facilitate these interactions through appropriate positioning. McDonald (1987) suggests that children with neuromotor disabilities be positioned so that they can see, feel, or hear the communication. If necessary, a mirror can be used so the child can read the facial expressions of communication partners, or others can see the child's face. In addition, by providing appropriate play materials, the teacher can also increase the possibilities for communicative interaction. In any case, it is essential that teachers encourage children with neuromotor disabilities to communicate with others and that the teachers themselves engage the children in communicative exchanges whenever possible.

For many children with neuromotor disorders, the use of augmentative communication devices will be an important option. When properly designed and used effectively, these devices can open up new worlds of communication to children who were previously unable to communicate. Chapter 15 provides more information about augmentative communication devices, but most important to this discussion is that the user be taught and encouraged to use the device for communication. Too often the child with an augmentative communication device sits idly in a classroom until called on to respond. Children who use such devices must continually be encouraged to use the device to initiate interaction and to respond appropriately.

Brain Injury and Language

Traumatic brain injury is a leading cause of death and disability in children and adolescents in the United States. Each year approximately 1,000,000 children receive medical attention because of a head injury and as many as 30,000 will have a permanently disabling condition (National Information Center for Children and Youth with Disabilities, 2006). Although most of these injuries are minor and leave no lasting problems, some result in significant impairments in motor, cognitive, and language functioning.

The Individuals with Disabilities Education Act (IDEA) includes traumatic brain injury (TBI) as a separate category of disability. It is defined as:

> An acquired injury to the brain caused by an external physical force, resulting in total or partial functional disability or psychosocial impairment, or both, that adversely affect a child's educational performance. The term applies to open and closed head injuries resulting in impairments in one or more areas, such as: cognition; language; memory; attention; reasoning; abstract thinking; judgment; problem-solving; sensory, perceptual, and motor abilities; psychosocial behavior; physical functions; information processing; and speech. The term does not apply to brain injuries that are congenital or degenerative, or brain injuries induced by birth trauma. (IDEA, 2004)

As the IDEA definition indicates, there are two types of head injuries. **Open-head injury** (also known as *localized*) is characterized by a visible injury, often a gunshot wound. The brain damage is usually confined to one portion of the brain. **Closed-head injury** is caused by a rapid acceleration and deceleration of the head, during which the brain bounces around inside the skull. Closed-head brain damage is most often caused by automobile accidents but can also be caused by falls and sports injuries. This is the type of injury suffered by Ethan, the boy in the case study, while he was riding his bicycle.

Head injuries can cause a variety of problems, depending on the location and severity of the injury and the age of the victim. Symptoms can include:

- *Physical impairments.* Speech, vision, hearing, and other sensory impairments; headaches, problems with coordination; spasticity and/or paralysis
- *Cognitive impairments.* Memory difficulties; slowness in thinking; problems concentrating; problems with perception and attention; problems planning and sequencing
- *Behavior and personality problems.* Fatigue; mood swings; anxiety; depression; difficulty with emotional control (NINDS, 2006; Telzrow, 1987)

In most cases, children with head injuries show improvement over time, but there may be lasting effects that can have an impact on classroom performance.

Outcomes of Traumatic Brain Injury

Traumatic brain injuries can have a significant impact on school performance and on life after school. Researchers have found that children with traumatic brain injury have difficulty in many functional areas, including cognitive performance and reading, social skills, and behavioral skills (Arroyos-Jurado et al., 2000). The result is that, in many cases, children with traumatic brain injury end up being referred to special education.

Researchers have been interested in discovering the factors that can predict the severity of disability following brain injury and the likelihood of recovery. A study by Arroyos-Jurado and colleagues (2000) examined the outcomes of traumatic brain injury on 43 children and adolescents. The children were tested shortly after their injury and 3, 12, and 24 months later. They found that the most important factor in explaining functioning after injury was the child's abilities prior to her or his injury. Although severity of injury was important, especially in behavioral functioning, it was the child's skills in reading and writing prior to injury that were most predictive of performance following the injury. That is, children with good skills in these domains tended to have better outcomes than children with poor skills prior to injury.

Language Characteristics

If a head injury affects the left hemisphere of the brain, there is likely to be an effect on language functioning. Children who lose language functioning as a result of brain injury are said to have *acquired aphasia*. In other words, they have lost some language functions that they had acquired earlier. Language difficulties resulting from traumatic brain injury can involve expressive language, receptive language, or both (Michaud & Duhaime, 1992). Some children with brain injury experience significant language losses, whereas others show little, if any, impairment (Cooper & Flowers, 1987).

There has been a big (and ongoing) debate among researchers about the effects of brain injury on language and about recovery of language skills. Briefly, the debate centers on the issues of *laterality* and *plasticity*. Lenneberg (1967), among others, argued that cerebral dominance is not established at birth but rather develops over time. He argued that children are better able to recover their language abilities after damage to the brain because uninjured areas of the brain take over the function of the damaged area (plasticity). Although it is true that children seem more capable of recovery of function than adults, other researchers (e.g., Kinsbourne & Hiscock, 1977) have claimed that cerebral dominance is largely established at birth.

Whatever the reason, children with brain injuries do frequently show marked improvements in their language abilities (Satz & Bullard-Bates, 1981). Campbell and Dollaghan (1990) investigated the phenomenon of language recovery by evaluating the language abilities of nine brain-injured children during the 13 months following their injuries. When first tested, the brain-injured children scored far below a group of nondisabled children matched for age and gender on all measures of expressive language. However, by the end of the 13-month period, the groups differed on only one measure—total number of utterances. There were, however, big differences in the language recovery of each of the brain-injured children. Two of the children showed no significant expressive language problems, even at the first session. Two other children eventually caught up to the nondisabled children their own age. But five of the brain-injured children never fully recovered their language skills, although they did show improvements. The results of this study show just how difficult it is to make generalizations about the recovery of children with brain injuries.

Although there is variability among brain-injured children, certain kinds of language impairments are more common in this population. For example, Ewing-Cobbs, Fletcher, Landry, and Levin (1985) found that most of a group of children with moderate to severe closed-head injury had little trouble understanding individual words, but many had difficulty understanding syntactically complex sentences. In their study of 15 children with acquired aphasia, Cooper and Flowers (1987) found that the greatest language deficiencies were in naming pictures, understanding paragraphs, and making word associations. They noted that no one pattern of language problems characterized the children, but that difficulties in later developing syntactic and metalinguistic abilities were most likely to occur. Reading and writing can also be impaired in children with brain injury.

Teachers can expect children with brain injuries to have a variety of language impairments. Some may have no obvious problems; others might have subtle language impairments that may only show up in conversation or in reading and writing; and still others might have significant difficulties, with word retrieval, speech fluency, and syntactic skills affected.

Intervention

The best intervention for head injury is prevention. Most head trauma is preventable. Use of seat belts, bicycle helmets, and appropriate sports equipment can reduce the incidence of head injury, as can efforts to reduce drunk driving and child abuse. Despite efforts aimed at prevention and education about brain injuries, they continue to occur at high rates.

With the high frequency of brain trauma and the trend toward inclusion of children with disabilities in regular education settings, most teachers are likely to have a brain-injured child in their classroom at some time. A child's return to school following a head injury can be very difficult for the child as well as the teacher. As Harrington (1990) put it, "The dilemma of returning to school after a traumatic brain injury is that life is just not the same" (p. 479). There can be changes in thinking, in behavior, in language, and in academic skills such as reading and writing. The child may also have physical problems such as headaches and difficulty staying alert.

Telzrow (1987) has suggested 10 elements that should be part of an educational program for children with traumatic brain injury. These include:

1. *Maximally controlled environment.* The child may need a highly structured environment where distraction is reduced.
2. *Low pupil-teacher ratio.* It may be necessary to provide a classroom aide or other assistant to work with the child.
3. *Intensive and repetitive instruction.* The brain-injured child often needs more time to learn. Reducing nonacademic activities and lengthening the school year can provide more learning time.
4. *Emphasis on process.* The child may need to be helped in learning how to learn. Instruction should include help in sustaining attention and on memory.
5. *Behavioral programming.* Instructional strategies that use task analysis and careful measurement of progress have been found to be successful.
6. *Integrated instructional therapies.* Integrate allied therapies such as speech and physical therapy into the student's primary instructional setting to facilitate generalization and transfer of skills.
7. *Simulation experiences.* Use simulations to enable the child to transfer skills to a new setting.

   8. *Cuing, fading, and shadowing.* Students may require cues to respond, which should be faded as soon as possible. When shadowing, the teacher closely monitors the child attempting a new task or moving to a new environment.
   9. *Readjustment counseling.* This may help the child adjust to his or her new environment and abilities.
   10. *Home-school liaison.* It is essential to build and maintain a strong link between parents and the school.

Some students with traumatic brain injury may need modifications to regular classroom instruction in order to become successful learners again. These may include relatively simple accommodations such as sitting near the teacher or a peer helper and frequent breaks for students who get tired easily. In some cases, more significant modifications may be needed (see Table 12.2).

For brain-injured children with language impairments, a range of services and methods may be necessary. Some will need speech and language therapy; others may need more help than most children do when learning (or relearning) to read and write; and still others will need augmentative communication devices to enable them to communicate effectively. Teachers can help by responding to the child and being alert to her or his language abilities. In some cases, teachers may need to adjust their language so the child can better understand directions and assignments. In addition, it may help to put the child in many situations where there are opportunities to interact with other children.

Teachers and other education professionals who work with children with traumatic brain injury must be prepared for just about anything. These children may have few problems or many disabilities. They may readily adjust to their disabilities or be emotionally upset. Parents may be overly protective of their child or deny that there are any problems. If teachers are aware of the range of needs and abilities that brain-injured children might bring to the classroom, they can better help these children reach their learning potential.

Summary

This chapter examined the impact of neuromotor disabilities and brain injury on language and communication development. Children with neuromotor disabilities such as cerebral palsy face a number of challenges. Often, their speech, language, and communication difficulties do not receive much attention. In some cases, this is because these problems are treated as secondary to the motor disabilities that are the primary focus for intervention. Language and communication deficits, however, play a significant role in the development of socialization and literacy skills that are critical for success in school and in the community.

Teachers and other education professionals need to understand the impact of neuromotor disabilities and brain injury on language, especially since so many children with these disabilities are being integrated into regular education settings. Impairments of mobility are certainly important and have an impact on instruction, but recognition of their associated speech and language impairments can also be critical to the academic and social success of children with neuromotor disabilities.

TABLE 12.2 Compensatory Aids and Strategies for Students with Traumatic Brain Injury (TBI)

Cognitive Impairment	External Aids	Teaching/Learning Strategies
Attention	Use FM unit or earplugs. Use a timer or alarm to focus attention. Place symbol or sign in an obvious location to remind student to attend.	Keep assignments and instructions simple and direct. Provide rest periods, breaks, or physical activity. Minimize distractions. Divide work into small sections. Use verbal, gestural, or visual cues to remind student to attend. Ask student to repeat or summarize instructions. Slow pace of instruction.
Memory	Use checklists, post-it notes, 3 × 5 cards. Keep appointment calendars, planners, electronic organizers, or dry-erase boards. Use memory log or card with personal information, map, schedule, etc. Set a timer or alarm to remind when a task needs to be done. Keep items in one designated location. Use tape recorders to review information. Provide photocopies of textbook pages for student to practice highlighting skills.	Ask student to repeat new information several times. Teach the use of visual imagery. Teach the use of mnemonic strategies. Simplify information to be remembered. Break each task into steps and teach each step separately. Teach study skills, note-taking techniques, and self-questioning. Test using multiple-choice format. Use fact cards and cue sheets to help recall. Teach student to rehearse or review notes immediately (within 1 hr.) after class.
Organization	Display pictorial or visual schedule of activities. Provide checklist with steps for completing tasks, or written outline of class lectures. Use a binder with subject sections and homework pockets. Use daily planner to record homework assignments. Use colored lines, highlighting, color-coding as cues for organization. Use graphic organizers to sequence thinking (time lines, outlines, flow charts, etc.).	Review daily routines with student. Teach use of student planner and cue student to record assignments in planner. Designate specific locations to turn in assignments/homework, use picture cues, or labels to identify place. Assign a peer buddy to assist with routines.
Writing and information-processing speed	Use tape recorders to record answers. Assign a peer note taker to take carbon paper notes. Use assistive devices such as a word processor, Dictaphone, or peer scribe.	Reduce amount of written work that is required and focus on mastery of critical information. Allow extra time to complete work or to verbally respond. Provide alternative forms of test taking. Enlarge the print on worksheets. Provide a make-up period at the end of the day. Present visual or verbal information at a slower pace.

Source: Bowen, J. M. (2005). "Classroom interventions for students with traumatic brain injuries." *Preventing School Failure, 49,* p. 38. Reprinted with permission of the Helen Dwight Reid Educational Foundation. Published by Heldref Publications, 1319 Eighteenth St., NW, Washington, DC 20036-1802. Copyright © 2005.

REVIEW QUESTIONS

1. Cerebral palsy is called a "nonprogressive" disorder. What does that mean? What is the implication for the development of language and cognition?

2. Why is intellectual ability difficult to assess in a person with cerebral palsy?

3. What factors affect the development of speech and language in children with cerebral palsy?

4. What did Bishop and colleagues (1990) discover about the ability of individuals with cerebral palsy to understand language?

5. What has research indicated about the language development of children with spina bifida and hydrocephalus?

6. Describe the specific communication deficits that have been found in some children with epilepsy.

7. Give three suggestions that teachers could use to enhance the language and communication of children with neuromotor disorders.

8. What factors are likely to affect the ability of children to recover from brain injuries?

9. What are some of the problems faced by children with traumatic brain injury as they return to school?

SUGGESTED ACTIVITY

1. If you have access to a person with a neuromotor impairment who also has significant difficulty with speech, you could evaluate this person's ability to comprehend language. You will need some pictures of action sequences (these could be pictures from books or magazines or be drawings or photographs). Develop a list of sentences describing the pictures—for example, *The girl is hitting the baseball.*

   Place three pictures in front of the person. Read a sentence that describes one of the pictures, then ask the person to touch or point to the picture that shows the action described by the sentence. If the person can neither touch nor point, you could point to each picture, in order, until he or she indicates the correct picture.

   What do the results indicate about the ability of persons with neuromotor disorders to understand language?

GLOSSARY

ataxic cerebral palsy: rare type of cerebral palsy that affects balance and depth perception

athetoid cerebral palsy: a type of cerebral palsy in which the limbs have involuntary movements; individuals seem to have little control over their movement and have difficulty balancing

closed-head injury: a type of brain injury caused by a rapid acceleration and deceleration of the head, during which the brain bounces around inside the skull; most often cased by automobile accidents

epilepsy: a condition that produces brief disturbances in the electrical functioning of the brain, causing seizures

hydrocephalus: a condition caused by the accumulation of fluid on the brain that, if untreated, can cause brain damage

hypertonia: a type of cerebral palsy characterized by significant limitations in the individual's range of motion; muscle tone is increased and the muscles contract; movement may be slow and jerky

mixed cerebral palsy: a type of cerebral palsy that is characterized by symptoms of two or more types of cerebral palsy

muscular dystrophy: a progressive disorder that produces weakness in muscles and eventually is fatal

myelomeningocele: a form of spina bifida in which damage to the spinal cord causes significant sensory and motor losses

open-head injury: a type of brain injury, usually confined to one portion of the brain, characterized by a visible injury, often a gunshot wound

rigidity: a type of cerebral palsy in which there is a simultaneous contraction of all muscle groups and movement is very limited

spina bifida: A group of conditions in which a portion of the spinal cord is not completely enclosed by the vertebrae in the spinal column

RESOURCES ON THE WEB

www.ninds.nih.gov/disorders/cerebral_palsy/cerebral_palsy.htm NINDS cerebral palsy information page

www.ucp.org/ United Cerebral Palsy Association

www.nichcy.org/pubs/factshe/fs2txt.htm NICHY fact sheet on cerebral palsy

www.cdc.gov/ncbddd/dd/ddcp.htm Centers for Disease Control information on cerebral palsy

www.biausa.org Brain Injury Association of America

www.ninds.nih.gov/disorders/tbi/tbi.htm NINDS Traumatic Brain Injury information page

www.neuro.pmr.vcu.edu/ National Resource Center for traumatic brain injury

REFERENCES

Arroyos-Jurado, E., Paulsen, J. S., Merrell, K. W., Lindgren, S. D., & Max, J. E. (2000). Traumatic brain injury in school-age children: Academic and social outcome. *Journal of School Psychology, 38,* 571–587.

Bax, M., Goldstein, M., Rosenbaum, P., & Paneth, N. (2005). Proposed definition and classification of cerebral palsy. *Developmental Medicine & Child Neurology, 47,* 571–576, 571.

Bax, M., Tydeman, C., & Flodmark, O. (2006). Clinical and MRI correlates of cerebral palsy. *Journal of the American Medical Association, 296,* 1602–1609.

Berninger, V., & Gans, B. (1986). Language profiles in nonspeaking individuals of normal intelligence with severe cerebral palsy. *Augmentative and Alternative Communication, 2,* 45–50.

Bigge, J. (1991). *Teaching individuals with physical and multiple disabilities.* New York: Macmillan.

Bishop, D., Brown, B., & Robson, J. (1990). The relationship between phoneme discrimination, speech production, and language comprehension in cerebral-palsied individuals. *Journal of Speech and Hearing Research, 33,* 210–219.

Bleck, E. (1982). Cerebral palsy. In E. Bleck & D. Nagel (Eds.), *Physically handicapped children: A medical atlas for teachers* (pp. 59–132). Orlando, FL: Grune & Stratton.

Bowen, J. M. (2005). Classroom interventions for students with traumatic brain injuries. *Preventing School Failure, 49,* 34–41.

Byrne, K., Abbeduto, L., & Brooks, P. (1990). The language of children with spina bifida and hydrocephalus: Meeting task demands and mastering syntax. *Journal of Speech and Hearing Disorders, 55,* 118–123.

Campbell, T., & Dollaghan, C. (1990). Expressive language recovery in severely brain-injured children and adolescents. *Journal of Speech and Hearing Disorders, 55,* 567–581.

Caplan, R., Guthrie, D., Komo, S., Siddarth, P., Chayasirisobhon, S., Kornblum, H., Sankar, R., Hansen, R., Mitchell, W., & Shields, W. D.

(2002). Social communication in children with epilepsy. *Journal of Child Psychology and Psychiatry, 43,* 245–253.

Cauley, K., Golinkoff, R., Hirsk-Pasek, K., & Gordon, L. (1989). Revealing hidden competencies: A new method for studying language comprehension in children with motor impairments. *American Journal of Mental Retardation, 94,* 55–63.

Cooper, J., & Flowers, C. (1987). Children with a history of acquired aphasia: Residual language and academic impairments. *Journal of Speech and Hearing Disorders, 52,* 251–262.

Ewing-Cobbs, L., Fletcher, J., Landry, S., & Levin, H. (1985). Language disorders after pediatric head injury. In J. Darby (Ed.), *Speech and language evaluation in neurology: Childhood disorders.* Orlando, FL: Grune & Stratton.

Dorman, C., Hurley, A., & D'Avignon, J. (1988). Language and learning disorders of older boys with Duchenne muscular dystrophy. *Developmental Medicine and Child Neurology, 30,* 316–327.

Hanzlik, J. R. (1990). Nonverbal interaction patterns of mothers and their infants with cerebral palsy. *Education and Training in Mental Retardation, 25,* 333–343.

Harrington, D. (1990). Educational strategies. In M. Rosenthal, E. Griftith, M. Bond, & J. Miller (Eds.), *Rehabilitation of the adult and child with traumatic brain injury* (pp. 476–493), Philadelphia: J. B. Lippincott.

Individuals with Disabilities Education Act. (2004). Washington, DC: U.S. Government Printing Office.

Karagan, N., & Zellweger, H. (1978). Early verbal disability in children with Duchenne muscular dystrophy. *Journal of Nervous and Mental Disease, 168,* 419–423.

Kennes, J., Rosenbaum, P., Hanna, S., Walter, S., Russell, D., Raina, P., Bartlett, D., & Galuppi, B. (2002). Health status of school-aged children with cerebral palsy: Information from a population-based sample. *Developmental Medicine & Child Neurology, 44,* 240–247.

Kinsbourne, M., & Hiscock, M. (1977). Does cerebral dominance develop? In S. Segalowitz & F. Gru-

ber (Eds.), *Language development and neurological theory.* New York: Academic Press.

Lenneberg, E. (1967). *Biological foundations of language.* New York: Wiley.

McDonald, E. (1987). *Treating cerebral palsy.* Austin, TX: Pro-Ed.

Michaud, L., & Duhaime, A. (1992). Traumatic brain injury. In M. Batshaw & Y. Perret (Eds.), *Children with disabilities: A medical primer* (pp. 525–546). Baltimore: Brookes.

National Information center for children and Youth with Disabilities. (2006). *Fact Sheet #18: Traumatic Brain Injury.* Retrieved from www.nichy.org/pubs/factshe/fs18txt.htm.

National Institute of Neurological Disorders and Stroke. (2006). *Cerebral palsy: Hope through research.* Bethesda, MD: National Institutes of Health.

Owens, R., Metz, D. E., & Haas, A. (2007). *Introduction to communication disorders,* 2rd ed. Boston: Allyn & Bacon.

Redmond, S. M., & Johnston, S. S. (2001). Evaluating the morphological competence of children with severe speech and physical impairments. *Journal of Speech, Language, and Hearing Research, 44,* 1362–1375.

Sandberg, A. D. (2001). Reading and spelling, phonological awareness, and working memory in children with severe speech impairments: A longitudinal study AAC. *Augmentative and Alternative Communication, 17,* 11–26.

Satz, P., & Bullard-Bates, C. (1981). Acquired aphasia in children. In M. Sarno (Ed.), *Acquired aphasia.* New York: Academic Press.

Smith, M. (2001). Simply a speech impairment? Literacy challenges for individuals with severe congenital speech impairments. *International Journal of Disability, Development and Education, 48,* 331–353.

Telzrow, C. (1987). Management of academic and educational problems in head injury. *Journal of Learning Disabilities, 20,* 536–545.

Tew, B. (1979). The "cocktail party syndrome" in children with hydrocephalus and spina bifida. *British Journal of Disorders of Communication, 14,* 89–101.

13 Assessing Language and Communication

Language assessment can serve several purposes. It can help determine what difficulties a child may have, what aspects of language are involved, and the degree of delay or the severity of the child's development problems. Assessment can help focus intervention, by identifying objectives for instruction and even indicating approaches that might be most successful, and, at times, it can even reveal the underlying causes of speech, language, or communication difficulty.

Unfortunately, assessment is also sometimes seen as a burdensome chore and a waste of time. Federal and state mandates require that particular areas be tested and, to some extent, dictate the types of assessment procedures that must be used. Assessment is sometimes viewed as a necessary evil—a way to comply with IEP requirements or to enable a child to receive services.

The goal of this chapter is to point out positive assessment practices. Specifically, the goal is to describe those assessment procedures that can reveal the most information about the language and communication of children with disabilities. Granted, assessment might be necessary to comply with legal mandates, but it will also be useful for teachers and other education professionals who make instructional decisions and evaluate the outcomes of instruction.

After completion of this chapter you should be able to:

1. List the purposes of language assessment.
2. Understand what should be included in a comprehensive assessment of language and how to make assessment decisions.
3. List some formal tests for assessing language skills.
4. Describe some informal techniques for language assessment.
5. Explain how to gather and analyze a language sample.
6. Describe some informal techniques for assessing specific language skills.
7. Understand classroom-based techniques for language.

Understanding Language Assessment

Language is one of the most difficult domains of human behavior to assess. There are many reasons why this is so. As we have seen throughout this book, the understanding of language and language acquisition is incomplete. It is hard to assess something that cannot be clearly defined. As Silliman and Diehl (2002) point out, language is not a unitary phenomenon—it is "multidimensional, complex, and dynamic; it involves many interrelated processes and abilities; and it changes from situation to situation" (p. 183). The sequence and timing of language development and the nature of language disorders can vary widely. Language disorders can range from mild to severe, from receptive to expressive, from speech production to conversational competence. The increasingly diverse school population also creates challenges in the assessment of language abilities and disabilities.

Knowing that language is difficult to assess does not, of course, absolve educators from doing so. It simply makes it all the more important to be clear about the purposes, the goals, and the means of language assessment. It is important to keep in mind the limitations of language assessment and the need to relate assessment in other domains (e.g., intelligence testing and testing of academic skills) to assessment of language.

Assessment of language is often seen as the domain of speech-language specialists. It is true that these professionals have significant training in the assessment of speech and language. But classroom teachers have an important role to play in language assessment. In most cases, they are the educators who see the child most often, in many different settings, interacting with a variety of communicative partners. They can help identify children at risk for language-learning disabilities and help focus assessment on specific areas of concern. In addition, classroom teachers can observe children's use of language in the classroom. Classroom teachers may be asked to complete questionnaires on the language of students in the classroom. In some cases, they plan and administer language assessments. Whatever the direct role that they play in language assessment, classroom teachers must be knowledgeable consumers of assessment information. They are an essential part of the team that must plan and carry out any program of language intervention, so it is essential that classroom teachers understand the purposes and methods of language assessment.

Purposes of Language Assessment

Silliman and Diehl (2002) have identified four purposes for assessment of language: *identification* of children suspected of having a language learning disability; *evaluation* to determine whether a language-learning disability is present; *intervention* assessment to determine whether an instructional program is appropriate for the individual child; and *functional outcomes* assessment to document the results of intervention.

The identification of children with language disorders usually includes two steps: screening and determining the nature of the disability. **Screening** involves the testing of a large number of children in order to identify those who may differ sufficiently in language functioning to warrant a more comprehensive assessment. The instruments that are used must be relatively brief and easy to administer and interpret. As a result, screening measures may overidentify or underidentify children. It is important for those using such tests to understand the limitations of the test itself. In addition, the variability in behavior of children during testing may be magnified by screening tests.

If screening suggests that a particular child may have a language learning disability, a more complete language *evaluation* is usually required. The purpose of this assessment is to determine whether a disability is present as defined by state and federal law. An assessment plan is developed on the basis of the screening results and observation of the child. Intensive, focused assessment is conducted. The results are reviewed by a team to determine whether the child is in need of and eligible for speech and/or language intervention.

Once eligibility for services is determined, the team can design appropriate language intervention programs, Assessment for *intervention* provides this information. Having information about how the child learns best and what instructional methods have been most successful are helpful to those planning language-intervention programs. Decisions about *where* to teach and *how* to teach should be made on the basis of assessment information.

It is essential that intervention outcomes be evaluated. How else can we know whether a particular instructional method is working and whether instructional objectives need to be changed? Silliman and Diehl (2002) point out the importance of assessing the child in a variety of settings, since generalization is such an important part of success in language.

What to Assess

What should be included in a comprehensive assessment of language? Although the answer to this question is affected by factors such as the characteristics of the child and the purposes for testing, there are some broad areas that should be included in most assessments of language. At the core of any assessment of language are the five basic elements of language discussed previously: phonology, morphology, syntax, semantics, and pragmatics. Both the child's understanding and production of each of these elements should be considered.

Phonology.   In examining the child's production of speech sounds, professionals listen for intelligibility of speech and accuracy of sound production. Specific areas examined might include phonological errors, including reduction of consonant clusters (*green* becomes *geen),* deletion of unstressed syllables *(banana* becomes *nana*), devoicing of the final consonant *(bed* becomes *bet),* and substitutions (*bus* becomes *but*). Phonological processing can also be assessed. Methods for the assessment of phonological awareness include the detection of rhyme, the division of words into sounds, and the detection of beginning and ending sounds.

Morphology.   We know from research discussed in Chapter 5 that there is a developmental sequence of morphology. For example, we know that the use of the *-ing* ending usually precedes the use of prepositions such as *in* and *on*. We also know that the use of the plural *s* generally emerges before the use of the regular past-tense *ed.* In assessing a child's morphological development, it is important to know which word endings and prefixes the child is using. It is also necessary to test the child's use of morphemes in both real and nonsense words. Children may correctly use constructions such as the past tense because they have heard them previously. By asking a child to use the correct morpheme with a nonsense word, we are assessing whether he or she has acquired the morphological rule.

Syntax.   Two general areas can be included in an assessment of syntactic development: use of phrase-structure rules and use of transformational rules. Phrase-structure rules are the fundamental building blocks of grammar. They include the basic syntactic elements (e.g., noun, verb, adjective) and the rules that govern word order (e.g., noun before verb). Assessment of syntax can include examining both the syntactic elements used by the child and the frequency of their usage, in addition to the types of sentences used by the child and the accuracy and frequency of their usage. For example, does the child use both simple and compound sentences? How frequently are compound sentences used? Are they used appropriately? One could also examine whether the child correctly produces and interprets a variety of types of sentences, including complex sentences and sentences that contain negation. Assessment of syntax might also include the use of transformational rules, such as in the understanding and use of questions, imperative sentences, and the passive voice.

Semantics.   The child's knowledge of meaning is typically assessed through examining vocabulary to see how many words and what types of words (e.g., objects, actions, social greetings) are in the child's vocabulary, as well as how quickly he or she can access words. Speed of processing is a critical factor in language usage. In addition, evaluations of the child's understanding of word meanings and he or his understanding and use of nonliteral language are used for some children. Does the child understand and use figures of speech such as metaphor? Does he or she understand proverbs and humor?

Pragmatics.   Assessment in pragmatics would help determine the child's understanding and use of a variety of speech acts and conversational rules. As a child develops, he or she uses an increasing variety of speech acts. Evaluating the child's use of speech acts—such as requesting, protesting, greeting, and answering—and the ability to understand both direct and indirect speech acts provides information on language development. Conversational rules include a number of aspects such as turn-taking, conversational repairs, topic setting and maintenance, and awareness of the need to vary one's language in different conversational situations. All of these elements and many more could be included in an assessment of pragmatic competence (see Table 13.1).

Bases of Language.   A comprehensive assessment of language might also include the evaluation of social, cognitive, and physiological bases of language. We know, for example, that typically developing children engage in a number of prelinguistic communicative routines with their parents. These include turn-taking exchanges, gaze behavior, and the like. Observation of these routines could be included in the assessment of a nonspeaking child. An evaluation of the child's level of cognitive development may provide helpful information on whether the child engages in symbolic play or whether the concept of object permanence seems to be established. Certainly, one

TABLE 13.1   Language Elements Used in Assessment

Element	Expressive	Receptive

Phonology	Articulation of speech sounds
	Phonological errors:
	    reduction
	    deletion
	    devoicing
	    substitution
		Phonological awareness:
		    rhyme
		    division of words into sounds
		    adding/deleting beginning and ending
		        sounds

Morphology	Use of grammatical morphemes in real and nonsense words	Identification of grammatical morphemes

Syntax	Use of basic sentence elements
	    (e.g., noun, verb)
	Use of sentence types (simple, complex)
	Use of transformational rules (question,
	    passive)
		Understanding and interpretation of
		    sentence types and transformational rules

Semantics	Vocabulary use:
	    amount
	    types
	Speed of word retrieval
	Use of figurative language
		Identification of words
		Comprehension of humor/proverbs

Pragmatics	Use of speech acts:
	    requesting
	    greeting
	    answering
	Use of conversational rules:
	    turn-taking
	    repairs
	    topic setting
		Understanding of direct and indirect speech
		    acts

would need to know whether the child's speech-processing abilities are intact. An examination of the child's mouth and teeth to determine whether they are healthy and intact may be necessary. In addition, a neurological evaluation may be necessary to determine whether the child is physically capable of using and understanding language.

Assessing Preschool Language Development

One of the most important and challenging problems in assessment of language and communication is the identification of young children with language and communication difficulties. It is important because of the increasing evidence that early intervention can be effective in reducing or eliminating language difficulties. However, there are special challenges when assessing young children. Some of them may produce little or no spoken language. Many will be intimidated by a testing situation or by an unknown evaluator. Despite these problems, the importance of early identification of language and communication difficulties makes early assessment an important activity.

A number of instruments have been developed to assess early language and communication development (see Table 13.2). Most of these instruments include observations and/or parent reports. As with any formal assessment, it is important to consider the reliability and validity of these instruments. **Reliability** refers to the consistency with which the instrument measures the target skill. In other words, reliability reflects the likelihood that, if repeated, the test results would be similar. **Validity** refers to the extent to which the instrument measures what it purports to measure.

Making Assessment Decisions

With so many possible elements to use in a comprehensive assessment of language, how is one to decide what to include? The choices can be determined by several factors. The first consideration is the purpose of the assessment. For example, as we have noted earlier in this chapter, screening techniques are used to identify children at risk for language and communication difficulties. A screening involves a quick examination of the child's language skills. Screening techniques should be easy and quick to administer to a large number of children. A screening may be administered to a group or to individuals and may be part of a more comprehensive assessment (e.g., a kindergarten screening). However, by their very nature, screening instruments are not very accurate. They may miss some children who need services or identify children as impaired who, in fact, are not. Therefore, it is essential that screening instruments be used only as a first step in the assessment process. A number of language and communication screening instruments are available. Table 13.3 lists some of the options.

A screening evaluation will likely include just a few of the major aspects of language. A more in-depth, **diagnostic assessment** should be used when a child is sus-

---

TABLE 13.2   Instruments Used for Assessing Early Language Skills

Test Name	Author(s) and Date of Publication	Publisher
Communication and Symbolic Publishing Behavior Scales	Wetherby & Prizant (1993)	Brookes
MacArthur Bates Communicative Development Inventories (2nd ed.)	Fenson, Marchman, Thal, Dale, Reznick, & Bates (2006)	Brookes
Preschool Language Scale–4	Zimmerman, Steiner, & Pond (2005)	Harcourt
Preschool Language Assessment Instrument–2nd ed. (PLAI-2)	Blank, Rose, & Berlin (2003)	Pro-Ed
Receptive-Expressive-Emergent Language Test–3rd ed. (REEL-3)	Bzoch, League, & Brown (2003)	Pro-Ed
Test of Early Language Development–3rd (TELD-3)	Hresko, Reid, & Hammill (1999)	Pro-Ed

TABLE 13.3   Examples of Language and Communication Screening Instruments

Test Name	Author(s)	Publisher
Fluharty Preschool Speech and Language Screening Test–2nd ed.	Fluharty (2000)	Pro-Ed.
Joliet 3-Minute Speech and Language Screen–Revised	Kinzler & Johnson (1993)	Harcourt
Kindergarten Language Screening Test, 2nd ed. (KLST-2)	Gauthier & Madison (1998)	Pro-Ed
Speech-Ease Screening Inventory	Speech-Ease (1985)	Pro-Ed
Adolescent Language Screening Test	Morgan & Guilford (1984)	Pro-Ed

pected of having significant difficulties with language and/or communication. Such assessment should be both more comprehensive and more thorough than screening.

The nature of the child is another important factor in determining what will be assessed. It should be obvious that it would not be appropriate to assess all elements of language in all children. Younger children and children with lower functional levels may need more comprehensive testing of phonological and morphological development, as well as language prerequisites. On the other hand, for older children and children at more advanced stages of development, assessment is likely to focus on the use of nonliteral language, complex sentences, and pragmatic skills.

It may also be useful to consider the child's language history and the results of observations of the child's use of language at home, in school, and/or in the community in making language assessment decisions for any particular child. Parents' reports of the child's language development, though often inaccurate, may give general information of the course and timing of language development in the child. The goal, of course, is to include just the right elements in the assessment—not so many that the child will become bored and noncompliant but enough to develop a comprehensive picture of the child's language abilities.

Assessment Methods

There are two basic types of assessment procedures: formal and informal. We will first examine formal procedures for evaluating language, including tests, checklists, and observation systems, and will then consider the many informal methods available.

Formal Procedures

Formal assessment procedures consist primarily of standardized tests—that is, tests that have a standard set of directions and format. Most standardized tests are also **norm referenced,** which means that the tests compare an individual's performance to that of a comparison population. Unfortunately, norms do not always include children from a variety of cultural and socioeconomic groups and often do not include children with disabilities.

Despite concerns about norms and test validity, use of formal, standardized tests of language continues. Therefore, it is important for practitioners to be aware of the great variety of language tests available, to keep in mind the limitations of these tests, and to learn about alternative assessment procedures—such as those discussed later in this chapter.

Formal tests of language can be divided into two main types: comprehensive measures and tests of specific language skills. The comprehensive tests of language are designed to test a broad range of language skills across a wide range of ages. For example, the Test of Language Development—Primary (Newcomer & Hammill, 1997) is designed to assess both expressive and receptive language in children from ages 4 to 9 and comprises nine subtests that cover the areas of phonology, syntax, and semantics. The subtests include:

1. *Picture vocabulary.* Choosing from a group of four pictures, the child points to the one that shows the stimulus word.
2. *Relational vocabulary.* Measures the child's ability to understand and express the relationships between two words. For example, the tester asks, "How are apples and oranges alike?"
3. *Oral vocabulary.* The tester reads a word. The child describes what the word means.
4. *Grammatic understanding.* The child selects from a group of three pictures the one that best represents a sentence read by the tester.
5. *Sentence imitation.* The child must repeat sentences that vary in length and grammatic complexity.
6. *Grammatic completion.* The child must complete a stimulus sentence by supplying the appropriate word (e.g., use of possessive, plural, tense).
7. *Word discrimination.* The child listens to pairs of words read by the tester and must say whether the words are the same or different from each other.
8. *Word articulation.* The child describes a picture. The examiner makes a phonetic transcription of the child's speech.
9. *Phonemic analysis.* The tester says a word, then asks the child to repeat it without one phonetic segment, e.g., "Say *cat* without the /k/."

Using scores for each subtest, practitioners can derive an overall language age, as well as gain composite scores for phonology, syntax, semantics, speaking, and listening. The test is relatively easy to administer and interpret. It requires no special training, other than requiring a very careful reading of the manual. Examples of other comprehensive tests of language skills can be found in Table 13.4.

Comprehensive tests of language skills have several advantages, the most important being that they give a reasonably complete picture of the child's language functioning. They provide information about the child's skills in syntax and semantics, and some (but not all) evaluate skills in phonology (e.g., the Test of Language Develop-

TABLE 13.4 Examples of Comprehensive Tests of Language

Test Name and Author(s)	Age Range (year, month)	Areas Assessed	
		Receptive	Expressive
Bankson Language Test–2 (Bankson, 1990)	3–0 to 6–11		syn, sem, prag
Clinical Evaluation of Language Fundamentals–4 (Semel, Wiig, & Secord, 2004)	6–0 to 21–0	syn, sem	syn, sem, pho, prag
Comprehensive Assessment of Spoken Language (CASL) (Carrow-Woolfolk, 1999)	3–0 to 21–0	sem, syn, prag	sem, syn, prag
Oral and Written Language Scales (OWLS) (Carrow-Woolfolk, 1995)	5–0 to 21–0	receptive lang.	expressive lang.
Test of Language Development–Primary (3rd ed.) (Newcomer & Hammill, 1997)	4–0 to 8–11	pho, syn, sem	pho, syn, sem
Test of Language Development–Intermediate (3rd ed.) (Hammill & Newcomer, 1997)	8–0 to 12–11	syn, sem	syn, sem
Test of Adolescent and Adult Language (4th ed.) (Hammill, Brown, Larsen, & Wiederholt, 2007)	12–0 to 24–11	syn, sem	syn, sem

Note: syn = syntax, sem = semantics, prag = pragmatics, pho = phonology

ment—Primary) and pragmatics (the Bankson Language Test). Most of these tests evaluate both receptive and expressive language skills. Because these tests evaluate a wide range of skills, the results reflect the child's skills in various domains of language. For example, look at the results below. What do they tell us about this child?

Test of Language Development—Primary

Name: Juanita M.
Chronological Age = 7 years, 4 months
Language Age = 6 years, 2 months
Subtests (standard scores: mean = 10, standard deviation 3)

Receptive

Picture Vocabulary = 10
Grammatic Understanding = 9
Relational Vocabulary = 9
Word Discrimination = 8

Expressive

Oral Vocabulary = 8
Sentence Imitation = 6
Grammatic completion = 5
Word Articulation = 7
Phonemic Analysis = 6

You can see that Juanita's overall language abilities are significantly below those of other children her age. Also, her scores are much lower for expressive than for receptive language. Vocabulary appears to be a relative area of strength, whereas syntax appears to be a special problem area.

Although these comprehensive tests of language can give us valuable information to use in making classification decisions, by their very nature they are limited in depth. Because they are designed to test a wide range of skills, they do not have a sufficient number of items for in-depth exploration of a specific language domain. Often such in-depth analysis is important for making instructional decisions because teachers need to know whether *specific* language structures are present or absent.

Tests of specific domains of language can provide more detailed information about a single area of language. These tests evaluate phonological, syntactic, semantic, or pragmatic skills in greater depth than most general tests of language can. Examples of these tests can be found in Table 13.5.

Formal, standardized tests can provide important information for making classification and instructional decisions. However, there are significant limitations to the use of standardized tests. Salvia and Ysseldyke (2001) note three particularly troubling issues regarding language assessment. First, standardized tests may not accurately reflect the child's spontaneous language abilities. Since standardized tests must be administered in a very particular way, they do not allow for spontaneous language expression. The child may talk incessantly before and after the testing session, but this cannot be counted as part of the test. A good tester, however, will be sure to note everything about the testing session. A second issue raised by Salvia and Ysseldyke involves problems associated with the use of test results to plan intervention. They note that many language tests do not easily translate into therapeutic goals. They also caution, as an aside here, that clinicians may be tempted to teach in ways that will improve test scores rather than focus on the skills the child needs for success in the classroom and the community. Third, there is a danger that tests may not adequately assess children from diverse social and cultural backgrounds. This is an especially important concern with language testing, since language is so closely intertwined with social and cultural norms.

Informal Procedures

Because of these and similar concerns, many researchers and clinicians have suggested that **informal assessment** of language be included in a comprehensive assessment of language (Lahey, 1988; Owens, 2004). Informal, nonstandardized assessment procedures range from relatively low-structured, spontaneous language samples to highly structured, elicited imitation tasks. Informal measures, even the more highly structured tasks, provide the clinician with greater opportunities to exercise judgment in the selection of assessment objectives and methods.

Language Sampling.   One very useful way to obtain information about a child's language abilities is by collecting and analyzing a sample of his or her language. Although language samples can be a rich source of information, they may also be seen as intim-

TABLE 13.5 Tests of Specific Language Skills

Test Name and Author(s)	Age Range (years, month)
Phonology	
Bankson-Bernthal Test of Phonology (Bankson & Bernthal, 1999)	3–0 to 9–0
Comprehensive Test of Phonological Processing (Wagner, Torgesen, & Rashotte, 1999)	5–0 to 24–11
Computerized Articulation and Phonology Evaluation (Masterson & Bernhardt, 2001)	2 to adult
Goldman-Fristoe Test of Articulation–2nd. ed. (Goldman & Fristoe, 2000)	2–21
Goldman-Fristoe-Woodcock Test of Auditory Discrimination (Goldman, Fristoe, & Woodcock, 1970)	4–70+
Lindamood Auditory Conceptualization Test–3rd ed. (Lindamood & Lindamood, 2004)	5–19
Wepman Auditory Discrimination Test–2nd ed. (Wepman, 1987)	5–8
Syntax	
Structured Photographic Expressive Language Test–3rd ed. (SPELT-3) (Dawson, Stout, & Eyer, 2005)	
Test of Auditory Comprehension of Language–3rd ed. (Carrow-Woolfolk, 1999)	3 to 9–11
Semantics	
Boehm Test of Basic Concepts–3 (Boehm, 2000)	K to grade 2
Comprehensive Receptive and Expressive Vocabulary Test–2nd. ed. (Wallace & Hammill, 2002)	5–0 to 17–11
Peabody Picture Vocabulary Test–4 (Dunn & Dunn, 2007)	2–6 to 90+
Expressive Vocabulary Test (Williams, 1997)	2–6 to 90+
Pragmatics	
Test of Pragmatic Language (Phelps-Teraski & Phelps-Gunn, 1992)	5–0 to 13–11

idating and difficult for teachers to collect and analyze. Because it is such a significant language assessment tool, it is important to know that there are readily applicable methods for collecting and analyzing language samples within school settings.

Owens (2004) noted that "good language samples do not just occur. They are the result of careful planning and execution" (p. 118). This is important to keep in mind. Since the goal of any language sampling is to get a representative sample of the child's language, one cannot just put a child at a table, turn on a tape recorder, and hope for a good sample of language. Accomplishing this goal requires careful planning of the *context, materials,* and *techniques* that will be used.

The best context in which to obtain a language sample is a realistic setting. In other words, the child's classroom, home, or lunchroom are ideal places to record the sample. If possible, the child should be engaged in real activities, such as recording a language sample from a group of three students with learning disabilities while they work together on a group science project. Recording the language sample in natural settings increases the likelihood that a representative sample of language will be obtained. This is especially true for young children. Research has found that younger children produce longer utterances when the speech sample is collected at home rather than in the clinic (Kramer, James, & Saxman, 1979).

Of course, each of these settings has some built-in limitations. Usually there are background noises and many other distractions in the classroom and the lunchroom; obtaining samples of language used at home may not be realistic for teachers and speech-language specialists. Therefore, the ideal of assessment in a natural setting must be balanced by the realities of the limitations. Sometimes it may be necessary to adapt the setting to make it more possible to record a language sample, for example, by bringing mom into a clinic room that is furnished in a homelike way or by sectioning off a portion of the classroom for language sampling.

The selection of materials used during the collection of the language sample is critical to the results. For young children, toys are often the most effective materials to use to elicit representative language samples. Owens (2004) suggests that blocks, dishes, and dolls work well for 2-year-olds, whereas 3-year-olds prefer books, clothes, and puppets. Sometimes pictures are used as the stimulus for a language sample. These, too, must be carefully selected. A single, static picture (e.g., a mountain and stream) is likely to elicit a brief, descriptive response (e.g., *there is a mountain* or *there is a stream).* Using a series of pictures showing action, such as a cartoon strip, for example, is the best way to elicit a variety of language. Whatever materials are used, it is essential that the items be interesting, age appropriate, and effective in eliciting language.

The choice of actual technique of language elicitation is as critical as the choice of context and the materials used. For example, children may be recorded during either spontaneous language situations, during structured activities, or during an interview. Each of these techniques has some advantages and weaknesses. A spontaneous language sample may be the ideal way to elicit the most representative sample of language, but it can be difficult to obtain. Participants may speak unnaturally if they know they are being observed or recorded, and unwanted interruptions can be problematic. An alternative is to use an activity or a material to elicit a structured language sample.

Coggins, Olswang, and Guthrie (1987) compared the results of using a low-structured observation to that of using an elicitation task in assessing the pragmatic skills of young children. In the elicitation condition, the children were presented with objects that they could not use by themselves (e.g., a plastic jar with a screw-on lid, a remote-control toy car). The examiner then waited for the child to make a request. In the low-structured condition, the examiner simply watched the child and mother as they played together. The researchers found that the two methods were complementary. For example, they discovered that the children produced very few spontaneous requests in the low-structured situation but produced numerous requests with the more structured task. The results of this study, as well other research (e.g., Wetherby & Rodriguez, 1992) suggest that it is best to use a variety of techniques to elicit a representative sample of language.

How long should the language sample be? There is no simple answer to this question. It depends, in part, on how talkative children are, the length of their utterances, and the number of conversational exchanges. Experts have suggested that 50 to 100 utterances is an optimal length (Lahey, 1988; Lee, 1974; Owens, 2004). Others have suggested that 30 minutes is a good length (Miller, 1981). Although there are no hard and fast guidelines, research by Cole, Mills, and Dale (1989) showed that it is important to get more than one sample of language and that several shorter samples over varying days and times give the most representative picture of the child's language.

After the language sample has been collected, it must be transcribed. This is a tedious task that must be performed with great accuracy. However, it is essential for the transcriber to record the language as accurately as possible. Utterances should never be interpreted or improved. Natural spoken language is a bit messy, with frequent stops and starts. Speakers frequently interrupt and overlap each other and sometimes stray from the topic. All these idiosyncrasies of language must be preserved in the language sample. There is often a great temptation on the part of the transcriber to edit or interpret the speech, thinking, "The child must have meant to say this, I'll just 'clean it up.'" The recorder must constantly listen for what was *actually* said rather than what *should* or *might* have been said. This is sometimes not as easy as it sounds. Look at the following, taken from a 7-year-old child with a severe expressive-language disorder:

NICK: Umm, army crows.

TEACHER: Tell me again?

N: Army crows.

T: An army crawl?

N.: Yeah.

T: I don't know what an army crawl is. Tell me about that.

N: Du dut craw on da mat.

When this exchange began, we did not know what Nicholas meant by an *army crow*. Later, it became more clear that he was talking about a way of crawling on your belly. It would have been easy to go back and "clean up" the transcript, but this sample shows just how difficult it is to understand Nick.

The next step in the language-sample assessment is to analyze the results. Syntactic analysis of language samples usually begins with calculation of *mean length of utterance (MLU),* which is a rough measure of the complexity of a child's language. It is derived by adding all the morphemes produced in a sample of language and dividing by the number of utterances. For example, if a child produced 125 morphemes in 50 utterances, the MLU would be 2.5 (125/50). The rules for counting morphemes can become rather complex. The best advice for anyone trying to calculate MLU is to be consistent in the decisions the person makes about counting morphemes. In addition to MLU, some of the following could be included in an analysis of the child's syntactic development:

- Word endings used (*-s, -ed, -ing*)
- Sentence types (declarative, question, imperative)
- Sentence complexity (simple, compound, embedded)
- Verb tenses (present, past, future)
- Advanced structures (gerunds, passive voice)

Like MLU, *type-token ratio (TTR)* is a rough measure of semantic development. Type-token ratio is calculated by counting the number of *different* words used in a language sample and dividing by the total number of words in the sample. For example, in the sentence *The dog chased the cat around the house,* there are eight words in the sentence but only six different words *(the, dog, chased, cat, around, house).* If the next sentence was *The dog caught the cat,* there would be only one new word *(caught).* In a language sample of 100 words with 50 different words, the type-token ratio would be .50. A language sample of 100 words with 80 different words would yield a TTR of .80. Thus, a higher type-token ratio indicates that a greater variety of words are being used in the language sample. This is an indicator of a larger vocabulary,

Other analyses of semantic skills are also possible, such as looking for overextensions and underextensions. For example, does the child use some words to stand for larger classes of things (e.g., *dog* for all domestic animals), or does the child use some words in a very narrow way (e.g., *cup* used only for a particular cup)? In addition, the child's use of figurative language (e.g., metaphor and humor) and the use of a variety of semantic functions (action, actor, state of being) could be examined. Of course, it is essential that words are used accurately—with correct meaning and in the appropriate context—and that notations are made of the speaker's violations of any of the rules of semantic relationships (for example, *the married bachelor is here*).

Language samples may also be analyzed for pragmatic as well as syntactic and semantic usage. Johnson, Johnston, and Weinrich (1984) reported a number of pragmatic-functioning problems that could be identified from samples of children's language. These included:

- Problems with topicalization
- Problems establishing the topic and making comments
- Problems in maintaining a topic
- Problems with conversation
- Difficulty in initiating and closing a conversation
- Inability to respond
- Not knowing how to take a conversational turn
- Problems with register
- Giving insufficient information to the listener
- Inability to adjust language to the listener

Each of these pragmatic trouble spots could be included in a language-sample analysis. In addition, one could look for the use of a variety of pragmatic functions. Halliday (1975) identified several ways in which language is used in young children (see Figure 13.1). Language samples can reveal which pragmatic functions are being used by the child. Other methods for examining pragmatic language include asking the child to teach a task to another, asking the child to request a cookie from different people (e.g., a friend, a teacher), and asking two children to act as host and guest on a talk-show (see Chapter 5).

Sometimes phonological development is examined via a language sample. A phonological analysis examining the child's use of speech sounds can reveal speech errors such as substitutions (*go* becomes *do*) and deletion of sounds (*banana* becomes *nana*) as well as whether errors usually appear in the initial, final, or middle position within words.

For a thorough analysis of phonological development, it is necessary to do a phonetic transcription of the language sample, rewriting each utterance using a standard sample of speech-sound coding. This is a laborious process that requires great expertise. Usually only a trained speech-language specialist can do a phonetic transcription.

It is possible to use a computer program to assist with language-sample analysis. The SALT program (Systematic Analysis of Language Transcripts) can calculate MLU and TTR, as well as many other measures of syntax, semantics, morphology, and pragmatics (for more information, go to www.languageanalysislab.com/). Although the computer can be very helpful, other judgments are required about the language sample itself, such as where utterances begin and end. Computer analysis of language samples can assist, but not replace, clinical judgment.

Language samples are a very good way to find out more about the language of a particular child. They can give a more realistic picture of the child's use of language in realistic conversational contexts. Careful analysis of the samples can yield information that can be used for instructional planning. One should be careful, however, when using language samples, not to compare children. Research has found that although language samples are reasonably consistent for any particular child, they are not a reliable way to compare the language performance of children (Cole et al., 1989).

FIGURE 13.1   Pragmatic Functions in Child Language

1. Instrumental-language used to satisfy needs and desires (*I want more milk*)
2. Regulatory-language used to control or regulate the actions of others (*Open the door*)
3. Interactional-language used to establish interactions (*Hi; Goodbye*)
4. Personal-language used to express personal feelings, attitudes, and interest (*I love you*)
5. Heuristic-language used to explore and organize the environment (*That's a kitty*)
6. Imaginative-language used to create an imaginary environment

Source: Adapted from Halliday (1975).

Language Elicitation Tasks.   Sometimes it is necessary to structure a language elicitation activity in a way that will prompt a certain kind of response. Let's say, for example, that you wanted to find out whether a child had developed the use of the past tense (*-ed*) ending. Although children just might use a few *-ed* endings in a spontaneous language sample, they would be unlikely to produce more than a few. Alternatively, you might want to use a task that prompts the use of *-ed* endings—for example, by showing a brief video of a cartoon character fishing and then asking questions about what the child saw. The responses should be mostly in the past tense.

One widely used method to elicit specific language responses is imitation. Using this technique, the examiner says a sentence and asks the child to repeat it. To prompt the use of the present progressive ending, the examiner might say *The girl is riding a bike.* The theory behind the use of imitation tasks is that children will be able to repeat only those language structures that they have already mastered (Menyuk, 1968). Research on the use of imitation tasks has yielded mixed results. Some studies have found imitation to be a poor way of measuring language performance (Connell & Myles-Zizter, 1982); others have found that the usefulness of these activities varied from child to child (Fujiki & Brinton, 1987). Although imitation tasks can be useful, they should be used in combination with other measures of language use, such as those that follow.

Morphology.   Berko (1958) developed a classic task that required children to complete a sentence that described a picture. For this task, the examiner prompts a response by saying *This is a wug. Now there are two of them. There are two _____.* The child has to fill in the blank. By using nonsense words, this task is able to assess the child's knowledge of morphological rules.

Syntax.   Owens (2004) gives two suggestions for eliciting negatives. He calls the first "The Emperor's New Clothes." The examiner makes an untrue statement *(Oh Shirley, what beautiful yellow boots),* which should prompt the child to respond with a negative *(I'm not wearing boots).* Owens calls the second technique "Screw-Up." The examiner makes a statement that does not match the action *(Here's your snack*—said as the examiner hands the subject a pencil). The subject should respond by saying *That's not a snack.* These examples show the creativity that teachers and others can apply to elicit specific syntactic structures. For example, to elicit the use of possessives, one could say *Who does that book belong to?* as a way to prompt the response, *It's Jack's book.*

Semantics.   Howell, Fox, and Morehead (1993, p. 281) present several ways to elicit vocabulary knowledge. One suggestion goes as follows:

> Target word: *drill*
> Directions: "Select the words which make sentence 2 most like sentence 1."
> Sentence 1: We need drill on our skills.
> Sentence 2: If we want to get better at our skills we should
>   . . . study them.
>   . . . put a hole in them.
>   . . . do them a lot.

Pragmatics. There are many ways to elicit aspects of pragmatics. For example, Owens (2004) suggested some of the following activities:

Target	Technique	Example
Requests for information	"Pass it on"	CLINICIAN: Max, do you know where Linda's project is? STUDENT: No. CLINICIAN: Oh, see if she does. STUDENT: Linda, where's your project?
Contingent query	"Mumble"	CLINICIAN (FINISHING A STORY): And so, just as the giant got to the door (mumble) STUDENT: What? (If the child makes no response, prompt with a question)
Initiating conversation	"Request for assistance"	CLINICIAN: Miguel, can you ask Keith to help me? STUDENT: Keith, can you help us?

The development of elicited language tasks is limited only by one's creativity and knowledge of language. These tasks can be fun for the child while also providing important information about the child's language development.

Curriculum-Based Assessment

Another informal approach to assessment that has become widely used in classrooms is **curriculum-based assessment (CBA).** The idea behind curriculum-based assessment is simple but powerful: Children should be assessed on what they have learned in the classroom (rather than on what "experts" think children should know). Nelson (1989) defines curriculum-based assessment of language as "the use of curriculum contexts and content for measuring a student's language intervention needs and progress" (p. 171). In other words, when using curriculum-based assessment to assess language skills, teachers can compare the child's language skills to those required by the curriculum in that classroom. Nelson suggests that teachers observe the child's ability to use the various language rule systems (phonological, morphological, and so on) in all modalities demanded by the curriculum (listening, speaking, reading, writing, and thinking). She also suggests that teachers pay attention to the child's ability to think about and use language (metalinguistic skills) (see Table 13.6).

In addition to simply observing children in their classrooms, teachers can gather informal, curriculum-based information about language use in many other ways—for instance, by participating with the child in answering questions at the end of a chapter. In this way, teachers can evaluate the ability of the child to understand text, to paraphrase, and to formulate a response. Other possibilities are to ask the student to retell a story or explain the steps to solving a math problem (Nelson, 1989). Each of these activities can yield important information about the child's ability to understand and use language in the classroom.

TABLE 13.6 Areas of Consideration for Curriculum-Based Language Assessment

Rule Systems	Modalities	Linguistic Levels	Contexts
Phonological	Listening	Sound	Formal tests
Morphological	Speaking	Syllable	Spontaneous samples
Syntactic	Reading	Word	Academic materials:
Semantic	Writing	Sentence	• workbook pages
Pragmatic	Thinking	Text	• reading text
			• science text
			• math activities

Source: Reprinted with permission from "Curriculum-Based Language Assessment and Intervention," by N. W. Nelson. *Language, Speech, and Hearing Services in Schools, 20,* 177. Copyright 1989 by American Speech-Language-Hearing Association. All rights reserved.

Portfolio assessment is another technique that can be used to apply a curriculum-based assessment approach to language (Kratcoski, 1998). Used properly, portfolio assessment should be more than accumulating a file of student papers. It should be a collection of work selected by the learner, speech-language pathologist, teacher, and other staff or communication partners that profiles the learner's use of targeted communication behaviors. Items in the portfolio might include writing samples, journal entries, projects, presentations, and the like.

In order for the portfolio to be useful as an assessment tool, the items in the portfolio must be analyzed. Holistic scoring can be applied to many writing and speaking assignments. In holistic scoring, the evaluator considers the language sample (spoken or written) as a whole. An overall score may be assigned to the sample based on a rubric that describes the target criteria (see Table 13.7).

In addition to holistic scoring, the teacher or speech-language specialist might also apply a descriptive analysis that focuses on specific structures that may be problematic for the child. For example, for a child who is having difficulty consistently using past-tense endings, the descriptive analyzed might focus on the accuracy and consistency of use of that structure.

Curriculum-based assessment is another informal approach that teachers and other professionals can use to assess language. As Kratcoski (1998) points out, it is useful both for determining the child's current status as well as looking at performance over time. Used properly, curriculum-based assessment can be a very useful source of information for guiding instruction.

Ecological Assessment

Ecological assessment examines the child's behavior in the context of environmental demands and expectations (McCormick, 2003) rather than comparing children to population norms. Ecological assessment is often used to evaluate students with severe dis-

TABLE 13.7   Example of a Holistic Scoring Rubric

Points	Criteria
3	An introduction is apparent. At least three supporting ideas are expressed. Each idea is elaborated. A closing is evident.
2	An introduction is apparent. At least one to two supporting ideas are expressed. Each idea is elaborated. A closing is evident.
1	The main topic is addressed. No supporting ideas are expressed. No closing is evident.
0	Off topic.

abilities because normed tests may not be useful with this population and functional goals may be of great importance.

The basic idea behind ecological assessment is to intensively evaluate the functioning of the individual in the real environments in which he or she must function. The results of this evaluation become the basis for functional intervention goals for the child and guide needed adaptations in the environment. McCormick (2003) has identified 10 steps in the ecological assessment process:

1. Get to know the student.
   - Identify the resources and supports available at home and in school.
   - Identify the student's strengths.
   - Develop goals for (and with) the student.
2. List activities/routines in a typical school day.
   - Observations and/or interviews can be conducted.
3. Prioritize activities/routines and develop a broad goal statement.
4. Observe and record the behavior of a nondisabled peer and/or conduct interviews to determine the key behavioral expectations for each activity/routine.
   - Nondisabled peers are observed in order to understand what skills the student with disabilities needs to perform the target task.
5. Observe and record the behavior of the student from initiation to completion of each activity/routine.
6. Compare the behavior of the student with expectations for each activity/routine.
   - Note when the student does not meet expectations to determine skills to be learned.
7. Highlight language and communication skills.
8. Try to ascertain why key language/communication behaviors are not demonstrated.

- The student may not recognize what he or she is supposed to do or say (strategy deficiency).
- The student may be unable to perform the skill.
- The student may be unmotivated to perform the skill.
- The student has never learned to perform the skill.
- The physical environment makes it difficult for the student to perform the skill.

9. State the language/communication objectives for each activity.
10. Develop an individualized instructional plan for each objective.

Ecological assessment can be a complex and difficult approach to assessment, but it can yield very useful results, especially for students for whom test norms may not be relevant. There is an inseparable relationship between assessment and instruction in the ecological approach (see Box 13.1).

BOX **13.1**

Example of an Ecological Assessment

Tricia is an 8-year-old student with cerebral palsy and mild cognitive disability who is placed in a regular education classroom. She is supported by a classroom aide.

Following a meeting with Tricia's classroom teacher, her aide, her parents, and Mrs. Kline, a special education teacher assigned to consult with the regular classroom teacher, it was determined that one of the priority goals for Tricia would be requesting food in the cafeteria.
(Steps 1, 2, and 3)

Observations of Tricia's peers indicate that, in most cases, they are asked by a cafeteria aide to make a verbal response to indicate their choice.
(Step 4)

Observation of Tricia by Mrs. Kline indicate that Tricia responds to the verbal prompt from the cafeteria aide by pointing. If the aide is not sure what Tricia wants, she points to various choices until Tricia nods her head.
(Step 5)

The language/communication goal for Tricia is for her to make a verbal request in response to the cafeteria aide's verbal prompt.
(Steps 6 and 7)

Mrs. Kline has determined that several of the common choices that Tricia needs to make are not currently available on her augmentative communication device.
(Step 8)

Requesting food choices is established as an instructional goal for Tricia. Common menu choices are added as options on her communication device and practiced with the classroom aide. Tricia is given several opportunities to practice this skill in the cafeteria with the cafeteria aide when her peers are not in the cafeteria. Her classroom aide observes and collects data on Tricia's performance of this goal.
(Steps 9 and 10)

Response to Intervention (RTI)

The traditional diagnostic-remedial model of assessment and intervention has been challenged recently by the **response to intervention** (RTI) initiative. In brief, RTI involves the assessment of students' responses to scientifically based instruction across education settings for the purpose of making decisions about students' needs (Graner, Faggella-Luby, & Fritschmann, 2005). The idea is that if all children are taught using scientifically validated instructional methods, then those children who do not "respond" to this instruction can be thought of as at risk for learning difficulties (for more on RTI, see Vaughn & Fuchs, 2003).

Response to intervention models use a multistep process to identify students with learning difficulties. In Tier I, students receive scientifically validated instruction from a general education teacher in the general education classroom. Assessment is continuously conducted on the overall level of achievement and on the rate of growth for all students in the classroom. Students identified by assessment in Tier I as "nonresponders" receive intervention instruction of a certain length of time, intensity, and duration in Tier II. A support teacher may provide this instruction, Students who still do not respond to intense intervention instruction may be eligible for more formal special education evaluation in Tier III. This is the point where additional assessment for eligibility determination may be conducted,

The RTI movement gained a great deal of impetus from the 2004 reauthorization of the Individuals with Disabilities Education Improvement Act (IDEA). The law states that for the purpose of determining whether a child has a specific learning disability, the school district "may use a process which determines if a child responds to a scientific, research based intervention as part of its evaluation procedures." Some school districts have interpreted this as a mandate for RTI but, in fact, the law only permits, not requires, the RTI approach.

It is too early to know the extent to which the response to intervention approach to assessment and intervention will replace the long-standing diagnostic-remedial model. Careful research will need to be conducted on the effectiveness of the model for identifying and treating children with learning difficulties. In the end, it is intervention outcomes that should determine which models are used.

Summary

In this chapter we have considered some of the challenges in assessing language and the many ways that language can be assessed. We examined formal, standardized language; language samples; and elicited language tasks. We also discussed alternative approaches to assessment, including curriculum-based assessment, ecological assessment, and response to intervention.

Development of a comprehensive plan of language assessment should include the following elements:

- Testing of hearing
- Examination of the child's mouth, teeth, and tongue to determine whether malformations may be affecting language production

- Assessment of cognitive functioning
- Observation of language use in school
- A language sample (or other functional assessment of language)
- Formal tests of language

The following case study illustrates how a variety of assessment procedures can be used to produce a comprehensive picture of an individual's language and literacy skills.

Marvin: A Case Study

Marvin is a 13-year-old, seventh-grade student in a public school district. He is currently included in regular education classes throughout the school day and receives support from a special education aide during language arts and math classes.

Marvin's parents report that in the home, their son shows a low tolerance for frustration. He frequently gives up easily on homework assignments and also seems to be easily distracted. However, they report no behavior problems. School reports indicate that Marvin is having difficulty in both language arts and math. Marvin enjoys sports and plays on several teams.

The results of a test of intelligence (WISC-IV) were as follows:

Subtests	Scaled Scores (10-average)
Verbal Comprehension Subtests	
Similarities	7
Vocabulary	10
Comprehension	10
Perceptual Reasoning Subtests	
Block Design	4
Picture Concepts	11
Matrix Reasoning	4
Working Memory Subtests	
Digit Span	8
Letter-Number Sequencing	8
Processing Speed Subtests	
Coding	7
Symbol Search	6

Verbal comprehension index: 95 (27th percentile) (90% confidence interval 86–97)

Perceptual Reasoning index: 77 (50th percentile) (90% confidence interval 86–97)

Working Memory index: 88 (42nd percentile) (90% confidence interval 86–97)

Processing Speed index: 80 (50th percentile) (90% confidence interval 86–97)

Full Scale Score: 81 (37th percentile) (90% confidence interval 86–97)

Marvin's overall level of cognitive development was at the 10th percentile, which places him in the low-average range. Within the verbal area, Marvin's scores clustered in the low-average to average range. His relative strengths were in word knowledge and in his ability to respond to practical problems. Overall, Marvin responses were often inconsistent and there was a great deal of variation among subtest scores.

The Woodcock Johnson III Test of achievement was administered to obtain standardized measures of academic achievement. The subtest scores were as follows:

Subtest	Standard Score (68% Confidence Band)		Percentile Rank
Letter-Word Identification	96	(85–90)	40
Reading Fluency	89	(91–95)	24
Story Recall	98	(93–107)	46
Calculation	83	(87–97)	13
Math Fluency	99	(82–89)	48
Spelling	99	(85–93)	46
Passage Comprehension	94	(87–94)	34
Applied Problems	95	(95–106)	37
Writing Samples	92	(99–116)	30
Reading Vocabulary	95	(77–86)	37
Handwriting	96	(79–91)	39

Marvin was administered the Peabody Picture Vocabulary test (PPVTIIIB). He obtained a scaled score of 90 (Mean = 100, SD = 15), which placed him at the 25th percentile. Marvin's vocabulary and word attack skills are areas of relative strength. He has difficulty understanding what he has read. Math calculation ability is significantly deficient. Marvin's inconsistent results and parental and school reports of distractibility and low frustration suggest that Marvin should be observed in the classroom with the Conners Hyperactivity Scale.

REVIEW QUESTIONS

1. What are some of the factors that make language especially difficult to assess?

2. Discuss the advantages and limitations of formal and informal methods of language assessment.

3. Calculate the mean length of utterance (MLU) for the following language-sample information:

Number of Morphemes	Number of Utterances	MLU
250	75	
327	90	
340	85	

4. What is type-token ratio? How is it calculated? What does it indicate about language development?

5. Compare the advantages and the limitations of two methods for eliciting language samples.

6. Describe an informal elicitation technique that could be used to prompt a child to ask questions.

7. Why is ecological assessment especially well suited for the assessment of students with severe disabilities?

SUGGESTED ACTIVITIES

1. Informal language elicitation tasks are designed to prompt a child to produce a specific language structure. Your task is to develop elicitation activities for the following language elements:

    Possessives *(his, yours, mine)*

    Multiple meaning words *(table, swing, left)*

    Use of politeness terms *(please, thank you)*

    You must select materials and formats that will cause the individual to produce the desired responses. Include in your report:

    a. A description of the materials and format you selected

    b. The age and disability (if any) of the individual being tested

    c. The results of your assessment

    d. Your interpretation of the results

2. Compare using two of the techniques for eliciting language samples (pictures, interviews, structured-task, spontaneous) discussed in the chapter. You will need to collect two language samples of approximately 50 utterances each (a total of 100 utterances) from one individual using each of the techniques. Analyze the resulting samples for the MLU, TTR, and language-complexity topics discussed. In your report, include the following:

    a. A description of the procedures used

    b. A description of the subject (e.g., age, disability, if any)

    c. A report of the results

    d. Your conclusion about what the results indicate about the two methods you used for eliciting language samples

GLOSSARY

curriculum-based assessment: an approach to assessment that utilizes classroom tasks as the basis for assessment

diagnostic assessment: assessment procedures that give in-depth information about a specific skill area

ecological assessment: examines the child's behavior in the context of environmental demands and expectations

formal assessment: published instruments that utilize a standard set of procedures to gather information to be used for assessment; can include tests, observation forms, rating scales, and so on

informal assessment: measures developed by teachers and other practitioners to directly evaluate the skills of children with whom they are working

norm referenced: norm-referenced tests compare an individual's performance to that of a comparison population

reliability: the consistency with which the instrument measures the target skill

response to intervention: assessment of students' responses to scientifically based instruction for the purpose of making decisions about students' needs

screening: an assessment procedure that is brief and easy to administer to a large number of individuals

validity: the extent to which the instrument measures what it purports to measure

RESOURCES ON THE WEB

www.proedinc.com Pro-Ed, test distributor and publisher

http://harcourtassessment.com/ Harcourt Assessment, source for the Psychological Corporation tests

www.ldaamerica.org/about/position/rti.asp Learning Disability Association of American position paper on response to intervention

www.brookespublishing.com/ Brookes Publishing, test distributor and publisher

REFERENCES

Bankson, N. (1990). *Bankson language test* (2nd ed.). Austin, TX: Pro-Ed.

Bankson, N., & Bernthal, J. (1999). *Bankson-Bernthal test of phonology.* Austin, TX: Pro-Ed.

Berko, J. (1958). The child's learning of English morphology. *Word, 14,* 150–177.

Blank, M., Rose, S. A., & Berlin, L. J. (2003). *Preschool language assessment instrument* (2nd ed.). Austin, TX: Pro-Ed.

Boehm, A. (2000). *Boehm test of basic concepts—Revised.* San Antonio, TX: Psychological Corporation.

Bzoch, K. R., League, R., & Brown, V. K. (2003). *Receptive-expressive-emergent language test* (3rd ed.). Austin, TX: Pro-Ed.

Carrow-Woolfolk, E. (1995). *Oral and written language scales.* Circle Pines, MN: American Guidance Service.

Carrow-Woolfolk, E. (1999). *Comprehensive assessment of language.* Circle Pines, MN: American Guidance Service.

Carrow-Woolfolk, E. (1999). *Test for auditory comprehension of language* (3rd ed.). Austin, TX: Pro-Ed.

Coggins, T., Olswang, L., & Guthrie, J. (1987). Assessing communicative intent in young children: Low structured observation or elicitation tasks? *Journal of Speech and Hearing Disorders, 52,* 44–49.

Cole, K., Mills, P., & Dale, P. (1989). Examination of test-retest and split-half reliability for measures derived from language samples of young handicapped children. *Language, Speech, and Hearing Services in Schools, 20,* 259–268.

Connell, P., & Myles-Zitzer, C. (1982). An analysis of elicited imitation as a language evaluation procedure. *Journal of Speech and Hearing Disorders, 47,* 390–396.

Dunn, L., & Dunn, L. (2007). *Peabody picture vocabulary test* (3rd ed.). New York: Pearson Assessments.

Fenson, L., Marchman, V. A., Thal, D. J., Dale, P. S., Reznick, S., & Bates, E. (2006). *Mac-Arthur-Bates Communicative Development Inventories.* (2nd ed.). Baltimore: Brookes.

Fluharty, N. B. (2000). *Fluharty preschool speech and language screening test.* Austin, TX: Pro-Ed.

Fujiki, M., & Brinton, B. (1987). Elicited imitation revisited: A comparison with spontaneous language production. *Language, Speech, and Hearing Services in Schools, 18,* 301–311.

Gauthier, S., & Madison, C. (1998). *Kindergarten Language Screening Test* (2nd ed.). Austin, TX: Pro-Ed.

Goldman, R., & Fristoe, M. (2000). *Goldman Fristoe test of articulation—Revised.* New York: Pearson Assessment.

Goldman, R., Fristoe, M., & Woodcock, R. (1970). *Goldman-Fristoe-Woodcock test of auditory discrimination.* New York: Pearson Assessment.

Graner, P. S., Faggella-Luby, M. N., & Fritschmann, N. S. (2005). An overview of responsiveness to intervention: What practitioners ought to know. *Topics in Language Disorders, 25,* 93–105.

Halliday, M. (1975). *Explorations in the function of language.* London: Edward Arnold.

Hammill, D., Brown, V., Larsen, S., & Wiederholt, J. (2007). *Test of adolescent and adult language* (4th ed.). Austin, TX: Pro-Ed.

Hammill, D., & Newcomer, P. (1997). *Test of language development—Intermediate* (3rd ed.). Austin, TX: Pro-Ed.

Howell, K., Fox, S., & Morehead, M. (1993). *Curriculum-based evaluation: Teaching and decision making* (2nd ed.). Pacific Grove, CA: Brooks/Cole.

Hresko, W., Reid, D., & Hammill, D. (1999). *Test of early language development* (3rd ed.). Austin, TX: Pro-Ed.

Johnson, A., Johnston, E., & Weinrich, B. (1984). Assessing pragmatic skills in children's language. *Language, Speech, and Hearing Services in Schools, 15,* 2–9.

Kinzler, M., & Johnson, C. (1993). *Joliet 3-minute speech and language Screen—Revised.* San Antonio, TX: Psychological Corporation.

Kramer, C., James, S., & Saxman, J. (1979). A comparison of language samples elicited at home and in the clinic. *Journal of Speech and Hearing Disorders, 44,* 321–330.

Kratcoski, A. M. (1998). Guidelines for using portfolios in assessment and evaluation. *Language, Speech, and Hearing Services in Schools, 29,* 3–10.

Lahey, M. (1988). *Language disorders and language development.* New York: Macmillan.

Lee, L. (1974). *Developmental sentence analysis.* Evanston, IL: Northwestern University Press.

Lindamood, C., & Lindamood, P. (2004). *Lindamood auditory conceptualization test.* New York: Pearson Assessments.

Masterson, J. & Bernhardt, B. (2001). *Computerized articulation and phonology evaluation.* San Antonio, TX: Psychological Corporation.

McCormick, L. (2003). Ecological assessment and planning. In L. McCormick, D. Loeb, & R. Schiefelbusch (Eds.), *Supporting children with communication difficulties in inclusive classrooms* (2nd ed.). Boston: Allyn & Bacon.

Menyuk, P. (1968). Children's learning and reproduction of grammatical and nongrammatical phonological sequences. *Child Development, 39,* 849–859.

Miller, J. (1981). *Assessing language production in children.* Baltimore: University Park Press.

Miller, J., & Chapman, R. (1985). *Systematic analysis of language transcripts.* Madison, WI: Weisman

Center on Mental Retardation and Human Development.

Morgan, D., & Guilford, A. (1984). *Adolescent Language Screening Test.* Austin, TX: Pro-Ed.

Nelson, N. W. (1989). Curriculum-based language assessment and intervention. *Language, Speech, and Hearing Services in Schools, 20,* 170–184.

Newcomer, P., & Hammill, D. (1997). *Test of language development—Primary* (3rd ed.). Austin, TX: Pro-Ed.

Owens, R. (2004). *Language disorders: A functional approach to assessment and intervention.* Boston: Allyn & Bacon.

Phelps-Teraski, D., & Phelps-Gunn, T. (1992). *Test of pragmatic language.* Austin, TX: Pro-Ed.

Salvia, J., & Ysseldyke, J. (2001). *Assessment* (8th ed.). Boston: Houghton-Mifflin.

Semel, E., Wiig, E., & Secord, W. (2004). *Clinical evaluation of language fundamentals* (3rd ed.). San Antonio, TX: Psychological Corporation.

Silliman, E. R., & Diehl, S. F. (2002). Assessing children with language learning disabilities. In D. Bernstein & E. Tiegerman (Eds.), *Language and communication disorders in children* (5th ed.) (pp. 182–255). Boston: Allyn & Bacon.

Speech-Ease (1985). *Speech-Ease, Screening Inventory.* Austin, TX: Pro-Ed.

Vaughn, S., & Fuchs, L. S. (2003). Redefining learning disabilities as inadequate response to instruction: The promise and potential problems. *Learning Disabilities Research & Practice, 18,* 137–146.

Wagner, R., Torgesen, J., & Rashotte, C. (1999). *Comprehensive test of phonological processing.* Austin, TX: Pro-Ed.

Wallace, G. & Hammill, O. (2002). *Comprehensive receptive and expressive vocabulary test* (2nd ed.). Austin, TX: Pro-Ed.

Wepman, J. (1987). *Wepman auditory discrimination test.* Los Angeles: Western Psychological Services.

Wetherby, A., & Prizant, B. (1993). *Communication and symbolic behavioral scales.* Chicago: Riverside.

Wetherby, A., & Rodriguez, G. (1992). Measurement of communicative intentions in normally developing children during structured and unstructured contexts. *Journal of Speech and Hearing Research, 35,* 130–138.

Williams, K. (1997). *Expressive vocabulary test.* Circle Pines, MN: American Guidance Services.

Zimmerman, I. L., Steiner, V. G., & Pond, R. E. (2005). *Preschool language scale* (4th ed.). San Antonio, TX: Harcourt.

14 Enhancing Language and Communication

As we know from the preceding chapters, there are children who, despite exposure to language, fail to develop language skills at the same rate or to the same extent as other children. Difficulty with the development and use of effective speech, language, and communication skills affects the ability of students to understand classroom instruction, socialize with their peers, and become full members of society. What are we to do about children with language learning disorders?

We could wait for them to catch up. Some may do so, but most children with language disorders do not catch up; in fact, they fall further and further behind. Since we cannot usually count on spontaneous recovery to take care of the problem, it is often necessary to develop strategies to help students with language disorders enhance their speech, language, and communication skills. These strategies may be of two types: instruction that is delivered in the classroom for the benefit of all children and intervention that focuses on the special needs of individuals.

In this chapter we will examine effective practices in language instruction and in intervention. Principles and guidelines for instruction, specific instructional approaches, and language-intervention procedures are discussed. The focus throughout is on effective, research-based techniques that can help children fully develop their language and communication skills.

After completion of this chapter, you should be able to:

1. Discuss the rationale for language instruction and intervention.
2. Discuss what type of language instruction works best in a variety of classroom settings.
3. Develop specific suggestions for enhancing language and communication skills of students at the preschool, elementary, and secondary levels.
4. Describe the skills needed for an effective collaboration with other professionals.
5. Understand the decisions that need to be made prior to language intervention.
6. Discuss the implications of research for making decisions about language instruction.

Rationale for Language Instruction

Young children with language disorders are much more likely to have academic, so-cial, and language difficulties later in life than are children with normally developing language (Aram & Nation, 1980; Aram, Ekelman, & Nation, 1984; King, Jones, & Laskey, 1982). If these children do not receive language intervention, their language disorders are likely to persist (Johnson et al., 1999; Law et al., 2000).

Fortunately, there is increasing evidence that early instruction that focuses on im-proving and communication skills can significantly enhance both language skills (e.g., Bryen & Joyce, 1985; Goldstein & Hockenberger, 1991; Law, Garrett, & Nye, 2004) and academic success of children, especially in reading (Moats, 2001). For this reason alone, it would be important to provide instruction in support of enhanced language and communication skills. But there are other reasons to intervene as well. Language is a critical skill for classroom interaction. If students are to fully participate, they must have the language and communication skills to understand classroom instruction and to ask and answer questions. Moreover, social skills are as important as (some would say more important than) academic skills in success during and after the school years.

Although there are a number of good reasons to provide language instruction, many children still do not receive the instruction they need. One explanation is that some educators still rely primarily on intervention provided by specialists as the major source of language and communication instruction for children. The term **intervention** suggests that this service takes place after a period of time in which the individual has been exposed to instruction. But some children have limited (or no) exposure to such instruction. Moats and Lyon (1996) note that many teachers lack the depth of under-standing of language and language instructional approaches that is necessary in order to deliver effective instruction. These teachers may not recognize the language and communication needs of their students. Even if they do recognize the need, they may not be able to provide effective instruction. Another reason is that instruction, when it occurs, may focus on the wrong skills. As Ferguson (1994) points out, in the past 20 years the focus of instruction has shifted from teaching people to speak (e.g., through speech therapy), to giving people language (e.g., sign language, symbol systems), to helping students communicate. Yet, sometimes language instruction continues to focus on the acquisition of speech sounds or language symbols without consideration of the purpose of language, which is communication.

In certain instances, effective instruction may not be enough. Some children need more focused and intensive instruction that can best be provided through intervention. Since intervention is a costly and limited commodity, it is important that it be delivered only when necessary and to those who need it most.

Whether teachers and other professionals are delivering instruction in a general education classroom or are providing intervention for students with disorders, it is es-sential that they use the most effective practices available. Increasingly, practitioners are urged to use **evidence-based practices** in delivering instruction. As Gillam and Gillam (2004) stated, until recently speech-language pathologists have been taught to consider their clients' wishes and their own experience in making clinical decisions. The same may be said about teachers. Although both speech and language specialists and teachers may have been knowledgeable about research, it rarely guided their day-to-day practice.

Slavin (2002) and others have noted that evidence-based practices are what have helped experts in fields as diverse as medicine and agriculture achieve the extraordinary progress they have made in the past century. Rather than basing practice largely on opinion or isolated experiences, evidence-based practices are developed from intensive, well-designed research that identifies practices that work and those that do not. The No Child Left Behind legislation calls for educators to use "scientifically based" practices in delivering education. In response, the U.S. Department of Education has established the Institute of Education Sciences to disseminate information about effective practices, and many professional organizations (including ASHA and CEC) are at work to identify and inform their members about educational practices that are supported by research.

In this chapter we will identify language instruction and intervention practices that have been supported by research. As Gillam and Gillam (2004) point out, however, research evidence is not always available regarding educational practices. Still, it is essential that teachers and other professionals attempt to utilize research-validated instructional practices and, when the research is not available, that they participate in studies of educational practices whenever feasible.

Language in the Classroom

Regular as well as special education classrooms can be a rich source of language experiences. Throughout the school day, teachers and children are engaged in communicative interaction. Whenever teachers give directions, ask a question, or provide verbal feedback to students, language is likely to be the mode of interaction. When students are asked to respond to questions, to work in groups, or to give reports, language is the means of expression. Many academic subject areas are directly dependent on language (e.g., reading and writing), while others rely on language in less obvious, but no less important, ways. For example, good language skills are necessary to understand the vocabulary and perform the complex problem solving required for success in math. Other language functions include structuring a lesson, delivering a lecture, organizing information, constructing knowledge, managing and clarifying information, developing and directing inquiry, and conversing with teachers and peers (Bashir & Scavuzzo, 1992).

Although the classroom can be a wonderful source for language stimulation and practice, it can be a minefield for children with language difficulties. Recall the example of what happened in the classroom of kindergarten-aged children with language disorders that was described in Chapter 2. When their teacher used an indirect request, the students looked puzzled and failed to respond. The actual interaction went like this:

TEACHER (directed to three children in the first row): Can you get your books and come here?

STUDENTS: (No response, puzzled looks on their faces)

TEACHER (RAISING HER VOICE): Can you come here?

STUDENTS: (More puzzled looks, still no response)

TEACHER (EXASPERATED):   Get your books and come here!

STUDENTS: (Picked up their books and walked to the teacher's desk)

What was going on here? It seems rather clear that the children were unable to understand the teacher's language. Because the teacher used an indirect request and gave multiple directions, the children were confused. They were not sure how to respond. When the teacher gave a direct command, the children responded appropriately. The teacher might have concluded that the children had hearing impairments or auditory perception problems, or even had emotional disturbances (resistance to authority).

This example is intended to show just how important it is for teachers to be aware of the language they direct toward students. At first, this teacher seemed to be unaware of the effect that her language was having on the students. Had she not modified her language, the students could have been left confused and may have missed an opportunity for learning. This teacher had the advantage of teaching in a classroom with a small number of children whom she had reason to believe had difficulties with language. In a regular education classroom with 25 or 30 children, the teacher may have been too busy helping other children to notice that some did not understand the directions.

Enhancing Language Skills in the Classroom

The classroom should be the primary locus of instruction in language and communication for most students. In this section we will identify techniques that can be used by teachers to enhance the language and communication of their students in the regular or special education classroom.

Enhancing Classroom Interaction

One of the most important things teachers can do is to teach in ways that will enhance the language and communication of children in their classroom. Sociolinguists who have carefully observed classroom interactions have found that teachers dominate the conversation, ask a lot of questions that require minimal responses (one-word answers), and initiate most of the interactions (Cazden, 1986). As a result, in the typical classroom, children are rather passive recipients of communication rather than active partners in such interaction. Even worse, many teachers actively discourage interaction between students and even between the student and the teacher. Of course, there is a limit to how much interaction can be tolerated, but if language learning is an important goal, some interaction should not only be tolerated but also encouraged. Without the chance to interact, children with language-learning difficulties will have little opportunity to develop crucial language skills.

Fortunately, it is possible to enhance classroom communication. After examining research on classroom language intervention, Dudley-Marling and Searle (1988) developed four recommendations that teachers can use to enhance the language-learning environment: (1) the physical setting must promote talk; (2) the teacher must provide opportunities for children to interact and use language as they learn; (3) the teacher needs to provide opportunities for children to use language for a variety of purposes, for a variety of audiences; and (4) the teacher needs to respond to student talk in ways that encourage continued talk. Let's look at each of these suggestions in more detail.

- *The physical setting must promote talk.* Dudley-Marling and Searle (1988) note that many classrooms are organized to discourage interaction. Individual work stations, carrels, and widely spaced rows are all designed to help students concentrate, but they also have the effect of reducing interaction. Certainly, there is a need for concentration, but many students also need opportunities to interact with their peers. Providing large tables where groups can work, learning centers, and interactive classroom displays can give students opportunities to interact in the classroom.

- *The teacher must provide opportunities for children to interact and use language as they learn.* Teachers can structure classroom conversation around academic tasks. For example, children reading a story about fishing can be encouraged to share their previous fishing experiences with the group. Teachers are sometimes reluctant to let students engage in these kinds of conversations because students may stray from the topic. If this happens, students can be redirected back to the topic. Remember, communication is a goal for many students and conversation is not an off-task behavior. Other examples of using instructional activities for language interaction are encouraging the students to say aloud their strategies for solving a math problem or having them read a story to the class.

- *The teacher needs to provide opportunities for children to use language for a variety of purposes, for a variety of audiences.* Teachers can encourage class decision making and problem solving and provide opportunities for discussion and sharing. Look at the following example from Lindfors (1987):

S1: Did even Martin Luther King have to sit in the back of the bus?

T: All black people did.

S2: That was really no fair.

S3: That reminds me. Why do we always have to sit at the same lunch table?

T: What would you rather do?

S3: Sit anywhere we want.

T: That might become confusing. Most people would rather know exactly where they sit.

S2: 1 don't would rather know.

T: How does everyone else feel about this?

In this example, the class went from discussing the life of Martin Luther King to talking about lunchroom seating. By pursuing the discussion, the students had the opportunity to really understand the concepts of freedom and responsibility. Teachers can provide opportunities for students to talk to each other, to younger children (through cross-age tutoring), and to adults (parents and visitors).

- *The teacher needs to respond to student talk in ways that encourage continued talk.* Teachers often ask questions in ways that give students little opportunity to respond. When students do reply, the teacher may not respond in ways that encourage further interaction. Dudley-Marling and Searle (1988) give an example of a teacher discouraging interaction:

S: Boy, you should have seen the neat stuff at the circus.

T: Really, James, you shouldn't say "neat stuff."

The authors suggest that this interaction could have been turned into a longer communicative interaction if the teacher had said something like, *Oh, you had a good time at the circus?* Consider another example of classroom interaction adapted from Lindfors (1987):

T: What does the earth revolve around?

S: The sun.

T: The sun. Right. But as it moves around the sun, it also keeps turning like this (turns ball) on its own . . .

S: Center.

T: Well, kind of. Its own . . .

S: Axis.

T: Its own axis, right.

Was this an effective instructional interaction? If we look just at the content of the lesson, it appears that the child knows the appropriate science facts. But, if communication is our concern, the interaction is not satisfactory. There was little opportunity for the child to participate in a prolonged interaction. The teacher asked questions that required only one-word answers. No discussion was required or expected.

Teachers should be careful not to dominate the conversation, and they should follow the child's lead in setting the conversational topic. One simple but effective strategy for increasing interaction is to pause several seconds for a response to a question. Research has found that teachers generally wait less than one second for a response (Rowe, 1974). Longer wait-time increases the likelihood that students will respond (Rowe, 1986).

Throughout the school day there are numerous opportunities for teachers to prompt interaction and respond to students in ways that encourage interaction. Two effective ways of increasing interaction are through use of self-talk and parallel talk. When using *self-talk,* teachers or speech-language specialists talk about what they are doing as they do it. For example, an adult playing with a set of farm animals might say, *Look, now I'm moving the horse. There goes the pig. Now, why did the chickens go over there?* With **parallel talk,** the adult describes the action for the child as the child performs the action. The adult might use language similar to the above as the child plays with the animals.

Norris and Hoffman (1990) give other examples of strategies derived from research that teachers and speech-language specialists can use to assist children. One example is **restating and rewording.** When using this technique, the adult acknowledges what the child has said and provides alternative models for communicating the same information. Norris and Hoffman give the following example:

CHILD: I want brush.

ADULT: Right, give me the brush. It's my turn. I want the brush now.

All of these techniques are designed to take naturally occurring classroom situations and turn them into opportunities for language teaching. As McCormick (1986) stated, the focus of instruction "should be on increasing the quantity and quality of child-initiated communications (verbal and nonverbal) to obtain desired objects and regulate the actions of others" (p. 124). McCormick gives five suggestions that teachers can use to enhance classroom communication:

1. Seek participation of as many persons as possible in language training (aides, volunteers, parents, related services personnel, peers).
2. Arrange opportunities for language training and practice in a range and variety of contexts.
3. Assure opportunities for language training and practice throughout the school day.
4. Accumulate an appealing assortment of materials.
5. Use natural, response-specific reinforcers.

Enhancing Communication in Specific Classroom Environments

The techniques considered so far for enhancing language and communication skills are useful in nearly any classroom. But there are some strategies that are more effective in particular classroom environments or with children at certain ages or developmental levels.

Preschool Classrooms

Language and communication development should be a major goal in preschool classrooms. Teachers of preschool children usually include many activities to involve their students in such interaction. For example, Watson, Layton, Pierce, and Abraham (1994) describe a preschool program for children with language disorders that incorporates instruction in emerging literacy skills into activities that most teachers of preschool children will recognize. These activities include:

1. *Circle time.* When the bell rings, children get their mats and bring them to the circle. Children must recognize their names in order to get their mats. After an opening song, children discuss the job chart that has jobs listed in print, supplemented by pictures. When there is a song, the words are written out on a poster board and the teacher points to the words as they are sung.

2. *Storytime.* Books that follow a classroom theme (animals, communities, etc.) are selected. As the teacher reads the story, each child is asked for some kind of response. In addition, there are opportunities for choral responding. Because repeated readings help children improve their comprehension skills, the story is reread at least three times in a week.

3. *Story-related group activity.* The teacher uses follow-up activities to reinforce concepts from the story. Children may role-play parts from the story or make puppets to represent characters from the story.

4. *Literacy-rich centers.* Watson and colleagues describe three literacy centers that are used in their classroom. At the *art and writing center,* children draw pictures related to the "story of the week" and tell about their picture. The *role-playing center* contains dress-up clothes, dolls, and toys that the children can use to act out action from the story or from their own scripts. During free time the children can go to the *book and library center* to look at books and listen to tapes.

5. *Snack time.* Often snack time is integrated with the weekly theme. Snack packaging may be used as reading material for the child.

6. *Gross motor play/Outdoor activities.* Even during gross motor activities there are opportunities to practice literacy skills. When teaching exercises, the teacher also introduces the written word (e.g., *arm, body).*

7. *Closing circle.* This provides a final opportunity during the day for children to recall and talk about their experiences. When children are given printed materials to take home, the child is told about the purpose of the message, reinforcing the idea that print has a purpose.

The preschool classroom provides many opportunities for language interaction and instruction. These opportunities can be enhanced by the use of carefully selected materials and activities and by adults who are ready to facilitate interaction with and among children. Ostrosky and Kaiser (1991) suggest seven strategies that they believe will increase the likelihood that children will show an interest in their environment and make communicative attempts, and that will increase the likelihood that the adult will prompt the use of language.

1. *Interesting materials.* Provide materials and activities that children enjoy. Children's preferences can be identified through observation during free-play times and from parents' reports. Rotating materials from time to time will keep the children interested.

2. *Out of reach.* Place some desired items in view but out of reach in order to prompt requests by the children. During snack time, for example, the teacher can place a cookie on the table out of reach from the child. If the child reaches for the

cookie, the teacher can prompt the child to make a request or, if the child is non-speaking, ask the child to point or use his or her communicative device to request.

3. *Inadequate portions.* Provide children with small or inadequate portions of a material, such as blocks. When the children need more, they are likely to make a request.

4. *Choice making.* Children can be prompted to make a choice by being presented with two objects and asked to make a choice. For example, during snack time the child may be asked to choose between a cookie and fruit. For children who are nonspeaking, pointing may be accepted. For other children, a verbalization may be required.

5. *Assistance.* Creating a situation in which the children will need assistance provides communicative opportunities. A wind-up toy or an unopened bottle of bubbles may provide opportunities for children to request adult assistance.

6. *Sabotage.* A "sabotage" is created when children are not provided with all the materials they need to complete a task. For example, students may be asked to cut out pictures and paste them on a chart but are given no paste. Alternatively, in a group setting each child may get some, but not all, of the needed materials. In order to complete the project, they will have to request materials from their peers.

7. *Silly situations.* Children may be prompted to communicate by creating silly or absurd situations. For example, during circle time the teacher may hold a picture upside down or place a weather symbol on the calendar instead of the date.

Each of these techniques is designed to increase communicative interaction. However, in many cases the goal is to move beyond interaction to more adult forms of communication. When materials and activities are carefully selected and adults are aware of and utilize effective techniques for enhancing communicative interaction, the preschool classroom can be a rich environment for language learning.

The development of literacy skills is another important goal of preschool education. According to the emergent literacy model (Chapter 5), literacy and language development are closely related. Language development enhances literacy, and experiences with books and writing enhance language. Dickinson (2001) observed teachers reading books in preschool classrooms and developed the following set of recommendations for teachers:

1. *Schedule sufficient time for book reading.* Teachers in full-day programs should read aloud at least three times a day for about 45 minutes total.

2. *Read and reread various types of books.* Rereading provides opportunities to extend children's understanding through questioning.

3. *Be thoughtful about book discussions.* Identify important concepts and vocabulary prior to reading the book. Encourage children to think by helping them relate the story to their own experiences.

4. *Enjoy reading and minimize time spent on organizational matters.* Establish routines for book reading that can be accomplished quickly and easily.

5. *Make books and book reading part of the full day.* Link books to themes. Set up listening centers with tapes of books previously read.

6. *Encourage parents to read to children at home.* Develop a classroom lending library.

Wasik, Bond, and Hindman (2006) demonstrated how relatively simple techniques to enhance book reading and classroom interaction can enhance the language of preschool-age children. Teachers in 10 Head Start classrooms (programs for children from high-poverty neighborhoods) were taught to use book reading and conversational strategies. Specifically, teachers were trained to use objects that represented a vocabulary word and ask open-ended questions such as, "What is this?" or "What do you call this?" For example, before the children listened to the book *The Carrot Seed* (Krauss, 1989), they talked about objects such as a shovel, rake, and gardening hose. In addition, teachers were provided with suggestions for extension activities that were designed to help children make connections between the book and vocabulary items. Teachers were also trained in the following conversational strategies:

1. *Active listening.* Teachers were trained to focus their attention on the child, wait for the child to speak, and respond in a meaningful way.

   Example: If a child said, "I see a dog," the teacher was trained to acknowledge and elaborate on the response by saying something like, "Yes, you see a big, black dog. What is the dog doing?"

   Students were also taught to listen to others, to raise a quiet hand if they wanted to talk, and to take turns speaking.
2. *Modeling language.* Teachers were taught to expand their use of vocabulary and provide more elaborate explanations and descriptions.

   Example: Rather than just saying, "Good job" in response to a child, the teacher might say, "I like the way you use the color blue to draw the sky."
3. *Provide feedback.* Teachers were taught to use three strategies:
   • *Informational talk.* An elaborated, rich description of activities or events
        Example: "You are putting the big rectangular block on the small square block."
   • ***Expansion.*** Repeating or requesting what the child said using more detail and greater vocabulary
        Example: If the child said, "I make a house," the teacher might respond by saying, "Yes, you built a house with ten blocks."
   • *Asking questions.* Teachers were trained to use questioning starters such as, "Tell me about it" and "I wonder how . . .?"

After nine months of using these simple techniques to enhance book reading and conversational interaction, the researchers compared the language of the children in these 10 classrooms with children from 6 other Head Start classrooms whose teachers did not receive this training. They found that the children in the experimental classrooms had improved in both expressive and receptive language much more than the children in the control-group classrooms. In addition, the teachers changed many of their questioning strategies during book reading and used many of the conversational techniques taught in the training. The results indicate that young children can be helped to enhance their language skills with relatively simple changes in the way that teachers interact with their preschool-age students.

Elementary Classrooms

Language development does not stop when children enter school. In Chapter 6 we reviewed research that described continuing growth in language development during the school years. This growth was in nearly all aspects of language. At the same time, students are continuing to develop their reading and writing skills. What can teachers and other education professionals in elementary classrooms do to support and extend language learning—oral and written?

As we have noted earlier in this book, there is considerable evidence that phonological processing abilities are related to initial success in reading. Many reading programs include activities to develop phonological skills, but many students need more practice on these skills than is generally provided by most basal reader series. Teachers can provide assistance by helping students identify words that begin with the same sound (not necessarily the same letter), pay attention to rhyme, and practice dividing words into parts and putting the parts back together to make words.

A number of phonological awareness instructional programs can be used as whole-classroom curricula. Some of these were mentioned in Chapter 7. They include the *Ladders to Literacy* program (Notari-Syverson, O'Connor, & Vadsey, 1998) and *Phonemic Awareness in Young Children* (Adams, Foorman, Lundberg, & Beeler, 1997). In addition, some programs that have been designed for remedial purposes can be adapted for whole-classroom use. For example, the Wilson reading program (Wilson, 1996), an intensive program that uses a 12-step approach to help children master decoding skills, has been successfully used to enhance the reading skills of all children in a regular first-grade classroom.

Research on the use of phonological training programs in elementary, general education classrooms has produced mixed results. In one large study (Hatcher, Hulme, & Snowling, 2004), children entering kindergarten were taught with one of four programs: Reading with Rhyme, Reading with Phoneme, Reading with Rhyme and Phoneme, or a general reading program. Contrary to their expectations, the study authors found that typically developing students did not benefit from a reading program that emphasized phonological skills. Although their phonological abilities did, indeed, improve, their reading scores were not significantly affected by the type of reading program. However, at-risk readers who were in classrooms that used the phonological training programs did have significantly better reading scores than their peers. Since prevention of reading difficulties is so critical, there may be considerable benefits to supplementing reading programs with additional practice on phonological skills.

Reading success requires more than just phonological awareness. Other language-based skills, such as vocabulary and concept knowledge, play an important role. The whole-language approach to reading instruction attempts to integrate literacy and language learning. Although this approach has fallen out of favor recently, there are many aspects of the whole-language model that are worth including in the elementary curriculum. Rather than presenting reading, writing, and language as separate units, teachers using whole-language instruction acknowledge the interrelationships between these domains. Reading becomes the basis for writing and language activities, discussions precede and follow reading, and writers talk before they write.

Kirkland and Patterson (2005) provide a number of suggestions for enhancing the language development of elementary-age children that are consistent with the whole-language approach to instruction. They recommend the following:

- *Classroom environment.* Classrooms should be rich with examples of the students' own language. Schedules for daily classroom activities should be posted with pictures and words so that children are capable of utilizing them independently. Areas of the room should be devoted to children's retellings of favorite stories. These areas might include dress-up areas, puppets, and stories on overhead transparencies, as well as listening centers.
- *Connections with literature.* Teachers should select books that provide opportunities for rich discussion in the classroom (see Box 14.1). It is also important to include books that offer "interesting" words to stretch the child's vocabulary. Book reading can be paired with other activities such as art, music, poetry, dance, and drama. For example, readers' theater has been found to build fluency for children who are low language learners or who are attempting to learn a new language (Manning, 2004).
- *Developmentally appropriate oral language activities.* Activities such as "Show and Tell" and "Daily News" can provide opportunities for language use. As children develop writing skills, daily news can move from a dictation activity to a more interactive writing activity.
- *Engaging curricula.* Techniques such as the "project approach" (Katz & Chard, 2000) or "theme immersion" (Manning, Manning, & Long, 1994) provide ways for teachers to utilize students' interests and questions in the curriculum.

How teachers present information in the classroom can have a significant impact on student learning. This is the conclusion of a study by Lapadat (2002). Second-grade students were asked to listen to taped lectures that varied in the pace of the delivery (slow to fast) and the amount of redundancy in the lecture (high or low). Lapadat found that students with greater language ability learned more, no matter how the lecture was delivered. Presentation style, however, did matter. Overall, slow-paced instructional language was positively related to learning, but students attended less to it than to fast-paced talk. For most students, slow-paced, nonredundant instruction seemed to work best. However, students with special needs learned best when instruction was faster paced. Perhaps the lesson for teachers from this research is to understand that the pace of a lesson matters considerably. Although the optimal pace may vary for different learners, teachers need to be aware of the effect of their instructional delivery on their students' learning.

Secondary Classrooms

During the secondary-school years, language continues to grow and develop (see Chapter 6). Development in advanced syntactic skills, in vocabulary, and in subtle

BOX **14.1**

Children's Literature to Promote Oral Language Development

Barber, T., Barber, R., & Burleigh, R. (2004). *By my brother's side.* New York: Simon & Schuster.

Blake, Q. (1996). *Clown.* New York: Henry Holt & Co., Inc.

Burton, V. L. (1978). *The little house.* Boston: Houghton Mifflin Co.

Bryan, A. (1989). *Porquoi tales: The cat's purr, why frog and snake never play together, the fire bringer.* Boston: Houghton Mifflin Co.

Cooper, M. (1997). *I got a family.* New York: Henry Holt & Co., Inc.

Cronin, D. (2002). *Giggle, giggle, quack.* New York: Simon & Schuster.

Defelice, C. (1997). *Willy's silly grandmamma.* London: Orchard Books.

Fleming, C. (2002). *When Agnes caws.* New York: Simon & Schuster.

Gag, W. (1977 [1928]). *Millions of cats.* New York: Putnam.

George, K. O. (1997). *The great frog race and other poems.* Boston: Houghton Mifflin Co.

Hodges, M. (1990). *Saint George and the dragon.* Boston: Little, Brown & Co.

Johnston, T. (1996). *The ghost of Nicholas Greebe.* New York: Penguin Group, Inc.

Kennedy, X. J. (1992). *Talking like the rain.* Boston: Little, Brown, & Co.

Lewin H. (1990). *Jafta.* Minneapolis, MN: Lerner Publications Co.

Long, M. (2003). *How I became a pirate.* San Diego, CA: Harcourt Brace.

Martin, B. Jr., & Archambault, J. (1989). *Chicka Chicka Boom Boom.* New York: Simon & Schuster.

McCloskey, R. (1976). *Make way for ducklings.* New York: Viking Penguin.

McKissack, P. (1986). *Flossie and the fox.* New York: Dial Books for Young Readers.

Merriam, E. (1998). *What in the world?* New York: Harper Collins.

Osborne, M. (2003). *Haunted castle on Hallow's Eve.* New York: Random House, Inc.

Polacco, P. (1998). *Chicken Sunday.* New York: Putnam.

Prelutsky, J. (2001). *Pizza the size of the sun.* New York: Green Willow Books.

Silverstein, S. (1981). *A light in the attic.* New York: Harper Collins.

Steig, W. (1969). *Sylvester and the magic pebble.* New York: Simon & Schuster.

Van Allsburg, C. (1996). *The mysteries of Harris Burdick.* Boston, MA: Houghton Mifflin.

Source: Lynn D. Kirkland and Janice Patterson. (2005). Developing Oral Language in Primary Classrooms. *Early Childhood Education Journal, 32* (6), p. 393. With kind permission of Springer Science and Business Media.

---

communicative skills is characteristic of the secondary years. Children with speech and language difficulties do not necessarily outgrow their problems (Aram et al., 1984). Instead, as they respond to the demands of the secondary setting, their problems may surface in new ways. Lecturing, note taking, and independent research projects pose difficult challenges to the student with language difficulties.

Buttrill, Niizawa, Biemer, Takahashi, and Hearn (1989) described a program they developed to support secondary-age students with language disorders. In the program, students attend a *language/study skills* class for one period a day; the remainder of the day they attend regular, general education classes. Seven major elements are included in the language/study skills curriculum:

1. *Academic organization.* Students are helped to organize their assignments, organize their time, and monitor their own performance.
2. *Study skills.* Students learn *how* to study, also receiving instruction in note taking, text reading, and test taking.
3. *Critical thinking.* Students are helped to enhance their ability to observe and describe, solve problems, and use inductive and deductive reasoning.
4. *Listening.* Students are given strategies for focusing their attention. They are taught to recognize lecture cues that will help them identify important information.
5. *Oral language.* Students are taught word-retrieval skills, helped with their use of figurative language, and given practice in being good listeners and effective speakers.
6. *Written language.* Students are given numerous opportunities to write. Writing includes note taking, use of computers, and research papers.
7. *Pragmatics.* Students learn about conversational roles. They role-play various conversational situations.

The special language problems of secondary-age students may sometimes be overlooked because of the emphasis put on content in secondary classrooms. The program described by Buttrill and colleagues reminds us that learning language does not stop at the preschool or elementary years but continues through adolescence and beyond. One of the critical skills for students at the secondary level is the acquisition of new vocabulary. Classroom lectures and texts often incorporate a wide range of new vocabulary in science, social studies, and literature. Many secondary-level students need help in acquiring these new concepts.

An instructional approach that has been used with success with secondary-age students is **learning strategies.** Many students lack an efficient strategy to use when they encounter unknown words. The learning strategies approach helps students recognize and use a strategy. For example, the DISSECT strategy was developed by Lenz and Hughes (1990) to help secondary students decode words. Students are taught to follow seven steps that require them to use context clues, break words into their constituents, and use additional resources when needed. The seven steps of the strategy are:

D: *Discover* the context. Students are reminded to use the context as an aid to identifying the target word.
I: *Isolate* the prefix. Students are instructed to find and separate the prefix and then try to say the word.
S: *Separate* the suffix. Students are instructed to find and separate the suffix and then try to say the word.
S: *Say* the stem. Once the prefix and suffix have been removed, what remains is the word stem. Students are now told to try to identify the stem.
E: *Examine* the stem. Students are taught to use the "rule of twos and threes" to identify the stem. That is, if the stem begins with a vowel, students pronounce

units of two letters. If the stem begins with a consonant, students separate and pronounce units of three letters.

C: *Check* with someone. If students have followed the first five steps and still do not recognize the word, they can check with a peer, teacher, or someone else.

T: *Try* the dictionary. Another (perhaps preferable) alternative is to check the dictionary.

In one study, DISSECT was found to significantly reduce the oral reading errors of eighth-grade students with learning disabilities after only six weeks of use (Lenz & Hughes, 1990). See Box 14.2 for another example of a learning strategy.

In addition to classroom skills, language is an essential part of social interaction. There is considerable research and clinical evidence that language skills play an important role in successful social interaction (Brinton & Fujiki, 1993). This is true for children at all ages, but, since social skills and social acceptance are such a crucial part of adolescence, the use of appropriate social language may be of even greater importance for secondary-age students. We have already discussed the changes in social interaction patterns that take place during adolescence (Chapter 6). The social skills that adolescents develop and practice are essential for success in school as well as in life outside of school.

Teachers can support the development of social interaction skills by providing opportunities for interacting with a variety of communicative partners during many different activities. Formal reports and presentations are one type of activity. These provide opportunities for teachers to give feedback on pragmatic skills such as introducing

---

BOX 14.2

The "Keyword" Method: An Example of a Strategy Approach to Instruction

The keyword method creates a concrete, acoustically similar keyword for the unfamiliar word to be learned. For example, a good keyword for the vocabulary word *jettison* could be *jet,* since it sounds like the first part of jettison and is easy to picture.

In the next step, the keyword is shown interacting with the definition. In the case of jettison (throwing overboard), a jet could be shown throwing overboard some cargo.

Students are told, when they hear the vocabulary word *(jettison),* think first of the keyword *(jet),* think back to the picture of the jet, remember what else was happening in the picture (throwing cargo overboard), and retrieve the answer (throw overboard).

Research has found the keyword method to be effective in improving learning and retention of verbal material by students with learning disabilities (Mastropieri & Scruggs, 1989; Scruggs & Mastropieri, 2000).

Source: "Keywords Make the Difference" by H. Z. Uberti, T. E. Scruggs, & M. A. Mastropieri, *Teaching Exceptional Children, 35,* 2004, 56–61. Copyright 2004 by The Council for Exceptional Children. Reprinted with permission.

a topic, taking the audience's perspective, elaborating on a theme, and providing an appropriate summary.

Although these are important skills for students to acquire, even more critical may be the opportunities for peer interaction. Group activities provide teachers with opportunities to observe their students in interaction with peers, model appropriate interaction, and assure that all students are given the opportunity to participate. Taking the time to set ground rules for interaction and discussing what the teacher has observed during group time can be as important as the content that the groups are assigned to complete.

Language skills continue to play an important role in learning at the secondary level. Unfortunately, in many cases students with language and communication difficulties fail to receive the instruction they need at the secondary level. The result is that some students continue to fall behind their peers and do not reach their potential. It is important for teachers and other education professionals to recognize the importance of language skills for the academic and social growth of secondary-age students and to attempt to enhance these skills in their students.

Instruction for Students with Severe Disabilities

As we have seen in earlier chapters of this book (e.g., Chapters 8 and 9), there are some new and promising ideas about teaching language skills to children with more severe disabilities. These new strategies emphasize the integration of students with disabilities into school and the community. They include an emphasis on functional skills, development of literacy skills, and the use of technology to enhance language skills.

Individuals with disabilities often have significant difficulty developing literacy skills. Until recently, these difficulties had been attributed largely to disabilities within the individual. But Koppenhaver, Pierce, Steelman, and Yoder (1995) suggest that literacy-learning difficulties may also be due to the way parents and professionals respond to individuals with disabilities and to learning contexts. For example, their research has shown that parents of children who use augmentative communication devices had relatively low expectations for their child's ability to acquire reading and writing skills (Light, Koppenhaver, Lee, & Riffle, 1994). Other research has discovered that children with severe disabilities are rarely exposed to text-length material. Most of their instruction is with isolated words and sentences.

Koppenhaver and Erickson (2003) described an approach to enhancing the language and literacy skills of students with severe disabilities in a preschool classroom. None of the children used speech. The authors worked with the teachers to use natural opportunities in the classroom to foster language and literacy skills. For example, they created an electronic writing center in the classroom that used a (previously unused) computer and a basic children's writing program. To enhance reading skills, they added a variety of reading materials to the classroom, including books with sound effects, wordless picture books, books on tape, and touch-and-feel books. Reading was also integrated into regular classroom activities. For example, at the beginning of each day the students took attendance by identifying pictures of their classmates. Name tags were added to the pictures so children would become familiar with the written form of their names. The children were also given increased opportunities for language interaction.

As an example, during drawing activities the teachers were encouraged to describe what the children were drawing. The authors reported that, as a result of these and other activities, the students showed much greater interest in reading and writing.

The development of powerful, portable, and relatively inexpensive computers and peripherals has the potential for significantly enhancing the learning of students with severe disabilities. Schery and O'Connor (1992) compared the outcomes of a computer-based language instruction program (Programs for Early Acquisition of Language) to regular classroom language instruction for 52 students with severe disabilities. The results indicated that the group that used the computer program outperformed the comparison group on a vocabulary posttest. In addition, the computer group also made significant gains in social and interpersonal behaviors. The authors caution that although computers are certainly not a panacea, they do represent an important instructional tool for students with severe disabilities, as evidenced by research results.

As technology advances, new techniques and devices have emerged. Blischak and Schlosser (2003) reported on research studies that have found that speech-generating devices and talking word-processing programs can be useful for enhancing the spelling skills of nonspeaking students. Lee and Vail (2005) developed a program to teach sight words to 6- and 7-year-old students with moderate to severe disabilities. The program combined a multimedia presentation with a constant-time-delay procedure. When a task direction (i.e., "Click the word__") was presented in the intervention program, a participant was given 5 seconds to initiate a response. One of five responses was possible:

1. A *correct response* was recorded when a participant clicked a correct word within 5 seconds after a task direction. Students received verbal praise for the response.
2. An *incorrect response* before a prompt was recorded when a participant clicked an incorrect word or did not click any word within 5 seconds after a task direction. The incorrect response resulted in a prompt screen, in which all letters in a target word appeared. The participant was given a second chance to identify the correct word after the prompt.
3. A *correct response after the prompt* was recorded when a participant identified a target word within 5 seconds after the prompt.
4. An *incorrect response after a prompt* was recorded when a participant clicked an incorrect word within 5 seconds after a prompt.
5. A *no-response* was recorded when a participant did not click any word within 5 seconds after a prompt.

Using this procedure, the children in the study were able to successfully learn the target words.

Expectations for students with moderate to severe disabilities are increasing. More of these children can be found in regular education settings, often in regular education classrooms. In response to these developments, new instructional approaches and technologies are emerging to enhance the language and literacy of students with significant disabilities so they can be more fully included in school and in society.

Specific Instructional Suggestions

The preceding sections have reviewed useful methods for enhancing classroom inter-action in a variety of environments, as well as strategies found effective in specific types of classrooms. Here are some activities that you may find helpful for enhancing language. They have been used by teachers and speech-language specialists in all kinds of classroom environments, but have not been systematically examined through re-search studies.

1. *Group decision making.* Assign a group of students to complete a project (such as making a poster to illustrate a science concept). Give the group some pictures from which they must select four to use on their poster. Encourage group discus-sion and decision making.

2. *Missing materials.* For younger children, set up a group project so that each member of the group has something that the other group members need. For ex-ample, one student has markers, one has crayons, one has scissors, and so on. En-courage the students to ask others when they need something. If necessary, provide a model for requesting.

3. *Rewriting.* One way to practice using different registers of communication is to rewrite a story for three different audiences. For example, one version could be for the students' peers, one for parents, and one for younger children.

4. *Classroom routines.* Teachers can use routine classroom tasks as the vehicle for classroom interaction. If your class has a snack time, for example, use this as a communication time. Even students with little or no spoken language can bene-fit from this activity. Students can be required to indicate either verbally or non-verbally which of two items they prefer. They get their snack only after making a response.

5. *Computers for socialization.* We don't usually think of computers as a forum for social interaction, but they can be. Computer programs that emphasize problem solving (e.g., Oregon Trail) are a great way to get a group talking to each other. You might group three students together and encourage them to come up with a group solution to the dilemmas posed by the software.

At times, it may be useful to focus instruction on specific aspects of language. A number of techniques, both formal and informal, for enhancing language elements are provided here. Some of these have been evaluated through research, some have not. However, the best activities are often those that the classroom teacher develops with the materials and situations that are natural to the classroom.

Phonology.   Mercer and Mercer (1993) suggest an activity called *phonetic bingo.* Each player receives a bingo card containing letters. The caller calls out a column num-ber and a phoneme (e.g., 4, t). The player having that phoneme in the correct column places a marker over the letter. The winner is the first player to cover five letters in a row.

Pro-Ed distributes a program titled Remediation of Common Phonological-Processes. With this program, 426 illustrated word-pair cards are provided to help teach children from preschool through grade 4 to hear minimal sound differences between words.

Morphology.   Following are two of Wiig and Semel's (1984) many suggestions for improving morphological skills. They suggest the following activity for practicing the use of the present progressive *(-ing)* ending:

The boy is _____.	*(walking/walks)*
The boy _____ every day.	*(walking/walks)*
The boy is _____.	*(sleeping/sleeps)*
During the night the boy _____.	*(walks/sleeps)*

Another technique to practice morphological skills is to reformulate sentences. For example:

Usually the boy eats cereal.
Yesterday _____.
Tomorrow _____.
Right now _____.

Teaching Morphology Developmentally (Communication Skill Builders) is an example of a commercially produced material that is designed to enhance skills in morphology. Color stimulus cards are provided to teach features such as the present progressive, past tense, and plurals to children between $2\frac{1}{2}$ and 10 years of age.

Syntax.   Hammill and Bartel (1995) suggest using a version of the children's game "I Spy" to teach the effective use of noun and verb phrases. One player must identify an object in the room by describing it *(I see two large red books and one large blue book).* The other player must guess what object the first player has in mind. The teacher can help by encouraging the students to use precise language (not just, *I see a book).*

Mercer and Mercer (1993) describe a self-correcting activity they call "Make It Say a Sentence" that can be used to practice sentence order. The student receives a card with a scrambled sentence *(ran school she was she since to late).* The student must unscramble the sentence, write down the correct word order, and then check for the correct answer from a list of the answers in an accompanying envelope.

There are many commercially available materials to teach syntax skills. One example is Syntax One and Syntax Two (Communication Skill Builders). Syntax One, designed to help students develop awareness of word order and word endings, uses a syntax wheel that rotates to reveal stimulus pictures designed to elicit specific syntactic forms. In Syntax Two, students are presented with problem-solving situations in which they must ask questions.

Semantics.   Atkinson and Longman (1985) suggest the use of sniglets to teach vocabulary development to adolescents and adults. *Sniglets* are words that do not appear in a dictionary but should. For example, *bathquake* means the loud sound you sometimes hear when the water faucet is turned on. By experimenting with *new* words and trying to define sniglets, students learn about word meaning.

Wiig and Semel (1984) also provide many suggestions for enhancing students' skills in semantics. For example, they suggest using verbal analogies *(Trees have leaves and birds _____ [feathers];* riddles *(You can ride on it. It rides on tracks. It has an engine. It has a caboose. It is a _____*); and the Twenty Question game.

The Peabody Language Development Kits (American Guidance Service) are probably the best known and most widely used materials for developing language skills. Although the kits focus on several aspects of language, they are especially useful for teaching semantic concepts. Three levels of kits span the age range from preschool to 7 years old and use a multimedia approach that includes picture cards, puppets, and posters. Children are taught to use receptive and expressive language as well as to develop thinking skills.

Pragmatics.   Hammill and Bartel (1995) suggest several role-playing activities designed to help students practice their communication skills. They suggest that students be assigned the role of speaker or responder in situations such as the following:

- The speaker (customer) is returning a defective appliance to the store. The speaker wants the responder (store representative) to refund the purchase price. The responder must try to implement the store policy, which is to make exchanges only.
- The speaker believes his or her examination has not been scored correctly. The speaker must try to convince the responder (teacher) to give him or her some extra points on an essay question.

Mercer and Mercer (1993) suggest providing students with a list (or tape recording) of sentences such as the following, to help them practice identifying indirect requests:

- What time is it?
- Can you shut the door?
- Can't you finish your work?
- Is the water running?
- Can't you sit still?

The student's job is to decide if each sentence is an indirect request or a question. An answer key could be provided so that students can check their work.

Let's Talk for Children (Psychological Corporation) is designed to help students from 4 to 9 years old acquire, maintain, and generalize communicative functions. Communication activity cards prompt children to use a variety of speech acts. A home activities manual provides suggestions for the generalization of skills that pertain to the home environment.

Delivering Language Instruction in the Classroom

In the last 10 years or so there have been great changes in the way that services are delivered to children with disabilities. These changes have occurred in special education and speech-language services as well as in many other professions that serve children with disabilities. The result of these changes has been that more children with disabilities are being served within the regular education classroom. At the same time, the role of speech and language specialists has changed. Cirrin and Penner (1995) noted that the profession of speech-language pathology has moved from reliance on pull-out services to delivery of speech and language intervention in the classroom. At the same time, intervention procedures for speech-language problems have changed from emphasizing voice and articulation goals to a greater emphasis on the use of language for communication and for literacy development. The result of these changes is that there is an increasing number of models for service delivery by speech and language professionals, including the following:

1. *The language specialist team teaches.* Team teaching may take place in a regular classroom with a regular education teacher, in a self-contained classroom with a special education or reading teacher, or in a resource setting with a special education teacher. Whatever the setting, the teachers should jointly plan, instruct, and evaluate.
2. *The language specialist provides one-to-one classroom-based intervention.* The language specialist can use actual classroom materials to help the child with significant difficulties improve his/her vocabulary, study skills, writing, and test-taking strategies. The language specialist must collaborate with the classroom teacher.
3. *The language specialist consults.* The language specialist provides information and support to the classroom teacher. The teacher is responsible for carrying out the mutually agreed on instructional strategies.
4. *The language specialist provides staff, curriculum, or program development.* The language specialist may provide in-service training, participate in curriculum development activities, and develop parent education programs (Owens, 2004).

Collaboration

A key to the effective delivery of classroom-based language and communication instruction is the ability of professionals to collaborate. Friend and Cook (1996) have defined collaboration as "a style for direct interaction between at least two coequal parties voluntarily engaged in shared decision making as they work toward a common goal" (p. 6). Successful collaboration can be difficult to achieve. It requires each participant to give up part of his or her traditional role while taking on aspects of the role of another. This is contrary to both the training and experience of most education professionals. Yet, collaboration is essential, especially for the delivery of effective instruction in language and communication.

In schools, collaboration is critical to the functioning of instructional planning teams and to the delivery of instruction in classrooms where two or more professionals are working together. Instructional teams, including IEP (individualized educational plan) teams and other planning groups must learn to interact in ways that respect the expertise of individuals while acknowledging the contribution that each person brings to the process. According to Thousand and Villa (1992), in order to be successful, a collaborative team must:

- Agree to coordinate their work to achieve common, agreed-on goals
- Hold a belief system that all members of the team have unique and needed expertise
- Demonstrate their belief in parity by alternately engaging in the dual roles of teacher and learner, expert and recipient, consultant and consultee
- Use a distributed functions theory of leadership wherein the task and relationship functions of the leader are distributed among all members of the group
- Use a collaborative teaming process that involves face-to-face interaction; positive interdependence; the performance, monitoring, and processing of interpersonal skills; and individual accountability

Collaborative teaching is becoming a very common way to deliver instruction. It is not uncommon to find two (or more) education professionals assigned to a classroom. Often, the team consists of a regular and special education teacher, but a reading professional, a speech-language specialist, and others may also be included. Collaborative teaching has the obvious advantage of providing additional professional help for any student in the classroom who requires assistance. In order for collaborative teaching to be successful, it is essential that professionals be willing to share instructional tasks and communicate effectively with each other. Friend and Cook (1996) suggest that coteachers ask themselves the following questions:

- How willing am I to let a colleague observe me teaching content with which I am not particularly familiar?
- How willing am I to consider and experiment with different ways of teaching?
- Am I willing to let someone take responsibility for tasks at which I am particularly skilled?
- What is my level of comfort about relying on someone else in a joint project?

Collaborative teaching can be a particularly effective model for supporting language and communication. With more professionals available, students can be assisted in classroom interaction and receive more immediate feedback for their communicative interaction. Additionally, when reading teachers and speech-language specialists are in the classroom, there are greater opportunities for coordinating instructional goals and delivering coordinated instruction. For example, for a child who is learning to identify the /b/ sound, reading a book about bats gives both the classroom teacher and the speech-language specialist the opportunity to teach and practice the target sound with the child.

Silliman, Ford, Beasman, and Evans (1999) describe the application of a collaborative teaching model in a regular education classroom that included children with language-learning disabilities. They identified the following factors as important to the success of collaborative teaching:

- *Empowerment as decision makers.* The teachers in this classroom made the decision to collaborate with support from their administration.
- *Personality characteristics.* Characteristics such as being open communicators, willingness to incorporate others' ideas into your own, and the commitment to stick it out were essential.
- *Parental support.* Although, at first, parents were skeptical, over time they saw positive results for their children.
- *Administrative support.* Support from school administrators was critical both to allow experimentation and to provide needed space and materials.
- *Flexibility in meeting individual student needs.* The collaborating professionals were willing to acknowledge that their classroom was not the best setting for service delivery for all their students. Some needed more intensive instruction than that which could be provided in their classroom.
- *Expectations for achievement.* All students were expected to achieve in the collaborative classroom.
- *Shared expertise.* The collaborating professionals found that they developed expertise from each other.

Clearly, there are challenges to making collaborative teaching work. All of the elements listed here may not be present in every situation. However, experience suggests that when education professionals are willing to work with each other for the shared goal of improved student achievement, they can solve the problems that may develop. The result can be enhanced performance for all students.

Language Intervention

In some cases, good instruction in language and communication skills is not enough. Some students will require the more intensive instruction that only language intervention services can provide. Language intervention, in the words of Olswang and Bain (1991), "is viewed as focused, intensive stimulation designed to alter specific behaviors" (p. 255). As they note, intervention involves more than monitoring or providing general suggestions to encourage communication. Intervention is targeted at specific language skills and is intensive enough to cause an improvement in these skills. As noted earlier, intervention is an expensive and therefore limited commodity. Thus, it is important to be able to identify those children who need and may benefit from intervention and to select intervention methods that have the greatest likelihood of success.

Developing a plan for language intervention requires addressing four questions. The first question is *when* to intervene. In order to answer this question, we need to know if there is a need for intervention. Answering this question might seem like a relatively simple task. By using the assessment procedures outlined in the previous chapter, we can establish that the child does, in fact, have a significant language disorder. Yet, this determination alone is not sufficient. Teachers and parents want to know whether the speech and/or language impairment is serious enough to justify intervention and if the problem will go away without intervention. In order to address these issues, we have to ask some more questions:

1. *Is the child having difficulty with academic tasks?* For example, does the child have difficulty with reading, spelling, or writing?
2. *Does the child have difficulty participating in classroom interactions?* Does the child have problems understanding directions, following discussions, or contributing to classroom interactions?
3. *Does the child have difficulty getting along with others?* Are language difficulties causing the child to be teased by others, be misunderstood, or be left out of social activities?
4. *Is the language problem getting worse, getting better, or staying about the same?* If the child is making steady progress, intervention may not be needed. Instead, the child may need to be carefully monitored for a while.

If the answer to at least one of the first three questions is yes, and the problem appears to be getting worse or not improving, the child should be considered for intervention for the speech or language difficulty.

Once a decision is made that the child needs intervention, the next question is *where* such intervention should take place. The answer to this question used to be easy. As Miller (1989) notes in her retrospective review of language intervention, until the 1970s, most language intervention was carried out in a speech clinic. The child was pulled out of the classroom for specialized—usually one-on-one—instruction. Miller points out that two developments changed this approach. First, theories of language began to put more emphasis on pragmatics—the use of language in natural contexts. Second was the realization that language is an integral part of classroom success. In addition, many researchers and practitioners were concerned about the stigma of removing children from their peers. As a result of these trends, the classroom-based, service-delivery model has become more widespread. With classroom-based intervention, the speech-language specialist becomes a partner with the classroom teacher in service delivery.

Even if the speech-language specialist is working one on one with the child in a corner of the room, there is an increased opportunity to observe the child in the natural setting of the classroom, for the child to immediately practice a new skill, and for the clinician to use actual curriculum materials from the classroom. So, the preferred location for service delivery today is in the child's classroom. Occasionally, it might be necessary to remove the child from the classroom. For example, when a new skill is being presented, the quiet and concentration available in a speech therapy room may be helpful. But these times should be limited in number and duration.

Answering the question about *where* intervention should take place suggests an answer to the third question—*who* should deliver intervention. With classroom-based intervention there is a greater role for the classroom teacher in the child's intervention. This is as it should be. After all, it is the classroom teacher who knows the child the best and will see that child for most of the school day. This is the professional who has the greatest opportunity to help the child improve his or her language skills. In classroom-based intervention models, the teacher becomes a significant partner in the intervention program. The speech-language specialist's role may be to act as a consulting or collaborating professional with the classroom teacher. As a consultant, the specialist can advise the teacher on the best methods and materials to help the child learn and practice the targeted language skill. In collaborative service-delivery models, the teacher and speech-language specialist divide their classroom responsibilities (Montgomery, 1992). As the teacher presents the lesson, the speech-language specialist may check for understanding or coach the child in how to respond. These roles may be difficult for teachers and speech-language specialists to accept at first, but the goal is to present a more natural setting for language intervention (see Table 14.1).

The fourth question is undoubtedly the most difficult—*how* to intervene. Earlier in this chapter we discussed the contemporary emphasis on evidence-based practices. What does the research say about the effectiveness of language intervention? Are some approaches more effective than others? What about the area of language that is the target of the intervention and characteristics of the child? How do these influence the effectiveness of language intervention?

Dimensions of Language Intervention Approaches

Language intervention methods can be characterized on two dimensions (see Figure 14.1). On one axis are programs that range from strongly emphasizing language development to those that utilize a functional approach to intervention. The other dimension contrasts highly structured approaches with those that use a more naturalistic approach. It is important to emphasize that these are not absolute differences. As we will see, many programs combine elements of several dimensions.

TABLE 14.1   Advantages/Limitations of Speech-Language Service-Delivery Models

Model	Advantages	Limitations
Pull-out	Specific skills can be focused on Distraction reduced for student	Student may be stigmatized No opportunity for realistic practice
In-class therapy	Opportunities for immediate application Availability of curricular materials	Distractions in classroom Stigma may still be attached
Consultation	Opportunity to share/discuss language goals for student Teacher involved as communicator	Relies on teacher's knowledge of language Need for planning time
Collaboration	Speech-language specialist can support instruction Language instruction embedded in classroom activities	Less focus, possibly, on language goals Need for planning time
Team teaching	Complete integration of language and academic goals No stigma for child	Less direct focus on language goals Need for planning time

FIGURE 14.1   Dimensions of Language Intervention Approaches

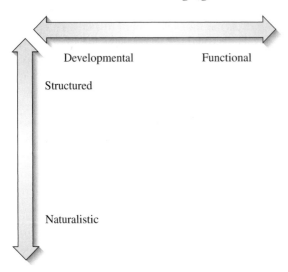

Developmental/Functional Approaches

One of the major questions in language instruction is how information about language acquisition can and should be used in planning therapy for children with language disorders. Knowledge of the usual steps and timing of typical language development provides a benchmark against which the language development of any individual child can be compared. Knowing what *should* come next can help in determining what should be taught next.

Since we know that children with disabilities often acquire language in the same sequence (although more slowly) as nondisabled children, it makes sense to follow developmental guidelines in planning language goals. This was the hypothesis tested by Dyer, Santarcangelo, and Luce (1987). In a series of studies, they taught phonetic sounds and syntactic structures to children with severe language disabilities. They found that earlier-emerging forms (e.g., /b/ sounds) were learned in fewer trials than were later-emerging forms (e.g., /z/ sounds). Moreover, later-emerging forms were never acquired unless the earlier forms had been learned. Here, using typical language development as a guideline turned out to be a useful way of planning instructional goals for these students with severe language disorders.

Although knowledge of normal language development can be helpful in planning language instruction, Owens (2004) suggests that we should be cautious in using development too strictly to guide intervention. He points out, for example, that it would be a mistake to teach children with language delays to go through all the steps that typically developing children use to get to the final form of a language structure. It is not necessary for a child to say *goded* before learning the correct irregular past-tense form, *went*. Owens suggests that developmental hierarchies can best be used as broad guidelines for instruction—for help in determining which structures are less complex—and should therefore be taught prior to more complex structures. Having knowledge of language development can also help the instructor avoid leaps that are too great for the child to master. Unfortunately, at times, developmental guidelines have been used as an argument to deny language intervention to students with disabilities. Language intervention was postponed until students developed some theoretical "prerequisites" that many children might never develop.

Largely as a result of concerns about the role of normal development in planning language instruction, some have suggested that instruction should focus on teaching specific skills that the children will need in their immediate environment. Sometimes called **functional approaches,** these instructional programs seek to identify skills that the children need in order to be successful in their present environment or in one that they will soon be entering.

To better understand how functional communication differs from nonfunctional, consider the situations that appear in Figure 14.2, described by Calculator and Jorgensen (1991). Calculator and Jorgensen use these situations as examples of what they call *integrated and nonintegrated objectives.* In the first example, the functional goal stipulates that John request an object (utensil) that he actually needs. The nonfunctional goal simply requires that John match pictures with objects. Similarly, in the other examples, the emphasis is on the utilization of skills that John actually needs to use rather

FIGURE 14.2   Examples of Functional (Integrated) and Nonfunctional (Nonintegrated) Objectives

Integrated (functional)
Given that John is seated at a table in the cafeteria and is missing an eating utensil that he needs, on three consecutive days he will request the utensil by pointing to the corresponding photograph on his communication board.

Given that John is dressing himself for school and requires assistance, on five consecutive days he will request his mother's attention and then point to the article of clothing with which he needs help.

Given that John is not feeling well, he will issue unambiguous yes/no responses 80 percent or more of the time to an adult who is attempting to identify what is wrong with him.

Nonintegrated (nonfunctional)
When seated at a table in the cafeteria, upon which is a spoon, a knife, and a fork, John will correctly place photographs of each of these three utensils on the corresponding object, with 80 percent or greater accuracy in three out of four consecutive sessions.

While getting dressed following gym class, upon his aide's request John will correctly point to his shoes, socks, shirt, and pants 80 percent or more of the time on two out of three consecutive days.

John will accurately indicate *yes* and *no* in his communication book 80 percent or more of the time, on two out of three consecutive days, in response to his mother's asking him a series of questions soliciting personal information.

Source: Adapted from Calculator & Jorgensen (1991).

then on performing a task that may be based on a developmental guideline. These examples demonstrate that it is possible to change a nonfunctional (developmental) objective to one that is integrated (or functional).

It is possible to combine a developmental approach to language instruction with a functional approach. Language development should be seen as a framework within which there can be considerable variation. This is true for normally developing children and even more true for children with disabilities. Information about typical language development should be used as a way to identify children at risk for language disorders and as a way to develop an overall sequence of skills. The child's age and status should most importantly determine how developmental guidelines are used. In general, developmental hierarchies are less valid for older children and children with more severe disabilities. These children are more likely to benefit from programs that focus on skills needed in their current environment, skills of functional communication and general literacy. But instructional objectives can always be put in functional terms. In other words, typical development can be used as a guideline for the selection of instructional objectives. The objectives themselves can be put in functional terms that will enable the child to enhance their functionality in natural settings.

The Intervention Continuum: From Structured to Naturalistic Approaches

Intervention methods represent a continuum from more highly structured to less structured approaches. Structured language instructional approaches are typically used with a standardized set of instructions and materials. They take the child through a highly structured sequence of steps toward a goal that is set prior to instruction. Although highly structured programs can work, they have been criticized for being unnatural (Goetz, Schuler, & Sailor, 1981); that is, the instructional procedures are unlike what the child is likely to encounter in the real world, and as a result, children may master *splinter* skills—skills that are relatively useless.

Naturalistic approaches emphasize the delivery of language intervention in natural settings, utilizing dispersed trials that follow the child's lead and use reinforcers indicated by the child's preferences (Warren & Kaiser, 1986). Although language-instruction goals may be set prior to instruction, the language facilitator is encouraged to be responsive to the child. The language facilitator may structure the environment in ways that will lead toward a language goal but should follow the child's lead and be responsive to the child rather than to a set of instructions (see Figure 14.3). Therefore, if the child uses structures that were not anticipated or wants to talk about topics that were not part of the plan, the facilitator should follow the child's lead.

A number of different instructional approaches can be grouped under the general heading of naturalistic instruction, including:

1. *Modeling.* A verbal model is presented that is related to the student's interests. The student is reinforced if a response occurs. If there is no response, the model is repeated. For example, if a child were playing with a favorite toy, the teacher might say, "Barney." If the child responds with the word, the teacher could ex-

FIGURE 14.3 Structured Instruction Contrasted with Naturalistic

Structured
Uses clinical setting
Uses drill and practice activities
Uses massed trials
Follows rigid hierarchy of goals
Uses reinforcers determined by instructor
Reinforces correct responding

Naturalistic
Uses natural environment contexts
Uses conversational activities
Uses dispersed trials
Follows child's lead
Uses reinforcers based on child's interest
Reinforces attempts at communication

Source: Adapted from Cole & Dale (1986), Warren & Kaiser (1986).

tend the conversation, such as, "I like Barney." If the child made no response, the teacher would repeat the sequence.

2. *Time delay.* When using this procedure, the language facilitator moves close to the child and looks at the child for 5 to 15 seconds while waiting for the child to talk. If the child does not initiate an interaction, the adult can provide a verbal prompt or model an initiation.

3. *Incidental teaching.* Warren and Kaiser (1986) describe incidental teaching as including the following elements:
   - Arranging the environment to increase the likelihood that the child will initiate to the adult
   - Selecting language targets appropriate for the child's skill level, interests, and environment
   - Responding to the child's initiations with requests for elaborated language
   - Reinforcing the child's communicative attempts with attention and access to the objects and activities with which the child has expressed interest

Research on Intervention Efficacy

In general, research has found that language intervention can be effective. A meta-analysis of a large number of studies found that language intervention was effective for children with phonological or vocabulary difficulties and somewhat effective for children with syntax difficulties. Intervention was not found to be effective for children with receptive language difficulties (Law, Garrett, & Nye, 2004).

Are some intervention methods more effective than others? Bryen and Joyce (1985) reviewed 43 published studies from the 1970s on the type and effectiveness of language-intervention programs for students with severe disabilities. They concluded that there were some methods that worked, and that successful intervention programs:

- Took into account the cognitive, social, motor, and language abilities of students prior to intervention
- Conducted intervention in an environment-based context
- Established goals that stressed the importance of spontaneous communication for a variety of purposes
- Used interactional methods of intervention (e.g., ongoing modeling, play, commenting, waiting, responsiveness to communicative intent)
- Viewed and measured the interdependence of the various communicative, cognitive, social, and environmental systems

How do the characteristics of the child influence the effectiveness of language intervention? Studies by Connell (1987) and Connell and Stone (1992) found that modeling correct language was sufficient to improve the language skills of typically developing children but did not have the same effect on the language of children with specific language impairments. However, research reported by Yoder and colleagues (1991) called into question the long-held assumption that direct, structured methods of language teaching are more effective for students with significant language disorders. In their study, Yoder and colleagues compared a less structured (milieu) approach to a more structured (communication training program) language-instruction program. They found that the milieu approach worked best for the children with the most serious language impairments. The more structured program worked best for the higher-functioning children. The authors speculated that one reason for their findings may have been that the lower-functioning children benefited more from a program that emphasized the generalization of language skills (the milieu approach).

The results of research on language intervention suggest that factors such as the child's age and degree of disability, as well as the aspect of language being taught, should be considered when making decisions about the goals and methods of intervention. Developmental guidelines seem to be most appropriate for younger children. Goals developed from the demands of the environment (functional goals) are also useful, especially for older students and students with more severe disabilities. Structured intervention procedures work best for teaching syntactic skills. Instruction that takes place in natural settings can be effective if there are clear goals. A number of commercially available language intervention programs and materials are available; some of these are listed in Table 14.2.

The ultimate goal of language intervention should always be to make the child a more effective communicator. Therefore, no matter what intervention method teachers choose to use, they should always consider that the skills taught should be generalized to new environments.

In addition to looking at what language interventions work, it can be instructive to examine those that do not work. Damico (1988) presented a case study of a therapy plan that failed. Debbie was referred to the speech-language pathologist at the age of 6 because of her "lack of pronouns and omission of words during conversation" (p. 52).

TABLE 14.2   Examples of language intervention programs/materials

Program/Material	Language Skill	Grade/Age Level	Publisher
100% Grammar	Syntax	Ages 9–14	Linguisystems
Language Skills Series	Grammar	Grades 1–6	Curriculum Associates
Build a Sentence	Syntax	Grades 1–4	Super Duper
Conversations	Pragmatics	Ages 11–18	Super Duper
Figurative Language	Semantics	Ages 10 and up	Super Duper
First Words, First Words II, First Verbs (software)	Semantics	Children with language learning disabilities	Laureate
Language: A Literacy Intervention Curriculum	Language, reading, writing	Grades 3–12	Sopris-West
Simple Sentence Structure (software)	Syntax	Children with language learning disabilities	Laureate
SPARC for Grammar	Syntax	Ages 4–10	Linguisystems
SPARC for Phonology	Phonology	Ages 4–10	Linguisystems
Swim, Swam, Swum	Irregular verbs	Children with language learning disabilities	Laureate
Vocabulary and Syntax Roundup	Semantics and syntax	PreK–grade 5	Super Duper
Working Out with: Phonological awareness Syntax Semantics	Phonology Syntax Semantics	PreK–grade 4	Super Duper

After extensive testing, she received about 7 months of group and individual therapy, at the end of which she was judged to have made sufficient progress to no longer need speech and language intervention. Six years later, Debbie was referred once again to the speech-language pathologist. Her problems were now worse than ever. She was shy and quiet, with poor social skills, and was reading four grade levels below the norm for her age. Language testing indicated that she had a severe language disorder. What went wrong?

Damico (1988) suggests five things that may have caused the failure of language intervention for Debbie:

1. *The fragmentation fallacy.* Speech and language therapy tends to focus on discrete aspects of language rather than on language as a whole. As a result, there was no focus on Debbie's ability to understand and use language in natural settings.

2. *Therapist bias.* In this case, the therapist was biased to perceive Debbie as successful. After all, she was a pretty, outgoing, and cooperative child from an upper-middle-class family. Test results were interpreted in the most positive light. Had the therapist been biased against Debbie, of course, Debbie might never have completed therapy.

3. *Acquiescence.* Parents and teachers acquiesced in response to the "expert"— the speech-language pathologist.

4. *Lack of follow-up.* Had there been a follow-up examination, Debbie's continuing problems might have been identified. But none was required and none was given.

5. *Bureaucratic policies and procedures.* Regulations required the use of tests that focused on discrete language skills. A large caseload contributed to the fact that Debbie was released from therapy so quickly and was not followed.

The factors cited by Damico for the failure of language intervention in Debbie's case are not uncommon in school environments. We would do well to be aware of these potential problems and do our best to avoid them.

Summary

In this chapter we have sampled the great variety of models and procedures that are available for enhancing language skills. The first part of the chapter focused on language instruction in the classroom. Techniques to enhance language skills in a variety of classroom environments were discussed, as was the importance of collaboration between teachers and language specialists. Language intervention methods were discussed in the second part of the chapter. Research on language intervention has suggested that the procedures that usually work best combine clearly stated outcomes with practice in natural settings. It is important that those planning instruction activities consider the characteristics of the individual child, as well as the various environments in which the child will have to apply her or his language skills. If research has done nothing else, it has made us aware that teaching isolated skills outside natural environments does not work.

R E V I E W   Q U E S T I O N S

1. Describe three ways that a classroom could be restructured to enhance language interaction.

2. Give an example of self-talk and discuss how it can be used to increase language interaction.

3. How could snack time in preschool classrooms be used as an opportunity for language interaction?

4. Describe three ways that speech-language specialists could work with regular or special education teachers to deliver services.

5. What are some of the limitations of the use of developmental guidelines for planning language intervention for children with language disabilities?

6. How can developmental and functional approaches be combined in an instructional program for language?

7. Contrast structured approaches to language intervention with naturalistic approaches.

SUGGESTED ACTIVITIES

1. Teachers often have to develop informal intervention activities using materials and methods readily available in the classroom. Develop informal intervention suggestions for the following language skills:

   - Understanding idioms *foot in your mouth, two left feet)*
   - Using conjunctions *(because, but)*
   - Developing turn-taking skills

2. Mercer and Mercer (1993) describe a technique that they call "Does It Mean the Same Thing?" This instructional method is designed to help students recognize the underlying (deep) structure of sentences. The student receives a card that contains two sentences. One is a simple sentence *(The boy hit the ball);* the other is a sentence with a more complex structure *(The ball was hit by the boy).* The student must indicate whether the two sentences have the *same* or *different* underlying meanings (deep structure). Your task is to make up additional sentences that include questions, embedded sentences, and passive constructions. Try to design this task so it is self-correcting.

3. If you have the opportunity to work with a young child (age 5 or younger) or a child with disabilities who is functioning at approximately this level, try to use *expansion.* You will need to set up a play activity that will give the child the opportunity to interact. As the child plays, ask questions to prompt a response. When the opportunity arises, use expansion to model a more adult form of language for the child. Try to video- or audiotape your play session.

GLOSSARY

evidence-based practices: instructional approaches that are based on an extensive base of research

expansion: a language instructional technique in which the adult takes a child's utterance and repeats it using a higher-level language model

functional approaches: intervention methods that identify skills that the children need in order to be successful in their present environment or in one that they will soon be entering

intervention: intensive instruction usually delivered after a period of time in which the individual has been exposed to instruction

naturalistic approaches: instructional approaches that utilize the natural environment as the basis for language instruction

learning strategies: instructional approaches that teach students to use a strategy to solve problems and carry out tasks

parallel talk: a language instructional technique in which the adult verbalizes action taken by the child

restating and rewording: a language instructional technique in which an adult acknowledges what the child has said and provides alternative models for communicating the same information

self-talk: a language instructional technique in which the adult verbalizes what action he or she is doing as he or she does it

RESOURCES ON THE WEB

www.ed.gov/about/offices/list/ies   U.S. Department of Education Institute of Education Sciences

www.curriculumassociates.com   Curriculum Associates Publishing Company with information on literacy instruction programs

www.laureatelearning.com   Laureate Learning Systems, manufacturer and publisher of language-intervention software

www.sopriswest.com/   Sopris-West, publisher of assessment and intervention materials

www.superduperinc.com   Super Duper Publications, publisher of language instruction materials

www.linguisystems.com   Linguisystems, Inc., publisher of materials for language instruction

REFERENCES

Adams, M., Foorman, B., Lundberg, I., & Beeler, C. (1997). *Phonemic awareness in young children: A classroom curriculum.* Baltimore: Brookes.

Aram, D. M., Ekelman, B. L., & Nation, J. E. (1984). Preschoolers with language disorders: 10 years later. *Journal of Speech and Hearing Research, 27,* 232–244.

Aram, D. M, & Nation, J. E. (1980). Preschool language disorders and subsequent language and academic difficulties. *Journal of Communication Disorders, 13,* 159–170.

Atkinson, R. H., & Longman, D. G. (1985). Sniglets: Give a twist to teenage and adult vocabulary instruction. *Journal of Reading, 29,* 103–105.

Bashir, A. S., & Scavuzzo, A. (1992). Children with language disorders: Natural history and academic success. *Journal of Learning Disabilities, 25,* 53–65.

Blischak, D. M., & Schlosser, R. W. (2003). Use of technology to support independent spelling by students with autism. *Topics in Language Disorders, 23,* 293–304.

Brinton, B., & Fujiki, M. (1993). Language, social skills, and socioemotional behavior. *Language, Speech, and Hearing Services in Schools, 24,* 194–198.

Bryen, D., & Joyce, D. (1985). Language intervention with the severely handicapped: A decade of research. *Journal of Special Education, 19,* 7–39.

Buttrill, J., Niizawa, J., Biemer, C., Takahashi, C., & Hearn, S. (1989). Serving the language learning disabled adolescent: A strategies-based model. *Language, Speech, and Hearing Services in Schools, 20,* 185–204.

Calculator, S. N., & Jorgensen, C. M. (1991). Integrating AAC instruction into regular education settings: Expounding on best practices. *Augmentative and Alternative Communication, 7,* 204–213.

Cazden, C. B. (1986). Classroom discourse. In M. C. Wittrock (Ed.), *Handbook of research on teaching* (pp. 432–464). New York: Macmillan.

Cirrin, F. M., & Penner, S. G. (1995). Classroom-based and consultative service delivery models for language intervention. In M. E. Fey, J. Windsor, & S. F. Warren (Eds.), *Language intervention: Preschool through the elementary years* (pp. 333–362). Baltimore: Brookes.

Cole, K. N., & Dale, P. (1986). Direct language instruction and interactive language instruction with language-delayed preschool children: A comparison study. *Journal of Speech and Hearing Research, 29,* 206–217.

Connell, P. J. (1987). A comparison of modeling and imitation teaching procedures on language-disordered children. *Journal of Speech and Hearing Research, 30,* 105–113.

Connell, P. J., & Stone, C. (1992). Morpheme learning of children with specific language impairments under controlled conditions. *Journal of Speech and Hearing Research, 35,* 844–852.

Damico, J. S. (1988). The lack of efficacy in language therapy: A case study. *Language, Speech, and Hearing Services in Schools, 19,* 51–66.

Dickinson, D. K. (2001). Book reading in preschool classrooms. In D. Dickinson & R. Tabors (Eds.), *Beginning literacy with language* (pp. 175–203). Baltimore: Brookes.

Dudley-Marling, C., & Searle, D. (1988). Enriching language learning environments for students with learning disabilities. *Journal of Learning Disabilities, 21,* 140–143.

Dyer, K., Santarcangelo, S., & Luce, S. (1987). Developmental influences in teaching language forms to individuals with developmental disabilities. *Journal of Speech and Hearing Disorders, 52,* 335–347.

Ferguson, D. (1994). Is communication really the point? Some thoughts on interventions and membership. *Mental Retardation, 32,* 7–18.

Friend, M., & Cook, L. (1996). *Interactions: Collaboration skills for school professionals.* White Plains, NY: Longman.

Gillam, S. L., & Gillam, R. B. (2006). Making evidence-based decisions about child language intervention in schools. *Language, Speech, and Hearing Services in Schools, 37,* 304–315.

Goetz, L., Schuler, A., & Sailor, W. (1981). Functional competence as a factor in communication instruction. *Exceptional Education Quarterly, 2,* 51–60.

Goldstein, H., & Hockenberger, E. H. (1991). Significant progress in child language intervention: An 11-year retrospective. *Research and Developmental Disabilities, 12,* 401–424.

Hammill, D. D., & Bartel, N. R. (1995). *Teaching students with learning and behavior problems.* Austin, TX: Pro-Ed.

Hatcher, P. J., Hulme, C., & Snowling, M. J. (2004). Explicit phoneme training combined with phonic reading instruction helps young children at risk of reading failure. *Journal of Child Psychology and Psychiatry, 45,* 338–358.

Johnson, C. J., Beitchman, J. H., Young, A., Escobar, M., Atkinson, L., Wilson, B., et al. (1999). Fourteen-year follow-up of children with and without speech/language impairments: Speech/language stability and outcomes. *Journal of Speech, Language, and Hearing Research, 42,* 744–761.

Katz, L., & Chard, S. (2000). *Engaging children's minds: The project approach* (2nd ed.). Stamford, CT: Ablex.

King, R., Jones, D., & Lasky, E. (1982). In retrospect: A fifteen year follow-up of speech-language-disordered children. *Language, Speech, and Hearing Services in Schools, 13,* 24–32.

Kirkland, L. D., & Patterson, J. (2005). Developing oral language in primary classrooms. *Early Childhood Education Journal, 32,* 391–395.

Koppenhaver, D. A., & Erickson, K. A. (2003). Natural emergent literacy supports for preschoolers with autism and severe communication impairments. *Topics in Language Disorders, 23,* 283–292.

Koppenhaver, D. A., Pierce, P. L., Steelman, J. D., & Yoder, D. E. (1995). Contexts of early literacy intervention for children with developmental disabilities. In M. E. Fey, J. Windsor, & S. R Warren (Eds.), *Language intervention: Preschool through the elementary years* (pp. 241–274). Baltimore: Brookes.

Krauss, R. (1989). *The carrot seed.* New York: Harper/Trophy.

Lapadat, J. C. (2002). Relationships between instructional language and primary students' learning. *Journal of Educational Psychology, 94,* 278–290.

Law, J., Garrett, Z., & Nye, C. (2004). The efficacy of treatment for children with developmental speech and language delay/disorder: A meta-analysis. *Journal of Speech, Language, and Hearing Research, 47,* 924–943.

Lee, Y., & Vail, C. O. (2005). Computer-based reading instruction for young children with disabilities. *Journal of Special Education Technology, 20,* 5–18.

Lenz, B. K., & Hughes, C. A. (1990). A word identification strategy for adolescents with learning disabilities. *Journal of Learning Disabilities, 23,* 149–158.

Light, J., Koppenhaver, D., Lee, E., & Riffle, L. (1994). *The home and school literacy experiences of students who use AAC systems.* Unpublished manuscript.

Lindfors, J. W. (1987). *Children's language and learning.* Englewood Cliffs, NJ: Prentice-Hall.

Manning, M. (2004, November/December). The fallacy of fluency. *Teaching Pre K–8.*

Manning, M., Manning, G., & Long, R. (1994). *Theme immersion: Inquiry-based curriculum in ele-*

mentary and middle schools. Portsmouth, NH: Heinemann.

Mastropieri, M. A., & Scruggs, T. E. (1989). Constructing more meaningful relationships: Mnemonic instruction for special populations. *Educational Psychology Review, 1,* 83–111.

McCormick, L. (1986, Winter). Keeping up with language intervention trends. *Teaching Exceptional Children, 18,* 123–129.

Mercer, C. D., & Mercer, A. R. (1993). *Teaching students with learning problems.* New York: Merrill.

Miller, L. (1989). Classroom-based language intervention. *Language, Speech, and Hearing Services in Schools, 20,* 153–169.

Moats, L. (2001, Summer). Overcoming the language gap and invest generously in teacher professional development. *American Educator,* 5–7.

Moats, L., & Lyon, G. R. (1996). Wanted: Teachers with knowledge of language. *Topics in Language Disorders, 16,* 73–86.

Montgomery, J. K. (1992). Perspectives from the field: Language, speech, and hearing services in schools. *Language, Speech, and Hearing Services in Schools, 23,* 363–364.

Norris, J. A., & Hoffman, P. R. (1990). Language intervention within naturalistic environments. *Language, Speech, and Hearing Services in Schools, 21,* 72–84.

Notari-Syverson, A., O'Connor, R. E., & Vadsey, P. F. (1998). *Ladders to literacy: A preschool activity book.* Baltimore: Brookes.

Olswang, L., & Bain, B. (1991). When to recommend intervention. *Language, Speech, and Hearing Services in Schools, 22,* 255–263.

Ostrosky, M., & Kaiser, A. (1991). Preschool classroom environments that promote communication. *Teaching Exceptional Children, 23,* 6–10.

Owens, R. E. (2004). *Language disorders: A functional approach to assessment and intervention* (4th ed.). Boston: Allyn & Bacon.

Rowe, M. (1974). Wait-time and rewards as instructional variables, their influence in language, logic, and fate control: Part I: Wait-time. *Journal of Research in Science Teaching, 11,* 81–94.

Rowe, M. (1986). Wait time: Slowing down may be a way of speeding up! *Journal of Teacher Education, 37,* 43–50.

Schery, T., & O'Conner, L. (1992). The effectiveness of school-based computer language instruction with severely handicapped children. *Language, Speech, and Hearing Services in Schools, 23,* 43–47.

Scruggs, T. E., & Mastropieri, M. A. (2000). The effectiveness of mnemonic instruction for students with learning and behavior problems: An update and research synthesis. *Journal of Behavioral Education, 10,* 163–173.

Silliman, E., Ford, C., Beasman, J., & Evans, D. (1999). An inclusion model for children with language learning disabilities: Building classroom partnerships. *Topics in Language Disorders, 19,* 1–18.

Slavin, R. E. (2002). Evidence-based education policies: Transforming educational practice and research. *Educational Researcher, 31,* 15–21.

Thousand, J., & Villa, R. (1992). Collaborative teams: A powerful tool in school restructuring. In R. Villa, J. Thousand, W. Stainback, & S. Stainback (Eds.), *Restructuring for caring and effective education* (pp. 73–108). Baltimore: Brookes.

Uberti, H. Z., Scruggs, T. E., & Mastropieri, M. A. (2004). Keywords make the difference: Mnemonic instruction in inclusive classrooms. *Teaching Exceptional Children, 35,* 56–61.

Warren, S. E., & Kaiser, A. P. (1986). Incidental language teaching: A critical review. *Journal of Speech and Hearing Disorders, 51,* 291–299.

Wasik, B. A., Bond, M. A., & Hindman, A. (2006). The effects of a language and literacy intervention on Head Start children and teachers. *Journal of Educational Psychology, 98,* 63–74.

Watson, L. R., Layton, T. L., Pierce, P. L., & Abraham, L. M. (1994). Enhancing emerging literacy in a language preschool. *Language, Speech, and Hearing Services in Schools, 25,* 136–145.

Wiig, E. H., & Semel, E. (1984). *Language assessment and intervention for the learning disabled.* Columbus, OH: Merrill.

Wilson, B. A. (1996). *Wilson Reading System: Instructor manual.* Millbury, MA: Wilson Language Training Corporation.

Yoder, P. J., Kaiser, A. P., & Alpert, C. L. (1991). An exploratory study of the interaction between language teaching methods and child characteristics. *Journal of Speech and Hearing Research, 34,* 155–167.

15 Augmentative and Alternative Communication

Some school-age children have significant disabilities that make it very difficult for them to develop spoken language. Until recently there was little that could be done for these children. They were often relegated to the back wards of institutions or employed in nonproductive sheltered workshop activities. Today new technologies offer hope for these individuals who previously lacked access to that most important human charac-teristic—communication. These new approaches are called augmentative and alterna-tive communication (AAC).

This chapter examines the rapidly developing field of augmentative and alterna-tive communication, describing a variety of approaches—from sign systems to sophis-ticated electronic devices. Most important, instructional methods that are designed to develop the functional use of AAC systems are discussed. The goal of this chapter is to help you become aware of the many options that are available for persons who do not speak and how to best utilize these procedures in classroom settings.

Specifically, after reading this chapter you should be able to:

1. Define *augmentative* and *alternative communication.*
2. Describe the options that are available to enhance the communication of non-speaking persons.
3. Understand the criteria for selecting AAC systems.
4. Know the outcomes that can be expected from the use of AAC procedures.
5. Describe methods found effective for enhancing the communicative interaction of AAC users.
6. Understand methods for successfully including students who use AAC systems.
7. Use methods to enhance the literacy skills of AAC users.

Howard, a student with Fragile-X syndrome, has severe articulation problems that make his speech very difficult to understand. He carries a communication wallet with pictures he shows others so they can understand what he is talking about. When he goes to McDonald's, he uses pictures from the wallet to help him order his meal.

Melissa, a 16-year-old girl with autism, rarely talks. She has learned to communi-cate with a Touch Talker. Now, she can respond to questions from her teacher by touch-ing a symbol on her display, activating a voice output device that serves as her voice.

Tony, a 9-year-old student with cerebral palsy, attends a regular education class-room. Because of his limited motor abilities, he uses a head pointer to touch an electronic keyboard to formulate written messages and produce a voice output.

Tamika, a student with Down syndrome, has learned a repertoire of eight signs that she uses to supplement her limited spoken output.

What all of these individuals have in common is that they are using some type of augmentative or alternative (AAC) procedure. For many, if not most, children with severe disorders of language and communication, AAC represents their best hope for the development of communication skills (Romski & Sevcik, 1988).

The American Speech-Language-Hearing Association (ASHA) cites estimates that 8 to 12 people per 1,000 experience severe communication impairments that require AAC. If accurate, that would mean that between 450,00 and 700,000 school-age children could benefit from the use of AAC systems (based on 2005 school population data). Although there is no accurate count of the number of school-age children who actually use augmentative and alternative communication, there are undoubtedly many children who could benefit from the use of AAC procedures but who do not yet have the opportunity to do so.

Recently, federal law in the United States has recognized the growing importance of augmentative and alternative communication systems by including provisions regarding the use of AAC in the Americans with Disabilities Act and the Individuals with Disabilities Education Act (IDEA). IDEA regulations now require that assistive technology be considered as part of the planning for children with disabilities. If it is determined that an assistive technology such as AAC is required, the school must purchase the device and train staff in its use.

Components of Augmentative and Alternative Communication

The American Speech-Language-Hearing Association (ASHA) defines *augmentative and alternative communication (AAC)* as, "an area of clinical practice that attempts to compensate (either temporarily or permanently) for the impairment and disability patterns of individuals with severe expressive communication disorders (i.e., the severely speech-language and writing impaired)." AAC may include existing speech or vocalizations, gestures, manual signs, and aided communication (Sevcik & Romski, 2007).

Augmentative and alternative communication systems typically are thought of as consisting of four components: *communication aids* (or *devices), communication techniques, symbol systems,* and *communication strategies* (Sevcik & Romski, 2007). Each of these components must be considered when an AAC procedure is being developed. Sometimes most attention is lavished on the communication device especially if it is a particularly high-tech system. Teachers and speech language specialists must be careful not to become so caught up in the technical sophistication of the device that they ignore the other components of AAC systems. After all, the device is of little use if the user cannot understand it or does not use it.

Techniques

There are two basic kinds of AAC techniques, aided and unaided. **Unaided techniques** do not require external support devices or procedures in order to operate. They include techniques such as speech, sign language, and facial expressions. Unaided techniques have the obvious advantages of portability and ease of use. With the exception of an occasional bout of laryngitis, the voice, hands, and facial expressions cannot be lost or broken. There are no concerns about electrical outlets or battery packs. The "device" is always ready for use. With spoken language or facial expressions, although the users may have difficulty expressing themselves, listeners are usually familiar with the means of communication (spoken or nonverbal language) being used. Of course, when a sign language is used as the mode of communication (e.g., American Sign Language or Signed English), there will be a more limited number of potential communication partners.

Aided techniques employ communication means that may be as simple as a communication board or as complex as a computer with a synthetic speech output device. They may be *electronic* or *nonelectronic,* and they employ *a selection procedure* and use some type of *symbol system.* Mustonen et al. (1991) note several advantages of electronic communication devices. For example, use of electronic devices can enable users to produce more complex messages than their own language skills allow. As an example, Mustonen et al. describe how by pressing a symbol for a soft drink, an electronic aid could produce the expression, *Gee, I'm thirsty. I'd like a medium Diet Cherry Coke.* If the device has voice output capabilities, there is the further advantage of communication from a distance. Another advantage of electronic devices is the capability to store messages for future use.

Four features are common to all communication aids, electronic or not: output, selection technique, vocabulary capability, and portability.

Output refers to the appearance of the display and how it enhances communication with a listener. Communication boards typically consist of a flat surface on which drawn or written symbols are displayed. They can be placed on a wheelchair lap tray, bound in a book, or folded into a wallet-sized container. The output is a visual display, which the user accesses by pointing. Electronic devices may use a visual display, a printed output, or a voice output. Visual displays allow listeners to check their understanding of the message and to even offer corrections or suggestions for extension of the communication. **Voice output communication aids (VOCAS)** have the advantage of being the closest approximation to natural speech and can be used at a distance.

The use of voice output systems has increased dramatically (Scherz & Beer, 1995). VOCAS range in complexity from simple devices with one message, such as the BIG-mack (AbleNet), to sophisticated devices with large capacities, such as the Vanguagrd (Prentke Romich) and the Dynavox V (Dynavox Systems). There are two types of voice output devices currently in use: *synthesized speech* and *digitized speech.* Synthesized speech devices generate speech-like sounds by electronically combining speech sounds. They can be used in text-to-speech applications where typed text is converted to vocal output. The intelligibility of synthesized-speech output devices can vary widely (Mirenda & Beukelman, 1990). Digitized voice-output systems are based on recorded human speech. They are nearly as intelligible as human speech (Mustonen et al., 1991) but, because of their high computer memory requirements, are not very useful for text-to-speech applications. Examples of devices that use digitized speech include the MaCaw (Zygo) and the Message Mate 40 (Words Plus).

A second common feature of communication aids is the **selection technique** employed. Users of a communication aid must indicate to their communication partner which letter or symbol they wish to select. Individuals with intact motor skills may use *direct selection.* In this case, the "speaker" simply points to a selected item. For those who have little or no voluntary control of their arms, adaptations can be used to allow them to make direct selections. These might be a head pointer (a rod attached to a headband) or an eye gaze system that identifies the selected item when the user looks at it for a period of time.

Direct selection is usually the fastest type of selection technique; however, some individuals with significant motor impairments need another type of selection method. *Scanning* is an alternative. Scanning involves making a selection from the presented choices. Rather than directly selecting the desired word or symbol, with scanning, choices are displayed for the individual. Typically, scanning is associated with electronic displays that present a blinking light (cursor) which moves from item to item on the display panel. The user selects an item by merely pressing a button (or a switch or pad), or making some other motor movement that stops the scanning. The cursor may move across the display in a linear motion, in up-and-down columns, or in any other preprogrammed way. Scanning devices can be coupled with various types of switches so that the individual who has any voluntary muscle control at all can operate a communication device.

Vocabulary capability is defined by Rounsefell et al. (1993) as "the capability of an aid to allow the individual to have the vocabulary that he or she wants displayed or stored in the aid" (p. 298). Communication boards can be designed with overlays that can be changed for various settings and activities. Most electronic devices can be reprogrammed and the overlay changed to meet changing communicative needs. The ease with which such changes can be made and the number and usefulness of the items on the display are factors that should be considered in the design or selection of a communication aid.

Portability is the final feature of communication aids discussed by Rounsefell et al. (1993). Portability is an important concern in an era when emphasis is on the integration of persons with disabilities into their schools and communities. As technology advances, the devices are becoming smaller and more powerful. Clearly, a communication device is of little help if it cannot be used in the settings where it is really needed. Therefore, it is essential that portability be considered when decisions about communication devices are being made.

There are advantages and limitations to the use of either aided or unaided procedures (see Table 15.1). Ideally, unaided communication techniques would be the choice for everyone. But there are many individuals who are unable to develop spoken language or understand and use nonverbal communication or sign language. For these persons, aided communication methods are the best alternative. When appropriately designed or selected, aided communication devices permit people with severe impairments in motor and/or cognitive abilities to communicate with others.

TABLE 15.1 Advantages and Disadvantages of Aided and Unaided AAC Systems

	Advantages	Disadvantages
Unaided Systems	No external support devices needed Portable No cost (other than training)	Potential communication partners limited Relies on user's memory ability Signs may be difficult to learn
Aided Systems	Can produce message that is more complex than user's own language Can communicate at a distance (with VOCAS)	Electronic device may break or lose power Portability may be limited May be expensive

Symbol Systems

Unaided AAC systems use language—spoken or signed. Studies examining the acquisition of sign systems by individuals with disabilities have generally found that such persons can acquire at least a basic sign vocabulary (Kiernan, 1983). Although a sign language system may be a useful form of communication for some students, for many students with disabilities, sign language is not an effective approach to the development of communication skills. Results of a survey reported by Bryen, Goldman, and Quinlisk-Gill (1988) indicated that despite years of training, few students with significant disabilities used signs in spontaneous conversation. In addition, with signing there is the obvious problem of the limited number of potential communication partners available. If the goal for persons with disabilities is community inclusion, sign language may not be the most effective approach. Therefore, many of these students require some sort of alternative approach that might include an aided AAC system.

Any AAC device must have some sort of symbol system as the mode of communication. For individuals with severe motor disorders but good literacy skills, letters and words can be the symbolic mode. But many users of AAC systems either have not had the opportunity to acquire literacy skills or have cognitive disabilities that impair their acquisition of written language. A variety of symbol systems ranging from real objects to photographs to abstract-symbol systems, have been developed to aid these persons in communicating with an AAC system.

Photographs have the advantage of clearly representing an item. Of course, the quality of the photograph will affect its usefulness. The context in which an item appears also affects its recognizability (Mustonen et al., 1991). Photos that include a contextual background (a spoon that appears next to a plate) are more recognizable. Additionally, in general, color photographs are more easily recognized than black-and-white photos (Mirenda & Locke, 1989). An alternative to photos is line drawings. These usually are composed of black lines drawn on a white background.

A number of abstract symbol-systems are available, including *Picture Communication Symbols (PCS)* (Johnson, 1981), *Picsyms* (Carlson, 1984), *Sigsymbols* (Creagan, 1982), and *Blissymbols* (Bliss, 1965). As illustrated in Figure 15.1, all of these graphic symbol systems include pictorial representations of the items they name. In

FIGURE 15.1   Examples of Line-Drawn Symbols

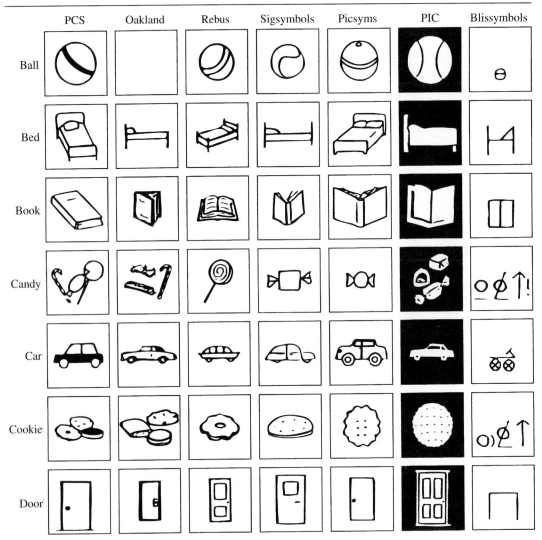

Source: Reprinted with permission from *Augmentative Communication: An Introduction,* S. W Blackstone, Ed. Rockville, MD: American Speech-Language-Hearing Association, p. 93.

addition, Sigsymbols include ideographs (ideas represented through graphic symbols) and Blissymbols include both ideographs and arbitrary symbols (ideas assigned arbitrary configurations of lines). *Rebus* symbols are another form of line drawing used with AAC systems. Rebuses use pictures of objects to replace the word in a sentence. A number of rebus systems are commercially available (e.g., Widgit Software).

Communication Skills

AAC procedures and devices present wonderful opportunities for nonspeaking persons to communicate with others. Yet, if the systems are not used or not used effectively, the intervention is of no use, no matter how high-tech the device. As Janice Light (1988) put it, "One of the most critical issues for clinicians in the field of augmentative and al-

FIGURE 15.2   Examples of Lexigrams

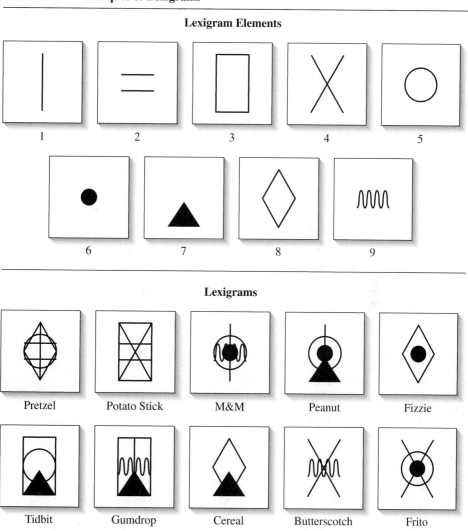

Source: Reprinted with permission from Establishment of Symbolic Communication in Persons with Severe Retardation, by M. A. Romski, R. A. Sevcik, and J. L. Pate. *Journal of Speech and Hearing Disorders, 53,* 98. Copyright 1998 by American Speech-Language-Hearing Association. All rights reserved.

ternative communication (AAC) is to determine how nonspeaking individuals can best facilitate their daily interactions in educational, vocational, community, and home environments" (p. 66).

Research on the use of AAC systems has found that users tend to be relatively passive communicative partners. They rely on their speaking listeners to direct the conversation and rarely initiate interaction themselves (Calculator & Dollaghan, 1982; Light, Collier, & Parnes, 1985; Mirenda & Iacono, 1990). Calculator (1988) has described many AAC users as "underfunctioning." That is, they are not expected to communicate effectively and tend to live down to these expectations. Instead of asking for more food, for example, a student may simply throw the plate on the floor. The staff member's response may be to simply clean up the mess, rather than ask the student why he or she threw the plate. Conversational partners tend to limit the interaction of AAC users in other ways. For example, they tend to ask questions that require only yes/no answers (Light et al., 1985) and initiate conversations that require no response (e.g., making a comment like "Nice work.") (Reichle, 1991).

In addition to their rarely initiating conversation, AAC users have been found to have difficulty terminating conversations (Reichle, 1991). Some simply do not know how to do this. Others want to extend the conversation as long as possible, even if the interaction is no longer meaningful. Some AAC users have even been reported to make untrue statements, simply to keep a conversation going (Reichle, 1991). While there is considerable variation in communicative abilities among AAC users (Light, 1988), the picture provided by most of the research suggests that most are not communicating effectively.

Implementing AAC Systems

Prerequisite Skills

One of the major issues in AAC involves prerequisites to its use. For many years it was claimed that in order to be successful, potential users of AAC systems had to have achieved certain cognitive and language prerequisites. Sometimes called the *candidacy model* (Mirenda & Iacono, 1990), this approach suggested that the potential AAC user should be able to demonstrate development to at least stage V (means-end relations) on Piaget's description of cognitive development and show evidence of intentional communication before being introduced to an AAC system. The idea that AAC users needed these cognitive and language prerequisites was based on data from spoken language acquisition in normally developing children. These data indicated that specific cognitive and communicative behaviors preceded the emergence of spoken language. However, as Romski and Sevcik (1988) have noted, the exact relationship between cognition and communication development, and language acquisition has never been clearly defined. Moreover, there is a rapidly expanding body of research that indicates that persons with disabilities can benefit from AAC systems even if they lack these cognitive and communicative prerequisites. For example, Reichle and Yoder (1985) were able to teach preschoolers who functioned at stage IV on a Piagetian scale to label objects using graphic symbols. Although the preschoolers were unable to generalize this skill to functional communication, such as commenting and requesting, they were able to label. Romski, Sevcik, and Pate (1988) taught young adults with severe mental retardation to request foods and objects by using graphic symbols on a computer display panel, despite the subjects' lack of spoken language comprehension skills.

Because of research such as that described above and the realization that research from normal language development is not always easily translated to individuals with disabilities, most clinicians and researchers are today suggesting a try-and-see, rather than a wait-and-see, model for potential AAC users (McGregor, Young, Gerak, Thomas, & Vogelsberg, 1992). Use of this approach requires a careful analysis of the communicative environments in which the AAC user functions and of what would be required to make it possible for the individual to communicate (Mirenda & Iacono, 1990).

Preassessment

As with any kind of intervention, the development of an AAC system begins with assessment. The most useful kind of assessment is one that is ecological in nature, that is, one that surveys the communicative environments and communicative needs in which the individual will function. McCormick and Wegner (2003) described a comprehensive assessment system for potential AAC users that includes the following elements:

- *The student:* They suggest that the assessment team ask questions such as:
  How does the student communicate now and for what purposes?
  What are the student's communication needs and goals?
  Where and with whom does the student need to communicate?
  What are the student's language, cognitive, sensory, and motor skills and capabilities?
  What are the potential barriers to the student communicating in his natural environment?
- *Mobility assessment:* Including, seating, positioning, and ambulation.
- *Motor assessment:* To what extent can the student use hands for signing, pointing, typing? Can the student have control over head movement, eye gaze, or other motor movements to communicate?
- *Communication assessment:* Interviews with teachers and family members and direct observation can address questions such as:
  How does the student currently communicate in different contexts?
  What communicative modes and functions does the student use?
  How effective are the student's present communication modes?
  What does the student communicate about?
  What motivational factors may have the potential to affect the student's communication?
- *Cognitive/linguistic assessment:* Including receptive language and cognitive development to determine:
  How does the student currently understand the world?

How can communication be best facilitated within this understanding?

To what extent can the student meet the cognitive demands of various symbol sets and systems?

- *Sensory/perceptual assessment:* How does the student process incoming information? Which sensory systems are intact?
- *Literacy assessment:* Including print and phoneme recognition, word recognition, reading comprehension, and spelling.
- *The environment:* What curricular and social activities could the student access with the use of an AAC system? Assessment should include:

Communicative preferences and skills of potential partners

Potential barriers in the environment such as attitudes, skills, and knowledge of teachers, support staff, and peers

Opportunities to use AAC systems in natural environments

Developing an AAC System

Using the results of assessment, the AAC development team needs to design a system that will help the user participate in academic, functional, and social activities in a variety of environments and improve the quality and quantity of the child's language and communication skills. Decisions need to be made about the *type* of system to be used (aided or unaided), the nature of the *symbol system* (e.g., gestural, pictorial, symbolic), and the communication instruction required.

Deciding the type of system to be used—aided or unaided—is the first decision needed in designing an AAC system. The provider must weigh the advantages and limitations of each type of system in combination with information about the learner and the communicative environment. Characteristics of the learner, such as sensory and motor skills, may determine what kind of system is possible. Similarly, environmental demands and opportunities will also have an impact on this decision. If potential communication partners are not familiar with American Sign Language, this might be a poor choice for an AAC system.

In many cases, the choice of a communication system is not as critical as it might seem. Frequently, a combination of communication systems, including both aided and unaided, are preferable. For example, Barrerra, Lobato-Barrera, and Sulzer-Azaroff (1980) found that a combined gestural and vocal mode intervention was more effective than either mode used alone. Keogh and Reichle (1985) suggested that a mixed mode, in which some vocabulary items are taught via one mode and others are taught in another, might be beneficial for some learners. Another alternative is to teach students to use two modes of communication. Depending on the situation, they can choose the method that works best. For example, signing may work well in school with a teacher who knows sign language but a communication wallet might be necessary when ordering at McDonald's (Reichle, Mirenda, Locke, Piche, & Johnston, 1992; Romski, Sevcik, Robinson, & Bakeman, 1994).

Once a method of communication (or combination of methods) has been selected, the next decision involves selection of an appropriate symbol system. For an un-

TABLE 15.2   Strategies for Selecting Signs

Strategy

Select contact signs over noncontact signs.
Select symmetric signs over asymmetric signs.
Select translucent signs over nontranslucent signs.
Select signs where there are maximal locational differences.
Select visible over invisible signs.
Select reduplicated over nonreduplicated signs.
Group signs to be taught in close proximity to each other into conceptually dissimilar sets.
Select single-handshape over multiple-handshape signs.
Select one-handed signs over two-handed signs.
Select single-movement over multiple-movement signs.

Interpretation

Contact signs are those where there is contact between the hands or between the hand and another part of the body.
Symmetric signs are those where each hand makes identical shapes or movements.
Translucent (or iconic) signs are those that resemble the item being signed.
Signs that are made in different locations relative to the signer's body are more easily learned (e.g., signs made at the side).
Visible signs are those that signers can easily see as they produce them.
Some signs are made out of the field of vision (e.g., from the top of one's head).
Reduplicated signs are those that are repeated two or more times.
Signs that differ in meaning may be learned more easily.

Source: Adapted from J. E. Doherty. (1985). The effects of sign characteristics on sign acquisition and retention: An integrative review of the literature. *Augmentative and Alternative Communication, 1,* 108–121.

aided communication procedure, the choice will be among the variety of gestural languages in existence. Research has found that some signs are easier to learn than others. Doherty (1985) has suggested several specific strategies for selecting signs. They are presented in Table 15.2.

Regardless of which communication system is selected, a decision must be made about which vocabulary items to include. Unfortunately, decisions about vocabulary are often based on what the teacher or clinician *thinks* the student needs to know rather than on what the environment demands (Reichle et al., 1992). In fact, when Reichle (1983) asked interventionists how they made decisions about vocabulary selection, he got the following responses (in order of frequency): (1) selected vocabulary that the interventionist thought would be important, (2) selected vocabulary from the first 50 word developmental data, (3) selected vocabulary from word lists obtained from surveying service providers, (4) selected vocabulary from word lists derived from vocabulary used by learners with developmental disabilities. A better strategy would be to select vocabulary demanded by the learner's environment. This vocabulary could be derived from the results of the preassessment ecological inventory.

Three factors should be considered when selecting AAC symbol systems: guessability, learnability, and generalization. Symbols range in **guessability** from those that are *very transparent* (easily guessed) to those that are *translucent* (need additional information to decode) (Mustonen et al., 1991). The term *iconic* is also used to describe guessability. Iconic symbols are similar in appearance to the items that they represent. For example, the drawings of the ball in Figure 15.1 are all reasonably transparent (or iconic); that is, naive viewers would likely call the drawing a ball. The Sigsymbol drawing of a cookie, however, may not be as readily guessable. In general, however, Picsyms and Rebus symbols have been found to be easier to guess than the meanings of Blissymbols (Musselwhite & Ruscello, 1984). Research by Mirenda and Locke (1989) on subjects with mild to severe mental retardation, found the following order of guessability: real objects, color photographs, black-and-white photographs, miniature objects, black-and-white line symbols (Picsyms, Picture Communication Symbols) (Mayer-Johnson Co., 1986), Rebuses, Self-Talk symbols (Johnson, 1986)), Blissymbols, and written words.

Learnability refers to the ease or difficulty of learning a particular symbol set. Generally, studies with nondisabled children have found that learnability is related to iconicity (guessability). Symbols that are more iconic (similar to the object being named) are more easily learned. Rebus symbols are easier to learn than Blissymbols, which are in turn easier to learn than Non-SLIP chips or words (Clark, 1981; Carrier & Peak, 1975). Research on persons with disabilities has found that, for them, matching photographs with objects is easier than matching line drawings with objects (Sevcik & Romski, 1986) and that Rebus symbols are also more easily learned than Blissymbols (Hurlbut, Iwata, & Green, 1982).

According to Mustonen et al. (1991) iconic symbols facilitate the acquisition, generalization, and maintenance of graphic communication systems. The researchers acknowledge, on the other hand, that for students who can acquire higher-order symbolic information, iconic symbols may not be necessary. Another consideration is determining the ease with which symbols can be combined to make sentences. Lexigrams and Blissymbols are readily combined into sentences. Of course, printed words are easily generalized, but lexigrams have been shown to be easier to discriminate than printed words for persons with severe mental retardation (Romski, Sevcik, Pate, & Rumbaugh, 1985).

When graphic symbols are selected for use with an AAC system, Reichle (1991) suggests that four questions should guide their selection:

- *What types of symbols should be used?* Choices include photographs, line drawings, abstract symbols, and the like. The selection should be made on the basis of what works for a particular learner.
- *How large will the symbols be?* Learners with poor visual acuity will require larger displays.
- *How will the learner select the symbols?* Direct selection, scanning, or a combination of these could be used.
- *How will the symbols be displayed?* A board (electronic or nonelectronic), wallet, or book could be used to display the symbols.

Enhancing Communication

Again, as with most decisions involving augmentative and alternative communication, the decision about which symbol system to use must include considerations of the abilities and needs of the individual student—the student's literacy skills, cognitive abilities, and potential communicative partners. Romski and Sevcik (1988) have suggested, however, that the most important decisions may regard the instructional strategies for enhancing communicative competence rather than the mode of communication employed.

Earlier in this chapter, we reviewed some of the research on the communication difficulties encountered by users of AAC and found that AAC users often lack opportunities to communicate. When they do communicate, they have been reported to have a lot of difficulty communicating effectively with others and are, therefore, relatively passive communicators who rarely initiate interactions.

A variety of techniques, from highly structured, direct-teaching procedures to more naturalistic methods, have been used to enhance the communication skills of AAC users. (Mirenda & Iacono, 1990). In reviewing the research on teaching conversational skills to students who have severe disabilities and are using AAC systems, Calculator (1988) identified two major approaches that appear to work: *teaching in natural environments* and *teaching functional skills.*

Natural environments have proven to be the best place to teach conversation skills. When instruction is designed so that students have opportunities to talk about real situations with conversational partners who actually exist in those settings, not only does interaction increase but there is a greater chance for generalization of the skill as well (Calculator, 1988). In addition to being provided with opportunities for interaction in natural environments, AAC users should be taught to use their systems for functional purposes—that is, to accomplish some real task in the environment rather than one contrived for instructional purposes. Calculator (1988) gives the following example of how instruction for 8-year-old nonspeaking Joshua was made more functional. For two years, Joshua's instructional program consisted of his teacher presenting two objects at a time and requesting that he indicate through eye gaze the one named by his teacher. Since, after two years of instruction Joshua still had not reached criterion levels, his program was redesigned to give him opportunities to use eye gaze during various activities in the school day. For example, at nap time Joshua was prompted to choose, using eye gaze, one of two locations for his nap. At snack time he selected between two snacks. Within six months, he was able to accurately indicate his preferences in a number of different contexts.

Spiegel, Benjamin, and Spiegel (1993) give another example of the integration of functional communication within natural environments. They taught a 19-year-old male with cerebral palsy and moderate mental retardation to increase his use of an AAC device (Touch Talker) (Prentke-Romich). Although the student had learned to use the Touch Talker, he used it infrequently for interaction with others. He learned to respond to conversational prompts that utilized sentences he had previously learned. For example, the student learned to produce the sentence *I need to go to the bank.* After demonstrating that he could produce this sentence, he was given the following prompt:

You just received your S.S.I. check in the mail. You want to put it in your savings account, and Ruby can drive you to the bank. Now, here comes Ruby to talk to you. The student was then expected to type his previously learned sentence. Using this procedure, the student not only learned to respond to the vignettes appropriately, but also increased his spontaneous use of his AAC device.

Merely teaching an individual to use an AAC device is not enough to ensure that the person will use it. The results of the Spiegel et al. (1993) study suggest this. So do the results of a training study conducted by Dattilo and Camarata (1991). They first taught two adults with severe motor impairments to use a Touch Talker. There was no significant increase in the initiation of interaction by either subject following this Touch Talker instruction. But when subjects were specifically taught to use their device to initiate conversations, the number of initiations increased rapidly. Johnston, Reichle, and Evans (2004) identified three major problems with the use of AAC systems:

- Students who do not use their systems
- Communication partners who do not participate fully with a person using an AAC system
- Students who use socially or contextually inappropriate strategies for communication

They reviewed research that has investigated solutions to each of these problems. This research is summarized in Table 15.3.

Not only the AAC user, but also the listener, requires training. Often, listeners have to be very patient as AAC users formulate their messages. But patience alone may not be enough. Researchers have found that instruction in understanding the speech produced by voice output communication devices can increase the responsiveness of listeners to AAC messages (Rounsefell, Zucker, & Roberts, 1993). Communication between AAC users and their conversational partners can also benefit from instruction given to the listener on how to elicit communication from others (Hunt, Alwell, & Goetz, 1991).

Calculator (1988) suggests the following guidelines for planning communication goals for AAC users:

- **Increase the environments in which AAC is used:** Students should have the opportunity to practice their skills in many different types of settings.
- **Engage in age-appropriate interactions:** Conversation should be consistent with that which would be expected with normally developing peers of the same age.
- **Increase opportunities for AAC use:** Students must be provided with both the vocabulary needed in the environments they are likely to encounter and the opportunities to use their conversational skills.
- **Focus conversation on topics valued by the individual:** When students have the opportunity to request desired things and reject items they really dislike, they tend to value their communication skills.
- **Focus conversation on topics valued by parents and guardians:** Parents must recognize the need for AAC and the value of communication that meets real needs.

TABLE 15.3   Challenges and Solutions for Supporting AAC Use

Challenge	Solutions

Learner doesn't use the AAC system	Response effort
	    Physical effort or cognitive effort required to use the AAC system should be minimized.
	Rate of reinforcement
	    The learner should be reinforced frequently for using the AAC system.
	Immediacy of reinforcement
	    The reinforcement received after using the AAC system is not delayed.
	Quality of reinforcement
	    The reinforcement provided for using the AAC system is motivating to the learner.
	Interaction of efficiency variables
	    The combined influence of response effort, rate of reinforcement, immediacy of reinforcement, and quality of reinforcement is considered.

Communication partners are not using the AAC system	Response effort
	    The physical or cognitive effort for interpreting the learner's communication via the AAC system is minimized.
	Rate of reinforcement
	    The communication partner is frequently reinforced for using the AAC system.
	Quality of reinforcement
	    The communication partner's use of the AAC system results in meaningful communicative interactions.
	Immediacy of reinforcement
	    The communication partner's use of the AAC system results in immediate communicative interactions.

Learner uses socially or contextually unacceptable communicative behaviors	Socially unacceptable communicative acts
	    Identify a communicative act that is more efficient than the unacceptable behavior.
	    Implement an intervention strategy that maximizes the efficiency of the new communicative act.
	    Implement an intervention strategy that minimizes the efficiency of the socially unacceptable behavior.
	Contextually unacceptable communicative acts
	    Identify the environmental contexts that should (and should not) elicit.
	    Implement an. intervention strategy that maximizes the efficiency of each communicative act in the appropriate environmental context.

- **Consider ease of acquisition:** Systems should be designed to be readily used so that students have the maximum opportunity for communication.
- **Consider enhancement of status for the AAC user:** Intervention should target skills that will enhance the status of the AAC users in their own eyes as well as in society's view.

There is increasing evidence that users of augmentative and alternative communication can be helped to be effective communicators. It seems clear, however, that general instruction in the use of an AAC system is not sufficient. Rather, AAC users have to be taught specifically to use their system in effective communication interactions. Instruction in natural environments on functional skills appears to be effective, as does instruction that considers the special needs of the listener.

To summarize, the process of planning an AAC instructional program consists of five steps:

1. **Preassessment,** including an ecological inventory and assessment of the learner
2. **Development of goals** that should enhance the child's ability to participate in all environments
3. **Selection of a mode of communication,** either aided, unaided, or a combination
4. **Selection of a symbol system,** gestural or graphic
5. **Selection of methods to enhance communication** for both the AAC user and communication partners

There is evidence from research that with careful planning and the use of effective instructional techniques, nonspeaking individuals can develop effective communication skills.

Integrating AAC Use into Regular Education Classrooms

As more and more students with severe disabilities, including students with severe communication disabilities, are included in regular education settings, it becomes increasingly important for teachers—both regular and special education—to be aware of methods that will help these students become more fully integrated. For those students who use AAC systems, there are many challenges. Not only may teachers and students be unfamiliar with AAC devices, but also many AAC users require a significant amount of help with their own communication skills.

Calculator and Jorgensen (1991) have provided some suggestions for integrating AAC users into regular education settings (see Table 15.4). They emphasize collaboration in planning for and teaching students with severe disabilities who use AAC systems. Since communication is a necessary skill in all the environments in which the student is expected to function, it is important that all staff be familiar with the AAC system used by the student. Both staff and student peers can benefit from instruction in the special listening skills required for augmentative and alternative communication.

Although most students with disabilities who use AAC systems can benefit from being included in regular education classrooms, they will not all be able to participate

TABLE 15.4 Suggestions for Integrating AAC Users into Regular Education Settings

1. Educational priorities should be established collaboratively with parents, advocates, and other team members (as opposed to discipline-referenced priorities).

2. Observation, assessment, and intervention should occur in the natural settings in which individuals spend their time.

3. Functional skills should be taught systematically throughout the day, rather than at designated times.

4. Anyone coming in contact with the augmented communicator is a potential instructor of communication skills.

5. The effectiveness of intervention procedures should be evaluated relative to individuals' performances in their natural settings.

6. Educational plans should specify desired communication behaviors relative to clusters of skills associated with the effective performance of a broader skill or activity.

Source: From Integrating AAC Instruction into Regular Education Settings: Expounding on Best Practices by Calculator, S. N., & Jorgensen, C. M. *Augmentative and Alternative Communication 1991, 7,* 204–212. Reprinted by permission of Taylor & Francis Ltd, http://www.informaworld.com.

equally. Beukelman and Mirenda (2005) describe three levels of participation to show how AAC users can participate in the regular education classroom:

Competitive Educational Participation: Students with disabilities participate in the same educational activities as their peers and are expected to meet the same academic standards, although they may not complete the same amount of work in the same amount of time (and with the same independence) as their peers. AAC users may require more time to complete assignments and tests.

Active Educational Participation: Students with disabilities participate in the same educational activities as their peers. However, the expected outcome is not the same as that of their peers. Their progress is evaluated according to individualized goals. Active students may receive supplementary instruction in specific skill areas. They usually benefit from adaptations or modifications to instruction.

Involved Educational Participation: Students with disabilities participate in the same educational activities as their peers but they are expected to learn in cross-curricular areas such as communication, social, and motor skills. Their progress is evaluated according to individualized goals. Such students may require extensive adaptations in order to participate with their peers (see Box 15.1).

The goal is for all students with disabilities to participate to the maximum extent possible with typically developing peers in the general education curriculum.

As team members responsible for working with students using AAC systems, special educators may be called on to perform a variety of functions. A survey conducted by Locke and Mirenda (1992) found that many of these functions are traditional teacher-related responsibilities: adapting the curriculum, preparing and maintaining documentation, and writing goals and objectives for AAC users. However, some of the

---

BOX **15.1**

Examples of Levels of Participation in the Regular Education Classroom

Coran: A Competitive Student

Coran is a student with cerebral palsy who uses a computer with a word prediction program to write. Coran is expected to meet the same educational goals as her peers. For example, on a social studies assignment, Coran is expected to read independently. She answers the assigned questions using her computer. When she takes a test, she receives additional time to complete the test.

Tim: An Active Student

Tim is a student with autism who uses a communication book based on the Picture Exchange Communication System (PECS) model. Tim participates in the same instructional activities as his classmates but with adaptations and modifications to instruction. For example, for a social studies reading assignment, Tim is assigned to read with a peer. The peer reads the selection aloud while Tim follows along with a partially completed outline. Tim and his classmate then complete the outline together. A classroom aide assesses Tim's knowledge of the reading by asking questions that Tim can answer by constructing picture "sentences."

Heather: An Involved Student

Heather is a student with significant intellectual disabilities who communicates primarily through vocalizations and by use of a simple voice output device. During social studies class, Heather participates in many of the same activities as her peers but her learning goals focus primarily on communication. For example, while the rest of the class is reading the assignment, Heather watches a brief video from an online social studies website, then answers "yes/no" questions posed by her instructional aide by using her communication device. Heather is evaluated on her level of participation in the activity and the number of times she correctly responds to the questions.

---

responsibilities are less traditional: identifying vocabulary, determining students' motivation and attitudes toward AAC techniques, and determining the communication needs of students. Two of the major concerns expressed by the teachers in this survey were the need for more training in AAC and the need for more time to work as a team.

Beukelman and Mirenda (2005) reviewed research that has identified a number of factors that contribute to the successful inclusion of AAC users with disabilities. These factors, include:

- Administrative support for and commitment to inclusion of all learners
- Availability of an AAC system with functions that are appropriate to meet individual student needs
- Attitudes among AAC team members that include creativity, flexibility, and open mindedness

- Willingness of the general education teacher to develop skills in both the use of AAC systems and inclusion
- A team whose members have a working knowledge of the general education curriculum as well as strategies for adapting/modifying the curriculum
- A team with expertise in assistive technology and other learning technologies
- A team with expertise in how to use inclusive educational practices
- A clear understanding of the roles and responsibilities of each AAC team member
- Sufficient time for AAC team members to meet regularly, in collaboration with parents

Literacy and Augmentative and Alternative Communication

As we have noted throughout this book, one of the key issues for all students is the development of literacy skills. Appropriate use of AAC systems in the classroom (and in the home) can enhance literacy skills. Unfortunately, many AAC users have limited access to and instruction in literacy skills. A review of the research on the literacy skills of AAC users showed that between 50 percent and 90 percent cannot read at all or read below age expectations (Koppenhaver & Yoder, 1992).

In addition to physical limitations, children who use AAC systems typically have reduced literacy-learning opportunities (Beukelman, Mirenda, & Sturm, 2005). Parents of children with severe speech and language impairments read aloud less often to their child. When they do read, they ask their child for fewer labels and make fewer requests for their child to point to pictures. Many parents of children with disabilities place more value on physical needs and on basic communication, rather than on the development of literacy skills (Light & Kelford Smith, 1993). In school, AAC users have been found to have more limited literacy-learning opportunities than their peers (Beukelman, Mirenda, & Sturm, 2005).

What can be done to provide children who use AAC systems with more and better opportunities for the development of reading and writing skills? Students with significant disabilities have been found to benefit from literacy instruction that includes the following components:

- Creation of a well-stocked, accessible library that includes both familiar and predictable books (those that include repeated passages and/or themes)
- Daily storybook readings in which children choose the book to be read
- Opportunities for children to write about functional and meaningful events
- Provision of a wide variety of reading and writing tools as well as time to explore use of those tools
- Adult scaffolding during storybook reading that draws attention to the form, content, and use of written language
- Routine integration of text into classroom routines
- Individual and small group activities that expose children to new reading and writing activities (Koppenhaver & Erickson, 2003).

The reading skills of AAC users can be enhanced by the use of communication tools that support their participation during reading. For example, communicative devices can be programmed to include symbols from a story. Students can comment on their reading by having access to multiple choice responses to questions (e.g., "I thought the book was:" funny/sad). Additionally, communication devices need to be designed to include letters and words that students are likely to encounter frequently.

In addition to reading, the writing skills of AAC users should also be a focus on instruction. Bedrosian et al. (2003) described a program to enhance the writing of a 14 year-old student with autism who used an AAC device (Lightwriter/Zygo) to communicate. At the beginning of the study the student had limited written language skills. The authors paired the student with autism with a typically developing peer. They used an additional AAC device (Alphatalker/Prentke-Romich) that was programmed with phrases designed to enhance communication between the students. In addition, they used a computer with story writing software ("My Words"/Hartley-Jostens Learning) to facilitate written language production. The students were taught to use these devices as well as story grammar maps and storyboards to plan and execute their writing. Using these techniques, the AAC user significantly improved his writing. The student took an active, even dominant, role in planning the stories. He learned to use a story map effectively to plan and write his stories. The typically developing peer reported that he enjoyed writing the stories with his disabled peer and would do so again.

Using techniques such as those described above, students who use AAC systems can more fully develop their literacy skills. Blischak (1995) described the case of Thomas, a 9-year-old boy with cerebral palsy and vision impairments. Thomas received early intervention for speech and language disabilities that included the development of an AAC system. In school, Thomas used an AAC device called a "Talking Screen" which enabled him to use his limited movement and vision skills to scan an array and produce a voice output. This system enabled Thomas to more fully participate in literacy activities. Using this device, Thomas was able to initiate interactions, answer questions, spell words, and write stories. For example, after listening to a story, questions were recorded by the teacher. Thomas was required to listen to the passage and use his Talking Screen to select and print answers.

Outcomes of AAC System Usage

One of the questions that must be asked about augmentative and alternative communication is, Does it work? Answering this question requires examining answers to three other questions. First, has the student increased communication ability? Second, what, if any, effects are there on other areas of functioning? And third, how is the AAC user accepted by others? All of these questions could be used in determining the success or failure of an AAC system.

The first question is, without a doubt, the most important one. After all, the primary reason for using an AAC system is to improve the communication skills of the student. There is considerable evidence from both research and clinical practice that augmentative and alternative communication, when properly instituted, can enhance the communication skills of nonspeaking individuals (Mirenda & Mathy-Laikko, 1989). In our brief review of the literature on AAC, we have seen that even students with severe mental retardation can learn to use symbols (Romski, Sevcik, & Pate, 1988). We have also reviewed evidence that AAC users, given instruction in communication skills, can become more effective communicators (McGregor et al., 1992).

There is also evidence that individuals who use AAC devices and systems can increase their production of spoken language. Many parents and professionals are concerned that using AAC systems with individuals who speak may reduce their spoken language, but a review of research on the speech production of AAC users found that, in nearly 90 percent of the studies AAC users increased their speech production (Millar, Light, & Schlosser, 2006). Moreover, there were no decreases in speech in subjects in any of the studies. This is powerful evidence that not only does AAC use not decrease spoken language, but also in most cases, it actually increases speech production.

There is also some research evidence that when students with challenging behaviors learn an alternative means of communication, their behavior can improve (Doss & Reichle, 1989). Durand (1993) reported on three cases of students who each had significant behavior problems, in combination with mental retardation and the absence of spoken language. Their behavior problems included crying, hitting, tantrums, and hair pulling. The parents and teachers of these students attended a series of workshops at which they learned about using assistive devices for functional communication. Following implementation of these procedures, the students increased their spontaneous communication and significantly decreased their challenging behaviors—by as much as 95 percent. These data and results from other studies suggest that when students are helped to improve their communication, the results can extend to other behaviors, as well.

The third area of consideration in evaluating the AAC system is acceptance by peers. If students with disabilities are to be fully included in school settings, it is essential that they become accepted by their peers. If speaking peers have negative attitudes toward them, nonspeaking AAC users may shy away from interacting with peers. Although there is little research on this issue, there is evidence that improved ability to communicate is associated with improved peer acceptance (Guralnick, 1986). When Blockenberger, Armstrong, O'Connor, and Freeman (1993) compared the attitudes of fourth-grade children toward a child using an alphabet board, an electronic device, and signing, they found that there was little difference in the children's reactions. Their research suggests that children are not heavily influenced by the type of AAC system used by another child. While there is clearly a need for more research in this area, teachers often report that children are more accepting of peers with disabilities than adults would expect.

Summary

Every child can communicate. Physical and cognitive limitations are no longer impenetrable roadblocks to the development of communication skills. The rapid development of augmentative and alternative communication procedures means that there are now a variety of options available to help nonspeaking persons develop communication skills.

Despite the rapid proliferation of AAC techniques, there are still many non-speaking persons who do not have access to communication aids. This may be due to factors such as lack of funding or lack of knowledge about augmentative and alternative communication on the part of teachers and clinicians. Whatever the reasons, to deny an individual access to effective means of communication is to deny that person the right to be part of the community. Therefore, it is incumbent upon teachers and clinicians to educate themselves about AAC and to advocate for the right of their students/clients to have access to AAC systems.

For those who need help getting started with augmentative and alternative communication, many states have an AAC resource center. If no center is listed for your state, you might try contacting a university medical center to see if they have someone with expertise in AAC systems.

REVIEW QUESTIONS

1. What is the difference between *alternative* and *augmentative* communication? Why is this distinction sometimes not important?

2. List and briefly describe the three components of AAC systems.

3. Compare the advantages and limitations of aided and unaided communication techniques.

4. What is scanning? How does it differ from direct selection?

5. What are some of the communication difficulties researchers have frequently described among AAC users?

6. Why has the candidacy model of AAC implementation been criticized?

7. List and briefly describe five learner characteristics that should be considered in choosing an AAC system.

8. Define *guessability* and *learnability* as applied to symbol systems.

9. Find the story of Joshua in the chapter. How was instruction redesigned to help Joshua become a more effective communicator?

10. What problems do you see that might inhibit the use of AAC systems?

11. Describe classroom-based techniques that could be used to enhance the reading and writing of AAC users.

SUGGESTED ACTIVITIES

1. Try interviewing a user of an AAC system. Find out about some of their experiences in using their system. What problems have they had? What are the reactions of other people? If the speaker has very limited communication skills, you might also have to interview a parent and/or staff member.

As you conduct the interview with the AAC user, note your own feelings. Do you find that you have any difficulty communicating with this person? What could be done to make the conversation flow more smoothly?

2. Try out an augmentative and alternative communication system yourself, an electronic device if possible. If you cannot get access to such a device, use a communication board or wallet. First, you will need to understand how the device works. Try it out. Then try to use it in a real environment (such as in a cafeteria or fast food restaurant).

How did you feel when you used the AAC system? How difficult was it to express yourself? How did others react to you? What could you have done to make the communicative exchanges work better?

3. Observe AAC users as they use their system. Note the following:

Do they appear to be familiar with their device/procedure?

With whom do they communicate?

How frequently do they initiate interaction?

How do others respond to them?

GLOSSARY

aided augmentative communication techniques: methods that utilize external support devices or procedures, for example, communication boards and voice output devices

augmentative communication: methods and devices that supplement existing verbal communication skills

guessability: refers to the degree of similarity in appearance between a symbol and the item it represents

learnability: refers to the ease with which a symbol system can be acquired

output: in AAC, the appearance of the display and how it enhances communication with a listener

selection technique: in AAC, the method used by an individual to select symbols on their communication device

unaided augmentative communication techniques: methods that do not require external support devices or procedures in order to operate, for example, speech, sign language, and facial expressions

voice output communication aids (VOCAS): communication devices that produce synthesized speech

RESOURCES ON THE WEB

www.ablenetinc.com Ablenet Corporation—manufacturer of AAC devices

www.ace-centre.org.uk Ace Centre—resource for information about AAC with links to AAC resources

www.closingthegap.com Closing The Gap—organization dedicated to providing information about and support for AAC users

www.dynavoxsys.com Dynavox Corporation—manufacturer of AAC devices

http://www.isaac-online.org/en/home.shtml International Society for Augmentative and Alternative Communication (ISAAC)

www.prentrom.com   Prentke Romich Company—manufacturer of AAC devices

www.resna.org   RESNA—the Rehabilitation Engineering and Assistive Technology Society of North America: includes information on AAC and links to other sites

http://www.ussaac.org/   United States Society for Augmentative and Alternative Communication

http://www.zygo-usa.com/   Zygo industries—AAC manufacturer

http://www.widgit.com/widgitrebus/   Widgit software—developers of the Widgit Rebus system

REFERENCES

Barrera, R. D., Lobato-Barrera, D., & Sulzer-Azaroff, E. (1980). A simultaneous treatment comparison of three expressive language training programs with a mute autistic child. *Journal of Autism and Developmental Disorders, 10,* 21–37.

Bedrosian, J., Lasker, J., Speidel, K., & Politsch, A. (2003). Enhancing the written narrative skills of an AAC student with autism: Evidence-based research issues. *Topics in Language Disorders, 23,* 305–324.

Beukelman, D. R., & Mirenda, P. (2005). *Augmentative and alternative communication.* Baltimore: Paul H. Brookes.

Beukelman, D. R., Mirenda, P., & Sturm, J. (2005). Literacy development of children who use AAC. In D. Beukelman & P. Mirenda (Eds.), *Augmentative and alternative communication* (pp. 351–390). Baltimore: Paul H. Brookes.

Blischak, D. M. (1995). Thomas the writer: Case study of a child with severe physical, speech, and visual impairments. *Language, Speech, and Hearing Services in Schools, 26,* 11–20.

Bliss, C. (1965). *Semantography.* Sydney, Australia: Semantography Publications.

Blockenberger, S., Armstrong, R. W., O'Connor, A., & Freeman, R. (1993). Children's attitudes toward a nonspeaking child using various augmentative and alternative communication techniques. *Augmentative and Alternative Communication, 9,* 243–250.

Bryen, D. N., Goldman, A. S., & Quinlisk-Gill, S. (1988). Sign language with severe/profound mental retardation: How effective is it? *Education and Training in Mental Retardation, 23,* 127–129.

Calculator, S. N. (1988). Promoting the acquisition and generalization of conversational skills by individuals with severe disabilities. *Augmentative and Alternative Communication, 4,* 94–103.

Calculator, S. N., & Dollaghan, C. (1982). The use of communication boards in a residential setting. *Journal of Speech and Hearing Disorders, 14,* 281–287.

Calculator, S. N., & Jorgensen, C. M. (1991). Integrating AAC instruction into regular education settings: Expounding on best practices. *Augmentative and Alternative Communication, 7,* 204–212.

Carlson, F. (1984). *Picsyms categorical dictionary.* Lawrence, KS: Baggeboda Press.

Carrier, J., & Peak, T. (1975). *Non-slip: Non-speech language initiation program.* Lawrence, KS: H & H Enterprises.

Clark, C. R. (1981). Learning words using traditional orthography and the symbols of Rebus, Bliss, and Carrier. *Journal of Speech and Hearing Disorders, 46,* 191–196.

Creagan, A. (1982). *Sigsymbol dictionary.* Hatfield, Hertsford, England: A. Creagan.

Dattilo, J., & Camarata, S. (1991). Facilitating conversation through self-initiated augmentative communication treatment. *Journal of Applied Behavior Analysis, 24,* 369–378.

Doherty, J. E. (1985). The effects of sign characteristics on sign acquisition and retention: An integrative review of the literature. *Augmentative and Alternative Communication, 1,* 108–121.

Doss, L. S., & Reichle, J. (1989). Establishing communicative alternatives to the emission of socially motivated excess behavior: A review. *Journal of the Association for Persons with Severe Handicaps, 14,* 101–112.

Durand, V. M. (1993). Functional communication training using assistive devices: Effects on challenging behavior and affect. *Augmentative and Alternative Communication, 9,* 168–176.

Guralnick, M. J. (1986). The peer relations of young handicapped and nonhandicapped children. In P. S. Strain, M. J. Guralnick, & H. M. Walker (Eds.), *Children's social behavior.* New York: Academic Press.

Hunt, R, Alwell, M., & Goetz, L. (1991). Interacting with peers through conversation turntaking with a communication book adaptation. *Augmentative and Alternative Communication, 7,* 117–126.

Hurlbut, B. I., Iwata, B. A., & Green, J. D. (1982). Nonvocal language acquisition in adolescents with severe physical disabilities: Blissymbol versus iconic stimulus formats. *Journal of Applied Behavior Analysis, 15,* 241–258.

Johnson, J. (1986). *Self-Talk: Communication boards for children and adults.* Tucson, AZ: Communication Skill Builders.

Johnson, R. (1981). *The picture communication symbols.* Salana Beach, CA: Mayer-Johnson.

Johnston, S. S., Reichle, J., & Evans, J. (2004). Supporting augmentative and alternative communication use by beginning communicators with severe disabilities. *American Journal of Speech-Language Pathology, 13,* 20–30.

Keogh, W. J., & Reichle, J. (1985). Communication intervention for the "difficult-to-teach" severely handicapped. In S. R. Warren & A. K. Rogers-Warren (Eds.), *Teaching functional language* (pp. 157–196). Austin, TX: Pro-Ed.

Kiernan, C. (1983). The use of nonvocal communication techniques with autistic individuals. *Journal of Child Psychology and Psychiatry, 24,* 339–375.

Koppenhaver, D. A., & Erickson, K. A. (2003). Natural emergent literacy supports for preschoolers with autism and severe communication impairments. *Topics in Language Disorders, 23,* 283–292.

Koppenhaver, D., & Yoder, D. (1992). Literacy issues in persons with severe physical and speech impairments. In R. Gaylord-Ross (Ed.), *Issues and research in special education* (Vol. 2, pp. 156–201). New York: Teachers College Press.

Light, J. (1988). Interaction involving individuals using augmentative and alternative communication systems: State of the art and future directions. *Augmentative and Alternative Communication, 4,* 66–82.

Light, J., Collier, B., & Parnes, P. (1985). Communication interaction between young nonspeaking physically disabled children and their primary caregivers: Part I: Discourse patterns. *Augmentative and Alternative Communication, 1,* 74–83.

Light, J., & Kelford Smith, A. (1993). The home literacy experiences of preschoolers who use augmentative communication systems and their nondisabled peers. *Augmentative and Alternative Communication, 9,* 10–25.

Locke, R. A., & Mirenda, P. (1992). Roles and responsibilities of special education teachers serving on teams delivering AAC services. *Augmentative and Alternative Communication, 8,* 200–210.

Mayor-Johnson Co. (1986). *The picture communication symbols, books I and 2.* Solana Beach, CA: Mayer-Johnson.

McCormick, L., & Wegner, J. (2003). Supporting augmentative communication. In L. McCormick, D. Loeb, & R. Schiefelbusch (Eds.), *Supporting children with communication difficulties in inclusive settings* (2nd ed.). Boston: Allyn & Bacon.

McGregor, G., Young, J., Gerak, J., Thomas, B., & Vogelsberg, R. T. (1992). Increasing functional use of an assistive communication device by a student with severe disabilities. *Augmentative and Alternative Communication, 8,* 243–250.

Millar, D. C., Light, J. C., & Schlosser, R. W. (2006). The impact of augmentative and alternative communication intervention on the speech production of individuals with developmental disabilities: A research review. *Journal of Speech, Language, and Hearing Research, 49,* 248–264.

Mirenda, P., & Beukelman, D. R. (1990). A comparison of intelligibility among natural speech and seven speech synthesizers with listeners from three age groups. *Augmentative and Alternative Communication, 6,* 61–68.

Mirenda, P., & Iacono, T. (1990). Communication options for persons with severe and profound disabilities: State of the art and future directions. *Journal of the Association for the Severely Handicapped, 15,* 3–21.

Mirenda, P., & Locke, P. A. (1989). A comparison of symbol transparency in nonspeaking persons with intellectual disabilities. *Journal of Speech and Hearing Disorders, 54,* 121–140.

Mirenda, P., & Mathy-Laikko, P. (1989). Augmentative and alternative communication applications for persons with severe congenital communication disorders: An introduction. *Augmentative and Alternative Communication, 7,* 3–21.

Musselwhite, C. R., & Ruscello, D. M. (1984). Transparency of three communication symbol systems. *Journal of Speech and Hearing Research, 27,* 436–443.

Mustonen, T., Locke, P., Reichle, J., Solbrack, M., & Lindgren, A. (1991). An overview of augmentative and alternative communication systems. In J. Reichle, J. York, & J. Sigafoos (Eds.), *Implementing augmentative and alternative communication: Strategies for learners with severe disabilities* (pp. 1–37). Baltimore: Paul H. Brooks.

Reichle, J. (1983). *A survey of professional serving persons with severe handicaps.* Unpublished manuscript, University of Minnesota, Minneapolis.

Reichle, J. (1991). Developing communicative exchanges. In J. Reichle, J. York, and J. Sigafoos (Eds.), *Implementing augmentative and alternative communication: Strategies for learners with severe disabilities* (pp. 123–156). Baltimore: Paul H. Brooks.

Reichle, J., Mirenda,. P., Locke, P., Piche, L., & Johnston, S. (1992). Beginning augmentative communication systems. In S. E. Warren and J. Reichle (Eds.), *Causes and effects in communication and language intervention* (pp. 121–156). Baltimore: Paul H. Brooks.

Reichle, J., & Yoder, D. E. (1985). Communication board use in severely handicapped learners. *Language, Speech, and Hearing Services in Schools, 16,* 146–167.

Romski, M. A., & Sevcik, R. A. (1988). Augmentative and alternative communication: Considerations for individuals with severe disabilities. *Augmentative and Alternative Communication, 4,* 83–93.

Romski, M. A., Sevcik, R. A., & Pate, J. L. (1988). Establishment of symbolic communication in persons with severe retardation. *Journal of Speech and Hearing Disorders, 53,* 94–107.

Romski, M. A., Sevcik, R. A., Pate, J. L., & Rumbaugh, D. M. (1985). Discrimination of lexigrams and traditional orthography by nonspeaking severely mentally retarded persons. *American Journal of Mental Deficiency, 90,* 185–189.

Romski, M. A., Sevcik, R. A., Robinson, B., & Bakeman, R. (1994). Adult-directed communications of youth with mental retardation using the system for augmenting language. *Journal of Speech and Hearing Research, 37,* 617–628.

Rounsefell, S., Zucker, S. H., & Roberts, I. G. (1993). Effects of listener training on intelligibility of augmentative and alternative speech in the secondary classroom. *Education and Training in Mental Retardation, 28,* 296–308.

Scherz, J. W., & Beer, M. M. (1995). Factors affecting the intelligibility of synthesized speech. *Augmentative and Alternative Communication, 11,* 74–85.

Sevcik, R. A., & Romski, M. A. (1986). Representational matching skills for persons with severe retardation. *Augmentative and Alternative Communication, 2,* 160–164.

Sevcik, R. A., & Romski, M. A. (2007). AAC: More Than Three Decades of Growth and Development. Retrieved from: http://www.asha.org/public/speech/disorders/Augmentative-and-Alternative.htm

Spiegel, B. B., Benjamin, B. J., & Spiegel, S. A. (1993). One method to increase spontaneous use of an assistive communication device: Case study. *Augmentative and Alternative Communication, 9,* 111–117.

Language, Culture, and English Language Learners

In this chapter, we will examine the influence of culture on language and the special problems posed by children learning to speak English—English language learners. Although most of these children do not have language disorders, many require help to achieve in school. We will consider the necessity of adjustments to assessment procedures in order to fairly and accurately assess this population, and we will also examine instructional approaches that can be used successfully with these children.

Some English language learners or students with dialect differences also have language disabilities. These children pose unique problems for educators. In this chapter, the special needs of this group of children are considered and recommendations for effective instructional practices are provided.

After completing this chapter, you should be able to:

1. Distinguish a dialect difference from a language disorder.
2. Understand the influence of culture on language.
3. Understand the special instructional needs of English language learners.
4. Select appropriate assessment procedures for children with language differences.
5. Describe effective programs for English language.
6. Understand the special problems of English language learners with disabilities.
7. Develop effective instructional practices for English language learners with disabilities.

Jeanne: A Case Study

Jeanne, a 10-year-old girl from Haiti, has been in the United States for less than a year. She is a student in a middle-class, suburban school district. Jeanne's first spoken language is Haitian Creole French. When she came to school, however, Jeanne was tested by a school psychologist who did not speak Haitian Creole and who determined Jeanne to have mental retardation. She was placed in a class for students with special needs. By January Jeanne's special education teacher realized that Jeanne had been inappropriately placed. She has acquired English quickly. Far from being mentally retarded, it is possible that Jeanne is, in fact, gifted. She now assists the teacher in helping other students. The teacher has requested a change of placement for Jeanne, but this cannot be done until next year.

Rosemary: A Case Study

Rosemary was born in Mexico and came to California at age 2. She entered school for the first time at age 7½ and was placed in a multigrade classroom in which English was the primary instruction language. Her teacher began to notice that Rosemary had learning difficulties and referred her for help in the special education resource room, but Rosemary continued to make poor progress. A speech evaluation that included testing in Spanish indicated that Rosemary had a four-year language delay and that her vocabulary was more developed in English than in Spanish. Rosemary was then placed in a special bilingual class for students with communication disabilities. (adapted from Ruiz, 1989)

According to the National Center for Education Statistics, the number of children who spoke a language other than English at home more than doubled between 1979 and 2004. There are now more than 10 million children attending school in the United States who speak a language other than English at home. While many of these children are competent English language users, the number of children who speak English with difficulty has been estimated at about 5 percent of the total school population (or about 3 million children). Hispanic students comprise 75 percent of all students in English as a Second Language (ESL), bilingual, and other English-language support programs while Asian English learners accounted for almost 10 percent of all English language learners (Echevarria, Short, & Powers, 2006).

The rise in the number of students with limited English proficiency (LEP) is related strongly to the increased immigrant population in the United States. The U.S. Census Bureau (Jamieson et al., 2001) determined that in 1999, 20 percent of school-aged children had at least one parent who was an immigrant, and 5 percent of the students were immigrants.

While changes in demographic patterns have an impact throughout society, they disproportionately affect schools. Younger people and people with families are more likely to emigrate to a new country, and higher birth rates for minority groups mean more children in the schools. So, in many parts of the United States, the schools have become the testing ground for our new society.

Cultural Diversity

As a nation of immigrants, the United States has been built on cultural diversity. Yet, there has always been a tension between the newer arrivals and those who were already here. Throughout most of the twentieth century, it was expected that immigrants would assimilate into the mainstream culture. In other words, they would give up their distinctive dress, food, and—most important—their language to become a part of "American" society. As a result, the myth of the "melting pot" developed. Many scholars now recognize that the United States is less a melting pot than a "tossed salad" of many different cultures living together (Emihovich, 1988; First, 1988). Terms such as multicultural and cultural pluralism have been coined to describe a society within which several subcultures exist. As Adler (1993) noted, there has been an ongoing debate between those who advocate assimilation of immigrant groups and those who urge the preservation of cultural diversity.

Whatever the outcome of the cultural diversity debate, educators have to deal with the reality of schoolchildren who hold varying cultural norms and speak many different languages. While this diversity can enrich our schools as well as our communities, it can also bring new problems. For example, a school district in New Jersey has struggled for years with how to celebrate holidays. Should it permit decorations for Christmas and Hanukkah? If so, what should it do about the Muslim, Hindu, and Buddhist children who have their own holidays? In this particular community (a midsized suburb), it is estimated that over a hundred languages are spoken.

Language poses one of the biggest dilemmas for educators. We may acknowledge and accept the desire of persons from different cultural groups to maintain their cultural heritage. But what about their language? After all, the language of instruction in U.S. schools is English. If children are to be successful in school, as well as in the larger community, won't they need to have good English-language skills? But what, then, do we do about their native language? Should we allow, or even encourage, students to use their first language? And what about children who speak English but in a different way? Should they be taught the "right" way to talk?

This is no mere theoretical issue. Some have responded to the increasing cultural and linguistic diversity in our society by calling for a declaration that English shall be the only language spoken in the United States. A number of states have adopted laws that make English the official language of the state; others are considering similar action. An organization called U.S. English has been lobbying Congress for an amendment to the Constitution to make English the official language of the United States. These developments indicate just how important language is to people and how strongly they feel about preserving their language.

These are a few of the problems posed by children from different cultural and language backgrounds. In addition, there is the issue of language disability. It is important to be able to distinguish children who talk differently from children with a language disorder. Yet, because of deficiencies in assessment materials and procedures, this is often difficult to do. As a result, some children are inappropriately referred to special education while others, who could use additional help, do not receive appropriate services (Gersten & Woodward, 1994).

Dialect Differences

A dialect is a variant of a particular language. Wolfram (1991) defined a dialect as "any variety of a language that is shared by a group of speakers." Dialects share most of the features of the main language but differ in pronunciation, vocabulary, and/or stylistic features. For example, in some parts of Boston, words that end with an "uh" sound, as *pizza*, are pronounced "er" (as in *pizzer*). President Kennedy, a Boston native, was faced with the challenge of the missile crisis in "Cuber." In some parts of the United States, the words *Mary, merry,* and *marry* are each pronounced the same. In other regions, they are differentiated from each other. In England, one works in a la-bor-a-tree, while in most regions of the United States, this word is pronounced lab-ra-tory. If you order a large sandwich on a roll, you get a *hoagie* in Philadelphia, a *torpedo* in some parts of the New York area, and a *grinder* in New England. People from the east and west coasts of the United States often feel that people from the South speak very slowly.

All of these are examples of regional dialect variations. Often these variations are minor; they may create brief moments of embarrassment or humor. However, some regional dialect differences are so great that it may be difficult for speakers and listeners to communicate easily. Some speakers from the Appalachian Mountains and those from isolated communities around the Chesapeake Bay area may use dialects that are very difficult to follow.

What we must keep in mind is that there is nothing "wrong" with these regional dialect differences. There is no one "right" way to talk, because the "right" way is different in different regions of the country. On the other hand, there is a widely held belief that there is (or should be) a standard dialect. A *standard dialect* is the one spoken by highly educated people in formal situations. The American Speech-Language-Hearing Association (ASHA, 2003) holds the position that each dialect is adequate as a functional and effective variety of American English and that dialect differences are not a sign of a language disorder.

Social Dialects

In addition to regional dialects, there are social dialects. Social dialects are ways of speaking that are associated with a particular social group. The haughty, sometimes mumbled speech of the "aristocrat" and the dropped endings (*I'm goin'*) often heard in the speech of working-class persons are both examples of social dialects. Some social dialects carry with them the stigma of discrimination and the widespread belief that some are inferior versions of English. Nowhere is this truer than in the case of African American English (AAE) (sometimes called "Ebonics" or "Black English").

The debate about social dialects, specifically African American English, heated up a few years ago when the Oakland, California, school board enacted a resolution directing teachers to recognize and appreciate the language used by their students (called **Ebonics**) and to use this language to help students make the transition to standard American English (SAE) (Applebome, 1996). The board's actions set off a wave of debate about language, dialects, and the role of education. The board was widely criticized for claiming that Ebonics was not a dialect at all but a separate language that was genetically programmed in African Americans, claims the board later dropped. However, the reaction to the board's actions shows just how sensitive issues of language and culture can be.

African American English is a dialect of English that is used by some, but not all, African American speakers. In actuality, there is a great deal of variation in language use within the African American community (Terrell & Terrell, 1993). Some scholars (e.g., Labov, 1972) have attempted to draw a distinction between the general term *Black English* and the distinctive language used largely by inner-city, low-socioeconomic-status, young African Americans. Labov called the latter dialect **Black English Vernacular (BEV).**

Black English Vernacular is the dialect that most people think of when they refer to African American English. BEV is characterized by differences in phonology, syntax, and pragmatics, as well as in aspects of conversational discourse (Cole & Taylor, 1990). Some of the unique features of BEV include: deletion or substitution of medial and final consonant sounds (*brother = brovah; walked = walk*), deletion of auxiliary verb (*The boy is running = The boy running*), deletion of the possessive suffix (*boy's = boy* as in *It is the boy ball*) (Walton, McCardle, Crowe, & Wilson, 1990; Terrell & Terrell, 1993) (see Table 16.1 for additional examples).

Even those African Americans who use Black English Vernacular do not do so at all times. They may use this type of language in some settings, with some people, but not in other situations. This phenomenon in which people switch from one language or one dialect to another is called **code switching.** It means that the individual is aware of environmental conditions that affect the choice of language.

Social dialects such as BEV are often considered inferior by speakers of a more standard form of a language. Not only do social dialects differ linguistically from the standard language, but also when used by people of color or by lower socioeconomic groups, they carry the additional stigma of racism and discrimination. The idea that social dialects are inferior forms of a standard language was reinforced by research on the language of lower socioeconomic groups that was conducted during the 1950s, 1960s, and 1970s. Today, most scholars agree that there is nothing inherently wrong with social dialects such as African American English. Despite a near unanimous consensus among researchers and clinicians that social dialects such as BEV are not inferior, concerns about what to do about speakers of these dialects continue to exist. Grossman

TABLE 16.1 Examples of Grammatical Features of Black English Vernacular

Grammatical Feature	Example
Deletion of past tense ending	cashed = cash
Variation in past tense of irregular verbs	saw = seen
	did = done
Use of double negatives	He didn't do nothing.
Use of *be* as a main verb	I be here in the evening.
Deletion of final *s* in third-person singular present tense	He walk.

Source: Adapted from S. L. Terrell and F. Terrell. (1993). African-American Cultures. In D. E. Battle (Ed.), *Communication disorders in multicultural populations* (pp. 3–37). Boston: Andover Medical Publishers.

(1995) notes three reasons for many educators' continued concerns about children who use nonstandard English dialects:

1. Although nonstandard English dialects are not substandard, they interfere with students' academic progress.
2. Competency in oral standard English is necessary for students to learn to write standard English.
3. Standard English is necessary for vocational success and in other areas in which nonstandard dialect speakers are branded as uneducated and ill prepared.

Although Grossman notes that there is little, if any, research that supports these concerns, some educators continue to hold these beliefs. Questions about whether to encourage or discourage students from using their particular dialect are haunted by issues of race and class. Later in this chapter we will examine the different approaches to teaching students with dialect differences.

Language and Culture

Language is an important part of one's culture. It unites groups of people and helps them form a common identity. At the same time, culture influences language. Children who speak a dialect other than "standard" English or who are English language learners may also have cultural differences that can have an impact on their ability to be understood and accepted by the mainstream culture.

For example, in some Asian cultures children are expected to be seen and not heard. Since they are discouraged from interrupting teachers, Asian students may appear passive and be slow to participate in the classroom (Cheng, 1987). In the Hispanic culture, physical proximity and touching during conversations is not uncommon (Cole, 1989). Some African American children have been taught that making eye contact is disrespectful (Terrell & Terrell, 1993). Table 16.2 gives additional examples of cultural differences in communication style and nonverbal behavior.

Making generalizations about any culture is risky. There are often differences within cultures that are caused by country of origin, exposure to different cultures, and other factors. The important point for teachers is to be aware of the cultural differences that may exist in students from their community.

For educators, gaining an awareness of cultural differences and respect for different cultural values can be an important first step in building a functional classroom environment. Students who are linguistically and culturally different from other students also are at risk for problems in socialization. There are many reasons why this may be so. For example, there are different cultural norms for social interaction. Children from diverse cultures can be expected to have different patterns of eye gaze, speaker distance, and use of facial expressions. Other factors, such as prejudice and language differences themselves, can also affect socialization (Damico & Damico, 1993).

TABLE 16.2   Some Cultural and Conversational Differences

Cultural Group	Cultural Norms	Conversational Characteristics
African Americans	Touching of someone's hair may be seen as offensive. Verbal abuse is not necessarily a precursor to violence. Asking personal questions of new acquaintances may be seen as improper.	Children may avoid eye contact with adults. Discourse may be loosely connected. Conversation may be emotionally intense.
Hispanics	Official or business conversations are preceded by lengthy greetings and pleasantries. Mexican-American children seldom ask for help. Students may deny responsibility for mistakes.	Respect is shown through use of formal language. Hissing to gain attention is proper. Avoidance of eye contact may be a sign of respect. Relative distance between speakers is close. Straightforward communication is impolite.
Asians	Touching or hand-holding between members of same sex is acceptable. A slap on the back is insulting.	Talk about sensitive or unacceptable topics is not proper.

Source: Adapted from H. Grossman. (1995). *Special education in a diverse society.* Boston: Allyn & Bacon and L. Cole. (1989). E pluribus pluribus: Multicultural imperatives for the 1990s and beyond. *ASHA, 31,* 65–70.

English Language Learners

Like children with dialect differences, children who come to school speaking a language other than English as their first language can pose significant challenges to teachers and other professionals. These children may be misunderstood as much for their cultural differences as their language differences. Sometimes these children are mislabeled as having disabilities and are inappropriately placed in special education. Often, they fail to achieve in school at anywhere near the rates that would be expected of them (Garcia, 1993). Our challenge as educators is to provide a program that will allow the child who speaks a language other than English to fully develop, both academically and socially.

There is not general agreement about what to call children who speak a language other than English. The terms *limited-English-proficient (LEP)* or *non-English proficient (NEP)* have sometimes been used to describe these children. Other terms like **ESL (English-as-a-second language)** students or *language-minority* students have sometimes been used. However, there seems to be a developing preference among researchers and practitioners alike to use the term, *English language learners (ELL).* This term has been defined as, "Students who speak another language other than English, who are in the process of acquiring English as a second language or additional language, and who have not yet achieved full English proficiency" (Klingner, Artiles, & Barletta, 2006, p. 126, note 1).

Bilingualism refers to the ability to understand and use two languages. Bilingualism is not an all-or-nothing principle, but ranges from minimal ability to complete fluency in more than one language (Baca & Almanza, 1991). Schiff-Myers (1992) distinguishes between three kinds of childhood bilinguality. One type is *infant bilinguality.* In this case, both languages are spoken to the child beginning in early infancy. When the child develops both languages simultaneously, that child's language competence in each language becomes similar to that of monolingual speakers. Most bilingual children learn to switch back and forth between their languages, depending on who they are talking to and what they are talking about. Schiff-Myers calls the other type of bilinguality *"early childhood."* Early childhood bilingual children hear one language in their home but are later exposed to a second language in the larger community and in school. A third type of bilingual child acquires a second language only after beginning school, The first type of bilinguality is sometimes called *simultaneous* while the other two kinds are called *sequential* or *consecutive.*

For teachers and other education professionals, it is important to keep in mind that while generalizations can be made about English language learners, they are still a heterogeneous group. They come to school with a variety of language and cultural experiences. Some are very familiar with the mainstream culture, while others are largely unfamiliar with any culture other than their native one. Some have good English language skills, while others have limited or nonexistent English language skills.

English Language Learners and Literacy

English language learners have been found to lag behind their peers in the development of academic skills—especially literacy skills (Echevarria et al., 2006). For example, on the 2005 National Assessment of Educational Progress (NAEP), English language learners at the fourth-grade level had a mean score of 187 in reading, while non–English language learners had a mean score of 222 (National Center for Education Statistics, 2005). While the data show that reading scores for English language learners have improved over the past eight years, they still lag far behind their peers. Similar results have been found for eighth-grade students. In 2002, only 11 percent of California seventh-grade English language learners scored at or above the 50th percentile on a statewide test of reading compared to 48 percent of all of the students who took the test (Echevarria et al., 2006).

Why do English language learners have difficulty acquiring literacy skills? This is a more complex question than it might appear at first. Are we interested in literacy in English-based text or in their first language? While it is true that many English language learners struggle with the acquisition of English reading and writing skills, there is no reason to believe that they are deficient in the acquisition of literacy in their first language. The English language learning population itself is diverse. It includes children from a variety of cultures, languages, and socioeconomic levels. Factors such as parents' educational levels, length of time that the family has been in the United States, and opportunities for education can influence the acquisition of literacy skills. However, even after considering all of these factors, we are left with the problem of explaining the significant lag in development of literacy skills among English language learners.

Obviously, skill in the English language is one factor. As we have noted earlier in this text, there is a close relationship between spoken language skill and reading and writing. It should not be surprising to find that children with limited English language skills may struggle with the development of reading and writing in English. Peregoy and Boyle (2000) note that even second language learners with good English skills have been found to read more slowly than native English speakers. Knowledge of English vocabulary has been found to be a particularly important predictor of reading success (Pollard-Durodola et al., 2006).

But, important as it is, English language skill does not fully explain the literacy deficiencies of English language learners. Cultural factors appear to play a role, as well. For example, the NAEP results also showed that Hispanic students lagged significantly behind white students in fourth and eighth grade reading but that Asian American students' scores were equivalent to those of white children. There is also evidence that quality of schooling may have a significant impact on the literacy development of English language learners. In one study, kindergarten reading and spelling performance differences between children learning English as a second language and native English-speaking children largely disappeared by second grade following implementation of an intensive phonological awareness training program (Lesaux & Siegel, 2003).

The development of literacy skills in the English language is a critical factor in the school success of English language learners. Unfortunately, many children with limited English proficiency lag behind in the development of reading and writing skills. Later in this chapter, we will examine instructional programs that have been developed to help English language learners improve their literacy skills.

English Language Learners and Special Education

Some students with limited English proficiency have such significant problems in learning and/or socialization that they require special education services. These children have needs that go beyond those of other ELL children because in addition to their learning or developmental disabilities, they also have language and cultural differences that may make it more difficult for them to learn. Rueda and Chan (1979) called children with disabilities and limited English proficiency "triple threat" students because they have three strikes against them before they even start school. Strike one is their behavioral and/or learning disability. Strike two is their limited English proficiency. Strike three is discrimination because of their race and/or social class.

One of the biggest challenges facing educators is appropriate identification of these students. Ironically, these students tend to be both overidentified and underidentified. Many researchers have found that children from language minority groups are overrepresented in special education classes (Ortiz & Yates, 1983; Artiles et al., 2005).

Use of identification practices that rely largely (or solely) on testing performed in English results in some children from language-minority groups being placed inappropriately into special education classes. A study by Artiles et al. (2005) found that English language learners in eleven urban school districts in California were overrepresented in special education classes by grade 5 and continued that way through grade 12. The study also found that ELLs in immersion programs (those that use little of the students' native language) were more likely to be referred to special education. At the same time, Klingner et al. (2006) note that general education teachers sometimes hesitate to refer English language learners to special education because they are not sure whether they have a learning problem or a language difference.

There is no inherent reason why second language learners should receive special education services more often than their peers. Yet, in some schools, this is the case. Conversely, English language learners can be expected to have learning difficulties at least as often as other children. It is incumbent on teachers and other education professionals to try to determine the factors that may be limiting the learning of individual children.

Appropriate Assessment

One of the great challenges for education professionals is to assess children from culturally and linguistically diverse backgrounds in a fair, appropriate, and accurate manner. As Campbell et al. (1997) noted, children from different ethnic, cultural, or economic backgrounds may perform poorly on tests because they lack experience with the test's format or stimuli. As a result, it becomes difficult to distinguish between children whose language differences reflect their differing experiences and backgrounds and children who have fundamental language disorders. In addition, norm-referenced tests have problems that affect the accuracy of their use with children from diverse language and cultural backgrounds. These problems include content bias (the assumption that all children have had similar life experiences), linguistic bias (differences between the child's language or dialect and the test), and disproportionate representation in normative samples of students with limited English proficiency (the fact that, until recently, most norm-referenced tests failed to include diverse samples in their norm sample) (Laing & Kamhi, 2003).

The Individuals with Disabilities Education Act (IDEA-2004) contains provisions that spell out the obligations of schools to conduct nonbiased assessments when evaluating children for special educational services. Among these provisions are the following:

- Testing and evaluation materials and procedures used for the purposes of evaluation and placement of handicapped children must be selected and administered so as not to be racially or culturally discriminatory.
- Testing and evaluation materials and procedures must be provided and administered in the language or other mode of communication in which the child is most proficient, unless it is clearly not feasible to do so.

- Tests must be administered to a child with a motor, speech, hearing, visual, or other communication disability, or to a bilingual child, so as to reflect accurately the child's ability in the area tested rather than the child's impaired communication skill or limited English language skill unless those are the factors the test purports to measure.

To summarize, IDEA requires that when students who are culturally or linguistically diverse are assessed for special education, testing must be culturally fair, conducted in the child's own language, and designed so that it examines the area tested rather than the child's communication skills in English.

These goals are supported by most educators who are interested in identifying those children from diverse backgrounds who need special education services. Unfortunately, these provisions of IDEA are often not followed (Figueroa, 1989). Among the reasons that testing regulations may not be followed are:

- Disagreement about what constitutes cultural bias in testing.
- A shortage of appropriate assessment materials for students from diverse cultural and linguistic backgrounds.
- A shortage of personnel trained in the assessment of children from diverse cultural and linguistic backgrounds.

Let's look at each of these problems in turn. First, although many educators are concerned about the possibility of bias in testing, the bias has often been difficult to prove. Court decisions have only added to the confusion. Throughout the 1970s, most court decisions supported the notion that there was bias inherent in standardized testing. But in *PASE* v. *Hannon* (1980) the court ruled that although black children were disproportionately represented in special education classes in the Chicago school system, there was little evidence that the tests used to determine placement were biased. The results of court decisions have caused continued disagreement about what constitutes fairness in testing. Even as the courts cannot agree on what constitutes bias in testing, many educators continue to have concerns about fairness in assessment procedures.

A second reason that the listed mandates of IDEA may not be carried out is that appropriate tests may not be available. For example, after an extensive review of the research literature, Figueroa (1989) concluded that psychological testing for children with varying levels of language proficiency and differing home backgrounds was inadequate. He criticized technical aspects of the tests, the knowledge base used for constructing psychological tests, and regulations regarding testing. Baca and Almanaza (1991) expressed similar concerns about educational testing. They noted that there is widespread concern about the content of test items, lack of cultural sensitivity by testers, and lack of test-taking strategies for students from diverse cultural and language backgrounds.

One solution to the problem of test fairness is to use a version of the test in the child's native language. Yet, even this is not always a totally satisfactory solution. Payan (1989) has pointed out that even if such tests are available, the test items may still be inappropriate for children from diverse cultural backgrounds. In addition, the tests are often translated into a standard dialect that may not be the one used by the child.

Cole and Taylor (1990) noted that researchers have often raised concerns about speech and language testing of African American children, claiming that few standardized tests of language contain items that are truly representative of the variety of dialects in use within the United States. When Cole and Taylor used three widely accepted tests of articulation in testing African American children, they found that the results varied considerably, depending on what norms were used. They suggest, then, that clinicians would get more reliable results by using language samples and other techniques that measure the *use* of language skills in communication rather than by using tests of specific language skills.

A third obstacle to the implementation of the IDEA testing requirements is a shortage of trained personnel. There are two problems related to personnel. One involves language abilities. It is often not possible to find a qualified test administrator who speaks a particular child's native language. Frequently, schools have to use a test administrator who is only familiar with standard English. The second problem involves possible bias. As Long (2005) pointed out, testers may construe cultural differences, such as lack of eye contact and unwillingness to respond as uncertainty, defiance, or disorder. Testers may also hold inaccurate expectations for children from particular cultural and language backgrounds and may interpret the test results to confirm those expectations.

In response to the serious problem of test adequacy for children from diverse cultural and language backgrounds, Fay Boyd Vaughn-Cooke (1983) has suggested seven principles that should be used in developing more appropriate testing (see Table 16.3).

Recommendations for Assessment

Considering all of the potential problems in testing children from diverse cultural and language backgrounds, what can educators do to try to fairly and accurately assess

---

TABLE 16.3   Principles for the Development of Appropriate Assessment of Children with Language Differences

1. Standardize existing tests on nonmainstream English speakers.
2. Include a small percentage of minorities in the standardization sample when developing a test.
3. Modify or revise existing tests in ways that will make them appropriate for nonmainstream speakers.
4. Utilize a language sample when assessing the language of nonmainstream speakers.
5. Use criterion-referenced measures when assessing the language of nonmainstream speakers.
6. Refrain from using all standardized tests that have not been corrected for test bias when assessing the language of nonmainstream speakers.
7. Develop a new test that can provide a more appropriate assessment of the language of nonmainstream English speakers.

Source: Adapted from F. B. Vaughn-Cooke. (1983). Improving language assessment in minority children. *ASHA, 25,* 29–33.

these children? One suggestion is to carefully consider the abilities and background knowledge of the child being tested. Baca and Almanza (1991) recommend consideration of the following factors:

- *Experiential background:* Including school attendance history, quality of prior instruction, family history, and medical history.
- *Culture:* Including family goals and expectations, religion, extent to which child has become acculturated, and the child's ability to function in more than one culture.
- *Language proficiency:* Including identification of the child's dominant and preferred language, the child's extent of exposure to each language, and the child's level of proficiency in both languages.
- *Learning style:* Identification of the child's preferred learning styles and the extent to which these require instructional accommodations.
- *Motivational influences:* Including the child's self-concept and the family's attitude toward education.

With these factors in mind, educators can proceed to actually conducting the assessment. Payan (1989) has suggested a seven-step process for the assessment of LEP students. Although her recommendations were designed specifically for the identification of children with special needs, the steps are appropriate for any child with limited or different English.

Step 1 is the *referral.* Payan (1989) provides a rather lengthy form that includes information about who referred the student for assessment, a description of the student's present program, and the student's language and communication abilities. This information is useful for planning the assessment, as well as for discouraging inappropriate referrals.

Step 2 is the *parent interview.* This is an especially important step for children who speak a language other than English at home. In order to completely understand the child's language and cultural background, the interviewer must ascertain what languages are spoken at home, who speaks them, and any concerns the parents may have about their child's language development. A parent interview is also an opportunity to find out about the cultural norms and cultural background of the family.

Step 3 is an assessment of *language proficiency.* Several standardized tests have been developed for the purpose of assessing the language skills of children with limited English (see Table 16.4). However, most of these tests have been developed for use with Spanish-speaking persons.

Step 4 is determining the *language for assessment.* The examiner should consider information from the parent interview and from assessment of the child's language in deciding in which language the assessment should be conducted.

Step 5 is an in-depth analysis of the child's *native language abilities,* including assessment of receptive and expressive skills in all areas of language.

Step 6 is a similar assessment of *English language skills.*

Finally, Payan (1989) recommends that in Step 7, the clinician *summarizes the results and makes recommendations.*

TABLE 16.4   Standardized Tests of Language Proficiency for Students with Limited English Proficiency

Name (Authors)	Ages or Grades	Language(s)	Oral Language Skills Assessed
Basic Inventory of Natural Language (CHECpoint Systems, 1991)	Gr. K to 12	Spanish and 31 other languages	A language sample is scored for fluency, complexity, and average sentence length
Bilingual Syntax Measure I and II (Harcourt Assessment, 1980)	Gr. pre-K to 12	Spanish, English	Expressive syntax
Dos Amigos Verbal Language Scales (Academic Communication Associates, 1999)	Ages 5 to 13	Spanish, English	Expressive vocabulary
Idea Proficiency Tests (Ballard & Tighe, 1994)	Gr. K to Adult	Spanish, English	Vocabulary, syntax, reading for understanding
Language Assessment Scales—Oral (CTB/McGraw-Hill, 1991)	Gr. 1 to 12	Spanish, English	Phonemic, lexical, syntactical, and pragmatic aspects of language
Woodcock-Munoz Language Survey	Ages 4 to 90	Spanish, English	Receptive and expressive semantics

Given the limitations of norm-referenced testing of English language learners and other children with cultural and/or linguistic differences, an alternative assessment model may be useful. One approach that has been used successfully with such children is called **dynamic assessment.**

Dynamic assessment evaluates how children learn during the assessment process. Gutiérrez-Clellen and Pena (2001) described three steps in implementing the model:

- *Testing the limits:* The goal is to find out what children really know and can do. For example, children might be provided feedback during testing, including explanations of why they got items wrong. Children might also be asked to explain how they arrived at their answers. This can help children realize why they are making mistakes and help them to self-correct.
- *Graduated prompting:* Responses are elicited through the use of increasingly more specific prompts. For example, a response may be *modeled* ("This is a baby"), *modeled with an elicitation question* ("This is a baby. What is it?"), or *modeled with an object obstacle* (withholding the object until the child attempted

to produce the word). The child's readiness to learn specific target items is determined by the level of prompting needed by the child.

- *Test-Teach-Retest:* Initial testing is used to determine what the child does (and does not know). Then intervention focuses on unknown items. Finally, the child is retested to see whether the child has acquired the newly taught information.

Gutiérrez-Clellen and Peña (2001) demonstrated that effective use of these techniques could provide more accurate information about the vocabulary knowledge of bilingual (Spanish/English) children than the standard administration of a norm-referenced test.

Criterion-referenced tests and informal procedures, such as language samples, are alternative means for assessing language proficiency. Other alternatives include dictation tasks in which the examiner says words or phrases from normal discourse and the student writes down the word or phrase; cloze procedure in which the child fills in (either orally or in written form) missing words in a passage; and an oral interview to assess the child's language skills (Oller, 1988).

Fair and accurate testing of linguistically and culturally diverse students, including those learning English, is a continuing and growing challenge for schools. Teachers and other professionals need to use a variety of techniques to assess such children and be willing to modify testing procedures to give children the opportunity to demonstrate what they really know. Only then will we be able to determine whether such children truly have learning difficulties or if their performance is largely the result of language or cultural differences.

Instructional Programs

In the previous section, we noted that children with language and cultural differences are a diverse group. They come to school with different degrees of skill in their first language and in English; they differ in their exposure to the mainstream culture; and they differ in their learning and social skills. Therefore, there is no one program that will suit everybody. The task for educators is to find the most effective program for each individual.

Although each individual's program of study may differ, certain broad goals are appropriate for all learners with language and/or dialect differences. One goal is to develop *competence* in English. But what is competence? Cummins (1980; 1984) describes two types of language skills: **basic interpersonal communicative skills (BICS)** and **cognitive/academic language proficiency (CALP).** Cummins cautions that children may develop BICS fairly quickly (one to two years) but that CALP takes much longer to develop (five to seven years). Thus, when we say that a child is competent in English, we should clarify whether we mean that the child is able to engage in interpersonal interaction or the more advanced skill of applying English language skills to academic tasks. There is a danger that some children will be transferred out of programs that help them develop their English skills because they are able to demonstrate basic communication skills. But many of these children will not be prepared to use their language for the complex learning tasks posed in the classroom. Handscombe (1994) has suggested that in addition to the development of skills in English, programs for children with language and/or cultural differences should also help students enhance their academic achievement and social integration.

Cummins (1994) reminds us that a number of factors are working against the development of effective programs for children who speak a language (or a dialect) other than standard English. These include government policies that ignore the research on second language learning, curriculum that is skewed toward white, middle-class values and experiences, and a shortage of professionals who share the language and/or cultural background of many of the students in today's schools. Despite these obstacles, effective programs have been developed. In subsequent sections of this chapter, we will examine programs for children with limited English proficiency, students with dialect differences, and students with special needs and language differences.

Instruction for English Language Learners

Students who come to school with competence in both their native language and English (bilingual) will usually not need any type of special program. But many children whose first language is other than English have limited skills in English, or limited English proficiency, and do need some type of instruction that helps them acquire the English skills they need for success in school. Instructional programs for English language learners range from those that require children to use English right from the beginning to those that emphasize the use of the child's native language. Rossell (2005) has described six types of programs that have been used in the United States to educate students learning English as a second language:

- *Structured immersion—or sheltered English immersion:* provides instruction almost entirely in English, but in a self-contained classroom consisting only of English language learners.
- *ESL pullout programs:* supplement regular, mainstream classroom instruction with instruction in a small-group setting outside the mainstream classroom aimed at developing English language skills.
- *The sink-or-swim approach:* provides mainstream classroom instruction with no special help or scaffolding.
- *Transitional bilingual education:* initially delivers instruction and develops students' literacy in the students' native language but puts a priority on developing students' English language skills.
- *Two-way bilingual education:* (also known as two-way immersion) is designed to develop fluency in both the students' first language and a second language; teachers deliver instruction in both languages to classes consisting of both native English speakers and speakers of another language (most commonly Spanish).
- *Bilingual maintenance programs:* generally consist of non-English speakers and, like two-way bilingual education programs, place equal emphasis on maintaining students' primary language and developing their English proficiency.

Which type of program is most successful? Unfortunately, there is no simple answer to this question. Research on the outcomes of bilingual education programs is limited by factors such as individual differences between students and variations in the ways that school districts choose to implement the basic models described above. Despite these limitations, some trends have emerged.

Reviews of research on the outcomes of bilingual education programs—programs that combined instruction in a first language with instruction in a second language—have generally found that such programs can work (Baca & Cervantes, 1989; Gersten & Woodward, 1994; Rossell, 2005). Most of the research has found that students in bilingual education programs perform as well as or better than their monolingual peers in assessments of academic, cognitive, and social functioning. This research has been conducted throughout the world, with speakers of a wide variety of languages.

Sheltered instruction (or **sheltered immersion**) programs have been found to be one the most successful programs for building both English language skills and content area knowledge in English language learners (Abadiano & Turner, 2002). Sheltered instruction programs are designed to help English language learners develop continued competence in English while learning in academic content areas, such as social studies, mathematics, and science. Instruction is delivered in English but usually at a slower pace and with more repetition than in typical content-area classrooms. Teachers in these classrooms are typically skilled in English as a second language techniques and use effective teaching strategies, such as visuals and demonstrations, scaffolded instruction, targeted vocabulary development, connections to student experiences, student-to-student interaction, adaptation of materials, and use of supplementary materials. Research on sheltered immersion programs has reported that students in such programs outperform their peers on expository writing assignments (Echevarria, Short, & Powers, 2006). While further research is needed, the sheltered immersion model is a promising approach to enhancing the language and academic skills of English language learners.

Despite strong evidence for the effectiveness of bilingual education programs that incorporate the child's minority language into instruction, many school districts choose other kinds of programs for these children. The reasons for such decisions often have more to do with politics than with educational outcomes. As Rossell (2005) notes, the "sink-or-swim" model is the most prevalent approach to educating English language learners, despite little research to support its effectiveness. Teachers and speech-language specialists should advocate for decisions based on the individual child's needs and program effectiveness rather than on factors such as prejudice, fear, and cost.

Gersten and Jimenez (1994) described the art of teaching English language learners as a "balancing act." The teacher must challenge the students but not frustrate them and help those who need it but also include all students in instruction. The researchers suggested that the following constructs be included in instructional programs for language-minority students:

1. *Challenge:* Including implicit challenges (such as the use of higher-order questions) and explicit challenges (high but reasonable expectations).
2. *Involvement:* All learners should be actively involved in instruction.

3. *Success:* Activities and tasks provided should be within students' abilities. Students should know when they are successful.
4. *Scaffolding/cognitive strategies:* The teacher uses instructional methods such as story maps, visual organizers, and think alouds to assist students in developing cognitive strategies for learning.
5. *Mediation/feedback:* Feedback should be frequent and understandable to the student.
6. *Collaborative/cooperative learning:* Learning in supportive groups.
7. *Techniques for second-language acquisition/sheltered English:* Including the incorporation of the students' primary language into instruction and the use of extended discourse.
8. *Respect for cultural diversity:* Teachers should be knowledgeable about the culture of their students and respectful toward cultural differences.

Instruction for Students with Dialect Differences

The question of how and what to teach children with dialect differences continues to be a very sensitive one. The issue clearly involves more than what is best in terms of language development or educational practice. It is closely related to our society's struggles with the issues of race, poverty, and equity.

In 1979, a United States district court judge ruled in favor of a group of African American children who had brought suit against the Ann Arbor, Michigan, school district. The suit claimed that these children were being denied an equal education because their school did not take into account their use of Black English. The judge noted that there was evidence that teachers had unconsciously indicated to the children that Black English is wrong. As a result, the judge argued, the children had been made to feel inferior and became disenchanted with school. The court ruled that teachers had to attend in-service education programs about nonstandard dialects and that a child's dialect had to be considered when the child was being taught to read and write (*Martin Luther King Jr. Elementary School* v. *Ann Arbor School District Board,* 1978).

This case caused many educators to rethink their attitudes toward dialect differences. In addition, it prompted debate (that continues even today) about the relationship between dialect differences and the development of literacy skills. Grossman (1995) described the debate as between those who argue for **bidialectalism** and those who argue for the *appreciation* of dialect differences.

Those who argue for a bidialectal approach to instruction for children who speak nonstandard dialects of English (such as Black English Vernacular [BEV]) contend that although there is nothing wrong with such dialects, they interfere with the child's ability to achieve success in the mainstream society. As Sol Adler, one of the advocates for a bidialectal approach, put it, "So long as linguistic and cultural prejudices dominate the thinking of these establishment members of our society, nonstandard speakers will continue to need to learn the language of the mainstream culture if they wish to have an equal opportunity to enter into the mainstream" (1993, p. 21). Adler argues that bidialectal programs must be mandatory, not voluntary, since most children will not pick up standard English without formal instruction.

Proponents of bidialectal programs generally give three reasons for the need for such programs (Adler, 1993):

1. *Educational reasons:* They cite evidence that the reading skills of speakers of BEV lag behind those of other children, both white and black. Furthermore, since "standard" English is the language of instruction in classrooms, speakers of BEV and other nonstandard dialects are at a disadvantage.
2. *Employment reasons:* They cite evidence that use of standard English is an important factor in hiring decisions. They argue that it is unfair to speakers of nonstandard dialects not to teach them the language skills they will need for employment.
3. *Ethical and pragmatic reasons:* Ethically, it is wrong to deny children the use of their dialect. But, it is equally wrong to deny them the opportunity to learn standard English. The pragmatic argument is that, like it or not, standard English is required for success in the United States and children must be given the opportunity to acquire the standard dialect.

The objectives of a bidialectal program are to create in students an awareness of the need to adjust language for different purposes, to help them understand the importance of communication skills, and to provide them with opportunities to develop and practice standard English while continuing to use their dialect (Harris-Wright, 1987). Many bidialectal programs use an instructional technique called *contrastive analysis,* in which children are given examples of nonstandard and standard English forms for communicating and are taught to analyze and recognize the differences between the two dialects.

The appreciation approach to dialect differences urges respect for dialect differences and the development of language skills in whatever dialect the child speaks. Grossman (1995) has summarized the arguments in support of the appreciation position:

1. Efforts to teach students to speak standard English do not work.
2. Dialect speakers who are required to speak standard English become less fluent and have difficulty expressing themselves.
3. Teaching students standard English before they are completely fluent in their original dialects stunts their language development.
4. It is not possible to encourage students to learn a second dialect without also communicating that their way of speaking is less desirable.
5. Acceptance and appreciation of nonstandard dialects by schools and teachers improves students' self-esteem.
6. Teaching standard English to nonstandard-dialect speakers is a form of political and cultural subjugation.

While the research base in support of many of these arguments is limited, the arguments do represent points of view that should be considered. At one time in the late 1960s and 1970s, some linguists were urging the development of Black English texts so that children who used this dialect would be less disadvantaged as they began to read (e.g., Baratz, 1969). Today, however, most educators recognize the need for all children to develop reading and writing skills in standard English.

Clearly the debate about what to do about children who speak nonstandard dialects of English, especially BEV, is about more than education. Issues of race and class inject highly emotional feelings into the debate. While most can agree that nonstandard dialects are not inferior forms of English and that speakers of such dialects deserve respect, they differ on the extent to which standard English should be taught. In making decisions about what kind of program to adopt, educators should consider the research base on nonstandard dialects and literacy, as well as the desires of parents, students, and the community as a whole.

Instruction for Students with Language Disorders and Language Differences

An earlier discussion in this chapter described a group of English language learners who also have disabilities affecting learning ability and/or social development. These students are sometimes *culturally and linguistically different exceptional (CLDE) students* (Baca & Almanza, 1991). These students often need special programs of instruction that will help them both develop their language skills and address their particular learning problems.

Baca and Almanza (1991) describe three types of instructional models for what they refer to as *culturally and linguistically different exceptional (CLDE)* students:

- *The bilingual support model:* Monolingual English special education teachers are teamed with native language tutors/paraprofessionals to provide special education services. The special education teacher provides ESL instruction.
- *The coordinated service model:* A monolingual special education teacher is teamed with a bilingual teacher. The special education teacher is responsible for providing ESL instruction and implementing IEP goals in English. The bilingual teacher provides academic instruction in the child's native language.
- *The integrated bilingual special education model:* A bilingual special educator is responsible for the implementation of the IEP. Teachers are trained in both bilingual education and special education.

Just as there is disagreement about what constitutes the best instructional program for English language learners, there is also great disagreement within the special education field about the most effective instructional practices. Often, this disagreement comes down to an argument between those who advocate a direct instruction approach versus those who favor instruction addressing cognitive learning processes. This debate is especially relevant with regard to English language learners with disabilities. Many educators have expressed concerns about the use of direct instruction techniques with these students (Cummins, 1984; Yates & Ortiz, 1991). They are concerned that programs focusing on the acquisition of specific language skills (such as phonics and vocabulary acquisition) may actually interfere with the child's acquisition of English. Some educators have suggested that programs that emphasize more naturalistic approaches may be more effective. At the same time, we cannot ignore the fact that many English language learners with disabilities will need extra help in identifying and correcting errors in language usage.

Cloud (1994) has suggested that educators consider the *whole* child when planning instruction for English language learners with special needs. She means that we should consider the child's *disability,* as well as the *language and cultural* differences; each should be given equal importance. Instruction should be based on a reciprocal-interaction model, where the teacher's task is to facilitate learning through modeling and sharing successful strategies for learning. In her review of effective practices for teaching English language learners with disabilities, Ruiz (1989) recommended that instructional programs:

1. Take into account students' sociocultural backgrounds and their effects on oral language, reading and writing, and second-language learning.
2. Take into account students' possible learning handicaps and their effects on oral language, reading and writing, and second-language learning.
3. Follow developmental practices in literacy acquisition.
4. Locate curriculum in a meaningful context where the communicative purpose is clear and authentic.
5. Connect curriculum with the students' personal experiences.
6. Incorporate children's literature into reading, writing, and ESL lessons.
7. Involve parents as active partners in the instruction of their children.
8. Give students experience with whole texts in reading, writing, and ESL lessons.
9. Incorporate collaborative learning whenever possible.

Literacy Instruction for Students with Limited English Language Proficiency

An important component of most instructional programs for English language learners is the development of literacy skills (reading, writing, and spoken language). As we noted earlier in this chapter, many English language learners lag behind their peers in the development of reading and writing skills. How can these students be helped in developing literacy skills?

One approach that has been successful is intensive instruction in phonological awareness skills. For example, Lesaux and Siegel (2003) studied the effects of combining an intensive phonological awareness training program with a balanced literacy instruction on English language learners at-risk for reading difficulties. The "at-risk" students (both those who spoke a language other than English and English-language proficient children) received intensive instruction in phonological awareness. By second grade the English language learners had caught up to (and, in some cases surpassed) the native English language speakers. Culatta, Reese, and Setzer (2006) reported the results of the use of the SEEL (Systematic and Engaging Early Literacy) instruction program with eleven English language learners from two kindergarten classrooms. The program utilizes meaning-based instruction to teach phonological skills in both English and Spanish, including:

- *Rhyming:* Activities designed to teach rhyme made the common word ending noticeable by (a) targeting one rhyme per activity, (b) highlighting the rime ending using intonation and stress, (c) providing multiple examples of target words, and (d) explicitly labeling the same word endings as rhyme.
- *Alliteration:* Instructors used the same techniques to highlight literacy targets as in the rhyming activities. When instructing in Spanish, they highlighted an initial syllable in an activity such as passing things that began with /pa/ (e.g., "Pasa la papa para papá con el papel o pala" ["Pass the potatoes to the father with a piece of paper or a shovel"]).
- *Sound Blending and Letter–Sound Associations:* Opportunities to segment and blend sounds and to make letter–sound associations were incorporated into the rhyme and alliteration activities.

Students who participated in the program made significant improvements on all of the skills taught by the program. Although the researchers did not evaluate whether the instruction led to better reading outcomes, they reported that the students were very motivated to participate.

Another approach to enhancing the literacy skills of English language learners has been to provide supplemental instruction. Linan-Thompson et al. (2003) provided supplemental reading instruction to second grade English language learners for thirty minutes a day, five times a week, for thirteen weeks. The instruction consisted of five components:

- *Fluent reading:* Repeated reading of familiar text designed to help students develop automatic recognition of words.
- *Phonological awareness:* Students were given the opportunity to blend, segment, delete, substitute, and manipulate phonemes in words. Teachers used picture cards to provide context for words.
- *Instructional-level reading:* Students read books at their instructional level. Teachers previewed vocabulary words and activated student's background knowledge.
- *Word study:* Students received specific instruction in word analysis strategies.
- *Writing:* Students wrote as many words as they could in one minute.

Most of the children who received this instruction made significant gains on measures of reading outcomes and continued those gains even after the supplemental instruction was discontinued. Similarly, Denton et al. (2004) studied the effects of providing tutoring to second through fifth grade English language learners. The tutoring sessions took place three times a week, for forty minutes a session, over ten weeks. The researchers compared two instructional programs: *Read Well* (Sprick, Howard, & Fidanque, 1998), in which students receive explicit, systematic instruction in English decoding, and *Read Naturally* (Ihnot, 1992), which uses a repeated reading approach. Students who received direct instruction in decoding (the *Read Well* program) made significant gains in reading. Most students in the *Read Naturally* program did not show improvement. The authors speculated that students may have not done as well in the latter program because they lacked the necessary vocabulary to be successful readers.

Hudelson (1994) described additional strategies for literacy development for second-language learners (see Table 16.5).

Hudelson's suggestions are based on a whole-language theory of instruction. While this approach can work for LEP students (Gersten & Woodward, 1994), Reyes (1992) cautions that this approach should be used with care. She suggests that literature-based programs must include literature from the cultural traditions of *all* of the students in the class. Furthermore, teachers should not be afraid to correct syntax and spelling when necessary. Reyes observed that modeling was not always adequate to teach English grammar rules to LEP students. In addition, Reyes suggests that second-language learners be given the opportunity to use their native language for both academic and nonacademic purposes.

Although research on effective literacy instruction for English language learners is still limited, it is becoming clear that early identification of children at-risk for reading and writing difficulties, coupled with intensive instruction that focuses on skills such as phonological awareness, can improve the literacy skills of these students.

TABLE 16.5   Strategies for Literacy Development of Second-Language Learners

- **Create a literate classroom environment:** The classroom should be a language-rich environment. Charts for attendance, favorite songs, and academic tasks; a classroom library; a writing center; and displays of children's written work can be used to enhance the classroom environment.
- **Encourage collaborative learning:** A collaborative learning environment has been found to be an important factor in the success of classrooms for linguistically diverse learners (Reyes & Laliberty, 1992). Children should be encouraged to work together, to rely on each other, and to support each other.
- **Utilize oral and written personal narratives:** Although second-language learners may take longer to feel comfortable producing personal narratives, this can be an effective procedure. Reyes (1992) notes that many second-language learners will need help with some of the mechanics of writing in order to be successful.
- **Utilize dialogic writing:** Dialogue journals enable students and teachers to communicate with each other in a nonjudgmental way. Second-language learners get the opportunity to see examples of standard written English.
- **Utilize predictable books:** Such books reinforce the idea that reading is a process of prediction. Students can be asked to predict what is likely to happen and to fill in missing words.
- **Include opportunities for self-selected reading:** Students need opportunities to select and read books of their own choice.
- **Include literacy development as a part of content study:** Content area study provides many opportunities for reading, researching, and writing. When students with limited English proficiency are grouped in classrooms with native English speakers, heterogeneous grouping can be used to give the LEP students an opportunity to be successful.

Source: Adapted from S. Hudelson. (1994). Literacy development of second language children. In F. Genesee (Ed.), *Educating second language children* (pp. 129–158). New York: Cambridge University Press.

Summary

In looking at the impact of language and cultural differences on schools and schooling, educators must have an awareness of the difference between a *language disability* and a *language difference.* Many children come to school speaking a dialect that differs from standard English or a language other than English. There is nothing "wrong" with most of these children, and most of them do not require special educational services. But many do need special programs that will allow them to retain their first language or dialect while learning standard English.

We have seen that most research favors a *holistic* approach that emphasizes the development of *literacy skills* through use of the child's *first language*—that students are then better able to make the transition to English. It is important that teachers show respect for the child's language and culture as they try to help the child make this transition.

Some children with language and cultural differences also have learning and/or behavior disabilities. These children not only need help in learning English but also need the intensive instructional support that can be provided through special education.

Teachers and other education professionals need to be aware of the special needs of children with language and cultural differences. They should also respect the contribution that cultural diversity makes to our society.

REVIEW QUESTIONS

1. Is there a "right" way to talk? Give arguments for and against this notion.

2. Give three examples of ways in which Black English Vernacular differs from standard English.

3. What is the effect of bilingualism on cognitive and language development?

4. What factors may contribute to the literacy difficulties experienced by many English language learners?

5. What are the three threats faced by English language learners with special needs?

6. List four ways that assessment can be modified to more fairly and accurately evaluate the abilities of English language learners.

7. Compare and contrast "sink or swim" programs with structured English immersion programs for English language learners, discussing both their instructional methods and their use of English and the child's first language.

8. Why do most educators who are interested in bilingual education support approaches emphasizing the development of competence in the child's first language?

9. What is the rationale for a bidialectal approach to teaching children with dialect differences?

SUGGESTED ACTIVITIES

1. Listen carefully to the language of teenagers. You will probably find dialect differences— the most apparent, in semantics. Often, different groups of students within a community can

have different dialects. For example, African American students can use a different dialect from white students. Try making a list of five to ten words that seem unique to one group of teenagers. Then ask another group to tell you what these words mean. What did you find? What do the results indicate about the ability of students from different social or cultural groups to understand each other?

2. If you have the opportunity to observe students who speak a language other than English, try to observe some nonverbal aspects of their interaction (you do not have to speak the language). Watch closely as they interact with their teacher. Also, try to observe as they interact with peers. Do you notice any differences in

distance between speakers?

facial expressions?

gestures?

lengths of conversation?

3. To find out about cultural differences, try asking a group of children or adults to share one thing from their culture that they think other people may not know about. This is a good opportunity to discuss the word *culture,* and some interesting (and enlightening) responses often surface.

GLOSSARY

basic interpersonal communicative skills (BICS): the ability to communicate with others using a second language

bidialectalism: an instructional approach that seeks to provide opportunities for students to develop and practice standard English while continuing to use their dialect

bilingualism: the ability to understand and use two languages

Black English Vernacular: (BEV) a dialect of English spoken by some African Americans that is characterized by differences in phonology, syntax, and pragmatics

code switching: changing from one language or dialect to another during conversation

cognitive/academic language proficiency (CALP): the ability to apply English language skills to academic tasks

dialect: systematic subvariants of a particular language that are spoken by a sizable group

dynamic assessment: evaluates how children *learn* during the assessment process

Ebonics: another name for Black English Vernacular, sometimes used to indicate a different language rather than a dialect difference

English as a Second Language (ESL): an instructional program in which students with limited English proficiency spend most of their day in a submersion classroom but receive some help with English

sheltered English immersion: type of program for English language learners that provides instruction almost entirely in English, but in a self-contained classroom consisting only of English language learners

RESOURCES ON THE WEB

http://www.cal.org/topics/dialects/aae.html Website of the Center for Applied Linguistics (information on Black English vernacular)

www.colorado.edu/education/bueno   Website of the Bueno Center for Multicultural Education at the University of Colorado-Boulder

http://www-rcf.usc.edu/~cmmr/   Website of the Center for Multilingual Multicultural Research at the University of Southern California

www.nabe.org   Website of the National Association for Bilingual Education

http://www.ncela.gwu.edu/   Website of the National Clearinghouse for English Language Acquisition and Language Instruction Educational Programs

http://www.ed.gov/about/offices/list/oela/index.html?src=mr   Website of the United States Office of English language acquisition

http://www.tesol.org/s_tesol/index.asp   Website of the Teachers of English to Speakers of Other Languages

http://www.cal.org/topics/ell/   Website of the Center for Applied Linguistics information page on English language learners

REFERENCES

Abadiano, H. R., & Turner, J. (2002). Sheltered instruction: An empowerment framework for English language learners. *NERA Journal, 38,* 50–55.

Adler, S. (1993). *Multicultural communication skills in the classroom.* Boston: Allyn & Bacon.

American Speech-Language-Hearing Association. (2003). *Technical Report: American English Dialects. ASHA, Supplement 23,* 2003.

Appelbome, P. (1996, December 20). School district elevates status of Black English. *New York Times,* p. 18.

Artiles, A. J., Rueda, R., Salazar, J. J., & Higareda, I. (2005). Within-group diversity in minority disproportionate representation: English language learners in urban school districts. *Exceptional Children, 71,* 283–300.

Baca, L. M., & Almanza, E. (1991). *Language minority students with disabilities.* Reston, VA: The Council for Exceptional Children. (ERIC Document Reproduction Services No. 339, 171).

Baca, L. M., & Cervantes, H. T. (1989). *The bilingual special education interface.* New York: Merrill.

Baratz, J. C. (1969). Linguistic and cultural factors in teaching reading to ghetto children. *Elementary English, 46,* 199–203.

Campbell, T., Dollaghan, C., Needleman, H., & Janosky, J. (1997). Reducing bias in language assessment: Processing dependent measures. *Journal of Speech, Language, and Hearing Research, 40,* 519–525.

Cheng, L. L. (1987). Cross-cultural and linguistic considerations in working with Asian populations. *Asha, 29,* 33–36.

Cloud, N. (1994). Special education needs of second language students. In F. Genesee (Ed.), *Educating second language children.* New York: Cambridge University Press.

Cole, L. (1989). *E pluribus pluribus:* Multicultural imperatives for the 1990s and beyond. *ASHA, 31,* 65–70.

Cole, P. A., & Taylor, O. L. (1990). Performance of working class African-American children on three tests of articulation. *Language, Speech, and Hearing Services in Schools, 21,* 171–176.

Culatta, B., Reese, M., & Setzer, L. A. (2006). Early literacy instruction in a dual-language (Spanish–English) kindergarten. *Communication Disorders Quarterly, 27,* 67–82.

Cummins, J. (1980). The cross-lingual dimensions of language proficiency: Implications for bilingual education and the optimal age issue. *TESOL Quarterly, 4,* 171–174.

Cummins, J. (1984). *Bilingualism and special education: Issues in assessment and pedagogy.* San Diego: College-Hill Press.

Cummins, J. (1994). Knowledge, power, and identity in teaching English as a second language. In F. Genesee (Ed.), *Educating second language children* (pp. 33–58). New York: Cambridge University Press.

Damico, J. S., & Damico, S. K. (1993). Language and social skills from a diversity perspective: Considerations for the speech-language pathologist. *Language, Speech, and Hearing Services in Schools, 24,* 236–243.

Denton, C. A., Anthony, J. L., Parker, R., & Hasbrouck, J. E. (2004). Effects of two tutoring programs in the English reading development of Spanish-English bilingual students. *Elementary School Journal, 104,* 289–305.

Echevarria, J., Short, D., & Powers, K. (2006). School reform and standards-based education: A model for English language learners. *Journal of Educational Research, 99,* 195–210.

Emihovich, C. (1988). Toward cultural pluralism: Redefining integration in American society. *Urban Review, 20,* 3–7.

Figueroa, R. A. (1989). Psychological testing of linguistic-minority students: Knowledge gaps and regulations. *Exceptional Children, 56,* 135–153.

First, J. M. (1988). Immigrant students in U.S. public schools: Challenges with solutions. *Phi Delta Kappan, 70,* 205–207.

Garcia, E. E. (1993). Language, culture, and education. In L. Darling-Hammond (Ed.), *Review of research in education* (vol. 19) (pp. 51–98). Washington, DC: AERA.

Gersten, R., & Jimenez, R. T. (1994). A delicate balance: Enhancing literature instruction for students of English as a second language. *The Reading Teacher, 47,* 438–448.

Gersten, R., & Woodward, J. (1994). The language-minority student and special education: Issues, trends, and paradoxes. *Exceptional Children, 60,* 310–322.

Grossman, H. (1995). *Special education in a diverse society.* Boston: Allyn & Bacon.

Gutiérrez-Clellen, V., & Peña, E. (2001). Dynamic assessment of diverse children: A tutorial. *Language, Speech, and Hearing Services in Schools, 32,* 212–224.

Handscombe, J. (1994). Putting it all together. In F. Genesee (Ed.), *Educating second language children.* New York: Cambridge University Press.

Harris-Wright, K. (1987). The challenge of educational coalescence: Teaching nonmainstream English-speaking students. *Journal of Childhood Communication Disorders, 11,* 209–215.

Hudelson, S. (1994). Literacy development of second language children. In F. Genesee (Ed.), *Educating second language children* (pp. 129–158). New York: Cambridge University Press.

Ihnot, C. (1992). *Read naturally.* St. Paul, MN: Read Naturally.

Jamieson, A., Curry, A., & Martinez, G. (2001). School enrollment in the United States—Social and economic characteristics of students. (Current Population Reports No. P20-533). Washington, DC: U.S. Government Printing Office.

Klingner, J. K., Artiles, A. J., and Barletta L. M. (2006). English language learners who struggle with reading: Language acquisition or LD? *Journal of Learning Disabilities, 39,* 108–128.

Labov, W. (1972). *Sociolinguistic patterns.* Philadelphia: University of Pennsylvania Press.

Laing, S. P., & Kamhi, A. (2003). Alternative assessment of language and literacy in culturally and linguistically diverse populations. *Language, Speech, and Hearing Services in Schools, 34,* 44–55.

Lesaux, N. K., & Siegel, L. S. (2003). The development of reading in children who speak English as a second language. *Developmental Psychology, 39,* 1005–1019.

Linan-Thompson, S., Vaughn, S., Hickman-Davis, P., & Kouzekanani, K. (2003). Effectiveness of supplemental instruction for second-grade English language learners with reading difficulties. *Elementary School Journal, 103,* 221–238.

Long, S. H. (2005). Language and linguistically-culturally diverse children. In V. A. Reed (Ed.), *An introduction to children with language disorders.* Boston: Allyn & Bacon.

Martin Luther King Junior Elementary School Children v. *Ann Arbor School District Board,* 1979. 473 R Suppl 1371.

National Center for Education Statistics. (2005). National assessment of educational progress. Available: http://www.nces.ed.gov.

Oller, J. (1988). Discrete point, integrative, or pragmatic tests. In P. A. Richard-Amato (Ed.), *Making it happen: Interaction in the second language classroom.* New York: Longman.

Ortiz, A. A., & Yates, J. R. (1983). Incidence among Hispanic exceptionals: Implications for manpower planning. *Journal of the National Association for Bilingual Education, 7,* 41–53.

PASE v. *Hannon,* 1980.506 F. Suppl. 831, N.D.Illinois.

Payan, R. M. (1989). Language assessment for the bilingual exceptional child. In L. M. Baca & H. T. Cervantes (Eds.), *The bilingual special education interface.* New York: Merrill.

Peregoy, S. F., & Boyle, O. F. (2000). English learners reading English: What we know, what we need to know. *Theory into Practice, 39,* 237–247.

Pollard-Durodola, S. D., Mathes, P. G., Vaughn, S., Cardenas-Hagan, E., & Linan-Thompson, S. (2006). *The role of oracy in developing comprehension in Spanish-speaking English language learners.* Topics in Language Disorders, 26, 365–384.

Reyes, M. de la Luz. (1992). Challenging venerable assumptions: Literacy instruction for linguistically different students. *Harvard Educational Review, 62,* 427–446.

Reyes, M. de la Luz, & Laliberty, E. (1992). A teacher's "Pied Piper" effect on young authors. *Education and Urban Society, 24,* 263–278.

Rossell, C. (2005). Teaching English through English. *Educational Leadership, 62,* 32–36.

Rueda, R., & Chan, K. (1979). Poverty and culture in special education: Separate but equal. *Exceptional Children, 45,* 422–431.

Ruiz, N. (1989). An optimal learning environment for Rosemary. *Exceptional Children, 56,* 130–134.

Schiff-Myers, N. B. (1992). Considering arrested language development and language loss in the assessment of second language learners. *Language, Speech, and Hearing Services in Schools, 23,* 28–33.

Sprick, M. M., Howard, L. M., & Fidanque, A. (1998). *Read well: Critical foundations in elementary reading.* Longmont, CO: Sopris West.

Terrell, S. L., & Terrell, F. (1993). African-American cultures. In D. E. Battle (Ed.), *Communication disorders in multicultural populations* (pp. 3–37). Boston: Andover Medical Publishers.

Vaughn-Cooke, E. B. (1983). Improving language assessment in minority children. *ASHA, 25,* 29–33.

Walton, J. H., McCardle, P., Crowe, T. A., & Wilson, B. E. (1990). Black English in a Mississippi prison population. *Journal of Speech and Hearing Disorders, 55,* 206–216.

Wolfram, W. (1991). *Dialects and American English* (pp. 7–22). Englewood Cliffs, NJ: Prentice Hall.

Yates, J. R., & Ortiz, A. A. (1991). Professional development needs of teachers who serve exceptional language minorities in today's schools. *Teacher Education and Special Education, 13,* 11–18.

AUTHOR INDEX

SUBJECT INDEX